MICROECONOMICS
A Contemporary Introduction

FIFTH EDITION

William A. McEachern

Professor of Economics

University of Connecticut

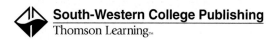
South-Western College Publishing
Thomson Learning™

Australia • Canada • Denmark • Japan • Mexico • New Zealand • Philippines
Puerto Rico • Singapore • South Africa • Spain • United Kingdom • United States

Acquisitions Editor:	Keri L. Witman
Developmental Editor:	Dennis Hanseman
Marketing Manager:	Lisa L. Lysne
Sr. Production Editor:	Sharon L. Smith
Manufacturing Coordinator:	Georgina Calderon
Internal Design:	A Small Design Studio/Ann Small
Cover Design:	Tin Box Studio
Cover Illustrator:	John Mattos
Photo Researcher:	Feldman & Associates, Inc.
Production House:	Pre-Press Company, Inc.
Printer:	Von Hoffmann Press, Inc.

Printed in the United States of America
4 02 01 00

For more information contact South-Western College Publishing, 5101 Madison Road, Cincinnati, Ohio, 45227. Or you can visit our Internet site at http://www.swcollege.com

For permission to use material from this text or product contact us by
• **telephone: 1-800-730-2214**
• **fax: 1-800-730-2215**
• **web: http://www.thomsonrights.com**

Library of Congress Cataloging-in-Publication Data
McEachern, William A.
　　Microeconomics: a contemporary introduction/William A. McEachern.—5th ed.
　　　　p. cm.
　　Includes bibliographical references and index.
　　1. Microeconomics. I. Title.
　　HB172.M393 1999   99-11641
　　338.5—dc21

ISBN: 0-538-88848-2

This book is printed on acid-free paper.

About the Author

William A. McEachern, Professor of Economics at the University of Connecticut, has taught principles of economics since 1973 and has offered teaching workshops since 1980. His research has appeared in a variety of journals, including *Economic Inquiry, National Tax Journal, Journal of Industrial Economics,* and *Public Choice.* He is Founding Editor of *The Teaching Economist,* a newsletter that focuses on teaching economics at the college level, and is Editor in Chief of *The Connecticut Economy: A University of Connecticut Quarterly Review.* Professor McEachern has advised federal, state, and local governments on policy matters and directed a bipartisan commission examining Connecticut's finances. Publications in which he has been quoted include the *New York Times, London Times, Wall Street Journal, Christian Science Monitor, USA Today,* and *Reader's Digest.* The University of Connecticut Alumni Association conferred on him its Faculty Award for Distinguished Public Service, and the Connecticut Academy of Arts and Sciences elected him to membership. He was born in Portsmouth, N.H., earned an undergraduate degree with honors from Holy Cross College and an M.A. and Ph.D. from the University of Virginia.

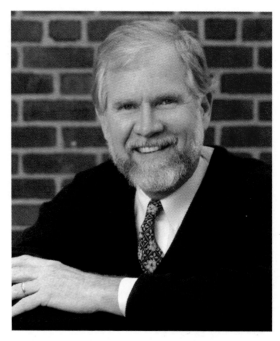

To Pat

Brief Contents

PART 1

INTRODUCTION TO ECONOMICS

1	The Art and Science of Economic Analysis	1
	Appendix: Understanding Graphs	18
2	Some Tools of Economic Analysis	25
3	The Market System	43
4	Economic Decision Makers: Households, Firms, Governments, and the Rest of the World	67

PART 2

INTRODUCTION TO THE MARKET SYSTEM

5	Elasticity of Demand and Supply	89
6	Consumer Choice and Demand	113
	Appendix: Indifference Curves and Utility Maximization	133
7	Production and Cost in the Firm	140
	Appendix: A Closer Look at Production and Costs	161

PART 3

MARKET STRUCTURE AND PRICING

8	Perfect Competition	166
9	Monopoly	196
10	Monopolistic Competition and Oligopoly	218

PART 4

RESOURCE MARKETS

11	Resource Markets	242
12	Labor Markets and Labor Unions	265
13	Capital, Interest, and Corporate Finance	288
14	Transaction Costs, Imperfect Information, and Market Behavior	308

PART 5

MARKET FAILURE AND PUBLIC POLICY

15	Economic Regulation and Antitrust Activity	328
16	Public Goods and Public Choice	351
17	Externalities and the Environment	371
18	Income Distribution and Poverty	395

PART 6

THE INTERNATIONAL SETTING

19	International Trade	417
20	International Finance	441
21	Developing and Transitional Economies	462

Contents

PART 1

INTRODUCTION TO ECONOMICS

CHAPTER 1
The Art and Science of Economic Analysis   1

The Economic Problem: Scarce Resources But Unlimited Wants   2
Resources 2   Goods and Services 3   Economic Decision Makers 4   Microeconomics and Macroeconomics 4

The Art of Economic Analysis   5
Rational Self-Interest 5   Economic Analysis Is Marginal Analysis 6   Choice Requires Time and Information 6   Normative Versus Positive 7

The Science of Economic Analysis   7
The Role of Theory 8   The Scientific Method 8   Economists Tell Stories 9   *Case Study: A Yen for Vending Machines* 9   Predicting Average Behavior 10   Some Pitfalls of Economic Analysis 11   If Economists Are So Smart, Whey Aren't They Rich? 11   *Case Study: College Major and Career Earnings* 12

Appendix: Understanding Graphs   18
Drawing Graphs 19   The Slopes of Straight Lines 20   The Slope, Units of Measurement, and Marginal Analysis 20   The Slopes of Curved Lines 21   Curve Shifts 22

CHAPTER 2
Some Tools of Economic Analysis   25

Choice and Opportunity Cost   26
Opportunity Cost 26   *Case Study: The Opportunity Cost of College* 26   Opportunity Cost Is Subjective 27   Sunk Cost and Choice 29

Specialization, Comparative Advantage, and Exchange   29
The Law of Comparative Advantage 29   Absolute and Comparative Advantage 30   Specialization and Exchange 31   Division of Labor and Gains from Specialization 32   *Case Study: Evidence of Specialization* 33

The Economy's Production Possibilities   33
Efficiency and the Production Possibilities Frontier 34   Inefficient and Unattainable Production 34   Shape of the Production Possibilities Frontier 35   What Can Shift the Production Possibilities Frontier? 36   What We Can Learn from the PPF? 38   Three Questions Each Economic System Must Answer 39

Economic Systems   39
Pure Market System 40   Pure Command System 41   Mixed and Transitional Economies 41   Economies Based on Custom or Religion 41

CHAPTER 3
The Market System   45

Demand   46
The Law of Demand 46   The Demand Schedule and Demand Curve 47

Changes in Demand   49
Changes in Consumer Income 49   Changes in the Prices of Related Goods 50   Changes in Consumer Expectations 51   Changes in the Number or Composition of Consumers 51   Changes in Consumer Tastes 51

Supply   52
The Supply Schedule and Supply Curve 52

Changes in Supply   54
Changes in Technology 54   Changes in the Prices of Relevant Resources 55   Changes in the Prices of Alternative Goods 55   Changes in Producer Expectations 55   Changes in the Number of Producers 55

Demand and Supply Create a Market   56
Markets 56   Market Equilibrium 56

Changes in Equilibrium Price and Quantity   58
Impact of Changes in Demand 58   Impact of Changes in Supply 59   Simultaneous Changes in Demand and Supply 60   *Case Study: The Market for Professional Basketball* 62

Disequilibrium Prices   63
Price Floors 63   Price Ceilings 64   *Case Study: Toys Are Serious Business* 65

CHAPTER 4
Economic Decision Makers: Households, Firms, Governments, and the Rest of the World 69

The Household 70
The Evolution of the Household 70   Households Maximize Utility 71   Households as Resource Suppliers 71   Households as Demanders of Goods and Services 72

The Firm 72
The Evolution of the Firm 72   Why Does Household Production Still Exist? 73   *Case Study: The Electronic Cottage* 74   Kinds of Firms 75   Nonprofit Institutions 76

The Government 76
The Role of Government 76   Government's Structure and Objectives 79   Size and Growth of U.S. Government 80   Sources of Government Revenue 80   Tax Principles and Tax Incidence 80

The Rest of the World 82
International Trade 82   Exchange Rates 83   Trade Restrictions 83   *Case Study: Wheel of Fortune* 83

The Circular Flow Model 84
Flows Between Households and Firms 84   Government-Related Flows 86   Flows To and From the Rest of the World 86

PART 2
INTRODUCTION TO THE MARKET SYSTEM

CHAPTER 5
Elasticity of Demand and Supply 89

Price Elasticity of Demand 90
Calculating Price Elasticity of Demand 91   Categories of Price Elasticity of Demand 92   Elasticity and Total Revenue 93   Price Elasticity and the Linear Demand Curve 93   Constant-Elasticity Demand 95

Determinants of the Price Elasticity of Demand 97
Availability of Substitutes 97   Proportion of the Consumer's Budget Spent on the Good 98   A Matter of Time 98   Elasticity Estimates 99   *Case Study: Deterring Young Smokers* 100

Price Elasticity of Supply 101
Categories of Supply Elasticity 102   Determinants of Supply Elasticity 104

Other Elasticity Measures 105
Income Elasticity of Demand 105   *Case Study: The Market for Food and "The Farm Problem"* 107   Cross-Price Elasticity of Demand 109

CHAPTER 6
Consumer Choice and Demand 113

Utility Analysis 114
Tastes and Preferences 114   The Law of Diminishing Marginal Utility 115

Measuring Utility 116
Units of Utility 116   Utility Maximization in a World Without Scarcity 117   Utility Maximization in a World of Scarcity 118   The Utility-Maximizing Conditions 119   *Case Study: Water, Water Everywhere* 120   The Law of Demand and Marginal Utility 121   Consumer Surplus 123   Market Demand and Consumer Surplus 125   *Case Study: The Marginal Value of Free Medical Care* 126

The Role of Time in Demand 127

Appendix: Indifference Curves and Utility Maximization 133
Consumer Preferences 133   The Budget Line 135   Consumer Equilibrium at the Tangency 136   Effects of a Change in Price 137   Income and Substitution Effects 137

CHAPTER 7
Production and Cost in the Firm 140

Cost and Profit 141
Explicit and Implicit Costs 141   Alternative Measures of Profit 142

Production in the Short Run 143
Fixed and Variable Resources 143   The Law of Diminishing Marginal Returns 144   The Total and Marginal Product Curves 145

Costs in the Short Run 146
Total Cost and Marginal Cost in the Short Run 147   Average Cost in the Short Run 149   The Relationship Between Marginal Cost and Average Cost 150   Summary of Short-Run Cost Curves 151

Costs in the Long Run 152
The Long-Run Average Cost Curve 152   Economies of Scale 154   Diseconomies of Scale 154   *Case Study: At the Movies* 155   Economies and Diseconomies of Scale at the Firm Level 156   *Case Study: Billions and Billions of Burgers* 156

Appendix: A Closer Look at Production and Costs 161
The Production Function and Efficiency 161   Isoquants 162   Isocost Lines 163   The Choice of Input Combinations 164   The Expansion Path 164

PART 3

MARKET STRUCTURE AND PRICING

CHAPTER 8
Perfect Competition   166

An Introduction to Perfect Competition   167
Perfectly Competitive Market Structure 167   Demand Under Perfect Competition 168

Short-Run Profit Maximization   169
Total Revenue Minus Total Cost 169   Marginal Cost Equals Marginal Revenue in Equilibrium 170   Economic Profit in the Short Run 172

Minimizing Short-Run Losses   173
Fixed Cost and Minimizing Losses 173   Marginal Cost Equals Marginal Revenue 173   Shutting Down in the Short Run 174   The Firm and Industry Short-Run Supply Curves 176   *Case Study: Auction Markets* 179

Perfect Competition in the Long Run   180
Zero Economic Profit in the Long Run 180   The Long-Run Adjustment to a Change in Demand 181

The Long-Run Industry Supply Curve   184
Constant-Cost Industries 184   Increasing-Cost Industries 185   Decreasing-Cost Industries 187

Perfect Competition and Efficiency   188
Productive Efficiency 188   Allocative Efficiency 188   What's So Perfect About Perfect Competition? 189   *Case Study: Experimental Economics* 190

CHAPTER 9
Monopoly   196

Barriers to Entry   197
Legal Restrictions 197   Economies of Scale 198   Control of Essential Resources 199   *Case Study: Are Diamonds Forever?* 199

Revenue for the Monopolist   200
Revenue Schedule 200   Revenue Curves 201

The Firm Costs and Profit Maximization   203
Profit Maximization 203   Short-Run Losses and the Shutdown Decision 206   Long-Run Profit Maximization 207

Monopoly and the Allocation of Resources   208
Price and Output under Perfect Competition 208   Price and Output Under Monopoly 209   Allocative and Distributive Effects 209

Problems Estimating the Welfare Cost of Monopoly   209
Why the Welfare Loss of Monopoly Might Be Lower 210   Why the Welfare Loss of Monopoly Might Be Higher 210   *Case Study: The Mail Monopoly* 211

Models of Price Discrimination   212
Conditions for Price Discrimination 212   Examples of Price Discrimination 212   A Model of Price Discrimination 213   Perfect Price Discrimination: The Monopolist's Dream 214

CHAPTER 10
Monopolistic Competition and Oligopoly   218

Monopolistic Competition   219
Characteristics of Monopolistic Competition 219   Product Differentiation 220   Short-Run Profit Maximization or Loss Minimization 220   Zero Economic Profit in the Long Run 222   *Case Study: Fast Forward* 224   Monopolistic Competition and Perfect Competition Compared 225

An Introduction to Oligopoly   226
Varieties of Oligopoly 226   *Case Study: The Unfriendly Skies* 227   Economies of Scale 228   High Cost of Entry 228

Models of Oligopoly   230
Collusion 230   Price Leadership 232   Game Theory 233   The Kinked Demand Curve 234   Summary of Oligopoly Models 237   Comparison of Oligopoly and Perfect Competition 237

PART 4

RESOURCE MARKETS

CHAPTER 11
Resource Markets   242

The Once Over   243
Resource Demand 243   Resource Supply 244

The Demand and Supply of Resources   244
The Market Demand for Resources 244   The Market Supply of Resources 246   Temporary and Permanent Resource Price Differences 246   Opportunity Cost and Economic Rent 248

A Closer Look at Resource Demand   251
The Firm's Demand for One Resource 251   Marginal Revenue Product 252   Marginal Resource Cost 254   Shifts in the Demand for Resources 255   *Case Study: The Derived Demand for Architects* 254   Optimal Use of More than One Resource 258   *Case Study: The McMinimum Wage* 259

Distribution of U.S. Resource Earnings   260

CHAPTER 12
Labor Markets and Labor Unions   265

Labor Supply   266
Labor Supply and Utility Maximization 266   Wages and Individual Labor Supply 269   Nonwage Determinants of Labor Supply 271   Market Supply of Labor 272   Why Wages Differ 272   *Case Study: Winner-Take-All Labor Markets* 275

Unions and Collective Bargaining 276
The Kinds of Unions 277   Collective Bargaining 277   The Strike 277

Union Wages and Employment   278
Inclusive, or Industrial, Unions 278   Exclusive, or Craft, Unions 280   Increasing Demand for Union Labor 281   Recent Trends in Union Membership   282   *Case Study: Hardball at Caterpillar* 284

CHAPTER 13
Capital, Interest, and Corporate Finance   288

The Role of Time in Consumption and Production   289
Production, Saving, and Time 289   Consumption, Saving, and Time 290   Optimal Investment 291   The Market for Loanable Funds 294   Why Interest Rates Differ 295   *Case Study: The Value of a Good Idea—Intellectual Property* 296

Present Value and Discounting   297
Present Value of Payment One Year Hence 297   Present Value for Payments in Later Years 298   Present Value of an Income Stream 299   Present Value of an Annuity 299   *Case Study: The Million-Dollar Lottery* 300

Corporate Finance   301
Corporate Stock and Retained Earnings 301   Corporate Bonds 302   Securities Exchanges 302

Corporate Ownership and Control   303
Managerial Behavior in Large Corporations 303   Constraints on Managerial Discretion 304

CHAPTER 14
Transaction Costs, Imperfect Information, and Market Behavior   308

Rationale for the Firm and the Scope of Its Operation   309
Firms Reduce Transaction Costs 309   The Bounds of the Firm 310   *Case Study: The Trend Toward Outsourcing* 314   Economies of Scope 315

Market Behavior with Imperfect Information   316
Optimal Search with Imperfect Information 316   The Winner's Curse 318

Asymmetric Information in Product Markets   319
Hidden Characteristics: Adverse Selection 319   Hidden Actions: Principal-Agent Problem 320

Asymmetric Information in Insurance Markets   321
Coping with Asymmetric Information 321   Asymmetric Information in Labor Markets 322   Adverse Selection Problems in Labor Markets 322   Signaling and Screening 323   *Case Study: The Reputation of a Big Mac* 324

PART 5

MARKET FAILURE AND PUBLIC POLICY

CHAPTER 15
Economic Regulation and Antitrust Activity   328

Business Behavior and Public Policy   329
Government Regulation of Business 329

Regulating Natural Monopolies   330
Unregulated Profit Maximization 330   Setting Price Equal to Marginal Cost 331   Subsidizing the Natural Monopolist 332   Setting Price Equal to Average Cost 332   The Regulatory Dilemma 332

Alternative Theories of Economic Regulation   333
Producers Have a Special Interest in Economic Regulation 333   *Case Study: Airline Regulation and Deregulation* 334   Antitrust Law and Enforcement 337   Origins of Antitrust Policy 337   Antitrust Law Enforcement 338   Per-se Illegality and the Rule of Reason 339   Mergers and Public Policy 339   Merger Movements 340

Competitive Trends in the U.S. Economy   342
Market Competition over Time 343   Recent Competitive Trends 344   Problems with Antitrust Legislation 345   *Case Study: Windows 98 Sold with Microsoft Browser* 346

CHAPTER 16
Public Goods and Public Choice   351

Optimal Provision of Public Goods   352
Private Goods, Public Goods, and In Between 352   Optimal Provision of Public Goods 354

Public Choice in a Representative Democracy   356
Median Voter Model 356   Goals of the Participants 357   Rational Ignorance 357   Distribution of Costs and Benefits 358   *Case Study: Farm Subsidies* 359   Rent Seeking 362   *Case Study: Campaign Finance Reform* 363   The Underground Economy   364

Bureaucracy and Representative Democracy   365
Ownership and Funding of Bureaus 365   Ownership and Organizational Behavior 367   Bureaucratic Objectives 367   Private Versus Public Production 367

CHAPTER 17
Externalities and the Environment   371

Externalities and the Common-Pool Problem   372
Renewable Resources 372   Resolving the Common Pool Problem 373

Optimal Level of Pollution   374
External Costs with Fixed Technology 375   External Costs with Variable Technology 376   *Case Study: Destruction of the Tropical Rain Forest* 379   The Coase Analysis of Externalities 380   A Market for Pollution Rights 382

Environmental Protection   384
Air Pollution 384   *Case Study: City in the Clouds* 385   Water Pollution 386   Hazardous Waste and the Superfund 387   Solid Waste: "Paper or Plastic?" 388

Positive Externalities   389

CHAPTER 18
Income Distribution and Poverty   395

The Distribution of Household Income   396
Income Distribution by Quintiles 396   A College Education Pays Relatively More 396   Problems with Distributional Benchmarks 398   Why Do Household Incomes Differ? 398

Poverty and the Poor   399
Official Poverty Level 399   Programs to Help the Poor 400

Who Are the Poor?   402
Poverty and Age 403   Poverty and Public Choice 403   The Feminization of Poverty 404   Poverty and Discrimination 406   Affirmative Action 407

Unintended Consequences of Income Assistance   408
Work Disincentives 408   Does Welfare Cause Dependency? 409

Welfare Reform   410
Recent Reforms 410   *Case Study: Is Welfare-to-Work Working?* 411   *Case Study: Oregon's Program of "Tough Love"* 413

PART 6

THE INTERNATIONAL SETTING

CHAPTER 19
International Trade   417

The Gains from Trade   418
A Profile of Imports and Exports 418   Production Possibilities Without Trade 419   Consumption Possibilities Based on Comparative Advantage 421   Reasons for International Specialization 423

Trade Restrictions   424
Consumer and Producer Surplus 424   Tariffs 425   Import Quotas 427   Quotas in Practice 429   Other Trade Restrictions 430   Freer Trade by Multilateral Agreement 430   *Case Study: The World Trade Organization* 431   Common Markets 432

Arguments for Trade Restrictions   433
National Defense Argument 433   Infant Industry Argument 433   Antidumping Argument 434   Jobs and Income Argument 434   Declining Industries Argument 435   Problems with Protection 436   *Case Study: Enforcing Trade Restrictions* 437

CHAPTER 20
International Finance   441

Balance of Payments   442
International Economic Transactions 442   Merchandise Trade Balance 443   Balance on Goods and Services 443   Unilateral Transfers 444   Capital Account 445   Statistical Discrepancy 445   Deficits and Surpluses 446

Foreign Exchange Rates and Markets   447
Foreign Exchange 447   Demand for Foreign Exchange 448   Supply of Foreign Exchange 449   Determining the Exchange Rate 450   Arbitrageurs and Speculators 451   Purchasing Power Parity 452   *Case Study: The Big Mac Index* 453   Flexible Exchange Rates 455   Fixed Exchange Rates 455

Development of the International Monetary System   455
The Bretton Woods Agreement 456   Demise of the Bretton Woods System 456   The Current System: Managed Float 457   *Case Study: The Asian Contagion* 458

CHAPTER 21
Developing and Transitional Economies   462

Worlds Apart   463
Developing and Industrial Economies 463   Health and Nutrition 464   High Birth Rates 467   Women in Developing Countries 468

Productivity: Key to Development   468
Low Labor Productivity 468   Technology and Education 469   Inefficient Use of Labor 469   Natural Resources 470   Financial Institutions 470   Capital Infrastructure 471   Entrepreneurial Ability 471   Government Monopolies 471   *Case Study: Crony Capitalism in Indonesia—All in the Family* 471

International Trade and Development   472
Import Substitution versus Export Promotion 473   Migration and the Brain Drain 474   Trade Liberalization and Special Interests 474

Foreign Aid and Economic Development   475
Foreign Aid 475   Does Foreign Aid Promote Economic Development? 475

Transitional Economies   476
Types of Economic Systems 476   Enterprises and Soft Budget Constraints 477   *Case Study: Ownership and Resource Use* 478

Markets and Institutions   479
Institutions and Economic Development 479   The Big Bang Versus Gradualism 480   Privatization 481   Transparent Finances 481   Institutional Requirements of Efficient Markets 481

Glossary   487

Index   497

Photo Credits   512

Preface

Economics has a short history but a long past. As a distinct discipline, economics has been studied for only a few hundred years, yet civilizations have confronted the economic problem of scarce resources but unlimited wants for millennia. Economics, the discipline, may be centuries old, but it is new every day as fresh evidence supports or reshapes economic theory. In *Microeconomics: A Contemporary Introduction*, I draw upon more than a quarter century of teaching experience to convey the vitality, timeliness, and evolving nature of economics.

LEADING BY EXAMPLE

Remember the last time you were in unknown parts and had to ask for directions? Along with the directions came the standard comment "You can't miss it!" So how come you missed it? Because the "landmark" that was obvious to the neighborhood resident who gave the directions might as well have been invisible to you, a stranger. Writing a principles text is much like giving directions. The author must be familiar with the material, but familiarity can also dull one's perceptions, making it difficult to see things through the fresh eyes of new students. Some authors try to compensate by telling all they know, in the process overwhelming students with so much detail that the central point gets lost. Other authors take a minimalist approach by offering little of what students may already know intuitively, and instead talking abstractly about good x and good y, units of labor and units of capital, or the proverbial widget. This turns economics into a foreign language.

Good directions rely on landmarks familiar to us all—a stoplight, a fork in the road, a white picket fence. Likewise, a good textbook builds bridges from the familiar to the new. How? In essence, I try to *lead by example*—I provide examples that draw on the students' common experience. I try to create graphic pictures that need little explanation, thereby eliciting from the reader that light of recognition, that "Aha!" Examples should be self-explanatory; they should convey the point quickly and directly. Having to explain an example is like having to explain a joke—the point gets lost. Throughout, I provide just enough intuitive information and institutional detail to get the point across without overwhelming the student. My emphasis is on economic ideas, not economic jargon.

Students arrive the first day of class with eighteen or more years of experience with economic choices, economic institutions, and economic events. Each student grew up in a household-the central economic institution. As consumers, students are familiar with fast-food restaurants, movie theaters, car dealerships, and dozens of stores at the mall. Most students have been resource suppliers—more than half held jobs while in high school. Students also have experience with government—they know about taxes, drivers' licenses, speed limits, and public education. And, from imported cars to the World Wide Web, students are becoming more familiar with the rest of the world.

Thus, students have abundant experience with the stuff of economics. They may not recognize the economic content of that experience, but they possess it nonetheless. Yet many principles authors neglect this rich lode of experience and, instead, try to create for the student a new world of economics. Such an approach fails to make the connection between economics and what Alfred Marshall called "the ordinary business of life."

Since instructors can cover only a fraction of the textbook material in class, principles texts should, to the extent possible, be self-explanatory, thereby providing instructors with greater flexibility to emphasize topics of special interest. My approach is to start where students are, not where we would like them to be. For example, to explain the division of labor, rather than refer to Adam Smith's pin factory, I call attention to the division of labor at McDonald's. To explain resource substitution, rather than referring to abstract units of labor and capital, I discuss a specific example, such as labor-capital combinations for washing a car—ranging from a drive-through car wash (much capital and little labor) to a Saturday-morning-send-the-band-to-Disney-World charity car wash (little capital and much labor). This edition is loaded with similar down-to-earth examples.

CLARITY BY DESIGN

In many principles textbooks, chapters are interrupted by boxed material, parenthetical explanations, qualifying footnotes, and other distractions that disrupt the flow of the material. Students remain uncertain about when or if such segregated elements should be read. In contrast, this book has a natural flow. Each chapter opens with a few questions aimed at stimulating interest, then tells a compelling story, using logical sections and subsections. Qualifying footnotes are used sparingly, and parenthetical explanations are used hardly at all. Moreover, case studies are not boxed off but appear in the natural sequence of the chapter. Students can thus read each chapter smoothly from the opening questions to the conclusion and summary. I also employ a "just-in-time" approach to introduce material just as it is needed to develop an argument. Overall, the Fifth Edition is a bit leaner, economic jargon has been reduced, and many tables have been converted to charts and graphs.

In most textbooks, the page design—the layout of the page and the use of color—is an afterthought, conceived without regard to how students learn. No element in the design of this book is wasted, and all elements work together for the maximum pedagogical value.

Page Design. By design, all elements of each chapter have been carefully integrated. Every effort has been made to present students with an open, readable page design. The size of the typeface, the length of the text line, and the amount of "white space" were all chosen to make learning easier. Graphs are uncluttered and are accompanied by captions explaining the key features. These features are all optimal for students encountering college textbooks for the first time.

Use of Color. Color is used systematically within graphs, charts, and tables to ensure that students quickly and easily see what's going on. Throughout the book, demand curves are blue and supply curves are red. In comparative statics examples, the curves determining the final equilibrium point are lighter than the initial curves. Color shading distinguishes key features of many graphs, such as measures of economic profit or loss, tax incidence, consumer and producer surplus, and the welfare effects of tariffs and quotas. In short, color is more than mere face entertainment—it is employed consistently and with forethought to help students learn.

THE FIFTH EDITION

I build on the success of earlier editions to make the material even more student-friendly through concrete examples, more questions along the way, and additional summaries as each chapter unfolds. And by making the material both more personal and more natural, I try to draw students into a collaborative discussion. I have also built on the success of the Fourth Edition's Internet support to make the use of technology even more innovative and helpful. This edition features an even tighter integration of text and technology.

Introductory Chapters Basic material on macroeconomics and microeconomics is covered in the first four chapters. Limiting the introductory material to four chapters saves precious class time.

Microeconomics Core My approach to microeconomics underscores the role of time and information in production and consumption. For example, both time and information are scarce resources and, as such, are valued by consumers and producers. The microeconomic presentation also reflects the growing interest in the economic institutions that underpin impersonal market activity. More generally, I try to convey the intuition that most microeconomic principles operate like gravity: Market forces work whether or not individual economic actors understand them.

At every opportunity, I turn the abstract into the concrete. For example, rather than talking in terms of an abstract monopolist, the monopoly chapter focuses throughout on the De Beers diamond monopoly. New material in this edition includes discussions of antitrust moves against Microsoft, the economics of tobacco legislation, winner-take-all labor markets, intellectual property, and welfare reform. To streamline the presentation of resource markets, I combine material on labor markets and on labor unions into a single chapter. And the chapter that had covered public choice now includes much more on public goods.

International Chapters This edition reflects the growing impact of the world economy on U.S. economic welfare. International issues are introduced early and discussed often. For example, the rest of the world is introduced in Chapter 1 and comparative advantage and the production possibilities frontier are each discussed from a global perspective in Chapter 2. International coverage is woven into the text. For example, students gain a better perspective about such topics as unionization trends, antitrust laws, pollution, environmental laws, tax rates, and the distribution of income if the U.S. experience is compared with that of other countries around the world.

New international material includes discussions of the euro, "crony capitalism," declining fertility rates around the world, and the painful progress of transitional economies. Although international references are scattered throughout the book, including a number of case studies, the final three chapters focus exclusively on international trade, international finance, and developing and transitional economies, respectively.

Case Studies. Some books use case studies as boxed-off asides to cover material that otherwise doesn't quite fit. I use case studies as real-world applications that reinforce ideas in the chapter and demonstrate the relevance of economic theory. My case studies are different enough to offer variety in the presentation yet are integrated enough into the flow of the chapter to let students know they should be read. This edition distinguishes among four categories of case studies: (1) "The World of Business" offers students a feel for the range of choices confronted by business decision makers today; (2) "The Information Economy" underscores the critical role of information in the new economy, from the computer revolution to the value of intellectual property; (3) "Other Times, Other Places" involves applications either from economic history or from other economies around the world; and (4) "Public Policy" cases highlight the trade-offs in the public sector. All case studies are supported by references and relevant Web addresses and are tied to further analysis on the Web with questions, navigation tips, and other information that can be accessed through the McEachern Interactive Study Center at http://mceachern.swcollege.com.

Net Bookmarks Each chapter includes a Net Bookmark. These margin notes identify interesting Web sites that illustrate real-world examples of chapter topics, giving students the opportunity to explore some of those sites and build their economic research skills. And they are extended on the Web with additional information on resources as well as step-by-step navigation hints. They can be accessed through the McEachern Interactive Study Center at http://mceachern.swcollege.com.

The *Wall Street Journal* Edition The Fifth Edition makes it easy to bring the real world into the classroom. This *Wall Street Journal* Edition provides numerous opportunities to relate economic concepts to late-breaking news stories. A special Preface guides students in their use of the *Wall Street Journal*. And there is a question at the end of each chapter that asks students to read and analyze information from the *Wall Street Journal*.

Experiential Exercises New to this edition are end-of-chapter questions that encourage students to develop their research and critical thinking skills. These Experiential Exercises ask students to apply what they have learned to real-world, hands-on economic analysis. Most of these exercises involve the Internet, the *Wall Street Journal*, or other media resources.

The Internet

As mentioned already, we devoted careful attention to capitalizing on the vast array of economic resources and alternative learning technologies the Internet can deliver. I gave much thought to two basic questions: What can this technology do that a textbook cannot do? And how can Web-based enhancements be employed to bring the greatest value to teaching and learning?

It's clear that students learn more when they are involved and engaged. The Internet provides a way to heighten student involvement while keeping the introductory economics course as current as today's news. With these ideas in mind, we have undertaken a major upgrading of our Web site to more tightly integrate the book and the Internet. We have done this in a way that exploits the comparative advantage of each medium, and in a structure that optimizes both teaching and learning experiences.

The McEachern Interactive Study Center (http://mceachern.swcollege. com) Through McEachern Interactive, students benefit from the best textual presentation as well as the most innovative on-line experience. This edition offers a structured approach to the Internet, providing a comprehensive chapter-by-chapter on-line study guide that includes graphical support, interactive quizzes, a glossary, updated and extended applications from the text, and numerous other features. Some highlights include:

> **Over 100 Examples and Exercises** The Internet-enhanced text features such as Net Bookmarks, Case Studies, and end-of-chapter Experiential Exercises are tied to the Study Center where students will find clear links to relevant Web sites. These applications are interesting and easy-to-use. All of the in-text features that are extended on the Web are indicated by a special McEachern Interactive icon. (Shown at left).
>
> **On-Line Graphing Tutorials** Key graphs from the text—also indicated by the McEachern Interactive icon—are brought to life as students explore interactive graphing tutorials that feature helpful audio explanations.
>
> **Interactive Quizzes** These multiple-choice on-line quizzes provide a perfect review resource and solid exam preparation. They feature detailed feedback for right and wrong answers as well as the option of e-mailing quiz results to the instructor.

It is important to note that none of these features requires detailed knowledge of the Internet. Nor are they required for a successful classroom experience if an instructor wants to assign only the materials contained within the text. The on-line enhancements simply offer optional paths for further study and exploration—new ways for students to employ their individual learning styles and new ways for instructors to experiment with technology and a wider range of assignment materials.

THE SUPPORT PACKAGE

The teaching and learning support package that accompanies *Economics: A Contemporary Introduction* provides instructors and students with focused, accurate, and innovative supplements to the textbook.

Student Supplements

Study Guide The *Study Guide* was written by John Lunn of Hope College. Each chapter of the *Study Guide* corresponds to a chapter in the text and offers:

(1) an introduction; (2) a chapter outline, with definitions of all terms; (3) a discussion of the chapter's main points; (4) a *lagniappe*, or bonus, which supplements material in the chapter and includes a "Question to Think About"; (5) a list of key terms; (6) a variety of true-false, multiple-choice, and discussion questions; and (7) answers to all these questions. Visit the McEachern Interactive Study Center at http://mceachern.swcollege.com. for more details.

Graphing Primer One of the most difficult challenges for many introductory economics students is working with graphs. The *Graphing Primer* is a print supplement that helps students create, interpret, and understand graphs.

McEachern Interactive CD-ROM This CD-ROM provides a powerful collection of electronic study tools:

> **PowerPoint Lecture Review Slides** Students can visually review key concepts and exhibits from each chapter, and print the slides to use as note-taking guides during class lectures.

> **South-Western Economics Tutorial Software** James T. Doak has developed tutorial software compatible with Microsoft Windows. It is organized around key topics, and correlated to relevant text chapters. Each topic provides a series of interactive graphing exercises that help students test their understanding of key concepts. Students can also track and record their progress.

> **McEachern Interactive Graphing Tutorials** The graphing tutorials found at the McEachern Study Center are also included on this CD-ROM.

Economics Guide **Tutorial Software** Robert Brooker, of Gannon University, has developed this economics tutorial software, compatible with Microsoft Windows. Through the use of a sophisticated testing engine, it presents students with an unlimited supply of quizzes over the topics covered in each chapter. Students are able to track and record their progress throughout the course. *Economics Guide* software is perfect for review or for test preparation

Microeconomics Alive! CD-ROM—Interactive Study Guide The *Microeconomics Alive!* CD-ROM, created by Willie Belton, Richard Cebula, and John McLeod, Jr. of the Georgia Institute of Technology, is compatible with Microsoft Windows and with the Apple Macintosh. This multimedia CD-ROM combines interactive lessons, graphing tools, and simulations to bring microeconomic concepts to life. To learn more about these CDs, visit the *Economics Alive!* Web site at http://econalive.swcollege.com.

The McEachern Web Site The McEachern Web Site at http://mceachern. swcollege.com. offers a variety of learning tools. In addition to the helpful tools available at the McEachern Interactive Study Center, students can also find summaries of current news stories, review current and historical economic data, keep up-to-date through current examples and policy applications, access information about saleable supplements, correspond with me, and take advantage of many other benefits.

Instructor Supplements

Instructor's Manual The *Instructor's Manual*, revised by Dorothy Siden of Salem State College, is keyed to the text. For each text chapter, it includes (1) a detailed lecture outline and brief overview; (2) a summary of main points; (3) pedagogical tips that expand on points raised in the chapter; and (4) suggested answers to all end-of-chapter questions and problems. New to this edition is a set of classroom economic experiments developed by Michael Haupert of the University of Wisconsin, La Crosse and Noelwah Netusil of Reed College. Each experiment comes with an abstract, an overview, a clear set of instructions for running the experiment, and forms for recording the results.

Teaching Assistance Manual I have revised my *Teaching Assistance Manual* to provides additional support beyond the Instructor's Manual. It is especially useful to new instructors, graduate assistants, and teachers interested in generating more class discussion. This manual offers: (1) overviews and outlines of each chapter; (2) chapter objectives and quiz material; (3) material for class discussion; (4) topics warranting special attention; (5) supplementary examples; and (6) "What if?" discussion questions. Appendices provide guidance on (a) presenting material; (b) generating and sustaining class discussion; (c) preparing, administering, and grading quizzes; and (d) coping with the special problems confronting foreign graduate assistants.

Test Bank Thoroughly revised for currency and accuracy, the *Microeconomics Test Bank* contains over 4,200 questions in multiple-choice and true-false formats. All multiple choice questions have five possible responses, and each is rated by degree of difficulty. For this edition, Nathan Eric Hampton of St. Cloud State University has thoroughly reworked the *Test Bank* and has grouped all questions according to chapter subheadings. This makes it easy to find just the questions you want and to make sure your questions are representative of material you teach in class.

Testing Tools—Computerized Testing Software *Testing Tools* is an easy-to-use test creation software package that is available in versions compatible with Microsoft Windows and with the Apple Macintosh. It contains all of the questions in the printed Test Banks. Instructors can add or edit questions, instructions, and answers, and select questions by previewing them on the screen and then choosing them by number, or at random. Instructors can also create and administer quizzes on-line, either over the Internet, through a local area network (LAN), or through a wide area network (WAN).

Microsoft PowerPoint Lecture Slides Tables and graphs from the text, as well as additional instructional materials, are available as PowerPoint slides to enhance lectures and help integrate technology into the classroom.

Transparency Acetates Most of the tables and graphs from this text are reproduced as full-color transparency acetates.

CNN Economics Video The CNN Economics Video provides a variety of brief video clips, taken from Cable News Network (CNN) programs, that illustrate various aspects of economics.

On-line Course Creation and Delivery Systems South-Western College Publishing now makes taking your course to the Web as easy as typing. Visit ITP Electronic Learning at http://www.itped.com to learn about simple-to-use options for creating an on-line course or a Web site for your traditional course.

The Teaching Economist For nearly a decade, I have edited *The Teaching Economist*, a newsletter aimed at making teaching more interesting and more fun. The newsletter discusses imaginative ways to present topics—for example, how to "sensationalize" economic concepts, useful resources on the Internet, economic applications from science fiction, and more generally, ways to teach just for the fun of it. A regular feature of *The Teaching Economist*, "The Grapevine," offers teaching ideas suggested by colleagues from across the country. The latest issue—and back issues—of *The Teaching Economist* are available on-line at http:// mceachern.swcollege.com.

ACKNOWLEDGEMENTS

Many people contributed to this book's development. I gratefully acknowledge the insightful comments of those who have reviewed chapters for the Fifth Edition. Their suggestions made me think more and made the book better.

Donna Anderson	University of Wisconsin, LaCrosse
Mohsen Bahmani	University of Wisconsin, Milwaukee
Jay Bhattacharya	Okaloosa Walton Community College
Doug Conway	Mesa Community College
Thomas Creahan	Morehead State University
Ron Elkins	Central Washington University
Roger Frantz	San Diego State University
J.P. Gilbert	MiraCosta College
Robert Gordon	San Diego State University
Fred Graham	American University
Nathan Eric Hampton	St. Cloud State University
Mehdi Haririan	Bloomsburg University
Julia Heath	University of Memphis
James Henderson	Baylor University
Bryce Kanago	Miami University
Robert Kleinhenz	California State University, Fullerton
Faik Koray	Louisiana State University
Marie Kratochvil	Nassau Community College
Jim Lee	Ft. Hays State University
Ken Long	New River Community College
Michael Magura	University of Toledo
Richard Martin	Agnes Scott College
KimMarie McGoldrick	University of Richmond
Mark McNeil	Irvine Valley College
Art Meyer	Lincoln Land Community College
Carrie Meyer	George Mason University
Bruce Mills	Troy State University
Shannon Mitchell	Virginia Commonwealth University

Maureen O'Brien	University of Minnesota, Duluth
Jaishankar Raman	Valparaiso University
Mitch Redlo	Monroe Community College
Simran Sahi	University of Minnesota, Twin Cities
George Santopietro	Radford University
Carol Scotese	Virginia Commonwealth University
Alden Shiers	California Polytechnic State University
Frederica Shockley	California State University, Chico
Gerald Simons	Grand Valley State University
Mark Stegeman	Virginia Polytechnic Institute
John Tribble	Russell Sage College
Robert Whaples	Wake Forest University
Mark Wheeler	Western Michigan University
Michael White	St. Cloud State University
Patricia Wyatt	Bossier Parish Community College

To practice what I preach, I relied on the division of labor based on comparative advantage to help put together the most complete teaching package on the market today. John Lunn of Hope College authored the *Study Guide*, which has been quite popular. Dorothy Siden of Salem State College authored the *Instructor's Manual*. And Nathan Eric Hampton of St. Cloud State University undertook a major reworking of the *Test Bank*. I thank them for their imagination and discipline.

The talented staff at South-Western College Publishing provided invaluable editorial, administrative, and sales support. I would especially like to single out the guidance of Dennis Hanseman, Development Editor and Ph.D. in economics, who helped me every step of the way, from the reviews of the previous edition to final proof pages. I also appreciate very much the excellent design work of Joe Devine, the superlative project coordination by Senior Production Editor Sharon Smith, the photography management of Cary Benbow, and the production assistance of Mary Ansaldo of Pre-Press Company, the production house for this edition. Kurt Gerdenich and Vicky True have been particularly helpful in developing the McEachern Interactive Study Center.

In addition I am most grateful to Bob Lynch, President of South-Western, Jack Calhoun, Publishing Team Director, Keri Witman, Acquisitions Editor, and especially Lisa Lysne, the Marketing Manager who knows the book inside and out. As good as the book is, all our efforts would be wasted unless students use it. To that end, I greatly appreciate South-Western's dedicated service and sales force, who have contributed in a substantial way to the success of previous editions.

Finally, I owe an abiding debt to my wife, Pat, who provided abundant encouragement and support along the way.

William A. McEachern

PREVIOUS EDITION REVIEWERS

Polly Reynolds Allen	University of Connecticut
Ted Amato	University of North Carolina, Charlotte
Richard Anderson	Texas A&M University
James Aylesworth	Lakeland Community College
Dale Bails	Christian Brothers College
Andy Barnett	Auburn University
Klaus Becker	Texas Tech University
David Brasfield	Murray State University
Jurgen Brauer	Augusta College
Gardner Brown, Jr.	University of Washington
Judy Butler	Baylor University
Charles Callahan III	SUNY College at Brockport
Giorgio Canarella	California State University, Los Angeles
Larry Clarke	Brookhaven College
Rebecca Cline	Middle Georgia College
Stephen Cobb	Xavier University
James P. Cover	University of Alabama
James Cox	DeKalb College
Jerry Crawford	Arkansas State University
Joseph Daniels	Marquette University
Elynor Davis	Georgia Southern University
Susan Davis	SUNY College at Buffalo
A. Edward Day	University of Central Florida
David Dean	University of Richmond
Janet Deans	Chestnut Hill College
David Denslow	University of Florida
John Edgren	Eastern Michigan University
Donald Elliott, Jr.	Southern Illinois University
G. Rod Erfani	Transylvania University
Gisela Meyer Escoe	University of Cincinnati
Mark Evans	California State University, Bakersfield
Eleanor Fapohunda	SUNY College at Farmingdale
Mohsen Fardmanesh	Temple University
Paul Farnham	Georgia State University
Rudy Fichtenbaum	Wright State University
T. Windsor Fields	James Madison University
Rodney Fort	Washington State University
Gary Galles	Pepperdine University
Edward Gamber	Lafayette College
Adam Gifford	California State University, Northridge
Robert Gillette	University of Kentucky
Art Goldsmith	Washington and Lee University
Philip Graves	University of Colorado, Boulder
Daniel Gropper	Auburn University
Simon Hakim	Temple University

Robert Halvorsen	University of Washington
William Hart	Miami University
Baban Hasnat	SUNY College at Brockport
James Hill	Central Michigan University
Jane Smith Himarios	University of Texas, Arlington
Dennis Hoffman	Arizona State University
Bruce Horning	Fordham University
Calvin Hoy	County College of Morris
Beth Ingram	University of Iowa
Joyce Jacobsen	Wesleyan University
Nancy Jianakoplos	Colorado State University
Nake Kamrany	University of Southern California
John Kane	SUNY College at Oswego
David Kennett	Vassar College
Joseph Kotaska	Monroe Community College
Joseph Lammert	Raymond Walters College
Dennis Leyden	University of North Carolina, Greensboro
C. Richard Long	Georgia State University
Thomas Maloy	Muskegon Community College
Gabriel Manrique	Winona State University
Robert Margo	Vanderbilt University
Wolfgang Mayer	University of Cincinnati
John McDowell	Arizona State University
James McLain	University of New Orleans
Martin Milkman	Murray State University
Milton Mitchell	University of Wisconsin, Oshkosh
Kathryn Nantz	Fairfield University
Reza Ramazani	St. Michael's University
Carol Rankin	Xavier University
Robert Rossana	Wayne State University
Mark Rush	University of Florida
Richard Saba	Auburn University
Rexford Santerre	Bentley College
Ted Scheinman	Mt. Hood Community College
Peter Schwartz	University of North Carolina, Charlotte
Roger Sherman	University of Virginia
William Shughart II	University of Mississippi
Calvin Siebert	University of Iowa
Phillip Smith	DeKalb College
V. Kerry Smith	Duke University
David Spencer	Brigham Young University
Jane Speyrer	University of New Orleans
Houston Stokes	University of Illinois, Chicago
Robert Stonebreaker	Indiana University of Pennsylvania
William Swift	Pace University
Lee J. Van Scyoc	University of Wisconsin, Oshkosh
Percy Vera	Sinclair Community College

Jin Wang   University of Wisconsin, Stevens Point
Gregory Wassall   Northeastern University
William Weber   Eastern Illinois University
David Weinberg   Xavier University
Donald Wells   University of Arizona
Richard Winkelman   Arizona State University
Kenneth Woodward   Saddleback College
Peter Wyman   Spokane Falls Community College
Mesghena Yasin   Morehead State University
Edward Young   University of Wisconsin, Eau Claire
William Zeis   Bucks Community College

THE WALL STREET JOURNAL.

DOW JONES

Educational Edition

What's News—

Business and Finance

World-Wide

How to Read Between the Lines

An Introduction to The Wall Street Journal

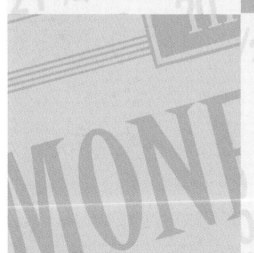

An invitation to learn more

about the world's business daily.

An opportunity to go behind

the scenes at America's most

important business publication.

THE WALL STREET JOURNAL.

DOWJONES

Educational Edition

The First Section

Columns 1 and 6: The Lead Stories

Column Six always provides the day's top business story about a company, industry or event, while Column One ranges further afield: It may take on politics, international affairs or social issues as well as business and finance.

Columns 2 and 3: What's News

"World-Wide" is a concise digest of the latest news developments from around the globe, while "Business and Finance" summarizes the top stories from those spheres.

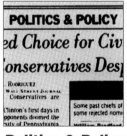

Column 4: Performance Graph

Each issue contains a different graph of a major economic indicator to help make the complex more easy to understand.

Column 4: The A-Hed

Ranging from silly to serious, quirky to downright bizarre, the A-Hed gives free rein to our reporters' imagination.

MONDAY:
The Outlook

Emphasizing markets and investing, reporters from every bureau contribute perspective and points of view on policy, trends and developments around the world.

Work Week

A Special News Report About Life On the Job — and Trends Taking Shape There

WORKPLACE ACCIDENTS can mean criminal charges for executives.
Prosecutors blame corporate managers for poor workplace safety. In Boston, Thomas E. Bowley, chief executive of Tewksbury Industries Inc., is indicted on manslaughter charges after two company workers were killed in separate accidents.

TUESDAY:
Work Week

Taking the broadest definition of work as its beat, this column charts the changing world of the office, factory and service sector.

ECONOMY

Economy

The Journal's economic news, on page A2, provides clear, straightforward stories about the latest news of inflation, unemployment, government announcements, Federal Reserve policy, economic forecasts, durable-goods prices and more. These complicated matters become understandable and meaningful as you realize how this news affects your life and your livelihood.

POLITICS & POLICY

Politics & Policy

The back page of our first section is home to a collection of wide-ranging articles on politics at every level, from local to state to federal. On any day, you might find exclusive Journal polls, in-depth personal profiles, innovative examples of municipal governance and informed commentary on administration initiatives.

Letters to the

The Editorial Pages

Daily, we publish the best of over 2,000 letters received weekly from prominent leaders in every field. Whether amplifying a comment, challenging an opinion, or debating with influential readers, they provide some lively writing. This creates the single most influential editorial page in the nation. Love it or hate it — but disregard it only at your peril.

The Marketplace

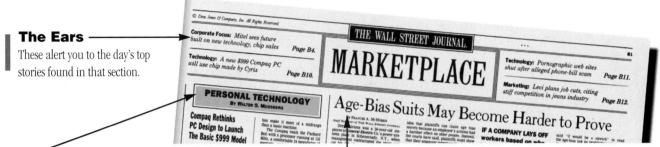

The Ears
These alert you to the day's top stories found in that section.

The Rotating Column
Here seasoned Journal writers, who are experts in their fields, inject personal opinion and informed judgements into their news stories.

MONDAY: **Health Journal**
TUESDAY: **Managing Your Career**
WEDNESDAY: **Work & Family, Business & Race**
THURSDAY: **Personal Technology**
FRIDAY: **The Front Lines**

The Top News
News with an individual perspective, you might find front-page articles about autos, travel, advertising, healthcare, pharmaceuticals, technology, law, marketing and the media.

Inside The Marketplace

Marketing & Media
Fifteen reporters and editors, focusing on the big stories first, cover all the news from the media, advertising and entertainment industries.

Net Interest/ Watching the Web
"Net Interest", a monthly column, takes a consumer's perspective to the Internet's promises, failures and personalities. "Watching the Web" is a directory of reviews that focus on must-visit or must-avoid sites.

Enterprise
Here you'll find news on trends, issues and legislation that affects small business, and illuminating news stories on why some small companies succeed while others fail.

Index to Business
Is there a company in which you're particularly interested? The Index, on page B2, lets you know at a glance if we've covered it in today's paper.

Inside The Marketplace (Continued)

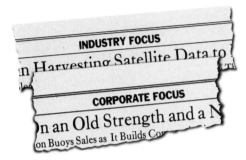

Industry/Corporate Focus

Every day, we take a detailed look at a specific corporation — its competitive situation, corporate strategy, problems and successes — or an entire industry. In the latter case, our reporters covering the beat put together an insightful overview of an industry's current situation and future prospects.

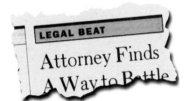

Law

Here's legal news from a unique perspective: In our daily "Legal Beat" column and feature articles, we write about the law as a service that most people need, sooner or later. And we do so with uncommon expertise, as four of our seven reporters on the beat are lawyers themselves.

Technology

Our technology coverage may be anchored on a Marketplace page — in columns such as "In the Lab", "Technology & Medicine" and "Technology & Environment" — but it is also found all throughout the publication, from the front page to the last.

Who's News

Make it big in business, and you might find your name and picture in this column, where we chart the comings and goings of the upper reaches of corporate management. If you're thinking of working for a company, or investing in it, you might do well to keep your eye here, to find out who's running it.

Digest of Earnings Report

Public corporations can satisfy their legal obligation to announce quarterly and annual figures by publishing them in the Journal. (Of course, we have to be satisfied of their veracity before we'll print them.) This extensive compilation, which can feature over 200 companies in a single issue, is a must for investors.

Money & Investing: All the Numbers

Expert analysis, straight-forward explanations and comprehensive statistics create an easy-to-navigate guide to the stock market and other markets that affect both America's business and your finances.

Markets Diary

A prominent display of Yesterday's results in the stock, bond and commodities markets as well as the previous week's activity, interest rates, and the performance of the U.S. dollar relative to other major currencies.

The Top News

Here you'll find feature stories that carry the hottest news from the world of finance.

Pan Markets

Here's where you'll find all of yesterday's activity from the stock, bond and dollar markets are brought together in a concise and comprehensive overview of what happened and what it means.

Money & Investing Columns

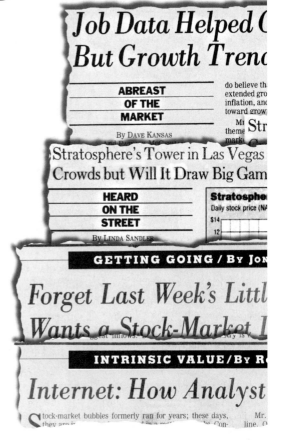

Abreast of the Market/Small Stock Focus

Look to these columns first, for the authoritative word that explains market activity. While "Abreast" trains its sights on large-capitalization stocks, "Small Stock" does the same for small and medium-cap issues. Together, they constitute the most respected daily analysis of the stock market in print.

Heard on the Street

Every day, "Heard" brings our readers the first word on subjects and stocks that Wall Street denizens are talking about among themselves.

Getting Going

Whether you've got $3,000 to invest or $3 million, "Getting Going" gets you started in the right direction. Because Jonathon Clements has a rare ability to explain the first principles of investing in simple terms. His column every Tuesday will help you learn the most important criteria by which to evaluate what kind of fund is right for you.

Intrinsic Value

Once you've got some trades under your belt, take a look at Roger Lowenstein's "Intrinsic Value", which appears on Fridays. It's a sophisticated analysis of the fundamentals underlying the numbers, written with obvious expertise and marked by a strong ethical underpinning.

Money & Investing Columns (Continued)

Annuities Watch

As more people take responsibility for their own retirement planning, annuities have rapidly grown in popularity. In response, the Journal introduced this column and an accompanying page of variable-annuity statistics.

Fund Track

The mutual fund, an essential financial instrument, is the centerpiece of our news coverage and analysis in "Fund Track." This major daily column's primary purpose is to break news on the industry, but it also takes an advisory tone on matters of personal finance.

Your Money Matters

"Your Money Matters" sticks to the basics of money management and, through the course of a year, covers virtually everything of importance to the individual, from buying a home to financing an education, from evaluating stocks to planning an estate.

World Markets

Sara Webb gained years of expertise covering global equities markets for The Asian Wall Street Journal and the Wall Street Journal/Europe. Now, American readers get the benefit of her insight.

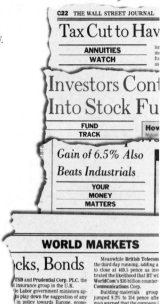

Money & Investing Statistics

The Journal's financial statistics are so comprehensive and extensive, it would take pages to introduce you to them in detail. Suffice it to say this: Whatever you need to know about the markets, either as an investment professional or individual investor, you'll find here. In most cases, you'll also find accompanying news columns that provide daily context and informed perspective on the movements of the particular market. Here's a brief look at some of the broad categories of data you'll find in "Money & Investing" every business day.

Stock Prices & the Stock Market

The Stock Market

The New York Stock Exchange, American Stock Exchange and Nasdaq National Market Issues lead the stock tables, but the Journal also includes regional and foreign stock exchange listings.

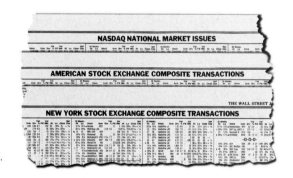

Stock Market Data Bank

Many analysts look at several indexes, not just the DJIA, and a variety of them are published at the top of the Stock Market Data Bank, which appears daily on page C2. Besides the Dow Jones Averages, there are the New York Stock Exchange indexes of all stocks traded on the exchange, and the NYSE indexes of major sectors. Indexes compiled by Standard & Poor's Corp. are market-weighted; the 500-stock index is often used as a benchmark of overall New York Stock Exchange performance. It is made up of 400 industrial, 20 transportation, 40 utility and 40 financial stocks. For each index, the Data Bank shows the latest day's closing level and changes from the previous day, a year earlier and the end of the previous year, both in absolute terms and as a percentage of the previous figure. The high and low for the latest 12 months also are shown. You can also find Nasdaq, American Stock Exchange, the 1,700-stock Value Line and the 5,000-stock Wilshire indexes.

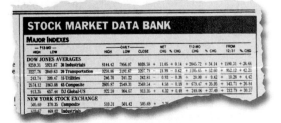

Understanding the Stock Market Tables

52 Week Hi and Lo:
Highest and lowest prices paid for the stock over the past 52 weeks, excluding the latest day's trading

Stock Symbol:
Used when looking up the stock on online systems

Dividend:
Stock's annual cash dividend, if any, based on the rate of the last quarterly payout to shareholders

Vol 100s:
Number of shares traded in each stock in the previous day, expressed in hundreds. Thus 57 means 5,700 shares were traded. Transactions generally take place in units of 100 shares. A "z" footnote before the volume figure means it represents the total shares traded; z57 means 57 shares were traded, not 5,700. Stocks with unusually high volume compared with that stock's average trading volume are underlined.

Stock Name

52 Weeks		Stock	Sym	Div	Yld %	PE	Vol 100s	Hi	Lo	Close	Net Chg
Hi	Lo										
42¾	28⅜	ColesMyer	CM	1.39e	3.6	↑...	38	39⅛	39¹⁄₁₆	39⅛	...
s78¹¹⁄₁₆	40¹³⁄₁₆	ColgatePalm	CL	1.10	1.7	29	9547	65¹¹⁄₁₆	64⁹⁄₁₆	64¾	− ⅜
12⅜	5½	CollnsAikman	CKC		...	5	340	11⁵⁄₁₆	11	11⁵⁄₁₆	+ ⁵⁄₁₆
s 28⁹⁄₁₆	16¹⁵⁄₁₆	ColBgp	CNB	.60	2.1	17	358	28	27½	27¹⁵⁄₁₆	...

Latest day's price data – high, low, close and change from the previous day's closing. If one of these is a record for the previous 52 weeks, a small up or down arrow will appear to the far left of that stock's listing that day. The new extreme will be reflected in the 52-week high or low for the next day. A special table lists new highs and lows of NYSE listed stocks established that day. The length of this list can be an indicator of the market's performance. When a lot of issues reach new highs, there probably is a lot of buying pressure in the market. A large number of new lows indicates a bearish tone. Stocks that close up or down more than 5% from the previous day's closing price are printed in boldface.

Yld %:
Yield Percentage is obtained by dividing the cash dividend by the closing price of the stock. This enables dividend yields to be compared with other stocks and with the interest paid on debt instruments.

PE:
The P-E ratio is used as an indicator of relative stock performance. High P-Es indicate a stock price that's a high multiple of a company's earnings – suggesting optimism about the stock. Low P-E stocks often represent lower investor favor, but there isn't any "best" ratio. Reasons for high and low P-Es include the company's growth outlook, the company's industry, accounting policies, riskiness or the stability of the earnings. P-E ratio is the result of dividing the latest closing price by the latest available earnings per share, based on primary per-share earnings for the most recent four quarters.

Footnote:
An explanation of the footnotes appears daily underneath the graphs of the Dow Jones Averages. This box also recaps the meaning of the numbers in each of the stock-listing columns. For example, an "n" indicates a new issue of stock.

Dow Jones Global Indexes

Nearly 3,000 companies from 16 countries and 120 industry groups go into the most extensive foreign listings in any U.S. publication. The groupings divide these stocks into nine sectors that reflect large segments of the world economy; these nine sectors are then further subdivided into more specific industries. Countries are being added to the index as the global economy evolves. Over time, it will include every country whose stocks are available to foreign investors. As investor interest in global markets continues to grow, the Dow Jones World Stock Index has become an increasingly crucial measurement of world-wide stock performance.

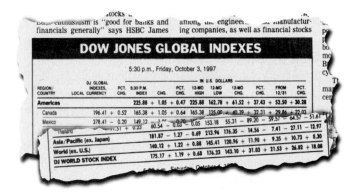

The Index offers superior measures of stock-market performance by providing investors with two comparative views: geographic and industrial. Investors can assess the political, economic and financial forces affecting the global market and measure how an individual issue has performed against its peers globally, regionally or nationally.

Dow Jones Averages

The universal standard barometer that charts the health of the market comes from Dow Jones & Company, the publisher of the Journal. When people ask "How's the market doing?" they usually mean the first of these indicators, the 30 stock Dow Jones Industrial Average. But there are indexes covering 20 transportation company stocks and 15 utility-company stocks, along with a composite index of the 65 stocks in the three indexes. The names of the stocks in each index appear daily next to the respective graph.

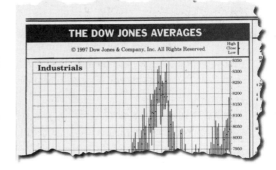

The daily graphs of the Dow Jones Averages are fairly self-explanatory. A vertical line, or bar, is drawn for each day. The top of the line represents the high of the day, the bottom the low. The small horizontal cross-bar represents the closing level of the day. Another bar chart below the three Averages' graphs depicts New York Stock Exchange volume for the days corresponding to the ones in the index charts.

The Dow Jones stock averages are price-weighted. This means a high-priced stock has a greater effect on the index than a low-priced one. There are other market indicators that attach weights to prices to give greater significance to stocks with greater market value. Market value is the price of a stock multiplied by the number of its shares outstanding. This system gives greater significance to larger companies. These are called market-weighted indexes.

You'll find the previous day's Dows detailed on page C3, along with other indexes of interest primarily to financial professionals.

Dow Jones Global Industry Groups

The Dow Jones Global Industry Group Table shows at a glance the relative performance of broad economic sectors both day-to-day and over the long term.

Unlike the Dow Jones Industrial Average, the World Stock Index World Industry Group Performance Table is market-weighted, not price-weighted – companies with large total-market values have the most effect on the movement of the indexes. They are all calculated based on a common value of 100 on June 30, 1982, so that their relative performance can be determined at a glance. Every day, the Journal reports on how each industry group fared compared with its close on the previous day, and the groups with the best and worst performance are displayed at the top of the Industry Group box along with the strongest and weakest stocks in each group.

Investment Funds

In many ways and for many reasons, the 1990s have seen America's first experiment with popular capitalism. In other words, investing is no longer just for the wealthy – it's become part of all our lives. One reason and result of this development is the explosive growth of investment funds, in which large and small investors pool their money and place it in the care of professional money managers. There are now thousands of funds with scores of investment objectives: growth funds, income funds, foreign-stock funds, bond funds...you get the picture. And you get all the data about all of them in the Journal. The best-known and most widely held, open-ended mutual and money-market funds are tracked daily. These funds continuously issue new shares if people wish to buy them back at prices based on the net asset value (NAV), or the value of the fund's portfolio less liabilities, divided by the number of shares outstanding. Unlike open-ended funds, closed-end funds offer a fixed number of shares–influenced by supply and demand but usually at prices that are very close to the net asset value. They trade on exchanges or over the counter; a table of closed-end funds is published on Mondays in the Journal. Each listing includes the closing NAV and exchange or over-the-counter price, the percentage difference and the market return for the latest 52-week period.

Mutual Funds

On Mondays through Thursdays, you'll find the fund's net asset value (NAV, or value per share); change from the previous day; and change for the year to date for every fund with assets of $25 million or more, or 1,000+ shareholders.

Mutual Funds–Friday

On Fridays, the listings expand to include the fund's investment objectives; total return over a month, year, three years and five years; its maximum load, or initial commission; and its annual expenses. In addition, each fund is ranked from A to E to compare its performance to other funds with the same objectives.

A charge, or sales commission of up to 8.5%, may apply to the mutual fund purchase price. Also, some funds may charge an exit fee when an investor redeems the shares. Other funds are sold on a no-load (NL) basis, i.e., without any sales commission. No-load shares usually are purchased directly from the fund, not through a broker. But these funds, like all others, usually charge an asset-management fee for investment advice or pay a fee to the outside firm that makes investment decisions for the fund. This annual fee is based on the average assets of the fund and typically averages less than 1% but can be higher.

Money Market Mutual Funds

Another type of open-ended fund is the money-market fund, which is limited to short-term instruments, such as CDs in large banks, commercial paper issued by major corporations and Treasury bills.

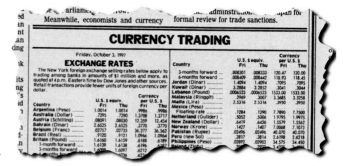

These money-market instruments often require a minimum investment of $100,000, but money-market funds allow smaller investors to participate in the higher interest rates offered by these instruments for a considerably smaller sum. But unlike bank deposits, money-market funds usually aren't guaranteed by the federal government.

Money-market fund quotes appear weekly on Thursdays. Each listing shows the average maturity for the portfolio in days, the average annual yield as a percentage based on the market for the past seven days, and total assets in millions of dollars.

Foreign Currency

Whether you're working at a company that does business overseas, or traveling to foreign shores, the foreign currency tables are the place to look for exchange rates, foreign currency futures prices and currency cross-rate tables that make it easy to convert one foreign currency into another.

Currency Trading Table

Gives the exchange rates prevailing at 3 p.m. Eastern time, expressed both as dollars per unit of foreign currency and as units of foreign currency per dollar. The former is the U.S. way of looking at things, the latter is the foreign way. Readers may encounter both ways. These rates apply to transactions among banks in amounts of $1 million or more. Rates for smaller transactions will be less favorable. Banks usually offer individuals better rates than commercial establishments do. Some currencies, such as the Belgian franc, have different rates for financial or commercial transactions. For some major currencies, such as the British pound and the German mark, rates also are given for future delivery.

At the bottom of the table is the conversion rate for the SDR, or Special Drawing Right, which is a reserve asset created by the International Monetary Fund for settlements among central banks. It also is used as a unit of account in international bond markets and by commercial banks. Based 42% on the U.S. dollar, 19% on the German mark and 13% each on the British pound, French franc and Japanese yen, the SDR's value fluctuates less than any single component currency. Also in the Journal every day is a currency cross-rates table that makes it more convenient to translate one foreign currency directly into another.

Exchange rates between important currencies used to be fixed, with sudden large changes forced only by the pressures of crises. Eventually the pressures became too great and too persistent, so rates now vary daily among major currencies. The system is known as floating exchange rates.

Since most international trade involves a delay between setting the price of a transaction and getting paid, this means at least one of the parties to such a transaction has a risk of losing money because the exchange rate may vary before payment is made.

This risk can be minimized by purchasing or selling foreign currency for future delivery at a specified exchange rate. For large amounts, this can be accomplished through banks in what is called the forward market; the 30-, 60-, 90- and 180-day rates in the Foreign Exchange table reflect this. Some foreign currencies also can be traded in futures markets, in smaller amounts; these are quoted daily (see "Futures above). There are also foreign currency options and futures options. The futures exchanges are increasingly providing a kind of secondary market in foreign exchange.

Money and Credit Markets *In other words (& very broadly): bonds, interest rates and the money supply.*

This can be a complicated world of secondary markets and over-the-counter trading among securities dealers, so let's just say this: This is the safest realm of investing, where the returns are lower but the security lets you sleep at night. Bonds and other instruments issued or backed by federal, state or local governments are considered virtually risk-free.

All types are covered thoroughly in our tables, with data that includes issue date, maturity, yield and asked/bid prices. We also include complete information on corporate bonds traded on the New York Stock Exchange and four major foreign-government bond markets.

Allied to these data is our information on the supply of and demand for money. The Federal Reserve Report, which we publish every Friday, gives important indicators for both, as do our daily Money Rates box (which lists the current prime lending rate) and the weekly Key Interest Rates table and Consumer Savings Rates List, which shows the rates paid by 100 banks in 10 large cities.

Treasury Issues

The Treasury issues instruments, due after various lengths of time, known as maturities. The shortest regularly issued maturities, three or six months, take the form of Treasury bills. These are issued every Monday in minimum denominations of $10,000 and in increments of $5,000 above the minimum. Investors bid for them at a discount, by offering, say $97.50 for every $100 of bills. At maturity, the investors will receive $100 for every $97.50 they paid. Yields are expressed on an annual basis.

Similar bills due in one year are sold monthly. The Treasury also issues cash-management bills on an irregular basis, generally for short periods, such as a few days. Treasury issues maturing in between one and 10 years are called notes. Those maturing in more than 10 years are called bonds. The process of selling these to the public takes place in the primary market, with the proceeds going to the issuer.

Secondary markets are made by securities dealers in all maturities of Treasury issues. In the secondary market, the prices of bills, notes and bonds fluctuate according to changes in interest rates. But, in one of the more confusing aspects of financial markets, the prices fluctuate inversely to the interest rates. Thus, when interest rates rise, bond prices go down, and when they fall, bond prices go up.

The rationale for this is as follows. Say the Treasury issues some 30-year bonds with an interest rate of 10%, or $10 of every $100. In time, interest rates may rise to 12%. Then, no one in the secondary market will want to pay full price for bonds paying 10% interest when they can buy new ones at 12%. However, they might be willing to pay less than $100 for every $100 of the old bonds. Tables and calculators exist which show the exact price to pay so the yield to maturity on a 10% bond is 12%, taking into account the time left to maturity when the purchase is made.

Similarly, when interest rates fall, bond prices will rise because sellers will hold out for a higher price to compensate for the higher-than-market interest paid on their holdings.

These changing prices are the basis of the Journal's tables for bonds and other debt securities. These issues are traded over the counter by securities dealers.

For bonds and notes, the price quotations are given per hundred dollars of face value.

Bonds issued some time ago may mature sooner than recently issued notes; this list is chronological. Some newer issues, designated "p", are exempt from withholding tax if held by nonresident aliens.

Month and Year of the security "n" designates notes; the rest are bonds.

The original interest rate.

Mid-afternoon bid price at which dealers were willing to buy the issue that day

Asked, or dealer, selling price

Changes in the bid price from the day before

Yield, or effective return on the investment. This is a calculation that takes into account the original interest rate, the current asked price and the amount of time left to maturity.

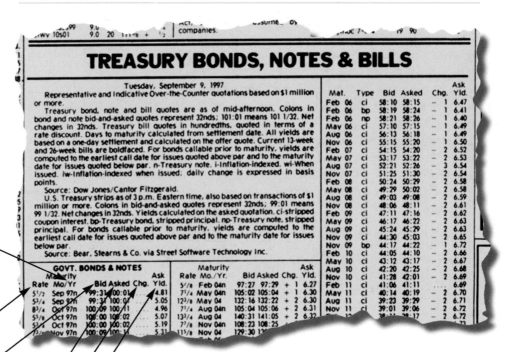

In the bond market, a price of 100 is called par and each one-hundredth of par is called a point. Normally, the minimum price fluctuation is 1/32nd of a point. To avoid repeating the figure 32 all the time, and to save space, there is a convention in the bond market that figures after a decimal point in a price represent 32nds. Thus, a quotation of 90.16 means 90 and 16/32nds or $90\frac{1}{2}$.

In the Treasury bill section of this table, however, the decimal takes on its customary meaning: 16.50 means 16µ. Maturities are given as months and dates; 5-28 means May 28. The quotations are for discounts, as explained above. The yield, as for longer-term issues, represents the effective total return and is used for comparison with other investments.

Corporate Bonds, There are three main types:

- Mortgage bonds: secured by real property, such as buildings
- Debentures: backed by a company's earning power rather than by specific hard assets
- Convertible bonds: can be exchanged for shares of the issue's stock.

Prices of a large number of corporate bonds are given in a table called New York Exchange Bonds. This covers bonds traded on the New York Stock Exchange, where only a small proportion of trading in these bonds takes place. Most bond trading is over the counter among securities dealers.

At the top of this table, there are data on the year's volume to date and a market diary. There is also a set of Dow Jones Averages for bond prices. The main index covers 20 bonds. There are component indexes for the 10 industrials and the 10 utilities. The New York table is followed by a short listing of bonds traded on the American Stock Exchange.

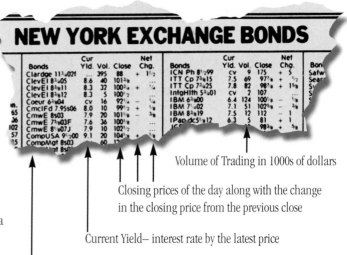

Volume of Trading in 1000s of dollars

Closing prices of the day along with the change in the closing price from the previous close

Current Yield– interest rate by the latest price

Name of the issuer, the original interest rate and the year of maturity, with an "s" where needed for ease of pronunciation.

Thus, 9s04 means "nines of oh-four," or 9% bonds due in 2004.

Other Government Bonds

Quotations for a selection of Government, Agency and miscellaneous securities are given in a separate table (at right), which is displayed much like Treasury bonds. Indexes measuring the performance of GNMA and FNMA issues are also included daily in the Bond Market Data Bank, as are prices and yields on representative individual mortgage-backed securities. Next to the Mortgage-Backed Securities list in the Data Bank, a small table lists the differential in yield between mortgage-backed securities and Treasury issues of comparable maturity.

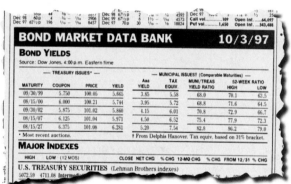

Municipal Bonds

Besides the U.S. government and its agencies, bonds may be issued by a variety of other government bodies that are lumped together under the heading "municipal," even though they include states, highway authorities and other noncity entities, as well as cities and their agencies. Usually, interest on these issues is exempt from income tax by the Federal government and by the state (and sometimes the city) in which the borrower is located. Because of this privilege, the issuer can apply a lower rate of interest, and investors have to consider the after-tax yield, based on their own income-tax situation, when comparing yields on these with those of other bonds. These bonds are also known as tax-exempts. The Journal prints a list of some of the most actively traded tax-exempts each day in the Bond Market Data Bank. The list is supplied by "The Bond Buyer," a New York trade publication.

Bond Market Data Bank

In addition to these market listings of individual bond prices, a further listing of the prices of 20 representative, actively traded corporate bonds is compiled by First Boston Corp. and appears daily in the Bond Market Data Bank. The Data Bank also lists the performance of several other indexes made up of various categories of corporate and convertible bond issues. The Merrill Lynch Corporate Master index, for example, represents a portfolio of about 4,400 nonconvertible bonds with remaining maturities of at least one year, a minimum of $1 million outstanding, and an average credit rating of A-1.

The Data Bank also lists bond prices and yields from four major foreign-government bond markets. All yields are semiannual, and compounded to maturity, to allow investors to make comparisons with domestic bonds. The Total Rates of Return box in the Data Bank provides an overall performance measure of the world's major bond markets.

Federal Reserve Report

One of the main influences on interest rates and the money markets is the supply of and demand for money. The Federal Reserve Report, published every Friday, gives important indicators of both. The level of commercial and industrial loans, for example, is an indicator of the demand for credit. In addition to the weekly report, a monthly chart shows the recent performance of the money supply indicators, compared with the Federal Reserve's targets. If one or more of the indicators is persistently outside the target range, the Fed may adjust its monetary policy and bring about a different level of interest rates.

Interest Rates

The Journal prints several features that track the levels of key interest rates affecting business and consumers. The daily Money Rates box lists the current prime lending rate as well as current yields and rates on a variety of short-term investments and loans. The weekly Key Interest Rates table is put together by the Federal Reserve Board and concentrates on returns for treasury issues. A weekly Consumer Savings Rates List shows the rates paid by 100 banks in 10 large metropolitan areas. Finally, on Wednesdays, the Banxquote Online deposits listings summarize rates paid on bank certificates of deposit.

THE WALL STREET JOURNAL.

WEEKEND JOURNAL.

All the Reasons You Work So Hard

It's Friday. The Wall Street Journal kicks off its shoes, and turns its attention to the world beyond Mondays-to-Fridays, 9-to-5. Every Friday, Journal subscribers smooth the transition from fast-paced to set-your-own speed with Weekend Journal, a regular section that celebrates the proposition that men and women do not thrive on work alone. Look inside, and you'll find great ideas on how to spend your well-earned time and money. If it's in your weekend, it's in Weekend Journal.

Inside Weekend Journal

Futures & Options

Diversions and Excursions. Weekly alerts on upcoming festivals, concerts, performances and gatherings. Previews of exceptional events throughout the U.S.

Travel

Weekend Journal's Travel page alerts you to the trends in airfares, critically examines vacation resorts and accommodations, from off-beat to the lap of luxury.

The Home Front

The Home Front page extols virtues (and vices) in personal real estate, offering one-of-a kind properties, valuable insight on the recoverable costs of improvements – and weekly data that reveals where prices are headed in communities across the country, courtesy of The Dow Jones Real Estate Index.

Sports

Sports page offers unique perspectives and postscripts on teams, individuals, tournaments, finals. You'll find surprising data and indices to change the way you think about, watch and participate in sporting events.

Entertainment

Weekend Journal looks behind the scenes and at the catalysts driving the entertainment business: performers, moguls, impresarios, marketing tie-ins. Reviews, alerts, cautions and catcalls for the performing arts on the road and in major cities.

Tastings

Tough-but-fair critics will get you to the bottom line: Is it worth $45 a bottle? Is it a find at $11? Are the entrees genuinely superb? Are you better served at home? Savory reports every week.

MICROECONOMICS
A Contemporary Introduction

Case Studies

Public Policy
Deterring Young Smokers, *page 100*
The Market for Food and the "Farm Problem," *page 107*
The Marginal Value of Free Medical Care, *page 126*
The Mail Monopoly, *page 211*
The McMinimum Wage, *page 259*
The Million-Dollar Lottery, *page 300*
Airline Regulation and Deregulation, *page 334*
Farm Subsidies, *page 359*
Campaign Finance Reform, *page 363*
Is Welfare-to-Work Working? *page 411*
Oregon's Program of "Tough Love," *page 413*

Other Times, Other Places
A Yen for Vending Machines, *page 9*
Destruction of the Tropical Rain Forest, *page 379*
City in the Clouds, *page 385*
The World Trade Organization, *page 431*
Enforcing Trade Restrictions, *page 437*
The Big Mac Price Index, *page 453*
The Asian Contagion, *page 458*
Crony Capitalism in Indonesia—All in the Family, *page 471*
Ownership and Resource Use, *page 478*

The World of Business
The Opportunity Cost of College, *page 26*
Evidence of Specialization, *page 33*
The Market for Professional Basketball, *page 62*
Toys Are Serious Business, *page 65*
Wheel of Fortune, *page 83*
Water, Water Everywhere, *page 120*
At the Movies, *page 155*
Billions and Billions of Burgers, *page 156*
Auction Markets, *page 179*
Experimental Economics, *page 190*
Are Diamonds Forever? *page 199*
Fast Forward, *page 224*
The Derived Demand for Architects, *page 254*
Winner-Take-All Labor Markets, *page 275*
Hardball at Caterpillar, *page 284*
The Trend Toward Outsourcing, *page 315*

The Information Economy
College Major and Career Earnings, *page 12*
The Electronic Cottage, *page 74*
The Value of a Good Idea,—Intellectual Property, *page 296*
The Reputation of a Big Mac, *page 324*
Windows 98 Sold With Microsoft Browser, *page 346*

The Art and Science of Economic Analysis

Visit the McEachern
Interactive Study Center
for this chapter at
ttp://mcisc.swcollege.com

Why are most comic strip characters, such as those in Hagar the Horrible, B.C., Cathy, and Peanuts, missing a finger? And how come Dilbert has no mouth? Why does Japan have twice as many vending machines per capita as does the United States and ten times as many as Europe? In what way are people who pound on vending machines relying on a theory? What's the big idea with economics? These and other questions are answered in this chapter, which introduces the art and science of economic analysis.

You have been reading and hearing about economic issues for years—unemployment, inflation, poverty, the federal budget, tuition, air fares, the stock market, computer prices, gas prices. When the explanations of these issues go into any depth, your eyes may glaze over and you may tune out the same way you do when a weather forecaster tries to provide an in-depth analysis of high-pressure fronts colliding with moisture carried in from the coast.

What many people fail to realize is that economics is much more lively than the dry accounts offered by the news media. Economics is about making choices, and you make economic choices every day—choices about whether to get a part-time job or focus on your studies, to live in a dorm or off-campus, to take a course in accounting or one in history, to pack a lunch or buy a Big Mac. You already know much more about economics than you realize. You bring to the subject a rich personal experience, an experience that we will tap throughout the book, to reinforce your understanding of the basic ideas. Topics discussed in this chapter include:

- The economic problem
- Marginal analysis
- Rational self-interest
- Scientific method
- Normative versus positive analysis
- Pitfalls of economic thinking

THE ECONOMIC PROBLEM: SCARCE RESOURCES BUT UNLIMITED WANTS

Would you like a new car, a nicer home, better meals, more free time, a more interesting social life, more spending money, more sleep? Who wouldn't? But even if you can satisfy some of these desires, others will pop up. *The problem is that, although your wants, or desires, are virtually unlimited, the resources available to satisfy these wants are scarce.* A resource is *scarce* when it is not freely available—that is, when its price exceeds zero. Because resources are scarce, you must choose from among your many wants and, whenever you choose, you must forgo satisfying some other wants. The problem of scarce resources but unlimited wants exists to a greater or lesser extent for each of the six billion people around the world. Everybody—taxicab drivers, farmers, brain surgeons, shepherds, students, politicians—faces the problem.

Economics examines how people use their scarce resources in an attempt to satisfy their unlimited wants. The taxicab driver uses the cab and other scarce resources, such as knowledge of the city, driving skills, and time, to earn income. The income, in turn, can be exchanged for housing, groceries, clothing, trips to Disney World, and thousands of other goods and services that help satisfy some of the driver's unlimited wants.

Let's pick apart the definition of economics, beginning with resources, next examining goods and services, and finally focusing on the heart of the matter: economic choice, which arises from scarcity.

Economics The study of how people use their scarce resources to satisfy their unlimited wants

Resources

Resources are the inputs, or factors of production, used to produce the goods and services that humans want. *Goods and services are scarce because resources are scarce.* We can divide resources into four general categories: labor, capital, land, and entrepreneurial ability. **Labor** is the broad category of human effort, both physical and mental. It includes the effort of the cab driver and the brain surgeon. Labor itself comes from a more fundamental resource: *time*. Without time we can accomplish nothing. We allocate our time to alternative uses: we can *sell* our time as labor, or we can *spend* our time doing other things such as sleeping, reading, or watching TV.

Resources The inputs, or factors of production, used to produce the goods and services that humans want; they consist of labor, capital, land, and entrepreneurial ability

Labor The physical and mental effort of humans used to produce goods and services

Capital includes human creations used to produce goods and services. We often distinguish between physical capital and human capital. *Physical capital* consists of factories, machines, tools, buildings, airports, highways, and other manufactured items employed to produce goods and services. Physical capital includes the driver's cab, the surgeon's scalpel, the farmer's tractor, the interstate highway system, and the building where your economics class meets. *Human capital* consists of the knowledge and skill people acquire to enhance their labor productivity, such as the taxi driver's knowledge of the city's streets and the surgeon's knowledge of human biology.

Land includes not only land in the conventional sense of plots of ground, but all other natural resources—all so-called *gifts of nature,* including bodies of water, trees, oil reserves, minerals, even animals.

A special kind of human skill called **entrepreneurial ability** is the talent required to dream up a new product or find a better way to produce an existing one. The entrepreneur tries to discover and act on profitable opportunities by hiring resources and assuming the risk of business success or failure. The largest firms in the world today, such as Ford, IBM, and Microsoft, each began as an idea in the mind of an individual entrepreneur.

Resource owners are paid **wages** for their labor, **interest** for the use of their capital, and **rent** for the use of their land. The entrepreneur's effort is rewarded by **profit,** which is the difference between *total revenue* from sales and the *total cost* of the resources employed. The entrepreneur claims what is left over after paying other resource suppliers. Sometimes the entrepreneur suffers a loss. Resource owners are usually paid for the *time* their resources are employed by entrepreneurs. Resource payments therefore have a time dimension, as in a wage of $10 *per hour,* interest of 6 percent *per year,* rent of $600 *per month,* or profit of $10,000 *per year.*

Goods and Services

Resources are combined in a variety of ways to produce goods and services. A farmer, a tractor, fifty acres of land, seeds, and fertilizer produce a good: corn. One hundred musicians, musical instruments, some chairs, a conductor, a musical score, and a music hall combine to produce a service: Beethoven's Fifth Symphony. Corn is a **good** because it is something we can see, feel, and touch; it requires scarce resources to produce; and it is used to satisfy human wants. The book you are now holding, the chair you are sitting in, the clothes you are wearing, and your next meal are all goods. The performance of the Fifth Symphony is a **service** because it is intangible, yet it uses scarce resources to satisfy human wants. Lectures, movies, concerts, phone calls, on-line computer services, piano lessons, dry cleaning, and haircuts are all services.

Because goods and services are produced using scarce resources, they are themselves scarce. A good or service is scarce if the amount people desire exceeds the amount that is available at a zero price. Since we cannot have all the goods and services we would like, we must continually choose among them. We must choose among more pleasant living quarters, better meals, nicer clothes, more reliable transportation, faster computers, and so on. Making choices in a world of **scarcity** means we must pass up some goods and services.

A few goods and services seem *free* because the amount freely available (that is, available at a zero price) exceeds the amount people desire. For example, air and seawater often seem free because we can breathe all the air we want and have

Capital The buildings, equipment, and human skill used to produce goods and services

Land Plots of ground as well as other natural resources used to produce goods and services

Entrepreneurial ability Managerial and organizational skills, combined with the willingness to take risks

Wages The payment that resource owners receive for their labor

Interest The payment that resource owners receive for the use of their capital

Rent The payment that resource owners receive for the use of their land

Profit The payment resource owners receive for their entrepreneurial ability; the total revenue from sales minus the total cost of resources employed by the entrepreneur

Good A tangible item that is used to satisfy human wants

Service An activity that is used to satisfy human wants

Scarcity When the amount people desire exceeds the amount available at a zero price all the seawater we can haul away. Yet, despite the old saying that "The best things in life are free," most goods and services are scarce, not free, and even those that appear to be free come with strings attached. For example, *clean* air and *clean* seawater have become scarce. *Goods and services that are truly free are not the subject matter of economics. Without scarcity, there would be no economic problem and no need for prices.*

Sometimes we mistakenly think of certain goods as free because they involve no apparent cost to us. Those subscription cards that fall out of magazines appear to be free. At least it seems we would have little difficulty rounding up about three thousand of them if necessary! Producing the cards, however, absorbs scarce resources, resources drawn away from competing uses, such as producing higher-quality magazines. You may have heard the expression "There is no such thing as a free lunch." There is no free lunch because all goods and services involve a cost to someone. The lunch may seem free to us, but it draws scarce resources away from the production of other goods and services, and whoever provides a free lunch likely expects something in return. A Russian proverb makes a similar point, but with a bit more bite: "The only place you find free cheese is in a mousetrap." Albert Einstein said, "Sometimes one pays the most for things one gets for nothing."

Economic Decision Makers

There are four types of decision makers, or participants, in the economy: households, firms, governments, and the rest of the world. The interaction between these decision makers determines how an economy's resources are allocated. *Households* play the leading role. As consumers, households demand the goods and services produced. As resource owners, households supply labor, capital, land, and entrepreneurial ability to firms, to governments, and to the rest of the world. *Firms, governments,* and *the rest of the world* demand the resources that households supply and use them to produce and supply the goods and services that households demand. The rest of the world includes foreign households, firms, and governments, which supply resources and products to U.S. markets and demand resources and products from U.S. markets.

Market A set of arrangements through which buyers and sellers carry out exchange at mutually agreeable terms

Markets are the means by which buyers and sellers carry out exchange; markets bring together the two sides of exchange—supply and demand—to determine price and quantity. Markets are often physical places, such as a supermarket, department store, shopping mall, or flea market. But markets also include the mechanisms by which buyers and sellers communicate, such as classified ads, radio and television ads, telephones, bulletin boards, the Internet, and face-to-face bargaining. These market mechanisms provide information about the quantity, quality, and price of products offered for sale. Goods and services are bought and sold in **product markets;** resources are bought and sold in **resource markets.** The most important resource market is the labor, or job, market. Think of your own experience looking for a job, and you get some idea of this market.

Product market A market in which a good or service is bought and sold

Resource market A market in which resources are bought and sold

Microeconomics and Macroeconomics

Although you have made thousands of economic choices, you probably have seldom thought about your own economic behavior. For example, why did you choose to spend your scarce resource—*time*—reading this book right now rather than doing something else?

Microeconomics The study of the economic behavior in particular markets, such as that for computers or for unskilled labor

Microeconomics is the study of your economic behavior and the economic behavior of others who make choices about such matters as what to buy and what to sell, how much to work and how much to play, how much to borrow and how much to save. Microeconomics examines the factors that influence individual economic choices and how the choices of various decision makers are coordinated by markets. For example, microeconomics explains how price and output are determined in individual markets, such as that for breakfast cereal, for sports equipment, or for Beanie Babies.

You have probably given little thought to the factors that influence your own economic choices. You have likely given even less thought to how your choices link up with those made by hundreds of millions of others in the U.S. economy to determine economy-wide sums such as total production, employment, and economic growth. **Macroeconomics** studies the performance of the economy as a whole. Whereas microeconomics studies the individual pieces of the economic puzzle, as reflected in particular markets, macroeconomics puts all the pieces together to focus on the big picture.

Macroeconomics The study of the economic behavior of entire economies

THE ART OF ECONOMIC ANALYSIS

An economy results from the choices that millions of individuals make in attempting to satisfy their unlimited wants. Because these choices lie at the very heart of the economic problem—coping with scarce resources but unlimited wants—they deserve a closer look. Developing an understanding of the forces that shape economic choice is the first step toward mastering the art of economic analysis.

Rational Self-Interest

A key economic assumption is that individuals, in making choices, rationally select alternatives they perceive to be in their best interests. By *rational,* economists mean simply that people try to make the best choices they can, given the available information. People may not know with certainty which alternative will turn out to be the best. They simply select the alternatives they *expect* will yield them the most satisfaction and happiness. *In general, rational self-interest means that individuals try to minimize the expected cost of achieving a given benefit or maximize the expected benefit achieved with a given cost.*

Rational self-interest should not be viewed as blind materialism, pure selfishness, or greed. We all know people who are tuned in to radio station WIIFM (What's In It For Me?). For most of us, however, self-interest often includes the welfare of our family, our friends, and perhaps the poor of the world. Even so, our concern for others is influenced by economic considerations. We may readily volunteer to drive a friend to the airport on Saturday afternoon, but we are less likely to offer a ride if the plane leaves at 6:00 A.M. We are more likely to donate old clothes rather than new ones to organizations such as Goodwill Industries. We tend to give more to our favorite charities if our contributions are tax deductible. TV stations are more likely to donate air time for public-service announcements during the dead of night than during prime time (in fact, 80 percent of such announcements air between 11:00 P.M. and 7:00 A.M.[1]). *The notion of self-interest does not rule out concern for others; it simply means that concern for others is to*

---

1 As reported in Sally Goll Beatty, "Media and Agencies Brawl Over Do-Good Advertising," *Wall Street Journal,* 29 September 1997.

some extent influenced by the same economic forces that affect other economic choices. The lower the personal cost of helping others, the more help we offer.

Economic Analysis Is Marginal Analysis

Economic choice usually involves some adjustment to the existing situation, or status quo. The software producer must decide whether to revise a word processing program. The town manager must decide whether to hire another worker for street maintenance. Your favorite jeans are on sale, and you must decide whether to buy another pair. You are wondering whether you should carry an extra course next term. You have just finished dinner and are deciding whether to have dessert.

Marginal Incremental, additional, or extra; used to describe the result of a change in an economic variable

Economic choice is based on a comparison of the *expected marginal cost* and the *expected marginal benefit* of the action under consideration. **Marginal** means incremental, additional, or extra. Marginal refers to a change in an economic variable, a change in the status quo. *You, as a rational decision maker, will change the status quo as long as your expected marginal benefit from the change exceeds your expected marginal cost.* For example, you compare the marginal benefit you expect from eating dessert (the added pleasure and satisfaction) with its marginal cost (the added money, time, and calories). Likewise, the software producer compares the marginal benefit expected from revising a software program (the added sales revenue) with the marginal cost (the added cost of the resources required).

Typically the change under consideration is small, but a marginal choice can involve a major economic adjustment, as in the decision to quit school and get a job. For a firm, a marginal choice might mean introducing a new product, building a plant in Mexico, or even filing for bankruptcy. By focusing on the effect of a marginal adjustment to the status quo, the economist is able to cut the analysis of economic choice down to manageable size. Rather than confront a bewildering economic reality head-on, the economist can begin with a marginal choice and then see how this choice affects a particular market and shapes the economic system as a whole. Incidentally, to the noneconomist, "marginal" usually means relatively inferior, as in "restaurant meals of marginal quality." Forget that meaning for this course and instead think of marginal as meaning incremental, additional, or extra.

Choice Requires Time and Information

Rational choice takes time and requires information, but time and information are scarce and valuable. If you have any doubts about the time and information required to make choices, talk to someone who recently purchased a home, a car, or a personal computer. Talk to a corporate official deciding whether to introduce a new product, build a new factory, or acquire another firm. Or think back to your own experience in selecting a college. You probably talked to friends, relatives, teachers, and guidance counselors. You likely looked at school catalogs and college guides. You may have visited campuses to meet with the admissions staff and anyone else willing to talk. The decision took time and money, and it probably involved aggravation and anxiety.

Because information is costly to acquire, we are often willing to pay others to gather and digest it for us. The existence of markets for college guidebooks, stock analysts, travel agents, real-estate brokers, career counselors, restaurant guidebooks, and *Consumer Reports* magazine indicates our willingness to pay for information that will improve our economic choices. *Rational decision makers will continue to acquire information as long as the expected marginal benefit from the information exceeds its expected marginal cost.*

Normative Versus Positive

Economists usually try to explain how the economy works. Sometimes they concern themselves not with how the economy *does* work but how it *should* work. Compare these two statements: "The U.S. unemployment rate is 5.1 percent" and "The U.S. unemployment rate should be lower." The first is called a **positive economic statement** because it is an assertion about economic reality that can be supported or rejected by reference to the facts. The second is called a **normative economic statement** because it reflects an opinion. And an opinion is merely that—it cannot be shown to be true or false by reference to the facts. Positive statements concern what *is;* normative statements concern what, in someone's opinion, *should be.* Positive statements need not necessarily be true, but they must be subject to verification or refutation by reference to the facts.

Theories are expressed as positive statements such as "If the price increases, then the quantity demanded will decrease." Most of the disagreement among economists involves normative debates—for example, the appropriate role of government—rather than statements of positive analysis. To be sure, many theoretical issues remain unresolved, but economists largely agree on most fundamental theoretical principles—that is, about positive economic analysis. For example, in a survey of 464 U.S. economists, only 6.5 percent disagreed with the statement "A ceiling on rents reduces the quantity and quality of housing available." This is a positive statement because it can be shown to be consistent or inconsistent with the evidence. In contrast, there was much less agreement on normative statements such as "The distribution of income in the United States should be more equal." Half the economists surveyed "generally agreed," a quarter "generally disagreed," and a quarter "agreed with provisos."[2]

Normative statements, or value judgments, have a place in policy debates about the proper role of government, provided that statements of fact are distinguished from statements of opinion. It's been said that "You are entitled to your own opinion, but you are not entitled to your own facts."

To review: The art of economic analysis focuses on how individuals use their scarce resources in an attempt to satisfy their unlimited wants. Rational self-interest guides individual choice. Choice involves a comparison of the marginal cost and marginal benefit of alternative actions, a comparison that requires time and information. Care must be taken to distinguish between positive statements, which focus on how the economy works, and normative statements, which represent people's opinions about how the economy should work.

THE SCIENCE OF ECONOMIC ANALYSIS

Economists use scientific analysis to develop theories, or models, that help explain how economic choices are made and how the economy works. An **economic theory,** or **economic model,** is a simplification of economic reality that *is used to make predictions about the real world.* A theory, or model, captures

Positive economic statement A statement that can be proved or disproved by reference to facts

Normative economic statement A statement that represents an opinion, which cannot be proved or disproved

Economic theory, economic model A simplification of reality used to make predictions about the real world

---

2   Richard M. Alston, et al., "Is There a Consensus Among Economists in the 1990s?," *American Economic Review* 82 (May 1992): pp. 203–209, Table 1.

the important elements of the problem under study; it need not spell out every detail and interrelation. In fact, the more details a theory contains, the more unwieldy it becomes and the less useful it may be. The world we live in is so complex that we must simplify if we want to make any sense of things. Similarly, comic strips simplify characters; most are missing fingers, and some lack other features (Dilbert has no mouth). You might think of economic theory as a stripped-down version of economic reality.

The Role of Theory

People often don't understand the role of theory. Perhaps you have heard "Oh, that's fine in theory, but in practice it's another matter." The implication is that the theory provides little aid in practical matters. People who say this fail to realize that they are merely substituting their own theory for a theory they either do not believe or do not understand. They are really saying "I have my own theory, which works better."

All of us employ theories, however poorly defined or understood. Someone who pounds on the Pepsi machine that just ate a quarter has a crude theory about how that machine works and what went wrong. One version of that theory might be "The quarter drops through a series of whatchamacallits, but sometimes the quarter gets stuck. *If* I pound on the machine, *then* I can free up the quarter and send it on its way." Evidently this theory is so prevalent that many people continue to pound on machines that fail to perform (a real problem for the vending machine industry and a reason why newer machines are fronted with glass). Yet, if you asked this mad pounder to explain the "theory" about how the machine operates, he or she would look at you as if you were crazy.

The Scientific Method

To study economic problems, economists employ a process of theoretical investigation called the *scientific method,* which consists of four steps.

Step One: Identify the Question and Define Relevant Variables. The first step is to identify the economic question and define the variables that are relevant to the solution. For example, the question might be "What is the relationship between the *price* of Pepsi and the *quantity* of Pepsi purchased." In this case the relevant variables are price and quantity. A **variable** is a measure that can take on different values. The variables of concern become the elements of the theory, so they must be selected with care.

Step Two: Specify Assumptions. The second step is to specify the assumptions under which the theory is to apply. One major category of assumptions is the **other-things-constant assumption**—in Latin, the *ceteris paribus* assumption. The idea is to identify the variables of interest, then to focus exclusively on the relations among them, assuming that nothing else of importance will change— that other things will remain constant. Again, suppose we are interested in how the price of Pepsi influences the amount purchased. To isolate the relation between the price of Pepsi and the quantity purchased, we assume that there are no changes in other relevant variables such as consumer income, the price of Coke, and the average temperature.

We also make assumptions about how people will behave; these are called **behavioral assumptions.** Perhaps the most fundamental behavioral assumption

Variable A measure, such as price or quantity, that can take on different possible values

Other-things-constant assumption The assumption, when focusing on key economic variables, that other variables remain unchanged

Behavioral assumption An assumption that describes the expected behavior of economic decision makers is rational self-interest. Earlier we assumed that individual decision makers pursue their self-interest rationally and make choices accordingly. Rationality implies that each consumer buys the products expected to maximize his or her level of satisfaction. Rationality also implies that each firm supplies the products expected to maximize that firm's profit. These kinds of assumptions are called behavioral assumptions because they specify how we expect economic decision makers to behave—what makes them tick, so to speak.

Step Three. The third step is to formulate a **hypothesis,** a theory about how key variables relate to each other. For example, one hypothesis holds that *if* the price of Pepsi goes up, other things constant, *then* the quantity purchased will decline. The hypothesis becomes a prediction of what will happen to the quantity purchased if the price goes up. The purpose of this hypothesis, like that of any theory, is to help make predictions about the real world.

Hypothesis A statement about relationships among key variables

Step Four. The validity of a theory is tested by comparing its predictions with evidence. To test a hypothesis, we must focus attention on the variables in question, while at the same time carefully controlling for other effects, which are assumed not to change. The test will lead us either to reject the theory as inconsistent with the evidence or to continue using the theory until a better one comes along. Even though a particular theory may not predict well at all times, it may still predict better than competing theories.

Economists Tell Stories

Despite economists' reliance on the scientific method for developing and evaluating theories, economic analysis is perhaps as much art as science. Formulating a question, isolating the key variables, specifying the assumptions, proposing a theory to answer the question, and devising a way to test the predictions all involve more than simply an understanding of economics and the scientific method.

Carrying out these steps requires good intuition and the imagination of a storyteller. Economists explain their theories by telling stories about how they think the economy works. To tell a compelling story, an economist relies on case studies, anecdotes, parables, and the personal experience of the listener. Throughout this book you will hear stories that bring you closer to the ideas under consideration. The story about the Pepsi machine mentioned earlier is one of those stories that help breathe life into economic theory and help you personalize abstract ideas. As an example, here is a case study about the popularity of vending machines in Japan.

CaseStudy

Other Times, Other Places

Speaking of storytelling, could an economist explain the arrangement of letters on your computer's keyboard? One story is told by David Tenenbaum in "Dvorak Keyboards" in *Technology Review* at http://www.techreview.com/articles/july96/trends.html.

A Yen for Vending Machines

In recent decades, the rate of unemployment has usually been lower in Japan than in other countries. Because of a declining birth rate, negligible immigration, and an aging population, Japan faces a steady drop in the number of people of working age. Because labor is relatively scarce in Japan, it is relatively costly. To sell products, Japanese retailers rely more on capital, particularly vending machines. Vending machines eliminate the need for a sales clerk.

Japan has more vending machines per capita than any other country in the world—more than twice as many as the United States and nearly ten times as many as Europe. Also vending machines in Japan are more sophisticated. For example, through a phone link, some vending machines tell vendors when more product or more change is needed, thereby eliminating unnecessary trips to restock the machines. Vending machines that sell cigarettes or alcohol now have a device that can verify a driver's license to check whether the customer is old enough to purchase these products legally. Robo Shop Super 24, a convenience store in Tokyo, is completely automated. After browsing long display cases, customers can make selections by punching product numbers on a keyboard. A bucket whirs around the store, rounding up the selections. Robo Shop is a giant vending machine.

A relatively low unemployment rate is not the only reason that vending machines are so popular in Japan. We already discussed how it is common practice in the United States to shake down vending machines that perform poorly. Such abuse increases the probability that the machines will malfunction in the future, leading to yet more abuse. In Japan, however, vending machines get more respect, in part because they are more sophisticated and more reliable and in part because of Japan's lower crime rate and greater respect for property. (For example, the automobile theft rate in Japan is only one-twentieth the U.S. rate.)

Japanese consumers use vending machines with great frequency. Sales per machine in Japan are double the U.S. level. Vending machines in Japan also sell a wider range of products, including videos, boxer shorts, stuffed animals, whisky, hot pizza, and even dating services. Some vending machines look like robots, which may seem natural in gadget-crazy Japan, where many childhood heroes are robotic characters. Despite the relative abundance of vending machines in Japan, their use is expected to grow even more, spurred on in part by technological innovations and a shrinking labor pool.

Sources: Nicholas Kristof, "In Japan, Chicken Little Lays the Golden Egg," *New York Times*, 30 July 1995; "The Coke Machine is Calling Again On Line 1," *The Nikkei Weekly*, 1 September 1997; "Economic Indicators," *The Economist*, 3 October 1997; and Serv-o-matic International, a worldwide seller of vending machines at http://www.ecity.net/~servom/.

This case study makes two points. First, producers combine resources in a way that conserves, or economizes on, the resource that is more costly, in this case labor. Second, the customs and conventions of the marketplace may differ across countries, and this may result in different types of economic arrangements, such as the more extensive use of vending machines in Japan.

Predicting Average Behavior

The task of an economic theory is to predict the impact of an economic event on economic choices and, in turn, the effect of these choices on particular markets or on the economy as a whole. Does this mean that economists try to predict the behavior of particular consumers or producers? Not necessarily, because any particular individual may behave in an unpredictable way. But the unpredictable actions of numerous individuals tend to cancel one another out, so the *average behavior* of groups can be predicted more accurately. For example, if the federal government cuts personal income taxes, certain households may decide to save the entire tax cut. On average, however, household spending in the economy will increase. Likewise, if Burger King cuts the price of Whoppers, the manager can better predict how much Whopper sales will increase than how a given customer will respond. *The random actions of individuals tend to offset one another, so the average behavior of a large group can be predicted more accurately than the behavior of a particular individual.* Consequently, economists tend to focus on the average, or typical, behavior of people in groups—for example, as average taxpayers or Whopper consumers—rather than on the specific behavior of a particular individual.

Some Pitfalls of Faulty Economic Analysis

Economic analysis, like other forms of scientific inquiry, is subject to common mistakes in reasoning that can lead to faulty conclusions. We will discuss three possible sources of confusion.

The Fallacy That Association Is Causation. Does something like this sound familiar: "The stock market was up today as traders reacted favorably to higher profits reported by Intel"? Although stock market analysts typically claim that millions of stock market transactions spring from a single event, such simplifications are often misleading and even wrong. To assume that event *A* caused event *B* simply because *B* followed *A* in time is to commit the **association-is-causation fallacy,** a common error. The fact that one event precedes another or that the two occur simultaneously does not necessarily mean that one causes the other. Remember: *Association is not necessarily causation.*

Association-is-causation fallacy The incorrect idea that if two variables are associated in time, one must necessarily cause the other

The Fallacy of Composition. Standing up at a football game to get a better view does not work if others stand as well. Arriving early to get in line for concert tickets does not work if many others have the same idea. Selling shares of stock before the price drops will not work if many others also try to sell. These are examples of the **fallacy of composition,** which is an erroneous belief that what is true for the individual or the part is also true for the group or the whole.

Fallacy of composition The incorrect belief that what is true for the individual or part must necessarily be true for the group or whole

The Mistake of Ignoring the Secondary Effects. In many cities, public officials, out of concern about rising rents, have imposed rent controls on apartments. The *primary effect* of this policy, the effect on which policy makers focus, is to keep rents from rising. Over time, however, fewer new apartments get built because the rental business becomes less profitable. Moreover, existing rental units deteriorate because owners have no incentive to pay for maintenance. Thus, the quantity and quality of housing may well decline as a result of what appears to be a reasonable measure to control rents. The policy makers' mistake was to ignore the **secondary effects,** or the *unintended consequences,* of their policy. Economic actions have secondary effects that often turn out to be more important than the primary effects. Secondary effects may develop more slowly and may not be obvious, but good economic analysis takes them into account.

Secondary effects Unintended consequences of economic actions that may develop slowly over time as people react to events

If Economists Are So Smart, Why Aren't They Rich?

Why aren't economists rich? Well, some of them are. Until his death, Taikichiro Mori, of Japan, a former economics professor, was reportedly the richest person in the world. Some economists earn as much as $25,000 per appearance on the lecture circuit. Others earn thousands of dollars a day as consultants. Economists have been appointed to the cabinet positions of Secretaries of Commerce, Defense, Labor, State, and Treasury. Economics is the only social science and the only business discipline for which the prestigious Nobel Prize is awarded, and pronouncements by economists are reported in the media daily.

A columnist for the *New York Times* wrote that business owners "employ economists in large numbers or consult them at high fees, believing that their cracked crystal balls are better than none at all. The press pursues the best-known seers. While many laymen may be annoyed by economists, other social scientists *hate* them—for their fame, Nobel Prizes, and ready access to political power."[3] A recent article in *The Economist,* a widely respected news weekly from London, argues that economic ideas have influenced policy "to a degree that would make other social scientists drool."[4]

Despite its critics, the economics profession thrives because its models usually do a better job of making economic sense out of a confusing world than do alternative approaches. But not all economists are wealthy, nor is personal wealth the objective of the discipline. In a similar vein, not all doctors are healthy; not all carpenters live in perfectly built homes; not all marriage counselors are happily married; and not all child psychologists have well-adjusted children. Still, those who study economics do reap rewards, as discussed in this closing case study, which looks at the link between earnings and the choice of a college major.

CaseStudy

The Information Economy

The Federal Reserve Bank of Minneapolis asked some Nobel Prize winners how they became interested in economics. Their stories can be found at http://woodrow.mpls.frb.fed.us/pubs/region/98-12/quotes.html.

College Major and Career Earnings

Earlier in the chapter, you learned that economic choice is based on a comparison of expected marginal cost and expected marginal benefit. Surveys show that students go to college because they believe a college diploma is the ticket to better jobs and higher pay. Put another way, for about two-thirds of high school graduates, college's expected marginal benefit seems to exceed its expected marginal cost. We'll discuss the cost of college in the next chapter; here let us focus on the benefits of college, particularly expected earnings.

Among college graduates, all kinds of factors affect earnings, such as general ability, choice of occupation, personal characteristics, college attended, college major, and highest degree earned. Until recently there had been little systematic evidence linking earnings to the college major, but then the National Science Foundation sponsored a huge survey of college graduates to examine that relationship. To isolate the effects of college major on earnings, the survey focused on people in specific age groups who worked full time in 1993 and who had earned a bachelor's degree as their highest degree.

Exhibit 1 shows the average earnings by major in 1993 for men and women aged 35 to 44. As a point of reference, the *median* annual earnings for men was $43,199. (Half earned more than $43,199 and half earned less.) The median earnings for women was $32,155, only 75 percent of the median for men. Among men, the top median pay was the $53,286 earned by engineering majors; that pay was 23 percent above the median for all men aged 35 to 44. Among women, the

3   Leonard Silk, *Economics in Plain English* (New York: Simon and Schuster, 1978), p. 17 (emphasis in original).
4   "The Puzzling Failure of Economics," *The Economist* 23 August 1997, p. 11.

EXHIBIT 1

**Median Annual Earnings
in 1993 of Those Age 35–44
with Bachelor's as Highest Degree by Major**

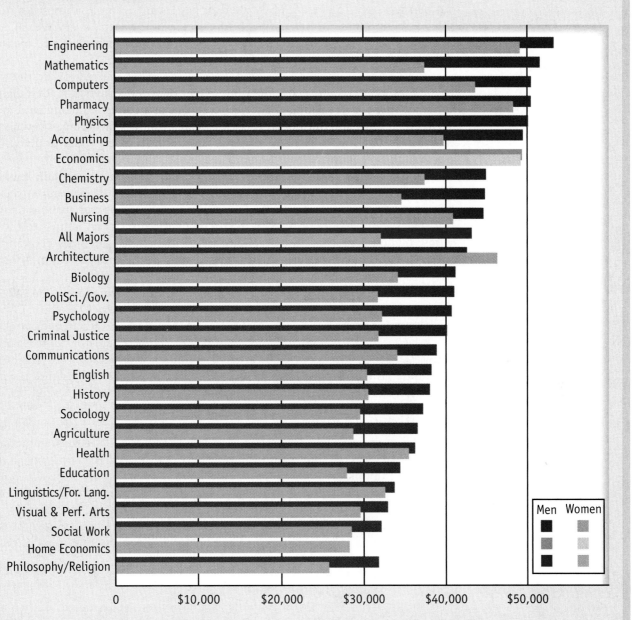

Source: Earnings based on figures reported by Daniel Hacker in "Earnings of College Graduates, 1993," *Monthly Labor Review*, December 1995, pp. 3–17.

top median pay was the $49,170 earned by economics majors; that pay was 53 percent above the median for all surveyed women aged 35 to 44.

Incidentally, men who majored in economics earned a median of $49,377, ranking them seventh among 27 majors and 14.3 percent above the median for all men aged 35 to 44 in the survey. Thus, even though the median pay for women was only 75 percent of the median pay for men, among those who majored in economics, women earned 99.6 percent of the men's salary. We can say that economics majors earned more than most, and they experienced little pay difference based on gender.

Notice that among both men and women, the majors ranked toward the top of the list tend to be those that are more quantitative and analytical. According to the study's author, "Employers may view certain majors as more difficult and may assume that graduates in these fields are more able and hard working, whereupon they offer them higher salaries." The selection of a relatively more challenging major such as economics sends a favorable signal to future employers.

The study also examined the kinds of jobs different majors actually found. Those who majored in economics became top and mid-level managers, executives, and administrators. They also found jobs in sales, computer analysis, financial analysis, and economic analysis. Remember, the survey was limited to those whose highest degree was the baccalaureate, so it excluded the many economics majors who went on to pursue graduate studies in law, business, economics, journalism, and other fields.

A number of world leaders majored in economics, including former Presidents Ford, Reagan, and Bush and Supreme Court Justice Sandra Day O'Connor. Other well-known economics majors include actor Arnold Schwarzenegger, rocker Mick Jagger, high-tech guru Esther Dyson, and "Dilbert" creator Scott Adams. Schwarzenegger, who reportedly earned $74 million in 1996 and 1997, has built an empire around his celebrity, including extensive real-estate holdings. Jagger, who attended the London School of Economics, heads what's been called "rock's most efficient corporation" (the Rolling Stones earned $68 million in 1996 and 1997). Both Schwarzenegger and Jagger rank among the dozen highest-paid entertainers in the world. Dyson, called by *The New York Times* "the most influential woman in all the computer world," authored *Release 2.0: A Design for Living in the Digital Age*, a book that helps people understand the wired world. She also publishes an influential high-tech newsletter and runs computer forums around the world. Adams has turned his "Dilbert" comic strip into a thriving industry including syndication in more than 1600 newspapers (in seventeen languages and thirty-nine countries), a TV program, best-selling books, plus dozens of tie-in products.

Sources: Scott Adams, *The Dilbert Principle* (New York, NY: HarperCollins, 1996); Daniel E. Hacker, "Earnings of College Graduates," *Monthly Labor Review*, December 1995; Robert La Franco, "The *Forbes* Top 40," *Forbes*, 22 September 1997; "The Accidental 'Techie'," *Newsweek*, 13 October 1997; Derek Bickerton, "Digital Dreams," *New York Times*, 30 November 1997.

CONCLUSION

This textbook describes how economic factors affect individual choices and how all these choices come together to shape the economic system. Economics is not the whole story, and economic factors are not always the most important. But economic considerations have important and predictable effects on individual choices, and these choices affect the way we live.

Sure, economics is a challenging discipline, but it is also an exciting and rewarding one. The good news is that you already know a great deal about economics. To use this knowledge, however, you must cultivate the art and science of economic analysis. You must be able to simplify the real world to formulate questions, isolate the relevant variables, and then tell a persuasive story about how these variables relate.

An economic relation can be expressed in words, represented as a table of quantities, described by a mathematical equation, or illustrated as a graph. The Appendix to this chapter provides an introduction to the use of graphs. You may find the Appendix unnecessary. If you are already familiar with graphs—such as relations among variables, slopes, tangents, and the like—you can probably just browse. If you have little recent experience with graphs, you may benefit from a more careful reading with pencil and paper in hand.

In the next chapter we will introduce some key ideas of economic analysis. Subsequent chapters will use these ideas to explore economic problems and to explain economic behavior that may otherwise appear puzzling. You must walk before you can run, however, and in the next chapter you will take those first wobbly steps.

SUMMARY

1. Economics is the study of how people choose to use their scarce and limited resources to produce, exchange, and consume goods and services in an attempt to satisfy their unlimited wants. The economic problem arises from the conflict between scarce resources and unlimited wants. If wants were limited or if resources were not scarce, there would be no need to study economics.

2. Economic resources are combined in a variety of ways to produce goods and services. Major categories of resources include labor, capital, land (representing all natural resources), and entrepreneurial ability. Because economic resources are scarce, only a limited number of goods and services can be produced with them; therefore, choices must be made.

3. Microeconomics focuses on choices made in households, firms, and governments and how these choices affect particular markets, such as the market for used cars. Each choice is assumed to be guided by rational self-interest. Choice typically requires time and information, both of which are scarce and valuable. Whereas microeconomics examines the individual pieces of the puzzle, macroeconomics steps back to look at the big picture—

the performance of the economy as a whole as reflected by such measures as total production, employment, the price level, and economic growth.

4. Economists use theories, or models, to help understand the effects of economic changes, such as a change in price or income, on individual choices and, in turn, how these choices affect particular markets and the economy as a whole. Economists employ the scientific method to study an economic problem by (1) formulating the question and isolating relevant variables, (2) specifying the assumptions under which the theory operates, (3) developing a theory, or hypothesis, about how the variables relate, and (4) testing that theory by comparing its predictions with the evidence. A theory may not work perfectly, but it will be useful as long as it predicts better than competing theories do.

5. Positive economics aims to discover how the economy works. Normative economics is concerned more with how, in someone's opinion, the economy should work. Those who are not careful can fall victim to the fallacy that association is causation, the fallacy of composition, and ignorance of the secondary effects.

QUESTIONS FOR REVIEW

1. *(Definition of Economics)* What determines whether or not a resource is scarce? Why is the concept of scarcity important to the definition of economics?

2. *(Resources)* To which category of resources does each of the following belong?
   a. A taxicab
   b. Computer software
   c. One hour of legal counsel
   d. A parking lot
   e. A forest
   f. The Mississippi River
   g. An individual introducing a new way to market products on the Internet

3. *(Goods and Services)* Explain why each of the following would *not* be considered "free" for the economy as a whole:
   a. Food stamps
   b. U.S. aid to developing countries
   c. Corporate charitable contributions
   d. Noncable television programs
   e. Public high school education

4. *(Economic Decision Makers)* Which group of economic decision makers plays the leading role in the economic system? Which groups play supporting roles? In what sense are they supporting actors?

5. *(Micro versus Macro)* Determine whether each of the following is primarily a microeconomic or a macroeconomic issue:

   a. Determining the price to charge for an automobile
   b. Measuring the impact of tax policies on total consumption spending in the economy
   c. A household's decisions about how to allocate its disposable income among various goods and services
   d. A worker's decision regarding how many hours to work each week
   e. Designing a government policy to affect the level of employment

6. *(Micro versus Macro)* Some economists believe that in order to really understand macroeconomics, you must fully understand microeconomics. How does microeconomics relate to macroeconomics?

7. *(Normative versus Positive Analysis)* Determine whether each of the following statements is normative or positive:
   a. The U.S. unemployment rate was below 5 percent in 1998.
   b. The inflation rate in the United States is too high.
   c. The U.S. government should increase the minimum wage.
   d. U.S. trade restrictions cost consumers $19 billion annually.

8. *(Role of Theory)* What good is economic theory if it cannot predict an individual's behavior?

PROBLEMS AND EXERCISES

9. *(Rational Self-Interest)* Discuss the impact of rational self-interest on each of the following decisions:
   a. Whether to attend college full time or enter the full-time workforce
   b. Whether to buy a new or a used textbook
   c. Whether to attend a local college or an out-of-town college

10. *(Rational Self-Interest)* If behavior is governed by rational self-interest, why do people make contributions to charity?

11. *(Marginal Analysis)* The owner of a small pizzeria is deciding whether to increase the radius of its delivery area by one mile. What considerations must be taken into account if such a decision is to contribute to profitability?

12. *(Time and Information)* It is often costly to obtain information necessary to make good decisions. Yet your own interests can be best served by rationally weighing all options available to you. This requires completely informed decision making. Does this mean that making uninformed decisions is irrational? How do you determine what amount of information is the right amount?

13. *(CaseStudy: A Yen for Vending Machines)* Do vending machines conserve on any resources other than labor? Does your answer offer any additional insight into the widespread use of vending machines in Japan?

14. *(CaseStudy: A Yen for Vending Machines)* Suppose you had the choice of purchasing identically priced lunches

from a vending machine or at a cafeteria. Which would you choose? Why?

15. *(Pitfalls of Economic Analysis)* Review the discussion of pitfalls in economic thinking in this chapter. Then identify the fallacy or mistake in thinking in each of the following statements:

    a. Raising taxes will always increase government revenues.

    b. Whenever there is a recession, imports decrease. Therefore, to stop a recession, we should increase imports.

    c. Raising the tariff on imported steel will help the U.S. steel industry. Therefore, the entire economy will be helped.

    d. Gold sells for about $300 per ounce. Therefore, the U.S. government could sell all of the gold in Fort Knox at $300 per ounce and eliminate the national debt.

16. *(Association versus Causation)* Suppose I observe that communities with lots of doctors tend to have relatively high rates of illness. I conclude that doctors cause illness. What's wrong with this reasoning?

EXPERIENTIAL EXERCISES

17. *(Microeconomics and Macroeconomics)* Go to the Bank of Sweden's page on the Nobel Prize in economic science at http://www.ee.nobel.se/prize/memorial.html. Review the descriptions of some recent awards and try to determine whether those particular awards were primarily for work in macroeconomics or in microeconomics.

18. *(CaseStudy: College Major and Career Earnings)* The Bureau of Labor Statistics maintains online copies of articles from their *Monthly Labor Review*. Go to the site http://stats.bls.gov/opub/mlr/mlrhome.htm, click on "Archives" and find the article by Daniel Hecker entitled "Earnings of College Graduates: Women versus Men" (March, 1998). What can you learn about the payoff to college education for both women and men? (Note: You will need an Adobe Acrobat reader to get the full text of this article. You can download a copy of the reader at http://www.adobe.com/prodindex/acrobat/.

19. *(Wall Street Journal)* Detecting economic fallacies is a key skill. Review the section titled "Some Pitfalls of Economic Analysis" in this chapter. Then use the *Wall Street Journal* to find at least one example of faulty reasoning. (Hint: Begin with the "Markets Diary" column in the "Money & Investing" section.)

Appendix

UNDERSTANDING GRAPHS

Take out a pencil, a ruler, and a blank piece of paper. Go ahead, do it. Put a point in the middle of the paper. This is our point of departure, called the **origin.** With your pencil at the origin, draw a three-inch straight line off to the right. This line is called the **horizontal axis.** The value of the variable x measured along the horizontal axis increases as you move to the right of the origin. Now mark off this line into increments of 5 units each, from 0 to 20. Returning to the origin, draw another three-inch line straight up. This line is called the **vertical axis.** The value of the variable y measured along the vertical axis increases as you move upward. Now mark off this line into increments of 5 units each, from 0 to 20.

Within the space framed by the axes, you can plot possible combinations of the variables measured along each axis. Each point identifies a value measured along the horizontal, or x, axis *and* a value measured along the vertical, or y, axis. For example, place point a in your graph to reflect the combination where x equals 5 units and y equals 15 units. Likewise, place point b in your graph to reflect 10 units of x and 5 units of y. Now compare your results with those shown in Exhibit 2.

A **graph** is a picture showing how variables relate, and a picture can be worth a thousand words. Take a look at Exhibit 3, which shows the U.S. annual unemployment rate since 1900. The year is measured along the horizontal axis and the unemployment rate along the vertical axis. Exhibit 3 is a **time-series graph** because it shows the value of a variable, in this case the unemployment rate, over time. If you had to describe the information presented in Exhibit 3 in words, the explanation could take pages and would be mind-numbing. The picture shows not only how one year compares to the next, but also how one decade compares to another and how the rate has trended over time. Your eyes can wander over the hills and valleys to observe patterns that would be hard to convey in words. The sharply higher unemployment rate during the Great Depression of the 1930s is unmistakable. *Graphs convey information in a compact and efficient way.*

This appendix shows how graphs express a variety of possible relations among variables. Most of the graphs of interest in this book reflect the relationship between two economic variables, such as the year and the unemployment rate, the price of a product and the quantity demanded, or the cost of production and the quantity supplied. Because we focus on just two variables at a time, we usually assume that other relevant variables remain constant.

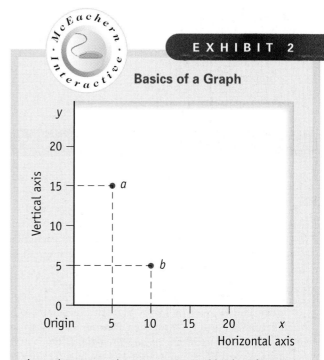

EXHIBIT 2

Basics of a Graph

Any point on a graph represents a combination of particular values of two variables. Here point a represents the combination of 5 units of variable x (measured on the horizontal axis) and 15 units of variable y (measured on the vertical axis). Point b represents 10 units of x and 5 units of y.

We often observe that one variable appears to depend on another. The time it takes you to drive home depends on your average speed. Your weight depends on how much you eat. The amount of Pepsi purchased depends on its price. A *functional relation* exists between two variables when the value of one variable *depends* on the value of another variable. The value of the **independent variable** determines the value of the **dependent variable**.

The task of the economist is to isolate economic relations and determine the direction of causality, if any. Recall that one of the pitfalls of economic thinking is the erroneous belief that association is causation. We cannot conclude, simply because two events are related in time, that the first event causes the second. There may be no relation between the two events.

EXHIBIT 3

U.S. Unemployment Rate Since 1900

A time-series graph depicts the behavior of some economic variable (here, the unemployment rate) over time.

Sources: *Historical Statistics of the United States*, 1970, and *Economic Report of the President*, February 1999.

DRAWING GRAPHS

Let's begin with a simple relation. Suppose you are planning to drive across country and want to determine how far you will travel each day. You estimate that your speed will average 50 miles per hour. Possible combinations of driving time and distance traveled appear in Exhibit 4. One column lists the hours driven per day, and the next column gives the number of miles traveled per day, assuming an average speed of 50 miles per hour. The distance traveled, the dependent variable, depends on the number of hours driven, the independent variable. We identify combinations of hours driven and distance traveled as *a, b, c,* and so on. We can plot these combinations as a graph in Exhibit 5, with hours driven per day measured along the horizontal axis and total distance traveled along the vertical axis. Each combination of hours driven and distance traveled is represented by a point in Exhibit 5. For example, point *a* shows that when you drive for only 1 hour, you travel only 50 miles. Point *b* indicates that when you drive for 2 hours, you travel 100 miles. By connecting the points, or combinations, we create a line running upward and

to the right. This makes sense because the longer you drive, the farther you travel. Held constant along this line is the average speed of 50 miles per hour.

EXHIBIT 4

Schedule Relating Distance Traveled to Hours Driven

	Hours Driven per Day	Distance Traveled per Day (miles)
a	1	50
b	2	100
c	3	150
d	4	200
e	5	250

EXHIBIT 5

Graph Relating Distance Traveled to Hours Driven

Points *a* through *e* depict different combinations of hours driven per day and the corresponding distances traveled. Connecting these points creates a graph.

Types of relations between variables include the following: (1) As one variable increases, the other increases, too—as in Exhibit 5; in this case there is a **positive, or direct, relation** between the variables; (2) as one variable increases, the other decreases; in this case there is a **negative, or inverse, relation;** and (3) as one variable increases, the other remains unchanged; in this case the two variables are said to be *independent, or unrelated.* One of the advantages of graphs is that they easily convey the relation between variables. We do not need to examine the particular combinations of numbers; we need only focus on the shape of the curve.

THE SLOPES OF STRAIGHT LINES

A more precise way to describe the shape of a curve is to measure its slope. The **slope** of a line indicates how much the vertical variable changes for a given increase in the horizontal variable. Specifically, the slope between any two points along any straight line is the vertical change between these two points divided by the horizontal increase, or

$$\text{Slope} = \frac{\text{Change in the vertical distance}}{\text{Increase in the horizontal distance}}$$

Each of the four panels in Exhibit 6 indicates a vertical change, given a 10-unit increase in the horizontal variable. In panel (a), the vertical distance increases by 5 units when the horizontal distance increases by 10 units. The slope of the line in panel (a) is therefore 5/10, or 0.5. Notice that the slope in this case is a positive number because the relation between the two variables is positive, or direct. This slope indicates that for every 1-unit increase in the horizontal variable, the vertical variable increases by 0.5 units. The slope, incidentally, does not imply causality; the increase in the horizontal variable does not necessarily *cause* the increase in the vertical variable. The slope simply indicates in a uniform way the relation between an increase in the horizontal variable and the associated change in the vertical variable.

In panel (b), the vertical distance declines by 7 units when the horizontal distance increases by 10 units, so the slope equals –7/10, or –0.7. The slope in this case is a negative number because the two variables have a negative, or inverse, relation. In panel (c), the vertical variable remains unchanged as the horizontal variable increases by 10, so the slope equals 0/10, or 0. These two variables are unrelated. Finally, in panel (d), the vertical variable can take on any value, although the horizontal variable remains unchanged. In this case any change in the vertical measure, for example a 10-unit change, is divided by 0, since the horizontal value does not change. Any change divided by 0 is infinitely large, so we say that the slope of a vertical line is infinite. Again, the two variables are unrelated.

THE SLOPE, UNITS OF MEASUREMENT, AND MARGINAL ANALYSIS

The mathematical value of the slope depends on the units of measurement on the graph. For example, suppose copper tubing costs $1 a foot to produce. Graphs depicting the relation between output and total cost are shown in Exhibit 7. In panel (a), total cost of production increases by $1 for each 1-foot increase in the amount of tubing produced. Thus, the slope in panel (a) equals 1/1, or 1. If the cost remains the same but the unit of measurement is not *feet* but *yards,* the relation between output and total cost is as depicted in panel (b). Now, total cost increases by $3 for each 1-yard increase in output, so the slope equals 3/1, or 3. Because of differences in the units used to measure copper tubing, the two panels reflect different slopes, even though the cost of tubing is $1 per foot in each panel. Keep in mind that *the slope will depend in part on the units of measurement.*

Economic analysis usually involves *marginal analysis,* such as the marginal cost of producing one more unit of output. The slope is a convenient device for measuring marginal effects because it reflects the change in total cost along the vertical axis for each 1-unit change along the horizontal axis. For example, in panel (a) of Exhibit 7, the marginal cost of

EXHIBIT 6

**Alternative Slopes
for Straight Lines**

The slope of a line indicates how much the vertically measured variable changes for a given increase in the variable measured on the horizontal axis. Panel (a) shows a positive relation between two variables; the slope is 0.5, a positive number. Panel (b) depicts a negative, or inverse, relation. When the *x* variable increases, the *y* variable decreases; the slope is –0.7, a negative number. Panels (c) and (d) represent situations in which two variables are unrelated. In panel (c), the *y* variable always takes on the same value; the slope is 0. In panel (d), the *x* variable always takes on the same value; the slope is infinite.

another *foot* of copper tubing is $1, which also equals the slope of the line. In panel (b), the marginal cost of another *yard* of tubing is $3, which again is the slope of that line. Because of its applicability to marginal analysis, the slope has special significance in economics.

THE SLOPES OF CURVED LINES

The slope of a straight line is the same everywhere along that line, but the slope of a curved line varies at different points along the curve, as in Exhibit 8. To find the slope of that

curved line at a particular point, draw a straight line that just touches the curve at that point but does not cut or cross the curve. Such a line is called a **tangent** to the curve at that point. The slope of the tangent is the slope of the curve at that point. Look at the line *AA*, which is tangent to the curve at point *a*. As the horizontal value increases from 0 to 10, the vertical value drops along *AA* from 40 to 0. Thus, the vertical change divided by the horizontal change equals –40/10, or –4, which is the slope of the curve at point *a*. This slope is negative because the curve slopes downward at that point. Along *BB*, a line drawn tangent to the curve at point *b*, the

EXHIBIT 7

Slope Depends on the Unit of Measure

(a) Measured in feet

Total cost

$6
5

$\text{Slope} = \dfrac{1}{1} = 1$

5 6

Feet of copper tubing

(b) Measured in yards

Total cost

$6

3

$\text{Slope} = \dfrac{3}{1} = 3$

1 2

Yards of copper tubing

The value of the slope depends on the units of measure. In panel (a), output is measured in feet of copper tubing; in panel (b), output is measured in yards. Although the cost of production is $1 per foot in each panel, the slope is different in the two panels because copper tubing is measured using different units.

slope again is the change in the vertical divided by the change in the horizontal, or −10/30, which equals −0.33. As you can see, the curve depicted in Exhibit 8 gets flatter as the horizontal variable increases, so the value of its slope approaches zero.

Other curves, of course, will reflect different slopes as well as different changes in the slope along the curve. Downward-sloping curves have a negative slope, and upward-sloping curves, a positive slope. Sometimes curves are more complex, having both positive and negative ranges, such as in the hill-shaped curve in Exhibit 9. For relatively small values of x, there is a positive relation between x and y, so the slope is positive. As the value of x increases, however, the slope declines and eventually becomes negative. We can divide the curve into two segments: (1) the segment between the origin and point a, where the slope is positive, and (2) the segment of the curve to the right of point a, where the slope is negative. The slope of the curve at point a is 0. The U-shaped curve in Exhibit 9 represents the opposite relation: x and y are negatively related until point b is reached; thereafter they are positively related. The slope equals 0 at point b.

CURVE SHIFTS

Let's go back to your cross country trip, where we were trying to determine how many miles you traveled per day. Re-

EXHIBIT 8

Slopes at Different Points on a Curved Line

The slope of a curved line varies from point to point. At a given point, such as a or b, the slope of the curve is equal to the slope of the straight line that is tangent to the curve at that point.

EXHIBIT 9

Curves with Both Positive and Negative Ranges

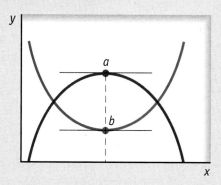

Some curves have both positive and negative slopes. The hill-shaped curve has a positive slope to the left of point *a*, a slope of 0 at point *a*, and a negative slope to the right of that point. The U-shaped curve starts off with a negative slope, has a slope of 0 at point *b*, and has a positive slope to the right of that point.

EXHIBIT 10

Shift in Curve Relating Distance Traveled to Hours Driven

Curve *T* appeared originally in Exhibit 5 to show the relation between hours driven per day and distance traveled per day, assuming an average speed of 50 miles per hour. If the average speed is only 40 miles per hour, the entire relation shifts to the right to *T'*, indicating that each distance traveled requires more driving time. For example, 200 miles traveled takes 4 hours of driving at 50 miles per hour, but that distance takes 5 hours at 40 miles per hour.

call that we measured hours driven per day on the horizontal axis and distance traveled per day on the vertical axis, assuming an average speed of 50 miles per hour. That same relation is shown as curve *T* in Exhibit 10. What if the average speed is not 50 miles per hour, but instead is 40 miles per hour? The entire relation between hours driven and distance traveled would change, as shown by the shift to the right in the curve to *T'*. With a slower average speed, any distance traveled per day now requires more driving time. For example, 4 hours of driving result in 200 miles traveled when the average speed is 50 miles per hour (as shown by point *d* on curve *T*), but that distance takes five hours when the speed averages 40 miles per hour (as shown by point *f* on curve

T'). Thus, *a change in the assumption about average speed changes the relationship between the two variables observed*. This changed relationship is expressed by a shift in the curve that shows how the two variables relate.

With this we close our once-over of graphs. Return to this appendix when you feel you need to review.

APPENDIX QUESTIONS

1. *(Understanding Graphs)* Look at Exhibit 3 and answer the following questions:
   a. In what year (approximately) was the unemployment rate the highest? In what year was it the lowest?
   b. In what decade, on average, was the unemployment rate highest? In what decade was it lowest?
   c. Between 1950 and 1980, did the unemployment rate *generally* increase, decrease, or remain about the same?

2. *(Drawing Graphs)* Sketch a graph to illustrate your idea of each of the following relationships. Be sure to label both axes appropriately. In each case, explain under what circumstances, if any, the curve could shift:
   a. The relationship between a person's age and height
   b. Average monthly temperature over the course of a year
   c. A person's income and the number of hamburgers consumed per month
   d. The amount of fertilizer added to an acre of land and the amount of corn grown on that land in one growing season
   e. An automobile's horsepower and its gasoline mileage (in miles per gallon)

3. *(Slope)* Suppose you are given the following data on wage rates and number of hours worked:

Point	Hourly Wage	Hours Worked Per Week
A	$ 0	0
B	5	0
C	10	30
D	15	35
E	20	45
F	25	50

   a. Construct and label a set of axes and plot these six points. Label each point. What variable do you think should be measured on the vertical axis, and which variable should be measured on the horizontal axis?
   b. Connect the points. Describe the curve you find. Does it make sense to you?
   c. Compute the slope of the curve between points A and B. Between points B and C. Between points C and D. Between points D and E. Between points E and F. What happens to the slope as you move from point A to point F?

Some Tools of Economic Analysis

W hy are you reading this book right now rather than doing something else?

What does college attendance cost you? Why will you eventually major in

one discipline rather than take courses in many different disciplines? Why is

fast food so fast? Why is there no sense crying over spilt milk? These and other

questions are addressed in this chapter, which introduces some tools of

economics—some tools of the trade.

The first chapter introduced the idea that scarcity forces us to make

economic choices, but the chapter said little about how to make good choices.

In this chapter we develop a framework for evaluating economic alterna-

tives. First, we think about the cost involved in selecting one alternative over

others. Next, we develop tools to explore the production choices available to individuals and to the economy as a whole. Finally, we examine the questions that different economies must answer—questions about what goods and services to produce, how to produce them and for whom. Topics discussed in this chapter include:

- Opportunity cost
- Division of labor
- Comparative advantage
- Specialization

- Production possibilities frontier
- Three economic questions
- Economic systems

CHOICE AND OPPORTUNITY COST

Think about a decision you just made: the decision to read this chapter right now rather than use the time to study for another course, play sports, watch TV, get some sleep, or do something else. Suppose your best alternative to reading right now is getting some sleep. The cost of reading is passing up the opportunity to sleep. Because of scarcity, whenever you make a choice, you must pass up another opportunity; you must incur an *opportunity cost*.

Opportunity Cost

Opportunity cost The value of the best alternative forgone when an item or activity is chosen

What do we mean when we talk about the cost of something? Isn't it what we have to give up—to sacrifice—to get that thing? The **opportunity cost** of the chosen item or activity is *the value of the best alternative that is forgone*. You might think of opportunity cost as the *opportunity lost*. Sometimes opportunity cost can be measured in terms of money, although, as we shall see, money is usually only part of the opportunity cost.

How many times have you heard people say they did something because they "had nothing better to do"? They actually mean they had no alternatives as attractive as the choice they selected. Yet, according to the idea of opportunity cost, people *always* do what they do because they have nothing better to do. The choice selected seems, at the time, preferable to any other possible choice. You are reading this chapter right now because you have nothing better to do. In fact, you are attending college for the same reason: College appears more attractive than your best alternative. In the following case study, consider the opportunity cost of attending college.

The Opportunity Cost of College

CaseStudy

The World of Business

Is college a sensible investment for you? Find out by trying Professor Jane Leuthold's COLLEGE CHOICE program at http://www.cba.uiuc.edu/college/econ/choice/choice.html.

What is your opportunity cost of attending college full time this year? What was the most valued alternative you gave up to attend college? If you had a job, you have a good idea of the income you gave up to attend college. Suppose you expected to earn $16,000 a year, after taxes, from a full-time job. As a college student, you can work part time during the school year and full time during the summer. Suppose you can earn a total of $7,000 throughout the year after taxes. Thus, by attending college this year you are giving up net earnings of $9,000 (= $16,000 − $7,000).

There is also the direct cost of college itself. Suppose you are paying $5,000 this year for tuition, fees, and books at a public college. This money is unavailable to you (or your family) to spend elsewhere. So the opportunity cost of paying for tuition, fees, and books is the value of the goods and services that money could have purchased. Tuition, fees, and books would be much higher at a private college—more like $15,000 to $20,000.

Expenses for room and board are not necessarily opportunity costs because, even if you were not attending college, you would still need to live somewhere and eat something (though these costs could be higher at college). Likewise, whether or not you attended college, you would still incur outlays for items such as entertainment, clothes, toiletries, and laundry. Such expenses do not represent an opportunity cost of attending college. They are personal upkeep costs that arise regardless of what you are doing. For simplicity, let's assume that room, board, and personal expenses are the same whether or not you attend college; so they are not an opportunity cost of college. Thus, the forgone earnings of $9,000 plus the $5,000 for tuition, fees, and books yield an opportunity cost of $14,000 for attending college this year at a public college (at a private college, your opportunity cost could be double that amount).

This analysis assumes that other things are constant. If, in your view, attending college is more of a pain than you expected the most valued alternative to be, the opportunity cost of attending college is even higher. In other words, if you are one of those people who find college difficult, often boring, and in most ways more unpleasant than a full-time job, then the cost in money terms understates your true opportunity cost. Not only are you incurring the expense of college, but you are forgoing a more pleasant quality of life. If, on the contrary, you think the wild and crazy life of a college student is more enjoyable than a full-time job, then $14,000 overstates your true opportunity cost, because the best alternative involves a less satisfying quality of life.

Evidently, you view college as a wise investment in your future, even though it is costly and perhaps even painful. In fact, a growing fraction of college students are willing to go into debt to finance their education. Some students, even those who attend public universities, graduate with debts exceeding $20,000.

Still, college is not for everyone. Some people find college less attractive than alternatives. Tiger Woods, once an economics major at Stanford, dropped out after two years to earn millions in professional golf. Some high school seniors who believe they are ready for professional basketball skip college altogether, as do most pro tennis players and many actors. (Tom Cruise even dropped out of high school.)

Sources: "Debt Load—Class of '96," *America's Best Colleges: 1998, U.S. News & World Report,* pp. 63–64; Ellen Graham, "Study Now, Pay Later: Students Pile on Debt," *Wall Street Journal,* 11 August 1995; and CollegeNET, the "Internet Guide to Colleges and Universities" at http://www.collegenet.com.

Opportunity Cost Is Subjective

Opportunity cost is subjective. Only the individual chooser can select the most attractive alternative. And the chooser seldom knows the actual value of the best alternative forgone, since that alternative is "the road not taken." (Incidentally, focusing on only the best alternative forgone makes all other alternatives irrelevant.) Thus, if you give up an evening of pizza and conversation with friends to work on a term paper, you will never know the exact value of what you gave up. You know only what you *expected*. Evidently you expected the value of working on that paper to exceed the value of the best alternative.

Calculating Opportunity Cost Requires Time and Information. We have assumed that people rationally choose the most valued alternative. This does not mean they exhaustively calculate the value of all possible alternatives. Since acquiring information about alternatives is costly and time consuming, people usually make choices based on limited or even incorrect information. Indeed, some choices may turn out to be poor ones (as examples, you went on a picnic and it rained; the movie you rented was boring; the shoes you bought gave you blisters). At the time you made the choice, however, you thought you were making the best use of all your scarce resources, including the time required to gather and evaluate information about your alternatives.

Time Is the Ultimate Constraint. The Sultan of Brunei is among the world's richest people, based on the huge oil revenues that flow into his tiny country. His palace has 2,000 rooms, with walls of fine Italian marble. His throne room is the size of a football field. He owns 150 Rolls Royces.[1] Supported by such wealth, he appears to have overcome the economic problem caused by scarce resources but unlimited wants. But even though the Sultan can buy whatever he wants, the *time* he has to enjoy his acquisitions is limited. If he pursues one activity, he cannot at the same time do something else, so each activity he undertakes has an opportunity cost. Consequently, the Sultan must choose from among the competing uses of his scarcest resource, time. Though your alternatives are not as exotic as the Sultan's, you, too, face a time constraint, especially toward the end of the college term.

Opportunity Cost May Vary with Circumstance. Opportunity cost depends on the value of your alternatives. This is why you are more likely to study on a Tuesday night than on a Saturday night. On a Tuesday night, the opportunity cost of studying is lower because you have fewer attractive alternatives than on a Saturday night, when more is happening. Suppose you choose a movie for Saturday night. The opportunity cost of the movie is the value forgone from your best alternative, which might be attending a sporting event. For some of you, studying on Saturday night may be well down the list of alternatives—perhaps ahead of reorganizing your closet, but certainly behind watching trucks being unloaded at the supermarket.

Opportunity cost is subjective, but in some circumstances money paid for goods and services is a good approximation of their opportunity cost. For example, the opportunity cost of the new CD player you bought is the value of spending that $300 on the best forgone alternative. However, sometimes the monetary-cost definition may leave out some important elements, particularly the time involved. For example, watching a video costs you not only the rental fee but also the time and travel expense to get it, watch it, and return it.

---

1 These figures are reported by Kieran Cooke in "Sultan's Swing to Reform," *London Financial Times,* 4 August 1995.

Sunk Cost and Choice

Suppose you have just finished shopping for groceries and are wheeling your grocery cart toward the row of checkout counters. How do you decide which line to join? You pick the line you think will involve the least time. Suppose, after waiting for 10 minutes in a line that barely moves, you notice that a cashier has opened another register and invites you to check out. Do you switch to the new line, or do you think, "Since I have already spent 10 minutes in this line, I'm going to stay here"? The 10 minutes you already waited represents a *sunk cost*, which is a cost that you cannot recover regardless of what you do. **Sunk costs** are costs that cannot be avoided, regardless of what you do in the future, because they have already been incurred. You should ignore sunk costs in making economic choices, because your choice has no impact on something that has already happened. Therefore, you should switch to the newly opened line.

Economic decision makers should consider only those costs that are affected by the choice. Sunk costs have already been incurred and thus are not affected by the choice, so they are irrelevant. Likewise, you should walk out on a boring movie even if the admission cost you $8. The irrelevance of sunk costs is underscored by the proverb is "There is no sense crying over spilt milk." Remember, you should ignore sunk costs because they have already been incurred; the milk has already spilled, so whatever you do now has no impact on those costs.

Sunk cost A cost that has already been incurred in the past and, hence, a cost that is irrelevant to present and future economic decisions

SPECIALIZATION, COMPARATIVE ADVANTAGE, AND EXCHANGE

Suppose you live in a dormitory. You and your roommate have such busy schedules that you each can spare only about an hour per week for such mundane tasks as typing and ironing. Each of you must turn in a three-page typed paper every week, and you each prefer to have your shirts ironed if you have the time. Suppose it takes you a half hour to type the three-page paper. Your roommate is from the hunt-and-peck school and takes about an hour to type the paper. But your roommate is talented at ironing and can iron a shirt in 5 minutes flat (or should that be, iron it flat in 5 minutes). You take about twice as long, or 10 minutes, to iron a shirt.

During the hour available each week for typing and ironing, the typing takes priority. If you each do your own typing and ironing, your roommate takes the entire hour to type the paper and so has no time left for ironing. You type your paper in a half hour and iron three shirts in the remaining half hour. Thus, with each of you performing your own tasks, the combined output is two typed papers and three ironed shirts.

The Law of Comparative Advantage

Before long, you each realize that total output would increase if you did all the typing and your roommate did all the ironing. In the hour available for these tasks, you type both papers and your roommate irons twelve shirts. As a result of specialization, total output increases by nine shirts! You strike a deal to exchange your typing for your roommate's ironing, so you each end up with a typed paper and six ironed shirts. Thus, *each of you is better off as a result of specialization*

Law of comparative advantage The individual, firm, region, or country with the lowest opportunity cost of producing a particular good should specialize in producing that good.

and exchange. By specializing in the task that you each do best, you both employ the **law of comparative advantage,** which states that the individual with the lower opportunity cost of producing a particular output should specialize in producing that output.

Absolute and Comparative Advantage

The gains from specialization and exchange in the previous example seem obvious. A more interesting case arises if you are not only a faster typist but also a faster ironer. Suppose we change the example so that your roommate takes 12 minutes to iron a shirt, compared to your 10 minutes. You now have an *absolute advantage* in both tasks, meaning each task takes you less time than it does your roommate. More generally, having an **absolute advantage** means being able to produce a product using fewer resources than other producers require.

Absolute advantage The ability to produce something using fewer resources than other producers use

Does your absolute advantage in both activities mean specialization is no longer a good idea? Recall that the law of comparative advantage states that the individual with *the lower opportunity cost* of producing a particular good should specialize in producing that good. You still take 30 minutes to type a paper and 10 minutes to iron a shirt, so your opportunity cost of typing a paper is ironing 3 shirts. Your roommate takes an hour to type a paper and 12 minutes to iron a shirt, so your roommate could iron 5 shirts in the time taken to type a paper. Hence your opportunity cost of typing a paper is ironing 3 shirts, and your roommate's opportunity cost is ironing 5 shirts. *Because your opportunity cost of typing is lower than your roommate's, you have a comparative advantage in typing.* Since you have a comparative advantage in typing, your roommate must have a comparative advantage in ironing (try working this out to your satisfaction). Hence you should do all the typing and your roommate, all the ironing. Although you have an absolute advantage in both tasks, your **comparative advantage** calls for specializing in the task for which you have the lower opportunity cost—in this case, typing.

Comparative advantage The ability to produce something at a lower opportunity cost than other producers face

If neither of you specialized, you could type one paper and iron three shirts; your roommate could still type just the one paper. Your combined output would be two papers and three shirts. If you each specialized according to comparative advantage, in an hour you could type both papers and your roommate could iron five shirts. Thus, specialization increases total output by two ironed shirts. Exhibit 1 summarizes this example. Even though you are better at both tasks than your roommate, you are comparatively better at typing. Put another way, your roommate, although worse at both tasks, is not quite as poor at ironing as at typing.

Don't think this is simply common sense. Common sense would lead you to do your own ironing and typing, since you are more skilled at both. *Absolute advantage focuses on who uses the fewest resources, but comparative advantage focuses on what else those resources could have been used to produce—that is, on the opportunity cost of those resources.* Comparative advantage is the better guide to who should do what.

The law of comparative advantage applies not only to individuals but also to firms, regions of a country, and entire nations. Those individuals, firms, regions, or countries with the lowest opportunity cost of producing a particular good should specialize in producing that good. Because of such factors as climate, the skills of the workforce, plus the capital and natural resources available,

EXHIBIT 1

CASE 1: You are a faster typist and your roommate is a faster ironer.

	Output per Hour			
	Each Does Own		Each Specializes	
	Typed Papers	Ironed Shirts	Typed Papers	Ironed Shirts
You	1	3	2	0
Roommate	1	0	0	12
Total	2	3	2	12

CASE 2: You are a faster typist and a faster ironer, but you are a comparatively faster typist.

	Output per Hour			
	Each Does Own		Each Specializes	
	Typed Papers	Ironed Shirts	Typed Papers	Ironed Shirts
You	1	3	2	0
Roommate	1	0	0	5
Total	2	3	2	5

Comparative Advantage: Maximizing Output

Cases 1 and 2 both show gains from specialization and exchange for you and your roommate. In both cases it takes you half an hour to type the paper and 10 minutes to iron one shirt. In both cases your roommate takes 1 hour to type the paper. But, whereas in Case 1 it takes your roommate only 5 minutes to iron a shirt, in Case 2 it takes 12 minutes to iron a shirt. In Case 1 you have an absolute advantage and a comparative advantage in typing, so total output is greater if you do all the typing and your roommate does all the ironing. In Case 2 you have an absolute advantage in both typing and ironing. But you have a comparative advantage only in typing because you have a lower opportunity cost of typing than does your roommate. So in Case 2 output is maximized if you do all the typing and your roommate does all the ironing.

certain parts of the country and certain parts of the world have a comparative advantage in producing particular goods. From Apple computers in California's Silicon Valley to oranges in sunny Florida, from VCRs in Korea to bananas in Honduras—*resources are allocated most efficiently across the country and around the world when production and trade conform to the law of comparative advantage.*

Specialization and Exchange

In the previous example, you and your roommate specialized and then exchanged your output. No money was involved. In other words, you engaged in barter. **Barter** is a system of exchange in which products are traded directly for other products. Barter works satisfactorily in very simple economies where there is little specialization and few different goods to trade. But for economies with greater specialization, *money* plays an important role in facilitating exchange. Money—coins, bills, and checks—serves as a *medium of exchange* because it is the one thing that everyone is willing to accept in return for all goods and services.

Barter The direct exchange of one good for another without the use of money

Because of specialization and comparative advantage, most people consume little of what they produce and produce little of what they consume. People specialize in particular activities, such as plumbing or carpentry, and they exchange their products for money, which in turn is exchanged for goods and services produced by others. Did you make any article of the clothing you are wearing? Probably not. Think about the degree of specialization that goes into your cotton shirt. Some farmer in a warm climate grew the cotton and sold it to someone who spun it into thread, who sold it to someone who wove it into fabric, who sold it to someone who sewed the shirt, who sold it to a wholesaler, who sold it to a retailer, who sold it to you. Your shirt was produced by many specialists.

Division of Labor and Gains from Specialization

Picture a visit to McDonald's: "Let's see, I'll have a Big Mac, an order of fries, and a chocolate shake." About a minute later your order is ready. It would take you about an hour to make a homemade version of this meal. Why is the McDonald's meal faster, cheaper, and—for some people—better tasting than one you could make yourself? Why is fast food so fast?

Division of labor Organizing production of a good into its separate tasks

McDonald's is taking advantage of the gains resulting from the **division of labor.** Rather than have each worker prepare an entire individual meal, McDonald's breaks down meal preparation into various tasks and has individuals specialize in these separate tasks. This division of labor allows the group to produce much more than it could if each person tried to prepare an entire meal. Instead of each of 10 workers doing it all and making a total of, say, 50 complete meals in an hour, workers specialize and produce more like 500 meals per hour.

How is this increase in productivity possible? First, the manager can assign tasks according to *individual preferences and abilities*—according to comparative advantage. The employee with the toothy smile and pleasant personality can handle the customers up front; the employee with the strong back but few social graces can do the heavy lifting out back. Second, a worker who performs the same task again and again gets better at it. Experience is a good teacher. The employee filling orders at the drive-through window, for example, becomes better at handling the special problems that arise in dealing with customers. Third, there is no time lost in moving from one task to another. Finally, and perhaps most important, the **specialization of labor** allows for the introduction of more sophisticated production techniques, techniques that would not make economic sense on a smaller scale. For example, McDonald's large shake machine would be impractical in the home. The specialization of labor allows for the introduction of specialized machines, and these machines make each worker more productive.

Specialization of labor Focusing an individual's efforts on a particular product or a single task

To review: The specialization of labor takes advantage of individual preferences and natural abilities, allows workers to develop more experience at a particular task, reduces the time required to shift between different tasks, and permits the introduction of labor-saving machinery. Specialization and the division of labor occur not only among individuals but also among firms, regions, and indeed entire countries. The clothing production mentioned earlier might involve growing cotton in one country, turning the cotton into cloth in another, sewing the clothing in a third country, and marketing that clothing in a fourth country.

We should also note that specialization can create problems, since doing the same thing all day often becomes tedious. Consider, for example, the assembly line worker whose task is to tighten a particular bolt. Such a job could drive that worker nuts. Repetitive motion can also lead to injury. Thus, the gains from breaking production down into individual tasks must be weighed against the problems caused by assigning workers to repetitive and tedious jobs. Specialization is discussed in the following case study.

Evidence of Specialization

CaseStudy

The World of Business

Economics is a subject that has benefited from specialization and the division of labor. To get a feel for the many different subjects that economists investigate, take a look at the *Journal of Economic Literature*'s classification system at http://www.econlit.org/elclasbk.htm.

Evidence of specialization is all around us. Dozens of "specialty stores" at the mall focus on products ranging from luggage to party supplies to pet products. Restaurants specialize in cuisine from soup to sushi. Let your fingers do the walking through the Yellow Pages, and you will find thousands of separate specializations. Listings under "Physicians" alone offer dozens of medical specialties. Without moving a muscle, you can witness the division of labor within a single industry; watch the credits roll at the end of a movie, and you will see dozens and sometimes hundreds of specialists are listed—everyone from the gaffer (lighting electrician) to the assistant location scout.

Perhaps the easiest way to explore specialization and the division of labor is on the Internet, where millions of individual sites offer specialized products or activities. For example, Cyberian Outpost sells computers around the world; its Web site takes orders in more than a dozen languages. BigBook, a huge on-line phone directly offering over 16 million business listings allows you to look up any specialty listing for any U.S. state or city. For example, South Carolina has only one tattoo parlor, whereas Oregon, a state with a smaller population, has 43.

With a search engine such as Lycos, you can identify the number of Web sites that reference any specialty. For example, at last count, "economist" yielded about 13,000 sites, compared to 11,000 for "accountant," 7,000 for "physicist," and 2,000 for "sociologist." "Economics" turns up about 100,000 sites. "Entrepreneurs" are found at over 12,000 sites. From "aardvark" to "zucchini," the Internet identifies more specialties than any other reference source in the world.

Sources: Lycos technology is developed and marketed by Lycos, Inc., an independent operating company of CMG Information Services; BigBook's address is http://www.bigbook.com.

THE ECONOMY'S PRODUCTION POSSIBILITIES

The focus to this point has been on how individuals choose to use their scarce resources to satisfy their unlimited wants or, more specifically, how they specialize based on comparative advantage. This emphasis on the individual has been appropriate because the economy is shaped by the choices of individual decision makers, whether they are consumers, producers, or public officials. Just as resources are scarce for the individual, they are also scarce for the economy as a whole (no fallacy of composition here). An economy has millions of different resources that can be combined in all kinds of ways to produce millions of possible goods and services. In this section, we step back from the immense complexity of the real economy to develop our first model, which presents the economy's production options.

Efficiency and the Production Possibilities Frontier

Let's develop a model to get some idea how much can be produced in the economy with the resources available. What is the economy's production capabilities? Here are the model's simplifying assumptions:

1. To reduce the analysis to manageable proportions, we limit the output to just two broad classes of products. In our example they are consumer goods, such as pizzas and haircuts, and capital goods, which includes physical capital such as tractors, and human capital, such as college education.
2. The focus is on production during a given time period—in this case, a year.
3. The resources available in the economy are fixed in both quantity and quality during the time period.
4. Society's knowledge about how these resources can be combined to produce output—that is, the available *technology*—does not change during the year.

The point of these assumptions is to freeze the economy in time and to focus on the economy's production alternatives based on the resources and technology available during that time.

Given the resources and the technology available in the economy, the **production possibilities frontier,** or **PPF,** identifies the various possible combinations of the two types of goods that can be produced when all available resources are employed efficiently. *Resources are said to be employed efficiently when there is no change in the way the resources are combined that could increase the production of one type of good without decreasing the production of the other type of good.* **Efficiency** involves getting the maximum possible output from available resources.

The economy's PPF for consumer goods and capital goods is shown by the curve *AF* in Exhibit 2. Point *A* identifies the amount of consumer goods produced per year if all the economy's resources are used efficiently to produce consumer goods, and *F* identifies the amount of capital goods produced per year if all the economy's resources are used efficiently to produce capital goods. Points along the curve between *A* and *F* identify possible combinations of the two types of goods that can be produced when all the economy's resources are used *efficiently*.

Inefficient and Unattainable Production

Points inside the PPF, including *G* in Exhibit 2, represent combinations that either do not employ resources fully or employ them inefficiently. Note that point *C* yields more consumer goods and no fewer capital goods than *G*. And point *E* yields more capital goods and no fewer consumer goods than *G*.

Production possibilities frontier (PPF) A curve showing alternative combinations of goods that can be produced when available resources are used efficiently

Efficiency The condition that exists when there is no way resources can be reallocated to increase the production of one good without decreasing the production of another

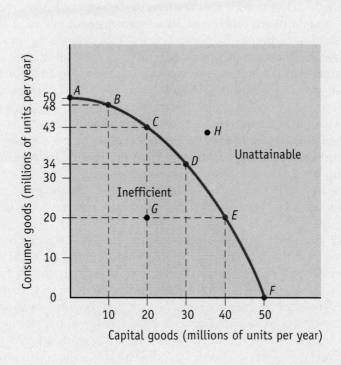

EXHIBIT 2

The Economy's Production Possibilities Frontier

If the economy uses its available resources and technology fully and efficiently in producing consumer goods and capital goods, it will be on its production possibilities frontier curve *AF.* The PPF is bowed out to illustrate the law of increasing opportunity cost: additional units of capital goods require the economy to sacrifice more and more units of consumer goods. Note that more consumer goods must be given up in moving from *D* to *E* than in moving from *A* to *B,* although in each case the gain in capital goods is 10 million units. Points inside the PPF, such as *G,* represent inefficient use of resources. Points outside the PPF, such as *H,* represent unattainable combinations.

Indeed, any point along the PPF between *C* and *E*, such as point *D*, yields both more consumer goods and more capital goods than *G*. Hence, point *G* is *inefficient*; by using resources more efficiently or by using previously idle resources, the economy can produce more of at least one good without reducing the production of the other good.

Points outside the PPF, such as *H* in Exhibit 2, represent *unattainable* combinations, given the resources and the technology available. Thus *the PPF not only reflects efficient combinations of production but also identifies the border between inefficient combinations inside the frontier and unattainable combinations outside the frontier.*

Shape of the Production Possibilities Frontier

Focus again on point *A* in Exhibit 2. Any movement along the PPF involves giving up some of one good to get more of the other. Movements down along the curve indicate that the opportunity cost of more capital goods is fewer consumer goods. For example, moving from point *A* to point *B increases* the amount of capital goods produced from none to 10 million units and *reduces* production of consumer goods from 50 million to 48 million units, a decline of only 2 million units. Increasing production of capital goods to 10 million units causes the production of consumer goods to fall just a little, because capital production initially draws upon resources (such as heavy machinery used to build factories) that add little to production of consumer goods but are quite productive in making capital goods.

As shown by the dashed lines in Exhibit 2, each additional 10 million units of capital goods reduces consumer goods by more and more. As more capital goods are produced, the resources drawn away from consumer goods are those that are better suited to producing consumer goods. *Opportunity cost increases as the economy produces more capital goods, because the resources in the economy are not all perfectly adaptable to the production of both types of goods.* The shape of the production possibilities frontier reflects the **law of increasing opportunity cost.** If the economy uses all resources efficiently, the law of increasing opportunity cost states that each additional increment of one good requires the economy to sacrifice successively larger and larger increments of the other good.

The PPF derives its bowed-out shape from the law of increasing opportunity cost. For example, whereas the first 10 million units of capital goods have an opportunity cost of only 2 million units of consumer goods, the final 10 million—that is, the increase from point *E* and point *F*—have an opportunity cost of 20 million units of consumer goods. Notice that the slope of the PPF shows the opportunity cost of an increment of capital. As we move down the curve, the curve becomes steeper, reflecting the higher opportunity cost of capital goods in terms of forgone consumer goods. The law of increasing opportunity cost also applies when moving from the production of capital goods to the production of consumer goods. Incidentally, if resources were perfectly adaptable to alternative uses, the PPF would be a straight line, reflecting a constant opportunity cost along the PPF.

What Can Shift the Production Possibilities Frontier?

When we construct the production possibilities frontier, we assume that resources available in the economy and the level of technology are fixed. Over time, however, the PPF may shift as a result of changes in resource availability or in technology. A shift outward in the PPF reflects **economic growth,** which shows an expansion in the economy's ability to produce goods and services.

Changes in Resource Availability. If people decide to work longer hours, the PPF will shift outward, as shown in panel (a) of Exhibit 3. An increase in the size or the health of the labor force, an increase in the skills of the labor force, or an increase in the availability of other resources, such as new oil discoveries, will also shift the PPF outward. In contrast, a decrease in the availability or the quality of resources will shift the PPF inward, as depicted in panel (b). For example, in 1990 Iraq invaded Kuwait, setting oil fields ablaze and destroying much of Kuwait's physical capital, thereby shifting Kuwait's PPF inward. In West Africa the encroaching sands of the Sahara cover and destroy thousands of square miles of productive farmland each year, shifting the PPF of that economy inward.

Law of increasing opportunity cost To produce each additional increment of a particular good, a successively larger increment of an alternative good must be sacrificed if the economy's resources are already being used efficiently

Economic growth A shift outward in the production possibilities frontier; an increase in the economy's ability to produce goods and services

EXHIBIT 3

Shifts in the Economy's Production Possibilities Frontier

(a) Increase in available resources

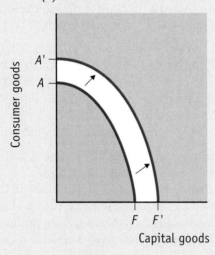

(b) Decrease in available resources

(c) Increase in resources or technological advance that benefits consumer goods

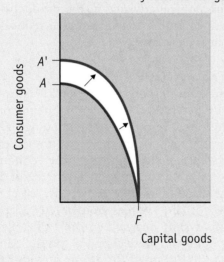

(d) Increase in resources or technological advance that benefits capital goods

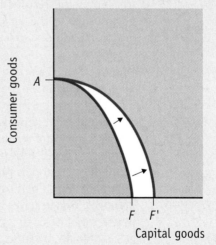

When the resources available to an economy change, the PPF shifts. If more resources become available, the PPF shifts outward, as in panel (a), indicating that more output can be produced. A decrease in available resources causes the PPF to shift inward, as in panel (b). Panel (c) shows a change affecting consumer goods production. More consumer goods can now be produced at any given level of capital goods. Panel (d) shows a change affecting capital goods production.

The new PPFs in both panels (a) and (b) appear to be parallel to the original PPF, indicating that the resource that changed could produce either good. For example, an increased supply of electrical power can be used in the production of both consumer goods and capital goods. If, however, a resource (such as farmland, for example) is suited only to the production of consumer goods, then an increase in the supply of that resource will shift the PPF more along the consumer goods axis than along the capital goods axis, as shown in panel (c). Panel (d) shows the effect of an increase in the supply of a resource (such as construction equipment) that is suited only to capital goods.

Increases in the Capital Stock. An economy's production possibilities frontier depends in part on the stock of human and physical capital. The more capital an economy accumulates during one period, the more output can be produced in the next period. Thus, increased production of capital goods this period (for example, by more machines in the case of physical capital or better education in the case of human capital) will shift out the economy's PPF next period.

Technological Change. Another type of change that could shift the economy's PPF outward is a technological discovery that employs available resources more efficiently. Some discoveries enhance the production of both products, such as an innovation that manages resources more efficiently. This is shown in panel (a) of Exhibit 3. The effect of a technological advance in the production of consumer goods, such as genetically altered seeds that double crop production, is reflected by a shift outward of the PPF along the consumer goods axis, as shown in panel (c) of Exhibit 3 (note that point *F* remains unchanged since the technological breakthrough does not affect the production of capital goods). Panel (d) shows the result of a technological advance in the production of capital goods, such as the development of improved software that reduces the cost of designing and manufacturing heavy machinery.

What We Can Learn from the PPF

The production possibilities frontier demonstrates several ideas introduced so far. The first is *efficiency*: The PPF describes the efficient combinations of output that are possible, given the economy's resources and technology. The second is *scarcity*: Given the resources and the technology, the economy can produce only so much. The PPF slopes downward, indicating that, as the economy produces more of one good, it produces less of the other good. This tradeoff demonstrates *opportunity cost*. The bowed-out shape of the PPF reflects the *law of increasing opportunity cost;* it arises because not all resources are perfectly adaptable to the production of each good. And a shift outward in the PPF reflects *economic growth*. Finally, because society must somehow choose a specific combination of output—a single point—along the PPF, the PPF also underscores the need for *choice*. That choice will determine not only current consumption but also the capital stock available next period. One thing the PPF does not tell us is which combination to choose; the PPF tells us only about the costs, not the benefits, of the two goods. To make a selection, we need information on both costs *and* benefits. How society goes about choosing a particular combination will depend upon the nature of the economic system, as we will see in the next section.

Three Questions Every Economic System Must Answer

Each point along the economy's production possibilities frontier is an efficient combination of output. Whether the economy produces efficiently and how the economy selects the most preferred combination will depend on the decision-making rules employed. Regardless of how decisions are made, each economy must answer three fundamental questions: What goods and services will be produced? How will they be produced? For whom will they be produced? An **economic system** is the set of mechanisms and institutions that resolve the *what, how,* and *for whom* questions. Some criteria used to distinguish among economic systems are (1) who owns the resources, (2) what decision-making process is used to allocate resources and products, and (3) what types of incentives guide the economic decision makers.

Economic system The set of mechanisms and institutions that resolve the what, how, and for whom questions

What Goods and Services Will Be Produced? Most of us take for granted the incredible number of choices that go into deciding what gets produced—everything from which new kitchen appliances are introduced and which aspiring novelists get published to which roads get built. Although different economies resolve these and millions of other questions using different decision-making rules and mechanisms, all economies must somehow make such choices.

How Will Goods and Services Be Produced? The economic system must determine how output is to be produced. Which resources should be used, and how should they be combined to produce each product? How much labor should be used, and at what skill levels? What kinds of machines should be used? What type of fertilizer should be applied to grow the best strawberries? Should the factory be built in the city or closer to the interstate highway? Millions of individual decisions determine which resources are employed and how these resources are combined.

For Whom Will Goods and Services Be Produced? Who will actually consume the goods and services produced? The economic system must determine how to allocate the fruits of production among the population. Should equal amounts be provided to everyone? Should the weak and the sick get more? Should those willing to wait in line the longest receive more? Should goods be allocated according to height? Weight? Religion? Age? Gender? Race? Looks? Strength? Political connections? The value of resources supplied? The question "For whom will goods and services be produced?" is often referred to as the *distribution question.*

ECONOMIC SYSTEMS

Although we discussed the three economic questions separately, they are closely interwoven. The answer to one depends very much on the answers to the others. For example, an economy that distributes goods and services in uniform amounts to all will, no doubt, answer the what-is-to-be-produced question differently than an economy that somehow allows each person to choose a unique mix of goods and services. Laws about resource ownership and the extent to which the government attempts to coordinate economic activity determine the "rules of the game"—the set of conditions that shape individual incentives and constraints. Along a spectrum ranging from the most free to the most regimented type of economic system, the *market system* would be at one end and the *command system* would be at the other end.

Pure Market System

Pure market system An economic system characterized by private ownership of resources and the use of prices to coordinate economic activity in unregulated markets

Under the **pure market system,** the rules of the game include the private ownership of all resources and the coordination of economic activity based on the price signals generated in free, unrestricted markets. Any income derived from supplying labor, capital, land, or entrepreneurial ability goes exclusively to the individual owners of those resources. Owners have *property rights* to the use of their resources and are therefore free to supply those resources to the highest bidder. Producers are free to make and sell whatever they think will be profitable. Consumers are free to buy whatever goods they can afford. All this voluntary buying and selling is coordinated by unrestricted markets, where buyers and sellers make their wishes known. Market prices guide resources to their highest-valued use and channel goods and services to consumers who value them the most.

Under the market system, markets answer the what, how, and for whom questions. Markets transmit information about relative scarcity, provide individual incentives, and distribute income among resource suppliers. No single individual or small group coordinates these activities. Rather, it is the voluntary choices of many buyers and sellers responding only to their individual incentives and constraints that direct resources and products to those who value them the most. According to Adam Smith (1723–1790), one of the first to explain the allocative role of markets, market forces coordinate as if by an "invisible hand"—an unseen force that harnesses the pursuit of self-interest to direct resources where they earn the greatest payoff. According to Smith, *although each individual pursues his or her self-interest, the "invisible hand" of markets promotes the general welfare.* The market system is sometimes called laissez-faire; translated from the French, this phrase means "to let do," or to let people do as they choose without government intervention. Thus, under the market system, voluntary choices based on rational self-interest are made in unrestricted markets to answer the questions what, how, and for whom.

As we shall see in later chapters, a pure market system has its flaws. The most notable market failures are the following:

1. There is no central authority that can protect property rights, enforce contracts, and otherwise ensure that the rules of the game are followed.
2. People with no resources to sell may starve.
3. Some producers may try to monopolize markets by eliminating the competition.
4. The production or consumption of some goods generates byproducts, such as pollution, that affect those not involved in the market transaction.
5. So-called *public goods*, such as national defense, will not be produced by private firms because private firms cannot prevent nonpayers from enjoying the benefits of public goods.

Because of these limitations, countries have modified the pure market system to allow a role for government. Even Adam Smith believed government should play a role. Hong Kong is perhaps the most market-oriented economy in the world today.

*Net*Bookmark

The Center for International Comparisons at the University of Pennsylvania at http://pwt.econ.upenn.edu/ is a good source of information on the performance of economies around the world.

Pure Command System

In a **pure command system,** resources are directed and production is coordinated based on the "command," or central plan, of government rather than by markets. At least in theory, there is public—communal—ownership of property. Government planners, as representatives of all the people, answer such questions as how much steel, how many cars, how many homes, and how many loaves of bread to produce. They also decide how to produce these goods and how to allocate them.

In theory, the pure command system incorporates individual choices into collective choices, which, in turn, are reflected in central planning decisions. In practice, the pure command system also has flaws. Most notably:

1. Running an economy is so complicated that some resources are used inefficiently.
2. Since nobody in particular owns resources, people have less incentive to employ them in their highest-valued use; so some resources are wasted.
3. Central plans may reflect more the preferences of central planners than those of society.
4. Since the central government is responsible for all production, the variety of products is much more limited than what is available in a competitive economy.
5. Each individual has less personal freedom in making economic choices.

Because of these limitations, countries have modified the pure command system to allow a role for markets. North Korea is perhaps the most centrally planned economy in the world today.

Pure command system An economic system characterized by public ownership of resources and centralized economic planning

Mixed and Transitional Economies

No country on earth exemplifies either type of economic system in its pure form. Economic systems have grown more alike over time, with the role of government increasing in market economies and the role of markets increasing in command economies. The United States represents a **mixed system,** with government directly accounting for about one-third of all economic activity. What's more, government regulates the private sector in a variety of ways. For example, local zoning boards determine lot sizes, home sizes, and the types of industries allowed. Federal bodies regulate workplace safety, environmental quality, competitive fairness, and many other activities.

Nearly all countries around the world have mixed economies. Countries with command systems are currently introducing more market incentives. For example, about 20 percent of the world's population live in the People's Republic of China, which grows more market oriented each day. The former Soviet Union dissolved into 15 independent republics; most are trying to privatize what had been state-owned enterprises. From Hungary to Mongolia, the transition to mixed economies now under way in former command economies will shape the 21st century.

Mixed system An economic system characterized by private ownership of some resources and public ownership of other resources; some markets are unregulated and others are regulated.

Economies Based on Custom or Religion

Finally, some economic systems are molded largely by custom or religion. For example, caste systems in India and elsewhere restrict occupational choice.

Family relations also play important roles in organizing and coordinating economic activity. Your own pattern of consumption and choice of occupation may be influenced by some of these factors.

CONCLUSION

Although economies can answer the three economic questions in a variety of ways, this book will focus primarily on the mixed market system found in the United States. This type of economy blends *private choice*, guided by the price system in competitive markets, with *public choice*, guided by democracy in political markets. The study of mixed market systems grows more relevant as former command economies try to develop market economies.

If you were to stop reading right now, you would already know more economics than most people. But to understand market economies, you must learn how markets work. You will do so in the next chapter, which introduces the market interaction of demand and supply.

SUMMARY

1. Resources are scarce, but human wants are unlimited. Since we cannot satisfy all wants, we must choose, and choice always involves an opportunity cost. The opportunity cost of the selected option is the value of the best alternative forgone.

2. The law of comparative advantage states that the individual, firm, region, or country with the lowest opportunity cost of producing a particular good should specialize in the production of that good. Specialization according to the law of comparative advantage promotes the most efficient use of resources.

3. The specialization of labor increases efficiency by (1) taking advantage of individual preferences and natural abilities, (2) allowing each worker to develop more experience at a particular task, (3) reducing the time required to move between different tasks, and (4) allowing for the introduction of more specialized capital and production techniques.

4. The production possibilities frontier shows the productive capabilities of an economy when all resources are used efficiently. The frontier's bowed-out shape reflects the law of increasing opportunity cost, which arises because some resources are not perfectly adaptable to the production of different goods. Over time, the frontier can shift in or out as a result of changes in the availability of resources or in technology. The frontier demonstrates several economic concepts, including efficiency, scarcity, opportunity cost, the law of increasing opportunity cost, economic growth, and the need for choice.

5. All economic systems, regardless of their decision-making processes, must answer three fundamental questions: What is to be produced? How is it to be produced? For whom is it to be produced? Economies answer the questions differently, depending on who owns their resources and how economic activity is coordinated.

QUESTIONS FOR REVIEW

1. *(Opportunity Costs)* Discuss the ways in which the following conditions might affect the opportunity cost of going to a movie tonight:
    a. You have a final exam tomorrow.
    b. School will be out for one month starting tomorrow.
    c. The same movie will be shown on TV next week.

2. *(Opportunity Costs)* Determine whether each of the following statements is true, false, or uncertain. Explain your answers:
    a. The opportunity cost of an activity is the total value of all the alternatives passed up.
    b. Opportunity cost is an objective measure of cost.

c. When making choices, people gather all available information about the costs and benefits of alternative choices.

d. A decision maker seldom knows the actual value of a forgone alternative and must base decisions on expected values.

3. *(Law of Comparative Advantage)* "You should never buy precooked frozen foods because you are paying for the labor costs of preparing food." Is this conclusion always valid, or can it be invalidated by the principle of comparative advantage?

4. *(Specialization and Exchange)* Explain how the specialization of labor can lead to increased productivity.

5. *(Production Possibilities)* Under what conditions is it possible to increase production of one good without decreasing production of another good?

6. *(Production Possibilities)* Under what conditions would an economy be operating inside its PPF? Outside its PPF?

7. *(Shifting Production Possibilities)* In response to an influx of illegal aliens, Congress made it a federal offense to hire them. How do you think this measure affected the U.S. production possibilities frontier? Do you think all industries were affected equally?

8. *(Production Possibilities)* "If society decides to use its resources fully (that is, to produce *on* its production possibilities frontier), then future generations will be worse off because they will not be able to use these resources." If this assertion is true, full employment of resources may not be a good thing. Comment on the validity of this assertion.

9. *(Economic Questions)* What basic economic questions must be answered in a barter economy? In a primitive economy? In a pure capitalist economy? In a command economy?

10. *(Economic Systems)* What are the major differences between a pure market system and a pure command system? Is the United States more like a pure market system or more like a pure command system?

PROBLEMS AND EXERCISES

11. *(Case**Study**: The Opportunity Cost of College)* During the Vietnam War, colleges and universities were overflowing with students. Was this bumper crop of students caused by a greater expected return on a college education or by a change in the opportunity cost of attending college? Explain.

12. *(Sunk Cost and Choice)* You go to a restaurant and buy an expensive meal. Halfway through, in spite of feeling full, you decide to clean your plate. After all, you think, you paid for the meal, so you are going to eat all of it. What's wrong with this thinking?

13. *(Comparative and Absolute Advantage)* You have the following information concerning the production of wheat and cloth in the United States and England:

Labor Hours Required to Produce One Unit

	England	United States
Wheat	2	1
Cloth	6	5

a. What is the opportunity cost of producing a unit of wheat in England? In the United States?

b. Which country has an absolute advantage in producing wheat? In producing cloth?

c. Which country has a comparative advantage in producing wheat? In producing cloth?

d. Which country should specialize in producing wheat? In producing cloth?

14. *(Case**Study**: Evidence of Specialization)* Provide some examples of specialized markets or retail outlets. What makes a medium like the World Wide Web conducive to specialization?

15. *(Shape of the PPF)* Suppose a production possibilities frontier includes the following data points:

Cars	Washing Machines
0	1,000
100	600
200	0

a. Graph the production possibilities frontier, assuming that it has no curved segments.

b. What is the cost of producing an additional car when 50 cars are being produced?

c. What is the cost of producing an additional car when 150 cars are being produced?

d. What is the cost of producing an additional washing machine when 50 cars are being produced? When 150 cars are being produced?

e. What do your answers tell you about opportunity costs?

16. *(Production Possibilities)* Suppose that there are two re-sources in the economy (labor and capital) that are used to produce two goods (wheat and cloth). Capital is rela-tively more useful in producing cloth, and labor is rela-tively more useful in producing wheat. If the supply of capital falls by 10 percent and the supply of labor increases by 10 percent, how will the PPF for wheat and cloth change?

17. *(Production Possibilities)* There's no reason why a produc-tion possibilities frontier could not be used to represent the situation facing an individual. Imagine your own PPF. Right now—today—you have certain resources—your time, your skills, perhaps some capital. And you can produce various outputs. Suppose you can produce combinations of two outputs, call them studying and partying.
   a. Draw your PPF for studying and partying. Be sure to label the axes of the diagram appropriately. Label the points where the PPF intersects the axes, as well as several other points along the frontier.

   b. Explain what it would mean for you to move up-ward and to the left along your personal PPF. What kinds of adjustments would you have to make in your life to make such a movement along the frontier?
   c. Under what circumstances would your personal PPF shift outward? Do you think the shift would be a "parallel" one? Why, or why not?

18. *(Shifting Production Possibilities)* Determine whether each of the following would cause the economy's PPF to shift inward, outward, or not at all:
   a. An increase in average length of annual vacations.
   b. An increase in immigration.
   c. A decrease in the average retirement age.
   d. The migration of skilled workers to other countries.

19. *(Economic Systems)* The United States is best described as having a "mixed" economic system. What are some ele-ments of command in the U.S. economy? What are some elements of tradition?

EXPERIENTIAL EXERCISES

20. *(Production Possibilities Frontier)* Here are some data on the U.S. economy taken from the *Economic Report of the President* at http://www.access.gpo.gov/eop/.

Year	Unemployment Rate	Real Government Spending (billions)	Real Civilian Spending (billions)
1982	9.7%	$ 947.7	$3,672.6
1983	9.6	960.1	3,843.6
1996	5.4	1,257.9	5,670.5
1997	4.9	1,270.6	5,920.8

   a. Sketch a production possibilities frontier for the years 1982 and 1983, showing the tradeoff be-tween public-sector (government) and private-sector (civilian) spending. Assume that resource availability and technology were the same in both years, but notice that the unemployment rate was relatively high.
   b. Sketch a PPF for the years 1996 and 1997. Assume that resource availability and technology were the same in both years, but higher than in 1982 and

1983. Note that the unemployment rate in the late 1990s was much lower than in the early 1980s.
   c. What lessons did you learn about the U.S. economy during the past 20 years?

21. *(Economic Systems)* The transitional economies of Eastern Europe are frequently in the news since they provide testing grounds for the transi-tion from socialist central planning to freer, more market-oriented economies. Take a look at the World Bank's *Transition Newsletter* at http://www.worldbank.org/html/prddr/trans/WEB/trans.htm. Choose a particular economy and try to determine how smoothly the tran-sition is proceeding. What problems is that nation encountering?

22. *(Wall Street Journal)* The ability to measure the true (op-portunity) cost of a choice is a skill that will pay you great dividends. Use any issue of the *Wall Street Journal*, and find an article that discusses a decision some firm has made. (Try the "Business Bulletin" column on the front page of Thursday's issue.) Then review this chap-ter's section titled "Choice and Opportunity Cost." Fi-nally, make a list of the kinds of opportunity costs in-volved in the firm's decision.

The Market System

Why do roses cost more on Valentine's Day than during the rest of the year? Why does TV advertising time cost more during the Super Bowl ($1.2 million for 30 seconds) than during *Nick-at-Nite* reruns. Why do hotel rooms in Phoenix cost more in February than in August? Why do surgeons earn more than butchers? Why do pro basketball players earn more than pro hockey players? Why do economics majors earn more than most other majors? Answers to these and most economic questions boil down to the workings of demand and supply, which will be examined in this chapter.

This chapter will introduce you to the underpinnings of demand and supply and show you how they interact in competitive markets. *Demand and supply are the most fundamental and the most powerful of all economic tools—important enough to warrant their own chapter.* Indeed, some believe that if you programmed a computer to respond "demand and supply" to every economic question, you could put many economists out of work. An understanding of the two concepts will take you far in mastering the art and science of economic analysis. As you will see, the correct analysis of demand and supply takes skill and care. This chapter uses graphs extensively, so you may want to refer to the Appendix of Chapter 1 for a refresher. Topics discussed in this chapter include:

- Demand and quantity demanded
- Supply and quantity supplied
- Markets
- Equilibrium price and quantity
- Changes in demand and in supply
- Disequilibrium

DEMAND

How much Pepsi will consumers buy each week if the price is $3 per six-pack? If the price is $2? If it's $4? The answers reveal the relationship between the price of Pepsi and the quantity purchased. Such a relationship is called the *demand* for Pepsi. **Demand** indicates the quantity of a product that consumers are both *willing* and *able* to buy at each possible price during a given period of time, other things constant. Because demand pertains to a specific period of time, such as a day, a week, or a month, think of demand as the desired *rate of purchase* per time period at each possible price. Also, note the emphasis on *willing* and *able*. You may be *able* to buy a motorcycle at a price of $4,000 because you can afford one, but you may not be *willing* to buy one if motorcycles don't interest you.

Demand A relation showing the quantities of a good that consumers are willing and able to buy at various prices during a given period of time, other things constant

The Law of Demand

In a remote region of western Pennsylvania is a poorly lit, run-down yellow building known as Pechin's Mart. The aisles are unmarked and strewn with half-empty boxes arranged in no apparent design. The sagging roof leaks when it rains. Why do shoppers come from as far away as Maryland and put up with the chaos and the grubbiness of Pechin's Mart to buy as many groceries as they can haul away? The store has violated nearly all the traditional rules of retailing, yet it thrives, with annual sales more than four times the national average. The store thrives because it reflects a rule merchants have known for thousands of years: Its prices are the lowest around.

As a consumer, you have little trouble understanding that people will buy more of a product at a lower price than at a higher price. Sell the product for less, and the world will beat a path to your door. This relation between the price of a product and the quantity demanded is an economic law. The **law of demand** states that the quantity of a product demanded during a given time period varies inversely with its price, other things constant. Thus, the higher the price, the smaller the quantity demanded; the lower the price, the greater the quantity demanded.

Law of demand The quantity of a good demanded in a given time period is inversely related to its price, other things constant

Demand, Wants, and Needs. Consumer *demand* and consumer *wants* are not the same thing. As we have seen, wants are unlimited. You may *want* a Mercedes-Benz 500-SL, but the $130,000 price is likely beyond your budget (that is, the quantity you demand at that price is zero). Nor is *demand* the same as *need*. You may *need* a new muffler for your car, but if the price is $200, you may decide

"I am not going to pay a lot for this muffler." Apparently, you have better ways to spend your money. If, however, the price of mufflers drops enough—say, to $90—then you become both willing and able to buy one.

The Substitution Effect of a Price Change. What explains the law of demand? Why, for example, is more demanded when the price is lower? The explanation begins with unlimited wants confronting scarce resources. Many goods and services are capable of satisfying particular wants. For example, you can satisfy your hunger with pizza, tacos, burgers, chicken, or dozens of other dishes. Similarly, you can satisfy your desire for warmth in the winter with warm clothing, a home-heating system, a trip to Hawaii, or many other ways. Clearly, some ways of satisfying your wants will be more appealing than others (a trip to Hawaii is more fun than warmer clothing). In a world without scarcity, everything would be free, so you would always choose the most attractive alternative. Scarcity, however, is a reality, and the degree of scarcity of one good relative to another helps determine each good's *relative* price.

Notice that the definition of demand includes the "other-things-constant" assumption. Among "other things" assumed to remain constant are the prices of other goods. When the price of pizza declines and other prices remain constant, pizza becomes relatively cheaper. Consumers are then more *willing* to purchase pizza when its relative price falls; they tend to substitute pizza for other goods. This is called the **substitution effect** of a price change. On the other hand, an increase in the price of pizza, other things constant, causes consumers to substitute other goods for the now higher-priced pizza. Remember, *it is the change in the relative price—the price of one good relative to the prices of other goods—that causes the substitution effect.* If all prices changed by the same percentage, there would be no change in relative prices and no substitution effect.

The Income Effect of a Price Change. A fall in the price of a product increases the quantity demanded for a second reason. Suppose you earn $30 a week from a part-time job and spend all your income on pizza, buying three a week at $10 per pizza. What if the price drops to $6? At that price you can now afford five pizzas a week with your income. The decrease in the price of pizza has increased your **real income**—that is, your income measured in terms of what it can buy. The price reduction, other things constant, increases the *purchasing power* of your income, thereby increasing your *ability* to purchase pizza. The quantity of pizza you demand will likely increase because of this **income effect** of a price decrease. You may not increase your quantity demanded to five pizzas, but you could. If you purchase four pizzas per week when the price drops to $6, you would have $6 left over to buy other goods. Thus, the income effect of a lower price increases your real income and thereby increases your ability to purchase all goods.

More generally, because of the income effect of a price decrease, other things constant, consumers typically increase their quantity demanded. Conversely, an increase in the price of a good, other things constant, reduces real income, thereby reducing the *ability* to purchase all goods. Because of the income effect of a price increase, consumers typically reduce their quantity demanded.

The Demand Schedule and Demand Curve

Demand can be expressed as a *demand schedule* or as a *demand curve*. Panel (a) of Exhibit 1 shows a hypothetical demand schedule for milk. When we describe

Substitution effect When the price of a good falls, consumers will substitute that good for other goods, which are now relatively more expensive

Real income Income measured in terms of the goods and services it can buy

Income effect A fall in the price of a good increases consumers' real income, making the consumers more able to purchase all goods; for normal goods, the quantity demanded increases

EXHIBIT 1

McEachern · Interactive

**The Demand Schedule
and Demand Curve for Milk**

(a) Demand schedule

	Price per Quart	Quantity Demanded per Month (millions of quarts)
a	$1.25	8
b	1.00	14
c	0.75	20
d	0.50	26
e	0.25	32

(b) Demand curve

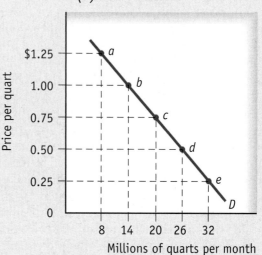

The market demand curve, D, shows the quantity of milk demanded, at various prices, by all consumers.

demand, we must specify the units being measured and the time period considered. In our example, the price is for a quart of milk, and the time period is a month. The milk is of uniform quality, in this case grade A homogenized whole milk. The schedule lists possible prices, along with the quantity demanded at each price. At a price of $1.25 per quart, for example, consumers demand 8 million quarts per month. As you can see, the lower the price, other things constant, the greater the quantity demanded. If the price drops as low as $0.25 per quart, consumers demand 32 million quarts per month. As the price of milk falls, consumers substitute milk for other goods. And as the price falls, the real income of consumers increases, causing them to increase the quantity of milk demanded.

Demand curve A curve showing the quantities of a particular good demanded at various possible prices during a given time period, other things constant

The demand schedule in panel (a) appears as a **demand curve** in panel (b), with price on the vertical axis and the quantity demanded per month on the horizontal axis. Each combination of price and quantity demanded listed in the demand schedule in panel (a) becomes a point in panel (b). Point a, for example, indicates that if the price is $1.25, consumers demand 8 million quarts per month. These points connect to form the demand curve for milk, labeled D. Note that the demand curve slopes downward, reflecting the *law of demand*: Price and quantity demanded are inversely related, other things constant. Assumed to be constant along the demand curve are the prices of other goods. Thus, along the demand curve for milk, the price of milk changes *relative to the prices of other goods*. The demand curve shows the effect of a change in the *relative price* of milk—that is, relative to other prices, which do not change.

Take care to distinguish between the *demand* for milk and the *quantity demanded*. The *demand* for milk is not a specific quantity, but rather the *entire relation* between price and quantity demanded—represented by the demand schedule or demand curve. An individual point on the demand curve shows the *quantity demanded* at a particular price. For example, at a price of $0.75 per quart, the quantity demanded is 20 million quarts per month. When the price of milk changes from, say, $0.75 to $1.00, this change is shown in Exhibit 1 by a movement along the demand curve—in this case from point *c* to point *b*. Any movement along a demand curve reflects a *change in quantity demanded*, not a change in demand.

The law of demand applies to the millions of products sold in grocery stores, department stores, clothing stores, drug stores, music stores, book stores, travel agencies, and restaurants, as well as through mail-order catalogues, the Yellow Pages, classified ads, the Internet, stock markets, real estate markets, job markets, flea markets, and all other markets. The law of demand applies even to choices that seem more personal than economic, such as whether or not to own a pet. For example, after New York City passed an anti-dog-litter law, owners had to follow their dogs around the city's sidewalks with scoopers, plastic bags, or whatever else would do the job. Because the law raised the cost, or price, of owning a dog, the quantity demanded decreased. The number of dogs left at animal shelters doubled. Many owners simply abandoned their dogs, raising the number of strays in the city. The law of demand predicts such behavior.

It is useful to distinguish between *individual demand*, which is the demand of an individual consumer, and *market demand*, which is the sum of the individual demands of all consumers in the market. In most markets, there are many consumers, sometimes millions. Unless otherwise noted, when we talk about demand, we will be referring to market demand, as in Exhibit 1.

CHANGES IN DEMAND

A demand curve isolates the relation between the price of a good and the quantity demanded, when other factors that could affect demand remain unchanged. What are these other factors, and how do changes in them affect demand? Variables that can affect market demand are (1) consumer income, (2) the prices of related goods, (3) consumer expectations, (4) the number and composition of consumers in the market, and (5) consumer tastes. Let's see how a change in each variable influences demand.

Changes in Consumer Income

Exhibit 2 shows the market demand curve for milk, *D*. This demand curve assumes a given level of consumer incomes. Suppose consumer incomes increase. Consumers will then be willing and able to purchase more milk at each price, so the demand for milk will increase; the demand curve shifts to the right from *D* to *D'*. For example, at a price of $1.00, the quantity demanded increases from 14 million to 20 million quarts per month, as indicated by the movement from point *b* on *D* to point *g* on *D'*.

An increase in the demand for milk also means that consumers are willing and able to pay a higher price for each *quantity* of milk. For example, consumers were initially willing and able to pay $1.00 per quart for 14 million quarts, as

EXHIBIT 2

An Increase in the Market Demand for Milk

An increase in the demand for milk is reflected by an outward shift in the demand curve. After the increase in demand, the quantity of milk demanded at a price of $1 per quart increases from 14 million quarts (point *b*) to 20 million quarts (point *g*). Another way to interpret the shift is to say that the maximum price consumers are willing to pay for 14 million quarts has increased from $1 per unit (at point *b*) to $1.25 per unit (at point *f*).

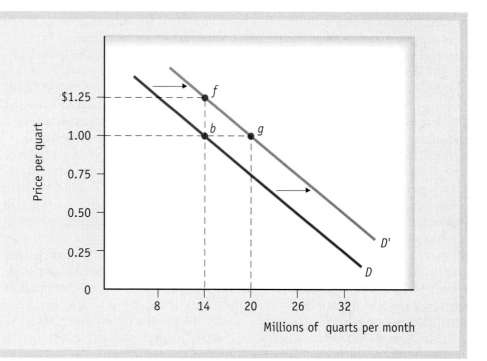

reflected by point *b*. After the increase in income, consumers are willing and able to pay $1.25 per quart for 14 million quarts, as reflected by point *f* on the new demand curve, which is directly above point *b* on the original demand curve. In short, *an increase in demand—that is, a shift to the right, or a shift upward, in the demand curve—means that consumers are willing and able to buy more units at each price and to pay more per unit at each quantity.*

We classify goods into two broad groupings, depending on how demand for the good responds to changes in income. The demand for **normal goods** increases as income increases. Because milk is a normal good, the demand for milk increases when consumer income increases. Most goods are normal goods. In contrast, the demand for **inferior goods** actually declines as income increases. Examples of inferior goods include ground chuck, trips to the laundromat, and bus rides. As income increases, consumers tend to switch from consuming these inferior goods to consuming normal goods (steak, their own washers and dryers, and automobile or plane rides), so the demand curves for inferior goods shift to the left.

Normal good A good for which demand increases as consumer incomes rise

Inferior good A good for which demand decreases as consumer incomes rise

Changes in the Prices of Related Goods

As we've seen, the prices of other goods are assumed to be constant along a given demand curve. Now let's bring these other prices into play. There are various ways of trying to satisfy any particular want. Consumers choose among substitutes partly on the basis of their relative prices. For example, milk and juice are substitutes. Obviously they are not perfect substitutes (you wouldn't pour juice on cereal or use it to make hot chocolate). Yet an increase in the price of juice, other things constant, will prompt some consumers to buy less juice and more milk. Two goods are **substitutes** if an increase in the price of one leads to an increase in the demand for the other and, conversely, if a decrease in the price of one leads to a decrease in the demand for the other.

Certain goods are used in combination to satisfy a want. Milk and chocolate chip cookies, computer hardware and software, popcorn and movies, and airline tickets and rental cars are complements. Two goods are **complements** if a decrease in the price of one leads to an increase in the demand for the other. For example, a decrease in the price of computers leads to an increase in the demand for software. Most pairs of goods selected at random are *unrelated*—for example, milk and housing, pizza and socks, dental floss and trail bikes.

Changes in Consumer Expectations

Another factor assumed to be constant along a given demand curve is consumer expectations about factors that influence demand, such as future income and the future price of the good. A change in consumer expectations can change demand. For example, a consumer who learns about a future pay increase may increase current demand well before that pay increase occurs. In anticipation of a steady paycheck, a college senior who lands a job may buy a new car even before graduation. Changes in price expectations can also affect demand. For example, if consumers come to believe that home prices will jump next year, some will increase their demand for housing this year, before prices go up. On the other hand, expectations of a lower price in the future will encourage some consumers to postpone current purchases, thereby reducing current demand.

Changes in the Number or Composition of Consumers

As mentioned earlier, market demand is the sum of the individual demands of all consumers in the market. If the number of consumers in the market changes, demand will change. For example, if the population grows, the demand for food will increase. Even if the total population remains the same, demand could change as a result of a change in composition of the population. For example, if the number of retired persons increases, the demand for recreational vehicles will probably increase. If the infant population booms, the demand for baby food, baby clothes, and playpens will jump.

Changes in Consumer Tastes

Do you like anchovies on your pizza or sauerkraut on your hot dog? How about tattoos and body piercing? Is music to your ears more likely to be rock, country, heavy metal, rap, reggae, jazz, or classical? Choices in food, body art, music, clothing, reading, movies, TV shows—indeed, all consumer choices—are influenced by consumer tastes. **Tastes** are nothing more than your likes and dislikes as a consumer. Tastes are assumed to be constant along a demand curve. What determines tastes? Who knows? Economists certainly don't, nor do they spend much time worrying about it. They recognize, however, that tastes are important in shaping demand.

Economists assume that tastes are relatively stable. Because a change in tastes is so difficult to isolate from other economic changes, we should be reluctant to attribute a change in demand to a change in tastes. In our analysis of consumer demand, *we will assume that tastes are given and are relatively stable over time.* We know, for example, that younger people usually prefer rock music, whereas older

Substitutes Goods that are related in such a way that an increase in the price of one leads to an increase in the demand for the other

Complements Goods that are related in such a way that an increase in the price of one leads to a decrease in the demand for the other

Tastes Consumer preferences; likes and dislikes in consumption people tend to prefer other kinds of music. The music piped into shopping malls tends to be so-called easy-listening music, intended to encourage older, higher-income customers to stay longer, be at ease, and spend more, while discouraging younger people from hanging out any longer than needed to do their shopping.

Remember, a movement along a given demand curve is called a **change in quantity demanded.** A change in quantity demanded results from a change in *price*, other things constant. A shift in the demand curve is called a **change in demand.** A change in demand results from a change in determinants of demand other than the price of the good—such as a change in income, a change in the price of related goods, a change in consumer expectations, a change in the number or composition of consumers, or a change in consumer tastes.

SUPPLY

Just as demand is a relation between price and quantity demanded, supply is a relation between price and quantity supplied. Specifically, **supply** indicates how much of a good producers are *willing* and *able* to offer for sale per period at each possible price, other things constant. The **law of supply** states that the quantity supplied is usually directly related to its price, other things constant. Thus, the lower the price, the smaller the quantity supplied; the higher the price, the greater the quantity supplied.

The Supply Schedule and Supply Curve

Exhibit 3 presents the market *supply schedule* and market **supply curve,** *S*, for milk. It shows the quantities of milk supplied per month at various possible prices by thousands of dairy farmers. As you can see, price and quantity supplied are directly, or positively, related. Producers offer more for sale at a higher price than at a lower price, so the supply curve slopes upward.

There are two reasons producers tend to offer more goods for sale when the price rises. First, as the price of a good increases, other things constant, a producer becomes more *willing* to supply the good. Prices act as signals to existing and potential suppliers about the rewards for producing various goods. An increase in the price of milk provides farmers with a profit incentive to shift some resources out of the production of other goods such as corn, for which the price is now relatively lower, and into milk, for which the price is now relatively higher. *A higher milk price attracts resources from lower-valued uses to the higher-valued use.*

A second reason the supply curve tends to slope upward is that higher prices increase the producer's *ability* to supply the good. The law of increasing opportunity cost, as noted in Chapter 2, states that the opportunity cost of producing more of a particular good rises as output increases—that is, the *marginal cost* of production increases as output increases. Since producers face a higher marginal cost for additional output, they must receive a higher price for that output in order to be *able* to increase the quantity supplied. For example, when milk production is low, farmers are able to employ resources that are well suited to the task. As output increases, however, producing the additional increments of milk draws on resources that may be better suited to producing other goods. To feed additional cows, for example, a farmer may have to convert a corn field

Change in quantity demanded A movement along the demand curve in response to a change in the price, other things constant

Change in demand A shift in a given demand curve caused by a change in any of the determinants of demand for the good other than its price

Supply A relation showing the quantities of a good producers are willing and able to sell at various prices during a given time period, other things constant

Law of supply The quantity of a product supplied in a given time period is usually directly related to its price, other things constant

Supply curve A curve showing the quantities of a good supplied at various prices, other things constant

EXHIBIT 3

**The Supply Schedule and
Supply Curve for Milk**

(a) Supply schedule

Price per Quart	Quantity Supplied per Month (millions of quarts)
$1.25	28
1.00	24
0.75	20
0.50	16
0.25	12

(b) Supply curve

The market supply curve, *S*, shows the quantity of milk supplied, at various prices, by all farmers.

into a pasture. Therefore, additional output has a higher opportunity cost. *Higher milk prices make farmers better able to draw resources away from alternative uses.* Similarly, a higher price for gasoline increased oil companies' ability to explore in less accessible locations, such as the remote jungles of the Amazon, the stormy waters of the North Sea, and the frozen tundra of Alaska and Siberia. On the other hand, a decade-long slide in the price of gold has shut down some gold mines that could no longer operate profitably.

Thus, a higher price makes producers more *willing* and more *able* to increase the quantity of goods offered for sale. Producers are more *willing* because production of the higher-priced good is now relatively more attractive than the alternative uses of the resources involved. Producers are more *able* because the higher price allows them to cover the higher marginal cost that typically results from a higher rate of production.

As with demand, we distinguish between *individual* supply and *market* supply. Market supply is the sum of the amounts supplied at each price by all the individual suppliers. Unless otherwise noted, when we talk about supply, we will be referring to market supply. We also distinguish between *supply* and *quantity supplied*. Supply is the relation between the price and quantity supplied, as reflected by the entire supply schedule or supply curve. Quantity supplied refers to a particular amount offered for sale at a particular price, as reflected by a point on a given supply curve.

CHANGES IN SUPPLY

The supply curve expresses the relation between the price of a good and the quantity supplied, other things constant. Assumed constant along a supply curve are the determinants of supply other than the price of the good, including (1) the state of technology, (2) the prices of relevant resources, (3) the prices of alternative goods, (4) producer expectations, and (5) the number of producers in the market. Let's see how a change in each of these determinants of supply will affect the supply curve.

Changes in Technology

Recall from Chapter 2 that the state of technology represents the economy's stock of knowledge about how to combine resources most efficiently. Along a given supply curve, technology is assumed to remain unchanged. If a more efficient technology is discovered, production costs will fall; so suppliers will be more willing and more able to supply the good at each price. Consequently, supply will increase, as reflected by a rightward shift of the supply curve. For example, suppose a new milking machine called The Invisible Hand has a soothing effect on cows; cows find the new machine so "udderly" delightful that they produce more milk. Such a technological advance increases the market supply of milk, as shown by the shift from *S* to *S'* in Exhibit 4.

EXHIBIT 4

An Increase in the Supply of Milk

An increase in the supply of milk is reflected by a shift to the right in the supply curve, from *S* to *S'*. After the increase in supply, the quantity of milk supplied at a price of $1 per quart increases from 24 million quarts (point *h*) to 28 million quarts (point *i*). Another way to interpret the shift is to say that it shows a reduction in the minimum price suppliers require in order to produce 24 million quarts. Previously, a price of $1 per quart was required (point *h*); after the increase in supply, suppliers require a price of only $0.75 per quart (point *j*).

Notice that, just as a change in demand can be interpreted in two different ways, so can a change in supply. First, an increase in supply means that dairy farmers supply more milk at each possible price. For example, when the price is $1.00 per quart, the amount of milk supplied increases from 24 million to 28 million quarts per month, as shown in Exhibit 4 by the movement from point *h* to point *i*. Second, an increase in supply means that farmers are willing and able to supply the same quantity at a lower price. For example, farmers originally supplied 24 million quarts when the price was $1.00 per quart; on the new supply curve, that same quantity is supplied for only $0.75 per quart, as shown by the movement from point *h* down to point *j*.

Changes in the Prices of Relevant Resources

Relevant resources are those employed in the production of the good in question. For example, suppose the price of cow fodder falls. This lower resource price reduces the cost of milk production. Dairy farmers are therefore more willing and better able to supply milk. The supply curve for milk shifts to the right or shifts down, as shown in Exhibit 4. On the other hand, an increase in the price of a relevant resource reduces supply. For example, higher electricity rates increase the cost of lighting the barn and operating the milking machines. These higher production costs decrease supply, meaning that supply shifts to the left, or shifts up.

Relevant resources Resources used to produce the good in question

Changes in the Prices of Alternative Goods

Nearly all resources have alternative uses. The farmer's labor, tractor, barn, field, and planning skills could produce a variety of crops. **Alternative goods** are those that use some of the same resources as are employed to produce the good under consideration. For example, as crop prices increase, so does the opportunity cost of dairy farming. Some farmers will shift out of dairy farming and into crop farming, so the supply of milk will decrease, or shift to the left. On the other hand, a fall in the price of an alternative good, such as crops, makes milk production relatively more attractive. As resources shift into milk production, the supply curve for milk will increase, or shift to the right.

Alternative goods Other goods that use some of the same resources as used to produce the good in question

Changes in Producer Expectations

Changes in producer expectations about market factors can change current supply. For example, a farmer expecting higher prices for milk in the future may begin to expand her dairy today, thereby increasing the current supply of milk and shifting the supply of milk to the right. When a good can be stored easily (crude oil, for example, can be left in the ground), expecting higher prices in the future prompts producers to *reduce* their current supply and await the higher price. Their decrease in supply is reflected by a shift to the left in the supply curve. Thus, an expectation of higher prices in the future could either increase or decrease the current supply, depending on the nature of the good under consideration. More generally, any change expected to affect future profitability, such as a change in business taxes, could change current supply.

Changes in the Number of Producers

Since market supply is the sum of the amounts supplied by all producers, market supply depends on the number of producers in the market. If the number of producers increases, supply will increase, or shift to the right; if the number decreases, supply will decrease, or shift to the left. For example, the number of coffee bars has more than quadrupled in the United States during the last decade, shifting the supply curve of coffee to the right.

Finally, note the distinction between (1) a **change in quantity supplied,** which is the producer response to a change in the *price* of the good, other things constant, and is represented as a movement along a given supply curve, and (2) a **change in supply,** which is the response to a change in one of the determinants of supply other than the price of good and is represented as a shift in the entire supply curve.

We are now ready to bring demand and supply together.

Change in quantity supplied A movement along the supply curve in response to a change in the price, other things constant

Change in supply A shift in a given supply curve caused by a change in one of the determinants of the supply of the good other than its price

DEMAND AND SUPPLY CREATE A MARKET

Suppliers and demanders have different views of price, because demanders pay the price and suppliers receive it. Thus, a higher price is bad news for consumers but good news for producers. As the price rises, consumers reduce their quantity demanded and producers increase their quantity supplied. How is this conflict between producers and consumers resolved?

Markets

A product's market sorts out the conflicting price perspectives of individual participants—suppliers and demanders. A *market*, as we know from Chapter 1, is the means by which individuals interact to buy or to sell; it is a mechanism that coordinates the independent intentions of buyers and sellers. A market represents all the arrangements used to buy and sell a particular good or service. Markets reduce the **transaction costs** of exchange—the costs of time and information required for exchange. For example, suppose you are looking for a summer job. One approach would be to go from employer to employer looking for openings. This approach would be time consuming and could involve extensive travel. A better strategy would be to pick up a copy of the local newspaper and read through the help-wanted ads. These ads, which are one element of the job market, reduce the transaction costs required to bring workers and employers together.

Transaction costs The costs of time and information required to carry out market exchange

The coordination that occurs through markets takes place not because of some central plan but because of Adam Smith's "invisible hand." For example, most of the auto dealers in your community tend to locate together, usually on the outskirts of town where land is cheaper. The dealers congregate, not because someone told them to or because they like one another's company, but because each wants to be where customers shop for cars—that is, near other dealers. Similarly, stores group together downtown and in shopping malls to be where shoppers shop. Disney World, Sea World, Universal Studios, and Universal City located together in Orlando to be where tourists tour. Theme parks cluster in the Los Angeles area for the same reason.

Market Equilibrium

To see how a market works, let's bring together market demand and market supply. Exhibit 5 shows the demand for and supply of milk, using schedules in panel (a) and curves in panel (b). To start, suppose the price initially is $1.00 per quart.

At that price, producers supply 24 million quarts per month, but consumers demand only 14 million quarts per month. The quantity supplied exceeds the quantity demanded, resulting in an *excess quantity supplied*, or a **surplus,** of 10 million quarts per month. This unsold milk tells producers that the price is too high. Unless the price falls, the surplus will continue and milk will sour on store shelves. The suppliers' desire to eliminate the surplus puts downward pressure on the price, as reflected by the arrow pointing downward in panel (b). As the price falls, producers reduce their quantity supplied and consumers increase their quantity demanded. As long as quantity supplied exceeds quantity demanded, the surplus will force the price lower.

   Alternatively, suppose the price is initially $0.50 per quart. You can see from Exhibit 5 that at this price consumers demand 26 million quarts per month but producers supply only 16 million quarts per month, resulting in an *excess*

Surplus An excess of quantity supplied compared to quantity demanded at a given price; a surplus puts downward pressure on the price

EXHIBIT 5

Equilibrium in the Milk Market

Market equilibrium occurs at a price at which the quantity demanded by consumers is equal to the quantity supplied by producers. This is shown at point *c*. At prices above the equilibrium price, the quantity supplied exceeds the quantity demanded; at these prices there is a surplus, and there is a downward pressure on the price. At prices below equilibrium, quantity demanded exceeds quantity supplied; the resulting shortage puts upward pressure on the price.

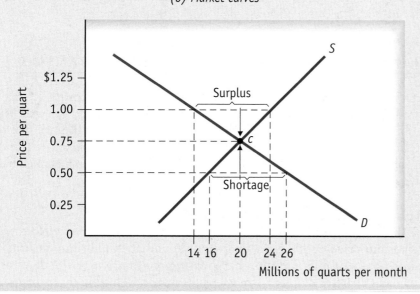

(a) Market schedules

Millions of Quarts per Month

Price per Quart	Quantity Demanded	Quantity Supplied	Surplus or Shortage	Price Will
$1.25	8	28	Surplus of 20	Fall
1.00	14	24	Surplus of 10	Fall
0.75	20	20	Equilibrium	Remain the same
0.50	26	16	Shortage of 10	Rise
0.25	32	12	Shortage of 20	Rise

(b) Market curves

Shortage An excess of quantity demanded compared to quantity supplied at a given price; a shortage puts upward pressure on price

quantity demanded, or a **shortage,** of 10 million quarts per month. Producers quickly notice that the quantity supplied has sold out and customers are grumbling because milk is no longer available. Empty store shelves, frustrated consumers, and the profit incentives of producers create market pressure for a higher price, as reflected by the arrow pointing upward in panel (b). As the price rises, producers increase their quantity supplied and consumers reduce their quantity demanded. The price will continue to rise as long as quantity demanded exceeds quantity supplied.

Thus, a surplus creates downward pressure on the price, and a shortage creates upward pressure on the price. So long as quantity demanded and quantity supplied differ, this difference will force a price change, which will change both quantity demanded and quantity supplied. Note that a shortage or a surplus must always be defined at a particular price. There is no such thing as a general shortage or a general surplus.

When the quantity that consumers are willing and able to buy equals the quantity that producers are willing and able to sell, the market is in equilibrium. In **equilibrium,** the independent plans of both buyers and sellers exactly match, so market forces will exert no pressure to change price and quantity. In panel (b) of Exhibit 5, the demand and supply curves intersect at the *equilibrium point*, identified as point *c*. The *equilibrium price* is $0.75 per quart, and the *equilibrium quantity* is 20 million quarts per month. At that price and quantity, the market *clears*. There is no shortage and no surplus, so there is no pressure for change.

Equilibrium The condition that exists in a market when the plans of the buyers match the plans of the sellers; the market clears

A market finds equilibrium through the independent actions of thousands, or even millions, of buyers and sellers. In one sense, the market is personal because each consumer and each producer makes a personal decision regarding how much to buy or sell at a given price. In another sense, the market is impersonal because it requires no conscious coordination among consumers or producers. *Impersonal market forces synchronize the personal and independent decisions of many individual buyers and sellers to determine equilibrium price and quantity.*

CHANGES IN EQUILIBRIUM PRICE AND QUANTITY

Recall that equilibrium is the combination of price and quantity at which the intentions of demanders and suppliers exactly match. Once a market reaches equilibrium, that price and quantity will continue to prevail until one of the determinants of demand or supply changes. A change in any one of these determinants will usually change equilibrium price and quantity in a predictable way, as we shall see.

Impact of Changes in Demand

In Exhibit 6, demand curve *D* and supply curve *S* intersect to yield the initial equilibrium price of $0.75 per quart and the initial equilibrium quantity of 20 million quarts of milk per month. Now suppose that one of the determinants of demand changes in a way that increases demand, shifting the demand curve to the right from *D* to *D'*. Any of the following changes could increase the demand for milk: (1) an increase in consumer income (since milk is a normal good); (2) an increase in the price of a substitute, such as juice, or a decrease in

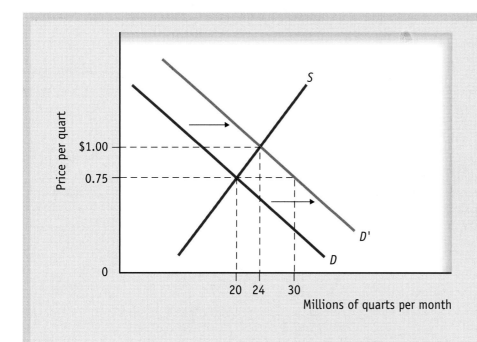

EXHIBIT 6

Effects of an Increase in Demand

After an increase in demand shifts the demand curve from *D* to *D'*, quantity demanded exceeds quantity supplied at the old price of $0.75 per quart. As the price rises, quantity supplied increases along supply curve *S*, and quantity demanded falls along demand curve *D'*. When the new equilibrium price of $1.00 per quart is reached, the quantity demanded will once again equal the quantity supplied. Both price and quantity are higher following the increase in demand.

the price of a complement, such as cereal; (3) a change in consumers' expectations that encourages them to buy more milk now; (4) an increase in the number of consumers; or (5) a change in consumer tastes—based, for example, on a discovery that milk consumption improves mental health.

After the increase in demand to *D'*, as reflected in Exhibit 6, the quantity demanded at the initial price of $0.75 is 30 million quarts, which exceeds the quantity supplied of 20 million quarts by 10 million quarts. This shortage puts upward pressure on the price. As the price increases, the quantity demanded decreases along the new demand curve, *D'*; and the quantity supplied increases along the existing supply curve *S* until the two quantities are equal in equilibrium once again. The new equilibrium price is $1.00 per quart, and the new equilibrium quantity is 24 million quarts per month. Thus, given an upward-sloping supply curve, an increase in demand increases both equilibrium price and quantity. A decrease in demand would lower both equilibrium price and quantity. We can summarize these results as follows: *Given an upward-sloping supply curve, any change in demand will change both equilibrium price and quantity in the same direction as the change in demand.*

Impact of Changes in Supply

Let's look now at the impact of a change in supply. In Exhibit 7, as before, we begin with demand curve *D* and supply curve *S* to yield the initial equilibrium price of $0.75 per quart and the initial equilibrium quantity of 20 million quarts per month. Suppose one of the determinants of supply changes, resulting in a supply increase from *S* to *S'*. Changes that could increase the supply of milk include: (1) a

EXHIBIT 7

Effects of an Increase in Supply

An increase in supply is depicted as a shift to the right in the supply curve, from *S* to *S'*. At the new equilibrium, quantity is greater and price is lower than before the increase in supply.

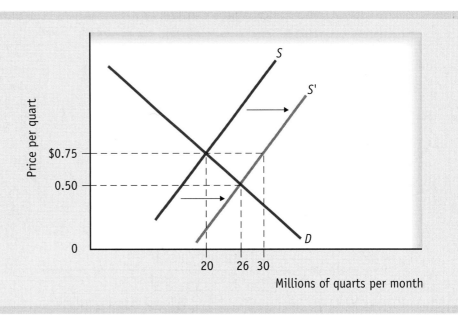

technological advance in milk production, such as development of milk-enhancing hormones; (2) a reduction in the price of a relevant resource, such as cow feed; (3) a decline in the price of an alternative good, such as corn; (4) a change in expectations that encourages farmers to supply more milk now, such as expectations of higher prices in the future; or (5) an increase in the number of dairy farmers.

After the increase in supply in Exhibit 7, the amount supplied at the initial equilibrium price of $0.75 increases from 20 million to 30 million quarts, resulting in a 10 million quart surplus. This surplus forces the price down. As the price falls, the quantity supplied declines along the new supply curve and the quantity demanded increases until a new equilibrium point is established. The new equilibrium price is $0.50 per quart, and the new equilibrium quantity is 26 million quarts. The increase in supply reduces the equilibrium price but increases the equilibrium quantity.

Alternatively, a reduction in supply—that is, a shift to the left in the supply curve—increases equilibrium price but reduces equilibrium quantity. Thus, *given a downward-sloping demand curve, a shift in the supply curve changes equilibrium quantity in the same direction as the change in supply but changes equilibrium price in the opposite direction.* An easy way to remember this is to picture the supply curve shifting along a given downward-sloping demand curve. If the supply curve shifts to the right, price decreases but quantity increases; if the supply curve shifts to the left, price increases but quantity decreases.

Simultaneous Changes in Demand and Supply

As long as only one curve shifts, we can say for sure what will happen to equilibrium price and quantity. If both curves shift, however, the outcome is less obvious. For example, suppose both demand and supply increase, as in Exhibit 8. Note that in panel (a) demand increases more than supply, and in panel (b) supply increases more than demand. In both panels, equilibrium quantity increases. The

EXHIBIT 8

**Indeterminate Effect of an
Increase in Both Supply
and Demand**

(a) Shift in demand dominates

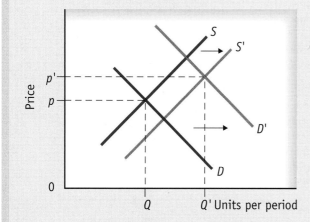

(b) Shift in supply dominates

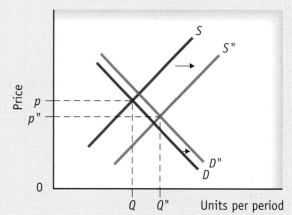

When both supply and demand increase, the quantity exchanged—the equilibrium quantity—also increases. The effect on price depends on which curve shifts farther. In panel (a), the shift in demand is greater than the shift in supply; as a result, the price rises. In panel (b), the shift in supply is greater, so the price falls.

change in equilibrium price, however, depends on the size of the increase in demand relative to the increase in supply. If the increase in demand is greater, as in panel (a), equilibrium price increases from p to p'. If the increase in supply is greater, as in panel (b), equilibrium price decreases from p to p''.

Conversely, if both demand and supply decrease, the equilibrium quantity decreases; but again we cannot say what will happen to the equilibrium price unless we examine the relative shifts. (You can use Exhibit 8 to examine decreases in demand and supply by viewing D' and S' as the initial curves.) If the decrease in demand exceeds the decrease in supply, the price will fall. If the decrease in supply exceeds the decrease in demand, the price will rise.

If demand and supply move in opposite directions, we can say what will happen to the equilibrium price. *The equilibrium price will increase if demand increases and supply decreases; the equilibrium price will decrease if demand decreases and supply increases.* Without reference to particular shifts, however, we cannot say what will happen to the equilibrium quantity.

These results are no doubt confusing, but Exhibit 9 summarizes the four possible combinations of changes. For example, the upper left-hand corner of Exhibit 9 shows the results just depicted with graphs in Exhibit 8. Using Exhibit 9 as a reference, work through some hypothetical shifts in demand and supply to develop an understanding of the results. Then evaluate the effect of an increase in demand for professional basketball in the following case study.

EXHIBIT 9

Effects of Changes in Both Supply and Demand

When the supply and de-mand curves shift in the same direction, equilibrium quantity also shifts in that direction; the effect on equi-librium price depends on which curve shifts more. If the curves shift in opposite directions, equilibrium price will move in the same direc-tion as demand; the effect on equilibrium quantity de-pends on which curve shifts more.

| | **Change in Demand** | |
	Demand increases	Demand decreases
Supply increases	Equilibrium price change is indeterminate. Equilibrium quantity increases.	Equilibrium price falls. Equilibrium quantity change is indeterminate.
Supply decreases	Equilibrium price rises. Equilibrium quantity change is indeterminate.	Equilibrium price change is indeterminate. Equilibrium quantity decreases.

Change in Supply

CaseStudy

The World of Business

The Busine$$ of Sport$ is a Web page devoted to eco-nomic issues surrounding (mainly) professional sports at http://www.bizsports.com/index.html. What is the latest on the market for pro basketball?

The Market for Professional Basketball

Toward the end of the 1970s, the National Basketball Association (NBA) seemed on the verge of collapse. Game attendance had sunk to only 58 percent of capacity. One-fifth of the teams were nearly bankrupt. The NBA champi-onship game did not even merit prime-time television coverage.

During the 1980s, however, three superstars turned the league around. Michael Jordan, Larry Bird, and Magic Johnson brought new life to the sagging game and attracted millions of new fans. Since 1980, total attendance has doubled, the number of NBA teams has increased from 22 to 29 (with new franchises selling for record amounts), and the value of television broadcast rights has jumped *35*-fold from $76 million in 1978–1982 to $2.64 billion in 1998–2002.

The NBA is more popular than ever, though a labor dispute during what would have been the 1998–99 season took some luster off that popularity. Celebrities such as Jack Nicholson and Spike Lee have become fixtures in court-side seats (seats that sell for as much as $500 per game). Basketball's popu-larity has also increased around the world. The NBA formed global marketing alliances with Coca-Cola, McDonald's, and IBM; and the 1998 NBA finals were televised in more than 165 countries.

The players are the key resource in the production of NBA games. The growth in demand for pro basketball, coupled with a collective bargaining agreement that gave players more than half of total revenue (in 1997–98 players were paid 57 percent of total league revenues), jacked up average player salaries from $170 thousand in 1980 to $2.5 million in 1997–98. Basketball players are now the highest-paid team professionals in the world; their average pay is more than double that in pro football and pro hockey.

The primary source of talent for the NBA is college basketball. College games, especially the NCAA tournament nicknamed "March Madness," serve to heighten interest in the NBA, because fans can follow top collegiate players into the professional ranks. Top college prospects sign multimillion-dollar contracts. Such numbers attract talented players earlier and earlier in their academic years, since top players who remain in school risk a costly injury. In 1997, Kevin Garnett, who entered the NBA right out of high school in 1995, signed a seven-year contract worth $121 million. Because of basketball's worldwide popularity, talented players who fail to make the NBA often can sign attractive contracts overseas.

The high pay earned by the top players stems from the limited supply of those with such talent, combined with a large and growing demand for that talent. But rare talent alone is not enough. For example, top rodeo riders, top bowlers, and top women basketball players also possess rare talent, but the demand for their talent is not great enough to support pay anywhere close to NBA levels. Both supply *and* demand determine the average pay level.

Sources: "Garnett Accepts $121 Million," *Hartford Courant*, 2 Oct. 1997; Anthony Bianco, "David Stern: This Time It's Personal," *Business Week*, 13 July 1998, pp. 114–118; *The American Almanac: Statistical Abstract of the United States: 1996–1997*, Bureau of the Census (Austin, Texas: Hoover's Business Press, 1996).

DISEQUILIBRIUM PRICES

A surplus exerts downward pressure on the price; a shortage exerts upward pressure on the price. Markets, however, do not always attain equilibrium quickly. During the time required for adjustment, the market is said to be in disequilibrium. **Disequilibrium** is usually a temporary phase when the market gropes for equilibrium. For example, popular toys, best-selling books, and chart-busting compact discs often sell out and are temporarily unavailable. On the other hand, some new products attract few customers and pile up unsold on store shelves, awaiting a "clearance sale." Sometimes, however, often as a result of government intervention in markets, disequilibrium can last a long time, as we will see next.

Disequilibrium A mismatch between quantity supplied and quantity demanded as the market seeks equilibrium

Price Floors

Sometimes public officials set prices above their equilibrium values. For example, the federal government often regulates the prices of some agricultural commodities in an attempt to ensure farmers a higher and more stable income than they would otherwise earn. To achieve higher prices, the federal government sets a **price floor,** or a *minimum* selling price above the equilibrium price. Panel (a) of Exhibit 10 shows the effect of a $1.00 per quart price floor for milk. At that price, farmers supply 24 million quarts of milk per month, but

Price floor A minimum legal price below which a good or service cannot be sold; to be effective, a price floor must be set above the equilibrium price

EXHIBIT 10

**Effects of a Price Floor
and a Price Ceiling**

(a) Price floor for milk

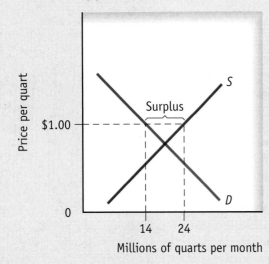

(b) Price ceiling for rent

If a price floor is established above the equilibrium price, a permanent surplus will result. A price floor established at or below the equilibrium price will have no effect. If a price ceiling is established below the equilibrium price, a permanent shortage will result. A price ceiling established at or above the equilibrium price will have no effect.

consumers demand only 14 million quarts. Thus the price floor results in a surplus of 10 million quarts. This surplus, unless somehow eliminated, will force the price down. So, as part of the price support program, the government usually agrees to buy the surplus milk to take it off the market. The federal government, in fact, has spent billions buying and storing surplus agricultural products.

Price Ceilings

Sometimes public officials try to keep prices below their equilibrium values by establishing a **price ceiling,** or a *maximum* selling price. For example, concern about the rising cost of rental housing in some cities prompted legislation to impose rent ceilings. Panel (b) depicts the demand and supply for rental housing in a hypothetical city; the vertical axis shows the monthly rent, and the horizontal axis shows the quantity of rental units. The equilibrium, or market-clearing, rent is $600 per month, and the equilibrium quantity is 50,000 housing units.

Suppose the government sets a maximum rent of $400 per month. At that ceiling price, 60,000 rental units are demanded, but only 40,000 are supplied, resulting in a housing shortage of 20,000 units. Because of such excess demand, the rental price no longer rations housing to those who value it the most. Other devices emerge to ration housing, such as waiting lists, political connections, and the willingness to pay under-the-table charges, such as "key fees," "finder's fees," higher security deposits, and the like.

Price ceiling A maximum legal price above which a good or service cannot be sold; to be effective, a price ceiling must be set below the equilibrium price

To have an impact, a price floor must be set above the equilibrium price. A price ceiling, to have an impact, must be set below the equilibrium price.[1] Effective price floors and ceilings distort market forces. Price floors above the equilibrium price create surpluses, and price ceilings below the equilibrium price create shortages. Various nonprice allocation devices emerge to cope with the disequilibrium resulting from the market interference.

Government intervention in the market is not the only source of disequilibrium, as shown in the following case study.

Toys Are Serious Business

CaseStudy

The World of Business

If you are interested in learning more about the serious business of toys, you can find a wealth of information at ToySource http://www.toysource.com/faq1.htm.

U.S. toy sales exceed $25 billion a year, but the business is not much fun for toy makers. Most toys don't make it from one season to the next, turning out to be costly duds. A few have staying power; for example, G.I. Joe could retire after more than 30 years of military service, Barbie is over 35 years old, and the Wiffle Ball is still a hit after 40 years.

Store buyers must order in February for Christmas delivery. Can you imagine the uncertainty of this market? Who, for example, could have anticipated the phenomenal success of Tickle-Me-Elmo, Beanie Babies, Teletubbies, or Furbies? How about the Cabbage Patch Kids frenzy that some of you experienced as toddlers? Over 20 million Kids were sold for about $30 each, and there was still a shortage at that price. The shortage attracted boatloads of counterfeit dolls from overseas. Some of these illegal aliens were detained at the border, but many more made it through.

A few years ago, the Mighty Morphin Power Rangers were the hot toy. Between 1993 and 1994, the manufacturer expanded production tenfold, with 11 new factories churning out nearly $1 billion worth of Rangers. Still, at a selling price of $13, the quantity demanded exceeded quantity supplied. A more recent hit toy was Tomagotchi, a virtual pet. The manufacturer had nine plants around the world turning them out.

Why didn't toy manufacturers simply allow the price to seek its market-clearing level? Suppose, for example, that the market-clearing price of Cabbage Patch Kids was $60, twice the actual price. Consumers may have resented paying such a high price for a doll, and Coleco, a producer of a variety of toys, may not have wanted to risk criticism for being opportunist, a "price gouger." After all, a firm's reputation is important. Suppliers who hope to retain customers over the long haul will often avoid appearing greedy. That's why the local hardware store doesn't raise the price of snow shovels after the first winter storm, why Wal-Mart doesn't jack up prices of air conditioners during the dog days of summer, and why Mercedes-Benz prefers long waiting lists to raising prices still higher for its new utility vehicle.

Eventually, market equilibrium is achieved. But in the meantime, disequilibrium prevails. Uncertainty abounds in the market for new products such as

---

1 Note that the terms "price floor" and "price ceiling" are used to describe situations in a way that is opposite from the way we usually think of the floor and ceiling of a room. A price floor is up high, where we find a room's ceiling, and a price ceiling is down low, where we find a room's floor.

toys. Suppliers can only guess what the demand will be, so they must feel their way in deciding how much to produce and what price to charge.

Sources: Patrice Apodaca, "Chicken Boom: Bandai Basks in Digital Pet Success," *Los Angeles Times*, 22 August 1997; Gretchen Morgenson, "Saturation Barbie?" *Forbes*, 20 Oct. 1997; and "Cabbage Patch Comeback Kids," *Business Week*, 14 August 1995;. Visit the Virtual Toy Store Directory at http://www.halcyon.com/uncomyn/ home.html; or visit FAO Schwarz at http://www.faoschwarz.com/.

CONCLUSION

Although a market usually involves the interaction of many buyers and sellers, few markets are consciously designed. Just as the law of gravity works whether or not we understand Newton's principles, market forces operate whether or not market participants understand demand and supply. These forces arise naturally, much the way car dealers cluster on the outskirts of town. Demand and supply are the foundation of a market economy.

Markets have their critics. Some observers are troubled, for example, that U.S. consumers spend billions each year on pet food, when some people do not have enough to eat. On your next trip to the supermarket, notice how much shelf space is devoted to pet products—often an entire aisle. Petsmart, a chain store for pet products, sells over 12,000 different items. Veterinarians charge up to $10,000 for cancer treatment, cataract removal, and other high-tech medical care for pets. Pet owners can even buy pet health insurance.[2] In the next chapter we'll discuss some limitations of market economies and introduce the role of government.

---

2 See Pamela Sebastian, "Canine Oncology and Other Advances Propel Costs and Insurance," *Wall Street Journal*, 23 October 1997.

SUMMARY

1. Demand is a relationship between the price of a good and the quantity consumers are willing and able to buy per time period, other things constant. According to the law of demand, the price of a good varies inversely with the quantity demanded, so the demand curve slopes downward.

2. A demand curve slopes downward for two reasons. A decrease in the price of a good (1) makes consumers more willing to substitute this good for other goods and (2) increases the real income of consumers, making them more able to buy the good.

3. Assumed to be constant along a demand curve are (1) consumer incomes, (2) the prices of related goods, (3) consumer expectations, (4) the number and composition of consumers in the market, and (5) consumer tastes. A change in any one of these could shift the demand curve.

4. Supply is a relationship between the price of a good and the quantity producers are willing and able to sell per period, other things constant. According to the law of

supply, price and quantity supplied are usually directly related, so the supply curve typically slopes upward. The supply curve slopes upward because higher prices (1) make producers more willing to supply this good rather than alternative goods and (2) make producers better able to cover the higher marginal cost associated with greater output rates.

5. Assumed to be constant along a supply curve are (1) the state of technology, (2) the prices of relevant resources, (3) the prices of alternative goods, (4) producer expectations, and (5) the number of producers. A change in any one of these could shift the supply curve.

6. Demand and supply come together in the market for a given product. Markets provide information about the price, quantity, and quality of the product for sale. They also reduce the transaction costs of exchange—the costs of time and information required to undertake exchange. The interaction of demand and supply guides resources and products to their highest-valued use.

7. Impersonal market forces reconcile the personal and independent intentions of buyers and sellers. Market equilibrium, once established, will continue unless there is a change in one of the determinants of demand or supply. Disequilibrium is usually a temporary phase while markets seek equilibrium, but sometimes it lasts a while.

QUESTIONS FOR REVIEW

1. *(Law of Demand)* What is the law of demand? Give two examples of how you have observed the law of demand at work in the "real world." How is the law of demand related to the demand curve?

2. *(Changes in Demand)* What variables influence the demand for a normal good? Explain why a reduction in the price of a normal good does not increase the demand for that good.

3. *(Substitution and Income Effects)* Distinguish between the substitution and income effects of a price change. If a good's price increases, does each effect have a positive or a negative impact on the quantity demanded?

4. *(Demand)* Explain the effect of an increase in consumer income on demand for a good.

5. *(Income Effects)* When moving along the demand curve, income must be assumed constant. Yet one factor that can cause a change in the quantity demanded is the "income effect." Reconcile these seemingly contradictory facts.

6. *(Supply)* What is the law of supply? Give an example of how you have observed the law of supply at work. What is the relationship between the law of supply and the supply curve?

7. *(Changes in Supply)* What kinds of changes in underlying conditions can cause the supply curve to shift? Give some examples and explain the direction in which the curve shifts.

8. *(Markets)* How do markets coordinate the independent decisions of buyers and sellers

9. *(Case**Study:** The Market for Professional Basketball)* In what sense can we speak of a market for professional basketball? Who are the demanders and who are the suppliers? What are some examples of how changes in supply or demand conditions have affected this market? (If you are interested in learning more about the economics of sports, visit the Busine$$ of Sport$ page at http://www.bizsports.com/index.html.

PROBLEMS AND EXERCISES

10. *(Shifting Demand)* Using supply and demand curves, show the effect of each of the following events on the market for cigarettes:
    a. A cure for lung cancer is found.
    b. The price of cigars increases.
    c. Wages increase substantially in states that grow tobacco.
    d. A fertilizer that increases the yield per acre of tobacco is discovered.
    e. There is a substantial increase in the price of matches and lighter fluid.
    f. More states pass laws restricting smoking in public places.

11. *(Substitutes and Complements)* For each of the following pairs, determine whether the goods are substitutes, complements, or unrelated:
    a. Peanut butter and jelly
    b. Private and public transportation
    c. Coke and Pepsi
    d. Alarm clocks and automobiles
    e. Golf clubs and golf balls

12. *(Equilibrium)* "If a price is not an equilibrium price, there is a tendency for it to move to its equilibrium value. Regardless of whether the price is too high or too low to begin with, the adjustment process will increase the quantity of the good purchased." Explain, using a supply and demand diagram.

13. *(Market Equilibrium)* Determine whether each of the following statements is true, false, or uncertain. Then provide a short explanation for your answer.
    a. In equilibrium, all sellers can find buyers.
    b. In equilibrium, there is no pressure on the market to produce or consume more than is being sold.
    c. At prices above equilibrium, the quantity exchanged exceeds the quantity demanded.
    d. At prices below equilibrium, the quantity exchanged is equal to the quantity supplied.

14. *(Supply and Demand)* How do you think each of the following affected the world price of oil? (Use basic supply and demand analysis.)

a. Tax credits were offered for expenditures on home insulation.
b. The Alaskan oil pipeline was completed.
c. The ceiling on the price of oil was removed.
d. Oil was discovered in Mexico and the North Sea.
e. Sport utility vehicles and minivans became popular.
f. The use of nuclear power decreased.

15. *(Equilibrium)* Consider the following graph in which demand and supply are initially *D* and *S*, respectively. What are the equilibrium price and quantity? If demand increases to *D'*, what are the new equilibrium price and quantity? What happens if the government does not allow the price to change when demand increases?

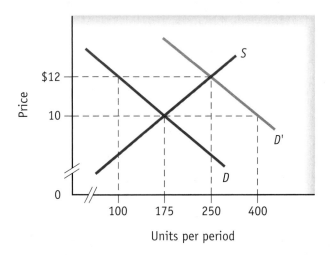

16. *(Demand and Supply)* What happens to the equilibrium price and quantity of ice cream in response to each of the following? Explain your answers.
a. The price of dairy cow fodder increases.
b. The price of beef decreases.
c. Concerns arise about the fat content of ice cream. Simultaneously, the price of sugar (used to produce ice cream) increases.

17. *(Changes in Equilibrium)* What are the effects on the equilibrium price and quantity of steel if the wages of steelworkers rise and, simultaneously, the price of aluminum rises?

18. *(Price Floor)* There is considerable interest in whether the minimum wage rate contributes to teenage unemployment. Draw a supply and demand diagram for the unskilled labor market, and discuss the effects of a minimum wage. Who is helped and who is hurt by the minimum wage?

19. *(Price Ceilings)* Suppose the supply and demand curves for rental housing units have the typical shapes and that the rental housing market is in equilibrium. Then, government establishes a rent ceiling below the equilibrium level.
a. What happens to the quantity of housing consumed?
b. Who gains from rent control?
c. Who loses from rent control?

20. *(CaseStudy: Toys Are Serious Business)* Use a supply and demand graph to describe developments in the market for Mighty Morphin Power Rangers toys. Keep in mind the shortage at the $13 selling price, the development of new factories, and the continued shortage.

EXPERIENTIAL EXERCISES

21. *(Market Demand)* Together with some other students in your class, determine your market demand for gasoline. Make up a chart listing a variety of prices per gallon of gasoline—$1.00, $1.25, $1.50, $1.75, $2.00, $2.25. Ask each student—and yourself—how many gallons *per week* they would purchase at each possible price. Then
a. Plot each student's demand curve. Check to see whether each student's responses are consistent with the law of demand.
b. Derive the "market" demand curve by adding up the quantities demanded by *all* students at each possible price.
c. What do you think will happen to that market demand curve after your class graduates and your incomes rise?

22. *(Price Floors)* The minimum wage is a price floor in a market for labor. The government sets a

minimum price per hour of labor in certain markets and no employer is permitted to pay a wage lower than that. Go to the Department of Labor's minimum wage page to learn more about the mechanics of the program http://www.dol.gov/dol/esa/public/minwage/main.htm. Then use a supply and demand diagram to illustrate the effect of imposing an above-equilibrium minimum wage on a particular labor market. What happens to quantity demanded and quantity supplied as a result of the minimum wage?

23. *(Wall Street Journal)* After reading this chapter, you have a basic understanding of how supply and demand determine market price and quantity. Find an article in the "first section" of today's *Wall Street Journal* and interpret the article, using a supply and demand diagram. Explain at least one case in which a curve shifts. What caused the shift, and how did it affect price and quantity?

Economic Decision Makers: Households, Firms, Governments, and the Rest of the World

I f we live in the age of specialization, then why haven't specialists taken over all

production—that is, why do most of you still do your own laundry and per-

form dozens of other tasks for yourself? If the "invisible hand" of competitive

markets is such an efficient allocator of resources, why did government get into

the act? Finally, how can it be said in economics that "what goes around comes

around"? Answers to these and other questions are addressed in this chapter,

which examines the four economic decision makers: households, firms, govern-

ments, and the rest of the world.

To develop a better understanding of how the economy works, you must

become more acquainted with these key players in the economy. You already

know more about them than you realize. You grew up in a household. You have dealt with firms all your life, from Wal-Mart to Subway. You know a lot about governments, from taxes to public education. And you have a growing awareness of the rest of the world, from foreign travel to the World Wide Web.

In this chapter you will draw on your abundant personal experience with economic decision makers to consider their structure, organization, and objectives. After considering all four groups, we will summarize how they interact. Topics discussed in this chapter include:

- Evolution of the household
- Evolution of the firm
- Household production versus firm production
- Role of government

- Government spending and taxation
- International trade and finance
- Trade restrictions
- Circular flow model

THE HOUSEHOLD

Households play the starring role in the economy. First, they demand goods and services from product markets and thereby help determine what gets produced. Second, households supply labor, capital, land, and entrepreneurial ability to resource markets and thereby make what gets produced. As demanders of goods and services and suppliers of resources, households make all kinds of choices, such as what to buy, how much to save, where to live, and where to work. Although a household usually consists of several individuals, we will think of each household as acting like a single decision maker; we will refer to that decision maker as the **householder.**

Householder The key decision maker in the household

The Evolution of the Household

In earlier times, when the economy was primarily agricultural, a farm household was largely self-sufficient. Individual family members specialized in specific farm tasks, such as making furniture, sewing clothes, tending livestock, and so on. These early households produced what they consumed and consumed what they produced. With the introduction of new seed varieties, fertilizers, and labor-saving machinery, farm productivity increased sharply. Fewer farmers were needed to grow enough food to feed a nation. Simultaneously, the growth of urban factories increased the demand for factory labor. As a result, many people moved from farms to cities, where they were far less self-sufficient.

Households have evolved in other ways. For example, in 1950 only about 15 percent of married women with children under 18 years of age were in the labor force. Since then, higher levels of education among married women and a growing demand for labor increased women's earnings, which raised their opportunity cost of working in the home. This rising opportunity cost likely contributed to growing labor participation.[1] Today more than half of married women with young children are in the labor force.

---

1 Professor Claudia Goldin, an economic historian from Harvard, argues that the increase in the wages, the growth of white-collar jobs, and the decline in the average work week increased the labor participation rate among women. See Goldin's *Understanding the Gender Gap: An Economic History of American Women* (New York: Oxford University Press, 1990).

The rise of two-earner households has affected the family as an economic unit. Less production occurs in the home, and more goods and services are demanded from the market. For example, child-care services and fast-food restaurants have displaced some household production. Most people eat at least one meal a day away from home. The rise in two-worker families has reduced the advantages of specialization within the household—a central feature of the farm family, where each family member specialized in particular tasks. Nonetheless, some production still occurs in the home, as we will explore in a later section.

Households Maximize Utility

There are more than 100 million households in the United States. All those who live under one roof are considered part of the same household. What exactly do householders attempt to accomplish in making decisions? Economists assume that people attempt to maximize their level of satisfaction, sense of well-being, or overall welfare. For the sake of brevity, we can say that householders attempt to maximize the household's **utility.** Householders, like other economic decision makers, are viewed as rational, meaning that they try to act in the household's best interests and would not deliberately make choices that are likely to make them worse off. Utility maximization depends on each household's subjective goals, not on some objective standard. For example, some households maintain a neat home with a well-groomed lawn; others pay no attention to their home and use the lawn as a junkyard.

Utility The satisfaction received from consumption; sense of well-being

Households as Resource Suppliers

Householders use their limited resources—labor, capital, land, and entrepreneurial ability—in an attempt to satisfy their unlimited wants. They can use these resources to produce goods and services in their homes. For example, they can prepare their own meals, mow the lawn, and fix that leaky roof. They can also sell these resources in the resource market and use the income to buy goods and services in the product market. The most valuable resource sold by most households is labor.

Exhibit 1 shows the sources of personal income received by U.S. households in 1998, when personal income totaled $7.3 trillion. As you can see, 63 percent, or nearly two-thirds, of personal income is from wages, salaries, and other labor income. Tied for second place at 11 percent each are interest earnings and transfer payments (to be discussed shortly), followed by proprietors' income at 8 percent. *Proprietors* are people who work for themselves rather than for employers; farmers, plumbers, and doctors are often self-employed. Only 5 percent of personal income comes from dividends and only 2 percent comes from rental income. *The majority of personal income in the United States is from labor earnings, rather than from the ownership of other resources such as capital or land.*

Because of a poor education, disability, discrimination, time demands of caring for small children, or bad luck, some households have few resources that are valued in the market. Society has made the political decision that individuals in such circumstances should receive short-term public assistance. Consequently, the government gives some households **transfer payments,** which are outright grants to certain households. *Cash transfers* are monetary payments, such as welfare benefits, unemployment compensation, and disability benefits. *In-kind* transfers, such as food stamps, Medicare, and Medicaid, provide specific goods and services.

Transfer payments Cash or in-kind benefits given to individuals as outright grants from the government

EXHIBIT 1

**Sources of U.S.
Personal Income
in 1998**

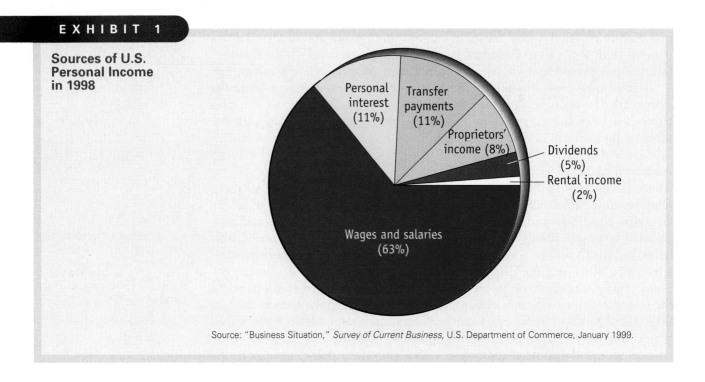

Source: "Business Situation," *Survey of Current Business*, U.S. Department of Commerce, January 1999.

Households as Demanders of Goods and Services

What happens to personal income, once it comes into the household? Personal income is allocated among personal consumption, saving, and taxes. On average, about 80 percent of U.S. personal income goes to personal consumption, about 5 percent is saved, and about 15 percent goes to taxes. Personal consumption sorts into three broad spending categories: (1) *durable goods*, such as automobiles and refrigerators, which are designed to last three years or more; (2) *nondurable goods*, such as food, clothing, and gasoline; and (3) *services*, such as haircuts, plane trips, and medical care. Durable goods make up 13 percent of U.S. personal consumption, nondurables make up 30 percent, and services make up 57 percent. The service sector is the fastest growing, because many activities—such as meal preparation and child care—that formerly were produced in the household are now often purchased in the market.

THE FIRM

Members of households once built their own homes, made their own clothes and furniture, grew their own food, and amused themselves. Over time, however, the efficiency arising from comparative advantage resulted in a greater specialization among resource suppliers. In this section, we take a look at firms, beginning with their evolution.

The Evolution of the Firm

For about 200 years, profit-seeking entrepreneurs relied on "putting out" raw material, such as wool and cotton, to rural households that turned this raw material into finished goods, such as woolen goods made from yarn. The system developed in the British Isles, where workers' cottages served as tiny factories. This approach to production, which came to be known as the *cottage industry system*, still exists in some parts of the world.

As the British economy expanded in the 18th century, entrepreneurs began to organize the various stages of production under one roof. Technological developments increased the productivity of each worker and contributed to the shift of employment from rural areas to urban factories. *Work, therefore, became organized in large, centrally powered factories that (1) promoted a more efficient division of labor, (2) allowed for the direct supervision of production, (3) reduced transportation costs, and (4) facilitated the use of machines far bigger than anything that had been used in the home.* The development of large-scale factory production, known as the **Industrial Revolution,** began in Great Britain around 1750 and spread to the rest of Europe, North America, and Australia.

Production, then, evolved from self-sufficient rural households, through the cottage industry system, where specialized production occurred in the household, to the current system of handling much production under one roof. Today, entrepreneurs combine resources in firms such as factories, mills, offices, stores, and restaurants. **Firms** are economic units formed by profit-seeking entrepreneurs who combine labor, capital, and land to produce goods and services. Just as we assume that householders attempt to maximize utility, we assume that firms attempt to *maximize profit*. Profit, the entrepreneur's reward, is total revenue minus the total cost of production.

Why Does Household Production Still Exist?

Why are such activities as house cleaning and meal preparation still undertaken primarily by households, not by firms? Some people fix their own cars, paint their own homes, and perform many other tasks that are also performed by firms. Why hasn't all production shifted to firms?

If a householder's opportunity cost of performing a task is below the market price of the task, then the householder usually performs that task. Thus, householders with a lower opportunity cost of time will tend to do more for themselves. For example, janitors typically mow their own lawns; physicians do not. Let's look at some reasons for household production.

No Skills or Specialized Resources Are Required. Some activities require so few skills or specialized resources that households find it cheaper to do these jobs themselves. Sweeping the floor requires only a broom and time, and so this job is usually performed by household members. Sanding the floor, however, involves costly machinery and special skills, so this service is usually purchased in the market. Similarly, although you wouldn't hire someone to brush your teeth each morning and evening, dental work is another matter. *Households usually perform tasks that demand neither particular skills nor specialized machinery.*

Household Production Avoids Taxes. Governments tax income, sales, and other market transactions. Suppose you are trying to decide whether to paint your home or hire a painter. If the income tax rate is one-third, a painter who requires $2,000 net of taxes to do the job must charge you $3,000 to net $2,000 after paying $1,000 in taxes. You must earn $4,500 before taxes in order to have $3,000 after taxes to pay the painter. Thus, you must earn $4,500 so that the painter can net

Industrial Revolution
Development of large-scale factory production that began in Great Britain around 1750 and spread to the rest of Europe, North America, and Australia

Firms Economic units, formed by profit-seeking entrepreneurs who employ resources to produce goods and services for sale

$2,000 after taxes. If you paint the house yourself, no taxes are imposed. *The tax-free nature of do-it-yourself activity favors household production over market purchases.*

Household Production Reduces Transaction Costs. Lining up bids from painting contractors, hiring a contractor, negotiating terms, and monitoring job performance all take time and require information. Doing the job yourself reduces these *transaction costs.* Household production also allows for more personal control over the final product than is usually available through the market. For example, some people prefer home-cooked meals to restaurant food, in part because home-cooked meals can be prepared according to individual tastes.

Technological Advances Increase Household Productivity. Technological breakthroughs are not confined to market production. Vacuum cleaners, dishwashers, microwave ovens, and other modern appliances reduce the time and often the skill required to perform household tasks. Also, modern technologies such as VCRs, CD players, cable TV, and computer games produce home entertainment. In fact, microchip-based technologies have shifted some production from the firm back to the household, as discussed in the following case study.

CaseStudy

The Information Economy

Economists have begun to study the economic implications of the virtual office and other virtual phenomena. Visit Yahoo! (http://www.yahoo.com/) and Excite (http://www.excite.com/) and search for the words "virtual" and "economics." Try it, and see what you find.

The Electronic Cottage

The Industrial Revolution shifted production from rural cottages to large urban factories. But the *Information Revolution* spawned by the invention of the microchip is decentralizing the acquisition, analysis, and transmission of information. These days people who say they work at a home office are often referring not to corporate headquarters, but to the room just off their kitchen. There are an estimated 8 to 11 million telecommuters in the United States, including nearly half the white-collar work force at AT&T. Merrill Lynch's Telecommuting Simulation Lab helps people learn how to work at home.

People with a personal computer, a modem, a fax machine, a cellular phone, and Internet access are ready for business. They can send a memo via fax or e-mail to colleagues around the corner, around the country, or around the globe. With the right software, they can write a document with coworkers scattered throughout the world. They can also buy or sell thousands of products from securities to hot sauce. And they can do all this without leaving home. An entire industry has sprung up to serve those who work at home, including magazines, newsletters, Web pages, even national conferences, such as the Telecommuting & Home Office Conference in San Francisco.

In fact, an office need not even be in a specific place. With chip-based technology, some people now work in a *virtual office*, which has no permanent location—"deals on wheels," so to speak. For example, accountants at Ernst & Young spend most of their time in the field. When workers need to return to company headquarters, they call a few hours ahead to reserve an office.

Newly developed software such as Netscape Virtual Office®, Virtual File Cabinet®, or Netopia Virtual Office® allows thousands of employees to share electronic files. When Anderson Consulting moved its headquarters from Boston to a suburb, the company got rid of 120 tons of paper, replacing it with a huge on-line data base accessible any time of the day or night from anywhere in the world. Computers have changed the world of work.

Sources: Gene Marcial, "Netopia: An Internet Sleeper," *Business Week*, 27 July 1998; "A Connected World," *The Economist*, 13 September 1997; Mark Davis, "Consulting Firm Puts Office Space Up for Grabs as Day-by-Day Commodity," *Kansas City Star*, 26 September 1997; Godfrey Nolan, "A Good Day at the Virtual Office," *The Irish Times*, 27 July 1997; and as an example of sales over the Internet, visit Hot Hot Hot, "the Net's coolest hot sauce shop" http://www.hot.presence.com/g/p/H3/.

Kinds of Firms

There are about 22 million for-profit businesses in the United States. Two-thirds of these are small retail businesses, small service operations, part-time home-based businesses, and small farms. Each year more than a million new businesses are started, many of which fail. Entrepreneurs organize firms in one of three ways: as a sole proprietorship, as a partnership, or as a corporation. Let's examine the advantages and disadvantages of each.

Sole Proprietorships. The simplest form of business organization is the **sole proprietorship,** a single-owner firm. Examples are a self-employed plumber, electrician, farmer, or family physician. To organize a sole proprietorship, the proprietor simply opens for business by, for example, taking out a classified ad announcing availability for carpentry, snow plowing, or lawn mowing. The owner is in complete control. But he or she faces *unlimited liability* for any business debts and could lose everything, including a home and other assets, as a result of a debt or claim against the business. Also, since the sole proprietor has no partners or other financial backers, raising enough money to get the business up and running can be difficult. One final disadvantage is that sole proprietorships usually go out of business upon the death of the proprietor. Still, they are the most common form of business organization, accounting most recently for 73 percent of all U.S. businesses. Because this type of firm is typically small, proprietorships generate a small portion of all U.S. business sales—only 6 percent.

Sole proprietorship A firm with a single owner who has the right to all profits and who bears unlimited liability for the firm's debts

Partnerships. A more complicated form of business organization is the **partnership,** which involves two or more individuals who agree to contribute resources to the business in return for a share of the profit or loss. Law, accounting, and medical partnerships typify this business form. Partners have strength in numbers and often find it easier than the sole proprietor to raise sufficient funds to get the business going. But the partners may not always agree. Also, each partner usually faces unlimited liability for all the debts and claims against the partnership, so one partner could lose everything because of another's foolish mistake. Finally, the death or departure of one partner may disrupt the firm's continuity and could require a complete reorganization. The partnership is the least common form of U.S. business organization, making up only 7 percent of all firms and accounting for just 5 percent of all business sales.

Partnership A firm with multiple owners who share the firm's profits and each of whom bears unlimited liability for the firm's debts

Corporations. By far the most important form of business organization is the corporation. The **corporation** is a legal entity established through articles of incorporation. The owners of a corporation are issued shares of stock entitling them to corporate profits in proportion to their stock ownership. A major advantage of the corporate form is that many individuals—hundreds, thousands,

Corporation A legal entity owned by stockholders whose liability is limited to the value of their stock even millions—can pool their money, so incorporating represents the easiest way to amass large sums of money to finance the firm. Also, stockholders have *limited liability*, meaning their liability for any losses is limited to the value of their stock. A final advantage of this form of organization is that the corporation has a life apart from those of the owners. The corporation continues to exist even if ownership changes hands, and it can be taxed and sued as if it were a person.

The corporate form has some disadvantages as well. A stockholder's ability to influence corporate policy is limited to voting for a board of directors, which oversees the operation of the firm. Each share of stock usually carries with it one vote; the typical stockholder of a large corporation owns only a tiny fraction of the shares and thus has little say. Whereas the income from sole proprietorships and partnerships is taxed only once, corporate income is taxed twice: first as corporate profits and second as stockholder income, either as corporate dividends or as realized capital gains. A *realized capital gain* is any increase in the market value of a share that occurs between the time the share is purchased and the time it is sold.

A hybrid type of corporation has evolved to take advantage of the limited liability feature of the corporate structure, while reducing the impact of double taxation. The *S corporation* provides owners with limited liability, but profits are taxed only once—as income on each shareholder's personal income tax return. To qualify as an S corporation, a firm must have no more than 35 stockholders and must have no foreign or corporate stockholders.

Corporations make up only 20 percent of all U.S. businesses, but because they tend to be much larger than the other two forms of business, corporate sales represent 89 percent of all business sales. Exhibit 2 shows, by type of U.S. firm, the percentage of firms and the percentage of total sales. *The sole proprietorship is the most important form in terms of total numbers, but the corporation is the most important in terms of total sales.*

Nonprofit Institutions

To this point we have considered firms that maximize profit. Some institutions, such as museums, ballet companies, nonprofit hospitals, the Red Cross, the Salvation Army, churches, synagogues, mosques, and perhaps the college you attend, are private organizations that do not have profit as an explicit objective. Yet even nonprofit institutions must somehow pay for the resources they employ. Revenue sources typically include some combination of voluntary contributions and service charges, such as college tuition and hospital bills. Although there are millions of nonprofit institutions, when we talk about firms in this book, we will be referring to for-profit firms.

THE GOVERNMENT

You might think that production by firms and by households could satisfy all consumer demands. Why must yet another economic decision maker get into the act?

The Role of Government

Sometimes the unrestrained operation of markets has undesirable results. Too many of some goods and too few of other goods may be produced. In this section we discuss the sources of **market failure** and how society's overall welfare could at times be improved through government intervention.

Market failure A condition that arises when unrestrained operation of markets yields socially undesirable results

EXHIBIT 2

Number and Sales of Each Type of Firm

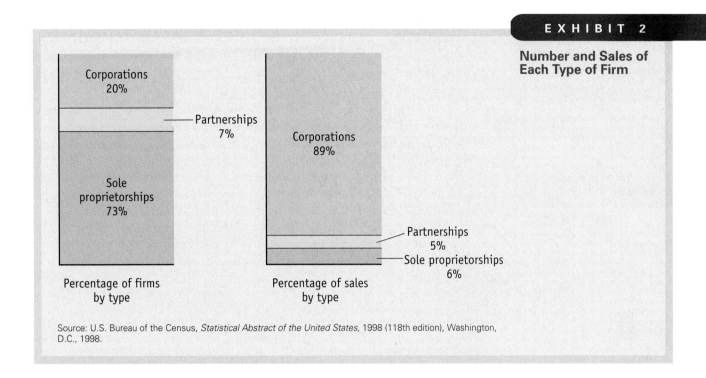

Percentage of firms by type
- Corporations 20%
- Partnerships 7%
- Sole proprietorships 73%

Percentage of sales by type
- Corporations 89%
- Partnerships 5%
- Sole proprietorships 6%

Source: U.S. Bureau of the Census, *Statistical Abstract of the United States,* 1998 (118th edition), Washington, D.C., 1998.

Establishing and Enforcing the Rules of the Game. Market efficiency depends on people like you using your resources to maximize your utility. But what if you were repeatedly robbed of your paycheck on your way home from work? Or what if, after you worked a month, your employer said you would not get paid? Why bother working? The system of private markets would break down if you could not safeguard your private property or if you could not enforce contracts. Governments play a role in *safeguarding private property* through police protection and in *enforcing contracts* through a judicial system. More generally, governments try to make sure that market participants play fair and abide by the "rules of the game." These rules are established through laws and through the customs and conventions of the market.

Promoting Competition. Although the "invisible hand" of competition usually promotes an efficient allocation of resources, some firms try to avoid competition through *collusion,* which is an agreement among firms to divide the market or to fix the market price. An individual firm may try to eliminate the competition by using unfair business practices. For example, to drive out local competitors, a large firm may temporarily sell at a price below its cost. *Government antitrust laws try to promote competition by prohibiting collusion and other anticompetitive practices.*

Regulating Natural Monopolies. Competition usually keeps the product price lower than it is when the product is sold by a **monopoly,** a sole supplier to the market. In rare instances, however, a monopoly can produce and sell the product for less than could several competing firms. For example, electricity is delivered more efficiently by a single firm that wires the community than by competing firms stringing their own wires. When it is cheaper for one firm to serve the market than for two or more firms to do so, that firm is called a **natural monopoly.**

Monopoly A sole producer of a product for which there are no close substitutes

Natural monopoly One firm that can serve the entire market at a lower per-unit cost than can two or more firms

Since a natural monopoly faces no competition, it maximizes profit by charging a higher price than is optimal from society's point of view. Therefore, the government usually regulates the natural monopoly, forcing it to lower the price.

Providing Public Goods. So far in this book, we have been talking about private goods, which have two important features. First, private goods are *rival* in consumption, meaning that the amount consumed by one person is unavailable for others to consume. For example, when you and a friend share a pizza, each slice your friend eats is one less slice available to you. Second, the supplier of a private good can easily exclude those who fail to pay. Only paying customers get a pizza. Thus, private goods are *exclusive*. In contrast, **public goods,** such as national defense and a system of justice, are *nonrival* in consumption. One person's consumption does not diminish the amount available to others. What's more, once produced, public goods are available to all. Suppliers cannot easily prevent consumption by those who fail to pay. For example, national defense is *nonexclusive*. It is available to all in the community, regardless of who pays for it and who does not. Because public goods are *nonrival* and *nonexclusive*, private firms cannot sell them profitably. The government, however, has the authority to collect taxes for public goods.

Dealing with Externalities. Market prices reflect the *private* costs and benefits of producers and consumers. But sometimes production or consumption imposes costs or benefits on third parties—on those who are neither suppliers nor demanders in a market transaction. For example, a paper mill fouls the air breathed by nearby residents, but the price of paper, as determined in the private market, fails to reflect the cost such pollution imposes on society. Since these pollution costs are outside, or *external* to, the market activity, they are called *externalities*. An **externality** is a cost or a benefit that falls on third parties. A *negative externality* imposes on third parties a cost such as factory pollution, jet noise, or auto emissions. A *positive externality* confers on third parties an external benefit, such as getting a flu shot so you will not contract and transmit the disease, observing traffic signs and speed limits so you don't hit other cars, and planting a flower garden in your front yard, where it beautifies the neighborhood.

Because market prices do not reflect externalities, governments often employ taxes, subsidies, and regulations to discourage negative externalities and to encourage positive externalities. For example, because education generates positive externalities (educated people are more apt to be able to read road signs and are less likely to resort to violent crime for income), government tries to encourage people to get more education. One approach is to pass laws requiring students to stay in school until they are 16 years old. Another approach is for taxpayers to fund education so the cost to students is minimal, as with free public schools, or to subsidize education, as with public higher education.

A More Equal Distribution of Income. As mentioned earlier, some people—because of a lack of education, mental or physical disabilities, or perhaps the need to care for small children—may be unable to earn enough to support themselves and their family. Since resource markets do not guarantee each household even a minimum level of income, transfer payments reflect society's attempt to provide a basic standard of living to all households. Nearly all citizens agree that, through government transfer payments, society should alter some of the results of the market by redistributing income to the poor. (Notice

---

Public good A good that, once produced, is available for all to consume, regardless of who pays and who does not

Externality A cost or a benefit that falls on third parties and is therefore ignored by the two parties to the market transaction

*Net*Bookmark

The annual *Economic Report of the President* is an invaluable source of information on current economic policy. It also contains many useful data tables. You can find it on-line at http://www.access.gpo.gov/eop/.

the normative nature of this statement.) But differences of opinion arise in deciding just how much redistribution should occur, what form it should take, who should receive the benefits, and how long those benefits should continue.

Full Employment, Price Stability, and Economic Growth. The government, through its ability to tax and spend and its control of the money supply, attempts to promote full employment, price stability, and an adequate rate of growth in the economy. The government's pursuit of these objectives through taxing and spending is called **fiscal policy** and pursuing them by regulating the money supply is called **monetary policy.** The study of macroeconomics examines these policies.

Government's Structure and Objectives

The United States has a *federal system* of government, meaning that responsibilities are shared across levels of government. State governments grant some powers to local governments and surrender some powers to the national, or federal, government. As the system has evolved, the federal government has assumed primary responsibility for national security and the stability of the economy. State governments fund public higher education, prisons and, with aid from the federal government, highways and welfare. Local government responsibilities include primary and secondary education, plus police and fire protection.

Difficulty in Defining Government Objectives. We assume that households maximize utility and firms maximize profit, but what about governments—or, more specifically, what about government decision makers? What do they maximize? One problem is that the federal system consists of many governments—more than 80,000 separate jurisdictions in all. What's more, because the federal government relies on offsetting, or countervailing, powers among the *executive*, *legislative*, and *judicial* branches, government does not act as a single, consistent decision maker. Even within the federal executive branch, there are so many agencies and bureaus that at times they seem to work at cross purposes. For example, at the same time as the U.S. Surgeon General requires health warnings on cigarettes, the U.S. Department of Agriculture subsidizes tobacco farmers. Given this thicket of jurisdictions, branches, and bureaus, one useful theory of government behavior is that elected officials try to maximize the number of votes they will get in the next election. Thus, we can assume that elected officials *maximize votes*. In this theory, vote maximization guides the decisions of elected officials who, in turn, control government employees.

Voluntary Exchange Versus Coercion. Market exchange relies on the voluntary behavior of buyers and sellers. If you don't like tofu, no problem—just don't buy any. But in political markets the situation is different. Any voting rule except unanimous consent will involve some government coercion. Public choices are enforced by the police power of the state. Those who fail to pay their taxes could go to jail, even though they may object to programs those taxes support.

Absence of Market Prices. Another distinguishing feature of governments is that the selling price of public output is usually either zero or some amount below its cost. If you are now attending a state college or university, your tuition probably covers less than half of the total cost of providing your education. Since the revenue side of the government budget is usually separate from the expenditure side, there is no necessary link between the cost and benefit of a

Fiscal policy The use of government purchases, transfer payments, taxes, and borrowing to influence aggregate economic activity

Monetary policy Regulation of the money supply in order to influence aggregate economic activity public program. In the private sector, however, marginal benefits are at least equal to marginal costs; otherwise, market exchange would not occur.

Size and Growth of U.S. Government

One way to track the role of government over time is by measuring government spending relative to the U.S. *gross domestic product,* or *GDP,* which is the total value of all final goods and services produced in the United States. In 1929, the year the Great Depression began, government spending, mostly by state and local governments, totaled just one-tenth the size of GDP. At that time, the federal government played a minor role. In fact, during the country's first 150 years, spending by the federal government, except during times of war, never exceeded 3 percent of the size of GDP.

The Great Depression, World War II, and a change in mainstream macro-economic thinking expanded the role of the federal government in the economy. By 1998, government spending was 32 percent as large as GDP, with 21 percent by the federal government and 11 percent by state and local governments. In comparison, government spending relative to GDP was 36 percent in Japan, 39 percent in the United Kingdom, 42 percent in Canada, 47 percent in Germany, 50 percent in Italy, and 54 percent in France. The average for 18 other industrial economies was 42 percent.[2]

Thus, government spending in the United States is small, compared to the rest of the industrialized world. Since 1960, defense spending has declined from over half of all federal spending to less than one-fifth today. Spending on Social Security and Medicare, programs aimed primarily at the elderly, has increased from about 10 percent of the federal budget in 1960 to about one-third today.

Sources of Government Revenue

Taxes provide the bulk of revenue at all levels of government. The federal government relies primarily on the individual income tax, state governments rely on income and sales taxes, and local governments rely on the property tax. In addition to taxes, other revenue sources include user charges, such as highway tolls, and borrowing. Some states also sell stuff, such as lottery tickets and liquor, to raise money.

Exhibit 3 focuses on sources of federal revenue since 1940. The individual income tax has accounted for about 45 percent of federal revenues since shortly after World War II. In the early 1950s, payroll taxes accounted for only about 10 percent of federal receipts, compared to 36 percent most recently. *Payroll taxes* are deducted from paychecks to support Social Security, unemployment benefits, and medical care for the elderly. Corporate income taxes and revenue from other sources, such as excise (sales) taxes and user charges, have declined as a share of the total since the 1950s.

Tax Principles and Tax Incidence

Ability-to-pay-tax principle Those with a greater ability to pay should pay more tax

The structure of a tax is often justified on the basis of one of two general principles. First, a tax could relate to the individual's **ability to pay,** so those with a greater ability pay more taxes. Income or property taxes often rely on this ability-to-pay principle. Alternatively, a tax could relate to the **benefits received** from the government activity funded by the tax. For example, the tax on gaso-

---

2 Figures for foreign countries are from the Organization for Economic Cooperation and Development (OECD).

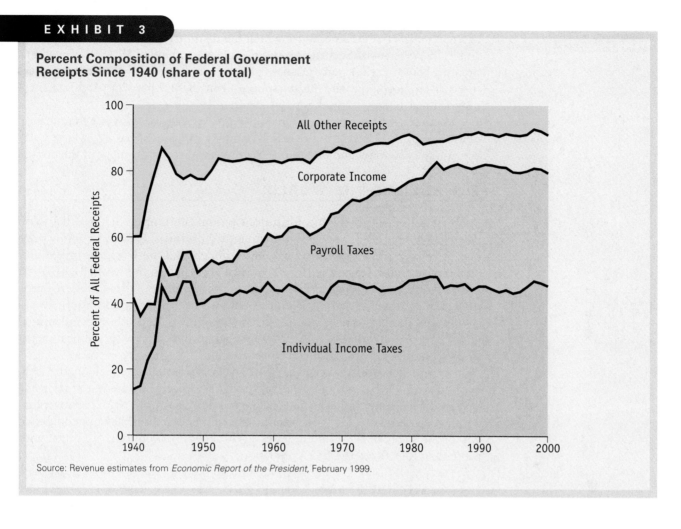

EXHIBIT 3

Percent Composition of Federal Government Receipts Since 1940 (share of total)

All Other Receipts

Corporate Income

Payroll Taxes

Individual Income Taxes

Percent of All Federal Receipts

Source: Revenue estimates from *Economic Report of the President*, February 1999.

line funds highway construction and maintenance, thereby linking tax payment to road use, since the more people drive, the more gas tax they pay.

Tax incidence indicates who actually bears the burden of the tax. One way to evaluate tax incidence is by measuring the tax as a percentage of income. Under **proportional taxation,** taxpayers at all income levels pay the same percentage of their income in taxes. A proportional income tax is also called a flat-rate tax, because the tax as a percentage of income remains constant, or flat, as income increases. Under **progressive taxation,** the percentage of income paid in taxes increases as income increases.

The **marginal tax rate** indicates the percentage of each additional dollar of income that goes to taxes. Because high marginal rates reduce the after-tax return from working or investing, they can reduce people's incentives to work and to invest. In 1999, there were 5 marginal rates under the U.S. federal personal income tax—15 percent, 28 percent, 31 percent, 36 percent, and 39.6 percent—so that tax is progressive. By way of comparison, the top marginal tax rate is 65 percent in Japan, 55 percent in England and Canada, and 53 percent in France and Germany.

Finally, under **regressive taxation,** the percentage of income paid in taxes decreases as income increases, so the marginal tax rate declines as income

Benefits-received tax principle Those who receive more benefits from the government program funded by a tax should pay more tax

Tax incidence The distribution of tax burden among taxpayers

Proportional taxation The tax as a percentage of income remains constant as income increases; also called a flat-rate tax

Progressive taxation The tax as a percentage of income increases as income increases

Marginal tax rate The percentage of each additional dollar of income that goes to taxes

Regressive taxation The tax as a percentage of income decreases as income increases

increases. Most U.S. *payroll taxes* are regressive, because they impose a flat rate up to a certain level of income, above which the marginal rate drops to zero. For example, in 1999, Social Security taxes were levied on the first $72,600 of workers' income. Half the 12.4 percent tax is paid by employers and half by employees (the self-employed pay the entire amount). But the 2.9 percent Medicare tax is proportional, because it applies to all earnings.

This discussion of revenue sources brings to a close, for now, our examination of the role of government in the U.S. economy. Government has a pervasive influence on the economy, and discussions of its role are woven throughout the book.

THE REST OF THE WORLD

Thus far we have focused on institutions within the United States—that is, on *domestic* households, firms, and governments. This initial focus was appropriate because our primary objective has been to understand the workings of the U.S. economy, which is by far the largest national economy in the world. But the rest of the world affects what U.S. households consume and what U.S. firms produce. For example, Asian economies such as those of Japan and South Korea supply U.S. markets with autos, electronic equipment, and other manufactured goods, thereby affecting U.S. prices, wages, and profits. Likewise, political unrest in the Persian Gulf can drive up the price of oil.

Foreign decision makers, therefore, have a significant effect on the U.S. economy—on what we consume and what we produce. The *rest of the world* consists of the households, firms, and governments in more than 200 sovereign countries throughout the world, ranging from countries with fewer people than any of the states in the United States to the People's Republic of China, with more than four times the U.S. population.

International Trade

In Chapter 2 you learned about comparative advantage and the gains from specialization. These gains explain why householders stopped trying to do everything for themselves and began to specialize. International trade arises for the same reasons. *International trade occurs because the opportunity cost of producing specific goods differs among countries.* Americans import raw materials such as crude oil, diamonds, and coffee beans and finished goods such as cameras, VCRs, and automobiles. U.S. producers export sophisticated products such as computer hardware and software, aircraft, and movies, as well as agricultural products such as wheat and corn.

International trade between the United States and the rest of the world has increased in recent decades. In 1970 U.S. exports of goods and services amounted to only 6 percent of gross domestic product. That figure has since more than doubled to 14 percent. Our chief U.S. trading partners in order of importance are Canada, Japan, Mexico, Great Britain, Germany, France, South Korea, and Taiwan.

Merchandise trade balance The value of a country's exported goods minus the value of its imported goods during a given time period

The **merchandise trade balance** equals the value of exported goods minus the value of imported goods. Goods in this case are distinguished from services, which show up in another trade account. For the last two decades, the United States has experienced a merchandise trade deficit, meaning that the value of goods imported into the U.S. has exceeded the value of U.S. goods exported. Just as a household must cover its spending, so too must a nation. The deficit in our merchandise trade balance must be offset by a surplus in one or more of the other *balance-of-*

payments accounts. A nation's **balance of payments** is the record of all economic transactions between its residents and the residents of the rest of the world.

Exchange Rates

The lack of a common currency complicates trade between countries. How many U.S. dollars buys a Porsche? An American buyer cares only about the dollar cost; the German car maker cares only about the *euros* received (the new common currency of 11 European countries). To facilitate trade when two currencies are involved, a market for foreign exchange has developed. **Foreign exchange** is a foreign currency needed to carry out international transactions. The supply and demand for foreign exchange come together in *foreign exchange markets* to determine an equilibrium exchange rate. The *exchange rate* measures the price of one currency in terms of another. For example, the exchange rate between the euro and the dollar might indicate that one euro exchanges for $1.10. At that exchange rate, a Porsche selling for 60,000 euros costs $66,000. The greater the demand for a particular foreign currency or the smaller the supply, the higher its exchange rate—that is, the more dollars it will cost. The exchange rate affects the prices of imports and exports and thus helps shape the flow of foreign trade.

Trade Restrictions

Although there are clear gains from international specialization and exchange, nearly all nations restrict trade to some extent. These restrictions can take the form of (1) **tariffs**, which are taxes on imports; (2) **quotas**, which are legal limits on the quantity of a particular good that can be imported; and (3) other restrictions, such as the voluntary agreement by Japanese automobile manufacturers to limit their exports to the United States.

If specialization according to comparative advantage is so beneficial, why do most countries restrict trade? Restrictions benefit certain domestic producers that lobby their governments for these benefits. For example, U.S. textile manufacturers have sought and received from Congress protective legislation restricting textile imports, thereby raising U.S. textile prices. These higher prices harm domestic consumers, but consumers are usually unaware of this harm. Trade restrictions interfere with the free flow of products across borders and tend to harm the overall economy. International trade in the auto industry is discussed in the following case study.

Wheel of Fortune

The U.S. auto industry is huge, with annual sales of more than $250 billion, an amount exceeding the gross domestic product of 90 percent of the world's economies. Imports accounted for only 0.4 percent of U.S. auto sales in the decade following World War II. In 1973, however, the suddenly powerful Organization of Petroleum Exporting Countries (OPEC) more than tripled oil prices. In response, Americans scrambled for more fuel-efficient automobiles, which at the time were sold primarily by foreign manufacturers, especially the Japanese. As a result, imports jumped to 21 percent of U.S. auto sales by 1980.

Balance of payments A record of all economic transactions between residents of one country and residents of the rest of the world during a given time period

Foreign exchange Foreign currency needed to carry out international transactions

Tariff A tax on imports or exports

Quota A legal limit on the quantity of a particular product that can be imported or exported

CaseStudy

The World of Business

The International Motor Vehicle Program at MIT maintains a Web page rich with links and other useful information about automobile production worldwide. You can find it at http://web.mit.edu/org/c/ctpid/www/imvp/IMVP-links.html.

In the early 1980s, at the urging of the Big Three auto makers (General Motors, Ford, and Chrysler), the Reagan administration persuaded Japanese producers to adopt "voluntary" import quotas limiting the number of Japanese automobiles they exported to the United States. The quotas, or supply restrictions, drove up the price of Japanese imports. U.S. auto producers used this as an opportunity to raise their own prices. Experts estimate that the so-called protection from foreign competition cost U.S. consumers over $15 billion.

The quotas had two effects on Japanese producers. First, faced with a strict limit on the number of cars they could export to the United States, they began shipping more upscale models instead of subcompacts. Second, the quotas encouraged Japanese producers to establish manufacturing plants in the United States. By making autos here, Japanese manufacturers also reduced the problem caused by fluctuations in the value of the yen relative to the dollar. Japanese-owned auto plants in the U.S. now account for more than one-quarter of car production in the United States. Two German auto makers, Mercedes and BMW, have also built plants here.

Imports still make up about one-quarter of U.S. car sales, with Japanese manufacturers accounting for most of that. Imports include cars produced abroad by foreign firms but sold under the names of U.S. firms. The Big Three also produce around the world. In fact, Ford is the largest auto maker in Australia, Great Britain, Mexico, and Argentina.

In China, India, and Latin America, the potential car market is enormous. Here's something to think about: There are more people in China under 26 years of age than the combined population of the United States, Japan, Germany, the United Kingdom, and Canada. Automobile production in China jumped from 23,500 in 1988 to about 2 million in 1998. Only about 100,000 vehicles were imported.

Sources: Rebecca Blumenstein and Gregory White, "In Aftermath of UAW Strikes, GM Seeks to Justify the Costs," *Wall Street Journal*, 30 July 1998; Walter Adams and James Brock, "Automobiles," in *The Structure of American Industry*, 9th ed. (Englewood Cliffs, N.J.: Prentice Hall, 1995): pp. 65–92; Michelle Krebs, "Heavy Traffic to the Third World," *The New York Times*, 3 Oct. 1997; Andrea Pulchalsky, "Camry Whizzes Past Taurus as Best-Selling Car in the U.S.," *Wall Street Journal*," 30 September 1997.

THE CIRCULAR FLOW MODEL

Circular flow model A diagram that outlines the flow of resources, products, income, and revenue among households, firms, governments, and the rest of the world

Now that we have examined each economic decision maker in detail, let's review how they interact. Such a picture is conveyed by the **circular flow model,** which describes the flow of resources, products, income, and revenue among households, firms, governments, and the rest of the world.

Flows Between Households and Firms

We begin with the most fundamental interaction in a market economy—that between households and firms. Exhibit 4 shows households on the left and firms on the right. Households supply labor, capital, land, and entrepreneurial ability to firms through resource markets, shown on the lower portion of the exhibit. In return, households demand goods and services from firms through product markets, shown on the upper portion of the exhibit. Viewed from the business end, firms supply goods and services to households through product markets, and they

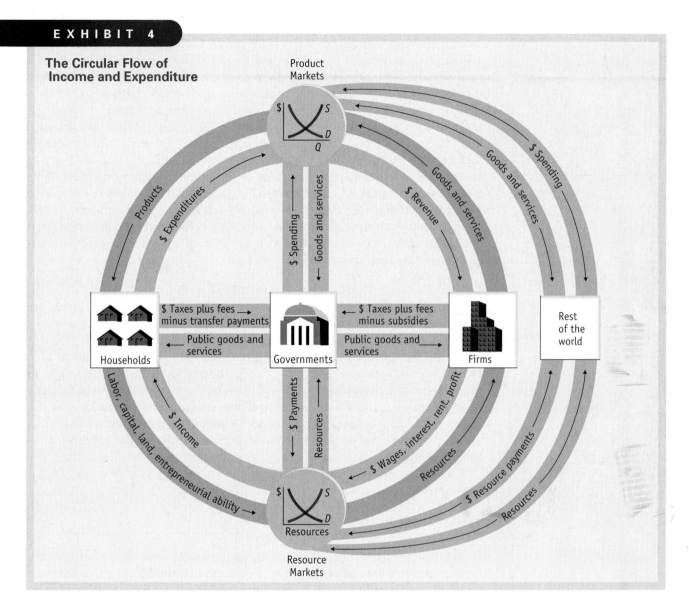

EXHIBIT 4

The Circular Flow of Income and Expenditure

Product Markets

Households

Governments

Firms

Rest of the world

Resource Markets

$ Taxes plus fees minus transfer payments

Public goods and services

$ Taxes plus fees minus subsidies

Public goods and services

$ Payments

Resources

$ Wages, interest, rent, profit

Resources

$ Resource payments

Resources

$ Spending

Goods and services

$ Revenue

Goods and services

Goods and services

$ Spending

Products

$ Expenditures

Labor, capital, land, entrepreneurial ability

$ Income

demand labor, capital, land, and entrepreneurial ability from households through resource markets. Resources and products flow in a counterclockwise direction.

In a barter economy, exchange is limited to physical flows of resources and products. But in nearly all economies of the world, the flows of resources and products are supported by flows of income and expenditure—that is, by the flow of money. So let's add money to the picture. Supply and demand in resource markets determine equilibrium wages, interest, rents, and profits, which—when multiplied by the quantity of resources supplied—flow as income to households. Supply and demand in product markets determine equilibrium prices for goods and services, which—when multiplied by the quantities of goods and services demanded—flow as revenue to firms. In the diagram note that resources and products flow in a counterclockwise direction, and that corresponding payments for these products and resources flow in a clockwise direction.

Government-Related Flows

Thus far we have focused on the private sector. But another decision maker is government. Governments are linked with all four elements discussed thus far in the circular flow: households, firms, resource markets, and products markets. Governments purchase resources such as labor from resource markets, and they purchase goods and services such as computer paper and phone service from product markets. Governments convert these into public goods and services, which they provide to households and firms. To finance this production, governments rely on the revenue received from households, firms, and the rest of the world. Government revenue consists of taxes and user fees. From this revenue, governments also make transfer payments (such as welfare payments) to certain households and provide subsidies (such as farm price supports) to certain firms. Thus, the net flow from households to governments equals taxes plus fees minus transfer payments, and the net flow from firms to governments equals taxes plus fees minus subsidies.

Flows To and From the Rest of the World

The discussion so far has been limited to the domestic economy. To complete the picture, we must add the flows to and from the rest of the world. The rest of the world supplies resources to our resource markets and demands resources from those markets. For example, foreigners sell specialized machines to U.S. firms and buy specialized machines from U.S. firms. Because resources flow in both directions, there is an arrow at both ends of the pipeline. Likewise, foreigners supply goods and services to U.S. product markets and demand goods and services from U.S. product markets. Again, to indicate the two-way nature of the flows, the arrows point in both directions. The same goes for the pipelines indicating the resource payments and product revenues.

Take a little time right now to review the big picture offered by the circular flow model in Exhibit 4.

CONCLUSION

In this chapter we examined four economic decision makers: households, firms, governments, and the rest of the world. Domestic households are by far the most important, for they, along with foreign households, supply the resources and demand the goods and services produced. In recent years, the U.S. economy has come to depend more on the rest of the world as a market for U.S. goods and as a source of products.

SUMMARY

1. Most household income arises from the sale of labor, and most household income is spent on personal consumption, which consists of spending on durable goods, nondurable goods, and services—the last being the fastest-growing portion of personal consumption. Income not spent on personal consumption is either saved or paid as taxes.

2. Members of households once built their own homes, made their own clothes and furniture, grew their own food, and amused themselves. Over time, however, the efficiency arising from comparative advantage resulted in a greater specialization among resource suppliers.

3. Firms bring together specialized resources. Firms can be organized in three different ways: as sole proprietorships, partnerships, or corporations. Because corporations are typically large, they account for the bulk of all sales by U.S. firms.

4. When private markets yield socially undesirable results, government may intervene to address these market failures. Government programs are designed to (1) protect private property and enforce contracts; (2) promote competition; (3) regulate natural monopolies; (4) provide public goods; (5) discourage negative externalities and encourage positive externalities; (6) provide for greater equality in the distribution of income; and (7) promote full employment, price stability, and growth.

5. In the United States, the federal government relies primarily on the personal income tax, the states rely on income and sales taxes, and the localities rely on the property tax. A tax is often justified by basing it on (1) the individual's ability to pay or (2) the benefits the taxpayer receives from the activities financed by the tax.

6. The rest of the world is also populated by households, firms, and governments. International trade takes advantage of the gains that arise from comparative. The balance of payments summarizes the transactions between the residents of one country and the residents of the rest of the world. Despite the benefits from comparative advantage, nearly all countries impose trade restrictions to protect specific domestic industries.

7. The circular flow model describes the flow of resources, products, income, and revenue among households, firms, governments, and the rest of the world.

QUESTIONS FOR REVIEW

1. *(Households as Demanders of Goods and Services)* Classify each of the following as a durable good, a nondurable good, or a service:
   a. A gallon of milk
   b. A lawn mower
   c. A videocassette recorder
   d. A manicure
   e. A pair of shoes
   f. An eye exam
   g. A personal computer
   h. A neighborhood teenager mowing a lawn

2. *(CaseStudy: The Electronic Cottage)* How has the development of personal computer hardware and software reversed some of the trends brought on by the Industrial Revolution?

3. *(Evolution of the Firm)* Explain how production after the Industrial Revolution differed from production under the cottage industry system.

4. *(Household Production)* What factors does a householder consider when deciding whether to produce a good or service at home or buy it in the marketplace?

5. *(Corporations)* Why did the institution of the firm appear after the advent of the Industrial Revolution? What type of business organization existed before this?

6. *(Sole Proprietorships)* What are the disadvantages of the sole proprietorship form of business?

7. *(Government)* Often it is said that government is necessary when private markets fail to work effectively and fairly. Based on your reading of the text, discuss how private markets might break down.

8. *(Externalities)* Suppose there is an external cost associated with production of a certain good. What's wrong with letting the market determine how much of this good will be produced?

9. *(Government Revenue)* What are the sources of government revenue in the United States? Which types of taxes are most important at each level of government? Which two taxes provide the most revenue to the U.S. federal government?

10. *(Objectives of the Economic Decision Makers)* In economic analysis, what are the assumed objectives of households, firms, and the government?

11. *(International Trade)* Why does international trade occur? What does it mean to run a deficit in the merchandise trade balance?

12. *(International Trade)* Distinguish between a tariff and a quota. Who benefits from and who is harmed by such restrictions on imports?

13. *(CaseStudy: Wheel of Fortune)* What factors led Japanese auto producers to build factories in the United States?

14. *(Circular Flow)* Review the illustration of the circular flow of income and expenditure in Exhibit 4. Which flows take the form of money, and which take the form of goods and services? What role does international trade play in this circular flow?

PROBLEMS AND EXERCISES

15. *(Evolution of the Household)* Determine whether each of the following would increase or decrease the opportunity costs for mothers who choose not to accept paid employment outside the home. Explain your answers.
    a. Higher levels of education for women
    b. Higher unemployment rates for women
    c. Higher average pay levels for women
    d. Lower demand for labor in industries that traditionally employ large numbers of women

16. *(Household Production)* Many households supplement their food budget by cultivating small vegetable gardens. Explain how each of the following might influence this kind of household production:
    a. Both husband and wife are professionals who earn high salaries.
    b. The household is located in a city rather than in a rural area.
    c. The household is located in a region where there is a high sales tax on food.
    d. The household is located in a region that has a high property tax rate.

17. *(Government)* Complete each of the following sentences:
    a. When the private operation of a market leads to overproduction or underproduction of some good, this is known as a(n) _____ .

    b. Goods that are nonrival and nonexcludable are known as _____ .
    c. _____ are cash or in-kind benefits given to individuals as outright grants from the government.
    d. A(n) _____ confers an external benefit on third parties that are not directly involved in a market transaction.
    e. _____ refers to the government's pursuit of full employment and price stability through variations in taxes and government spending.

18. *(Tax Rates)* Suppose taxes are related to income level as follows:

Income	Taxes
$1,000	$200
$2,000	$350
$3,000	$450

    a. What percent of income is paid in taxes at each level?
    b. Is the tax rate progressive, proportional, or regressive?
    c. What is the marginal tax rate on the first $1,000 of income? The second $1,000? The third $1,000?

EXPERIENTIAL EXERCISES

19. *(The Evolution of the Firm)* Get a library copy of *The Wealth and Poverty of Nations* by David Landes and read pages 207–210. How would you interpret Landes' story about mechanization using the ideas developed in this chapter?

20. *(The Evolution of the Firm)* The Center for Research on Contracts and the Structure of Enterprise at the University of Pittsburgh http://crcse.business.pitt.edu/ maintains lots of interesting information about the evolution of the firm. Visit that site to familiarize yourself with the kinds of issues economists are studying.

21. *(International Trade)* Visit McEachern Interactive Web Site http://mceachern.swcollege.com and click on EconDebates Online. Review the materials on "Does the U.S. Economy Benefit from Foreign Trade?" What are some of the benefits of international trade—not just to the U.S., but to all nations?

22. *(Wall Street Journal)* The household is the most important decision-making unit in our economy. Look through the rotating columns (e.g., "Work and Family," and "Personal Technology") in the *Wall Street Journal* this week. Find a description of some technological change that might affect household production. Explain how production would be affected.

Elasticity of Demand and Supply

hy did visits to Microsoft's on-line magazine, *Slate*, drop 95 percent when the access charge increased from zero to $20 a year? Why did total usage by subscribers of America Online explode when the company switched from an hourly charge to a flat monthly fee? Why do higher cigarette taxes cut teenage smoking more than smoking by other groups? Why is a bountiful harvest often bad news for farmers? Answers to these and other questions are explored in this chapter, which considers the effects of price changes on quantity demanded and quantity supplied.

As we learned back in Chapter 1, macroeconomics concentrates on aggregate markets—on the big picture. But the big picture is a mosaic pieced together from individual decisions made by households, firms, governments, and the rest of the world. To understand how a market economy works, we must take a closer look at these individual decisions, especially at the role played by prices. In a market economy, prices inform producers and consumers about the relative scarcity of products and resources.

A downward-sloping demand curve and an upward-sloping supply curve combine to form a powerful analytical tool. But to make best use of this tool, you must learn more about the shapes of demand and supply curves. The more you know about their shapes, the better you can predict the effects of a change in the price on quantity demanded or supplied. Decision makers are willing to pay dearly for such information. For example, Taco Bell would like to know what happens to taco sales if the price decreases. Public officials would like to know the effect of higher cigarette taxes on teenage smoking. College officials would like to know how tuition hikes affect enrollments. And public transportation officials would like to know the impact of fare cuts on ridership. To answer such questions, we must determine how *responsive* consumers and producers are to price changes. *Elasticity* is a tool used to measure such *responsiveness*. Topics discussed in this chapter include:

- Price elasticity of demand
- Determinants of price elasticity
- Price elasticity and total revenue
- Price elasticity of supply
- Income elasticity of demand
- Cross-price elasticity of demand

PRICE ELASTICITY OF DEMAND

Just before a recent Thanksgiving weekend, Delta Airlines, in an attempt to boost ticket sales, announced fare cuts of up to 50 percent. Was this a good idea? For Delta's total revenue to increase, the growth in the number of tickets sold would have to more than offset the decline in ticket prices. A firm's success or failure often depends on how much it knows about the market for its product.

Likewise, the operators of Taco Bell would like to know what would happen to sales if the price of a taco increased from, say, $0.90 to $1.10. The law of demand says that a higher price will reduce quantity demanded, but by how much? How sensitive is quantity demanded to a change in price? Would the number sold decline by only a little or by a lot? After all, if quantity demanded declined just a little, a price increase might be a profitable move for Taco Bell.

Price elasticity of demand
A measure of the responsiveness of quantity demanded to a price change; the percent change in quantity demanded divided by the percent change in price

Let's get more specific about the sensitivity of changes in quantity demanded to changes in price. Consider the two demand curves in Exhibit 1. In each panel, we begin with a price of $0.90 per taco and a quantity demanded of 105,000 tacos per day. Now suppose the taco price increases to $1.10. Note that quantity demanded decreases to 95,000 tacos per day in panel (a), where the demand is less responsive, but to 75,000 tacos per day in panel (b). In response to the price increase, consumers in panel (b) cut their quantity demanded more than do consumers in panel (a). The numerical measure of this responsiveness is called the **price elasticity of demand.** *Elasticity* is simply another word for *responsiveness*.

EXHIBIT 1

Demand Curves of Different Elasticities

For a given change in price, the less elastic the demand, the smaller the change in quantity demanded. In panel (a), a 20 percent increase in price leads to a 10 percent decrease in quantity demanded. In panel (b), with more elastic demand *D'*, the same 20 percent price increase leads to a 33 percent decrease in quantity demanded.

Calculating Price Elasticity of Demand

In simplest terms, the price elasticity of demand is the percent change in quantity demanded divided by the percent change in price, or

$$\text{Price elasticity of demand} = \frac{\text{percent change in quantity demanded}}{\text{percent change in price}}$$

Recall that the law of demand states that price and quantity demanded are inversely related, so the change in price and the change in quantity demanded will move in opposite directions. Hence in the elasticity formula the numerator and the denominator have opposite signs, so the price elasticity of demand has a negative sign.

To compute the percent change in price or in quantity demanded, we use as a base the average of the initial value and the new value. For example, in Exhibit 1, the price increases from $0.90 to $1.10, an increase of $0.20. The base used to calculate the percent change is the average of $0.90 and $1.10, which is $1.00. The percent change in price is therefore $0.20/$1.00, or 20 percent.

The same holds for changes in quantity demanded. In panel (a), the quantity demanded decreases from 105,000 to 95,000 tacos per day, so the base used to calculate the percent change is the average, or 100,000. The percent change in quantity demanded is therefore $-10,000/100,000$, or -10 percent. The resulting price elasticity of demand is the percent change in quantity demanded, -10 percent, divided by the percent change in price, 20 percent, or $-10\%/20\%$, which is -0.5. So in panel (a) the price elasticity of demand between points *a* and *b* is -0.5.

If the quantity demanded falls from 105,000 to 75,000 tacos per day, as it does in panel (b), the base used for computing the percent change is 90,000, which is the average of 105,000 and 75,000. So the percent change in quantity demanded is $-30,000/90,000$, or -33 percent. The resulting price elasticity of demand is $-33\%/20\%$, or -1.65. Demand in panel (b) is about three times more responsive to the price increase than is demand in panel (a).

Note that elasticity expresses a relationship between two amounts: the percent change in quantity demanded and the percent change in price. Since the focus is on the percent change, we need not be concerned with how output or price is measured. For example, suppose the good in question is apples. It makes no difference in the elasticity formula whether the measure of apples is in pounds, bushels, or even tons. All that matters is the percent change in quantity demanded, not how quantity demanded is measured. Nor does it matter whether we measure the price in U.S. dollars, Mexican pesos, French francs, or Botswanan thebes. All that matters is the percent change in price.

Let's develop a more general price elasticity formula. Suppose that if the price increases from p to p', the quantity demanded decreases from q_D to q_D'. The **price elasticity formula** for calculating the price elasticity of demand, E_D, between the two points is the percent change in quantity demanded divided by the percent change in price, or

$$E_D = \frac{q_D' - q_D}{(q_D' + q_D)/2} \div \frac{p' - p}{(p' + p)/2}$$

> **Price elasticity formula** Percent change in quantity divided by the percent change in price; the average quantity and the average price are used as bases for computing percent changes in quantity and in price

The 2s cancel out to yield

$$E_D = \frac{q_D' - q_D}{q_D' + q_D} \div \frac{p' - p}{p' + p}$$

Incidentally, because the average quantity and average price are used as a base for computing percent change, the same elasticity measure results whether the change is from the higher price to the lower price or the other way around.

Categories of Price Elasticity of Demand

Price elasticity of demand can be divided into three general categories, based on how responsive quantity demanded is to a change in price. In terms of absolute values, if the percent change in quantity demanded is smaller than the percent change in price, the resulting price elasticity has a value between 0 and -1.0. That portion of the demand curve is said to be **inelastic,** meaning that quantity demanded is relatively *unresponsive* to a change in price. For example, the elasticity derived in Exhibit 1 (a) between points *a* and *b* is -0.5, so that portion of the demand curve is inelastic. If the percent change in quantity demanded just equals the percent change in price, the resulting price elasticity has a value of -1.0, and that portion of the curve is said to exhibit unit elastic demand. Finally, if the percent change in quantity demanded exceeds the

> **Inelastic demand** The type of demand that exists when a change in price has relatively little effect on quantity demanded; the percent change in quantity demanded is less than the percent change in price

percent change in price, the resulting price elasticity is more negative than −1.0, and that portion of the demand curve is said to be **elastic.** For example, the elasticity derived in panel (b) of Exhibit 1 is −1.65, so between points *a* and *c*, the demand curve is elastic. In summary, *the price elasticity of demand is inelastic if it is between 0 and −1.0, unit elastic if equal to −1.0, and elastic if more negative than −1.0.*

Elasticity and Total Revenue

Knowledge of price elasticity is especially valuable to producers because it tells them what happens to their total revenue when the price changes. **Total revenue** (*TR*) is the price multiplied by the quantity sold at that price, or $TR = p \times q$. What happens to total revenue when the price decreases? Well, according to the law of demand, if the price falls, the quantity demanded increases. The lower price means producers get less per unit, which tends to decrease total revenue. But the increased quantity demanded that results from a lower price tends to increase total revenue. The overall change in total revenue resulting from a lower price is the net result of these opposite effects. *If the positive effect of a greater quantity demanded exceeds the negative effect of a lower price, total revenue will rise.* More specifically, when demand is *elastic*, the percent increase in quantity demanded exceeds the percent decrease in price, so total revenue increases. When demand is *unit elastic*, the percent increase in quantity demanded just offsets the percent decrease in price, so total revenue remains unchanged. Finally, when demand is *inelastic*, the percent increase in quantity demanded is less than the percent decrease in price, so total revenue decreases.

Price Elasticity and the Linear Demand Curve

The price elasticity of demand usually varies along a demand curve. An examination of the elasticity along a particular type of demand curve, the linear demand curve, will tie together the concepts examined thus far. A **linear demand curve** is simply a straight-line demand curve. Panel (a) of Exhibit 2 presents a linear demand curve, and panel (b) shows the total revenue generated at each price-quantity combination along the demand curve. Recall that total revenue equals price times quantity.

Since the demand curve in panel (a) is linear, the slope is constant, so a given decrease in price always causes the same unit increase in quantity demanded. For example, a $10 drop in price always increases quantity demanded by 100 units. But *the price elasticity of demand is greater on the higher-price end of the demand curve than on the lower-price end.* Here is why. Because quantity demanded is smaller at the upper end of the demand curve than at the lower end, a 100-unit increase in quantity demanded represents a greater percent change in quantity demanded at the upper end than at the lower end. And because the price is higher at the upper end than at the lower end of the curve, a $10 decrease in price represents a smaller percent change in price at the upper end than at the lower end. Thus at the upper end of the demand curve, the percent increase in quantity demanded is relatively large and the percent decrease in price is relatively small, so the price elasticity of demand is relatively large. At the lower end of the demand curve, the percent increase in quantity demanded is relatively small and the percent decrease in price is relatively large, so the price elasticity of demand is relatively small.

Elastic demand The type of demand that exists when a change in price has a relatively large effect on quantity demanded; the percent change in quantity demanded exceeds the percent change in price

Total revenue Price multiplied by the quantity sold at that price

Linear demand curve A straight-line demand curve; such a demand curve has a constant slope

EXHIBIT 2

Demand, Price Elasticity, and Total Revenue

Where demand is elastic in panel (a), total revenue in panel (b) increases following a price decrease. Total revenue attains its maximum value at the level of output where demand is unit elastic. Where demand is inelastic, further decreases in price cause total revenue to fall.

Consider a movement from point *a* to point *b* on the upper end of the demand curve in Exhibit 2. The 100-unit increase in quantity demanded is a percent change of 100/150, or 67 percent. The $10 price drop is a percent change of −10/85, or about −12 percent. Therefore, the price elasticity of demand between points *a* and *b* is 67%/−12%, which equals −5.6. Between points *d* and *e* on the lower end, however, the 100-unit quantity increase is a percent change of 100/850, or only 12 percent, and the $10 price decrease is a percent change of −10/15, or −67 percent. The price elasticity of demand is 12%/−67%, or −0.18. In other words, *if the demand curve is linear, consumers are more responsive to a given price change when the initial price is high than when the price is low.*

Demand becomes less elastic as we move down the curve. At a point halfway down the linear demand curve in Exhibit 2, the elasticity is equal to −1.0. *This halfway point divides a linear demand curve into an elastic upper half and an inelastic lower half.* You can observe the clear relationship between the elasticity of demand in the upper diagram and total revenue in the lower diagram. Note that where demand is elastic, a decrease in price will increase total revenue because the gain in revenue from selling more units (represented by the large blue rectangle in the top panel) exceeds the loss in revenue from selling at the lower price (the small red rectangle). Where demand is inelastic, a price decrease reduces total revenue because the gain in revenue from selling more units (the small blue rectangle) is less than the loss in revenue from selling at the lower price (the large red rectangle). Where demand is unit elastic, the gain and loss of revenue exactly cancel each other out, so total revenue at that point remains constant (hence, total revenue "peaks" in the lower portion of the exhibit).

In summary, total revenue increases as the price declines until the midpoint of the linear demand curve is reached, where total revenue peaks. In Exhibit 2, total revenue peaks at $25,000 when quantity demanded equals 500 units. Below the midpoint of the demand curve, total revenue declines as the price falls. More generally, regardless of whether the demand curve is a straight line or a curve, there is a relationship between the price elasticity of demand and total revenue: A price decline *increases* total revenue if demand is elastic, *decreases* total revenue if demand is inelastic, and *has no effect* on total revenue if demand is unit elastic. Finally, note that a downward-sloping linear demand curve has a constant slope but a varying elasticity, so *the slope of a demand curve is not the same as the price elasticity of demand.*

Constant-Elasticity Demand

Again, price elasticity measures the responsiveness of consumers to a change in price. This responsiveness varies along a linear demand curve unless the demand curve is horizontal or vertical, as in panels (a) and (b) of Exhibit 3. These two demand curves, along with the special demand curve in panel (c), are called *constant-elasticity demand curves* because the elasticity does not change along the curves.

Perfectly Elastic Demand. The horizontal demand curve in panel (a) indicates that consumers will demand all that is offered for sale at the given price *p*. If the price rises above *p*, however, the quantity demanded drops to zero. This demand curve is said to be **perfectly elastic**, and its numerical elasticity value is minus infinity, a number too negatively large to be defined. You may think this is an odd sort of demand curve: Consumers, as a result of a small increase in price, go from demanding as much as is available to demanding nothing. Consumers are so sensitive to price changes that they cannot tolerate any increase. As you will see later, this reflects the demand for the output of any individual producer when many producers are selling identical products. The shape of the demand curve for a firm's product is an important ingredient in the pricing and output decision.

Perfectly Inelastic Demand. The vertical demand curve in panel (b) of Exhibit 3 represents the situation in which quantity demanded does not vary at all when the price changes. This demand curve expresses consumers' sentiment that "price is no object." For example, if you were very rich and needed insulin injections to stay alive, price would be no object. No matter how high the price, you would continue to demand the amount necessary to stay well. As Ben Franklin said, "Necessity never made a good bargain." And if the price of insulin

Perfectly elastic demand curve A horizontal line reflecting a situation in which any price increase reduces quantity demanded to zero; the elasticity value is minus infinity

EXHIBIT 3

Three Constant-Elasticity Demand Curves

(a) Perfectly elastic   *(b) Perfectly inelastic*   *(c) Unit elastic*

Along the perfectly elastic (horizontal) demand curve of panel (a), consumers will purchase all that is offered for sale at price *p*. Along the perfectly inelastic (vertical) demand curve of panel (b), consumers will purchase quantity *Q* regardless of price. Along the unit-elastic demand curve of panel (c), total revenue is the same for every price-quantity combination.

Perfectly inelastic demand curve A vertical line reflecting a situation in which price change has no effect on the quantity demanded; the elasticity value is zero

dropped, you would not demand any more of it. Vertical demand curves are called **perfectly inelastic** because price changes do not affect quantity demanded, at least not over the range of prices shown by the demand curve. Since the percent change in quantity demanded is zero for any given percent change in price, the numerical value of the price elasticity is zero.

Unit-elastic demand The type of demand that exists when a percent change in price causes an equal (but of opposite sign) percent change in quantity demanded; the elasticity value is minus one

Unit-Elastic Demand. Panel (c) in Exhibit 3 presents a demand curve that is unit elastic everywhere. **Unit-elastic demand** means that a percent change in price will always result in an identical percent change in quantity demanded but of opposite sign. Because percent changes in price and in quantity will be equal and offsetting, total revenue will be the same for every price-quantity combination along the curve. For example, when the price falls from $10 to $6, the quantity demanded increases from 60 to 100 units. The red shaded rectangle represents the loss in total revenue because all units are sold at the lower price; the blue shaded rectangle represents the gain in total revenue because more units are sold when the price drops. Because the demand curve is unit elastic, the revenue gained by selling more units just equals the revenue lost by lowering the price on all units, so total revenue is unchanged at $600. A demand curve that is unit elastic everywhere would actually be quite rare.

Constant-elasticity demand curve The type of demand that exists when price elasticity is the same everywhere along the curve; the elasticity value is constant

Each of the demand curves in Exhibit 3 is called a **constant-elasticity demand curve** because the elasticity is the same all along the curve. In contrast, the downward-sloping linear demand curve examined earlier had a different elasticity value at each point along the curve. Exhibit 4 lists the values of the five categories of price elasticity we have discussed, summarizing the varying

EXHIBIT 4

Effects of a 10 Percent Increase in Price

Price Elasticity Value	Type of Demand	What Happens to Quantity Demanded	What Happens to Total Revenue
$E_D = 0$	Perfectly inelastic	No change	Increases by 10 percent
$-1 < E_D < 0$	Inelastic	Drops by less than 10 percent	Increases by less than 10 percent
$E_D = -1$	Unit elastic	Drops by 10 percent	No change
$-\infty < E_D < -1$	Elastic	Drops by more than 10 percent	Decreases
$E_D = -\infty$	Perfectly elastic	Drops to 0	Drops to 0

effects of a 10 percent increase in the price on quantity demanded and on total revenue. Give this exhibit some thought, and see if you can draw a demand curve to reflect each type of elasticity.

DETERMINANTS OF THE PRICE ELASTICITY OF DEMAND

Thus far we have explored the technical properties of demand elasticity. But we have not yet considered why price elasticities of demand vary for different goods. Several characteristics influence the price elasticity of demand for a good. We will examine each of these in detail.

Availability of Substitutes

As we saw in Chapter 3, your particular wants can be satisfied in a variety of ways. A rise in the price of pizza makes other foods relatively cheaper. If close substitutes are available, an increase in the price of pizza will encourage consumers to shift to these substitutes. But if nothing else satisfies like pizza, the quantity of pizza demanded will not decline as much. *The greater the availability of substitutes for a good and the closer these substitutes, the more elastic the demand.*

The number and similarity of substitutes depend on how we define the good. *The more broadly we define a good, the fewer substitutes there will be and the less elastic the demand will be.* For example, the demand for shoes is less elastic than the demand for running shoes because there are few substitutes for shoes but several substitutes for running shoes, such as sneakers, tennis shoes, cross-trainers, and the like. The demand for running shoes, however, is less elastic than the demand for Nike running shoes because the consumer has more substitutes for Nikes, including Reeboks, New Balance, and so on. Finally, the demand for Nike running shoes is less elastic than the demand for a specific model of Nikes, such as Visi-Zoom Air or Air Max Triax Plus.

For some goods, such as insulin for a diabetic, there are simply no close substitutes. The demand for such goods tends to be less elastic than for goods with close substitutes. Much advertising is aimed at establishing in the consumer's mind the uniqueness of a particular product—an effort to convince consumers "to accept no substitutes." Why might a firm want to make the demand for its product less elastic?

As an example of the substitute principle, consider the pattern of commercial breaks during TV movies. When the movie first begins, viewers have several possible substitutes for it, including other shows and perhaps movies on other channels. To keep viewers from switching channels, the first movie segment is longer than usual, perhaps 20 or 30 minutes without a commercial break. But after viewers get hooked on the movie, shows on other channels are no longer close substitutes, so broadcasters inject commercials with greater frequency without fear of losing many viewers.

Proportion of the Consumer's Budget Spent on the Good

Recall that a higher price reduces quantity demanded in part because a higher price causes consumers' real spending power to decline. A demand curve reflects both the *willingness* and *ability* to purchase a good at alternative prices. Because spending on some goods represents a large share of the consumer's budget, a change in the price of such a good has a substantial impact on the quantity that consumers are *able* to purchase. An increase in the price of housing, for example, reduces consumers' ability to purchase housing. The income effect of a higher price reduces the quantity demanded. In contrast, the income effect of an increase in the price of, say, paper towels is trivial because paper towels represent such a small proportion of any budget. *The more important the item is as a proportion of the consumer's budget, other things constant, the greater will be the income effect of a change in price, so the more elastic will be the demand for the item.* The smaller the spending on the item as a proportion of the budget, other things constant, the smaller the income effect of a change in price, so the less elastic is the demand for the item. Hence the quantity of housing demanded will be more responsive to a given percentage change in price than the quantity of paper towels demanded.

A Matter of Time

Consumers can substitute lower-priced goods for higher-priced goods, but finding substitutes usually takes time. Suppose your college announces a substantial increase in room and board fees, effective immediately. Some students will move off campus as soon as they can; others will wait until the next school year. And, over time, fewer students may apply for admission, and more incoming students will choose off-campus housing. Thus *the longer the adjustment period allowed, the greater is consumers' ability to substitute away from relatively higher-priced products toward lower-priced substitutes. Hence, the longer the period of adjustment, the more responsive the change in quantity demanded is to a given change in price.* As another example, between 1973 and 1974, the OPEC cartel raised the price of oil sharply. As a result, the price of gasoline increased 45 percent, but the quantity demanded decreased by only 8 percent. As more time passed, however, people purchased smaller cars and made more use of public transportation. Since the price of oil used to fire power generators and to heat homes had increased as well, people bought more energy-efficient appliances and added more insulation to their homes. Again, the change in quantity demanded was greater as consumers had more time to respond to the price increase.

Exhibit 5 demonstrates how demand becomes more elastic over time. Given an initial price of $1.00, let D_w be the demand curve one week after a price change; D_m, one month after; and D_y, one year after. If the price increases from $1.00 to $1.25, the more time consumers have to respond to the price increase, the greater the reduction in quantity demanded. For example, the demand curve D_w shows that one week after the price increase, the quantity demanded per day has not declined much—in this case, from 100 to 95. The demand curve D_m indicates a reduction to 75 after one month, and demand curve D_y shows a reduction to 50 after one year. Notice that among these demand curves and over the range starting from the point of intersection, the flatter the demand curve, the more price elastic the demand. Here elasticity appears to be linked to the slope because we are starting from the same point—the same price-quantity combination.

Elasticity Estimates

Let's review some estimates of the price elasticity of demand for particular goods and services. As we have noted, the substitution of relatively lower-priced goods for a good whose price has just increased often takes time. Thus, when estimating price elasticity, economists often distinguish between a period during which consumers have little time to adjust—let's call it the *short run*—and a period during which consumers can fully adjust to a price change—let's call it the *long run*. Exhibit 6 provides some short-run and long-run price elasticity estimates for selected products.

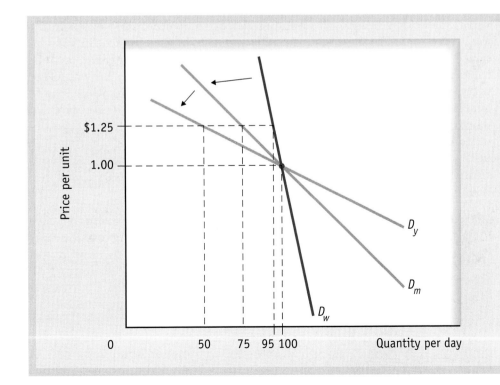

EXHIBIT 5

Demand Becomes More Elastic over Time

D_w is the demand curve one week after a price increase from $1.00 to $1.25. Along this curve, quantity demanded per day falls from 100 to 95. One month after the price increase, quantity demanded has fallen to 75 along D_m. One year after the price increase, quantity demanded has fallen to 50 along D_y. At any given price, D_y is more elastic than D_m, which is more elastic than D_w.

EXHIBIT 6

Selected Price Elasticities of Demand

Sources: F. Chaloupka, "Rational Addictive Behavior and Cigarette Smoking," *Journal of Political Economy*, (August 1991); Hsaing-tai Cheng and Oral Capps, Jr., "Demand for Fish," *American Journal of Agricultural Economics* (August 1998); J. Johnson et al., "Short-Run and Long-Run Elasticities for Canadian Consumption of Alcoholic Beverages," *Review of Economics and Statistics* (February 1992); R. Archibald and R. Gillingham, "The Review of the Short-Run Consumer Demand for Gasoline Using Household Survey Data," *Review of Economics and Statistics* 62 (November 1980); J. Griffin, Energy Conservation in the OECD, 1980–2000 (Cambridge, Mass.: Balinger, 1979); H. Houthakker and L. Taylor, *Consumer Demand in the United States: Analysis and Projections*, 2nd ed. (Cambridge, Mass.: Harvard University Press, 1970); and G. Lakshmanan and W. Anderson, "Residential Energy Demand in the United States," *Regional Science and Urban Economics* 10 (August 1980).

Product	Short Run	Long Run
Cigarettes (among adults)	—	−0.4
Electricity (residential)	−0.1	−1.9
Air travel	−0.1	−2.4
Medical care and hospitalization	−0.3	−0.9
Gasoline	−0.4	−1.5
Milk	−0.4	—
Fish (cod)	−0.5	—
Wine	−0.7	−1.2
Movies	−0.9	−3.7
Natural gas (residential)	−1.4	−2.1
Automobiles	−1.9	−2.2
Chevrolets	—	−4.0

The price elasticity is greater in the long run because consumers have more time to adjust. For example, if the price of electricity rose today, consumers in the short run might cut back a bit in their use of electrical appliances, and those with electric heat might lower the thermostat a bit in winter. Over time, however, consumers would switch to more energy-efficient appliances and might convert from electric heat to oil or natural gas. So demand is more elastic in the long run than in the short run, as is reflected in Exhibit 6. In fact, in every instance where values for both the short run and the long run are listed, the long run is more elastic than the short run. Notice also that the long-run price elasticity of demand for Chevrolets exceeds the price elasticity for automobiles in general. There are many more substitutes for Chevrolets than for automobiles. There are no close substitutes for cigarettes, even in the long run, so the demand for cigarettes among adults is price inelastic. Such elasticity measures can be of more than just academic interest, as discussed in the following case study.

Deterring Young Smokers

CaseStudy

Public Policy

Smoking rates among teens are higher in Alaska than in the rest of the U.S., and are even higher for Native Alaskans according to "Tobacco Use among Alaska Youth," an article in the State of Alaska's

As the U.S. Surgeon General warns on each pack of cigarettes, smoking can be hazardous to your health. Researchers estimate that smoking causes many times more deaths than traffic accidents do. Deaths from lung cancer have doubled among older women since 1980. A recent federal study found that cigarette smoking costs the U.S. economy $130 billion a year: $80 billion in foregone output because of smoking-related illness and death and $50 billion because of health care costs resulting from smoking-related disease. That's more than was spent on all U.S. public higher education in 1998.

Health-related issues and the addictive nature of cigarettes have created a growing public policy concern about smoking, especially smoking by young people, which jumped one-third during the 1990s. A federal study of 16,000 U.S. students in grades 9 through 12 found cigarette smoking rose from 27.5 percent of those surveyed in 1991 to 36.4 percent in 1997. Among black youths, the rate nearly doubled from 12.6 percent to 22.7 percent. Reasons offered for the jump include a stable price for cigarettes (prices did not increase between 1992 and 1997) and the greater glamorization of smoking in movies and television. (For example, in the movie *Titanic*, the two young, attractive, leading characters smoked cigarettes.)

One way to reduce smoking is to raise the price of cigarettes through higher cigarette taxes. Researchers have found the price elasticity of demand for cigarettes among young smokers to be −1.3, so a 10 percent increase in the price of cigarettes would reduce smoking by 13 percent. As noted earlier, among adult smokers, the estimated price elasticity of demand was only −0.4.

Why are teenagers more responsive to price changes than adults? *First*, recall that one of the factors affecting price elasticity of demand is the importance of the item in the consumer's budget. The proportion of income that a young smoker spends on cigarettes usually exceeds the proportion for adult smokers. *Second*, peer pressure is much more influential in the young person's decision to smoke than in an adult's decision to continue smoking. (If anything, adults face negative peer pressure.) Because of peer pressure, the effects of higher price get multiplied among young smokers because a higher price reduces smoking by peers. With fewer peers smoking, there is less pressure to smoke. And *third*, since smoking is addictive, young people who are not yet hooked are more sensitive to price increases than are adult smokers who are already hooked. Addicts by definition are less sensitive to a price change than those not addicted.

If a price elasticity of −1.3 remains constant over the relevant range of price changes, a price increase of $1.80 per pack would reduce smoking among young people by 60 percent. To be fully effective, the price increase must be introduced quickly, not, as was proposed in Congress, phased in over five years. The experience from other countries supports the effectiveness of higher prices. For example, a large tax increase on cigarettes in Canada during the 1980s cut youth smoking by two thirds.

Sources: David Wessel and Jeanne Cummings, "U.S. to Release Analysis Showing Smoking Costs $130 Billion a Year," *Wall Street Journal* (25 March 1998); Sheryl Gay Stolberg, "Smoking by Black Youths Is Up Sharply, Study Finds," *New York Times* (3 April 1998); Marlene Cimons, "Tobacco Use Soars Among Teenagers," *Hartford Courant* (3 April 1998); "Prepared Statement of Frank J. Chaloupka, Ph.D., Before the Senate Judiciary Committee," *Federal News Service* (29 October 1997).

Epidemiology Bulletin at http://www.epi.hss.state.ak.us/bulletins/topics/docs/b1997_05.htm. The report uses estimates of elasticity to predict decreases in smoking as a result of increases in cigarette taxes. What missteps can you detect in the way in which the report uses price elasticity? Alaska did increase the tax on a pack of cigarettes to $1.

Let's turn now to the price elasticity of supply.

PRICE ELASTICITY OF SUPPLY

Prices are signals to both sides of the market about the relative scarcity of products; high prices discourage consumption but encourage production. The price elasticity of demand measures how responsive consumers are to a price change.

Price elasticity of supply
A measure of the responsiveness of quantity supplied to a price change; the percent change in quantity supplied divided by the percent change in price

Similarly, the **price elasticity of supply** measures how responsive producers are to a price change. This elasticity is calculated in the same way as price elasticity of demand, but by using the percent change in quantity supplied instead of the percent change in quantity demanded. In simplest terms, the price elasticity of supply equals the percent change in quantity supplied divided by the percent change in price. Since the higher price usually results in an increased quantity supplied, the percent change in price and the percent change in quantity supplied move in the same direction, so the price elasticity of supply is usually positive.

Exhibit 7 depicts a typical upward-sloping supply curve. As you can see, if the price increases from p to p', the quantity supplied increases from q_S to q'_S. Price and quantity supplied move in the same direction. Let's look at the elasticity formula for the supply curve. The price elasticity of supply, E_S, is

$$E_S = \frac{q'_S - q_S}{(q'_S + q_S)/2} \div \frac{p' - p}{(p' + p)/2}$$

Again, the 2s cancel out so the formula reduces to

$$E_S = \frac{q'_S - q_S}{(q'_S + q_S)} \div \frac{p' - p}{(p' + p)}$$

Categories of Supply Elasticity

The terminology for supply elasticity is the same as for demand elasticity: If supply elasticity is less than 1.0, supply is *inelastic*; if its value is equal to 1.0, supply is

EXHIBIT 7

Price Elasticity of Supply

If the price increases from p to p', the quantity supplied increases from q_s to q'_s. Price and quantity supplied move in the same direction, so the price elasticity of supply is a positive number.

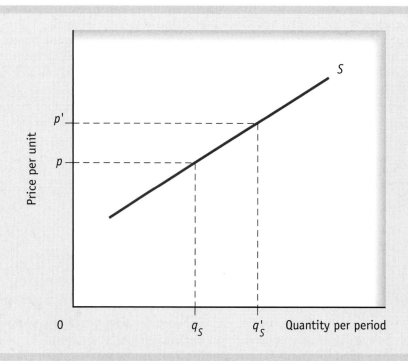

unit elastic; and if its value is greater than 1.0, supply is *elastic.* There are also some special values of supply elasticity to consider.

Perfectly Elastic Supply. At one extreme is the horizontal supply curve, such as supply curve S in panel (a) of Exhibit 8. In this case, producers will supply none of the good at a price below *p* but will supply any amount at a price of *p*. The quantity actually supplied at price *p* will depend on the amount demanded at that price. Because a tiny increase from a price just below *p* to a price of *p* will result in an unlimited quantity supplied, this curve is said to reflect **perfectly elastic supply,** which has a numerical value of infinity. As individual consumers, we typically face perfectly elastic supply curves. When we go to the supermarket, we usually can buy as much as we want at the prevailing price but none at a lower price. This is not to say that all consumers together could buy an unlimited amount at the prevailing price. (Recall the fallacy of composition: What is true for any individual consumer is not necessarily true for all consumers as a group.)

Perfectly elastic supply curve A horizontal line reflecting a situation in which any price decrease reduces the quantity supplied to zero; the elasticity value is infinity

Perfectly Inelastic Supply. The most unresponsive relationship between price and quantity supplied is the one in which there is no change in the quantity supplied regardless of the price. Such a case is represented by the vertical supply curve S' in panel (b) of Exhibit 8. Because the percent change in quantity supplied is zero, regardless of the change in price, the value of the supply elasticity equals zero. This curve reflects **perfectly inelastic supply.** Any good that is in fixed supply, such as Picasso paintings or 1978 Dom Perignon champagne, will have a perfectly inelastic supply curve.

Perfectly inelastic supply curve A vertical line reflecting a situation in which a price change has no effect on the quantity supplied; the elasticity value is zero

EXHIBIT 8

Three Constant-Elasticity Supply Curves

(a) Perfectly elastic   *(b) Perfectly inelastic*   *(c) Unit elastic*

Supply curve *S* in panel (a) is perfectly elastic (horizontal). Along *S*, firms will supply any amount of output demanded at price *p*. Supply curve *S'* is perfectly inelastic (vertical). *S'* shows that the quantity supplied is independent of the price. In panel (c), *S"* is a ray, which has a unit-elastic price elasticity of supply. Any percentage change in price will result in the same percentage change in quantity supplied.

Unit-elastic supply curve
A percent change in price causes an identical percent change in quantity supplied; depicted by a supply curve that is a straight line from the origin; the elasticity value is one

Unit-Elastic Supply. Any supply curve that can be represented as a straight line from the origin—such as *S*" in panel (c) of Exhibit 8—is a **unit-elastic supply curve.** This means that a percent change in price will always result in an identical percent change in quantity supplied. For example, along *S*" a doubling of the price results in a doubling of the quantity supplied. Note that unit elasticity is determined not by the slope of the line but by the fact that the linear supply curve emanates from the origin.

Determinants of Supply Elasticity
The elasticity of supply indicates how responsive producers are to a change in price. Their responsiveness depends on how easy or difficult it is to alter output as a result of a change in price. If the cost of supplying an additional unit rises sharply as output expands, then a higher price will elicit little increase in quantity supplied, so supply will tend to be inelastic. But if the additional cost rises slowly as output expands, the lure of a higher price will prompt a large increase in output. In this case, supply will tend to be more elastic.

One determinant of supply elasticity is the length of the adjustment period under consideration. Just as demand becomes more elastic over time as consumers adjust to price changes, supply also becomes more elastic over time as producers adjust to price changes. The longer the time period under consideration, the more able producers are to adjust to changes in relative prices. Exhibit 9 presents a different supply curve for each of three time periods. *S*_w is the supply curve when the period of adjustment is a week. As you can see, a higher price will not elicit much of a response in quantity supplied because firms have little time to adjust. Thus such a supply curve will tend to slope steeply, reflecting inelastic supply.

EXHIBIT 9

Market Supply Becomes More Elastic over Time

The supply curve one week after a price increase, *S*_w, is less elastic, at a given price, than the curve one month later, *S*_m, which is less elastic than the curve one year later, *S*_y. Given a price increase from $10 to $12, quantity supplied per day increases to 55 units af-ter one week, to 70 units after one month, and to 100 units after one year.

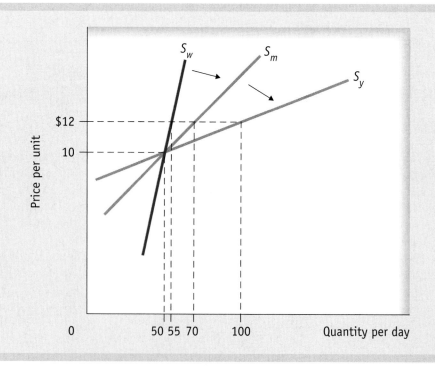

S_m is the supply curve when the adjustment period under consideration is a month. In a month, firms can more easily adjust the rate at which they employ some resources. As a result, firms have a greater ability to vary output. Thus supply is more elastic when the adjustment period is a month than when it is a week. Supply is even more elastic when the adjustment period is a year, as is shown by S_y. If firms can vary all inputs in a year, they can more easily respond to a higher price.

So a given price increase will elicit a greater quantity supplied, the longer the adjustment period. For example, if the price of oil increases, oil producers in the short run can try to pump more from existing wells, but in the long run they can try to discover more oil in the remote jungles of the Amazon or the stormy waters of the North Sea. Empirical research confirms the positive link between the price elasticity of supply and the length of the adjustment period. *The elasticity of supply is typically greater the longer the period of adjustment.* Firms' ability to alter quantity supplied in response to price changes differs across industries. The response time will be slower for producers of electricity, oil, and timber—where production capacity may take years to develop—than for window washing, lawn maintenance, and hot-dog vending—where a production capacity can be increased overnight.

OTHER ELASTICITY MEASURES

The price elasticities of demand and supply are frequently used in economic analysis, but other elasticities also provide useful information—information about how demand responds to a change in consumer income or to a change in the price of a related good.

Income Elasticity of Demand

What happens to the demand for new cars, garden supplies, or computer software if consumer income increases by, say, 10 percent? The answer to this question is of great interest to producers of these goods because it helps them predict the effect of changing income on quantity sold and on total revenues. The **income elasticity of demand** measures how consumer demand at a given price changes in response to a change in income. More specifically, *the income elasticity of demand measures the percent change in demand divided by the percent change in income that caused it.*

> **Income elasticity of demand** The percent change in demand (at a given price) divided by the percent change in income

As we noted in Chapter 3, the demand for some products, such as bus rides and laundromat services, actually declines as income increases. Thus, the income elasticity of demand for such products will be negative. Goods with an income elasticity less than zero are called *inferior goods.* The demand for most goods increases as income increases. These goods are called *normal goods,* and they have an income elasticity greater than zero.

Let's take a closer look at normal goods. Suppose demand increases as income increases but by a smaller percent than income increases. In such cases the value of income elasticity is greater than zero but less than 1. For example, people buy more food as their incomes rise, but the percent increase in demand is less than the percent increase in income. Normal goods with an income elasticity less than 1 are said to be *income inelastic. Necessities* such as food, housing, and clothing often have an income elasticity less than 1.

Goods with an income elasticity greater than 1 are said to be *income elastic*. *Luxuries*, such as fine cars, vintage wine, and meals at fancy restaurants, have an income elasticity greater than 1. For example, during 1990 and 1991, the U.S. economy experienced a recession, meaning that national income declined; as a result, the demand for meals at fancy restaurants declined, and some restaurants went out of business. During the same period, the demand for basic foods such as bread, sugar, and cheese changed very little. Incidentally, the terms *inferior goods*, *necessities*, and *luxuries* are not meant to imply some value judgment about the merit of particular goods; these terms are simply convenient definitions economists use to classify economic behavior.

Exhibit 10 presents some income elasticity estimates for various goods and services. The figures indicate that as income increases, consumers spend proportionately more on items such as private education, automobiles, wine, owner-occupied housing, furniture, dental service, and restaurant meals. For items such as food, cigarettes, gasoline, rental housing, and beer, consumer spending increases as income increases, but less than proportionately. So as income rises, the demand for owner-occupied housing increases more in percentage terms than the demand for rental housing and the demand for wine increases more in percentage terms than the demand for beer. Flour has negative income elasticity, indicating that the demand for flour declines as income increases. As income increases, consumers switch from home baking to purchasing baked goods.

As we have seen, the demand for food is income inelastic. The demand for food also tends to be price inelastic. This combination of income inelasticity

EXHIBIT 10

Selected Income Elasticities of Demand

Product	Income Elasticity	Product	Income Elasticity
Private education	2.46	Physicians' services	0.75
Automobiles	2.45	Coca-Cola	0.68
Wine	2.19	Beef	0.62
Owner-occupied housing	1.49	Food	0.51
Furniture	1.48	Coffee	0.51
Dental service	1.42	Cigarettes	0.50
Restaurant meals	1.40	Gasoline and oil	0.48
Shoes	1.10	Rental housing	0.43
Chicken	1.06	Beer	0.27
Spirits ("hard" liquor)	1.02	Pork	0.18
Clothing	0.92	Flour	−0.36

Sources: F. Gasmi et al., "Econometric Analyses of Collusive Behavior in a Soft-Drink Market," *Journal of Economics and Management Strategy* (Summer 1992); J. Johnson et al., "Short-Run and Long-Run Elasticities for Canadian Consumption of Alcoholic Beverages," *Review of Economics and Statistics* (February 1992); H. Houthakker and L. Taylor, *Consumer Demand in the United States: Analyses and Projections,* 2d ed. (Cambridge, Mass.: Harvard University Press, 1970); C. Huang et al., "The Demand for Coffee in the United States, 1963–77," *Quarterly Review of Economics and Business* (Summer 1980); and G. Brester and M. Wohlgenant, "Estimating Interrelated Demands for Meats Using New Measures for Ground and Table Cut Beef," *American Journal of Agricultural Economics* (November 1991).

and price inelasticity creates special problems in agricultural markets, as described in the following case study.

The Market for Food and "The Farm Problem"

Despite decades of federal support through various farm-assistance programs, the number of farmers continues to drop. Farm employment dropped by more than two-thirds from 10 million in 1950 to about 3 million today. The demise of the family farm can be traced to the price and income elasticities of demand for farm products and to technological breakthroughs that increased production.

Many of the forces that determine farm production are beyond the farmer's control. Temperature, rain, insects, and other external forces affect crop size and quality. For example, 1995 offered especially favorable growing conditions and crop production increased by 16 percent. Such swings in production create special problems for farmers because the demand for most farm crops, such as milk, eggs, corn, potatoes, oats, sugar, and beef, is price inelastic.

The effect of inelastic demand on farm revenue is illustrated in Exhibit 11. Suppose that in a normal year, farmers supply 10 billion bushels of grain at a market price of $5 per bushel. Annual revenue, which is price times quantity, totals $50 billion in our example. What if more favorable growing conditions increase crop production to 11 billion bushels, an increase of 10 percent? Because demand is price inelastic, the average price in our example must fall by

CaseStudy

Public Policy

What are the forces shaping U.S. agriculture today? The Economics Research Service of the U.S. Dept. of Agriculture provides some answers with its briefing book at http://www.econ.ag.gov/briefing/forces/. Check to find out what the latest edition says about the current state of the American farm family. How have farm size and the number of family farms been changing? How does farm family income compare to average household income? What percent of farm income is a result of government farm support policies?

EXHIBIT 11

The Demand for Grain

The demand for grain tends to be price inelastic. As the market price falls, total revenue also falls.

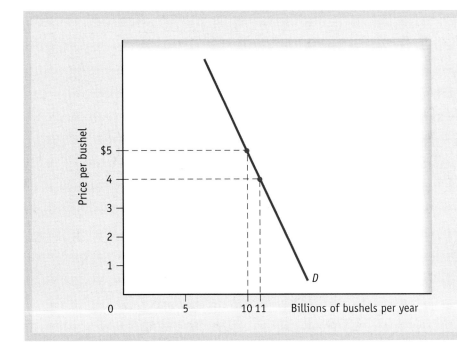

more than 10 percent to, say, $4 per bushel, in order to clear the market of the additional billion bushels. Thus the 10 percent increase in farm production can be sold only if the price drops by 20 percent.

Because, in percentage terms, the drop in price exceeds the increase in output, total revenue declines from $50 billion to $44 billion. So farm revenue drops by over 10 percent, despite the 10 percent increase in production. *Since demand is price inelastic, an increase in output reduces total revenue.* Of course, for farmers, the up side of inelastic demand is that a lower-than-normal crop results in a proportionately higher price and a higher total revenue. For example, because of the drought of 1988, corn prices rose by more than 50 percent and net farm income was up sharply. So weather-generated changes in farm production create substantial year-to-year swings in farm revenue.

Problems created by fluctuations in farm revenue are compounded in the long run by the *income inelasticity* of demand for grain and, more generally, for food. As household incomes grow over time, spending on food may increase because people substitute prepared foods and restaurant meals for home cooking. But this switch has little effect on the total demand for farm products. Thus, as the economy grows over time and real incomes rise, the demand for farm products tends to increase but by less than the increase in real income. This is reflected by the shift of the demand curve from *D* to *D'* in Exhibit 12.

Because of technological improvements in production, the supply of farm products has increased sharply. Farm output per worker is about *eight times* greater now than in 1950 because of such factors as more sophisticated machines, better fertilizers, and healthier seed strains. Exhibit 12 shows the supply of grain increasing from *S* to *S'*. Since the increase in supply exceeds the increase in demand, the price of grain has declined. And because the demand for

EXHIBIT 12

The Effect of Increases in Supply and Demand on Farm Revenue

Over time, technological advances in farming have sharply increased the supply of grain. In addition, increases in household income over time have increased the demand for farm products. But because increases in the supply of grain have exceeded increases in demand, the combined effect has been a drop in the market prices and a fall in total farm revenue.

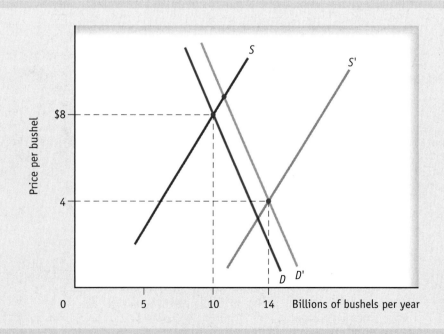

grain is price inelastic, the percent drop in price exceeds the percent increase in output. The combined effect in our example is lower total farm revenue. In fact, net income (adjusted for inflation) to all U.S. farmers combined is now only half what it was in the early 1950s.

Another wild card in the farm-revenue equation is unstable foreign demand. Foreign demand for U.S. crops depends on foreign production and prices, on the exchange rate between the dollar and foreign currencies, and on public policy with regard to foreign trade. Thus many of the forces that shape the market for farm products are beyond the farmer's control. And demand that is both price inelastic and income inelastic means that greater farm output may result in lower total revenue.

Sources: Bruce L. Gardner, "Changing Economic Perspective on the Farm Problem," *Journal of Economic Literature* 30 (March 1992): 62–105; Ching-Fun Cling and James Peale, "Income and Price Elasticities," in *Advances in Econometrics Supplement*, Henri Theil, ed. (Greenwich, Conn.: JAI Press, 1989); and *Economic Report of the President*, February 1999, Tables B–97 to B–102.

Cross-Price Elasticity of Demand

Since a corporation often produces an entire line of products, it has a special interest in how a change in the price of one product will affect the demand for another. For example, the Coca-Cola Corporation needs to know how changing the price of Cherry Coke will affect sales of Classic Coke. Similarly, Procter & Gamble wants to know how changing the price of Safeguard soap will affect sales of its Ivory soap. The responsiveness of the demand for one good to changes in the price of another good is called the **cross-price elasticity of demand**. It is defined as the percent change in the demand of one good (holding the price constant) divided by the percent change in the price of another good. Its numerical value can be positive, negative, or zero, depending on whether the two goods in question are substitutes, complements, or unrelated, respectively.

Cross-price elasticity of demand The percent change in the demand of one good as a result of the percent change in the price of another good

Substitutes. If an increase in the price of one good leads to an increase in the demand for another good, the value of their cross-price elasticity is positive, and the goods are considered *substitutes*. For example, an increase in the price of Coke, other things constant, will increase the demand for Pepsi, reflecting the fact that the two are substitutes. In fact, the cross-price elasticity between Coke and Pepsi is about 0.7, indicating that a 10 percent increase in the price of one will increase the demand for the other by 7 percent.[1]

Complements. If an increase in the price of one good leads to a decrease in the demand for another good, the value of their cross-price elasticity is negative, and the goods are considered *complements*. For example, an increase in the price of gasoline, other things constant, will reduce the demand for tires because people will drive less and so will replace their tires less frequently. Gasoline and tires have a negative cross-price elasticity and are complements.

In summary, when the change in demand for one good has the same sign as the change in price of another good, the two goods are substitutes; when the change in demand for one good has the opposite sign from the change in price

---

1 This estimate was reported in F. Gasmi, J. Laffont, and Q. Vuong, "Econometric Analysis of Collusive Behavior in a Soft-Drink Market," *Journal of Economics and Management Strategy* (Summer 1992).

of another good, the goods are complements. Most pairs of goods selected at random are *unrelated*, so the value of their cross-price elasticity is approximately zero.

CONCLUSION

Because this chapter has been more quantitative than earlier chapters, you may have been preoccupied with the mechanics of the calculations and thus may have overlooked the intuitive appeal and the neat simplicity of the notion of elasticity. *An elasticity measures the willingness and ability of buyers and sellers to alter their behavior in response to a change in their economic circumstances.* For example, if the price of a good falls, consumers may be able but not willing to increase their consumption of the good. In that case the demand would be perfectly inelastic.

Firms try to estimate the price elasticity of demand for their products. Since a corporation often produces an entire line of products, it also has a special interest in certain cross-price elasticities. Governments also have an ongoing interest in various elasticities. For example, state governments want to know the effect of a 1 percent increase in the sales tax on total tax receipts, and local governments want to know how an increase in income will affect the demand for real estate and, hence, the revenue generated by a property tax. International groups are interested in elasticities; for example, the Organization of Petroleum Exporting Countries (OPEC) is concerned about the price elasticity of demand for oil. Many questions can be answered by referring to particular elasticities. Some corporate economists estimate elasticities for a living.

SUMMARY

1. The price elasticities of demand and supply show how sensitive buyers and sellers are to changes in the price of a good. More elastic means more responsive, and less elastic means less responsive.

2. If demand is price elastic—that is, if the percent change in quantity demanded exceeds the percent change in price—a price increase will reduce total revenue and a price decrease will increase total revenue. If demand is price inelastic—that is, if the percent change in quantity is less than the percent change in price—then a price increase will increase total revenue and a price decrease will reduce total revenue. And if demand is unit elastic—that is, if the percent change in quantity just equals the percent change in price—a price change will not affect total revenue.

3. Along a linear, or straight-line, downward-sloping demand curve, the elasticity of demand falls steadily as the price falls. But constant-elasticity demand curves have the same elasticity everywhere.

4. Demand will be more elastic (1) the greater the availability of substitutes and the more closely they resemble the good in question; (2) the more narrowly the good is defined; (3) the larger the proportion of the consumer's

budget spent on the good; and (4) the longer the time allowed for adjustment to a change in price.

5. The price elasticity of supply uses a similar approach to the price elasticity of demand, but since price and quantity supplied are directly related, price elasticity of supply is a positive number. Price elasticity of supply depends on how quickly production cost changes as output changes. If such cost rises sharply as output expands, quantity supplied will be less responsive to price increases and, hence, less elastic. The longer the time period producers have to adjust to price changes, the more elastic the supply.

6. The income elasticity of demand measures the responsiveness of demand to changes in consumer income. This elasticity is positive for normal goods and negative for inferior goods.

7. The cross-price elasticity of demand measures the responsiveness of demand to changes in the price of another product. Two goods are defined as substitutes, complements, or unrelated, depending on whether the value of their cross-price elasticity of demand is positive, negative, or equal to zero, respectively.

QUESTIONS FOR REVIEW

1. *(Categories of Price Elasticity of Demand)* For each of the following values of price elasticity of demand, indicate whether demand is elastic, inelastic, perfectly elastic, perfectly inelastic, or unit elastic. In addition, determine what would happen to total revenue if a firm raised its price in each elasticity range identified.
   a. $E_D = -2.5$
   b. $E_D = -1.0$
   c. $E_D = -\infty$
   d. $E_D = -0.8$

2. *(Elasticity and Total Revenue)* Explain the relationship between the price elasticity of demand and total revenue.

3. *(Price Elasticity and the Linear Demand Curve)* How is it possible for many price elasticities to be associated with a single demand curve?

4. *(Determinants of Price Elasticity)* Why is the price elasticity of demand for Coca-Cola greater than the price elasticity of demand for soft drinks generally?

5. *(Determinants of Price Elasticity)* What factors help determine the price elasticity of demand? What factors help determine the price elasticity of supply?

6. *(Cross-Price Elasticity)* Using supply and demand curves, predict the impact on the price and quantity demanded of Good 1 of an increase in the price of Good 2 if the two goods are substitutes. What if the two goods are complements?

7. *(Other Elasticity Measures)* Complete each of the following sentences:
   a. The income elasticity of demand measures, for a given price, the _____ in quantity demanded divided by the _____ income from which it resulted.
   b. If a decrease in the price of one good causes a decrease in demand for another good, the two goods are _____.
   c. If the value of the cross-price elasticity of demand between two goods is approximately zero, they are considered _____.

PROBLEMS AND EXERCISES

8. *(Calculating Price Elasticity of Demand)* Suppose that 50 units of a good are demanded at a price of $1 per unit. A reduction in price to $0.20 results in an increase in quantity demanded to 70 units. Show that these data yield a price elasticity of -0.25. By what percentage would a 10 percent rise in the price reduce the quantity demanded assuming price elasticity remains constant along the demand curve?

9. *(Price Elasticity and Total Revenue)* Fill in values for each point listed in the following table. What relationship have you depicted?

P	Q	Price Elasticity	Total Revenue
$8	2	_____	_____
7	3	_____	_____
6	4	_____	_____
5	5	_____	_____
4	6	_____	_____
3	7	_____	_____
2	8	_____	_____

10. *(Income Elasticity of Demand)* Calculate the income elasticity of demand for each of the following goods:

	Quantity Demanded When Income = $10,000	Quantity Demanded When Income = $20,000
Good 1	10	25
Good 2	4	5
Good 3	3	2

11. *(Price Elasticity of Supply)* Calculate the price elasticity of supply for each of the following combinations of price and quantity supplied. Determine whether supply is elastic, inelastic, perfectly elastic, perfectly inelastic, or unit elastic in each case.
   a. Price falls from $2.25 to $1.75; quantity supplied falls from 600 units to 400 units.
   b. Price falls from $2.25 to $1.75; quantity supplied falls from 600 units to 500 units.
   c. Price falls from $2.25 to $1.75; quantity supplied remains at 600 units.
   d. Price increases from $1.75 to $2.25; quantity supplied increases from 466.67 units to 600 units.

Use the following diagram to answer the next two questions.

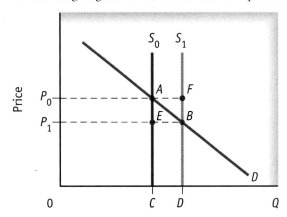

12.   *(CaseStudy: The Demand for Food and "The Farm Problem")* Interpret this diagram as showing the market supply and demand curves for agricultural products. Suppose that supply increased from S_0 to S_1 and that demand is inelastic over the relevant range of

prices. What areas in the figure would you use to illustrate the net change in farmers' total revenue as a result of the increase in supply?

13.   *(CaseStudy: The Demand for Food and "The Farm Problem")* Again suppose that this diagram represents the market for agricultural products and that supply has increased from S_0 to S_1. To aid farmers, the federal government decides to stabilize the price at P_0 by buying up surplus farm products. Show on the diagram how much this would cost the government. By how much would farm income change compared to what it would have been without government intervention?

14.   *(Cross-Price Elasticity)* Rank the following in order of increasing (from negative to positive) cross-price elasticity of demand with coffee. Explain your reasoning.

Bleach
Tea
Cream
Cola

EXPERIENTIAL EXERCISES

15.   *(CaseStudy: Deterring Young Smokers)* Policy.com has a Web page devoted to tobacco-related policy issues. Review the articles at their site at http://policy.com/issues/issue 126.html. Choose one and interpret the analysis using supply and demand curves and the concept of elasticity. For additional background information in the form of the transcript of a five-part television series, check *The Tobacco Wars* by Walter Adams and James Brock (Cincinnati, OH: South–Western College Publishing Co., 1999).

16.   *(CaseStudy: The Demand for Food and the "Farm Problem")* Farm problems are not unique to the United States. Alan Matthews at Trinity College, Dublin has an interesting Web page devoted to "The Farm Problem and Farm Policy Objectives" at http://www.economics.tcd.ie/amtthews/AgEcCourse/FarmProblem/pagetwo.html. Review the material presented there and determine to what extent agricultural issues in

the European Union (EU) are similar to those experienced in the United States. What role does economics play in the analysis of EU farm policy?

17.   *(Wall Street Journal)* In the computer industry, cross-elasticities of demand are quite important. For example, we know that computers and computer software are complements, and the cross-elasticity of demand would tell us how strong that relationship is. Read the "Personal Technology" column in Thursday's *Wall Street Journal* and find a story that describes pricing of computer hardware or software. Based on what you know about the relationships among different types of computers, among different types of software, and between computers and software, try to predict the effects of the price change. How will the change affect the quantity demanded of the item described? How will it affect the demand for substitutes and complements to that item?

Consumer Choice and Demand

W hy does Universal Studios in Orlando offer second-day admission free? Why are newspapers sold in vending machines that allow you to take more than one copy? How much do you eat when you can eat all you want? What's a cure for spring fever? Why is water cheaper than diamonds even though water is essential to life? To answer these and other questions, we take a closer look at the law of demand, a key building block in economics.

You have already learned two reasons why demand curves slope downward. The first is the *substitution effect* of a price change. When the price of a good falls, consumers substitute that now-cheaper good for other goods. The second is the *income effect* of a price change. When the price of a good falls, the real incomes of consumers increase, so they will purchase more of the good as long as the good is normal.

Demand is so important that we must know more about it. In this chapter, we develop the law of demand based on the satisfaction derived from consumption. As usual, we assume that consumer choice in a world of scarcity is motivated by the desire to maximize satisfaction. The point of this chapter is not to tell you how to maximize satisfaction. That comes naturally. But understanding the theory behind this behavior helps us understand the implications of that behavior, making predictions more accurate. Topics discussed in this chapter include:

- Total and marginal utility
- The law of diminishing marginal utility
- Measuring utility

- Utility-maximizing conditions
- Consumer surplus
- The role of time in demand
- Money price and time price

UTILITY ANALYSIS

Suppose you and a friend dine together. After dinner, your friend asks how you liked your meal. You might say, "It was delicious," or "I liked it better than my last meal here." You would not say, "I liked mine twice as much as you liked yours." Nor would you say, "It deserves a rating of 86 on the consumer satisfaction index." The utility, or satisfaction, you derived from that meal cannot be measured objectively. You cannot give your meal an 86 satisfaction rating and your friend's meal a 43. Although you can't make comparisons with other people's experience, you can say whether one of your personal experiences was more satisfying than another, and we can draw inferences from your behavior. For example, we can conclude that you like apples more than oranges if, when the two are priced the same, you always buy apples.

Tastes and Preferences

Tastes A consumer's preferences for different goods and services

As was mentioned in Chapter 4, *utility* is the sense of pleasure, or satisfaction, that comes from consumption. Utility is subjective. The utility you derive from consuming a particular good depends on your **tastes,** which are your attitudes toward and preferences for different goods and services—your likes and dislikes in consumption. Some goods are extremely appealing to you and others are not. You may not understand, for example, why someone would pay good money for raw oysters, chicken livers, polka music, martial arts movies, the Psychic Friends Network, or an Electric Tongue Cleaner from Sharper Image. Why are nearly all baby carriages sold in the United States navy blue, whereas they are yellow in Italy and chartreuse in Germany? And why do Australians like chicken-flavored potato chips and chicken-flavored salt?

Economists actually have little to say about the origin of tastes or why tastes seem to differ across individuals, across households, across regions, and across countries. *Economists assume simply that tastes are given and are relatively stable—that is, different people may have different tastes but an individual's tastes are not constantly in flux.* To be sure, tastes for some products do change over time (for example, hiking and work boots are replacing running shoes as preferred footwear among college students), but economists believe tastes to be stable enough to allow for the study of such matters as the relationship between price and quantity demanded. If tastes were not reasonably stable, then we could not make the assumption in demand analysis that "other things remain constant."

The Law of Diminishing Marginal Utility

Suppose it's a hot summer day and you are extremely thirsty after jogging four miles. You pour yourself a glass of cold water. That first glass is wonderful, and it puts a serious dent in your thirst; the next one is not quite as wonderful, but it is still pretty good; the third is just fair; and the fourth glass you barely finish. Let's talk about the *utility,* or satisfaction, you get from consuming water.

We want to distinguish between total utility and marginal utility. **Total utility** is the total satisfaction a consumer derives from consumption. For example, total utility is the total satisfaction you get from consuming the four glasses of water. **Marginal utility** is the change in total utility resulting from a one-unit change in consumption of a good. For example, the marginal utility of the third glass of water is the change in total utility resulting from consuming that third glass of water.

Your experience with water reflects a basic principle of utility analysis: the **law of diminishing marginal utility.** This law states that the more of a good an individual consumes per time period, other things constant, the smaller the increase in total utility from additional consumption—that is, the smaller the marginal utility of each additional unit consumed. The marginal utility you derive from each additional glass of water declines as your consumption increases. You enjoy the first glass a lot, but each additional glass provides less and less marginal utility. If someone forced you to drink a fifth glass, you probably would not have enjoyed it; your marginal utility from a fifth glass would likely have been negative.

Diminishing marginal utility is a feature of all consumption. A second Big Mac may provide some marginal utility, but, for most people, the marginal utility of a third one during the same meal would be slight or even negative. You may still enjoy a second video movie on Friday night, but a third and fourth one would be numbing. More generally, the expression "Been there, done that" conveys the idea that, for many activities, things start to get old after the first time.

Marginal utility does not always decline right away or very quickly. For example, you may eat many potato chips before the marginal utility of additional chips begins to fall. After a long winter, that first warm day of spring is something special and is the cause of "spring fever." The fever is "cured" by many warm days like the first. By the time August rolls around, people attach much less marginal utility to yet another warm day. For some goods, the drop in marginal utility with additional consumption is more pronounced. A second copy of the same daily newspaper would likely provide you with no marginal utility (in fact, the design of newspaper vending machines relies on the fact that you will not want to take more than one paper).[1] Likewise, a second viewing of the same movie at one sitting usually yields no additional utility. A second day at Orlando's Universal Studios may provide few additional thrills, which is why the theme park can safely offer the second day free without being overrun with people.

Total utility The total satisfaction a consumer derives from consumption; it could refer either to the total utility of consuming a particular good or the total utility from all consumption

Marginal utility The change in total utility derived from a one-unit change in consumption of a good

Law of diminishing marginal utility The more of a good consumed per period, the smaller the increase in total utility from consuming one more unit, other things constant

---

1 This example appeared in Marshall Jevons, *The Fatal Equilibrium* (Cambridge, MA: MIT Press, 1985).

MEASURING UTILITY

So far our descriptions of utility have used such words as "wonderful," "good," and "fair." We cannot push the analysis very far if we limit ourselves to such subjective language. If we want to predict behavior based on changes in the economic environment, we must develop a consistent way of viewing utility.

Units of Utility

Let's go back to the water example. Although there really is no objective way of measuring utility, if pressed you might be able to be more specific about how much you enjoyed each glass of water. For example, you might say the first glass was twice as good as the second, the second was twice as good as the third, the third was twice as good as the fourth, and you passed up a fifth glass because you expected no additional utility. In order to get a handle on this description of your satisfaction, let's assign arbitrary numbers to the amount of utility from each quantity consumed, so that the pattern of numbers reflects the pattern of your satisfaction. Let's say the first glass of water provides you with 40 units of utility, the second glass yields 20, the third yields 10, and the fourth yields 5. A fifth glass, if you were forced to drink it, would yield negative utility, in this case, say, -2 units of utility. *Developing numerical values for utility allows us to be more specific about the utility derived from consumption.* If it would help, you could think of units of utility more playfully as kicks, thrills, or jollies—as in, getting your jollies from consumption.

By attaching a numerical measure to utility, we can compare the total utility a particular consumer gets from different goods as well as the marginal utility that same consumer gets from additional consumption. Thus we can employ units of utility to evaluate a consumer's preferences for various units of a good or even various units of different goods. Note, however, that we should not try to compare units of utility across consumers. *Each individual has a uniquely subjective utility scale.*

The first column of Exhibit 1 lists possible quantities of water you might consume after running four miles on a hot day; the second column presents the total utility derived from that consumption; and the third column shows the

EXHIBIT 1

Utility You Derive from Water After Jogging Four Miles

Units of Water Consumed (8-ounce glass)	Total Utility	Marginal Utility
0	0	—
1	40	40
2	60	20
3	70	10
4	75	5
5	73	−2

marginal utility of each additional glass of water consumed. Recall that marginal utility is the change in total utility that results from consuming an additional unit of the good. You can see from the second column that total utility increases with each of the first four glasses, but by smaller and smaller amounts. The third column shows that the first glass of water yields 40 units of utility, the second glass yields an additional 20 units, and so on. Marginal utility declines after the first glass of water, becoming negative with the fifth glass. At any level of consumption, marginal utilities up to and including that level sum to total utility. Total utility is graphed in panel (a) of Exhibit 2. Again, because of diminishing marginal utility, each glass adds less to total utility, so total utility increases for the first four glasses but at a decreasing rate. Marginal utility is presented in panel (b).

Utility Maximization in a World Without Scarcity

Economists assume that your purpose for drinking water, as with all consumption, is to *maximize total utility*. So how much water do you consume? If the price of water is zero, you drink water as long as each additional glass increases

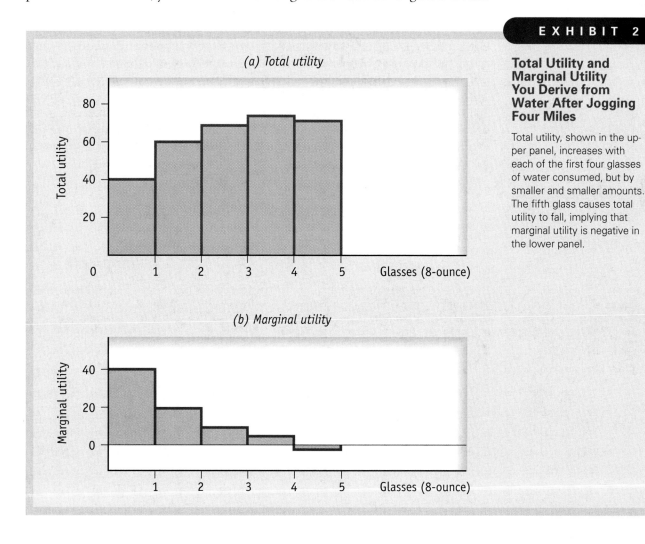

EXHIBIT 2

Total Utility and Marginal Utility You Derive from Water After Jogging Four Miles

Total utility, shown in the upper panel, increases with each of the first four glasses of water consumed, but by smaller and smaller amounts. The fifth glass causes total utility to fall, implying that marginal utility is negative in the lower panel.

total utility, which means you consume four glasses of water. *So when a good is free, you increase consumption as long as additional units provide positive marginal utility.*

Let's extend the analysis of utility to discuss the consumption of pizza and video rentals. We will continue to translate the relative satisfaction you receive from consumption into units of utility. Given your tastes and preferences, suppose your total and marginal utility from consumption are as presented in Exhibit 3. The first four columns apply to pizza and the second four to videos. Please spend a little time right now becoming familiar with each column.

Notice from columns (3) and (7) that both goods exhibit diminishing marginal utility. Given this set of preferences, how much of each good would you consume? At a zero price, you would increase consumption as long as you derived positive marginal utility from additional units of each good. Thus you would consume at least the first six pizzas and first six videos per week because both generate positive marginal utility at that level of consumption. Did you ever go to a party where the food and drinks were free? How much did you eat and drink? You probably ate and drank until you didn't want any more—that is, until the marginal utility of each good consumed declined to zero.

Utility Maximization in a World of Scarcity

Alas, scarcity is our lot, so we should focus on how a consumer chooses when goods are not free. Suppose the price of a pizza is $8, the rental price of a movie video is $4, and your income is $40 per week. You still want to maximize utility, but now subject to the conditions that income is limited and prices are greater than zero. Under these conditions, the utility you receive from different goods relative to their prices determines how you allocate your income. In the real world, consumption depends on tastes (as reflected by the marginal utilities), prices, and your income.

EXHIBIT 3

Total and Marginal Utility from Pizza and Video Rentals

Pizzas Consumed per Week (1)	Total Utility of Pizza (2)	Marginal Utility of Pizza (3)	Marginal Utility of Pizza per Dollar Expended (price = $8) (4)	Video Rentals per Week (5)	Total Utility of Videos (6)	Marginal Utility of Videos (7)	Marginal Utility of Videos per Dollar Expended (price = $4) (8)
0	0	—	—	0	0	—	—
1	56	56	7	1	40	40	10
2	88	32	4	2	68	28	7
3	112	24	3	3	88	20	5
4	130	18	$2\frac{1}{4}$	4	100	12	3
5	142	12	$1\frac{1}{2}$	5	108	8	2
6	150	8	1	6	114	6	$1\frac{1}{2}$

How do you allocate income between the two goods so as to maximize utility? Suppose you start off with some combination of pizzas and videos. If you can increase your utility by reallocating expenditures, you will do so, and you will continue to make adjustments as long as you can increase your utility. There may be some trial and error at first, but, by learning from your mistakes, you move toward the utility-maximizing position. When no further utility-increasing moves are possible, you have settled on the combination that maximizes your utility, given your tastes, prices, and your income—*you have arrived at the equilibrium combination.* Once you achieve this utility-maximizing equilibrium, you will maintain this consumption pattern unless there is a change in your tastes, your income, or the prices you face.

To get the process rolling, suppose you start off spending your entire budget of $40 on pizza, purchasing 5 pizzas a week, which yields a total of 142 units of utility a week. You soon realize that if you buy one less pizza, you free up enough income to rent 2 movies. Would total utility increase? You give up 12 units of utility, the marginal utility of the fifth pizza, to get 68 units of utility from the first 2 videos. Total utility thereby increases from 142 to 198 units of utility per week. Then you notice that if you reduce purchases to 3 pizzas, you give up 18 units of utility from the fourth pizza but gain 32 units of utility from the third and fourth videos. This is another utility-increasing move. Further reductions in pizza, however, would reduce your total utility because you would give up 24 units of utility from the third pizza but gain only 14 units of utility from the fifth and sixth videos. Thus, by trial and error, you find that the utility-maximizing equilibrium combination is 3 pizzas and 4 videos per week, for a total utility of 212. This involves an outlay of $24 on pizza and $16 on videos. *You are in equilibrium when consuming this combination because any affordable change would reduce your total utility.* Note that you consume fewer units now than when they were free.

The Utility-Maximizing Conditions

As you can see from the previous example, once equilibrium has been achieved, any shift in spending from one good to another will decrease utility. *Once a consumer is in equilibrium, there is no way to increase utility by reallocating the budget.* We will now examine a special property of the utility-maximizing combination: In equilibrium, the last dollar spent on each good yields the same utility. More specifically, *utility is maximized when the budget is completely spent and the marginal utility of a good divided by its price is identical for the last unit of each good purchased.* In short, the consumer gets the same bang per last buck spent on each good.

Let's see how this works. Columns (4) and (8) in Exhibit 3 indicate the marginal utility of each dollar's worth of pizza and videos, respectively. Column (4) shows the marginal utility of pizza divided by its price of $8. Column (8) shows the marginal utility of videos divided by its price of $4. You can see that the equilibrium choice of 3 pizzas and 4 videos exhausts the $40 budget and yields 3 units of utility for the last dollar spent on each good. **Consumer equilibrium** is achieved when the budget is completely spent and the last dollar spent on each good yields the same utility, or the marginal utility of pizza divided by its price equals the marginal utility of videos divided by its price. This equality can be expressed as

Consumer equilibrium
The condition in which an individual consumer's budget is completely spent and the last dollar spent on each good yields the same marginal utility; therefore, utility is maximized

$$\frac{\mathrm{MU}_p}{p_p} = \frac{\mathrm{MU}_v}{p_v}$$

where MU_p is the marginal utility of pizza, p_p is the price of pizza, MU_v is the marginal utility of videos, and p_v is the price of videos. Although we have considered only two goods, the logic of utility maximization applies to any number of goods. The consumer will reallocate spending until the last dollar spent on each product yields the same marginal utility.

In equilibrium, higher-priced goods must yield more marginal utility than lower-priced goods—enough additional utility to compensate for their higher price. In our example, since a pizza costs twice as much as a video, the marginal utility of the final pizza purchased must, in equilibrium, be twice that of the final video rented. In fact, 24 units of utility, the marginal utility of the third pizza, is twice as much as 12 units of utility, the marginal utility of the fourth video rented. Economists do not claim that you consciously equate the ratios of marginal utility to price, but they do claim that you act as if you had made such calculations. *Thus, you decide how much of each good to purchase by considering your relative preferences for the alternative goods, the prices of the alternative goods, and your income.*

Thus consumers maximize utility by equalizing the marginal utility per dollar of expenditure across goods. This equality resolved what had been an economic puzzle, as discussed in the following case study.

CaseStudy

The World of Business

Almost any question you might have about water supply and use in the United States can be answered by visiting the Water Q&A at the U.S. Geological Survey's Web site at http://wwwga.usgs.gov/edu/qausage.html. Various terms are linked to pages with additional information. What is the number one use of water in the U.S.? How does domestic use rate in importance? From which sources is most of the water in your state drawn—surface or groundwater supplies? How does water supply and use in the U.S. compare with the rest of the world. Find the answer in "Water: Critical Shortages Ahead?" from the World Resources Institute at http://www.wri.org/wr-98-99/water.htm.

Water, Water, Everywhere

Centuries ago economists puzzled over the price of diamonds relative to the price of water. Diamonds are mere baubles—certainly not a necessity of life in any sense. Water is essential to life and has a huge number of uses. Yet diamonds are expensive, while water is cheap. For example, the $10,000 spent on a one-carat diamond could instead buy about ten million gallons of municipally-supplied water (which typically sells for about 10 cents per hundred gallons). However measured, diamonds are extremely expensive relative to water. For the price of a one-carat diamond, you could buy enough water to last four lifetimes.

How can the price of something as useful as water be so much lower than something of such limited use as diamonds? Adam Smith discussed in 1776 what has come to be called the *diamonds-water paradox*. What explains this paradox? Because water is so essential to life, the total utility derived from water greatly exceeds the total utility derived from diamonds. But the market value of a good is based, not on its total utility, but on what consumers are willing and able to pay for an additional unit of the good—that is, on its marginal utility. Since water is so abundant in nature, the marginal utility of the last gallon purchased is relatively low. Since diamonds are so scarce in nature, the marginal utility of the last diamond purchased is relatively high. Thus water is cheap and diamonds expensive.

Speaking of water, let's examine the recent surge in the demand for bottled water. In the past decade, sales of bottled water gushed 144 percent—faster than any other beverage segment—creating a $4 billion industry in the United States. Annual consumption of bottled water increased from 5 gallons to 11 gallons per capita. The United States offers the world's largest market for bottled water—some of it imported from places such as Italy, France, Sweden, Wales, even Fiji. And there are even "water bars" in Boston, New York and Los Angeles, where the primary attraction is bottled water.

Why would consumers pay a premium for bottled water when they can draw water from the tap for virtually nothing? First, many people do not view the two options as good substitutes. About half of respondents in a recent Gallup Poll said they won't drink water straight from the tap. They have concerns about the safety of tap water, such as possible contamination by e-coli bacteria, and they view bottled water as a healthy alternative. Second, even those who have no problem with tap water consider bottled water a convenient alternative when away from home.

According to the theory of utility maximization, people who buy bottled water apparently feel the additional benefit offsets the additional cost. Bottled-water sales are expected to continue growing. Pepsi's Aquafina brand is sold around the country, and Coke is launching its own brand.

Sources: Corby Kummer, "What's In the Water?" *New York Times Magazine*, 30 (August 1998), pp. 38, 42, 59, 61; Christopher Williams "US Filter, Water Stocks Up; New Report on Drinking Water Cited," Dow Jones Newswire, 21 (October 1998); "Lax Oversight Raises Tap Water Risks," *USA Today*, 21 (October 1998); and Nikhil Deogun, "The Really Real Thing: Coke to Peddle Brand of Purified Bottled Water in U.S." *Wall Street Journal*, 3 (November 1998). The Web site for the International Bottled Water Association is www.bottledwater.org.

The Law of Demand and Marginal Utility

The purpose of utility analysis is to provide information about quantity demanded. How does the previous analysis relate to your demand for pizza? It yields a single point on your demand curve for pizza: At a price of $8, you demand 3 pizzas per week. This point is based on a given income of $40 per week, a given rental price of $4 per video, and the tastes reflected by your utility schedules in Exhibit 3.

This single point, in itself, offers no inkling about the shape of your demand curve. To generate another point, let's change the price of pizza, keep other things constant (such as income, tastes, and the price of videos), then see what happens to the quantity demanded. Suppose the price of a pizza drops from $8 to $6. What will happen to your consumption, given the preferences already outlined in the discussion of Exhibit 3? Exhibit 4 is the same as Exhibit 3, except the price per pizza has been reduced from $8 to $6.

Your original choice was 3 pizzas and 4 video rentals. At that combination and with the price of pizza now $6, the marginal utility per dollar expended on the third pizza is 4, but the marginal utility per dollar spent on the fourth video is 3. The marginal utilities of the last dollar spent on each good are no longer equal across goods. What's more, if you maintained the original combination, you would have $6 remaining in your budget because you would be spending only $18 on pizza. So you could still buy your original bundle but have $6 left over (this, incidentally, is the income effect of a lower price of pizza). You can increase your utility by consuming a different bundle.

EXHIBIT 4

Total and Marginal Utility from Pizza and Video Rentals After Price of Pizza Decreases from $8 to $6

Pizzas Consumed per Week (1)	Total Utility of Pizza (2)	Marginal Utility of Pizza (3)	Marginal Utility of Pizza per Dollar Expended (price = $6) (4)	Video Rentals per Week (5)	Total Utility of Videos (6)	Marginal Utility of Videos (7)	Marginal Utility of Videos per Dollar Expended (price = $4) (8)
0	0	—	—	0	0	—	—
1	56	56	$9\frac{1}{3}$	1	40	40	10
2	88	32	$5\frac{1}{3}$	2	68	28	7
3	112	24	4	3	88	20	5
4	130	18	3	4	100	12	3
5	142	12	2	5	108	8	2
6	150	8	$1\frac{1}{3}$	6	114	6	$1\frac{1}{2}$

Take a moment to see if you can figure out what the new equilibrium bundle should be.

In light of your utility schedules in Exhibit 4, you would increase your consumption to 4 pizzas per week. This increase exhausts your budget and equates the marginal utilities of the last dollar expended on each good. Your video purchases remain the same (although they could have changed due to the income effect of the price change). But as your consumption increases to 4 pizzas per week, the marginal utility of the fourth pizza, 18, divided by the price of $6, yields 3 units of utility per dollar of expenditure, which is the same as for the fourth video. You are in equilibrium once again. Your total utility increases by the 18 units of utility you receive from pizza. Hence you are clearly better off as a result of the price decrease.

We now have a second point on your demand curve for pizza—when the price of pizza is $6, your quantity demanded is four pizzas. The two points are presented as *a* and *b* in Exhibit 5. We could continue to change the price of pizza and thereby generate additional points on the demand curve, but you get some idea of the demand curve's downward slope from these two points. The shape of the demand curve for pizza conforms to our expectations based on the law of demand: Price and quantity demanded are inversely related. (Try to estimate the price elasticity of demand between points *a* and *b*. Hint: What does total expenditure tell you?)

We have gone to some length to see how you (or any consumer) maximize utility. Given prices and your income, your tastes and preferences naturally guide you to the most preferred bundle. You are not even conscious of your behavior. The urge to maximize utility is like the force of gravity—both work whether or not you understand them. Even animals seem to behave in a way that appears consistent with the law of demand.

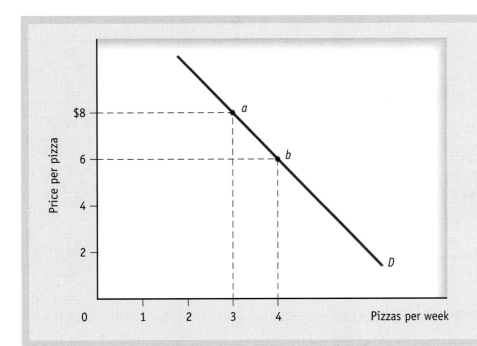

EXHIBIT 5

Demand for Pizza Generated from Marginal Utility

At a price of $8 per pizza, the consumer is in equilibrium when consuming 3 pizzas (point *a*). Marginal utility per dollar is the same for all goods consumed. If the price falls to $6, the consumer will increase consumption to 4 pizzas (point *b*). Points *a* and *b* are two points on this consumer's demand curve for pizza.

Certain animal behavior in the wild appears consistent with the idea that resources are valued more when they are relatively scarce. When food is naturally abundant in the environment, some species devote little or no energy to establishing and defending food sources. Wolves, for example, exhibit no territorial concerns when game is plentiful. But when game is scarce, wolves carefully mark their territory and defend it against interlopers.

Now that you have some idea of utility, let's consider an application of utility analysis.

Consumer Surplus

In our earlier example, total utility increased when the price of pizza fell from $8 to $6. In this section, we'll take a closer look at how consumers benefit from a lower price. Suppose your demand for foot-long Subway sandwiches is as shown in Exhibit 6, which measures on the horizontal axis the number of Subways you are willing and able to buy each month. Recall that in constructing an individual's demand curve, we hold tastes, income, and the prices of related goods constant; only the price of Subways varies.

At a price of $8 or above, you find that the marginal utility of other goods that you could buy for $8 is higher than the marginal utility of a Subway. Consequently, you buy no Subways. At a price of $7, you are willing and able to buy one per month, so the marginal utility of that first Subway exceeds the marginal utility you expected from spending that money on your best alternative—say, a movie ticket. A price of $6 prompts you to buy two Subways a month. The second is worth at least $6 to you. At a price of $5, you buy three Subways, and at $4, you buy four. *In each case, the value to you of the last Subway purchased must at least equal the price; otherwise, you wouldn't buy it.* Along the

EXHIBIT 6

Consumer Surplus from Subway Sandwiches

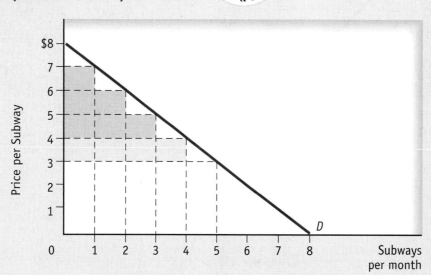

At a given quantity of Subway sandwiches, the height of the demand curve shows the value of the last one purchased. The area under the demand curve up to a specific quantity shows the total value the consumer places on that quantity. At a price of $4, the consumer purchases four Subways. The first one is valued at $7, the second at $6, the third at $5, and the fourth at $4. The consumer values four at $22. Since the consumer pays $4 per Subway, all four can be obtained for $16. The difference between what the consumer would have been willing to pay ($22) and what the consumer actually pays ($16) is called consumer surplus. When the price is $4, the consumer surplus is represented by the dark shaded area under the demand curve above $4. When the price of Subways falls to $3, consumer surplus increases by $4, as is reflected by the lighter shaded area.

Marginal valuation The dollar value of the marginal utility derived from consuming each additional unit of a good

Consumer surplus The difference between the maximum amount that a consumer is willing to pay for a given quantity of a good and what the consumer actually pays

demand curve, therefore, the price reflects your **marginal valuation** of the good, or the dollar value of the marginal utility derived from consuming each additional unit.

Notice that when the price is $4, you can purchase each of the four Subways for that price even though you would have been willing to pay more than $4 for each of the first three Subways. The first sandwich provides marginal utility that you value at $7; the second, marginal utility valued at $6; and the third, marginal utility valued at $5. In fact, if you had to, you would have been willing to pay $7 for the first, $6 for the second, and $5 for the third. The value of the total utility of the first four sandwiches is $7 + $6 + $5 + $4 = $22. But when the price is $4, you get all four for $16. Thus, a price of $4 confers a **consumer surplus,** or a consumer bonus, equal to the difference between the maximum amount you would have been willing to pay ($22) rather than go without Subways and what you actually paid ($16). When the price is $4, your consumer surplus is $6, as shown by the six darker shaded blocks in Exhibit 6. The consumer surplus equals the total utility you receive from consuming the sandwiches minus your total spending on them. Consumer surplus is the area under the demand curve but above the price.

If the price falls to $3, you purchase five Subways a month. Evidently you feel that the marginal benefit you receive from the fifth one is worth at least $3. The lower price means that you get to buy all five for $3 each even though most are worth more to you than $3. Your consumer surplus when the price is $3 is the value of the total utility conferred by the first five, which is $7 + $6 + $5 + $4 + $3 = $25, minus your cost, which is $3 × 5 = $15. Thus, your consumer surplus totals $25 − $15 = $10, as indicated by both the dark and the light shaded blocks in Exhibit 6. If the price declines to $3, you are able to purchase all Subways for less, so your consumer surplus increases by $4, as reflected by the four lighter-shaded blocks in Exhibit 6. You can see how consumers benefit from lower prices.

Market Demand and Consumer Surplus

Let's talk more generally now about the market demand for a good, assuming the market consists of you and two other consumers. *The market demand curve is simply the horizontal sum of the individual demand curves for all consumers in the market.* Exhibit 7 shows how the demand curves for three consumers in the market for Subway sandwiches are summed horizontally to yield the market demand. At a price of $4, for example, you demand 4 Subways per month, Brittany demands 2, and Chris demands none. The market quantity demanded at a price of $4 is therefore 6 sandwiches. At a price of $2, you demand 6 per month, Britanny, 4, and Chris, 2, for a market quantity demanded of 12 sandwiches. *The market demand curve shows the total quantity demanded per period by all consumers at various prices.*

The idea of consumer surplus can be used to examine market demand as well as individual demand. *At a given price, consumer surplus for the market is the difference between the amount consumers are willing to pay for that quantity and the total amount they do pay.*

EXHIBIT 7

Summing Individual Demands to Derive the Market Demand for Subway Sandwiches

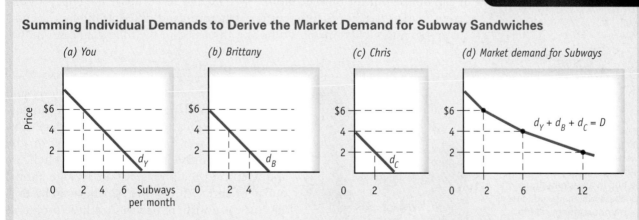

At a price of $4 per Subway, you demand 4 per month, Brittany demands 2, and Chris demands none. Total market demand at a price of $4 is 4 + 2 + 0 = 6 Subways per month. At a lower price of $2, you demand 6, Brittany demands 4, and Chris demands 2. Market demand at a price of $2 is 12 Subways. The market demand curve *D* is the horizontal sum of individual demand curves d_Y, d_B, and d_C.

EXHIBIT 8

Market Demand and Consumer Surplus

Consumer surplus at a price of $2 is shown by the darker area. If the price falls to $1, consumer surplus increases to include the lighter area.

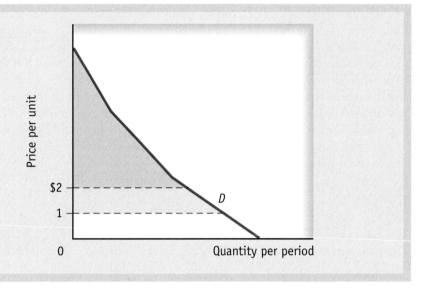

Instead of just three consumers in the market, suppose there are many. Exhibit 8 presents market demand for a good when there are millions of consumers. If the price is $2 per unit, each person adjusts his or her quantity demanded until the marginal valuation of the last unit purchased equals $2. But each consumer gets to buy all the other units for $2 as well. In Exhibit 8, the dark shading, bounded above by the demand curve and below by the price of $2, depicts the market consumer surplus when the price is $2. The light shading shows the increase in consumer surplus if the price drops to $1. Note that if this good were given away, the consumer surplus would not be that much greater than when the price is $1.

Consumer surplus is the net benefit consumers get from market exchange. It can be used to measure economic welfare and to compare the effects of different market structures, different tax structures, and different public expenditure programs, such as medical care, as is discussed in the following case study.

CaseStudy

Public Policy

This case study points out that patients have little incentive to monitor physician behavior when they do not pay the bill. In an attempt to control costs Medicare reduces the reimbursement rate for services provided by the physicians. How do you suppose that they respond? The Health Care Financing Administration's auditors examined physician behavior and found

The Marginal Value of Free Medical Care

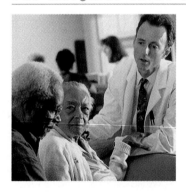

Certain Americans, such as the elderly and those on welfare, are provided government-subsidized medical care. State and federal taxpayers spent over $400 billion in 1998 on the medical care provided to 75 million Medicare and Medicaid recipients, for an average annual outlay of about $5,000 per beneficiary. The dollar cost to most beneficiaries of these programs was usually little or nothing. The problem with giving something away is that beneficiaries consume it up to the point where their marginal benefit from the final unit is zero, although the marginal cost to taxpayers can be substantial.

This is not to say that beneficiaries derive no benefit from free medical care. Even though they may attach little or no value to marginal units, they likely derive a substantial consumer surplus from the other units they consume. For example, suppose that the previous exhibit, Exhibit 8, represents the demand for medical care by Medicare and Medicaid beneficiaries. If the price to them is zero, they consume up to the point where the demand curve intersects the horizontal axis, so their consumer surplus is the entire area under the demand curve.

One way to reduce the taxpayer cost of such programs without significantly harming beneficiaries is to charge a nominal price—say $1 per physician visit. As a result, beneficiaries would eliminate visits they value less than $1. This would yield significant savings to taxpayers, yet would still leave beneficiaries with adequate health care and with a substantial consumer surplus (measured in Exhibit 8 as the area under the demand curve but above the $1 price). As a case in point, one Medicaid experiment in California required a group of beneficiaries to pay $1 per visit for their first two office visits per month (after two visits, the price of additional visits reverted to zero). Few could argue that a cost of at most $2 per month represents a substantial burden on recipients. A control group continued to receive completely free medical care. The $1 charge reduced office visits by 8 percent compared to the control group.

Medical care, like other goods and services, is also sensitive to the time component of the cost (a topic to be examined in the next section). For example, a 10 percent increase in the average travel time required to visit a free outpatient clinic reduced visits by 10 percent. Similarly, when the relocation of a free clinic at one college campus increased students' walking time by ten minutes, student visits declined by 40 percent.

These findings do not mean that certain groups do not deserve low-cost medical care. The point is that when something is free, people consume it until their marginal valuation is zero. Even a modest money or time cost will reduce consumption yet will still leave beneficiaries with a substantial consumer surplus. A second problem with giving something away is that beneficiaries are less vigilant about getting honest value for their money when they pay little or nothing for the good. This increases the possibility of fraud and abuse by health care providers. According to experts, about 10 percent of government spending on health care is wasted because of padded bills, fake claims, and other activities that would be less tolerated if the beneficiaries were paying their own bills. For example, in one case the government was billed for round-the-clock cardiac monitoring when the patient was in fact monitored only 30 minutes a month. Such abuse by health care providers translates into a waste of at least $40 billion per year.

Sources: Steven Rhoads, "Marginalism," *The Fortune Encyclopedia of Economics*, D. R. Henderson, ed. (New York: Warner Books, 1993): 31–33; Joseph White, "Paying the Right Prices: What the United States Can Learn from Health Care Abroad," *Brookings Review* (Spring 1994) 6–11; Paul Gertler and Jacques van der Gaag, *The Willingness to Pay for Medical Care* (Baltimore: Johns Hopkins University Press, 1990); and L. J. Davis, "Medscam," *Mother Jones* (March/April 1995).

that they increase the volume and intensity of work in response to declining prices in order to maintain revenue. Their easy-to-read report on physician response, which includes several real examples, can be found at http://www.hcfa.gov/pubforms/behavoff/behavoff.htm.

THE ROLE OF TIME IN DEMAND

Because consumption does not occur instantaneously, time also plays an important role in demand analysis. Consumption takes time and, as Benjamin Franklin said, time is money—time has a positive value for most people. Consequently,

*Net*Bookmark

For an example of pricing that uses the law of marginal utility, visit the on-line ticket purchase page for Universal Studios Florida at http://www.usf.com/tickets/index_2dfree.html. Find the prices for one-day, two-day and three-day passes. How much does each additional day cost? What special promotions are being offered? What restrictions are there on getting a second day free? Compare these to the restrictions on using the second day of a two-day pass. Also try comparing a three-day pass to an annual pass. Which is cheaper?

the cost of consumption has two components: the *money price* of the good and the *time price* of the good. Goods are demanded because of the benefits they offer. Your demand for medicine is based on its ability to cure you; your interest is not in the medicine itself but in the benefit it provides. Thus, you may be willing to pay more for medicine that works more quickly. Similarly, it is not the microwave oven, personal computer, or airline trip that you value, but the benefits they provide. Other things constant, the good that provides the same benefit in less time is preferred. That's why we are willing to pay more for seedless grapes, seedless oranges, and seedless watermelon.

Your willingness to pay a premium for time-saving goods and services depends on the opportunity cost of your time. Differences in the value of time among consumers help explain differences in the consumption patterns observed in the economy. Consider the alternative ways to get to Europe. You could, for example, take the Concorde or a regular airline. Your mode of travel will depend in part on your opportunity cost of time. The Concorde takes less than half the time of other flights, but because the Concorde is much more expensive, only travelers with an extremely high opportunity cost of time, such as busy corporate executives and celebrities, will pay such a premium for faster service. Students on their summer vacations are more inclined to opt for some discount excursion fare or even standby status; for them, the lower money cost more than compensates for the higher time cost.

A retired couple is likely to have a lower opportunity cost of time and so will purchase fewer time-saving goods, such as microwave ovens and frozen dinners, than a working couple in the fast lane. The retired couple may clip coupons and search the newspapers for bargains, sometimes going from store to store for particular grocery items on sale that week. The working couple will usually ignore the coupons and sales and will often eat out or purchase items at convenience stores, where they pay extra for the "convenience." The retired couple will be more inclined to drive across the country on vacation, whereas the working couple will fly to a vacation destination.

Just inside the gates at Anaheim's Disneyland, Orlando's Disney World, and Orlando's Universal Studios are signs posting the waiting times of each attraction and ride. Since, at that point, the dollar cost of admission has already been paid, the dollar cost of each ride and attraction is zero. The posting of waiting times offers menus of the time costs of each ride or attraction. Incidentally, people who are willing to pay up to $55 an hour at Disney World and $60 an hour at Disneyland (plus the price of admission) can take VIP tours that eliminate the lines.[2]

Differences in the opportunity cost of time among consumers shape consumption patterns and add another dimension to our analysis of demand.

CONCLUSION

We have developed a utility-based analysis of consumer choice. Our focus was on the utility, or satisfaction, that consumers receive from consumption. In observing consumer behavior, we assume that for a particular individual, utility

---

2   Nancy Keates, "Tourists Learn How to Mouse Around Disney's Long Lines," *Wall Street Journal* (27 March 1998).

can be measured in some systematic way, even though different consumers' utility levels cannot be compared. Our ultimate objective is to predict how consumer choice is affected by such variables as a change in price. We judge a theory not by the realism of its assumptions but by the accuracy of its predictions. Based on this criterion, the theory of consumer choice presented in this chapter has proven to be quite useful.

Again, we stress that consumers do not have to understand the material presented in this chapter in order to maximize utility. Economists assume that rational consumers attempt to maximize utility naturally and instinctively. In this chapter, we simply tried to analyze that process using a model of consumer choice based on utility analysis. A more general approach to consumer choice and utility analysis, an approach that does not require a specific measure of utility, is developed in the appendix to this chapter.

SUMMARY

1. Utility is the sense of pleasure or satisfaction that comes from consumption; it is the want-satisfying power of goods, services, and activities. The utility you receive from consuming a particular good depends on your tastes. We distinguish between the total utility derived from consuming a good and the marginal utility derived from consuming one more unit of that good. The law of diminishing marginal utility says that the greater the amount of a particular good consumed per time period, other things constant, the smaller the increase in total utility received from each additional unit consumed.

2. Any assessment of the want-satisfying power of consumption must be made by each individual consumer—utility is subjective. By translating an individual's subjective measure of satisfaction into units of utility, we can predict the effect of a change in price on quantity demanded.

3. The consumer's objective is to maximize utility within the limits imposed by income and prices. In a world without scarcity, utility would be maximized by consuming goods until the marginal utility of the last unit of each good consumed was zero. In the real world, a world shaped by scarcity, utility is maximized when the final unit of each good consumed yields the same utility

per dollar spent. Put another way, utility is maximized when the marginal utility divided by the price is identical for each good consumed.

4. Utility analysis can be used to construct an individual consumer's demand curve. By changing the price and observing the utility-maximizing levels of consumption, we can generate points along the demand curve.

5. When the price of a good drops, other things constant, the consumer is able to buy all units of the good at the lower price. Consumers typically receive a surplus, or a bonus, from consumption, and this surplus grows as the price falls.

6. The market demand curve is simply the horizontal sum of the individual demand curves for all consumers in the market. Consumer surplus for the market demand curve can be measured as the difference between the maximum amount consumers would pay for a given quantity of the good and the amount paid.

7. There are two components to the cost of consumption: the money price of the good and the time price of the good. People with a higher opportunity cost of time will pay a higher money price for goods and services that save time.

QUESTIONS FOR REVIEW

1. *(Law of Diminishing Marginal Utility)* Some restaurants offer "all you can eat" meals. How is this practice related to diminishing marginal utility? What restrictions must the restaurant impose on the customer in order to make a profit?

2. *(Law of Diminishing Marginal Utility)* Complete each of the following sentences:
   a. Your tastes determine the _____ you derive from consuming a particular good.

b. _____ utility is the change in _____ utility resulting from a _____ change in the consumption of a good.

c. As long as marginal utility is positive, total utility is _____ .

d. The law of diminishing marginal utility states that as an individual consumes more of a good during a given time period, other things constant, total utility _____ .

3. *(Marginal Utility)* Is it possible for marginal utility to be negative while total utility is positive? If yes, under what circumstances is it possible.

4. *(Utility-Maximizing Conditions)* For a particular consumer, the marginal utility of cookies equals the marginal utility of candy. If the price of a cookie is less than the price of candy, is the consumer in equilibrium? Why or why not? If not, what should the consumer do to attain equilibrium?

5. *(Utility-Maximizing Conditions)* Suppose that marginal utility of Good X = 100, the price of X is $10 per unit, and the price of Y is $5 per unit. Assuming that the consumer is in equilibrium and is consuming both X and Y, what must the marginal utility of Y be?

6. *(Utility-Maximizing Conditions)* Suppose that the price of X is twice as high as the price of Y. You are a utility maximizer who allocates your budget between those two goods. What must be true about the equilibrium relationship between the marginal utility levels of the last unit consumed of each good? What must be true about the equilibrium relationship between the marginal utility levels of the last dollar spent on each good?

7. *(Consumer Surplus)* The height of the demand curve at a given quantity reflects the marginal valuation of the last unit of that good consumed. For a normal good, an increase in income will shift the demand curve to the right and therefore increase its height at any quantity. Does this mean that consumers get greater marginal utility from each unit of this good than they did before? Explain.

8. *(Consumer Surplus)* Suppose that a good is in perfectly elastic supply at a price of $5. The market demand curve for this good is linear, with zero quantity demanded at a price of $25. If the slope of this linear demand curve is −0.25, draw a supply and demand graph to illustrate the consumer surplus that occurs when the market is in equilibrium.

9. *(CaseStudy: The Marginal Value of Free Medical Care)* Medicare recipients pay a monthly premium for coverage, must meet an annual deductible, and have a copayment for doctor's office visits. There is no coverage for prescription medications. What impact would an increase in the monthly premium have on their consumer surplus? What would be the impact of a reduction in their copayments? What would be the impact on the quantity demanded and consumer surplus if Medicare started providing coverage for prescription medications?

10. *(Role of Time in Demand)* In many amusement parks, you pay an admission fee to the park but you do not need to pay for individual rides. How do people choose which rides to go on?

11. *(CaseStudy: Water, Water Everywhere)* What is the diamonds–water paradox, and how is it explained? Use the same reasoning to explain why bottled water costs so much more than tap water?

PROBLEMS AND EXERCISES

12. *(Utility Maximization)* The following tables illustrate Eileen's utilities from watching first-run movies in a theater and from renting movies from a video store. Suppose that she has a monthly entertainment budget of $36, each movie in a theater costs $6, and each video rental costs $3.

Movies in a Theater

Q	TU	MU	MU/P
0	0	———	———
1	200	———	———
2	290	———	———
3	370	———	———
4	440	———	———
5	500	———	———
6	550	———	———
7	590	———	———

Movies from a Video Store

Q	TU	MU	MU/P
0	0	———	———
1	250	———	———
2	295	———	———
3	335	———	———
4	370	———	———
5	400	———	———
6	425	———	———
———	———	———	

a. Complete the tables.
b. Do these tables show that Eileen's preferences obey the law of diminishing marginal utility? Explain your answer.
c. How much of each good will Eileen consume in equilibrium?
d. Suppose the prices of both types of movies drop to $1 while Eileen's entertainment budget shrinks to $10. How much of each good will she consume in equilibrium?

13. *(Utility Maximization)* Suppose that a consumer has a choice between two goods, X and Y. If the price of X is $2 per unit and the price of Y is $3 per unit, how much of X and Y will the consumer purchase, given an in-come of $17? Use the following information about marginal utility:

Units	MU_X	MU_Y
1	10	5
2	8	4
3	2	3
4	2	2
5	1	2

14. *(The Law of Demand and Marginal Utility)* Daniel allocates his budget of $24 per week among three goods. Use the following table of the marginal utilities for Good A, Good B, and Good C to answer the questions below:

Q_A	MU_A	Q_B	MU_B	Q_C	MU_C
1	50	1	75	1	25
2	40	2	60	2	20
3	30	3	40	3	15
4	20	4	30	4	10
5	15	5	20	5	7.5

a. If the price of A is $2, the price of B is $3, and the price of C is $1, how much of each will Daniel purchase in equilibrium?
b. If the price of A rises to $4 while other prices and Daniel's budget remain unchanged, how much of each will he purchase in equilibrium?
c. Using the information from parts (a) and (b), draw the demand curve for Good A. Be sure to indicate the price and quantity demanded for each point on the curve.

15. *(Consumer Surplus)* Suppose the linear demand curve for shirts slopes downward and that consumers buy 500 shirts per year when the price of a shirt is $30 and 1,000 shirts per year when their price is $25.
a. Compared to the prices of $30 and $25, what can you say about the marginal valuation that consumers place on the 300th shirt, the 700th shirt, and the 1,200th shirt they might buy each year?
b. With diminishing marginal utility, are consumers deriving any consumer surplus if the price is $25 per shirt? Explain.
c. Use a market demand curve to illustrate the change in consumer surplus if the price drops from $30 to $25.

EXPERIENTIAL EXERCISES

16. *(Consumer Surplus)* Access a copy of "Creating Value and Destroying Profits? Three Measures of Information Technology's Contributions," by Loren Hitt and Erik Brynjolfsson at http://ccs.mit.edu/CCSWP183.html. Use your "find" function to search for the words "consumer surplus" in this paper. How do Hitt and Brynjolfsson use the concept of consumer surplus to measure the value of information technology?

17. *(CaseStudy: The Marginal Value of Free Medical Care)* To learn more about economic issues related to health care, visit the McEachern Web page http://mceachern.swcollege.com, click on Econ-Debate Online, and find the debate "Is there a need for health care reform?" What are some economic issues related to health care reform?

18. *(The Role of Time in Demand)* To learn more about the economics of consumption, read Jane Katz's "The Joy of Consumption: We Are What We Buy," in the Federal Reserve Bank of Boston's *The Region* at http://www.bos.frb.org/economic/nerr/katz97_1.htm. What evidence does Katz cite about how the rising value of time has affected consumer spending patterns?

19. *(Wall Street Journal)* In this chapter, you learned that the cost of consumption involves both a money price and a time price. Turn to the Wednesday *Wall Street Journal* and find the "Work and Family" column. See if you can find some examples of changes in new goods, services, government policies, or institutional arrangements that work by reducing the time price of a product. How do you think that change will affect the demand for the product? Will demand for any related products be affected?

Appendix

INDIFFERENCE CURVES AND UTILITY MAXIMIZATION

The approach used in the main part of the chapter, marginal utility analysis, requires some numerical measure of utility in order to determine the optimal bundle of goods and services. Economists have developed another, more general, approach to utility and consumer behavior, one that does not require that numbers be attached to specific levels of utility. All the new approach requires is that consumers be able to rank their preferences for various combinations of goods. For example, the consumer should be able to say whether combination A is preferred to combination B, combination B is preferred to combination A, or both combinations are equally preferred. This approach is more general and more flexible than the approach developed in the body of the chapter. We begin by examining consumer preferences.

CONSUMER PREFERENCES

Indifference curve analysis is an approach to the study of consumer behavior that does not require a numerical measure of utility. An **indifference curve** shows all combinations of goods that provide the consumer with the same satisfaction, or the same utility. Thus the consumer finds all combinations on a curve equally preferred. Since each of the alternative bundles of goods yields the same level of utility, the consumer is *indifferent* about which combination is actually consumed. We can best explain the use of indifference curves through the following example.

In reality consumers choose from among thousands of goods and services, but to keep the analysis manageable, suppose there are only two goods available: pizzas and movie videos. In Exhibit 9, the horizontal axis measures the quantity of pizzas you consume per week, and the vertical axis measures the quantity of videos you rent per week. Point *a,* for example, shows the consumption bundle consisting of 1 pizza and 8 video rentals. Suppose you are given a choice of the combination at point *a* or some other combination along the curve. The question is: Holding your total utility constant, how many video rentals would you be willing to give up to get a second pizza? As we can see, in moving from point *a* to point *b,* you are willing to give up 4 videos to get a second pizza. Total utility is the same at points *a* and *b.* The marginal utility of that additional pizza per week is just sufficient to compensate you for the utility lost from decreasing your video watching by 4 movies per week. Thus, at point *b,* you are eating 2 pizzas and watching 4 movies a week and are indifferent between this combination and the combination represented by point *a,* since total utility is the same at both points.

EXHIBIT 9

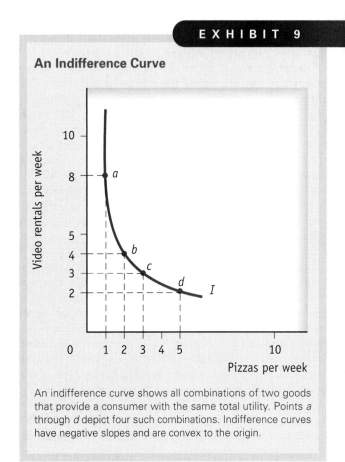

An Indifference Curve

An indifference curve shows all combinations of two goods that provide a consumer with the same total utility. Points *a* through *d* depict four such combinations. Indifference curves have negative slopes and are convex to the origin.

In moving from point *b* to point *c,* again total utility is constant; you are now willing to give up only 1 video to get another pizza. At point *c,* your consumption bundle consists of 3 pizzas and 3 videos. Once at point *c,* you are willing to give up another video only if you get two more pizzas in return. Combination *d* therefore consists of 5 pizzas and 2 videos.

Points *a, b, c,* and *d* are connected to form an indifference curve, *I,* which represents possible combinations of pizza and videos that would keep you at the same level of total utility. Since points on the curve offer the same total utility, you are indifferent among them—hence the name *indifference curve.* Note that we don't know, nor do we need to know, the value you attach to the utility reflected by the indifference curve—that is, there is no particular number attached to the total utility along *I. Combinations of goods along an indifference curve reflect some constant, though unspecified, level of total utility.*

For you to remain indifferent among consumption combinations, the decrease in your utility from watching fewer videos must be just offset by the increase in your utility from eating more pizza. Thus, along an indifference curve, there is an inverse relationship between the quantity of one good consumed and the quantity of another consumed. Because of this inverse relationship, *indifference curves slope downward.*

Indifference curves are also *convex to the origin,* which means that they are bowed inward toward the origin. The curve gets flatter as you move down it. Here is why. Your willingness to substitute pizza for videos depends on how much of each is in your current consumption bundle. At combination *a,* for example, you rent 8 videos and eat only 1 pizza, so there are many videos relative to pizza. Because movies are relatively abundant in your consumption bundle, you are willing to give up watching 4 movies to get another pizza. Once you reach point *b,* your pizza consumption has doubled, so you are not quite so willing to give up movie-watching to get a third pizza. In fact, you will forgo only 1 video to get 1 more pizza. This moves you from point *b* to point *c.*

The **marginal rate of substitution,** or **MRS,** between pizza and video rentals indicates the number of videos that you are willing to give up to get one more pizza, neither gaining nor losing utility in the process. Because the MRS measures your willingness to trade videos for pizza, it depends on the amount of each good you already have at the time. Mathematically, the MRS is equal to the absolute value of the slope of the indifference curve. Recall that the slope of any line is the vertical change between two points on the line divided by the corresponding horizontal change. For example, in moving from combination *a* to combination *b* in Exhibit 9, you are willing to give up 4 videos to get 1 more pizza; the slope between those two points equals -4, so the MRS is 4. In the move from *b* to *c,* the slope is -1, so the MRS is 1. And from *c* to *d,* the slope is $-\frac{1}{2}$, so the MRS is $\frac{1}{2}$.

The **law of diminishing marginal rate of substitution** says that as your consumption of pizza increases, the number of videos that you are willing to give up to get another pizza declines. This law applies to most pairs of goods. Because your marginal rate of substitution of videos for pizza declines as your pizza consumption increases, the indifference curve has a diminishing slope, meaning that it is convex when viewed from the origin. As you move down the indifference curve, your pizza consumption increases, so your marginal utility of additional pizza decreases. Conversely, the number of movies you rent decreases so your marginal utility of movies increases. Thus, in moving down the indifference curve, you require more pizza to offset the loss of each video.

We have focused on a single indifference curve, which indicates some constant but unspecified level of utility. We can use the same approach to generate a series of indifference

curves, called an **indifference map**. An indifference map is a graphical representation of a consumer's tastes. Each curve in the indifference map reflects a different level of utility. Part of such a map is shown in Exhibit 10, where indifference curves for a particular consumer, in this case you, are labeled I_1, I_2, I_3, and I_4. Each consumer has a unique indifference map based on his or her preferences.

Because both goods yield utility, you, the consumer, prefer more of each, rather than less. Thus, curves farther from the origin represent greater consumption levels and, therefore, higher levels of total utility. The total utility level along I_2 is higher than that along I_1. I_3 reflects a higher level of utility than I_2, and so on. We can show this best by drawing a ray from the origin and following it to higher indifference curves. Such a ray has been included in Exhibit 10. By following that ray to higher and higher indifference curves, we can see that the combination on each successive indifference curve reflects greater amounts of *both* goods. Since you value both goods, the greater amounts of each good reflected on higher indifference curves represent higher levels of utility.

Indifference curves in a consumer's indifference map do not intersect. Exhibit 11 shows why. If indifference curves crossed, as at point *i,* then every point on indifference

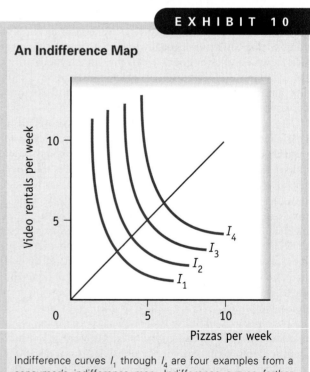

An Indifference Map

Indifference curves I_1 through I_4 are four examples from a consumer's indifference map. Indifference curves farther from the origin depict higher levels of utility. A ray intersects each higher indifference curve, reflecting more of both goods.

EXHIBIT 11

Indifference Curves Do Not Intersect

If indifference curves crossed, as at point *i*, then every point on indifference curve *I* and every point on curve *I'* would have to reflect the same level of utility as at point *i*. But point *k* is a combination with more pizza and more videos than point *j* and so must represent a higher level of utility. This contradiction means that indifference curves cannot intersect.

THE BUDGET LINE

The **budget line** depicts all possible combinations of pizza purchases and movie rentals, given prices of pizzas and videos and your budget. Suppose a pizza sells for $8, movies rent for $4, and your budget, or income, for these items is $40 per week. If you spend the entire $40 on videos, you can afford to watch 10 videos per week. Alternatively, if you spend the entire $40 on pizzas, you can afford to eat 5 per week. In Exhibit 12, your budget line meets the vertical axis at 10 video rentals and meets the horizontal axis at 5 pizzas. We can connect the axis intercepts to form the budget line. You can purchase any combination on your budget line, or your budget constraint. You might think of the budget line as your *consumption possibilities frontier*.

Let's find the slope of the budget line. At the point where the budget line meets the vertical axis, the maximum number of videos you can rent equals your income divided by the video rental price, or I/p_v, where I is income and p_v is the rental price. At the point where the budget line meets the horizontal axis, the maximum quantity of pizzas that you can

curve *I* and every point on curve *I'* would have to reflect the same level of utility as at point *i*. But point *k* in Exhibit 11 is a combination with more pizza and more videos than point *j* and so must represent a higher level of utility. This contradiction means that indifference curves cannot intersect.

Let's summarize the properties of indifference curves.

1. *A particular indifference curve reflects a constant level of utility, so the consumer is indifferent among all consumption combinations along a given curve.*
2. *If total utility is to remain constant, an increase in the consumption of one good must be offset by a decrease in the consumption of the other good, so each indifference curve slopes downward.*
3. *Because of the law of diminishing marginal rate of substitution, indifference curves are bowed in toward the origin.*
4. *Higher indifference curves represent higher levels of utility.*
5. *Indifference curves do not intersect.*

Given a consumer's indifference map, how much of each good will be consumed? To determine that, we must consider the relative prices of the goods and the consumer's income. In the next section we focus on the consumer's budget.

EXHIBIT 12

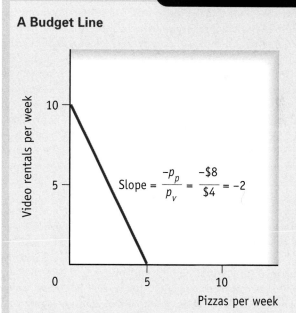

A Budget Line

$$\text{Slope} = \frac{-p_p}{p_v} = \frac{-\$8}{\$4} = -2$$

The budget line shows all combinations of pizza and videos that can be purchased at fixed prices with a given amount of income. If all income is spent on vidoes, 10 can be purchased. If all income is spent on pizzas, 5 can be purchased. Points between the vertical intercept and the horizontal intercept represent combinations of some pizza and some videos. The slope of the budget line is −2, illustrating that the cost of 1 pizza is 2 videos.

purchase equals your income divided by the price of a pizza, or I/p_p, where p_p is the price of pizza. The slope of the budget line between the vertical intercept in Exhibit 12 and the horizontal intercept equals the vertical change, or $-I/p_v$, divided by the horizontal change, or I/p_p:

$$\text{Slope of budget line} = -\frac{I/p_v}{I/p_p} = -\frac{p_p}{p_v}$$

In our example it is $-\$8/\$4$, which equals -2. The slope of the budget line indicates what it costs you in terms of forgone video rentals to get another pizza. You must give up 2 videos for each additional pizza. *Note that the income term cancels out, so the slope of a budget line depends only on relative prices, not on the level of income.*

The indifference curve indicates what you are *willing* to buy. The budget line shows what you are *able* to buy. We must therefore bring together the indifference curve and the budget line to find out what quantities of each good you are both *willing* and *able* to buy.

CONSUMER EQUILIBRIUM AT THE TANGENCY

As always, the objective of consumption is to maximize utility. We know that indifference curves farther from the origin represent higher levels of utility. You, as a utility-maximizing consumer, therefore will select a combination along the budget line in Exhibit 13 that lies on the highest attainable indifference curve. Given prices and income, you maximize utility at the combination of pizza and videos depicted by point e in Exhibit 13, where indifference curve I_2 just touches, or *is tangent to*, your budget line. At point e, you buy 3 pizzas at $\$8$ each and rent 4 videos at $\$4$ each. You thereby spend your budget of $\$40$ per week. Other attainable combinations along the budget line reflect lower levels of utility. For example, point a is on the budget line and is therefore a combination you are *able* to purchase, but a is on a lower indifference curve, I_1. Other, "better," indifference curves, such as I_3, lie completely above the budget line and are thus unattainable.

Since you maximize your utility at point e, that combination becomes an equilibrium outcome. Note that the indifference curve is tangent to the budget line at the equilibrium point, and at the point of tangency the slope of a curve equals the slope of a line drawn tangent to that curve. At point e, the slope of the indifference curve equals the slope of the budget line. Recall that the absolute value of the slope of the indifference curve is your marginal rate of substitution, and the absolute value of the slope of the budget line equals the price ratio. In equilibrium, therefore, your marginal rate of substitution between video rentals and pizza, MRS, must equal the ratio of the price of pizza to the price of video rentals, or

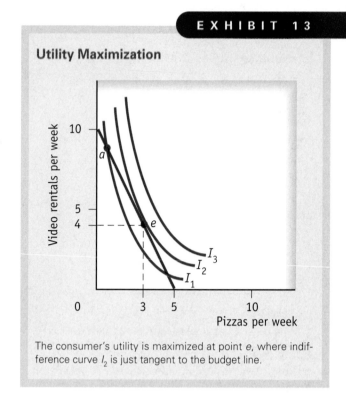

EXHIBIT   13

Utility Maximization

The consumer's utility is maximized at point e, where indifference curve I_2 is just tangent to the budget line.

$$\text{MRS} = \frac{p_p}{p_v}$$

What is the relationship between indifference curve analysis and the marginal utility theory introduced in the chapter? The marginal rate of substitution of pizza for video rentals can also be found from the marginal utilities of pizza and videos presented in the chapter. Exhibit 3 indicated that, at the consumer equilibrium, the marginal utility you derived from the third pizza was 24 and the marginal utility you derived by the fourth video was 12. Since the marginal utility of pizza (MU_p) is 24 and the marginal utility of videos (MU_v) is 12, in moving to that equilibrium, you were willing to give up 2 videos to get 1 more pizza. Thus, the marginal rate of substitution of pizza for videos equals the ratio of pizza's marginal utility (MU_p) to video's marginal utility (MU_v), or

$$\text{MRS} = \frac{MU_p}{MU_v}$$

In fact, the absolute value of the slope of the indifference curve equals MU_p/MU_v. Since the absolute value of the slope of the budget line equals p_p/p_v, the equilibrium condition for the indifference curve approach can be written as

$$\frac{MU_p}{p_p} = \frac{MU_v}{p_v}$$

This equation is the same equilibrium condition for utility maximization presented in the chapter using marginal utility analysis. The equality says that in equilibrium—that is, when the consumer maximizes total utility—the last dollar spent on each good yields the same marginal utility. If this equality does not hold, the consumer can increase total utility by adjusting consumption until the equality occurs.

EFFECTS OF A CHANGE IN PRICE

What happens to your equilibrium consumption when there is a change in price? The answer can be found by deriving the demand curve. We begin at point *e,* our initial equilibrium, in panel (a) of Exhibit 14. At point *e,* you eat 3 pizzas

EXHIBIT 14

Effect of a Drop in the Price of Pizza

A reduction in the price of pizza rotates the budget line outward in panel (a). The consumer is back in equilibrium at point *e"* along the new budget line. Panel (b) shows that a drop in the price of pizza from $8 per unit to $6 per unit leads to an increase in quantity demanded from 3 to 4. Price and quantity demanded are inversely related.

and watch four videos per week. Suppose that the price of pizzas falls from $8 to $6 per unit, other things constant. The price drop means that if the entire budget were devoted to pizza, you could purchase 6.67 pizzas (40/6). Since the rental price of videos has not changed, however, 10 remains the maximum number you can rent. Thus the budget line's vertical intercept remains fixed at 10 videos, but the lower end of the budget line rotates out.

After the price of pizza changes, the new equilibrium position occurs at *e"*, where pizza purchases increase from 3 to 4, and, as it happens, video rentals remains at 4. Thus, price and the quantity of pizza demanded are inversely related. The demand curve in panel (b) of Exhibit 14 shows how price and quantity demanded are related. Specifically, when the price of pizza falls from $8 per unit to $6 per unit, other things constant, your quantity demanded increases from 3 to 4. Since you are on a higher indifference curve at *e"*, you are clearly better off after the price reduction (your consumer surplus has increased).

INCOME AND SUBSTITUTION EFFECTS

The law of demand was originally explained in terms of an income effect and a substitution effect. You now have the analytical tools to examine these two effects more precisely. Suppose the price of pizza falls from $8 to $4, other things constant. You can now purchase a maximum of 10 pizzas with a budget of $40 per week. As shown in Exhibit 15, the budget line intercept rotates out from 5 to 10 pizzas. After the price change, the quantity of pizzas demanded increases from 3 to 5. The increase in utility shows that you benefit from the price decrease.

The increase in the quantity of pizzas demanded can be broken down into the substitution effect and the income effect of a price change. When the price of pizza falls, the change in the ratio of the price of pizza to the price of video rentals shows up through the change in the slope of the budget line. In order to derive the substitution effect, let's assume that you must maintain the same level of utility after the price change as before. In other words, let's suppose your utility level has not yet changed but the relative prices you face have changed. We want to learn how you would adjust to the price change. A new budget line reflecting just the change in relative prices, not a change in utility, is shown by the dashed line, *CF*, in Exhibit 15. Given the new set of relative prices, you would increase the quantity of pizzas demanded to the point on indifference curve *I* where the indifference curve is just tangent the dashed budget line. That tangency keeps utility at the initial level but reflects the new set of relative prices. Thus we adjust your budget line to correspond to the new relative prices, but adjust your income level so that your utility remains unchanged.

EXHIBIT 15

Substitution and Income Effects of a Drop in the Price of Pizza from $8 to $4 Each

A reduction in the price of pizza moves the consumer from point *e* to point *e**. This movement can be decomposed into a substitution effect and an income effect. The substitution effect (from *e* to *e'*) reflects a reaction to a change in relative prices along the original indifference curve. The income effect (from *e'* to *e**) moves the consumer to a higher indifference curve at the new relative price ratio.

You move down along indifference curve *I* to point *e'*, renting fewer videos but buying more pizza. These changes in quantity demanded reflect the *substitution effect* of lower pizza prices. The substitution effect always increases the quantity demanded of the good whose price has dropped. Since consumption bundle *e'* represents the same level of utility as consumption bundle *e*, you are neither better off nor worse off at point *e'*.

But at point *e'*, you have not spent your full budget. The drop in the price of pizza has increased the quantity of pizza

you can buy, as shown by the expanded budget line that runs from 10 video rentals to 10 pizzas. Your *real income* has increased because of the lower price of pizza. As a result, you are able to attain point *e** on indifference curve *I**. At this point, you buy 5 pizzas and rent 5 videos. Because prices are held constant during the move from *e'* to *e**, the change in consumption is due solely to a change in real income. Thus, the change in the quantity of pizza demanded reflects the *income effect* of the lower pizza price.

We can now distinguish between the substitution effect and the income effect of a drop in the price of pizza. The substitution effect is shown by the move from point *e* to point *e'* in response to a change in the relative price of pizza, with your utility held constant along *I*. The income effect is shown by the move from *e'* to *e** in response to an increase in your real income, with relative prices held constant.

The overall effect of a change in the price of pizza is the sum of the substitution effect and the income effect. In our example, the substitution effect accounts for a one-unit increase in the quantity of pizza demanded, as does the income effect. Thus, the income and substitution effects combine to increase the quantity of pizza demanded by 2 units when the price falls from $8 to $4. The income effect is not always positive. For inferior goods, the income effect is negative, so as the price falls, the income effect can cause consumption to fall, offsetting part or even all of the substitution effect. Incidentally, notice that as a result of the increase in your real income, video rentals increase as well—from 4 to 5 rentals per week in our example, though it will not always be the case that the income effect is positive.

CONCLUSION

Indifference curve analysis does not require us to attach numerical values to particular levels of utility, as marginal utility theory does. The results of indifference curve analysis confirm the conclusions drawn from our simpler models. Indifference curves provide a logical way of viewing consumer choice, but consumers need not be aware of this approach in order to make rational choices. The purpose of the analysis in this chapter is to predict consumer behavior—not to advise consumers how to maximize utility.

APPENDIX QUESTIONS

1. *(Consumer Preferences)* The absolute value of the slope of an indifference curve equals the marginal rate of substitution. If two goods were *perfectly* substitutable, what would the indifference curves look like? Explain.

2. *(Effects of a Change in Price)* Chris has an income of $90 to allocate between Goods A and B. Initially, the price of A is $3 and the price of B is $4.
   a. Draw Chris's budget line, indicating its slope if units of A are measured on the horizontal axis and units of B are on the vertical axis.
   b. Add an indifference curve to your graph and label the point of consumer equilibrium. Indicate Chris's consumption levels of A and B. Why is this a consumer equilibrium?
   c. Now assume that the price of A rises to $4. Draw the new budget line, a new point of consumer equilibrium, and the consumption levels of Goods A and B. What is Chris's marginal rate of substitution at the new equilibrium point?
   d. Draw the demand curve for good A, labeling the different price and quantity demanded combinations determined in parts (b) and (c).

Production and Cost in the Firm

Visit the McEachern
Interactive Study Center
for this chapter at
http://mcisc.swcollege.com

Why is fast food is so fast? Why do too many cooks spoil the broth? Why do movie theaters have so many screens? Why don't they add even more? If you go into business for yourself, how much must you earn just to break even? Why might your grade point average fall even though your grades improved from the previous term? Answers to these and other questions are discovered in this chapter, which introduces production and cost in the firm.

The previous chapter explored the consumer behavior underlying the demand curve. This chapter examines the producer behavior underlying the supply curve. More specifically, we will examine a firm's production and cost of operation as a prelude to our analysis of supply. In the previous chapter, you were asked to think like a consumer, or demander. In this chapter, you must think like a producer, or supplier. You may feel more natural as a consumer (after all, you *are* a consumer), but you know more about producers than you may realize. You have been around producers all your life—bookstores, video stores, department stores, grocery stores, doughnut shops, convenience stores, dry cleaners, gas stations, auto dealers, restaurants, farms, factories, offices, and thousands of other producers in the *Yellow Pages* and on the Internet.

Although you may not yet have been a producer yourself, you already have some idea how businesses operate. They all have the same goal: *maximum profit.* Profit equals revenue minus cost. In this chapter we introduce the cost side of the profit equation. Topics discussed in this chapter include:

- Explicit and implicit costs
- Economic and normal profit
- Increasing and diminishing returns
- Short-run costs
- Long-run costs
- Economies and diseconomies of scale

COST AND PROFIT

When we examined demand, we assumed that consumers try to maximize utility, a goal that provides the motivation for consumer behavior. When we turn to supply, we assume that producers try to maximize *profit*—that is, the difference between the total revenue from the sale of output and the opportunity cost of resources. Over time, the firms that survive and grow are those that are the most profitable. Firms that are unprofitable year after year eventually fail.

Firms transform inputs or resources into outputs or products to earn a profit. Each year throughout the world, millions of new firms enter the marketplace, and nearly as many leave. The firm's decision makers must choose what goods and services to produce and what resources to employ. They must make plans while confronting uncertainty about consumer demand, resource availability, and the intentions of other firms in the market. *The lure of profit is so strong, however, that eager entrepreneurs are always ready to pursue their dreams.*

Explicit and Implicit Costs

To hire resources, producers must pay resource owners at least their *opportunity cost*—that is, what the resources could earn in their best alternative use. For resources purchased in resource markets, the corresponding cash payments approximate the opportunity cost. For example, the $3 per pound that Domino's Pizza pays for cheese reflects a price the cheese supplier could get elsewhere. Some resources, however, are owned by the firm (or the firm's owners), so there are no direct cash payments for their use. For example, the firm pays no rent to operate in a company-owned building. Similarly, the owner and operator of the corner dry cleaner usually does not pay himself or herself an hourly wage. But these resources are not free. *Whether resources are hired in resource markets or owned by the firm, resources have an opportunity cost.* The company-owned building could likely be sold or rented to another user; the dry cleaner could find another job.

A firm's **explicit costs** are its actual cash payments for resources purchased in resource markets: wages, rent, interest, insurance, taxes, and the like. In addition to these direct cash outlays, or explicit costs, the firm also faces **implicit costs,** which are the opportunity costs of using resources owned by the firm or

Explicit cost Opportunity cost of a firm's resources that takes the form of cash payments

Implicit cost A firm's opportunity cost of using its own resources or those provided by its owners without a corresponding cash payment provided by the firm's owners. Examples include the use of a company-owned building, use of company funds, or the time of the firm's owners. Like explicit costs, implicit costs are opportunity costs. But unlike explicit costs, implicit costs require no cash payment and no entry in the firm's *accounting statement,* which records its revenues, explicit costs, and accounting profit.

Alternative Measures of Profit

A particular example may help clarify the distinction between implicit and explicit costs. Meet Wanda Wheeler, an aeronautical engineer who earns $40,000 a year working for the Skyhigh Aircraft Company. On her way home from work one day, she gets an idea for a rounder, more friction-resistant airplane wheel. She decides to quit her job and start a business, which she calls Wheeler Dealer. To buy the necessary machines and equipment, she withdraws savings of $20,000 from her bank account, where it had been earning interest of $1,000 a year. She hires an assistant and starts producing the wheel in a spare bay in her garage, a bay that she had been renting to a neighbor for $100 per month.

Sales are slow at first—people keep telling her she is just trying to reinvent the wheel—but her wheel eventually gets rolling. When Wanda and her accountant examine the firm's performance after the first year, they are quite pleased. As you can see in the top part of Exhibit 1, company revenue in 1999 was $95,000. After paying the assistant's salary and the cost of materials and equipment, the firm shows an accounting profit of $54,000. **Accounting profit** equals total revenue minus explicit costs. This is the profit used by accountants to determine a firm's taxable income.

Accounting profit A firm's total revenue minus its explicit cost

But accounting profit ignores the opportunity cost of Wanda's own resources used in the firm. First is the opportunity cost of her time. Remember, she quit a $40,000-a-year job to work full time on her business, thereby forgoing that salary. Second is the $1,000 annual interest she passes up by financing the operation with her own savings. And third, by using the spare bay in her garage for the business, she forgoes $1,200 per year in rental income. The forgone salary, interest, and rental income are implicit costs because, although Wanda makes no explicit payment for the resources, she no longer earns income generated from

EXHIBIT 1

Accounts of Wheeler Dealer, 1999

Total revenue		$95,000
Less explicit costs:		
Assistant's salary	−21,000	
Material and equipment	−20,000	
Equals accounting profit		$54,000
Less implicit costs:		
Wanda's forgone salary	−$40,000	
Forgone interest on savings	−1,000	
Forgone garage rental	−1,200	
Equals economic profit		$11,800

their best alternative uses. **Economic profit** equals total revenue minus all costs, both implicit and explicit; *economic profit takes into account the opportunity cost of all resources used in production.* In Exhibit 1, accounting profit of $54,000 less implicit costs of $42,200 equals economic profit of $11,800.

What would happen to the accounting statement if Wanda decided to pay herself a salary of $40,000 per year? Explicit costs would increase by $40,000, implicit costs would decrease by $40,000, and accounting profit would decrease by $40,000. Economic profit would not change, however, since it already reflects both implicit and explicit costs.

There is one other important profit measure to consider: the accounting profit required to induce the firm's owners to employ their resources in the firm. The accounting profit just sufficient to ensure that *all* resources used by the firm earn their opportunity cost is called a **normal profit.** Wanda's firm earns a normal profit when accounting profit equals the sum of the salary she gave up at her regular job ($40,000), the interest she gave up by using her own savings ($1,000), and the rent she gave up on her garage ($1,200). Thus, if the accounting profit is $42,200 per year—the opportunity cost of resources Wanda supplies to the firm—the company earns a normal profit. *Any accounting profit in excess of a normal profit is economic profit.*

If accounting profit is large enough, it can be divided into normal profit and economic profit. The $54,000 in accounting profit earned by Wanda's firm consists of (1) a normal profit of $42,200, which just covers the opportunity cost of Wanda's resources supplied to the firm, and (2) an economic profit of $11,800, which is over and above what these resources could earn in their best alternative use. As long as economic profit is positive, Wanda is better off running her own firm than working for the Skyhigh Aircraft Company. If total revenue had been only $50,000, accounting profit of only $9,000 would cover less than one-fourth of Wanda's salary, to say nothing of her forgone rent and interest. Since Wanda would not be earning even a normal profit, she would be better off back in her old job.

To understand profit maximization, you must develop a feel for both revenue and cost. In this chapter, we will begin learning about the cost of production, beginning first with the relationship between inputs and outputs.

Economic profit A firm's total revenue minus its explicit and implicit costs

Normal profit The accounting profit required to persuade a firm's owners to employ their resources in the firm; the accounting profit earned when all resources used by the firm earn their opportunity cost

PRODUCTION IN THE SHORT RUN

We shift now from a discussion of profit to a discussion of how firms operate. Suppose a new McDonald's has just opened in your neighborhood and business is booming far beyond expectations. The manager responds to the unexpected demand by quickly hiring more workers. But cars are still backed up into the street waiting for a parking space. The solution is to add a drive-through window, but such an expansion takes time.

Fixed and Variable Resources

Some resources, such as labor, are called **variable resources** because they can be varied quickly to change the output rate. Adjustments in some other resources, however, take more time. The size of the building, for example, cannot easily be altered. Such resources are therefore called **fixed resources.** When considering the time required to alter the quantity of resources employed,

Variable resource Any resource that can be varied in the short run to increase or decrease the rate of output

Fixed resource Any resource that cannot be varied in the short run

Short run A period during which at least one of a firm's resources is fixed

Long run A period during which all resources under the firm's control are variable

economists distinguish between the short run and the long run. In the **short run,** at least one resource is fixed. In the **long run,** no resource is fixed.

Output can be changed in the short run by adjusting variable resources, but the size, or *scale,* of the firm is fixed in the short run. In the long run, however, all resources can vary. The length of the long run differs from industry to industry because the nature of the production process differs. For example, the size of a McDonald's restaurant can be increased more quickly than can the size of an electric power plant. Thus, the long run for McDonald's is shorter than the long run for an electric company. As the length of time required to plan and construct a new building increases, so does the length of the long run.

The Law of Diminishing Marginal Returns

Let's focus on the short-run link between resource use and the rate of production by considering a hypothetical moving company called Smoother Mover. Suppose the company's fixed resources are already in place and consist of a warehouse, a moving van, and moving equipment. In this example, labor will be the only variable resource.

Exhibit 2 relates the amount of labor employed to the amount of output produced. Labor is measured in worker-days, which is one worker for one day, and output is measured in tons of furniture moved per day. The column to the left shows the amount of labor employed, which ranges from 0 to 8. The center column shows the tons of furniture moved, or the **total product**, at each rate of employment. The relationship between the amount of resources employed and total product is called the firm's *production function.* The right column shows the **marginal product** of each worker—that is, the amount by which the total product changes with each additional unit of labor, assuming all other resources remain unchanged. Spend a little time acquainting yourself with each column.

Increasing Marginal Returns. Without labor, nothing gets moved, so when the quantity of labor is 0, the total product is 0. Now look what happens when labor gets into the act. If only one worker is employed, that worker alone must do all

Total product The total output produced by a firm

Marginal product The change in total product that occurs when the use of a particular resource increases by one unit, all other resources constant

EXHIBIT 2

The Short-Run Relationship Between Units of Labor and Tons of Furniture Moved

Units of the Variable Resource (worker-days)	Total Product (tons moved per day)	Marginal Product (tons moved per day)
0	0	—
1	2	2
2	5	3
3	9	4
4	12	3
5	14	2
6	15	1
7	15	0
8	14	−1

the driving, packing, crating, and moving. Some of the larger pieces of furniture, such as couches and beds, cannot easily be moved by one worker. Still, in our example one worker manages to move 2 tons of furniture per day.

When a second worker is hired, some division of labor in packing is possible, and two workers can lift the larger household items much more easily than just the one worker could, so total production more than doubles, reaching 5 tons per day. The marginal product resulting from adding a second worker is 3 tons per day. Adding a third worker allows for a better division of labor, which contributes to increased output. For example, one worker can specialize in packing fragile objects while the other two do the heavy lifting. The total product of three workers is 9 tons per day, which is 4 tons more than that of two workers. Because the marginal product increases, the firm experiences **increasing marginal returns** to labor as each of the first three workers is added. Marginal returns to labor increase because additional workers can specialize and can thereby make more efficient use of the fixed resources.

Diminishing Marginal Returns. The addition of a fourth worker adds to the total product, but not as much as was added by a third worker. Adding still more workers increases total product by successively smaller amounts, so the marginal product in Exhibit 2 declines after three workers. With four workers, the **law of diminishing marginal returns** takes hold. This law states that as additional quantities of the variable resource are combined with a given amount of fixed resources, a point is eventually reached where each additional unit of the variable resource yields a smaller marginal product. *The law of diminishing marginal returns is the most important feature of production in the short run.*

As additional units of the variable resource are added, total output may eventually turn negative. For example, when Smoother Mover hires eight workers per day, the working area becomes so crowded that workers get in each other's way. Transporting so many people to and from moving sites cuts into production because workers take up valuable space in the moving van. As a result, the total product actually declines if an eighth worker is added, so the marginal product turns negative. Likewise, a McDonald's outlet can add only so many workers before congestion in the work area causes marginal product to decline. As more workers are added, marginal product will at some point turn negative. ("Too many cooks spoil the broth.")

The Total and Marginal Product Curves

Panels (a) and (b) of Exhibit 3 illustrate the relationship between total product and marginal product, using the data from Exhibit 2. Note that because of increasing marginal returns, marginal product in panel (b) increases as each of the first three workers is added. With marginal product increasing, total product in panel (a) increases at an increasing rate (although this is hard to see). But when decreasing marginal returns set in, which occurs with the fourth worker, marginal product begins to decline. Total product continues to increase, although at a decreasing rate. As long as marginal product is positive, total product increases. At the output rate where marginal product turns negative, total product begins to decrease.

Note that Exhibit 3 sorts production into three ranges: increasing marginal returns, diminishing but positive marginal returns, and negative marginal returns. These ranges correspond with total product that increases at an increasing rate, total product that increases at a decreasing rate, and total product that declines.

Increasing marginal returns Marginal product increases experienced by a firm when another unit of a particular resource is employed, all other resources constant

Law of diminishing marginal returns When more and more of a variable resource is added to a given amount of a fixed resource, the resulting change in output will eventually diminish and could become negative

The Total and Marginal Product Labor

When marginal product is rising, total product is increasing by increasing amounts. When marginal product is decreasing but is still positive, total product is increasing by decreasing amounts. When marginal product equals 0, total product is at a maximum. Finally, when marginal product is negative, total product is falling.

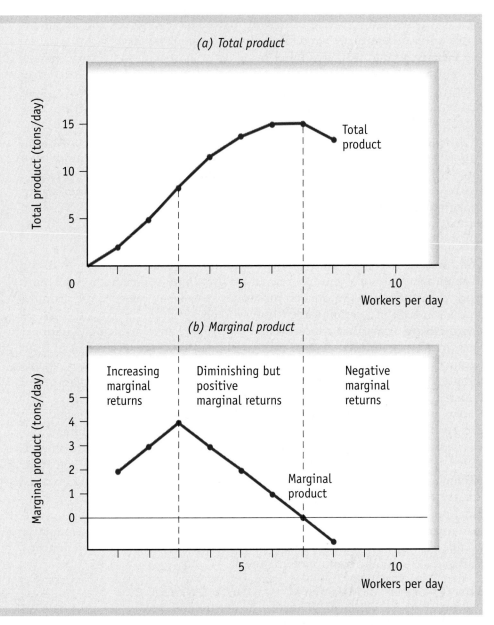

(a) Total product

(b) Marginal product

COSTS IN THE SHORT RUN

Now that we have examined the relationship between the amount of resources used and the rate of output, we can consider how the firm's cost of production varies as its rate of output varies. Short-run cost is divided into two categories: fixed cost and variable cost. Simply put, fixed cost is incurred for fixed resources and variable cost is incurred for variable resources. A firm must pay a **fixed cost** even if no output is produced. Even if Smoother Mover hires no labor and moves no furniture, it must pay for property taxes, insurance premiums, vehicle registration, and maintenance, plus principal and interest on any loans for its

Fixed cost Any production cost that is independent of the firm's rate of output warehouse, van, and equipment. By definition, fixed cost is just that: fixed—it does not vary with output in the short run. Another name for fixed cost is *sunk cost* because this cost is incurred in the short run even if the firm decides to produce nothing. Let's assume that the firm's *fixed cost* amounts to $200 per day.

Variable cost, as the name implies, is the cost of variable resources. When no variable resource is employed, output is 0, as is variable cost. As more variable resources are employed, output increases, as does variable cost. The amount by which variable cost increases depends on the amount of variable resources employed and the prices of those resources. In our example, variable cost consists of labor cost. Suppose the firm can hire labor at a cost of $100 per worker-day. This firm's *variable cost*, therefore, equals $100 times the quantity of labor employed.

Variable cost Any production cost that changes as output changes

Total Cost and Marginal Cost in the Short Run

Exhibit 4 presents cost data for Smoother Mover. The table lists the daily cost of production associated with alternative rates of output per day. Column (1) shows possible rates of output in the short run, measured in tons of furniture moved per day.

Total Cost. Column (2) indicates the fixed cost (*FC*) for each rate of output. Note that fixed cost remains constant at $200 per day regardless of the rate of output. Column (3) shows the amount of labor required to produce each rate of output and is based on the productivity measures reported in the previous two exhibits. (Only the first 6 units of labor are listed because units 7 and beyond added nothing to total product.) For example, moving 2 tons requires one worker, 5 tons requires two workers, and so on. Column (4) lists variable cost (*VC*) per day, which equals $100 times the number of workers. For example, the variable cost of moving 9 tons of furniture per day is $300, since three workers are employed. Column (5) lists the **total cost** (*TC*) of each rate of output, which is the sum of fixed cost and variable cost: $TC = FC + VC$. Note that at 0 units of output, variable cost is $0, so total cost equals only the fixed cost of $200. Since total cost is the opportunity cost of all resources employed by the firm, total cost includes a normal profit.

Total cost The sum of fixed cost and variable cost; the opportunity cost of all resources employed by the firm

EXHIBIT 4

Short-Run Cost Data for Smoother Mover

Tons Moved per Day (q) (1)	Fixed Cost (FC) (2)	Workers per Day (3)	Variable Cost (VC) (4)	Total Cost (TC = FC + VC) (5)	Marginal Cost $\left(MC = \dfrac{\Delta TC}{\Delta q} \right)$ (6)
0	$200	0	$ 0	$200	——
2	200	1	100	300	$ 50.00
5	200	2	200	400	33.33
9	200	3	300	500	25.00
12	200	4	400	600	33.33
14	200	5	500	700	50.00
15	200	6	600	800	100.00

Marginal cost The change in total cost resulting from a one-unit change in output; the change in total cost divided by the change in output

Marginal Cost. Of special interest to the firm is how total cost changes as output changes. More specifically, what is the marginal cost of producing another unit? The **marginal cost** of production listed in column (6) is simply the change in total cost divided by the change in output, or $MC = \Delta TC/\Delta q$, where Δ means "change in". For example, increasing output from 0 to 2 tons increases total cost by \$100 (= \$300 − \$200). The marginal cost of each of the first 2 tons is the change in total cost, \$100, divided by the change in output, 2 tons, or \$100/2, which equals \$50. The marginal cost of each of the next 3 tons is \$100/3, or \$33.33.

Notice in column (6) that marginal cost first decreases, then increases. *Changes in marginal cost reflect changes in the marginal productivity of the variable resource employed.* Recall from Exhibit 2 that the first three workers contributed to increasing marginal returns, with each additional worker producing more than the last. This greater productivity of labor results in a falling marginal cost for the output produced by the first three workers. As more labor is hired beyond three workers, however, the firm experiences diminishing marginal returns to labor, so the marginal cost of output increases. *When the firm experiences increasing marginal returns, the marginal cost of output decreases; when the firm experiences diminishing marginal returns, the marginal cost of output increases.*

Thus, the marginal cost in Exhibit 4 first falls and then rises, because of first increasing and then diminishing marginal returns. The labor employed by Smoother Mover shows increasing marginal returns for the first 9 tons of furniture moved and decreasing marginal returns thereafter.

Total and Marginal Cost Curves. Exhibit 5 shows the cost curves for the data in Exhibit 4. Since fixed cost does not vary with output, the fixed cost curve is a horizontal line at the \$200 level in panel (a). Variable cost is \$0 when output is 0, so the *variable cost curve* starts from the origin. For reasons that we will get to soon, variable cost increases slowly at first, then increases sharply. The *total cost curve* is derived by *vertically* summing the variable cost curve and the fixed cost curve. Because a constant amount of fixed cost is added to variable cost, the total cost curve is the variable cost curve shifted vertically by the amount of fixed cost.

We have already discussed the reasons for the pattern of marginal cost. In panel (b) of Exhibit 5, marginal cost declines until the ninth unit of output and then increases, reflecting labor's increasing and then diminishing marginal returns. There is a geometric relationship between panels (a) and (b) because the change in total cost resulting from a one-unit change in production equals the marginal cost. With each successive unit of output, the total cost increases by the marginal cost of that unit. Thus, *the slope of the total cost curve at each rate of output equals the marginal cost at that rate of output.* The total cost curve can be divided into two sections, based on what happens to marginal cost:

1. Because of increasing marginal returns from the variable resource, marginal cost at first declines, so total cost initially increases by successively smaller amounts and the total cost curve gets flatter.
2. Because of diminishing marginal returns from the variable resource, marginal cost begins to increase after the ninth unit of output, leading to a steeper total cost curve.

Keep in mind that economic analysis is marginal analysis. Marginal cost is key to economic decisions made by firms. The firm operating in the short run has

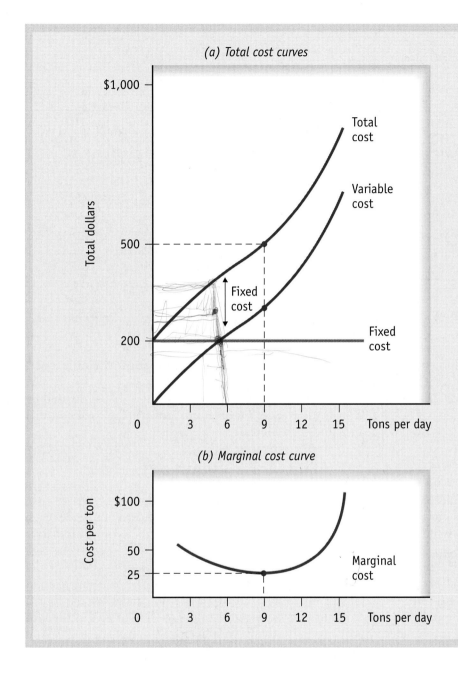

(a) Total cost curves

EXHIBIT 5

Total and Marginal Cost Curves for Smoother Mover

In panel (a), fixed cost is constant at all levels of output. Variable cost starts from the origin and increases slowly at first as output increases. When the variable resource generates diminishing marginal returns, variable cost begins to increase more rapidly. Total cost is the vertical sum of fixed cost and variable cost. In panel (b), marginal cost first declines, reflecting increasing marginal returns, and then increases, reflecting diminishing marginal returns.

(b) Marginal cost curve

no control over its fixed cost, but, by varying output in the short run, the firm alters its variable cost and hence its total cost. *Marginal cost indicates how much total cost will increase if one more unit is produced or how much total cost will drop if production is reduced by one unit.*

Average Cost in the Short Run

Although total cost and marginal cost are of the greatest analytical interest, the average cost per unit of output is also useful. There are average cost measures corresponding to variable cost and to total cost. These average costs are shown

EXHIBIT 6

Short-Run Cost Data for Smoother Mover

Tons Moved per Day (q) (1)	Variable Cost (VC) (2)	Total Cost $(TC = FC + VC)$ (3)	Marginal Cost $\left(MC = \dfrac{\Delta TC}{\Delta q}\right)$ (4)	Average Variable Cost $\left(AVC = \dfrac{VC}{q}\right)$ (5) = (2)/(1)	Average Total Cost $\left(ATC = \dfrac{TC}{q}\right)$ (6) = (3)/(1)
0	$ 0	$200	$ 0	——	∞
2	100	300	50.00	$50.00	$150.00
5	200	400	33.33	40.00	80.00
9	300	500	25.00	33.33	55.55
12	400	600	33.33	33.33	50.00
14	500	700	50.00	35.71	50.00
15	600	800	100.00	40.00	53.33

Average variable cost Variable cost divided by output

Average total cost Total cost divided by output

in columns (5) and (6) of Exhibit 6. Column (5) lists **average variable cost,** or AVC, which equals variable cost divided by output, or $AVC = VC/q$. The final column lists **average total cost,** or ATC, which is total cost divided by output, or $ATC = TC/q$. Both average variable cost and average total cost first decline as output expands and then increase.

The Relationship Between Marginal Cost and Average Cost

To understand the relationship between marginal cost and average variable cost, let's begin with an analogy of college grades. Think about how your grades each term, which we can think of as your marginal grades, affect your cumulative grade point average, or your average grades. Suppose you do well your first term, starting your college career with a grade point average of 3.4. Your grades for the second term drop to 2.8, reducing your average to 3.1. You slip again in the third term to 2.2, lowering your average to 2.8. Your grades for the fourth term improve a bit to 2.4, but your average continues to slide to 2.7. In the fifth term, your grades improve to 2.7, leaving your average unchanged at 2.7. And in the sixth term, you get a 3.3, boosting your average to 2.8.

Notice that when your term grades are below your average grades, your average falls. When your performance for the term improves, your average does not improve until your term grades *exceed* your average grades. Your term grades at first pull down your average and then pull up your average.

Let's now take a look at the relationship between marginal cost and average cost. In Exhibit 6, marginal cost has the same relationship to average cost as your term grades have to your grade point average. You can observe this marginal-average relationship in columns (4) and (5). Because of increasing marginal returns from the first three workers, the marginal cost falls for the first 9 tons of furniture moved. Where marginal cost is below average cost, marginal cost pulls

EXHIBIT 7

Average and Marginal Cost Curves for Smoother Mover

Average variable cost and average total cost drop, reach low points, and then rise; overall, they take on U shapes. When marginal cost is below average variable cost, average variable cost is falling. When marginal cost equals average variable cost, average variable cost is at its minimum value. When marginal cost is above average variable cost, average variable cost is increasing. The same relationship holds between marginal cost and average total cost.

down average cost. Marginal cost and average cost are equal where output equals 12 tons, and marginal cost exceeds average cost where output exceeds 12 tons, so marginal cost pulls up average cost.

Exhibit 7 shows the same marginal cost curve first presented in Exhibit 5, along with average cost curves based on data in Exhibit 6. At low rates of output, marginal cost declines as output expands because of increasing marginal returns. As long as marginal cost is below average cost, average cost falls as output expands. At higher rates of output, marginal cost increases because of diminishing marginal returns. Where marginal cost exceeds average cost, marginal cost pulls up the average. Because marginal cost first pulls down average cost and then pulls up average cost, this explains why the average cost curves have a U shape. The shape of the average variable cost curve and average total cost curve are determined by the shape of the marginal cost curve, and each is shaped by increasing and diminishing marginal returns.

Notice also that the rising marginal cost curve intersects both the average variable cost curve and the average total cost curve where these average curves are at their minimum. This occurs because the marginal pulls down the average where the marginal is below the average and pulls up the average where the marginal is above the average. One more thing: The distance between the average variable cost curve and the average total cost curve is *average fixed cost*, which gets smaller as the rate of output increases.

Summary of Short-Run Cost Curves

The law of diminishing marginal returns and the prices of resources determine the shape of short-run cost curves. The shape of the marginal product curve discussed earlier in the chapter determines the shape of the marginal cost curve. And the shape of the marginal product curve is determined by the law of diminishing marginal productivity, which is the relationship between the variable resource and output. Thus, the marginal cost curve depends ultimately on how much each unit of the variable resource, in this case labor, produces. When the marginal product of labor increases, the marginal cost of output must fall. Conversely, once diminishing marginal returns set in, the marginal cost of output must rise. Thus marginal cost first falls, then rises. And the marginal cost curve dictates the shapes of the average variable cost and average total cost curves. When marginal cost is less than average cost, average cost falls; when marginal cost is above average cost, average cost rises.

COSTS IN THE LONG RUN

Thus far our analysis has focused on how costs vary as the rate of output expands in the short run for a firm of a given size. In the long run, all inputs that are under the firm's control can be varied, so there is no fixed cost. The long run is not just a succession of short runs. The long run is best thought of as a *planning horizon*. In the long run, the choice of input combinations is flexible, but this flexibility is available only to a firm that has not yet acted on its plans. Firms plan for the long run, but they produce in the short run. Once the size of the plant has been selected and the concrete has been poured, the firm has fixed costs and is once again back in the short run. We turn now to long-run cost curves.

The Long-Run Average Cost Curve

Suppose that, because of the special nature of technology in the industry, a firm's plant can be one of only three possible sizes: small, medium, or large. Exhibit 8 presents this simple case. The short-run average total cost curves for the three

---

EXHIBIT 8

Short-Run Cost Curves and the Long-Run Planning Curve

Curves *SS'*, *MM'*, and *LL'* show short-run average total costs for smal, medium, and large plants, respectively. For output less than q_a average cost is lowest when the plant is small. Between q_a and q_b cost is lowest with a medium-size plant. If output exceeds q_b the large plant is best. The long-run average-cost curve is *SabL'*.

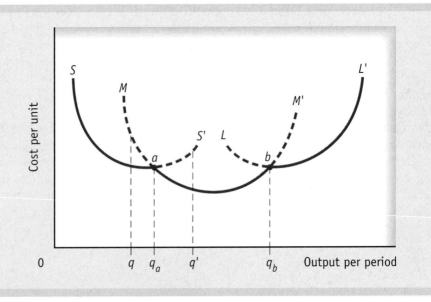

plant sizes are *SS'*, *MM'*, and *LL'*. Which size plant should the firm build to minimize the average cost of production? The appropriate size, or scale, for the plant depends on how much the firm wants to produce. For example, if q is the desired production rate in the long run, the average cost per unit will be lowest with a small plant. If the desired output rate is q', the medium plant size ensures the lowest average cost.

More generally, for any output less than q_a, average cost of output is lowest when the plant is small. For output rates between q_a and q_b, the average cost is lowest when the plant is of medium size. And for output rates that exceed q_b, the average cost is lowest when the plant is large. The **long-run average cost curve** connects portions of the three short-run average cost curves that are lowest for each output rate. In Exhibit 8, that curve consists of the line segments connecting *S*, *a*, *b*, and *L'*.

Now suppose there are many possible plant sizes. Exhibit 9 presents a sample of possible short-run average total cost curves. The long-run average cost curve is created by connecting the points on the various short-run average cost curves that represent the lowest per-unit cost for each rate of output. Each of the short-run cost curves is tangent to the long-run average cost curve, which is sometimes called the firm's *planning curve*, or *envelope curve*. An envelope curve is the long-run curve tangent to each of a family of short-run curves. If we could display enough short-run cost curves, we would have a different plant size for each rate of output. *These points of tangency represent the least-cost way of producing each particular rate of output, given the technology and resource prices.* For example, the short-run average cost curve ATC_1 is tangent to the planning curve at point *a*, indicating that the least-cost way of producing output rate q is with the plant size associated with ATC_1. No other size plant would produce output rate q at as low a cost per unit. Note, however, that other output rates along ATC_1

Long-run average cost curve A curve that indicates the lowest average cost of production at each rate of output when the firm's size is allowed to vary; also called the planning curve and the envelope curve

EXHIBIT 9

Family of Many Short-Run Cost Curves Forming a Firm's Long-Run Planning Curve

With many possible plant sizes, the long-run average cost curve is the envelope of portions of the short-run average cost curves. Each short-run curve is tangent to the long-run average cost curve, or long-run planning curve. Each point of tangency represents the least-cost way of producing a particular level of output.

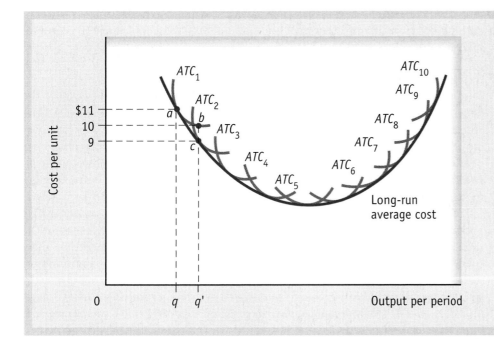

have a lower average cost of production. In fact, for output rate q' at point b, the average cost per unit is only $10, compared to an average cost per unit of $11 for producing q at point a. Point b depicts the lowest average cost along ATC_1. So although the point of tangency represents the least-cost way of producing a particular rate of output, it does not in this case represent a least-cost output rate for this particular plant size.

If the firm decides to produce output rate q', which size plant should it choose to minimize the average cost of production? Output rate q' could be produced at point b, which represents the minimum average cost along ATC_1. However, the firm could achieve a lower average cost with a larger plant. Specifically, if the firm built a plant of the size associated with ATC_2, the average cost of producing q' would be minimized at $9 per unit at point c. *Each point of tangency between a short-run average cost curve and the long-run average cost curve, or planning curve, represents the least-cost way of producing that particular rate of output.*

Economies of Scale

Economies of scale Forces that cause a reduction in a firm's average cost as the scale of operation increases in the long run

Like short-run average cost curves, the long-run average cost curve is U-shaped. Recall that the shape of the short-run average total cost curve is determined primarily by the law of diminishing marginal returns. A different principle shapes the long-run cost curve. A firm experiences **economies of scale** if long-run average cost falls as output expands. Consider some sources of economies of scale. *A larger size often allows for larger, more specialized machines and greater specialization of labor.* For example, compare a household-sized kitchen of a small restaurant with the kitchen at McDonald's. At low rates of output, say 15 meals a day, the smaller kitchen produces meals at a lower average cost than does McDonald's. But if production in the smaller kitchen increases beyond, say, 100 meals per day, a kitchen on the scale of McDonald's would have a lower average cost. Thus, because of economies of scale, the long-run average cost for a restaurant may fall as firm size increases. A larger scale of operation allows firms to employ larger, more efficient, machines and allows workers a greater degree of specialization.

Diseconomies of Scale

Diseconomies of scale Forces that cause a firm's average cost to increase as the scale of operation increases in the long run

Often another force, called **diseconomies of scale**, eventually takes over as the firm expands, increasing long-run average cost as output expands. As the amount and variety of resources employed increase, so does the *task of coordinating all these inputs.* As the work force grows, additional layers of management are needed to monitor production. In the thicket of bureaucracy that develops, *communication may become garbled.* The top executives have more difficulty keeping in touch with the shop floor because information is distorted as it passes through the chain of command. Indeed, in very large organizations, rumors may become a primary source of information, thereby reducing the efficiency of the organization and increasing average cost. For example, IBM undertook a massive restructuring program because the firm was experiencing diseconomies of scale, particularly in management. IBM's solution was to decentralize into six smaller decision-making groups. *Note that diseconomies of scale result from a larger firm size, whereas diminishing marginal returns result from using more variable resources in a firm of a given size.*

In the long run, the firm can vary the inputs under its control. Some inputs, however, are not under the firm's control, and the inability to vary these inputs may be a source of diseconomies of scale. Consider economies and diseconomies of scale at the movies in the following case study.

At the Movies

Movie theaters experience both economies and diseconomies of scale. A movie theater with one screen needs someone to sell tickets, someone to operate the concession stand (concession stand sales, incidentally, account for well over half the profit at most theaters), and someone to operate the projector. If another screen is added, the same staff can perform these tasks for both screens. Thus the ticket seller becomes more productive by selling tickets for both movies. Furthermore, construction costs per screen are reduced because only one lobby and one set of rest rooms are required. The theater can run bigger, more noticeable, newspaper advertisements and can spread the cost over more films. This is why we see theater owners adding more and more screens at the same location; they are taking advantage of economies of scale. In the last decade the number of screens in the United States increased from 18,000 to 27,000, or by 50 percent, a rate of increase that exceeded the growth rate in the number of theater locations.

But why stop at, say, 12 screens per movie theater? Why not 20 or 30 screens, particularly in thickly populated urban areas with sufficient demand for such a high rate of output? One problem with expanding the number of screens is that the public roads leading to the theaters are a resource that theaters cannot control. The congestion around the theater grows with the number of screens at that location. Also, the supply of popular films may not be sufficiently large at any one time to fill so many screens.

Finally, time itself is a resource that the firm cannot easily control. Only certain hours are popular with moviegoers. Scheduling becomes more difficult because the manager must space out starting and ending times to avoid the road congestion that occurs when too many customers arrive and depart at the same time. No more additional "prime time" can be created. Thus theater owners lack control over such inputs as the size of public roads, the supply of films, and the amount of "prime time" in the day, and this lack of control may contribute to an increase in the long-run average cost as output expands, or to diseconomies of scale.

Sources: Leonard Klady, "Theaters Scramble to Fit in Summer Pix," *Variety* (6 August 1995); Bruce Orwall, "Cineplex-Leows Merger Is Backed By Regulators, with Theater Sales," *Wall Street Journal* (17 April 1998); William Echikson, "Europe's Film Industry Could Use a Dose of Realism," *Business Week*, International Edition (9 March 1998); and *Statistical Abstract of the United States 1997*, Bureau of the Census, (Hoover's Business Press, 1997), Tables 408 and 418.

CaseStudy

The World of Business

With substantial economies of scale in the movie theater industry, a few chains now operate thousands of theaters. Their corporate Web sites provide information on current plans and include histories of how they grew to be so large. Browse through the following sites: AMC theatres at http://www.amctheatres.com/amc_info/index.html, General Cinema at http://www.generalcinema.com/default.asp?ID=0801, and Regal Cinemas at http://www.regalcinemas.com/corporate/facts.html. Can you find the average number of screens per theater for each corporation? What is a megaplex? Where can megaplexes be found?

It is possible for average cost to neither increase nor decrease with changes in firm size. If neither economies of scale nor diseconomies of scale are apparent, the firm experiences *constant long-run average costs*. Perhaps economies and diseconomies of scale exist simultaneously in such a firm but have offsetting effects.

EXHIBIT 10

A Firm's Long-Run Average Cost Curve

Up to output level *A*, the long-run average cost curve has a negative slope; the firm is experiencing economies of scale. Output level *A* is the minimum efficient scale—the lowest rate of output at which the firm takes full advantage of economies of scale. Between *A* and *B*, the average cost is constant. Beyond output level *B*, the long-run average cost curve has a positive slope, reflecting diseconomies of scale.

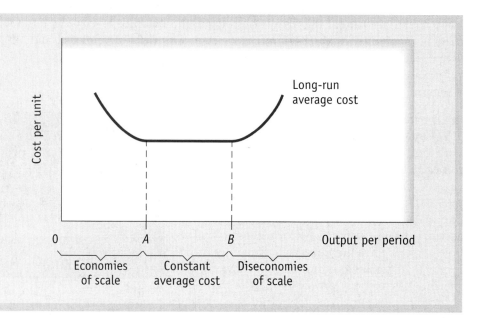

Minimum efficient scale
The lowest rate of output at which a firm takes full advantage of economies of scale

Exhibit 10 presents a firm's long-run average cost curve, which is divided into segments reflecting economies of scale, constant long-run average cost, and diseconomies of scale. The rate of production must reach quantity *A* for the firm to achieve the **minimum efficient scale**, which is the lowest rate of output at which long-run average cost is at a minimum. From output rate *A* to rate *B*, average cost is constant. Beyond output rate *B*, diseconomies of scale increase long-run average cost.

Economies and Diseconomies of Scale at the Firm Level

Our discussion so far has referred to a particular plant—a movie theater or a restaurant, for example. But a firm could also be a collection of plants, such as the thousands of McDonald's restaurants. More generally, we can distinguish between economies and diseconomies of scale at the *plant level*—that is, at a particular location—and at the *firm level*, where the firm is a collection of plants. We'll explore issues of multi-plant scale economies and diseconomies in the following case study.

Billions and Billions of Burgers

CaseStudy

The World of Business

McDonald's uses the term "corporate alliances" to describe its placement of restaurants in service stations and Wal-marts. View the Web page devoted to this new strategy

McDonald's experiences economies of scale at the plant, or restaurant, level because of its specialization of labor and machines, but it also benefits from economies of scale at the company level. Experience gained from decades of selling hamburgers can be shared with new managers through centralized management training programs. More efficient production techniques can be shared across thousands of locations. For example, the new campaign "Made for you . . . at the speed of McDonald's," involves new high-tech holding cabinets with special moisture controls to keep cooked beef and chicken patties hot and juicy for up to 20 minutes (it took three years to decide on an exact temperature for the holding cabinets). And the cost of advertising and promoting McDonald's can be spread across the more than 13,000 U.S. locations and the more than 10,000 locations in 110 foreign countries.

Some diseconomies also arise in such large-scale operations. The fact that the menu must be reasonably uniform across thousands of locations means that if customers in some parts of the country or the world do not like a product, it may not get on the menu regardless of its popularity elsewhere. Another problem with a uniform menu is that the ingredients must be available around the world and cannot be subject to droughts or sharp swings in price. One burger chain decided not to add bacon strips as an option on its burgers because the price of pork bellies fluctuated so much.

Because McDonald's has moved aggressively overseas (10 percent of the beef sold in Japan is in McDonald's hamburgers), menu planning has grown increasingly complex. For example, when McDonald's went into Russia, the company had to develop supply sources for beef, potatoes, lettuce, and other ingredients. In some cases, the company had to train farmers to grow products to specifications. Thus when a firm expands to multiple firms and to multiple countries, it experiences both economies of scale and diseconomies of scale.

Change comes slowly in large firms, but it does come. McDonald's in 1997 reorganized its U.S. operation into five regions, allowing managers in each region more leeway in pricing and promotion. McDonald's has also become more flexible by putting mini-restaurants in airports, gas stations, and Wal-Marts. These so-called satellite restaurants recently accounted for half of the company's new U.S. outlets openings. This flexibility in product and pricing across regions and in restaurant structure is an effort by McDonald's officials to overcome some diseconomies of scale.

Sources: Bruce Horovitz, "Re-inventing McDonald's Fast-Food Giant's New Plan: Hot Juicy, Made to Order," *USA Today* (20 February 1998); Richard Gibson and Matt Moffitt, "McDonald's to Expand Overseas, Making a Dynamic Market Push," *Wall Street Journal* (23 October 1997); "McDonald's Testing 'Big Xtra' Hamburger," *Reuters* (27 December 1997); and *Golden Arches East: McDonald's in East Asia*, James L. Watson, ed. Palo Alto, CA: Stanford University Press, 1998). An Internet site featuring McDonald's restaurants in Austria is at http://www.mcdonalds.co.at/mcdonalds/.

at http://www.mcdonalds.com/corporate/alliances/index.html. How many alliances has it developed? McDonald's now reaches the four corners of the globe. Surf the world of McDonald's at http://www.mcdonalds.com/surftheworld/index.html. Since tastes vary, so does the McDonald's menu. Can you find the country where they serve the Rhode Island McFeast Menu? If you can read a foreign language, try to find a McDonald's page for a country where it is spoken.

CONCLUSION

By considering the relationship between production and cost, we have developed the foundations for a theory of firm behavior. The chapter appendix presents an alternative way of determining a firm's most efficient combination of resources. Despite what may appear to be a tangle of short-run and long-run cost curves, *only two relationships between resources and outputs underlie all the curves. In the short run, it is increasing and diminishing returns to the variable resource. In the long run, it is economies and diseconomies of scale.* If you understand the sources of these two phenomena, you have grasped the central ideas of the chapter. Our examination of the relationship between resource use and the amount produced in both the short run and the long run will help us derive an upward-sloping supply curve in the next chapter.

SUMMARY

1. Explicit costs are opportunity costs of a firm's resources that take the form of cash payments. Implicit costs are the opportunity costs of using resources owned by the firm or provided by the firm's owners. A firm is said to be earning a normal profit if total revenue just covers all implicit and explicit costs. Economic profit equals total revenue minus both explicit and implicit costs.

2. Resources that can quickly be varied to increase or decrease the output level are called variable resources. In the short run, at least one resource is fixed. In the long run, all resources are variable.

3. Short-run increases in a variable resource initially may result in increasing marginal returns as the firm takes advantage of increased specialization of the variable resource. The law of diminishing marginal returns indicates that a point is eventually reached where additional units of the variable resource, combined with the fixed resources, yield an ever-smaller marginal product.

4. The law of diminishing marginal returns is the most important feature of production in the short run and explains why the marginal cost curve eventually slopes upward as output expands. The law of diminishing mar-

ginal returns also explains why average cost eventually increases as output increases in the short run.

5. In the long run, all inputs under the firm's control are variable, so there are no fixed costs. The firm's long-run average cost curve is an envelope formed by a series of short-run average total cost curves. The long run is best thought of as a planning horizon.

6. In the long run, the firm selects the most efficient size for the desired rate of output. Once the size of the firm has been selected and resources have been committed, some resources become fixed, so the firm is back operating in the short run. Thus the firm plans for the long run but produces in the short run.

7. The long-run average cost curve, like the short-run average total cost curve, is U-shaped. As output expands, average cost at first declines because of economies of scale—a larger plant size allows for more specialized machinery and a more extensive division of labor. Eventually, average cost stops falling. Average cost may be constant over some range. If output expands still further, the plant may encounter diseconomies of scale as the cost of coordinating resources grows.

QUESTIONS FOR REVIEW

1. *(Explicit and Implicit Costs)* Amos McCoy is currently raising corn on his 100-acre farm and earning an accounting profit of $100 per acre. However, if he raised soybeans, he could earn $200 per acre. Is he currently earning an economic profit? Why or why not?

2. *(Explicit and Implicit Costs)* Determine whether each of the following is an explicit or an implicit cost:
   a. Payments for labor purchased in the labor market
   b. A firm's use of a warehouse that it owns and that could be rented to another firm
   c. Rent paid for the use of a warehouse not owned by the firm
   d. The wages that owners could earn if they did not work for themselves

3. *(Alternative Measures of Profit)* Calculate the accounting profit or loss as well as the economic profit or loss in each of the following situations:
   a. A firm with total revenues of $150 million, explicit cost of $90 million, and implicit costs of $40 million

   b. A firm with total revenues of $125 million, explicit cost of $100 million, and implicit costs of $30 million
   c. A firm with total revenues of $100 million, explicit cost of $90 million, and implicit costs of $20 million
   d. A firm with total revenues of $250,000, explicit cost of $275,000, and implicit costs of $50,000

4. *(Alternative Measures of Profit)* Why is it reasonable to think of normal profit as a type of cost to the firm?

5. *(Short Run Versus Long Run)* What distinguishes a firm's short-run period from its long-run period?

6. *(Law of Diminishing Marginal Returns)* As a farmer, you must decide how many times during the year you will plant a new crop. Also, you must decide how far apart to space the plants. Will diminishing returns be a factor in your decision making? If so, how will it affect your decisions?

7. *(Marginal Cost)* What is the difference between fixed cost and variable cost? Do both types of costs affect short-run marginal cost? If yes, explain how each affects marginal cost. If no, explain why each does or does not affect marginal cost.

8. *(Marginal Cost)* Explain why the marginal cost of production *must* increase if the marginal product of the variable resource is decreasing.

9. *(Costs in the Short Run)* What effect would each of the following have on a firm's short-run marginal cost curve and its total fixed cost curve?
    a. An increase in the wage rate
    b. A decrease in property taxes
    c. A rise in the purchase price of new capital
    d. A rise in energy prices

10. *(Costs in the Short Run)* Identify each of the curves in the following graph:

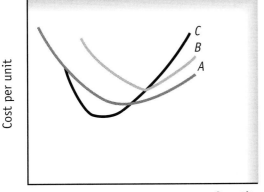

11. *(Marginal Cost and Average Cost)* Explain why the marginal cost curve must intersect the average total cost curve and the average variable cost curve at their minimum points. Why do the average total cost and average variable cost curves approach one another as output increases?

12. *(Marginal and Average Cost)* In Exhibit 7 in this chapter, the output level where average total cost is at a minimum is greater than the output level where average variable cost is at a minimum. Why is this the case?

13. *(Long-Run Average Cost Curve)* What types of changes could shift the long-run average cost curve? How would these changes also affect the short-run average total cost curve?

14. *(Long-Run Average Cost Curve)* Explain the shape of the long-run average cost curve. What does "minimum efficient scale" mean?

15. *(CaseStudy: At the Movies)* The case study notes that the concession stand accounts for well over half the profits at most theaters. Given this, what are the benefits of the staggered movie times allowed by multiple screens? What is the benefit to a multiscreen theater of locating at a shopping mall?

16. *(CaseStudy: Billions and Billions of Burgers)* How does having a menu that is uniform around the country provide McDonald's with economies of scale? Why is menu planning made more complex by expanding into other countries?

PROBLEMS AND EXERCISES

17. *(Production in the Short Run)* Complete the following table. At what point do diminishing marginal returns set in?

Units of the Variable Resource	Total Product	Marginal Product
0	0	—
1	10	_____
2	22	_____
3	_____	9
4	_____	4
5	34	_____

18. *(Total Cost and Marginal Cost)* Complete the following table, assuming that each unit of labor costs $75 per day.

Quantity of Labor per Day	Output per Day	Fixed Cost	Variable Cost	Total Cost	Marginal Cost
0	_____	$300	$_____	$_____	$_____
1	5	_____	75	_____	15
2	11	_____	150	450	12.5
3	15	_____	_____	525	_____
4	18	_____	300	600	25
5	20	_____	_____	_____	37.5

a. Graph the fixed cost, variable cost, and total cost curves for these data.
b. What is the marginal product of going from two to three units of labor?
c. What is average total cost when output is 18 units per day?

19. (*Total Cost and Marginal Cost*) Complete the following table, where L is units of labor, Q is units of output and MP is the marginal product of labor.

L	Q	MP	VC	TC	MC	ATC
0	0	___	$ 0	$12	___	___
1	6	___	3	15	___	___
2	15	___	6		___	___
3	21	___	9		___	___
4	24	___	12		___	___
5	26	___	15		___	___

a. At what level of labor input do the marginal returns to labor begin to diminish?
b. What is the average variable cost when $Q = 24$?
c. What is this firm's fixed cost?
d. What is the wage rate?

20. (*Relationship Between Marginal Cost and Average Cost*) Assume that labor and capital are the only inputs used by a firm. Capital is fixed at 5 units, which cost $100 each. Workers can be hired for $200 each. Complete the following table to show average variable cost (AVC), average total cost (ATC), and marginal cost (MC).

Quantity of Labor	Total Output	AVC	ATC	MC
0	0	___	___	___
1	100	___	___	___
2	250	___	___	___
3	350	___	___	___
4	400	___	___	___
5	425	___	___	___

21. (*Long-Run Costs*) Suppose that a firm has only three possible scales of production, as shown below.

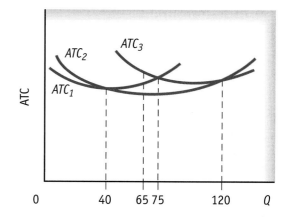

a. Which scale of production is best when $Q = 65$?
b. Which scale of production is best when $Q = 75$?
c. Trace out the long-run average cost curve on the diagram.

EXPERIENTIAL EXERCISES

22. (*Short- and Long-Run Costs*) The terms "diminishing returns" and "economies of scale" are often referred to in everyday discussions and in the popular press. Using an Internet search engine, search for the "diminishing returns" or for "economies of scale." Check the first five sites you find and, in each case, decide whether the term is being used correctly or incorrectly. If the latter, see if you can determine the nature of the writer's confusion. For example, check "The Concepts of Diminishing and Increasing Returns" (http://www.useit.com/alertbox/increasingreturns.html), in which the author manages to compare a short-run concept—diminishing (marginal) returns—with a long-run concept—increasing returns (to scale).

23. (*Costs in the Long Run*) Find Erik Brynjolfsson and Shinkyu Yang's "Information Technology and Productivity: A Review of the Literature," available on-line at http://ccs.mit.edu/ccswp202/. Using the concepts you learned in this chapter, try to explain the expected long-run impact of information technology on productivity and costs.

24. (*Wall Street Journal*) A firm's cost curves are based on the prices of the inputs it uses and on the firm's technology. Technology is the way the inputs are combined to produce a product. The "Technology" column in the Marketplace section of the *Wall Street Journal* describes many interesting technological innovations. Pick one and see if you can determine how it might affect a firm's cost curves. Will it cause one resource to be substituted in place of another? Try to guess both the short-run and long-run effects.

Appendix

A CLOSER LOOK AT PRODUCTION AND COSTS

This appendix develops a model for determining how a profit-maximizing firm will combine resources to produce a particular amount of output. The quantity of output that can be produced with a given amount of resources depends on the existing *state of technology,* which is the prevailing knowledge of how resources can be combined. Therefore, let's begin by considering the technological possibilities available to the firm.

THE PRODUCTION FUNCTION AND EFFICIENCY

The ways in which resources can be combined to produce output are summarized by a firm's production function. The *production function* identifies the maximum quantities of a particular good or service that can be produced per time period with various combinations of resources, for a given level of technology. The production function can be presented as an equation, a graph, or a table.

The production function summarized in Exhibit 11 reflects, for a hypothetical firm, the output resulting from particular combinations of resources. This firm uses only two resources: capital and labor. The amount of capital used is listed in the left-hand column of the table, and the amount of labor employed is listed across the top. For example, if 1 unit of capital is combined with 7 units of labor, the firm can produce 290 units of output per month.

The firm produces the maximum possible output given the combination of resources employed; that same output could not be produced with fewer resources. Since the production function combines resources efficiently, 290 units is the most that can be produced with 7 units of labor and 1 unit of capital. Thus we say that production is **technologically efficient.**

We can examine the effects of adding additional labor to an existing amount of capital by starting with any level of capital and reading across the table. For example, when 1 unit of capital and 1 unit of labor are employed, the firm produces 40 units of output per month. If the amount of labor is increased by 1 unit and the amount of capital employed is held constant, output increases to 90 units, so the marginal product of labor is 50 units. If the amount of labor employed increases from 2 to 3 units, other things constant, output goes to 150 units, yielding a marginal product of 60 units. By reading across the table, you will discover that the marginal product of labor first rises, showing increasing marginal returns from the variable resource (labor), and then declines, showing diminishing marginal returns. Similarly, by holding the amount of labor constant and following down the column, you will find that the marginal product of capital also reflects first increasing marginal returns, then diminishing marginal returns.

EXHIBIT 11

A Firm's Production Function Using Labor and Capital: Production per Month	Units of Capital Employed per Month	Units of Labor Employed per Month						
		1	2	3	4	5	6	7
	1	40	90	150	200	240	270	290
	2	90	140	200	250	290	315	335
	3	150	195	260	310	345	370	390
	4	200	250	310	350	385	415	440
	5	240	290	345	385	420	450	475
	6	270	320	375	415	450	475	495
	7	290	330	390	435	470	495	510

ISOQUANTS

Notice from the tabular presentation of the production function in Exhibit 11 that some different combinations of resources yield the same rate of output. For example, several combinations of labor and capital yield 290 units of output per month. (Try to find all four combinations.) Some of the information provided in Exhibit 11 can be presented more clearly in graphical form. In Exhibit 12, the quantity of labor employed is measured along the horizontal axis and the quantity of capital along the vertical axis. Combinations that yield 290 units of output are presented in Exhibit 12 as points *a, b, c,* and *d*. These points can be connected to form an *isoquant, Q_1,* which shows the possible combinations of the two resources that produce 290 units of output per month. Likewise, Q_2 shows combinations of inputs that yield 415 units of output, and Q_3 shows combinations that yield 475 units of output. (The colors of the isoquants match those of the corresponding entries in the production function table in Exhibit 11.)

An **isoquant,** such as Q_1 in Exhibit 12, is a curve that shows all the technologically efficient combinations of two resources, such as labor and capital, that produce a certain rate of output. *Iso* is from the Greek word meaning "equal," and *quant* is short for "quantity"; so *isoquant* means "equal quantity." Along a particular isoquant, such as Q_1, the rate of output produced remains constant, in this case 290 units per month, but the combinations of resources vary. To produce a particular rate of output, the firm can use resource combinations ranging from much capital and little labor to much labor and little capital. For example, a paving contractor can put in a new driveway with 10 workers using shovels, wheelbarrows, and hand rollers; the same job can also be done with only 2 workers, a road grader, and a paving machine. A Saturday-afternoon charity car wash to raise money to send the school band to Disney World is labor-intensive, involving perhaps a dozen workers per car, plus buckets, sponges, and hose. In contrast, a professional car wash is fully automated, requiring only one worker to turn on the machine and collect the money. An isoquant shows such alternative combinations of resources for producing the same rate of output. Let's consider some properties of isoquants.

Isoquants Farther from the Origin Represent Greater Output Rates   Although we have included only three isoquants in Exhibit 12, there is a different isoquant for every quantity of output depicted in Exhibit 11. Indeed, there is a different isoquant for every output rate the firm could possibly produce, with isoquants farther from the origin indicating higher rates of output.

Isoquants Slope Down to the Right   Along a given isoquant, the quantity of labor employed is inversely related to the quantity of capital employed, so isoquants have negative slopes.

Isoquants Do Not Intersect   Since each isoquant refers to a specific rate of output, no two isoquants intersect, for such an intersection would indicate that the same combination of resources could, with equal efficiency, produce two different amounts of output.

Isoquants Are Usually Convex to the Origin   Isoquants are usually convex to the origin, meaning that any isoquant gets flatter as you move down along the curve. The slope of an isoquant measures the ability of additional units of one resource—in this case, labor—to substitute in production for another—in this case, capital. As noted already, the isoquant has a negative slope. The absolute value of the slope of the isoquant is the **marginal rate of technical substitution,** or **MRTS,** between two resources. The MRTS is the rate at which labor can be substituted for capital without affecting output. When much capital and little labor are used, the marginal productivity of labor is relatively great and the marginal productivity of capital is relatively small, so one unit of labor will substitute for a relatively large amount of capital. For example, in moving from point *a* to *b* along isoquant Q_1 in Exhibit 12, 1 unit of labor substitutes for 2 units of capital, so the MRTS between points *a* and *b* equals 2. But as more labor and less capital are employed, the marginal product of labor declines and the marginal product of capital increases,

EXHIBIT 12

Isoquants

Isoquant Q_1 shows all technologically efficient combinations of labor and capital that can be used to produce 290 units of output. Isoquant Q_2 is drawn for 415 units, and Q_3 for 475 units. Each isoquant has a negative slope and is convex to the origin.

so it takes more labor to make up for a one-unit reduction in capital. For example, in moving from point c to point d in Exhibit 12, 2 units of labor substitute for 1 unit of capital; hence, the MRTS between points c and d equals $\frac{1}{2}$.

The extent to which one input substitutes for another, as measured by the marginal rate of technical substitution, is directly linked to the marginal productivity of each input. For example, between points a and b, 1 unit of labor replaces 2 units of capital, yet output remains constant. So labor's marginal product, MP_L—that is, the additional output resulting from an additional unit of labor—must be twice as large as capital's marginal product, MP_C. In fact, *anywhere along the isoquant, the marginal rate of technical substitution of labor for capital equals the marginal product of labor divided by the marginal product of capital, which also equals the absolute value of the slope of the isoquant.* Thus we can say that

$$|\text{Slope of isoquant}| = \text{MRTS} = MP_L/MP_C$$

where the vertical lines on either side of "Slope of isoquant" mean the absolute value. For example, between points a and b the slope equals -2, which has an absolute value of 2, which equals the marginal rate of substitution of labor for capital and the ratio of marginal productivities. Between points b and c, 3 units of labor substitute for 3 units of capital, while holding output constant at 290. Thus, the slope between b and c is $-3/3$, for an absolute value of 1. Note that the absolute value of the isoquant's slope declines as we move down the curve because larger increases in labor are required to offset the decline in capital. Put another way, as less capital is employed, its marginal product increases, and as more labor is employed, its marginal product decreases.

If labor and capital were perfect substitutes in production, the rate at which labor substituted for capital would remain fixed along the isoquant, so the isoquant would be a downward-sloping straight line. Since most resources are *not* perfect substitutes, however, the rate at which one substitutes for another changes along an isoquant. As we move down along an isoquant, more labor is required to offset each 1-unit decline in capital, so the isoquant gets flatter, yielding an isoquant that is convex to the origin.

Let's summarize the properties of isoquants.

1. *Isoquants farther from the origin represent higher rates of output.*
2. *Isoquants slope downward.*
3. *Isoquants never intersect.*
4. *Isoquants are bowed toward the origin.*

ISOCOST LINES

Isoquants graphically illustrate a firm's production function for all quantities of output the firm could possibly produce. Given these isoquants, how much should the firm produce? But here we are interested in what combination of resources should be

employed to minimize the cost of producing a given rate of output. The answer depends on the cost of resources.

Suppose a unit of labor costs the firm $1,500 per month, and a unit of capital costs $2,500 per month. The total cost (TC) of production is

$$TC = (w \times L) + (r \times C)$$
$$= \$1,500L + \$2,500C$$

where w is the monthly wage rate, L is the quantity of labor employed, r is the monthly cost of capital, and C is the quantity of capital employed. An **isocost line** identifies all combinations of capital and labor the firm can hire for a given total cost. Again, *iso* is Greek for "equal," so an isocost line is a line representing resource combinations of equal cost. In Exhibit 13, for example, the line $TC = \$15,000$ identifies all combinations of labor and capital that cost the firm a total of $15,000. The entire $15,000 could pay for 6 units of capital per month; if the entire budget is spent on only labor, 10 workers per month could be hired; or the firm could employ any other combination of resources along the isocost line.

Recall that the slope of any line is the vertical change between two points on the line divided by the corresponding horizontal change. At the point where the isocost line meets the vertical axis, the quantity of capital that can be purchased equals the total cost divided by the monthly cost of a unit of

EXHIBIT 13

Firm's Isocost Lines

$$\text{Slope} = -\frac{w}{r} = -\frac{\$1,500}{\$2,500} = -0.6$$

$TC = \$22,500$
$TC = \$19,000$
$TC = \$15,000$

Units of capital per month (vertical axis)
Units of labor per month (horizontal axis)

Each Isocost line shows combinations of labor and capital that can be purchased for a fixed amount of total cost. The slope of each is equal to minus the wage rate divided by the rental rate of capital. Higher levels of cost are represented by isocost lines farther from the origin.

capital, or TC/r. At the point where the isocost line meets the horizontal axis, the quantity of labor that can be hired equals the firm's total cost divided by the monthly wage, or TC/w. The slope of any isocost line in Exhibit 13 can be calculated by considering a movement from the vertical intercept to the horizontal intercept. That is, we divide the vertical change $(-TC/r)$ by the horizontal change (TC/w), as follows:

$$\text{Slope of isocost line} = -\frac{TC/r}{TC/w} = -\frac{w}{r}$$

The slope of the isocost line equals minus the price of labor divided by the price of capital, or $-w/r$, which indicates the relative prices of the inputs. In our example, the absolute value of the slope of the isocost line equals w/r, or

$$|\text{Slope of isocost line}| = w/r$$
$$= 1{,}500/2{,}500$$
$$= 0.6$$

The wage rate of labor is 0.6 of the monthly cost of a unit of capital, so hiring one more unit of labor, without incurring any additional cost, implies that the firm must employ 0.6 fewer units of capital.

A firm is not confined to a particular isocost line. This is why in Exhibit 13 we include three isocost lines, each corresponding to a different total budget. In fact, there is a different isocost line for every possible budget. *These isocost lines are parallel because each reflects the same relative resource price.* Resource prices in our example are assumed to be constant regardless of the amount of each resource the firm employs.

THE CHOICE OF INPUT COMBINATIONS

We bring the isoquants and the isocost lines together in Exhibit 14. Suppose the firm has decided to produce 415 units of output and wants to minimize the total cost of doing so. It could select point *f*, where 6 units of capital are combined with 4 units of labor. This combination, however, would cost $21,000 at prevailing prices. Since the profit-maximizing firm wants to produce its chosen output at the minimum cost, it tries to find the isocost line closest to the origin that still touches the isoquant. At a point of tangency, a movement in either direction along an isoquant shifts the firm to a higher cost. So *the point of tangency between the isocost line and the isoquant shows the minimum cost required to produce a given output.*

Look at what's going on at the point of tangency. At point *e* in Exhibit 14, the isoquant and the isocost line have the same slope. As mentioned already, the absolute value of the slope of an isoquant equals the *marginal rate of technical substitution* between labor and capital, and the absolute value of the slope of the isocost line equals the *ratio of the input prices.* So when a firm produces output in the least costly way,

EXHIBIT 14

Optimal Combinations of Inputs

At point *e*, isoquant Q_2 is tangent to the isocost line. The optimal combination of inputs is 6 units of labor and 4 units of capital. The maximum output that can be produced for $19,000 is 415 units. Alternatively, point *e* determines the minimum-cost way of producing 415 units of output.

the marginal rate of technical substitution must equal the ratio of the resource prices, or

$$\text{MRTS} = w/r = 1{,}500/2{,}500 = 0.6$$

This equality shows that the firm adjusts resource use so that the rate at which one input can be substituted for another in production—that is, the marginal rate of technical substitution—equals the rate at which one resource can be exchanged for another in resource markets, which is w/r. If this equality does not hold, the firm could adjust its input mix to produce the same output for a lower cost.

THE EXPANSION PATH

Imagine a set of isoquants representing each possible rate of output. Given the relative cost of resources, we could then draw isocost lines to determine the optimal combination of resources for producing each rate of output. The points of tangency in Exhibit 15 show the least-cost input combinations for producing several output rates. For example, output rate Q_2 can be produced most cheaply using *C* units of capital and *L* units of labor. The line formed by connecting these tangency points is the firm's **expansion path**. The expansion path need not be a straight line, although it will generally slope upward, implying that firms will expand the use of both resources in

EXHIBIT 15

Isoquants

The points of tangency between isoquants and isocost lines each show the least expensive way of producing a particular level of output. Connecting these tangency points gives the firm's expansion path.

output. The firm's expansion path and the firm's long-run average cost curve represent alternative ways of portraying costs in the long run, given resource prices and technology.

We can use Exhibit 15 to distinguish between short-run and long-run adjustments in output. Let's begin with the firm producing Q_2 at point b, which requires C units of capital and L units of labor. Now suppose that in the short run, the firm wants to expand output to Q_3. Since capital is fixed in the short run, the only way to expand output to Q_3 is by increasing the quantity of labor employed to L', which requires moving to point e in Exhibit 15. Point e is not the cheapest way to produce Q_3 in the long run, for it is not a tangency point. In the long run, capital usage is variable, and if the firm wishes to produce Q_3, it should adjust capital and shift from point e to point c, thereby minimizing the total cost of producing Q_3.

One final point: If the relative prices of resources change, the least-cost combination of those resources will also change, so the firm's expansion path will change. For example, if the price of labor increases, capital becomes cheaper relative to labor. The efficient production of any given rate of output will therefore call for less labor and more capital. With the cost of labor higher, the firm's total cost for each rate of output rises. Such a cost increase would also be reflected by an upward shift in the average total cost curve.

SUMMARY

A firm's *production function* specifies the relationship between resource use and output, given prevailing technology. An *isoquant* is a curve that illustrates the possible combinations of resources that will produce a particular rate of output. An *isocost* line presents the combinations of resources the firm can employ, given resource prices and the firm's total budget.

For a given rate of output—that is, for a given isoquant—the firm minimizes its total cost by choosing the lowest isocost line that just touches, or is tangent to, the isoquant. The least-cost combination of resources will depend on the productivity of resources and the relative cost of resources.

the long run as output increases. Note that we have assumed that the prices of inputs remain constant as the firm varies output along the expansion path, so the isocost lines at the points of tangency are parallel—that is, they have the same slope.

The expansion path indicates the lowest long-run total cost for each rate of output. For example, the firm can produce output rate Q_2 for TC_2, output rate Q_3 for TC_3, and so on. Similarly, the firm's long-run average cost curve indicates, at each rate of output, the total cost divided by the rate of

APPENDIX QUESTIONS

1. *(Choice of Input Combination)* Suppose that a firm's cost per unit of labor is $100 per day and its cost per unit of capital is $400 per day.
    a. Draw the isocost line for a total cost per day of $2000.
    b. If this firm is producing efficiently, what is the marginal rate of technical substitution between labor and capital?
    c. Demonstrate your answer to part (b) using isocost lines and isoquant curves.

2. *(The Expansion Path)* How are the expansion path and the long-run average cost curve related?

Perfect Competition

Visit the McEachern
Interactive Study Center
for this chapter at
http://mcisc.swcollege.com

What does a bushel of wheat have in common with a share of Amazon.com stock? Why might a firm continue to operate even though it's losing money? Why do firms, even in the most competitive of industries, sometimes earn economic profit? In what sense can it be said that the more competitive the industry, the less individual firms compete with each other? To answer these and other questions, we examine our first market structure, perfect competition.

The previous chapter developed cost curves for an individual firm in both the short run and the long run. In light of these costs, how much should a firm produce and what price should it charge? To discover the firm's profit-maximizing output and price, we revisit an old friend: demand. Demand and production costs, or supply, together guide the firm to maximum economic profit.

In the next few chapters we will examine how firms respond to their economic environments in deciding what to produce, in what quantities, and at what price. No matter what the market structure, we assume that firms try to maximize economic profit. Topics discussed in this chapter include:

- Market structure
- Price takers
- Marginal revenue
- Golden rule of profit maximization
- Loss minimization
- Firm and industry short-run supply curve
- Industry's long-run supply curve
- Competition and efficiency
- Producer surplus
- Gains from exchange

AN INTRODUCTION TO PERFECT COMPETITION

First, a few words about terminology. An industry consists of all firms that supply output to a particular market, such as the auto market, the shoe market, or the wheat market. The terms *industry* and *market* are used interchangeably throughout this chapter. Many of the firm's decisions depend on the structure of the market in which it operates. **Market structure** describes the important features of a market, such as the number of firms (are there many or few?), the product's degree of uniformity (do firms in the market supply identical products or are there differences across firms?), the ease of entry into the market (can new firms enter easily or are they blocked by natural or artificial barriers?), and the forms of competition among firms (do firms compete only through prices or are advertising and product differentiation common as well?). The various features will become clearer as we examine each type of market structure in the next few chapters.

Market structure Important features of a market, such as the number of firms, uniformity of product among firms, ease of entry and exit, and forms of competition

Perfectly Competitive Market Structure

We begin with **perfect competition,** in some ways the most basic of market structures. A *perfectly competitive* market is characterized by the following: (1) there are many buyers and sellers, so many that each buys or sells only a tiny fraction of the total amount exchanged in the market; (2) firms sell a standardized, or *homogeneous,* product such as bushels of wheat or a share of Amazon.com stock; (3) buyers and sellers are fully informed about the price and availability of all resources and products; and (4) firms and resources are freely mobile—that is, over time they can easily enter or leave the industry, with no obstacles to block entry or exit, such as patents, licenses, high capital costs, or ignorance about available technology.

Perfect competition A market structure in which there are large numbers of fully informed buyers and sellers of a homogeneous product, with no obstacles to entry or exit of firms in the long run

If these conditions are present in a market, individual participants have no control over the price. Price is determined by market supply and demand. A perfectly competitive firm is called a **price taker** because it must "take," or accept, the market price—as in "take it or leave it." Once the market establishes the price, each individual firm is free to supply whatever amount maximizes that firm's profit. A perfectly competitive firm is so small relative to the size of the market that the firm's choice of what quantity to supply has no perceptible effect on the market price.

Price taker A firm that faces a given market price and whose actions have no effect on that market price

Examples of perfectly competitive markets include markets for stocks and bonds; markets for basic commodities such as gold and silver; markets for foreign exchange; and markets for most agricultural products such as wheat, corn, and livestock. Again, there are so many buyers and sellers that the actions of any one cannot influence the market price. For example, about 150,000 farmers in the United States raise hogs.

The model of perfect competition allows us to make a number of predictions that hold up when we examine the real world. Perfect competition is also an important benchmark for evaluating the efficiency of other types of markets. Let's look at demand under perfect competition.

Demand Under Perfect Competition

Suppose the market in question is the world market for wheat and the firm in question is a wheat farm. In the world market for wheat, there are tens of thousands of farms, so any one farm produces only a tiny fraction of market output. For example, the thousands of wheat farmers in Kansas together produce less than 3 percent of the world's supply of wheat.

In Exhibit 1, the market price of wheat of $5 per bushel is determined in panel (a) by the intersection of the market demand curve, *D*, and the market supply curve, *S*. Once the market price is established, any farmer can sell all he or she wants at that market price. *The demand curve as it appears to an individual farmer is therefore a horizontal line drawn at the market price.* In our example, the demand curve facing the farmer, identified as *d* in panel (b), is drawn at the market price of $5 per bushel, indicating that this farmer can sell any quantity he or she desires at the market price. Thus each farmer faces a horizontal, or *perfectly elastic*, demand curve.

Each farm is so small relative to the market that each has no impact on the market price; each farmer is a *price taker*. Because all farmers supply identical goods, bushels of wheat in this case, anyone who charges more than the market

EXHIBIT 1

Market Equilibrium and the Firm's Demand Curve in Perfect Competition

(a) Market equilibrium

(b) Firm's demand

In panel (a), the market price of $5 is determined by the intersection of the market demand and supply curves. The individual perfectly competitive firm can sell any amount at that price. The demand curve facing the competitive firm is horizontal at the market price, as shown by demand curve *d* in panel (b).

price will sell no output. For example, if a farmer charged $5.25 per bushel, buyers would simply turn to other suppliers. Of course, any farmer is free to charge less than the market price, but why do that when all wheat can be sold at the market price? Farmers are not stupid; if they were, they would not last long.

It has been said, "In perfect competition there is no competition." Ironically, two neighboring wheat farmers in perfect competition are not really rivals. They both sell as much wheat as they want to at the market price. The amount one sells has no effect on the price the other receives.

SHORT-RUN PROFIT MAXIMIZATION

We assume that firms (farms are the firms in this example) try to maximize economic profit. Firms that ignore this strategy will not be around long. Economic profit equals total revenue minus total opportunity cost, including both explicit and implicit costs. Implicit cost, you will recall, is the opportunity cost of resources owned by the firm and includes a normal profit; economic profit is any profit above normal profit. How do firms maximize profit? You have already learned that the perfectly competitive firm has no control over price. What the firm does control is the amount produced, the rate of output. The question then boils down to: *What rate of output will maximize economic profit?*

Total Revenue Minus Total Cost
The firm maximizes economic profit by finding the rate of output at which total revenue exceeds total cost by the greatest amount. Total revenue for a perfectly competitive firm is simply the rate of output times the price per unit. Column (1) in Exhibit 2 shows an individual farmer's output possibilities in bushels of wheat per day. Column (2) shows the market price per bushel of $5, a price that does not vary with output. Column (3) shows total revenue, which is output times price, or column (1) times column (2). And column (4) shows the total cost of output. Total cost already includes a normal profit, so total cost includes all opportunity costs. Although the exhibit does not distinguish between fixed and variable costs, fixed cost must equal $15 per day, since total cost is $15 when output is zero. The fact that this farm incurs a fixed cost indicates that at least one resource must be fixed, so the farm must be operating in the short run.

Total revenue in column (3) minus total cost in column (4) yields the economic profit or economic loss per period, which is presented in column (7). As you can see, at low and high rates of output, total cost exceeds total revenue, so the farm incurs an *economic loss* at low and high rates of output. Between 7 and 14 bushels per day, total revenue exceeds total cost, so the farm earns an *economic profit*. Economic profit is maximized at $12 per day when the farm produces 12 bushels of wheat per day (the $12 and 12 bushel combination is just a coincidence).

These results are graphed in panel (a) of Exhibit 3, which shows the total revenue and total cost curves. As output increases by 1 bushel, total revenue increases by $5, so the farm's total revenue curve is a straight line emanating from the origin, with a slope of 5. The short-run total cost curve has a backward S shape reflecting first increasing marginal returns, then diminishing marginal returns from changes in the amount of variable resource employed. Total cost

EXHIBIT 2

Short-Run Costs and Revenues for a Perfectly Competitive Firm

Bushels of Wheat per day (q) (1)	Marginal Revenue (Price) (p) (2)	Total Revenue ($TR = q \times p$) (3) = (1) × (2)	Total Cost (TC) (4)	Marginal Cost $\left(MC = \dfrac{\Delta TC}{\Delta q}\right)$ (5)	Average Total Cost $\left(ATC = \dfrac{TC}{q}\right)$ (6) = (4) ÷ (1)	Economic Profit or Loss $= TR - TC$ (7) = (3) − (4)
0	—	$ 0	$15.00	—	∞	−$15.00
1	$5	5	19.75	$ 4.75	$19.75	−14.75
2	5	10	23.50	3.75	11.75	−13.50
3	5	15	26.50	3.00	8.83	−11.50
4	5	20	29.00	2.50	7.25	−9.00
5	5	25	31.00	2.00	6.20	−6.00
6	5	30	32.50	1.50	5.42	−2.50
7	5	35	33.75	1.25	4.82	1.25
8	5	40	35.25	1.50	4.41	4.75
9	5	45	37.25	2.00	4.14	7.75
10	5	50	40.00	2.75	4.00	10.00
11	5	55	43.25	3.25	3.93	11.75
12	**5**	**60**	**48.00**	**4.75**	**4.00**	**12.00**
13	5	65	54.50	6.50	4.19	10.50
14	5	70	64.00	9.50	4.57	6.00
15	5	75	77.50	13.50	5.17	−2.50
16	5	80	96.00	18.50	6.00	−16.00

always increases as the rate of output expands. Note that the shape of the total cost curve is independent of the market structure.

Comparing total revenue and total cost is one way to find the profit-maximizing rate of output. At rates of output less than 7 bushels or greater than 14 bushels, total cost exceeds total revenue, resulting in an economic loss, which is measured by the vertical distance between the two curves. Total revenue exceeds total cost between 7 and 14 bushels per day; at these rates of output the farm earns an economic profit. *Profit is maximized at the rate of output where total revenue exceeds total cost by the greatest amount.* We already know that profit is greatest when 12 bushels are produced per day.

Marginal Cost Equals Marginal Revenue in Equilibrium

Both total revenue and total cost change when output changes, which is why the profit-maximizing choice is not immediately apparent. A second way to find the profit-maximizing rate of output is to focus on marginal revenue and marginal

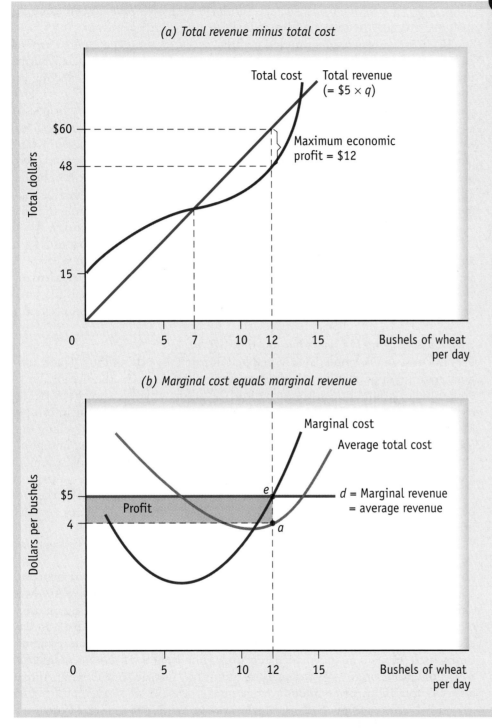

(a) Total revenue minus total cost

Total cost   Total revenue (= $5 × q)

$60
48
15

Maximum economic profit = $12

Total dollars

0   5   7   10 12   15   Bushels of wheat per day

(b) Marginal cost equals marginal revenue

Marginal cost
Average total cost

$5
4

e
Profit
a

d = Marginal revenue = average revenue

Dollars per bushels

0   5   10 12   15   Bushels of wheat per day

EXHIBIT 3

Short-Run Profit Maximization

In panel (a), the total revenue curve for a competitive firm is a straight line with a slope equal to the market price of $5. Total cost increases with output, first at a decreasing rate and then at an increasing rate. Profit is maximized at 12 bushels of wheat per day, where total revenue exceeds total cost by the greatest amount. In panel (b), marginal revenue is a horizontal line at the market price of $5. Profit is maximized at 12 bushels of wheat per day, where the marginal cost equals marginal revenue (point *e*). Profit per day is output (12 bushels) multiplied by the difference between price ($5) and average total cost ($4), as shown by the shaded rectangle.

cost. Column (2) of Exhibit 2 presents the farm's marginal revenue schedule. **Marginal revenue** is the change in total revenue divided by the change in output, or $MR = \Delta TR/\Delta q$. In perfect competition each firm is a price taker, so if one

Marginal revenue The change in total revenue resulting from a one-unit change in sales; in perfect competition, marginal revenue equals the market price

more unit is sold, total revenue increases by an amount equal to the market price. Thus, *in perfect competition, marginal revenue equals the market price.* In this example, marginal revenue, the revenue from selling one more bushel of wheat, is $5.

In the previous chapter you learned that *marginal cost* is the change in total cost divided by the change in output. Column (5) of Exhibit 2 presents the farm's marginal cost of each bushel of wheat. Marginal cost first declines, reflecting increasing marginal returns in the short run as more of the variable resource is employed. Marginal cost then increases, reflecting diminishing marginal returns.

The firm will expand output as long as each additional unit sold adds more to total revenue than to total cost—that is, as long as marginal revenue exceeds marginal cost. Comparing columns (2) and (5) in Exhibit 2, we see that marginal revenue exceeds marginal cost for each of the first 12 units of output. The marginal cost of bushel 13, however, is $6.50, compared to its marginal revenue of $5. Producing the thirteenth bushel would reduce economic profit by $1.50. Since we assume the goal is maximum profit, the farm will limit its output rate to 12 bushels per day.

A firm will expand output as long as marginal revenue exceeds marginal cost, and it will stop expanding before marginal cost rises above marginal revenue. A shorthand expression for this approach is the **golden rule of profit maximization,** which states that the firm produces where marginal cost equals marginal revenue. The golden rule flows from our assumption about profit maximization.

Golden rule of profit maximization To maximize profit or minimize loss, a firm should produce at the rate of output at which cost equals marginal revenue; this rule holds for all market structures.

Economic Profit in the Short Run

Per-unit cost and revenue data are graphed in panel (b) of Exhibit 3. Since marginal revenue in perfect competition equals the market price, the marginal revenue is a horizontal line at the market price of $5, which is also the perfectly competitive firm's demand curve. Since the perfectly competitive firm can get $5 for each bushel sold, the price of $5 is the marginal revenue from selling one more bushel and also the average revenue for each bushel sold. At any point along the demand curve, marginal revenue equals the price. Because the perfectly competitive firm can sell all output for the same market price, marginal revenue equals **average revenue,** which is the total revenue divided by the rate of output. Regardless of the rate of output, therefore, the following equality holds at all points on a perfectly competitive firm's demand curve:

Average revenue Total revenue divided by output; in all market structures, average revenue equals the market price

$$\text{market price} = \text{marginal revenue} = \text{average revenue}$$

The marginal cost curve intersects the marginal revenue (and demand) curve at point *e,* where the rate of output is about 12 bushels per day. At lower rates of output, marginal revenue exceeds marginal cost, so the farm could increase profit by expanding output. At higher rates of output, marginal cost exceeds marginal revenue, so the farm could increase profit by reducing output. Profit itself appears as the shaded rectangle. The height of that rectangle, *ea,* equals the price, or average revenue, $5, minus the average total cost, $4, at that rate of output. Thus, price minus average total cost yields an average profit of $1 per bushel. Profit per day, $12, equals the average profit per bushel, $1 (denoted by *ea*), times the 12 bushels produced.

Note that with total cost and total revenue curves, we measure economic profit by the vertical *distance* between the two curves. But with per-unit curves, we measure economic profit by an *area*—that is, by multiplying the average profit of $1 per bushel times the 12 bushels sold.

MINIMIZING SHORT-RUN LOSSES

An individual firm in perfect competition has no control over the market price. Sometimes the price is so low that no rate of output will yield an economic profit. Faced with losses at all rates of output, the firm can continue to produce at a loss or can temporarily shut down production, such as when an auto plant responds to slack demand by temporarily halting production for weeks or months, or when Dairy Queen shuts down for the winter. Even if the firm shuts down, it cannot in the short run go out of business or produce something else. The short run is by definition a period too short to allow existing firms to leave or new firms to enter this industry. In a sense, firms are trapped in this industry in the short run.

Fixed Cost and Minimizing Losses

Your instincts probably tell you that, rather than produce at a loss, the firm should shut down. But it's not that simple. Keep in mind that the firm has two types of cost in the short run: fixed cost, which must be paid in the short run even if the firm produces nothing, and variable cost, which depends on the rate of output. If the firm shuts down, it must still pay fixed costs, such as property taxes, fire insurance, interest on any loans, and other expenses incurred, even though output is zero. *There may be some positive rate of output at which the firm's revenue will not only cover variable cost but also cover a portion of fixed cost.* A firm will produce if the revenue thus generated exceeds the variable cost of production; revenue in excess of variable cost is used to pay a portion of fixed cost.

Consider the same cost data presented in Exhibit 2, but now suppose the market price has fallen from $5 to $3 per bushel of wheat. This new situation is presented in Exhibit 4. Because of the lower price, total revenue and economic profit are lower at all rates of output. Column (8) indicates that each output rate results in a loss. If the firm produces nothing, its loss is the fixed cost of $15 per day. But if it produces between 6 and 12 bushels per day, it loses less than $15 per day. From column (8), you can see that the loss is minimized at $10 per day when 10 bushels are produced, so the farmer minimizes the loss by producing 10 units per day rather than shutting down. Total cost per day increases from $15 at zero output to $40 at 10 bushels. So total cost increases by $25, which is the variable cost of producing 10 bushels. Since total revenue from selling 10 bushels is $30, the farmer covers the variable cost of $25, leaving $5 toward fixed cost.

Panel (a) of Exhibit 5 presents the firm's total cost and total revenue curves from the data in Exhibit 4. The total cost curve has not changed and remains the same as in Exhibit 3. The drop in price from $5 to $3 per unit changes the slope of the total revenue curve from 5 to 3, so the curve is now flatter than in Exhibit 3. Notice that the total revenue curve now lies below the total cost curve at all output rates. The vertical distance between the two curves measures the loss at each rate of output. If the farmer produces nothing, the loss is the fixed cost of $15 per day. The vertical distance between the two curves is minimized at an output rate of about 10 bushels, where the loss is $10 per day.

Marginal Cost Equals Marginal Revenue

We get the same result using marginal analysis. The per-unit data from Exhibit 4 are presented in panel (b) of Exhibit 5. *The firm will produce rather than shut down if marginal cost equals marginal revenue at a rate of output where the price exceeds or is equal*

EXHIBIT 4

Minimizing Losses in the Short Run

Bushels of Wheat per day (q) (1)	Marginal Revenue (Price) (p) (2)	Total Revenue (TR = q × p) (3) = (1) × (2)	Total Cost (TC) (4)	Marginal Cost $\left(MC = \frac{\Delta TC}{\Delta q}\right)$ (5)	Average Total Cost $\left(ATC = \frac{TC}{q}\right)$ (6) = (4) ÷ (1)	Average Variable Cost $\left(AVC = \frac{TVC}{q}\right)$ (7)	Economic Profit or Loss = TR − TC (8) = (3) − (4)
0	—	$ 0	$15.00	—	∞	—	−$15.00
1	$3	3	19.75	$ 4.75	$19.75	$4.75	−16.75
2	3	6	23.50	3.75	11.75	4.25	−17.50
3	3	9	26.50	3.00	8.83	3.83	−17.50
4	3	12	29.00	2.50	7.25	3.50	−17.00
5	3	15	31.00	2.00	6.20	3.20	−16.00
6	3	18	32.50	1.50	5.42	2.92	−14.50
7	3	21	33.75	1.25	4.82	2.68	−12.75
8	3	24	35.25	1.50	4.41	2.53	−11.25
9	3	27	37.25	2.00	4.14	2.47	−10.25
10	**3**	**30**	**40.00**	**2.75**	**4.00**	**2.50**	**−10.00**
11	3	33	43.25	3.25	3.93	2.57	−10.25
12	3	36	48.00	4.75	4.00	2.75	−12.00
13	3	39	54.50	6.50	4.19	3.04	−15.50
14	3	42	64.00	9.50	4.57	3.50	−22.00
15	3	45	77.50	13.50	5.17	4.17	−32.50
16	3	48	96.00	18.50	6.00	5.06	−48.00

to the average variable cost. In Exhibit 5, the marginal cost and marginal revenue curves intersect at point *e,* where the output rate is about 10 bushels per day and the price of $3 exceeds the average variable cost per bushel of $2.50.

Because the price of $3 per bushel exceeds average variable cost, the farmer is able to cover variable cost and a portion of fixed cost. Specifically, $2.50 of the price pays the average variable cost, and $0.50 covers a portion of the average fixed cost of $1.50 (average fixed cost is average total cost of $4.00 minus average variable cost of $2.50). This still leaves a loss of $1 per bushel. A loss of $1 per bushel multiplied by 10 bushels yields an economic loss of $10 per day, which is identified in panel (b) by the shaded rectangle. Why is the farmer better off operating with this loss rather than shutting down?

Shutting Down in the Short Run

As long as the loss that results from producing is less than the shutdown loss, the farmer will remain open for business in the short run. You may have read or heard about firms that report a loss; most firms reporting a loss continue to op-

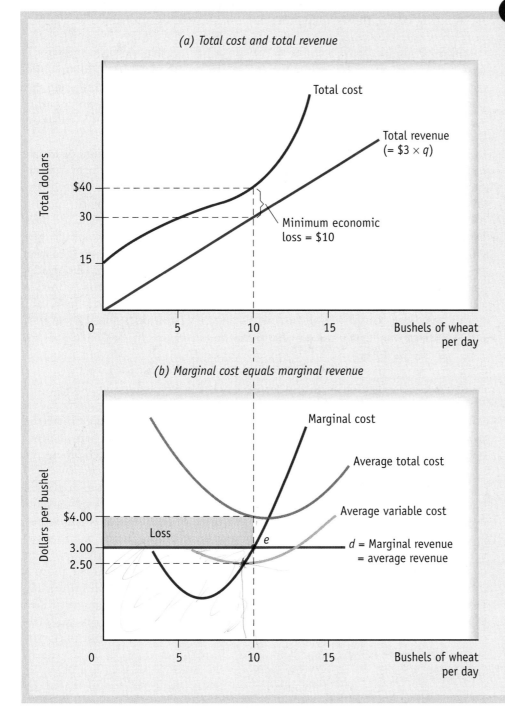

(a) Total cost and total revenue

Total cost

Total revenue
(= $3 × q)

Total dollars

$40

30

15

Minimum economic
loss = $10

0   5   10   15   Bushels of wheat
per day

(b) Marginal cost equals marginal revenue

Marginal cost

Average total cost

Average variable cost

Dollars per bushel

$4.00

Loss

3.00

2.50

e

d = Marginal revenue
= average revenue

0   5   10   15   Bushels of wheat
per day

EXHIBIT 5

Minimizing Short-Run Losses

Since total cost always exceeds total revenue in panel (a), the firm suffers a loss at every rate of output. The loss is minimized at 10 bushels per day. Panel (b) shows that marginal cost equals revenue at point *e*. The loss is equal to output (10) multiplied by the difference between average total cost ($4) and price ($3). Since price exceeds average variable cost ($2.50), the firm is better off continuing to produce in the short run.

erate. In fact, most new firms lose money for the first year or two. But *if the average variable cost of production exceeds the price at all rates of output, the firm will shut down*. After all, why produce if doing so only increases the short-run loss? For example, suppose the price of wheat falls to $2 per bushel. As you can see from column (7) of Exhibit 4, average variable cost exceeds $2 at all rates of output. By shutting down, the farmer must pay only fixed cost, not fixed cost plus a portion of variable cost.

From column (7) of Exhibit 4 you can also see that the lowest price at which the farmer would cover average variable cost is $2.47 per bushel, which is the average variable cost when output is 9 bushels per day. At this price, the farmer will be indifferent between producing and shutting down, since either way the loss is the outlay of $15 for fixed cost. Any price above $2.47 will allow the farmer, by producing, to cover some portion of fixed cost.

Note that shutting down is not the same as going out of business. In the short run, a firm keeps its productive capacity intact—paying the rent, fire insurance, and property taxes, keeping water pipes from freezing in the winter, and so on. (Think, again, about Dairy Queen shutting down for the winter months.) The firm does not escape fixed cost by shutting down, since fixed cost, by definition, is cost that does not vary with output. If prices should rise enough or costs should fall enough, the firm will resume operation. If market conditions look grim and are not expected to improve, the firm will consider going out of business, but that's a long-run decision. The short run is defined as a period during which some resources and some costs are fixed, so a firm cannot escape those costs in the short run, no matter what it does. *Fixed cost is sunk cost in the short run, no matter what decision the firm makes.*

The Firm and Industry Short-Run Supply Curves

A firm will vary its rate of output as the market price changes. As long as the price exceeds average variable cost, the firm will produce where marginal cost equals marginal revenue. But if average variable cost is everywhere above the price, the firm will shut down. The effects of various prices on the firm's output decision are summarized in Exhibit 6. Points 1, 2, 3, 4, and 5 indicate where the marginal cost curve intersects various demand, or marginal revenue, curves.

At a price as low as p_1, the firm will shut down rather than produce at point 1 because no output rate generates revenue sufficient to cover average variable cost; so the loss-minimizing output rate at a price of p_1 is zero, as identified by q_1. At a price of p_2, the firm will be indifferent between producing q_2 and shutting down because either way the loss will equal fixed cost since the price just covers average variable cost. Point 2 is called the *shutdown point*. If the price is p_3, the firm will produce q_3 to minimize its loss. At p_4, the firm will produce q_4 to earn just a normal profit, since price equals average total cost. Point 4 is called the *break-even point*. If the price rises to p_5, the firm will earn a short-run economic profit by producing q_5 (see if you can identify economic profit in the diagram when price is p_5).

The Short-Run Firm Supply Curve. As long as the price is high enough to cover average variable cost, the firm will supply the quantity resulting from the intersection of its upward-sloping marginal cost curve and its marginal revenue, or demand, curve. Thus, that portion of the firm's marginal cost curve that intersects and rises above the lowest point on its average variable cost curve becomes the **short-run firm supply curve.** *In Exhibit 6, the short-run supply curve is the upward-sloping portion of the marginal cost curve, beginning at point 2, the shutdown point.* The solid short-run supply curve indicates the quantity the firm is willing and able to supply in

Short-run firm supply curve A curve that indicates the quantity a firm supplies at each price in the short run; that portion of a firm's marginal cost curve that intersects and rises above the low point on its average variable cost curve

EXHIBIT 6

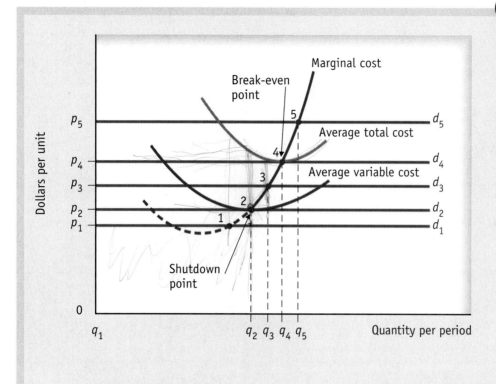

Summary of Short-Run Output Decisions

At price p_1, the firm produces nothing because p_1 is less than the firm's average variable cost. At price p_2, the firm is indifferent between shutting down and producing q_2 units of output, because in either case the firm would suffer a loss equal to its fixed cost. At p_3, it produces q_3 units and suffers a loss that is less than its fixed cost. At p_4, the firm produces q_4 and just breaks even, since p_4 equals average total cost. Finally, at p_5, the firm produces q_5 and earns an economic profit. The firm's short-run supply curve is that portion of its marginal cost curve at or rising above the minimum point of average variable cost (point 2).

the short run at each alternative price. The quantity supplied when the price is p_2 or higher is determined by the intersection of the firm's marginal cost curve and its demand, or marginal revenue, curve. The firm shuts down if the price is below p_2.

The Short-Run Industry Supply Curve. Exhibit 7 presents an example of how supply curves for just three firms with identical marginal cost curves can be summed horizontally to form the short-run industry supply curve. (In perfectly competitive markets, there will be many more firms.) The **short-run industry supply curve** is the horizontal sum of all firms' short-run supply curves. At a price below p, no output is supplied. At a price of p, 10 units are supplied by each of the three firms, for a market supply of 30 units. At a price above p, say p', 20 units are supplied by each firm, so the market supply is 60 units.

Firm Supply and Industry Equilibrium. Exhibit 8 shows the relationship between the short-run profit-maximizing output of the individual firm and market equilibrium price and quantity. We assume there are 100,000 identical wheat farmers in this industry. Their individual supply curves (represented by the portions of the marginal cost curve at or rising above the average variable cost) are summed horizontally to yield the market, or industry, supply curve shown in panel (b), where the market price of $5 per bushel is determined. At that market

Short-run industry supply curve A curve that indicates the quantity supplied by the industry at each price in the short run; the horizontal sum of each firm's short-run supply curve

EXHIBIT 7

Aggregating Individual Supply to Form Market Supply

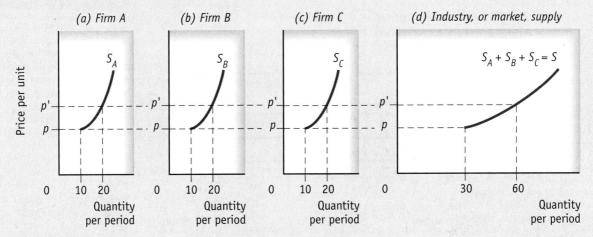

At price *p*, firms A, B, and C each supply 10 units of output. Total market supply is 30 units. In general, the market supply curve, panel (d), is the horizontal summation of the individual firm supply curves S_A, S_B, and S_C.

EXHIBIT 8

Relationship Between Short-Run Profit Maximization and Market Equilibrium

The market supply curve *S* in panel (b) is the horizontal sum of the supply curves of all firms in the industry. The intersection of *S* with the market demand curve *D* determines the market price, $5. That price, in turn, determines the height of the perfectly elastic demand curve facing the individual firm in panel (a). That firm produces 12 bushels per day (where marginal cost equals marginal revenue of $5) and earns an economic profit of $1 per bushel, or $12 in total per bushels per day.

price, each farmer supplies 12 bushels per day, as shown in panel (a), for a total quantity supplied of 1,200,000 bushels per day, as shown in panel (b). Each farmer in the short run earns an economic profit of $12 per day, represented by the shaded rectangle in panel (a).

In summary, *a perfectly competitive firm selects the short-run output rate that maximizes profit or minimizes loss. When confronting a loss, a firm either will produce an output that minimizes that loss or will shut down temporarily.*

Given the conditions for perfect competition, the market will converge toward equilibrium. But how is that equilibrium actually reached? In the real world, markets operate based on customs and conventions, which vary across markets. For example, the rules acceptable on the New York Stock Exchange are not the same as those followed in the market for flowers. In the following case study, we consider one of the oldest market mechanisms for reaching equilibrium—auctions.

Auction Markets

Five days a week in a huge building ten miles outside Amsterdam, some 2,500 buyers gather to participate in the world's largest flower auction. About 14 million flowers from 5,000 growers are auctioned off each day in the largest commercial building in the world, spread across the equivalent of 100 football fields. Flowers are grouped and auctioned off by type—long-stemmed roses, tulips, and so on. Hundreds of buyers are seated in the theater-like setting with their fingers on buttons. Once the flowers are presented, a clock-like instrument starts ticking off descending prices until a buyer stops it by pushing a button. The winning bidder gets to choose how many and which items to take. The clock starts again until another buyer stops it, and so on, until all flowers are sold. Flower auctions occur swiftly; on average a transaction occurs every four seconds.

This is an example of a *Dutch auction,* which starts at a high price and works down. Dutch auctions are more common when there are multiple lots of similar, though not identical, items to be sold, such as flowers in Amsterdam, tobacco in Canada, and fish in seaports around the world. Because there is some difference among the products for sale in a given market—for example, some flower lots are in better condition than others—this is not quite perfect competition, since perfectly competitive markets sell homogeneous products.

More common than the Dutch auction is the *English open outcry auction,* where bidding opens at a low price and moves up until only one buyer remains. Products sold this way include stocks, bonds, wine, art, antiques, livestock, and automobiles. For example, on commodity markets, such as the Chicago Board of Trade, market prices for homogeneous commodities like coffee, wheat, and gold are continuously determined in the trading pits using variations of an open outcry auction.

The birth of the Internet has breathed new life into auctions. Web sites such as eBay, Auction Interactive 2000, Onsale, Internet Auction List, Z Auction, and hundreds more hold on-line auctions. Individual sites specialize in old maps, used computers, wine, airline tickets, antiques, military memorabilia, comic books, paperweights, Beanie Babies, you name it. The largest auction site is eBay, which sells more than one thousand categories in a forum that mimics a live auction. Internet auctions allow specialized sellers to reach a world of customers.

Computers are taking over markets in other ways. In New York, Chicago, Philadelphia, London, and Frankfurt, hand-waving traders in what seem like mosh pits are gradually being replaced by electronic trading. On the Matif, the French futures exchange, when electronic trading was added as an option to the open-outcry system, electronic trading dominated within a matter of months.

Sources: Ken Bensinger and Dustan Prial, "On-Line Auction Sites Gain in Credibility and Popularity," *Wall Street Journal* (31 July 1998); Saul Hansell, "Auctions of Goods and Services Thrive on Internet," *New York Times* (2 April 1998); and David Barboza, "Cold, Efficient Screens Threaten Traditional 'Outcry' Trading," *New York Times* (12 June 1998). On the Internet, eBay's address is http://www.ebay.com.

NetBookmark

Quick links to numerous on-line auctions, such as eBay, can be found at the most popular search engines. Excite offers auctions at http://www.classifieds2000.com/, Lycos has http://www.lycos.com/auctions/ and Yahoo! presents http://auctions.yahoo.com/. HotBot offers a list of particular on-line auctions at http://shop.hotbot.com/index.html?section=auction. What are the most frequently listed types of goods available through on-line auctions? Are these the types of goods you would expect to find offered in a perfectly competitive market? Can you distinguish which goods are fads? Some of the search engines bring you directly to auctions for particular goods, but are they running the auction? Who is "powering" the auction processes? Does the auctioning business appear to be perfectly competitive?

PERFECT COMPETITION IN THE LONG RUN

In the short run, variable resources can be altered, but other resources, which mostly determine firm size, are fixed. In the long run, however, firms have time to enter and exit and to adjust their size—that is, to adjust the scale of their operations. In the long run, there is no distinction between fixed and variable costs because all resources under the firm's control are variable.

Short-run economic profit will attract new entrants and will encourage existing firms to expand the scale of their operations. Economic profit will attract resources from industries where firms are earning only normal profit or may be suffering losses. An increase in the number and size of firms will increase market supply in the long run, and an increase in market supply will reduce the price. New firms will continue to enter a profitable industry and existing firms will continue to increase in size as long as economic profit is positive. Entry and expansion will stop only when the increase in supply has reduced the market price to the point where economic profit is zero. *Short-run economic profit will attract new entrants and may cause existing firms to expand; market supply will thereby increase, driving down the market price until economic profit is eliminated.*

On the other hand, a short-run loss will prompt some firms to leave the industry or to reduce their scale of operation. In the long run, departures and reductions in scale will reduce market supply and increase market price until remaining firms just break even—that is, earn just a normal profit.

Zero Economic Profit in the Long Run

In the long run, firms in perfect competition will earn just a normal profit, which means zero economic profit. Exhibit 9 shows the individual firm and the market in long-run equilibrium. In the long run, market supply adjusts as firms enter or leave the market or change the scale of their operations; *this process continues until the market supply curve intersects the market demand curve at a price that equals the lowest point on each firm's long-run average cost curve, or LRAC curve.* A higher price would generate economic profit in the short run and would therefore attract new entrants in the long run. In the case of wheat farming, economic profit encourages existing farmers to expand the scale of their operation and will

EXHIBIT 9

Long-Run Equilibrium for the Firm and the Industry

(a) Firm

(b) Industry, or market

In long-run equilibrium, the firm produces *q* units of output per period and earns a normal profit. At point *e*, price, marginal cost, short-run average total cost, and long-run average cost are all equal. There is no reason for new firms to enter or for existing firms to leave the market. Thus, the market supply curve, *S*, in panel (b) does not shift. As long as market demand, *D*, is stable, the industry will continue to produce a total of *Q* units of output at price *p*.

attract new wheat farmers, perhaps some who had been raising other crops. A lower price would create a loss in the short run, causing some farmers in the long run to scale back their wheat production or give up wheat farming altogether.

Perfect competition in the long run cuts economic profit to zero. Because the long run is a time period during which all resources under the firm's control are variable and because firms try to maximize profit, *firms in the long run will adjust their scale of operation until their average cost of production is minimized.* Firms that fail to minimize costs will not survive in the long run. At point *e* in panel (a) of Exhibit 9, the firm is in equilibrium, producing *q* units and earning just a normal profit. At point *e*, price, marginal cost, short-run average total cost, and long-run average cost are all equal. No firm in the market has any reason to alter its output and no outside firm has any incentive to enter this industry, since each firm in the market is earning normal, but not economic, profit.

The Long-Run Adjustment to a Change in Demand

To explore the long-run adjustment process, let's consider how a firm and an industry respond to an increase in market demand. This firm is representative of all firms in the industry. Assume that the costs facing each individual firm do not depend on the number of firms in the industry (this assumption will be explained soon).

Effects of an Increase in Demand. Exhibit 10 shows a perfectly competitive firm and industry in long-run equilibrium, with the market supply curve intersecting the market demand curve at point *a* in panel (b). The market-clearing price is

EXHIBIT 10

Long-Run Adjustment to an Increase in Demand

(a) Firm

(b) Industry, or market

An increase in market demand from *D* to *D'* in panel (b) moves the short-run equilibrium point from *a* to *b*. Output rises to Q_b and price increases to *p'*. The rise in market price causes the demand curve facing the firm to rise from *d* to *d'* in panel (a). The firm responds by increasing output to *q'* and earns an economic profit, identified by the shaded rectangle. With existing firms earning economic profit, new firms enter the industry in the long run. Market supply shifts out to *S'* in panel (b). Output rises further, to Q_c, and price falls back to *p*. In panel (a), the firm's demand curve shifts back to *d*, eliminating economic profits. The short-run adjustment is from point *a* to point *b* in panel (b), but the long-run adjustment is from point *a* to point *c*.

p and the market quantity is Q_a. The individual firm, shown in panel (a), supplies *q* units at that market price, earning a normal profit in long-run equilibrium. This representative firm produces where price, or marginal revenue, equals marginal cost, short-run average total cost, and long-run average cost. (Remember, a normal profit is included in the firm's average total cost curve.)

Now suppose the market demand for this product increases from *D* to *D'* in panel (b), causing the market price to increase in the short run to *p'*. Each firm responds to the higher price by expanding output along its short-run supply, or marginal cost, curve until the quantity supplied increases to *q'*. At that rate of output, the firm's marginal cost curve intersects the new marginal revenue curve, which is also the firm's new demand curve, *d'*. Because all firms expand production, industry output increases to Q_b, where the change in industry output is the sum of the changes of all the individual firms in the industry. Note that in the short run, each firm is now earning economic profit, shown by the shaded rectangle in panel (a).

In the long run, economic profit attracts new firms. Their entry adds additional supply to the market, shifting out the market supply curve, which causes the market price to fall. Firms continue to enter as long as they can earn economic profit. The market supply curve eventually shifts out to S', where it intersects D' at point c, returning the price to its initial equilibrium level, p. The decline in the market price has dropped the demand curve facing the individual firm from d' back down to d. As a result, each firm reduces output from q' back to q and once again each earns just a normal profit. Notice that although industry output increases from Q_a to Q_c, each firm's output returns to q. In this case, the additional output comes from new firms attracted to the industry rather than from greater output by existing firms, since existing firms could not expand without increasing their long-run average costs.

New firms are attracted to the industry by short-run economic profits arising from the increase in demand. The resulting increase in market supply, however, forces the price down until economic profit disappears. In Exhibit 10(b), the short–run adjustment to increased demand is from point a to point b; in the long run, market equilibrium moves to point c.

Effects of a Decrease in Demand. Next, let's consider the effect of a decrease in demand on the long-run market adjustment process. The initial long-run equilibrium situation in Exhibit 11 is the same as in Exhibit 10. Market demand and supply curves intersect at point a in panel (b), yielding an equilibrium price of p and an equilibrium quantity of Q_a. The firm in panel (a) earns a normal profit

EXHIBIT 11

Long-Run Adjustment to a Decrease in Demand

A decrease in demand to D'' in panel (b) disturbs the long-run equilibrium at point a. Prices are driven down to p'' in the short run; output falls to Q_f. In panel (a), the firm's demand curve shifts down to d''. Each firm reduces its output to q'' and suffers a loss. As firms leave the industry in the long run, the market supply curve shifts left to S''. Market prices rise to p as output falls further to Q_g. At price p, the remaining firms once again earn zero economic profit. Thus, the short-run adjustment is from point a to point f in panel (b); the long-run adjustment is from point a to point g.

in the long run by producing output rate *q,* where price, or marginal revenue, equals marginal cost, short-run average cost, and long-run average cost.

Now suppose that the demand for this product declines, as reflected in panel (b) by the shift to the left in the market demand curve, from *D* back to *D"*. In the short run, this decline in demand reduces the market price to *p"*. As a result, the demand curve facing each individual firm drops from *d* to *d"*. Each firm responds in the short run by cutting its output to *q"*, where marginal cost equals the now-lower marginal revenue, or price. Market output falls to Q_f. Since the lower market price is below short-run average total cost, each firm operates at a loss. This loss is shown in panel (a) by the shaded rectangle (although the price must still be above average variable cost, since the firm's short-run supply curve, *MC,* is defined as that portion of the firm's marginal cost curve at or above its average variable cost curve).

In the long run, continued losses force some firms out of the industry. As firms leave, market supply decreases so the market price increases. Firms continue to leave until the market supply curve decreases to *S"*, where it intersects *D"* at point *g*. Market output has fallen to Q_g, and price has returned to *p*. With the price back up to *p*, the remaining firms once again earn a normal profit. At the conclusion of the adjustment process, each remaining firm produces *q,* the initial equilibrium quantity, but because some firms have left the industry, market output has fallen from Q_a to Q_g. Note, again, that the adjustment process involves the departure of firms from the industry rather than a reduction in the scale of firms; a reduction in scale would have increased each firm's long-run average cost.

THE LONG-RUN INDUSTRY SUPPLY CURVE

Thus far, we have looked at firm and industry responses to changes in demand, distinguishing between a short-run adjustment and a long-run adjustment. In the short run, firms alter quantity supplied by moving up or down their marginal cost curves (that portion at or rising above average variable cost) until marginal cost equals marginal revenue, or price. If price does not cover minimum average variable cost, firms shut down in the short run. The long-run adjustment, however, involves the entry or exit of firms until the resulting equilibrium price provides remaining firms with a normal profit.

In Exhibits 10 and 11, we began with an initial long-run equilibrium point and were able to identify two more long-run equilibrium points generated by the intersection of the shifted demand curve and the shifted short-run market supply curve. In each case, the price remained the same in the long run, but industry output increased in Exhibit 10 and decreased in Exhibit 11. Connecting these long-run equilibrium points yields the *long-run industry supply curve,* labeled *S★* in Exhibits 10 and 11. The **long-run industry supply curve** shows the relationship between price and quantity supplied once firms fully adjust to any short-term economic profit or loss resulting from a shift in market demand.

Constant-Cost Industries

The industry we have studied thus far is called a **constant-cost industry** because the firm's long-run average cost curve does not shift up or down as industry output changes. Resource prices and other production costs remain

Long-run industry supply curve A curve that shows the relationship between price and quantity supplied by the industry once firms fully adjust to any change in market demand

Constant-cost industry An industry that can expand or contract without affecting the long-run, per-unit cost of production; the long-run industry supply curve is horizontal constant in the long run as industry output increases or decreases. In a constant-cost industry, each firm's per-unit production costs are independent of the number of firms in the industry, so a firm's long-run average cost curve remains constant in the long run as firms enter or leave the industry. *The long-run supply curve for a constant-cost industry is horizontal,* as is depicted in Exhibits 10 and 11.

A constant-cost industry is most often characterized as one that uses such a small portion of the resources available in resource markets that increasing industry output does not bid up resource prices. For example, output in the pencil industry can expand without bidding up the prices of wood, graphite, and synthetic rubber, since the pencil industry uses such a small share of the market supply of these resources.

Increasing-Cost Industries

The firms in some industries encounter higher average costs as industry output expands in the long run. Firms in these **increasing-cost industries** find that expanding output bids up the prices of some resources or otherwise increases per-unit production costs, and these higher production costs shift each firm's cost curves upward. For example, an industry-wide expansion of oil production could bid up the price of drilling equipment and the wages of petroleum engineers and geologists, raising per-unit production costs for each firm. Likewise, more housing construction could bid up what building contractors must pay for land, lumber, other building materials, and carpenters.

To illustrate the equilibrium adjustment process for an increasing-cost industry, we begin again in long-run equilibrium in panel (b) of Exhibit 12, where the industry demand curve, D, intersects the short-run industry supply curve, S, at equilibrium point a to yield the market price p_a and the market quantity Q_a. When the price is p_a, the demand (and marginal revenue) curve facing each firm is d_a in panel (a). The firm produces the rate of output at which marginal cost equals marginal revenue, shown by point a in panel (a). At the firm's equilibrium rate of output, q, average total cost is at a minimum, so average total cost equals the price and the firm earns no economic profit in this long-run equilibrium.

Suppose an increase in the demand for this product shifts the market demand curve to the right from D to D' in panel (b). The new demand curve intersects the short-run market supply curve S at point b, yielding the short-run equilibrium price p_b and quantity Q_b. With an increase in the equilibrium price, each firm's demand curve shifts from d_a up to d_b in panel (a). The new short-run equilibrium occurs at point b in panel (a), where the marginal cost curve intersects the new demand curve, which is also the marginal revenue curve. Each firm produces output q_b. In the short run, each firm earns an economic profit equal to q_b times the difference between the price, p_b, and the average total cost at that rate of output. So far, the sequence of events is the same as for a constant-cost industry.

Economic profit attracts new entrants like bears to honey. Because this is an increasing-cost industry, the new entrants' increased demand for resources drives up the cost of production, raising each firm's marginal and average cost curves. In panel (a) of Exhibit 12, MC and ATC shift up to MC' and ATC'. (We assume for simplicity that the new average cost curves are parallel to the old curves, so the minimum efficient plant size remains the same.)

Increasing-cost industry
An industry that faces higher per-unit production costs as industry output expands in the long run; the long-run industry supply curve slopes upward

EXHIBIT 12

An Increasing-Cost Industry

(a) Firm

(b) Industry, or market

An increase in demand to *D'* in panel (b) disturbs the initial equilibrium at point *a*. A short-run equilibrium is established at point *b*, where *D'* intersects the short-run market supply curve, *S*. At the higher price p_b, the firm's demand curve shifts up to d_b, and its output increases to q_b in panel (a). At point *b*, the firm is earning an economic profit. New firms enter to try to capture some of the profits. As they do so, input prices are bid up, so each firm's marginal and average cost curves rise. The intersection of the new market supply curve, *S'*, with *D'*, determines the market price, p_c. At p_c, individual firms are earning zero economic profit. Point *c* is a point of long-run equilibrium. By connecting long-run equilibrium points *a* and *c* in panel (b), we obtain the upward-sloping long-run market supply curve, *S**, for this increasing-cost industry.

The entry of new firms also shifts the short-run industry supply curve outward, thus reducing the market price of output. *New firms enter the industry until the combination of a higher production cost and a lower output price squeezes economic profit to zero.* This long-run equilibrium occurs when entry of new firms has shifted the short-run industry supply curve out to *S'*, which lowers the price until it equals the minimum on each firm's new average total cost curve. The market price does not fall back to the initial equilibrium level because each firm's average total cost curve has shifted up. The intersection of the new short-run market supply curve, *S'*, and the new market demand curve, *D'*, determines the new long-run market equilibrium point, identified as point *c* in panel (b). Points *a* and *c* are on the *upward-sloping* long-run supply curve, denoted as *S** for this increasing-cost industry.

In constant-cost industries, each firm's costs depend simply on the scale of its plant and its rate of output. For firms in increasing-cost industries, costs depend also on the number of firms in the market. By bidding up the price of resources, long-run expansion increases each firm's average cost. The long-run supply curve for an increasing-cost industry slopes upward, like $S\star$ in Exhibit 12.

Decreasing-Cost Industries

Firms in some industries may experience a lower average cost as output expands in the long run, although this is considered rare. Firms in **decreasing-cost industries** find that as industry output expands, the per-unit cost of production falls, causing a downward shift in each firm's cost curves. For example, in the coal-mining industry, a major production cost is pumping ground water from the mine shafts. As more mines in the same area operate pumps, the water table in the area falls, so each mine's pumping costs go down.

An increase in market demand results in a higher price in the short run, so firms earn economic profit. This profit attracts new entrants in the long run, reducing average cost for all firms in the industry. Decreasing-cost industries have long-run supply curves like the one depicted in Exhibit 13, where point *a* is the initial equilibrium, point *b* is the short-run adjustment to an increase in demand, and point *c* is the long-run equilibrium adjustment as new firms are attracted by short-run profits. In the long run, the price, p_c, falls below the initial price, p_a. Entry eliminates economic profit by driving down the price.

In summary, firms in perfect competition can earn an economic profit, a normal profit, or an economic loss in the short run, but in the long run the entry or exit of firms drives economic profit to zero, so firms earn only a normal profit. This is true whether the industry in question exhibits constant costs, increasing costs, or decreasing costs in the long run. Notice that, regardless of

Decreasing-cost industry The rare case in which an industry faces lower per-unit production costs as industry output expands in the long run; the long-run industry supply curve slopes downward

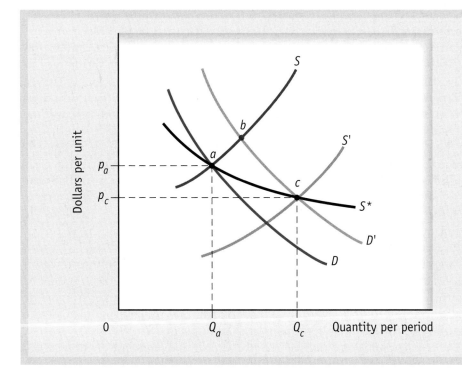

EXHIBIT 13

A Decreasing-Cost Industry Adjusts to an Increase in Demand

An increase in market demand moves the industry from starting point *a* to short-run equilibrium at point *b*. With each firm earning an economic profit, new firms begin to enter. If entry drives down the average cost of production, long-run equilibrium will be reestablished at point *c*, with a lower price than at point *a*. Connecting long-run equilibrium points *a* and *c* yields the downward-sloping long-run market supply curve, $S\star$ for this decreasing-cost industry.

the nature of costs in the industry, the industry supply curve is less elastic in the short run than in the long run. In the long run, firms can adjust all their resources, so they are better able to respond to changes in price.

As mentioned at the outset, perfect competition serves as a useful benchmark for evaluating the efficiency of markets. Let's examine the qualities of perfect competition that make it so useful.

PERFECT COMPETITION AND EFFICIENCY

How does perfect competition perform in terms of the efficient allocation of resources? There are two concepts of efficiency used in judging market performance. The first, called *productive efficiency,* refers to producing output at the least possible cost. The second, called *allocative efficiency,* emphasizes producing the output that consumers value the most. Perfect competition guarantees both productive efficiency and allocative efficiency.

Productive Efficiency

Productive efficiency The condition that exists when output is produced with the least-cost combination of inputs, given the level of technology

Productive efficiency occurs when the firm produces at the minimum point on its long-run average-cost curve, so the market price equals the minimum average total cost. In the long run in perfect competition, the entry and exit of firms and any adjustment in the scale of each firm ensure that each firm produces at the minimum point on its long-run average cost curve. Firms whose size does not reach minimum long-run average cost must either change their size or leave the industry to avoid continued losses. Thus, the long-run industry output in perfect competition is produced at the least possible cost per unit.

Allocative Efficiency

Allocative efficiency The condition that exists when firms produce the output that is most preferred by consumers; the marginal cost of each good just equals the marginal benefit that consumers derive from that good

Allocative efficiency occurs when firms produce the output that is most preferred by consumers. How do we know that perfect competition guarantees allocative efficiency? The answer lies with the market demand and supply curves. You'll recall that the demand curve reflects the marginal value that consumers attach to each unit, so the market price is the amount of money that people are willing and able to pay for the final unit they consume. We also know that, in both the short run and the long run, the equilibrium price in perfect competition equals the marginal cost of supplying the last unit sold. Marginal cost measures the opportunity cost of using resources employed by the firm. Thus the supply and demand curves intersect at the combination of price and quantity at which the marginal value, or the marginal benefit, that consumers attach to the last unit of output purchased just equals the opportunity cost of the resources employed to produce that unit of output.

As long as marginal cost equals marginal benefit, the last unit produced is valued as much as, or more than, any other good that could have been produced using those same resources. There is no way to reallocate resources to increase the value of output. Thus, there is no way to reallocate resources to increase the total utility or total benefit consumers reap from production. *When the marginal cost of producing each good equals the marginal benefit that consumers derive from that good, the market is said to be allocatively efficient.*

What's So Perfect About Perfect Competition?

If the marginal cost to firms of supplying the good just equals the marginal benefit to consumers, does this mean that market exchange confers no net benefits on participants? No. Market exchange usually benefits both consumers and producers. Recall that consumers garner a surplus from market exchange because the maximum amount they would be willing to pay for each unit of the good exceeds the amount they in fact pay. Exhibit 14 depicts a market in short-run equilibrium. The *consumer surplus* in this exhibit is represented by the blue shaded area, which is the area below the demand curve but above the market-clearing price of $10.

Producers in the short run also usually derive a net benefit, or a surplus, from market exchange, because the amount they receive for their output exceeds the minimum amount they would require to supply that amount in the short run. Recall that the short-run market supply curve is the sum of that portion of each firm's marginal cost curve at or above the minimum point on its average variable cost curve. Point *m* in Exhibit 14 is the minimum point on the market supply curve; it indicates that at a price of $5, firms are willing to supply 100,000 units. At prices below $5, quantity supplied is zero because firms could not cover variable costs and would shut down. At point *m*, firms in this industry gain no net benefit from production in the short run, because the total industry revenue derived from selling 100,000 units at $5 each just covers the variable cost incurred by producing that amount of output.

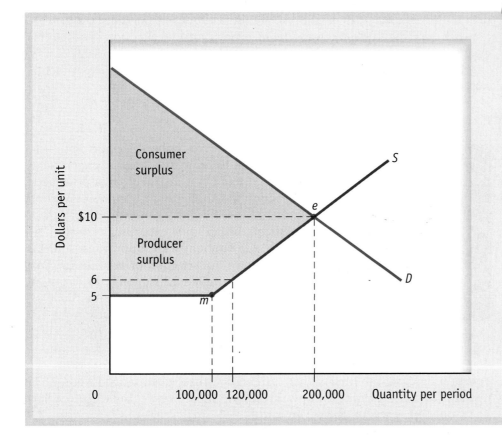

EXHIBIT 14

Consumer Surplus and Producer Surplus for a Competitive Market in the Short Run

Consumer surplus is represented by the area above the market-clearing price of $10 per unit and below the demand curve; it is shown as a blue triangle. Producer surplus is represented by the area above the short-run market supply curve and below the market-clearing price of $10 per unit; it is shown by the gold shading. At a price of $5 per unit, there is no producer surplus. At a price of $6 per unit, producer surplus is the shaded area between $5 and $6.

If the price increases to $6, firms increase their quantity supplied until their marginal cost equals $6. Market output increases from 100,000 to 120,000 units, and total revenue increases from $500,000 to $720,000. Part of the increased revenue covers the higher marginal cost of production. But the balance of the increased revenue is a bonus to producers, who would have been willing to supply 100,000 units for only $5 each. When the price is $6, they get to sell these 100,000 units for $6 each rather than $5 each. Thus producer surplus at a price of $6 is the shaded area between $5 and $6.

Producer surplus The amount by which total revenue from production exceeds total variable cost

In the short run, **producer surplus** is the total revenue producers are paid minus their total variable cost of production. In Exhibit 14, the market-clearing price is $10 per unit, and the producer surplus is depicted by the shaded area under the price but above the market supply curve. That area represents the market price minus the marginal cost of each unit produced.

The combination of consumer surplus and producer surplus shows the gains from voluntary exchange. Productive and allocative efficiency in the short run occurs at point *e*, which is the combination of price and quantity that maximizes the sum of consumer surplus and producer surplus. Even though marginal cost equals marginal benefit in equilibrium, both consumers and producers usually get a surplus, or bonus, from market exchange.

Note that producer surplus is not the same as economic profit. Any price that exceeds average variable cost will result in a short-run producer surplus, even though that price could result in a short-run economic loss. The definition of producer surplus ignores fixed cost, because fixed cost is irrelevant to the firm's short-run production decision. Fixed cost is *sunk* in the short run because the firm must pay it whether or not production occurs. Only variable cost matters. For each firm, the marginal cost is the increase in total variable cost as output increases, and the sum of the marginal costs for all units is the total variable cost.

The gains from market exchange have been examined in an experimental setting, as is discussed in the following case study.

Experimental Economics

Economists have limited opportunities to carry out the kind of controlled experiments available in the physical and biological sciences. But about four decades ago, Professor Vernon Smith (pictured at left), now at the University of Arizona, began some experiments to see how quickly and efficiently a group of test subjects could achieve market equilibrium. His original experiment involved 22 students, 11 of whom were designated as "buyers" and 11 as "sellers." Each buyer was given a card indicating the value of purchasing one unit of a hypothetical commodity; these values ranged from $3.25 downward to $0.75, forming a downward-sloping demand curve. Each seller was given a card indicating the cost of providing one unit of that commodity; these costs ranged from $0.75 upward to $3.25, forming an upward-sloping supply curve. Buyers and sellers knew only what was on their own cards.

To provide market incentives, participants were told they would receive a cash bonus at the end of the experiment based on the difference between their cost or their value and the price they negotiated in the open market. As a way of trading, Smith employed a system in which any buyer or seller announced a bid or an offer to the entire group—a system called a *double continuous auction*—based on rules similar to those governing stock markets and commodity exchanges. A transaction occurred whenever any buyer accepted an offer or when any seller accepted a bid. *Smith found that the price quickly converged to the market-clearing level,* which in his experiment was $2.00.

Economists have since performed thousands of experiments testing the properties of markets. The experiments show that under most circumstances, markets are extremely efficient in moving goods from the lowest-cost producers to the consumers who place the highest value on the goods. This maximizes the sum of consumer and producer surplus and thus maximizes social welfare. One surprising finding is how few participants are required to establish a market price. Market experiments sometimes use only four buyers and four sellers, each capable of trading several units. Some experiments use only two sellers, yet the competitive equilibrium model performs quite well under double-auction rules.

Incidentally, most U.S. retail markets, such as supermarkets and department stores, use *posted-offer pricing*—that is, the price is marked, not negotiated. Experiments show that posted pricing does not adjust to changing market conditions as quickly as does a double-continuous auction. Despite their slow response times, posted prices may be the choice for large, relatively stable markets, because such pricing involves low transaction costs. In contrast, continuous-auction pricing involves high transaction costs, requiring in the case of stock and commodity markets thousands of people in full-time negotiations to maintain prices at their equilibrium levels (although, as discussed in the previous case study, the Internet has reduced the transaction costs of establishing prices through continuous auctions).

Experiments have provided empirical support for economic theory and have yielded insights about how market rules affect market outcomes. They have also helped shape markets that did not exist, such as the market for pollution rights or for broadcast spectrum rights. Finally, experiments offer a safe and inexpensive way for those in emerging market economies, such as Poland, Russia, and Hungary, to learn how markets work.

Sources: Vernon Smith and Arlington Williams, "Experimental Market Economics," *Scientific American* (December 1992): 116–121; Vernon Smith, "Experimental Methods in Economics," *The New Palgrave Dictionary of Economics*, Vol. 2, J. Eatwell et al., eds. (New York: Stockton Press, 1987): 241–249; Vernon Smith, "Economics in the Laboratory," *Journal of Economic Perspectives* 8 (Winter 1994): 113–134; and T. C. Bergstrom and J. H. Miller, *Experiments with Economic Principles* (New York: McGraw-Hill, 1997).

Plott, an early innovator of experimental economics. Be sure to check out the Jaws animation, a QuickTime video presentation of changing equilibrium prices. Charles Holt of the University of Virginia, an innovator in using games in the classroom maintains a Web site with instructions and game sheets for some experiments at http://theweb.badm.sc.edu/laury/games.html.

CONCLUSION

Let's review the assumptions of a perfectly competitive market and see how they relate to ideas developed in this chapter. *First,* there must be many buyers and many sellers. This is necessary so that no individual buyer or seller is large enough to influence the price (although recent experiments show that the large-number assumption may be stronger than is necessary). *Second,* firms must produce a homogeneous product. If consumers could distinguish among the output of different producers, they might prefer one firm's product even at a higher price, so different producers could sell at different prices. In that case, not every firm would be a price taker—that is, each firm's demand curve would no longer be horizontal. *Third,* all market participants must have full information about all prices and all production processes. Otherwise, some producers could charge more than the market price, and some uninformed consumers would pay that higher price. Also, through ignorance, some firms might select outdated technology or fail to recognize the opportunity for short-run economic profits. *Fourth,* all resources must be mobile in the long run, and there must be no obstacles preventing new firms from moving into profitable markets. Otherwise, some firms could earn economic profit in the long run.

Perfect competition is not the market structure most commonly observed in the real world. The markets for agricultural products, stocks, commodities such as gold and silver, and foreign exchange come close to being perfect. But even if not a single example of perfect competition could be found, the model would be a useful tool for analyzing market behavior. As you will see in the next two chapters, perfect competition provides a valuable benchmark for evaluating the efficiency of other market structures.

SUMMARY

1. Market structure describes important features of the economic environment in which firms operate. These features include the number of buyers and sellers, the ease or difficulty of entering the market, the similarities or differences in the output that is produced by each firm, and the forms of competition among firms. As we will see in the next two chapters, there are four types of market structure. This chapter examined perfect competition.

2. Perfectly competitive markets are characterized by (1) a large number of buyers and sellers, each too small to influence market price; (2) production of a homogeneous product; (3) full information about the availability and prices of all resources, goods, and technologies; and (4) free and complete mobility of resources in the long run. Firms in such markets are said to be price takers because no individual firm can influence the price. Individual firms can vary only the amount they choose to sell at the market price.

3. The market price in perfect competition is determined by the intersection of the market demand and market supply curves. Each firm then faces a demand curve that is a horizontal line drawn at the market price. Because this demand curve is horizontal, it represents the average revenue and the marginal revenue the firm receives at

each rate of output. Firms in perfect competition are price takers.

4. That portion of the firm's marginal cost curve at or above the average variable cost curve is the perfectly competitive firm's short-run supply curve. The horizontal summation of all firms' supply curves forms the market supply curve. Each perfectly competitive firm maximizes profit or minimizes loss by producing where marginal cost equals marginal revenue. Fixed costs are irrelevant to the short-run production decision.

5. Because firms are not free to enter or leave the market in the short run, economic profit or loss is possible in the short run. In the long run, however, some firms will adjust their scale of operations and other firms will enter or leave the market until economic profit or loss is driven to zero. In the long run, each firm will produce at the lowest point on its long-run average cost curve. At this rate of output, marginal cost, marginal revenue, price, and average total cost are all equal. Firms that fail to produce at this least-cost combination will not survive in the long run.

6. In the short run, a firm alters quantity supplied in response to a change in price by moving up or down its marginal cost curve. The long-run industry adjustment

to a change in demand involves firms entering or leaving the market until the remaining firms in the industry earn just a normal profit. As the industry expands or contracts in the long run, the long-run industry supply curve has a shape that reflects either increasing costs, constant costs, or decreasing costs.

7. Perfectly competitive markets exhibit both productive efficiency, because output is produced using the most ef-ficient combination of resources available, and allocative efficiency, because the goods produced are those most valued by consumers. In equilibrium, perfectly competitive markets allocate goods so that the marginal cost of the last unit produced equals the marginal value that consumers attach to that last unit purchased. Voluntary exchange in competitive markets maximizes the sum of consumer surplus and producer surplus.

QUESTIONS FOR REVIEW

1. *(Market Structure)* Define "market structure." What factors are considered in determining the market structure of a particular industry?

2. *(Demand Under Perfect Competition)* What type of demand curve does a perfectly competitive firm face? Why?

3. *(Total Revenue)* Look back at Exhibit 3(a) in this chapter. Explain why the total revenue curve is a straight line from the origin, whereas the slope of the total cost curve changes.

4. *(Profit in the Short Run)* Look back at Exhibit 3(b) in this chapter. Why doesn't the firm choose the output that maximizes average profit (i.e., the output for which average cost is the lowest)?

5. *(The Short-Run Firm Supply Curve)* An individual competitive firm's short-run supply curve is the portion of its marginal cost curve that equals or rises above the average variable cost. Explain why.

6. *(CaseStudy: Auction Markets)* Which of the characteristics of the perfectly competitive market structure are found in the Amsterdam flower market?

7. *(Long-Run Industry Supply)* Why does the long-run industry supply curve for an increasing-cost industry slope upward? What causes the increasing costs in an increasing-cost industry?

8. *(Perfect Competition and Efficiency)* Define productive efficiency and allocative efficiency. What conditions must be met in order to achieve them?

9. *(CaseStudy: Experimental Economics)* In the University of Arizona experiment, which "buyers" ended up with a surplus at the market-clearing price of $2? Which "sellers" had a surplus? Which "buyers" or "sellers" did not engage in a transaction?

PROBLEMS AND EXERCISES

10. *(Short-Run Profit Maximization)* A perfectly competitive firm has the following fixed and variable costs in the short run. The market price for the firm's product is $150.

Output	FC	VC	TC	TR	Profit/ Loss
0	$100	$ 0	____	____	____
1	100	100	____	____	____
2	100	180	____	____	____
3	100	300	____	____	____
4	100	440	____	____	____
5	100	600	____	____	____
6	100	780	____	____	____

a. Complete the table.
b. At what output rate does the firm maximize profit or minimize loss?
c. What is the firm's marginal revenue at each positive level of output? Its average revenue?
d. What can you say about the relationship between marginal revenue and marginal cost for output rates below the profit-maximizing (or loss-minimizing) rate? For output rates above the profit-maximizing (or loss-minimizing) rate?

11. *(The Short-Run Firm Supply Curve)* Use the following data to answer the questions below:

Q	TVC	MC	AVC
1	$10	——	——
2	16	——	——
3	20	——	——
4	25	——	——
5	31	——	——
6	38	——	——
7	46	——	——
8	55	——	——

    a. Calculate the marginal cost and average variable cost for each level of production.

    b. How much would the firm produce if it could sell its product for $5? for $7? for $10?

    c. Explain your answers.

    d. Assuming that its fixed cost is $3, calculate the firm's profit at each of the production levels determined in part (c).

12. *(The Short-Run Firm Supply Curve)* Each of the following situations could exist for a firm in the short run. In each case, indicate whether the firm should produce in the short run or shut down in the short run, or whether additional information is needed to determine what it should do in the short run.

    a. Total cost exceeds total revenue at all output levels.

    b. Total variable cost exceeds total revenue at all output levels.

    c. Total revenue exceeds total fixed cost at all output levels.

    d. Marginal revenue exceeds marginal cost at the current output level.

    e. Price exceeds average total cost at all output levels.

    f. Average variable cost exceeds price at all output levels.

    g. Average total cost exceeds price at all output levels.

13. *(Perfect Competition in the Long Run)* Draw the short- and long-run cost curves of a competitive firm in long-run equilibrium. Indicate the long-run equilibrium price and quantity.

    a. Discuss the firm's short-run response to a reduction in the price of a variable resource.

    b. Assuming that this is a constant-cost industry, describe the process by which the industry returns to long-run equilibrium following a change in market demand.

14. *(The Long-Run Industry Supply Curve)* A normal good is being produced in a constant-cost, perfectly competitive industry. Initially, each firm is in long-run equilibrium.

    a. Graphically illustrate and explain the short-run adjustments of the market and the firm to a decrease in consumer incomes. Be sure to discuss any changes in output levels, prices, profits, and the number of firms.

    b. Next, show on your graph and explain the long-run adjustment to the income change. Be sure to discuss any changes in output levels, prices, profits, and the number of firms.

15. *(The Long-Run Industry Supply Curve)* The following graph shows possible long-run market supply curves for a perfectly competitive industry. Determine which supply curve indicates a constant-cost industry, an increasing-cost industry, and a decreasing-cost industry.

    a. Explain the difference between a decreasing-cost industry and an increasing-cost industry.

    b. Distinguish between the long-run impact of an increase in market demand in a decreasing-cost industry and the impact in an increasing-cost industry.

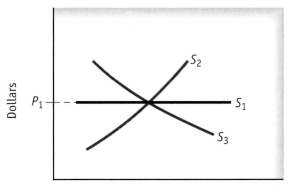

16. *(What's So Perfect About Perfect Competition)* Use the following data to answer the questions.

Quantity	Marginal Cost	Marginal Valuation
0	—	—
1	$ 2	$10
2	3	9
3	4	8
4	5	7
5	6	6
6	8	5
7	10	4
8	12	3

a. For the product shown, assume that the minimum point of each firm's average variable cost curve is at $2. Construct a supply and demand diagram for the product and indicate the equilibrium price and quantity.

b. On the graph, label the area of consumer surplus as *f*. Label the area of producer surplus as *g*.

c. If the equilibrium price were $2, what would be the amount of producer surplus?

EXPERIENTIAL EXERCISES

17. Economics America's EconEd link has an interesting module on the economics of Internet access at http://www.economicsamerica.org/econedlink/newsline/internet/index.html. Review the materials provided (including video if you have the right software available). Is provision of Internet access a competitive industry? How would you use the tools of supply and demand to model recent developments in Internet pricing?

18. *(CaseStudy: Auction Markets)* Rent the movie *Trading Places*, starring Eddie Murphy and Dan Ackroyd. Enjoy the movie and pay special attention to the scene near the end when Billy Ray and Louis participate in an auction of orange-juice futures. How does the arrival of new information affect the price of those futures contracts? Try to model the situation, using supply and demand curves.

19. *(Wall Street Journal)* Financial markets are quintessential examples of perfectly competitive markets. And, of course, the *Wall Street Journal* features in-depth coverage of these markets. Turn to the Money and Investing section of today's *Wall Street Journal* and choose one or two articles that seem interesting to you. Then, try to determine how financial markets contribute to productive and allocative efficiency in the U.S. economy.

Monopoly

Why aren't all markets monopolized? Why don't monopolies charge the highest price possible? Why don't most monopolies last? Why do some firms offer discounts to students, senior citizens, and other groups? Why do airlines charge less if you stay over Saturday night? Why are diamonds so expensive even though they aren't especially rare either in nature or in jewelry stores? These and other questions are answered in this chapter, which examines monopoly—a market structure quite different from perfect competition.

Monopoly is from the Greek, meaning "one seller." In some parts of the country, monopolists sell electricity, cable TV service, and local phone service. Monopolists also sell postage stamps, food at sports arenas, patented products, and other goods and services with no close substitutes. You have probably heard about the evils of monopoly. You may have even played the board game, Monopoly, on a rainy day.

Like perfect competition, pure monopoly is not as common as other market structures. But by understanding monopoly, you will grow more familiar with the market structures that lie between the two extremes of perfect competition and pure monopoly. In this chapter we examine (1) the sources of monopoly power, (2) how a monopolist maximizes profit, (3) the difference between monopoly and perfect competition in terms of efficiency, and (4) why a monopolist often charges different prices for the same product. Topics discussed in this chapter include:

- Barriers to entry
- Price elasticity and marginal revenue
- Economic profit in the short run and the long run

- Monopoly and resource allocation
- Welfare cost of monopoly
- Price discrimination
- Perfect price discrimination

NetBookmark

For more information about patents—their purpose, what can be patented, how to apply, what rights are included—go to the Patent Office's Web page on General Information Concerning Patents at http://www.uspto.gov/web/offices/pac/doc/general/. How does the Patent Office treat the information provided about a new invention? Why do you suppose that some firms prefer not to seek patent protection for new inventions? What types of intellectual property, other than new machines and processes, can be protected by patents?

BARRIERS TO ENTRY

As noted in Chapter 4, a *monopoly* is the sole supplier of a product with no close substitutes. Why do some markets come to be dominated by a single supplier? Perhaps the most important characteristic of a monopolized market is *barriers to entry*—new firms cannot profitably enter that market in the long run. **Barriers to entry** are restrictions on the entry of new firms into an industry. We will examine three types of barriers: legal restrictions, economies of scale, and the monopolist's control of an essential resource.

Legal Restrictions

One way to prevent new firms from entering a market is to make entry illegal. Patents, licenses, and other legal restrictions imposed by the government provide some producers with legal protection against competition.

Patents and Invention Incentives. In the United States, a **patent** awards an inventor the exclusive right to produce a good or service for 20 years. Originally enacted in 1790, the patent laws encourage inventors to invest the time and money required to discover and develop new products and processes. If others could simply copy successful products, inventors would be less inclined to incur the up-front costs of developing new products. Patents also provide the stimulus to turn an invention into a marketable product, a process called **innovation.**

Licenses and Other Entry Restrictions. Governments often confer monopoly status by awarding a single firm the exclusive right to supply a particular good or service. Federal licenses give certain firms the right to broadcast radio and TV signals. State licenses are required to provide services such as medical care, haircuts, and legal assistance. A license is not a monopoly, but it often confers the ability to charge a price above what would be the competitive level; hence, a license can serve as an effective barrier to new firms. Governments confer monopoly rights to sell hot dogs at civic auditoriums, collect garbage, provide bus and cab service in and out of town, and supply services ranging from electricity to cable TV. The government itself may claim the right to provide

Barrier to entry Any impediment that prevents new firms from competing on an equal basis with existing firms in an industry

Patent A legal barrier to entry that conveys to its holder the exclusive right to supply a product for 20 years

Innovation The process of turning an invention into a marketable product certain products by outlawing competitors. For example, many states are monopoly sellers of liquor and lottery tickets, and the U.S. Postal Service has the exclusive right to deliver first-class mail.

Economies of Scale

A monopoly sometimes emerges naturally when a firm experiences *economies of scale,* as reflected by the downward-sloping, long-run average cost curve shown in Exhibit 1. When this is the case, a single firm can satisfy market demand at a lower average cost per unit than could two or more firms operating at smaller rates of output. Thus a single firm will emerge from the competitive process as the sole seller in the market. Even though the production of electricity has grown more competitive, the *transmission* of electricity still exhibits economies of scale. Once wires are run throughout the community, the marginal cost of linking additional households to the power source is relatively small. Consequently, the average cost per household declines as more and more households are wired for electricity.

Because such a monopoly emerges from the nature of supply, it is called a *natural monopoly,* to distinguish it from the artificial monopolies created by government patents, licenses, and other legal barriers to entry. A new entrant cannot sell enough output to experience the economies of scale enjoyed by an established natural monopolist, so entry into the market is naturally blocked. We will have more to say about the regulation of natural monopolies in a later chapter, where we examine government regulation of markets.

EXHIBIT 1

Economies of Scale as a Barrier to Entry

A monopoly sometimes emerges naturally when a firm experiences economies of scale as reflected by a downward-sloping, long-run average cost curve. An individual firm can satisfy market demand at a lower average cost per unit than could two or more firms operating at smaller rates of output.

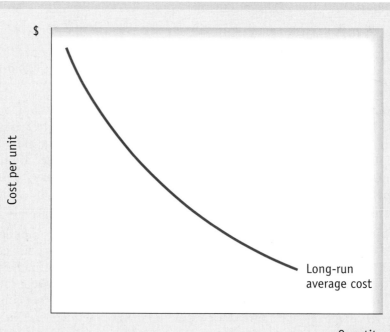

Control of Essential Resources

Sometimes the source of monopoly power is a firm's control over some nonre-producible resource critical to production. For example, professional sports leagues try to block the formation of competing leagues by signing the best athletes to long-term contracts and by seeking the exclusive use of sports stadiums and arenas. Likewise, Alcoa was the sole U.S. manufacturer of aluminum from the late 19th century until World War II; its monopoly power was initially due to production process patents that expired in 1909, but for the next three decades its monopoly power stemmed from its control of U.S. bauxite supplies. Similarly, the world's diamond trade is operated primarily by De Beers Consolidated Mines, which controls most of the world's supply of rough diamonds, as is discussed in the following case study.

Are Diamonds Forever?

In 1866, a child walking along the Orange River in South Africa picked up an interesting-looking pebble that turned out to be a 21-carat diamond. That discovery on a farm owned by Johannes De Beers sparked the development of the largest diamond mine in history. De Beers Consolidated Mines eventually expanded from mining diamonds to buying rough diamonds mined elsewhere around the world. By controlling the supply of rough diamonds, De Beers has tried to maintain a worldwide monopoly for more than six decades.

De Beers now controls three-quarters of the world's diamond trade—not quite a monopoly, but close to it. The company keeps prices high by carefully limiting supply and promoting market demand through advertising. Several times a year, De Beers invites wholesalers to London, where they are offered a box of diamonds for a set price—no negotiating. If the box of diamonds is not purchased, the buyer may not be invited back next time. Because De Beers tries to reduce market competition, the company cannot operate in the United States due to antitrust legislation (which is why U.S. buyers go to London).

It may surprise you that diamonds are not rare gems, either in nature or in jewelry stores. Nearly all jewelry stores offer more diamonds for sale than any other gem. Diamonds may be the most common natural cut gemstone. Jewelers are willing to hold large inventories of diamonds because they are confident that, because of De Beers' supply controls and marketing efforts, the price will not plummet tomorrow. De Beers' slogan "A diamond is forever" implies both that diamonds retain their value and that diamonds should stay in the family. This slogan helps keep secondhand diamonds, which are good substitutes for newly cut diamonds, off the market, where they could otherwise increase supply and drive down the price. De Beers spends over $200 million a year convincing people that diamonds are scarce and valuable. One promotional coup was to persuade the producers of "Baywatch," a TV show viewed widely around the world, to devote an entire episode to a story about the purchase of a

CaseStudy

The World of Business

At www.adiamondisforever.com you can learn about buying diamonds but you will not learn much about the sponsoring firm—De Beers. For information about the company check http://www.edata.co.za./DeBeers/ from E-Data. In particular, look at the Primary Activities section and the Corporate Report supplied by Financial Mail, a South African business newspaper. What are the current prospects for De Beers' grip on the diamond market? De Beers is not standing idly by while Canadian diamonds come into the market. The company has set up operations in Canada. What have they accomplished there? Find out at the De Beers Canada Web site at http://www.debeers.ca/index.html.

diamond engagement ring. The story played up the company line that the ring should cost two months' salary.

But De Beers has recently lost control of some rough diamond suppliers and the average price has declined. Russians have apparently been selling half their diamonds to independent dealers. A major diamond mine in Australia has also broken away from De Beers. And in October 1998, Canada began operations expected eventually to mine 10 percent of the world's gem-quality diamonds; the prospecting company has not yet promised to sell to De Beers. A monopoly that relies on the control of a key resource, as De Beers does, loses its monopoly status once that control slips away. Perhaps reflecting the growing uncertainty in this monopoly's grip, prices of some diamonds have slipped lately, and De Beers's stock price dropped by 40 percent between mid-1997 and April 1999.

Sources: Jon Ashworth, "Diamond Chief Looks Forward to Keeping the Dream Alive," *Times* (24 January 1998); "Glass with Attitude," *Economist* (20 December 1997); and "First World-Class Diamond Mine in North America," *Journal Inquirer* (17 June 1998). The De Beers home page is at http://www.adiamondisforever.com/.

Local monopolies are more common than national or international monopolies. In rural areas, monopolies may include the only grocery store, movie theater, or restaurant for miles around. But long-lasting monopolies are rare because, as we will see, a profitable monopoly attracts competitors offering close substitutes. Also, over time, technological change tends to break down barriers to entry. For example, the development of wireless transmission of long-distance telephone calls attracted competitors to AT&T. Wireless transmission will soon erase the monopoly held by local cable TV providers and even local phone service. Likewise, fax machines, e-mail, the Internet, and firms such as Federal Express now compete with the U.S. Postal Service's monopoly on first-class mail, as we will see in a later case study. And the ability to produce synthetic diamonds will eventually create additional problems for De Beers.

REVENUE FOR THE MONOPOLIST

Because a monopoly, by definition, supplies the entire market, the demand for goods or services produced by a monopolist is also the market demand. The demand curve for the monopolist's output therefore slopes downward, reflecting the law of demand—price and quantity demanded are inversely related. Let's first take a look at the monopolist's revenue schedule and revenue curves.

Revenue Schedule

Suppose that De Beers controls the entire diamond market, and the market demand for 1-carat diamonds is as presented in the first two columns of Exhibit 2. The first column lists the quantity of diamonds demanded per day, and the second column lists the corresponding price, or average revenue. The two columns together represent the demand schedule facing De Beers for 1-carat diamonds. The monopolist's *total revenue,* which equals price times quantity, appears in the third column. Notice that total revenue increases for the first 15 diamonds sold per day, but then tops out and begins to decline with 17 diamonds.

Marginal revenue, the change in total revenue as a result of selling one more diamond, is listed in the fourth column. For all units of output except the first,

EXHIBIT 2

1-Carat diamonds per day (Q) (1)	Price (average revenue) (p) (2)	Total Revenue (TR = Q × p) (3) = (1) × (2)	Marginal Revenue $\left(MR = \dfrac{\Delta TR}{\Delta Q} \right)$ (4)	Revenue for De Beers, a Monopolist
0	$7,750	0	—	
1	7,500	$ 7,500	$7,500	
2	7,250	14,500	7,000	
3	7,000	21,000	6,500	
4	6,750	27,000	6,000	
5	6,500	32,500	5,500	
6	6,250	37,500	5,000	
7	6,000	42,000	4,500	
8	5,750	46,000	4,000	
9	5,500	49,500	3,500	
10	5,250	52,500	3,000	
11	5,000	55,000	2,500	
12	4,750	57,000	2,000	
13	4,500	58,500	1,500	
14	4,250	59,500	1,000	
15	4,000	60,000	500	
16	3,750	60,000	0	
17	3,500	59,500	−500	

marginal revenue is less than the price, and the gap between the two grows larger as the price declines. As the price declines, marginal revenue falls for two reasons: (1) the amount of revenue received from selling another diamond declines (since the price drops), and (2) the revenue forgone by selling all diamonds at this lower price increases. For example, to sell a second diamond, the price must drop from $7,500 to $7,250. Total revenue from selling two diamonds is $14,500 and marginal revenue is $7,000 (= $14,500 − $7,500), so marginal revenue is below the price of $7,250.

Revenue Curves

The data in Exhibit 2 are graphed in Exhibit 3, which shows the demand and marginal revenue curves in the upper panel and the total revenue curve in the lower panel. Total revenue, recall, equals price times quantity. Note that the marginal revenue curve is below the demand curve and that total revenue is at a maximum when marginal revenue is zero. Take a minute to study these relationships—they are important.

Total revenue divided by quantity is *average revenue per unit.* Average revenue equals the price for any level of sales, so *the demand curve is also the*

EXHIBIT 3

Monopoly Demand and Marginal and Total Revenue

Where demand is price elastic, marginal revenue is positive, so total revenue increases as the price falls. Where demand is price inelastic, marginal revenue is negative, so total revenue decreases as the price falls. Where demand is unit elastic, marginal revenue is zero, so total revenue is at a maximum, neither increasing nor decreasing.

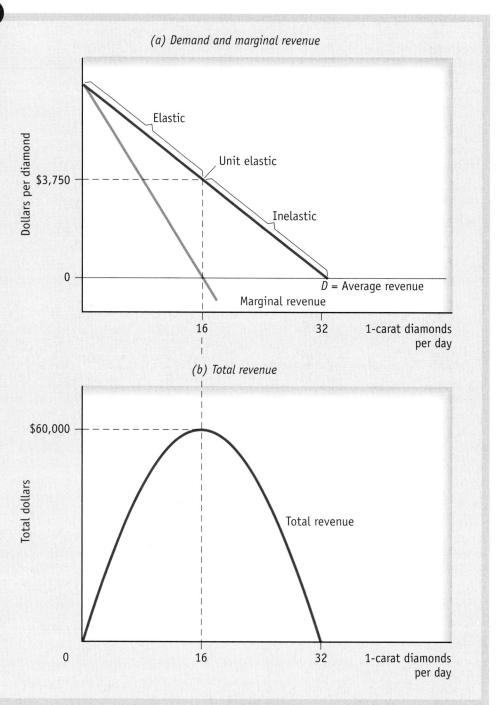

(a) Demand and marginal revenue

(b) Total revenue

monopolist's average-revenue curve (just as the perfectly competitive firm's demand curve is also that firm's average-revenue curve). Earlier you learned that the price elasticity for a straight-line demand curve decreases as you move down the curve. Where demand is elastic—that is, where the percent increase in quantity demanded more than offsets the percent decrease in price—a decrease in price will increase total revenue. Therefore, *where demand is elastic, marginal revenue is positive, so in that region total revenue increases as the price falls.* On the other hand, where demand is inelastic, the increase in quantity demanded from a lower price is not enough to make up for the loss in revenue resulting from selling all diamonds for the lower price, so total revenue will decline if the price falls. *Where demand is inelastic, marginal revenue is negative, so total revenue decreases as the price falls.* From Exhibit 3, you can see that marginal revenue becomes negative if the price drops below $3,750, indicating an inelastic demand at prices below $3,750.

In this example, demand is unit elastic at the price of $3,750. At that price, marginal revenue is zero and total revenue is at a maximum. Your understanding of elasticity will help as we discover the price and output combination that maximizes the monopolist's profit.

THE FIRM'S COSTS AND PROFIT MAXIMIZATION

Given the demand curve, the important question is: How will this monopolist choose among the price-quantity alternatives? We assume that the objective of De Beers, like that of other firms, is to *maximize economic profit.* In the case of perfect competition, the firm's choice is confined to *quantity* because the price is already determined by the market. The perfect competitor is a *price taker.* The monopolist, however, can choose either the price or the quantity, but choosing one determines the other. Because the monopolist can select the price that maximizes profit, we say the monopolist is a *price searcher.* More generally, any firm that has some control over the price it charges is a **price searcher.**

Price searcher A firm that has some control over the price it charges because its demand curve slopes downward

Profit Maximization

Exhibit 4 repeats the revenue data from Exhibits 2 and 3 and also includes short-run cost data reflecting costs similar to those already introduced in the two previous chapters. Please take a little time right now to become familiar with Exhibit 4. Then ask yourself what price-quantity combination maximizes profit.

There are two approaches to profit maximization—the total approach and the marginal approach.

Total Revenue Minus Total Cost. The profit-maximizing monopolist employs the same decision rule as the competitive firm. *The monopolist must find the production rate where total revenue exceeds total cost by the greatest amount.* Economic profit appears in the right-hand column of Exhibit 4. As you can see, the maximum profit is $12,500 per day, which occurs when output is 10 diamonds per day and price is $5,250. At that rate of output, total revenue is $52,500 and total cost is $40,000.

Marginal Cost Equals Marginal Revenue. De Beers, as a profit-maximizing monopolist, increases output as long as selling additional diamonds adds more to total revenue than to total cost. So De Beers expands output as long as marginal revenue exceeds marginal cost but will stop before marginal cost exceeds marginal revenue. Again, profit is maximized at $12,500 when output is 10 diamonds per day. The marginal revenue from the 10th diamond is $3,000; its marginal cost

EXHIBIT 4

Short-Run Costs and Revenue for a Monopolist

Diamonds per day (Q) (1)	Price (average revenue) (p) (2)	Total Revenue (TR = Q × p) (3) = (1) × (2)	Marginal Revenue $\left(MR = \frac{\Delta TR}{\Delta Q}\right)$ (4)	Total Cost (TC) (5)	Marginal Cost $\left(MC = \frac{\Delta TC}{\Delta Q}\right)$ (6)	Average Total Cost $\left(ATC = \frac{TC}{Q}\right)$ (7)	Total Profit or Loss = TR − TC (8)
0	$7,750	0	—	$15,000	—	—	−$15,000
1	7,500	$ 7,500	$7,500	19,750	$ 4,750	$19,750	−12,250
2	7,250	14,500	7,000	23,500	3,750	11,750	−9,000
3	7,000	21,000	6,500	26,500	3,000	8,830	−5,500
4	6,750	27,000	6,000	29,000	2,500	7,750	−2,000
5	6,500	32,500	5,500	31,000	2,000	6,200	1,500
6	6,250	37,500	5,000	32,500	1,500	5,420	5,000
7	6,000	42,000	4,500	33,750	1,250	4,820	8,250
8	5,750	46,000	4,000	35,250	1,500	4,410	10,750
9	5,500	49,500	3,500	37,250	2,000	4,140	12,250
10	**5,250**	**52,500**	**3,000**	**40,000**	**2,750**	**4,000**	**12,500**
11	5,000	55,000	2,500	43,250	3,250	3,930	11,750
12	4,750	57,000	2,000	48,000	4,750	4,000	9,000
13	4,500	58,500	1,500	54,500	6,500	4,190	4,000
14	4,250	59,500	1,000	64,000	9,500	4,570	−4,500
15	4,000	60,000	500	77,500	13,500	5,170	−17,500
16	3,750	60,000	0	96,000	18,500	6,000	−36,000
17	3,500	59,500	−500	121,000	25,000	7,120	−61,500

is $2,750. Because an 11th diamond has a marginal cost of $3,250 but a marginal revenue of only $2,500, producing that additional unit would lower profit from $12,500 to $11,750. As you can see, at output rates in excess of 10 diamonds per day, marginal cost exceeds marginal revenue. For simplicity, we say that *the profit-maximizing output occurs where marginal cost equals marginal revenue,* which, you will recall, is the golden rule of profit maximization.

Graphical Solution. The cost and revenue data in Exhibit 4 are reflected in Exhibit 5, with per-unit cost and revenue curves in the upper panel and total cost and revenue curves in the lower panel. The intersection of the two marginal curves at point *e* in the upper panel indicates that profit is maximized when 10 diamonds are sold. At that rate of output, we move up to the demand curve to find the profit-maximizing price of $5,250. The average total cost of $4,000 is

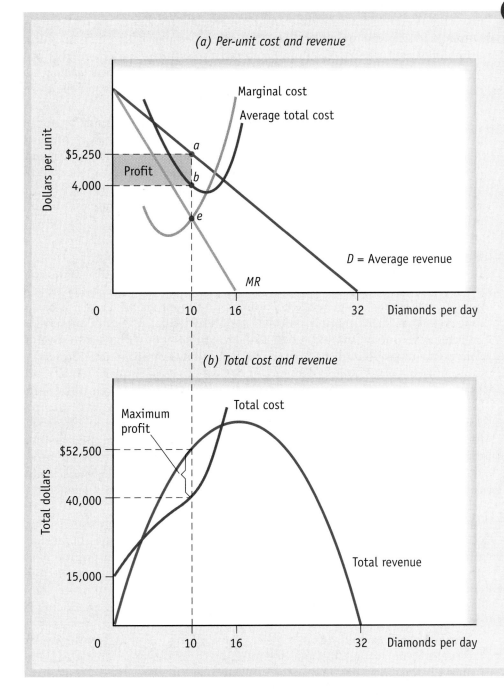

(a) Per-unit cost and revenue

EXHIBIT 5

Monopoly Costs and Revenue

The monopolist produces 10 diamonds per day and charges a price of $5,250. Total profit, shown by the blue rectangle in panel (a), is $12,500, the profit per unit multiplied by the number of units sold. In panel (b), profit is maximized where total revenue exceeds total cost by the greatest amount, which occurs at an output rate of 10 diamonds per day. Profit is total revenue ($52,500) minus total cost ($40,000), or $12,500.

identified by point *b*. The average profit per diamond equals the price of $5,250 minus the average total cost of $4,000. Economic profit is the average profit per unit of $1,250 multiplied by the 10 units sold, for a total profit of $12,500 per day, as identified by the shaded rectangle. *So the profit-maximizing rate of output is found where the rising marginal cost curve intersects the marginal revenue curve.*

In the lower panel, the firm's profit or loss is measured by the vertical distance between the total revenue and total cost curves. De Beers will expand output as long as the increase in total revenue that results from selling one more diamond exceeds the increase in total cost that results from producing that diamond. *The profit-maximizing firm will produce the rate of output where total revenue exceeds total cost by the greatest amount.* Again, profit is maximized where De Beers produces 10 diamonds per day.

One common myth about monopolies is that they will charge as high a price as possible. But the monopolist is interested in maximizing profit, not price. The amount the monopolist can charge is limited by consumer demand. De Beers could charge a price of $7,500 per diamond, but only one would be purchased at that price. Indeed, the monopolist could charge $8,000 or $10,000 per diamond, but none would be purchased. So charging the highest possible price is not consistent with maximizing profit.

Short-Run Losses and the Shutdown Decision

Being a monopolist provides no guarantee of profit. A monopolist is the sole producer of a good with no close substitutes, but the demand for that good may not be great enough to generate economic profit in either the short run or the long run. After all, many new products are protected from direct competition by patents, yet most patented products fail to attract enough buyers to survive. And even a monopolist that is initially profitable may eventually suffer losses because of rising costs, falling demand, or market entry of similar products. For example, Coleco, the original mass producer of Cabbage Patch dolls, went bankrupt after that craze died down. And Cuisinart, the company that introduced the food processor in the early 1980s, soon faced many imitators and filed for bankruptcy before the end of the decade. In the short run, the loss-minimizing monopolist, like the loss-minimizing perfect competitor, must decide whether to produce or to shut down. *If the price covers average variable cost, the firm will operate. If no price covers average variable cost, the firm will shut down, at least in the short run.*

Loss minimization is illustrated graphically in Exhibit 6, where the marginal cost curve intersects the marginal revenue curve at point *e*. At the equilibrium rate of output, *Q*, the price, *p*, is read off the demand curve at point *b*. That price exceeds average variable cost (found at point *c*) but is below average total cost (found at point *a*). Since price covers average variable cost and makes some contribution to average fixed cost, this monopolist loses less by producing *Q* than by shutting down. The loss per diamond is *ab*, which is the average total cost minus the average revenue, or price. The total loss, identified by the shaded rectangle, is the average loss per diamond, *ab*, times the number sold, *Q*. The firm will shut down if the average variable cost curve is above the demand curve, or average revenue curve, at all output rates.

Recall that for a perfectly competitive firm, that portion of the marginal cost curve at or above the average variable cost curve shows how much the firm supplies at each price. Thus that portion of the marginal cost curve represents a perfect competitor's supply curve. For the monopolist, unlike the perfectly competitive firm, marginal revenue does not equal the price. The price at the profit-maximizing (or loss-minimizing) rate of output is found on the demand

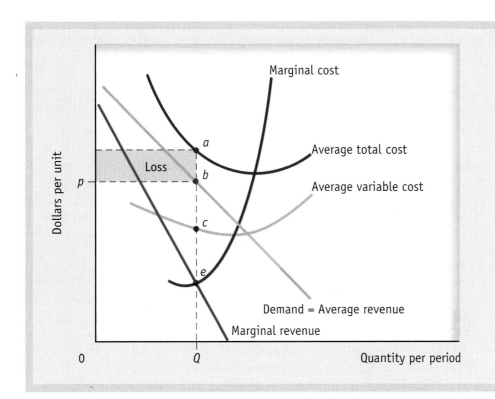

EXHIBIT 6

The Monopolist Minimizes Losses in the Short Run

Marginal cost equals marginal revenue at point *e*. At quantity *Q*, price *p* (at point *b*) is less than average total cost (at point *a*), so the monopolist is suffering a loss. The monopolist will continue to produce in the short run because price is greater than average variable cost (at point *c*).

curve, which lies *above* the marginal revenue and marginal cost curves at that quantity. The intersection of a monopolist's marginal cost and marginal revenue curves identifies the profit-maximizing (or loss-minimizing) quantity, but the price must be read off the demand curve. So each point along the monopolist's marginal cost curve does not identify a price-quantity combination, as was the case for a perfectly competitive firm. Hence, there is no curve that reflects combinations of price and quantity the monopolist is willing and able to supply, so *there is no monopolist supply curve.*

Long-Run Profit Maximization

For perfectly competitive firms, the distinction between the short run and the long run is important, because in the long run entry and exit of firms can occur, erasing any economic profit or loss. For the monopolist, the distinction between the short and long run is less important. *If a monopoly is insulated from competition by high barriers that block new entry, then economic profit can persist in the long run.*

Yet short-run profit is no guarantee of long-run profit. For example, if the monopoly power rests on a patent, patents last only a specified time and even while a product is under patent, the monopolist often must defend the patent in court (patent litigation has increased by more than half in the last decade).

A monopolist that earns economic profit in the short run may find that profit can be increased in the long run by adjusting its scale of production.

A monopolist that suffers a loss in the short run may be able to eliminate that loss in the long run by adjusting to a more efficient size or by trying to increase demand through advertising (most start-up firms lose money initially). A monopolist that is unable to erase a loss in the long run will leave the market.

MONOPOLY AND THE ALLOCATION OF RESOURCES

If monopolists are no more greedy than perfectly competitive firms (since both maximize profit), if monopolists do not charge the highest possible price, and if monopolists are not guaranteed a profit, then what's the problem? To get a handle on the problem, we will compare monopoly with that benchmark established in the previous chapter: perfect competition.

Price and Output Under Perfect Competition

Let's begin with the long-run equilibrium price and output for a perfectly competitive market. Suppose the long-run market supply curve in perfect competition is horizontal, as shown by S_c in Exhibit 7. Since this is a constant-cost industry, the horizontal long-run supply curve also shows marginal cost and average total cost at each rate of output.

Long-run equilibrium in perfect competition occurs at point c, where market demand and market supply intersect to yield price p_c and quantity Q_c. Remember, the demand curve reflects the marginal benefit from each unit purchased. In competitive equilibrium, this marginal benefit also equals the marginal cost to society of producing the final unit sold. Because consumers are able to purchase Q_c units at price p_c, they enjoy a net benefit from con-

EXHIBIT 7

Perfect Competition and Monopoly

A perfectly competitive industry would produce output Q_c, determined at the intersection of market demand curve D and supply curve S_c. The price would be p_c. A monopoly that could produce output at the same minimum average cost would produce output Q_m, determined at point b, where marginal cost and marginal revenue intersect. It would charge price p_m. Hence, output is lower and price is higher under monopoly than under perfect competition.

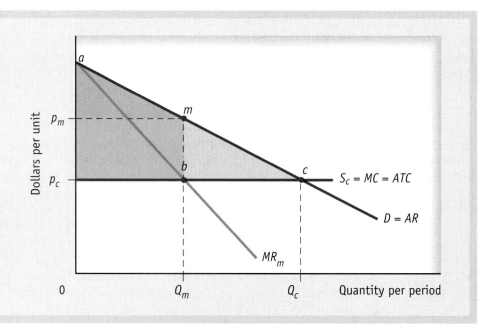

sumption, or a consumer surplus, which is measured by the entire shaded triangle acp_c.

Price and Output Under Monopoly

When there is only one firm in the industry, the industry demand curve becomes the monopolist's demand curve, so the price the monopolist charges determines how much is sold. Because the monopolist's demand curve slopes downward, the marginal revenue curve also slopes downward, as is indicated by MR_m in Exhibit 7. Suppose the monopolist can produce at the same constant long-run average cost as can the competitive industry. The monopolist maximizes profit in the long run by equating marginal cost with marginal revenue. Marginal cost equals marginal revenue at point b, yielding equilibrium output Q_m at price p_m. The consumer surplus at that price is triangle amp_m. The consumers' marginal benefit, identified as point m, exceeds the monopolist's marginal cost, identified as point b. Society would be better off if output were expanded beyond Q_m, because the marginal value consumers attach to additional units exceeds the marginal cost of producing those additional units.

Allocative and Distributive Effects

Consider the allocative and distributive effects of monopoly versus perfect competition. In Exhibit 7, the monopolist earns economic profit equal to the rectangle $p_m mbp_c$. Consumer surplus under perfect competition was the large triangle acp_c; under monopoly, it shrinks to the smaller triangle amp_m, which in this example is only one-fourth as large. By comparing the situation under monopoly with that under perfect competition, you can see that economic profit comes entirely from what was consumer surplus under perfect competition. Because the profit rectangle reflects a transfer from consumer surplus to monopoly profit, this amount is not lost to society and so is not considered a welfare loss of monopoly.

Notice, however, that consumer surplus has been reduced by more than the profit rectangle. Consumers have also lost the triangle *mcb*, which was part of the consumer surplus under perfect competition. The *mcb* triangle is called the **deadweight loss,** or *welfare loss,* of monopoly because it is a loss to consumers that is a gain to nobody. *The triangle* mcb *measures the welfare loss arising from the higher price and reduced output of the monopolist.* This triangle is a deadweight loss because it represents consumer surplus forgone on units of output that are not produced. Empirical estimates of the U.S. annual welfare cost of monopoly have ranged from about 1 percent to about 5 percent of national income. Applied to national income data for 1999, these estimates imply a welfare cost that could range from about $90 billion to $440 billion.

Deadweight loss A loss of consumer surplus and producer surplus that is not transferred to anyone else; it can result from monopolization of an industry

PROBLEMS ESTIMATING THE WELFARE COST OF MONOPOLY

The actual cost of monopoly could differ from the welfare loss described in the previous section. We will first consider why the welfare loss of monopoly might be lower than that measured in Exhibit 7 and then consider why it might be higher.

Why the Welfare Loss of Monopoly Might Be Lower

If firms in an industry experience economies of scale, a monopolist may be able to produce output at a lower cost per unit than could competitive firms. Therefore, the price, or at least the cost of production, could be lower under monopoly than under competition. If there are no economies of scale, the monopolist may still keep the price below the profit-maximizing level to avoid attracting new competitors. For example, before World War II, Alcoa was the only U.S. manufacturer of aluminum. Some observers claim the company kept prices low to discourage potential rivals from entering the industry.

The welfare loss shown in Exhibit 7 may also overstate the true cost of monopoly because monopolists may, in response to public scrutiny and political pressure, keep prices below what the market could bear. Although monopolists would like to earn as great an economic profit as possible, they realize that if the public outcry over high prices and high profits grows loud enough, some sort of government intervention could reduce or even eliminate profits. For example, the prices and profits of drug companies, which individually are monopoly producers of patented medicines, came under scrutiny by President Clinton, who threatened to regulate drug prices. Firms may try to avoid such treatment by keeping prices below the level that would maximize economic profit.

Why the Welfare Loss of Monopoly Might Be Higher

Another line of thought suggests that the welfare loss of monopoly may, in fact, be greater than shown in our simple diagram. *If resources must be devoted to securing and maintaining a monopoly position, monopolies may involve more of a welfare loss than simple models suggest.* For example, consider radio and TV broadcasting rights, which confer on the recipient the exclusive right to use a particular band of the scarce broadcast spectrum. In the past, these rights have been given away by government agencies to the applicants deemed most deserving. Because these rights are so valuable, numerous applicants spend a bundle on lawyers' fees, lobbying expenses, and other costs associated with making themselves appear the most deserving. The efforts devoted to securing and maintaining a monopoly position are largely a social waste because they use up scarce resources but add not one unit to output. Activities undertaken by individuals or firms to influence public policy in a way that will directly or indirectly redistribute income to themselves are referred to as **rent seeking.**

Rent seeking Activities undertaken by individuals or firms to influence public policy in a way that will directly or indirectly redistribute income to them

The monopolist, insulated from the rigors of competition in the marketplace, may also grow fat and lazy—and become inefficient. Since some monopolies could still earn an economic profit even if output were not produced at the least possible cost, corporate executives may waste resources in creating a more comfortable life for themselves. Long lunches, afternoon golf, plush offices, corporate jets, and extensive employee benefits may make company life more enjoyable, but these additional expenses also increase the average cost of production.

Monopolists have also been criticized for being slow to adopt the latest production techniques, being reluctant to develop new products, and generally lacking innovativeness. Because monopolists are largely insulated from the rigors of competition, they may take it easy. It's been said that "The best of all monopoly profits is a quiet life." The following case study discusses the performance of one of the oldest monopolies in the United States, the U.S. Postal Service.

The Mail Monopoly

The U.S. postal monopoly was established in 1775 and has operated under federal protection ever since. In 1971, Congress converted the Post Office Department into an independent agency called the U.S. Postal Service, with revenue of about $60 billion in 1998. It has a legal monopoly in delivering first-class letters; it also has the exclusive right to the use of the space inside mailboxes. The 760,000 Postal Service employees handle over half a billion pieces of mail a day—nearly half the world's total.

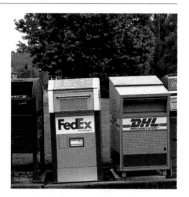

The Postal Service monopoly has suffered in recent years because of higher postal rates and competition from new technologies. The price of a first-class stamp climbed from 6 cents in 1970 to 33 cents by 1999, more than double the increase in inflation and triple the increase in telephone rates. Emerging technologies such as fax machines and e-mail also compete with the Postal Service (e-mail messages now greatly outnumber first-class letters).

The United Parcel Service (UPS) is more mechanized and more containerized than the Postal Service and thus has lower costs and less breakage. The Postal Service has tried to emulate UPS, but with only limited success. Postal employees are also paid more on average than employees at UPS or other private-sector delivery services, such as Federal Express.

Despite threatened legal actions by the Postal Service, Federal Express and others have captured 90 percent of the overnight mail business. Since the Postal Service has no monopoly except for regular first-class mail, it has lost huge chunks of the other classes to private firms offering lower rates and better service. For example, in the last 20 years, UPS and others have taken away 95 percent of fourth-class mail—parcel post business. When the Postal Service recently raised third-class ("junk" mail) rates, third-class mailers shifted to other forms of advertising, including cable TV and telemarketing. The Postal Service is losing its first-class monopoly because of competition from overnight mail and from new technologies. Things could be worse: Russia's Post Office went broke in 1998, and trainloads full of mail were held hostage by the state Railway Ministry waiting to get paid.

Source: Richard John, *Spreading the News: The American Postal System from Franklin to Morse* (Harvard University Press, 1996); Matt Lake, "Focus on Productivity and Profit at Internet World," *New York Times* (9 October 1998); and Michael Wines, "At Russian Post Office, Check Isn't in the Mail," *New York Times* (3 October 1998). The home page of the U.S. Postal Service is at http://www.usps.com/welcome.htm.

CaseStudy

Public Policy

How has the Postal Service dealt with competition and change? A chapter in its online history, at http://www.usps.gov/history/his3_5.htm#CHANGE, describes the reforms made in the 1990s to compete with for-profit firms and e-mail. How does the Postal Service set rates now that it is no longer a monopoly? The process is described at http://www.usps.gov/fyi/welcome.htm. What role do forces of competition play in rate setting? On-line cost calculators are provided by both USPS at http://www.usps.gov/business/calcs.htm and UPS (United Parcel Service) at http://www.usps.gov/business/calcs.htm. Try finding the cost of sending a letter to Uruguay. Which is cheaper? Why?

Not all economists believe that monopolies, especially private monopolies, manage their resources with any less vigilance than perfect competitors do. Some argue that because monopolists are protected from rivals, they are in a good position to capture the fruits of any innovation and therefore will be more innovative than competitive firms. Other economists believe that if a private monopolist strays from the path of profit maximization, the value of the firm's stock will drop. This lower stock price provides an incentive for outsiders to buy a controlling share of the firm's stock, shape up the operation, and watch profits—as well as the value of the firm's stock—grow. This market for corporate control is thus said to direct monopolists along the path of efficient production.

MODELS OF PRICE DISCRIMINATION

In the model of monopoly developed so far, to sell more output, a monopolist must lower the price for all output sold. In reality, a monopolist can sometimes increase economic profit by charging higher prices to people who value the output more. This practice of charging different prices to different consumers for identical output is known as **price discrimination.** For example, some firms offer discounts to senior citizens. Children pay lower admission prices to sporting events, movies, plays, and other shows. As a student, you also qualify for reduced prices for a variety of products. Firms offer certain groups reduced prices because doing so enhances profits. Let's see how and why.

Price discrimination Increasing profit by selling the same good for different prices to different consumers for reasons unrelated to cost

Conditions for Price Discrimination

To practice price discrimination, certain conditions must exist. First, the demand curve for the product must slope downward, indicating that the producer is a price searcher—the producer has some market power, some control over the price. Second, there must be at least two classes of consumers, with different price elasticities of demand. Third, the producer must be able, at little cost, to identify each class of consumers and charge them different prices. Finally, the producer must be able to prevent those who pay the lower price from reselling the product to those who pay the higher price.

Examples of Price Discrimination

Let's consider some examples of price discrimination. Because businesspeople face unpredictable yet urgent demands for travel and communication, and because such expenses are paid by the company, businesspeople are less sensitive to changes in the price of travel and communication than are householders. In other words, businesspeople have a less elastic demand for business travel and telephone use than do householders, so airlines and telephone services try to maximize profits by charging business customers higher rates than residential customers.

But how do firms distinguish between classes of customers? Telephone companies are able to sort out their customers by charging different rates based on the time of day. Long-distance charges are often higher during normal *business* hours than during evenings and weekends, when householders, who presumably have a higher price elasticity of demand, make social calls. Airlines try to distinguish between business customers and household customers based on the terms under which tickets are purchased. Householders plan their trips well in advance and often stay over Saturday night. They have more flexibility about when they travel and are more sensitive to price than are business travelers. Business travel, on the other hand, is more unpredictable, more urgent, and seldom involves a weekend stay. The airlines separate business travelers from vacationers by requiring purchasers of "super-saver" fares to buy tickets well in advance and to stay over Saturday.

Major amusement parks, such as Disney World, often think of customers as falling into two distinct groups with different elasticities: local residents and out-of-towners. Out-of-towners typically spend a substantial amount on airlines and lodging just to get there, so they are less sensitive to the price of admission than are local residents, who can go any time. The problem is how to charge a lower price to local residents. The parks do this by making discount coupons available at local businesses, such as dry cleaners, which tourists are not likely to visit.

A Model of Price Discrimination

Exhibit 8 shows the effects of price discrimination. Consumers are divided into two groups with distinctly different demands. *At a given price level,* the price elasticity of demand in panel (b) is greater than that in panel (a). Think of panel (b) as reflecting the demand of college students, senior citizens, or some other group that tends to be more sensitive to the price.

The exhibit also shows the marginal cost curve. For simplicity, we assume that the monopolist produces at a constant long-run average cost of $1 and that this cost is the same for both groups. The monopolist maximizes profit by finding the output in each market that equates marginal cost with marginal revenue. In panel (a), the resulting price is $3 per unit; in panel (b), that price is $1.50 per unit. So profit maximization results in charging a lower price to the group with more elastic demand. Note that, despite the price difference, the monopolist collects the same marginal revenue from the last unit sold to each group.

EXHIBIT 8

Price Discrimination with Two Groups of Consumers

A monopolist that faces two groups of consumers with different demand elasticities may be able to practice price discrimination. With marginal cost the same in both markets, the firm sells 400 units to the high-marginal-value consumers in panel (a) and charges them a price of $3 per unit. It sells 500 units to the low-marginal-value consumers in panel (b) and charges them a price of $1.50.

Perfect Price Discrimination: The Monopolist's Dream

The demand curve shows the marginal value of each unit consumed, which is also the maximum amount consumers would pay for each unit. If the monopolist could charge a different price for each unit sold—a price reflected by the height of the demand curve—the firm's marginal revenue from selling one more unit would equal the price of that unit. Thus, the demand curve would become the firm's marginal revenue curve. The **perfectly discriminating monopolist** charges a different price for each unit of the good.

In Exhibit 9, the monopolist is assumed to produce at a constant average cost in the long run. A perfectly discriminating monopolist, like any producer, would maximize profit by finding the output rate where marginal cost equals marginal revenue. Since the demand curve is now the marginal revenue curve, the profit-maximizing output occurs at the point where the demand curve intersects the marginal cost curve, identified at point *e* in Exhibit 9. Price discrimination is a way of increasing profit. The perfectly discriminating monopolist's economic profit is defined by the area of the shaded triangle *aec*.

By charging a different price for each unit of output, the perfectly discriminating monopolist is able to convert every dollar of consumer surplus into economic profit. Although it may seem unfair to consumers, perfect price discrimination gets high marks based on allocative efficiency. In fact, because we have assumed that this is a constant-cost industry, *Q* is the same rate of output that would result from perfect competition (though under perfect competition, consumer surplus would equal the triangle *aec*). As in the perfectly competitive outcome, the marginal cost of the last unit of output produced just equals the marginal benefit consumers attach to that unit. And although perfect price discrimination yields no consumer surplus, the total benefits consumers derive from consumption just equal the total amount they paid for the good. Note also that because the mo-

Perfectly discriminating monopolist A monopolist who charges a different price for each unit of the good

EXHIBIT 9

Perfect Price Discrimination

If a monopolist can charge a different price for each unit sold, it may be able to practice perfect price discrimination. By setting the price of each unit equal to the maximum amount consumers are willing to pay for that unit (shown by the height of the demand curve), the monopolist can achieve a profit equal to the area of the shaded triangle. Consumer surplus is zero.

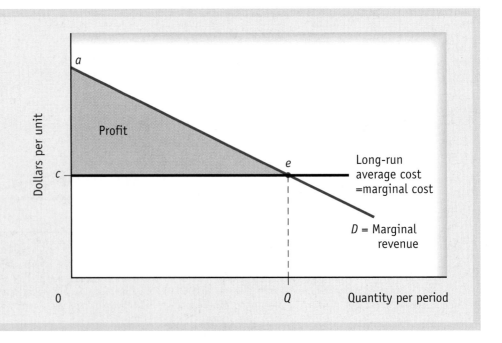

nopolist does not restrict output, there is no deadweight loss of monopoly—no welfare-loss triangle. Hence perfect price discrimination enhances social welfare when compared with monopoly output in the absence of price discrimination. The problem is that the monopolist reaps all net gains from production and consumers just break even, since their total cost equals their total benefit.

CONCLUSION

Pure monopoly, like perfect competition, is not that common. Perhaps the best examples are firms producing patented items with unique characteristics, such as certain prescription drugs. Some firms may have monopoly power in the short run, but the lure of economic profit encourages rivals to hurdle seemingly high entry barriers. Changing technology also works against monopoly in the long run. The railroad monopoly was erased by the interstate highway system. AT&T's monopoly on long-distance phone service crumbled as microwave technology replaced copper wire. The U.S. Postal Service's legal monopoly on first-class mail delivery is being eroded by express delivery, fax machines, and e-mail. And cable TV may soon lose its local monopoly status to technological breakthroughs in fiber-optics technology and wireless communications.

Although perfect competition and pure monopoly are relatively rare, our examination of them yields a framework that will help us view market structures that lie between the two extremes. As we will see, many firms have some degree of monopoly power—that is, they face downward-sloping demand curves. In the next chapter, we will consider two market structures that lie in the gray region between perfect competition and monopoly.

SUMMARY

1. A monopolist sells a product with no close substitutes. Economic profit earned by a monopolist can persist in the long run only if the entry of new firms into the market is blocked. Three barriers to entry are (1) legal restrictions, such as patents and operating licenses; (2) economies of scale, which lower average cost as output expands in the long run; and (3) control over a key resource.

2. Because a monopolist is the sole supplier, the monopolist's demand curve is also the market demand curve. Since the monopolist can sell more only if the price falls, the marginal revenue is less than the price. When demand is elastic, marginal revenue is positive and total revenue increases as the price falls. When demand is inelastic, marginal revenue is negative and total revenue decreases as the price falls.

3. If, at some positive rate of output, the monopolist can at least cover variable cost, profit is maximized or loss is minimized in the short run by finding the output rate that equates marginal cost with marginal revenue.

4. In the short run, the monopolist, like the perfect competitor, can earn economic profit but will shut down unless price is at or above average variable cost. In the long run, the monopolist, unlike the perfect competitor, can continue to earn economic profit as long as the entry of new firms is blocked.

5. Resources are not allocated as efficiently under unregulated monopoly as under perfect competition. If costs are similar, the monopolist will charge a higher price and supply less output than will a perfectly competitive industry. Monopoly usually results in a net welfare loss when compared to perfect competition because the loss in consumer surplus under monopoly exceeds the gain in monopoly profit.

6. To increase profit through price discrimination, the monopolist must have at least two identifiable types of consumers with different elasticities of demand and must be able to prevent those consumers charged the lower price from reselling to those charged the higher price. A perfect price discriminator charges a different price for each unit of the good, thereby converting all consumer surplus into economic profit. Perfect price discrimination seems unfair because the monopolist "cleans up," but it gets high marks in terms of allocative efficiency.

QUESTIONS FOR REVIEW

1. *(Barriers to Entry)* Complete each of the following sentences:
   a. Patents and licenses are examples of government-imposed _____ that prevent entry into an industry.
   b. A U.S. _____ awards inventors the exclusive right to production for 20 years.
   c. When economies of scale make it possible for a single firm to satisfy market demand at a lower cost per unit than could two or more firms, the single firm is considered a _____.
   d. A potential barrier to entry is a firm's control of a(n) _____ resource critical to production in the industry.

2. *(Barriers to Entry)* Explain how economies of scale can be a barrier to entry.

3. *(CaseStudy: Are Diamonds Forever?)* How does the De Beers cartel maintain control of the price in the diamond market? How might this control be threatened?

4. *(Revenue for the Monopolist)* How does the demand curve faced by a monopolist differ from the demand curve faced by a perfectly competitive firm?

5. *(Revenue Schedule)* Explain why the marginal revenue curve for a monopolist lies below its demand curve, rather than coinciding with the demand curve, as is the case for a perfectly competitive firm. Is it ever possible for a monopolist's marginal revenue curve to coincide with its demand curve?

6. *(Revenue for the Monopolist)* Why is it impossible for a profit-maximizing monopolist to choose any price *and* any quantity it wishes?

7. *(Revenue Curves)* Why would a monopoly firm never knowingly produce on the inelastic portion of its demand curve?

8. *(Profit Maximization)* Review the following graph (upper right) showing the short-run situation of a monopolist. What output level will the firm choose in the short run? Why?

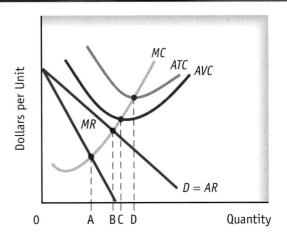

9. *(Allocative and Distributive Effects)* Why is society worse off under monopoly than under perfect competition, even if both market structures face the same constant long-run average cost curve?

10. *(Welfare Cost of Monopoly)* Explain why the welfare loss of a monopoly may be smaller or larger than the loss shown in Exhibit 7 in this chapter.

11. *(CaseStudy: The Mail Monopoly)* Can the U.S. Postal Service be considered a monopoly in first-class mail? Why or why not? What has happened to the price elasticity of demand for first-class mail in recent years?

12. *(Conditions for Price Discrimination)* What conditions must be met in order for a monopolist to price discriminate successfully?

13. *(Price Discrimination)* Explain how it may be profitable for South Korean manufacturers to sell new autos at a lower price in the United States than in South Korea, even with transportation costs included.

14. *(Perfect Price Discrimination)* Why is the perfectly discriminating monopolist's marginal revenue curve identical to the demand curve it faces?

PROBLEMS AND EXERCISES

15. *(Short-Run Profit Maximization)* Answer the following questions on the basis of the monopolist's situation illustrated in the following graph.
    a. At what output level and price will the monopolist operate?
    b. In equilibrium, what will be the firm's total cost and total revenue?
    c. What will be the firm's profit or loss in equilibrium?

16. *(Monopoly)* Suppose that a certain manufacturer has a monopoly on the sorority and fraternity ring business (a constant-cost industry) because it has persuaded the "Greeks" to give it exclusive rights to their insignia.
    a. Using demand and cost curves, draw a diagram depicting the firm's profit-maximizing price and output level.
    b. Why is marginal revenue less than price for this firm?
    c. On your diagram, show the deadweight loss that occurs because the output level is determined by a monopoly rather than by a competitive market.
    d. What would happen if the Greeks decided to charge the manufacturer a royalty fee of $3 per ring?

EXPERIENTIAL EXERCISES

17. *(The Welfare Cost of Monopoly)* In many larger U.S. cities monopoly owners of sports franchises have been lobbying local governments for new, publicly financed sports stadiums. Is this a form of rent seeking? Go to the Heartland Institute's Sports Stadium Madness page at http://www.heartland.org/studies/sports/index.html and look at one of the papers collected there. Is there convincing evidence of rent seeking? If so, how does that relate to the welfare cost of monopoly?

18. *(Price Discrimination)* The Robinson-Patman Act is a federal statute that outlaws certain forms of price discrimination. Review the main provisions of the Act as outlined by RPAMall http://www.lawmall.com/rpa/. Then visit a local supermarket and look for evidence of price discrimination. Are the conditions for price discrimination, as outlined in this chapter, met there? Do you think the forms of price discrimination you found are legal under the Robinson-Patman Act?

19. *(Wall Street Journal)* The Legal Beat column, found in the Marketplace section of the *Wall Street Journal* chronicles court decisions and legal trends that affect American businesses. In the legal arena, firms and the government often struggle over monopoly power. Find an article describing a firm seeking to restrict competition or a government action aimed at reducing monopoly power. See if you can use the monopoly model to understand the issues involved.

Monopolistic Competition and Oligopoly

hy are some panty hose sold in egg-shaped cartons? Why do some pizza makers deliver? Why is some shampoo sold only in beauty salons? Why do airlines sometimes engage in airfare warfare? Why was the oil cartel, OPEC, created and why has it failed? To answer these and other questions, we turn in this chapter to the vast gray area that lies between perfect competition and monopoly.

Perfect competition and pure monopoly represent the two extreme market structures. Under perfect competition, many suppliers offer a homogeneous commodity to a market where firms in the long run can enter and leave the industry with ease. A monopoly sells a product with no close substitutes; would-be competitors are blocked by natural or artificial barriers to entry. These polar market structures are logically appealing and are useful in describing the workings of some markets observed in the economy.

But most firms operate in markets that are not well described by either model. Some firms are in markets that have many sellers producing goods that vary slightly, such as the many radio stations that vie for your attention or the video rental stores that abound. Other firms are in markets consisting of a small number of sellers that in some cases produce homogeneous goods (such as the markets for oil, steel, or aluminum) and in other cases produce differentiated goods (such as the markets for automobiles, breakfast cereals, or cigarettes). In this chapter, we examine the two additional market structures that together include the majority of firms in the economy. Topics discussed in this chapter include:

- Monopolistic competition
- Product differentiation
- Excess capacity
- Models of oligopoly
- Firm interdependence
- Mergers

MONOPOLISTIC COMPETITION

During the 1920s and 1930s, economists began formulating models to fit between perfect competition and pure monopoly. Two models of *monopolistic competition* were developed independently. In 1933 at Harvard University, Edward Chamberlin published *The Theory of Monopolistic Competition*. Across the Atlantic that same year, Cambridge University's Joan Robinson published *The Economics of Imperfect Competition*. Although the theories differed, their underlying principles were similar. We will discuss Chamberlin's approach.

Characteristics of Monopolistic Competition

As the expression **monopolistic competition** suggests, this market structure contains elements of both monopoly and competition. Chamberlin used the term to describe a market in which many producers offer products that are close substitutes but are not viewed as identical by consumers. Examples include the many convenience stores scattered throughout a metropolitan area or the dozens of radio stations vying for listeners. Because the products of different suppliers differ slightly—for example, some convenience stores are closer to you than others—the demand curve for each is not horizontal but rather slopes downward. Each producer therefore has some power over the price it charges. Thus the firms that populate this market are not *price takers,* as they would be under perfect competition, but are *price searchers.*

Monopolistic competition A market structure characterized by a large number of firms selling products that are close substitutes, yet different enough that each firm's demand curve slopes downward

Because barriers to entry are low, firms in monopolistic competition can enter or leave the market with ease. Consequently, there are enough sellers that they behave competitively. There are also enough sellers that each tends to get lost in the crowd. For example, in a large metropolitan area, an individual restaurant, gas station, drugstore, video rental store, dry cleaner, or convenience store tends to act *independently*. In other market structures, there may be only two or three sellers in each market, so they keep an eye on one another; they act *interdependently*. You will understand the significance of the distinction between independent and interdependent behavior later in the chapter.

Product Differentiation

In perfect competition, the product is homogeneous, such as a bushel of wheat or a share of stock. In monopolistic competition, the product differs among sellers, as with the difference between a Big Mac and a Whopper or between one rock radio station and another. Sellers differentiate their products in four basic ways.

Physical Differences. The most obvious way products differ is in their physical appearance and their qualities. Product differentiation is seemingly endless: size, weight, color, taste, texture, and so on. Shampoos, for example, differ in color, scent, thickness, lathering ability, and bottle design. Particular brands aim at consumers with dandruff and those whose hair is normal, dry, or oily. Packaging is also designed to make a product stand out in a crowded field, such as panty hose in a plastic egg shell (L'Eggs®), instant soup in a cup (Cup O' Soup®), and base-ball cards in a can (Pinnacle®).

Location. The number and variety of locations where a product is available are another means of differentiation. Some products seem to be available everywhere, including the Internet; finding other products requires some search and travel. If you live in a metropolitan area, you are no doubt accustomed to a large number of convenience stores. Each wants to be closest to you when you need that gallon of milk or bag of Doritos—hence the proliferation of stores. As the name says, these mini grocery stores are selling *convenience.* Their prices are higher and their selections are more limited than those of regular grocery stores, but they are likely to be nearer customers, don't have long lines, and stay open later.

Services. Products also differ in terms of their accompanying services. For example, some pizza sellers, such as Domino's, and some booksellers, such as Amazon, deliver; others do not. Some retail stores offer helpful product demonstrations by a well-trained sales staff; other stores are essentially self-service. Some products come with on-line support and toll-free numbers; other products leave you on your own. Some offer a money-back guarantee; others say "no returns."

Product Image. A final way products differ is in the image the producer tries to foster in the consumer's mind. For example, footwear and clothing producers often rely on endorsements from athletes and other celebrities. Some producers try to demonstrate high quality based on where products are sold, such as shampoo that is sold only in beauty salons. Some products try to appeal to environmental concerns by emphasing the use of recycled packaging material.

Short-Run Profit Maximization or Loss Minimization

Because each monopolistic competitor offers a product that differs somewhat from other products in the industry, each seller has some control over the price charged. This *market power* means that the product's demand curve for the product slopes downward. Since many firms are selling close substitutes, any firm that raises its price can expect to lose some (but not all) customers to rivals. By way of comparison, a monopolist has no close rivals and loses fewer customers when the price increases, whereas a perfect competitor who raises the price can expect to lose *all* customers. Therefore, a monopolistic competitor faces a demand curve that is more elastic than a monopolist's and less elastic than a perfect competitor's.

Recall that the number and similarity of available substitutes for a given product are important determinants of the price elasticity of demand. Therefore, the elasticity of the monopolistic competitor's demand depends on (1) the number of rival firms that produce similar products and (2) the firm's ability to differentiate its product from those of its rivals. *A firm's demand curve will be more elastic the greater the number of competing firms and the less differentiated the firm's product.*

Marginal Cost Equals Marginal Revenue. From our study of monopoly, we know that the downward-sloping demand curve means the marginal revenue curve also slopes downward and lies below the demand curve. Exhibit 1 depicts demand and marginal revenue curves for a monopolistically competitive firm. The exhibit also presents cost curves. Remember that the forces that determine the cost of production are independent of the forces that shape demand, so there is nothing special about a monopolistic competitor's cost curves.

In the short run, if a firm can at least cover its variable cost, it will increase output as long as marginal revenue exceeds marginal cost. A monopolistic competitor maximizes profit in the short run just as a monopolist does: *the profit-maximizing rate of output occurs where marginal cost equals marginal revenue; the profit-maximizing price is found on the demand curve at that rate of output.* Exhibit 1 shows the price and output combinations that maximize short-run profit in panel (a) and minimize short-run loss in panel (b). In each panel, the marginal

EXHIBIT 1

The Firm in Monopolistic Competition in the Short Run

The monopolistically competitive firm produces the level of output at which marginal cost equals marginal revenue (point *e*) and charges the price indicated by point *b* on the downward-sloping demand curve. In panel (a), the firm produces *q* units, sells them at price *p*, and earns a short-run economic profit equal to (*p* − *c*) multiplied by *q*, shown by the blue rectangle. In panel (b), the average total cost exceeds the price at the optimal level of output. Thus the firm suffers a short-run loss equal to (*c* − *p*) multiplied by *q*, represented by the red rectangle.

cost and marginal revenue curves intersect at point *e,* yielding equilibrium output *q,* equilibrium price *p,* and average total cost *c.* Demand is greater in panel (a) than in panel (b).

Maximizing Profit or Minimizing Loss in the Short Run. Recall that the short run is a period too brief to allow firms to enter or leave the market. The demand and cost conditions shown in panel (a) of Exhibit 1 indicate that this firm will earn an economic profit in the short run. At the firm's profit-maximizing rate of output, average total cost, measured as *c* on the vertical axis, is below the price, *p.* As noted earlier, the difference between the two is the firm's profit per unit, which, when multiplied by the quantity sold, yields the economic profit, shown by the blue shaded rectangle in panel (a). Again, quantity supplied is found by the intersection of the marginal cost and marginal revenue curves, and the price is found on the demand curve at that quantity. Hence a monopolistic competitor, like a monopolist, has no supply curve—that is, *there is no curve that uniquely relates price and quantity supplied.*

The monopolistic competitor, like other firms, has no guarantee of earning economic profit. The firm's demand curve is the same in panel (b) as in panel (a), but the average total cost curve is higher in panel (b). Because the firm's average total cost curve lies above the demand curve, no rate of output would allow the firm to break even. In such a situation, the firm must decide whether to produce or to shut down temporarily. The rule here is the same as with perfect competition and monopoly: As long as the price is at or above average variable cost, the firm should produce in the short run, thereby covering its variable cost and at least a portion of its fixed cost. If the price fails to cover average variable cost, the firm should shut down. Recall that the halt in production may be only temporary; shutting down is not the same as going out of business. However, firms that expect economic losses to persist in the long run will leave the industry.

Short-run profit maximization in monopolistic competition is quite similar to that under monopoly. But the stories differ in the long run, as we'll see next.

Zero Economic Profit in the Long Run

Since there are no barriers to entry in monopolistic competition, short-run economic profit will attract new entrants in the long run. Because new entrants offer products that are similar to those offered by existing firms, they draw some customers away from existing firms, thereby reducing the demand facing each firm and increasing the elasticity of demand. Entry will continue in the long run until the demand facing each firm falls enough to erase economic profit. *Because of the ease of entry, monopolistically competitive firms will tend toward zero economic profit in the long run.*

If they incur short-run losses, some monopolistic competitors will leave the industry in the long run, redirecting their resources to activities that are expected to earn at least a normal profit. As firms leave the industry, their customers will switch to the remaining firms, increasing the demand for each remaining firm's product. Firms will continue to leave in the long run until the remaining firms have enough customers to earn normal profit but not economic profit (since economic profit would attract more firms to the industry).

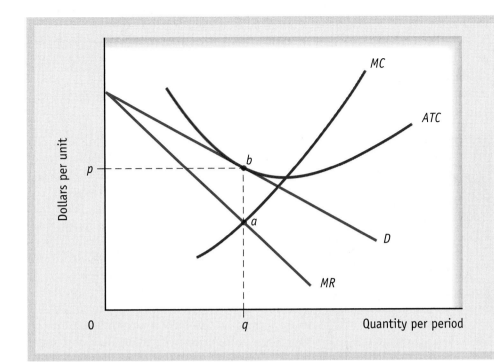

Long-run Equilibrium in Monopolistic Competition

If existing firms are earning economic profits, new firms will enter the industry. The entry of firms reduces the demand facing each firm. In the long run, demand is reduced until marginal revenue equals marginal cost (point *a*) and the demand curve is tangent to the average total cost curve (point *b*). Profit is zero at output *q*. With zero economic profit, no new firms enter, so the industry is in long-run equilibrium.

Exhibit 2 shows the long-run equilibrium for a typical monopolistic competitor. In the long run, entry and exit will alter each firm's demand curve until economic profit disappears—that is, until average total cost equals the price. This long-run outcome is shown in Exhibit 2, where the marginal cost curve intersects the marginal revenue curve at point *a*. At the equilibrium rate of output, *q*, the average total cost curve is tangent to the demand curve at point *b*. Since average total cost equals the price, *p*, the firm earns no economic profit.[1] At all other rates of output, the firm's average total cost is above its demand curve, so the firm would lose money if it reduced or increased its output.

Thus if entry is easy, short-run economic profit will draw new entrants into the industry in the long run. The demand curve facing each firm shifts left until economic profit disappears and firms earn only a normal profit. A short-run economic loss will prompt some firms to leave the industry in the long run. The demand curve facing each firm shifts right until the loss disappears and remaining firms earn just a normal profit. In summary, *monopolistic competition is like pure monopoly in the sense that firms in both industries face demand curves that slope*

---

1 You may wonder why average cost equals the price at the same rate of output where marginal cost equals marginal revenue. The explanation relies on total cost and total revenue curves, which are not shown. Recall that the slope of the total cost curve equals the firm's marginal cost, and the slope of the total revenue curve equals the firm's marginal revenue. Where average cost equals price, the firm earns a normal profit but no economic profit. Where there is no economic profit, the total cost curve is tangent to the total revenue curve, so both total curves have the same slope at that rate of output. Therefore, marginal cost must equal marginal revenue at that rate of output.

downward. Monopolistic competition is like perfect competition in the sense that easy entry and exit eliminate economic profit or economic loss in the long run.

One way to understand how short-run economic profit can be competed away by new firms in the long run is to consider the evolution of a newly emerging industry, as is discussed in the following case study.

Fast Forward

CaseStudy

The World of Business

A history of Blockbuster Video is maintained by the firm at http://www. blockbuster.com/company/. A FORTUNE magazine profile of Bill Fields, the person chosen to be Blockbuster's CEO in 1996, is at http://www. pathfinder.com/fortune/1996/ 961125/blo.html. Try reading both of these to get a feel for how the firm has developed. When did Blockbuster's rapid growth grind to a halt? What were Fields' plans for reviving the company? How long did he remain CEO? What change of direction can you discern following the hiring of John Antioco as CEO?

Video recorders have now become standard equipment in the typical American home. These recorders fueled demand for videotaped movies. The first videotape rental outlets required tape deposits, imposed membership fees of up to $100, and rented tapes for as much as $5 per day. Despite the high prices and high fees, the exploding number of VCRs allowed these early rental stores to thrive. What's more, part of the initial surge in rental demand came from consumers who were catching up on older movies they had missed at the theaters. In the beginning, most rental stores faced no competition in their area, and most earned short-run economic profit.

But this profit attracted competitors. Since entry was relatively easy, many new rental stores opened for business. Other types of stores—convenience stores, grocery stores, bookstores, even drugstores—also began renting tapes as a sideline. The growth rate of new rental outlets soon exceeded the growth rate of VCRs. Between 1982 and 1987, for example, the number of outlets renting tapes increased fourfold. And once consumers caught up with the backlog of movies, demand came to focus primarily on new releases.

Thus, the supply of rental movies increased faster than the demand. Worse yet for video stores, cable television with 40 to 50 channels and pay-per-view options plus direct sale of movie videos to consumers all substituted for video rentals. The greater supply of rentals along with the increased availability of substitutes had the predictable effect on market prices. Rental rates dropped sharply—to as little as 99 cents per night—and membership fees and tape deposits disappeared. Some rental stores could not survive at such a low price, and they folded. In fact, so many failed that a market developed to buy and resell their tape inventories. The "shakeout" in the industry is still going on—tape rental revenue declined 3 percent industry-wide in 1997. Many existing rental stores will fail. As the market evolves, one large firm, Blockbuster, has grown to over 4000 U.S. stores, accounting for 25 percent of market rentals in 1998. If that firm comes to dominate the market, tape rentals could change from monopolistic competition to oligopoly, a market structure to be examined later in the chapter. But Blockbuster faces its own growing pains, including an "excess inventory" of tapes and a failed effort to sell books, magazines, and snacks at its rental stores.

Sources: John Kirkpatrick, "Troubles Cut Blockbuster Performance," *Dallas Morning News* (2 July 1997); Chris Olson, "Curtain to Rise on Video Sites," *Omaha World-Herald* (6 August 1997); Eban Shapiro, "Blockbuster's Chief Executive Says the Viacom Unit Is on Fast Forward," *Wall Street Journal*, (7 April 1998); and Ed Hulse, "Roaming the Aisles," *Video Business* (29 September 1997).

Monopolistic Competition and Perfect Competition Compared

How does monopolistic competition compare with perfect competition in terms of efficiency? In the long run, neither a perfect competitor nor a monopolistic competitor can earn economic profit, so what's the difference? The difference arises because of the different demand curves facing individual firms in each of the two market structures. Exhibit 3 presents the long-run equilibrium price and quantity for firms in each of the two market structures, assuming the two firms have identical cost curves. In each case, the marginal cost curve intersects the marginal revenue curve at the rate of output where the average total cost curve is tangent to the demand curve faced by the firm.

The demand curve for the firm in perfect competition is a horizontal line drawn at the market price, as shown in panel (a). This demand curve is tangent to the lowest point of the long-run average total cost curve. Thus a perfect competitor produces at the lowest possible average cost in the long run. In panel (b), a monopolistic competitor faces a downward-sloping demand curve because its product differs somewhat from that of other producers. In the long run, the monopolistic competitor produces less than the amount necessary to achieve the lowest possible average cost. Thus, the price and average cost under monopolistic competition, identified in panel (b) as p', exceed the price and average cost under perfect competition, identified in panel (a) as p. *If firms have the same*

EXHIBIT 3

Monopolistic Competition Versus Perfect Competition

(a) Perfect competition

(b) Monopolistic competition

The perfectly competitive firm of panel (a) faces a demand curve that is horizontal at market price p. Long-run equilibrium occurs at output q, where the demand (average revenue) curve is tangent to the average total cost curve at its lowest point. The monopolistically competitive firm of panel (b) is in long-run equilibrium at output q', where demand is tangent to average total cost. However, since the demand curve slopes downward, the tangency does not occur at the minimum point of average total cost. Hence the monopolistically competitive firm produces less output at a higher price than does a perfectly competitive firm facing the same cost conditions.

cost curves, the firm under monopolistic competition produces less and charges more than the firm under perfect competition.

Firms in monopolistic competition do not produce at minimum average cost. They are said to have **excess capacity,** since production is short of the rate that would achieve the lowest average cost. Excess capacity means that producers could easily satisfy a greater demand and in the process would lower the average cost of production. Because the marginal value of production exceeds the marginal cost of production, then the marginal value of increased output would exceed its marginal cost, thereby increasing economic welfare. Such excess capacity exists with gas stations, drugstores, convenience stores, restaurants, motels, bookstores, flower shops, and firms in other monopolistic competitive industries. A good example is the funeral home business. Industry analysts argue that the nation's 23,000 funeral homes could efficiently handle 4 million funerals a year, but only about 2.5 million people die. So the industry operates at only about 60 percent of capacity, resulting in a higher average cost per funeral because valuable resources are idle much of the time.

There is another difference between perfect competition and monopolistic competition that does not show up in Exhibit 3. Although the cost curves drawn in each panel of Exhibit 3 are identical, firms in monopolistic competition in fact spend more on advertising and other promotional expenses to differentiate their products than do firms in perfect competition. These higher costs shift up their average cost curves.

Some economists have argued that monopolistic competition results in too many suppliers and in product differentiation that is often artificial. The counter argument is that consumers are willing to pay a higher price for having a greater selection. According to this latter view, consumers benefit from the wider choice among gas stations, restaurants, convenience stores, clothing stores, drugstores, economics textbooks, and many other goods and services. For example, what if half of the restaurants were to close just so the remaining ones could operate at full capacity? Some consumers would be disappointed if their favorite or most convenient restaurant went out of business.

Excess capacity　The difference between the rate of output at a firm's minimum average cost and the profit-maximizing rate of output

AN INTRODUCTION TO OLIGOPOLY

Perfect competitors and monopolistic competitors are so numerous in their respective markets that an action by any one of them has little effect on the behavior of others in the market. Another important market structure in the gray area between perfect competition and monopoly is *oligopoly,* a Greek word meaning "few sellers." When you think of "big business," you are thinking of **oligopoly,** a market dominated by just a few firms. Perhaps three or four firms account for more than half the market output. Many industries, including steel, automobiles, oil, breakfast cereals, and tobacco, are *oligopolistic.* Because an oligopolistic market has only a few firms, each firm must consider the effect of its own policies on competitors' behavior. Oligopolists are therefore *interdependent.*

Oligopoly　A market structure characterized by a small number of firms whose behavior is interdependent

Varieties of Oligopoly

In some oligopolistic industries, such as steel and oil, the product is homogeneous—an ingot of steel or a barrel of oil. In other industries, such as automobiles and breakfast cereal, the product is differentiated across producers—Ford versus Toyota or Wheaties versus Kellogg's Corn Flakes. The more homogeneous the products, the greater the interdependence among the few dominant firms in the industry. For example, because steel ingots are essentially identical, steel producers are quite sensitive to each other's pricing policies. A small rise in the one producer's price will send customers to a rival. But in markets where the product is differentiated, such as the auto industry, producers are not quite as sensitive about each other's pricing policies as are steel producers.

Because of this interdependence among firms in an industry, the behavior of any particular firm is difficult to analyze. *Each firm knows that any changes in its product quality, price, output, or advertising policy may prompt a reaction from its rivals. And each firm may react if another firm alters any of these features.* Monopolistic competition is like a golf tournament, where each player is striving for a personal best; oligopoly is more like a tennis match, where each player's actions depend on how and where the opponent hits the ball.

Why have some industries evolved into an oligopolistic market structure, dominated by only a few firms, whereas other industries have not? Although the reasons are not always clear, *an oligopolistic market structure can often be traced to some form of barrier to entry, such as economies of scale, legal restrictions, brand names built up by years of advertising, or control over an essential resource.* In the previous chapter, we examined barriers to entry as they applied to monopoly. The same principles apply to oligopoly. In the following case study, we consider some barriers to entry in the airline industry.

The Unfriendly Skies

At one time, airline routes were straight lines from one city to another. Now they radiate like the spokes of a wagon wheel from a "hub" city. From 29 hub airports across the country, the airlines send out planes along the spokes to about 400 commercial airports, then quickly bring them back to the hubs. The major airlines dominate hub airports. For example, American and United dominate Chicago's O'Hare International, which is a big, centrally located airport. A new airline trying to enter the industry would have to secure a hub airport as well as landing rights at crowded airports around the country—not an easy task, since all the viable hubs are taken, as are the landing rights at those airports. So landing rights are the first barrier to entry in the airline industry. Studies show that ticket prices involving airports dominated by a single airline average about 5 percent higher than tickets at more competitive airports.

Another barrier to entry is frequent flyer mileage programs. The biggest airlines fly more national and international routes, so they offer greater opportunities to accumulate frequent flyer miles and to use the accumulated mileage for free flights. Hence the biggest airlines have the most attractive programs.

These factors—landing slots and frequent flyer programs—create barriers for potential entrants and create barriers to expansion for smaller airlines already

CaseStudy

The World of Business

The Government Accounting Office (GAO) prepares reports on competition in the domestic airline industry. For example, read "Barriers to Entry Continue to Limit Benefits of Airline Deregulation" at http://www.bts.gov/ntl/data/rc97120t.pdf. This report includes data on the concentration of ownership of landing slots at the major U.S. airports. What particular barriers to entry does GAO cite? Current statistics on air travel are available in the annual reports of the Air Transport Association at http://www.air-transport.org/data/ff.htm. Try clicking through the series of graphs showing recent trends in the airline industry. What trends do you find in prices, number of passengers, and percent of Americans who have never flown?

in the industry. Five airlines now dominate the U.S. market. American, United, Delta, USAir, and Northwest handle about 70 percent of all traffic and control 80 percent of the hubs. The dominance of U.S. carriers is enhanced by federal regulations that prevent foreign airlines from flying between U.S. cities.

Until quite recently, another barrier to entry was the computerized reservation systems used by travel agents. American Airlines offered the Sabre system and United the Apollo system. These two airlines have now spun off their computer systems into separate entities, so the systems are available to all airlines. Airline Internet sites also allow individuals to buy tickets on-line.

Sources: "US Airways Plans Computer Deal with Sabre," *Los Angeles Times* (29 January 1998); "Medium-sized Airports Need Landing Slots, Gates, Terminals," *Business Wire* (25 June 1997); Kenneth Li, "Web's Got the Ticket," *New York Daily News* (9 November 1997); Matthew Wald, "U.S. Seeks to Curb Unfair Practices of Major Airlines," *Wall Street Journal* (7 April 1998); and Steven Morrison and Clifford Winston, *The Evolution of the Airline Industry*, (Washington, D.C.: Brookings Institution, 1995).

Economies of Scale

Perhaps the most significant barrier to entry is economies of scale. Recall that the minimum efficient scale is the lowest rate of output at which the firm takes full advantage of economies of scale. If a firm's minimum efficient scale is relatively large compared to industry output, then only a few firms are needed to produce the total output demanded in the market. A good example is the auto industry. Research shows that an automobile plant of minimum efficient scale could produce enough cars to supply nearly 10 percent of the U.S. market. If there were 100 auto plants, each would supply such a tiny portion of the market that the average cost per car would be higher than if only 10 plants manufactured autos.

In the automobile industry, economies of scale are a barrier to entry. To compete with existing producers, a new entrant must sell enough automobiles to reach a competitive scale of operation. Exhibit 4 presents the long-run average cost curve for a typical firm in the industry. If a new entrant sells only S cars, the average cost per unit, c_a, far exceeds the average cost, c_b, of a firm that has reached the rate of output, M, achieved at the minimum efficient size. If autos sell for a price less than c_a, a potential entrant can expect an economic loss, and this prospect will discourage entry.

High Cost of Entry

Potential entrants into oligopolistic industries may face another problem. The total investment needed to reach the minimum efficient size is often gigantic (a new auto plant or new semiconductor plant can cost over $1 billion). The average cost of developing and testing a new drug exceeds $300 million. Advertising a new product enough to compete with established brands may also require an enormous initial outlay. High start-up costs and established brand names can create substantial barriers to entry, especially since the fortunes of a new product are uncertain. In fact, eight of ten new consumer products don't survive. An unsuccessful attempt at securing a place in the market could result in crippling losses for upstart firms. The prospect of such losses turns away many potential entrants. Most new products come from existing firms, which can better with-

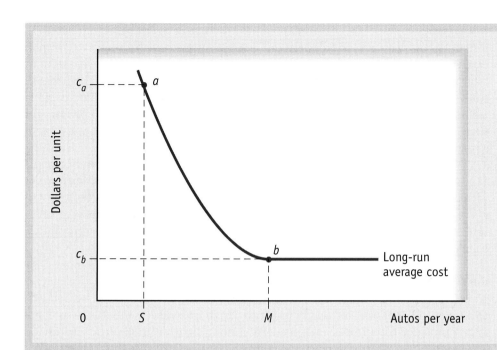

EXHIBIT 4

Economies of Scale as a Barrier to Entry

At point b, an existing firm can produce M automobiles at an average cost of c_b. A new entrant that can hope to sell only S automobiles will incur a much higher average cost of c_a at point a. If cars sell for less than c_a, the new entrant will suffer a loss. In this case, economies of scale serve as a barrier to entry, protecting the existing firms from new competitors.

stand the possible losses. For example, Colgate–Palmolive spent $100 million introducing Total toothpaste, as did McDonald's in its failed attempt to sell America the Arch Deluxe. And Unilever lost $160 million when its new detergent, Power, failed to crack into the market.

In perfect competition, all firms sell identical products. There is no incentive to advertise or to promote a particular product since consumers know that all products are the same. Moreover, producers already can sell all they want at the prevailing market price, so why advertise? In an oligopoly, however, firms often spend millions and sometimes billions differentiating their products. Some of these expenditures have the beneficial effects of providing valuable information to consumers and offering them a wider array of products. But some forms of product differentiation are of little value. Slogans such as "Generation Next" or "Always Cola-Cola" convey little information, yet Pepsi and Coke have spent huge sums on such messages (Coke spent $1.6 billion on advertising in 1997).

Product differentiation expenditures create barriers to entry. Oligopolies often compete with existing rivals and try to block new entry by offering a variety of models or products. For example, several cereal makers offer more than a dozen products each, and seven of the top-selling cereals are from Kellogg.[2] One study of 25,500 new products introduced in 1996 found only 7 percent really offered new or added benefits.[3] With the proliferation of brands, retail shelf space grows scarce, blocking out potential competitors.

---

2 Rankings are for 1997 sales according to the Food Marketing Policy Center at the University of Connecticut.
3 The study was carried out by Market Intelligence Service and was reported in "Market Makers," *The Economist* (14 March 1998).

MODELS OF OLIGOPOLY

Since oligopolists are interdependent, analyzing their behavior gets complicated. Because of this interdependence, we should not expect any *one* model of oligopoly theory to explain all oligopoly behavior. At one extreme, the firms in the industry may try to coordinate their behavior so they act collectively as a single monopolist, forming a cartel, such as the Organization of Petroleum Exporting Countries (OPEC). At the other extreme, oligopolists may compete so fiercely that price wars erupt, as with airfare warfare and cigarette price wars.

Many theories have been developed to explain oligopoly pricing behavior. We will study four of the better-known models: (1) cartels, (2) price leadership, (3) game theory, and (4) the kinked demand curve. As you will see, each model has some relevance in explaining observed behavior, although none is entirely satisfactory as a general theory of oligopoly. Thus *there is no general theory of oligopoly, but a set of theories, each based on the diversity of observations.*

Collusion

In an oligopolistic market there are few firms; hence, they may try to *collude*, or to agree on price and output rates, in order to decrease competition and increase profit. **Collusion** is an agreement among firms in the industry to divide the market up and fix the price. A **cartel** is a group of firms that agree to collude so they can act as a single monopolist and earn monopoly profits. Cartels are more likely when the good supplied is homogeneous, as with oil or steel. A cartel provides benefits to member firms—greater certainty about the behavior of "competitors," an organized effort to block new entry, and, as a result, increased profit. Colluding firms, when compared to competing firms, usually reduce output, increase price, and block the entry of new firms. Consumers suffer because prices are higher as a result of limited output, and potential entrants suffer because of lost opportunities for profit. Collusion and cartels are both illegal in this country; some other countries are more tolerant. Some countries even promote cartels, as with OPEC.

Monopoly profit can be so tempting that U.S. firms sometimes break the law. During the 1950s, for example, there was evidence of extensive collusion among electrical equipment producers, and some executives went to jail for their participation in the scheme. Some cartels are worldwide in scope, such as the now-familiar oil cartel, OPEC. If OPEC held a meeting in the United States, its members would be arrested for price fixing. Cartels can operate worldwide (even though they are outlawed in some countries) because there are no international laws to stop them.

Suppose that the firms in an industry establish a cartel. The market demand curve, *D*, appears in Exhibit 5. What price will maximize the cartel's profit, and how will market output be divided among participating firms? The first task of the cartel is to determine the marginal cost of production for the cartel as a whole. Since the cartel acts as if it were a single monopoly operating many plants, the marginal cost curve in Exhibit 5 is the horizontal sum of the marginal cost curves of all firms in the cartel. The cartel's marginal cost curve intersects the marginal revenue curve to determine the price and output that maximize the cartel's profit. This intersection yields price *p*, industry output *Q*, and marginal cost of production, identified as *c*. So far, so good. To maximize

---

Collusion An agreement among firms to divide the market or to fix the market price to maximize economic profit

Cartel A group of firms that agree to coordinate their production and pricing decisions to maximize cartel profits, thereby behaving as a monopolist

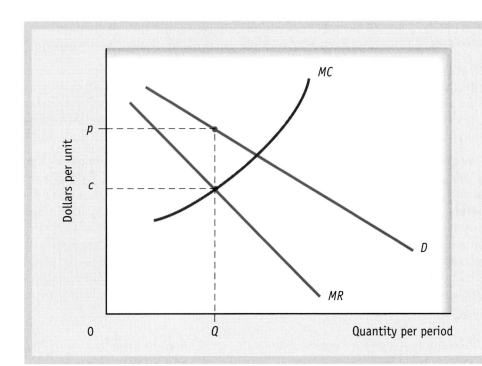

EXHIBIT 5

Cartel Model Where Firms Act as a Monopolist

A cartel acts like a monopolist. Here *D* is the market demand curve, *MR* the associated marginal revenue curve, and *MC* the horizontal sum of the marginal cost curves of cartel members. Cartel profits are maximized when the industry produces quantity *Q* and charges price *p*.

cartel profits, output *Q* must be allocated among firms so that each cartel member's marginal cost equals *c*; otherwise some firms would be producing where the marginal cost of output exceeds *c*, and this higher marginal cost would lower cartel profits. Thus *for cartel profit to be maximized, output must be allocated so that the marginal cost of production is identical across firms.* All this is easier said than done. Let's look at the problems with maintaining a successful cartel.

Differences in Cost. If all firms have identical cost curves, output and profit are easily allocated across firms (each firm produces the same output), but if costs differ, as they usually do, problems arise. The greater the differences in average costs across firms, the greater will be the differences in economic profits among firms. If cartel members try to equalize each firm's total economic profit, a high-cost firm would need to sell more than a low-cost firm. But this allocation scheme would violate the profit-maximizing condition for the cartel, which is that the marginal cost be identical across firms. Thus, *if average costs differ across firms, the quantity allocation that maximizes cartel profit will yield unequal profit across cartel members.* If the cartel allocates less output to high-cost firms than they want, they could drop out of the cartel, thereby undermining it. Usually, the allocation of output is the result of haggling among cartel members. Firms that are more influential or more adept at bargaining will get a larger share of output. Allocation schemes are sometimes based on geography or on the historical division of output among firms. OPEC allocates output among member countries based on their estimated oil reserves.

Number of Firms in the Cartel. The greater the number of firms in the industry, the more difficult it is to negotiate an acceptable allocation of output among them.

Consensus becomes harder to achieve as the number of firms in the industry grows. And the more firms there are in the industry, the greater the chances are that one or more firms will become dissatisfied with the cartel and break with the agreement.

New Entry into the Industry. If a cartel cannot block the entry of new firms into the industry, new entry will eventually force the price down, squeezing economic profit. The profit of the cartel attracts entry, entry increases market supply, and increased supply forces the price down. A cartel's continued success therefore depends on barriers that block the entry of new firms.

Cheating. Perhaps the biggest problem in keeping the cartel running smoothly is the powerful temptation to cheat on the agreement. By offering a price slightly below the established price, a firm can usually increase its sales and economic profit. Because oligopolists usually operate with excess capacity, some may cheat on the established price. Even if cartel members keep an eagle eye on each firm's price, a firm, rather than lowering the price, can increase sales by offering extra services, rebates, or other concessions. The incentive to cut prices is particularly strong when industry sales are in a slump. Typically, when production is low, so is the marginal cost of producing more output. Cartel agreements collapse if cheating becomes widespread.

In summary, *establishing and maintaining an effective cartel will be more difficult (1) if the product is differentiated among firms, (2) if costs differ among firms, (3) if there are a large number of suppliers in the industry, (4) if entry barriers in the industry are low, and (5) if cheating on the agreement becomes widespread.* The problems of establishing and maintaining a cartel are reflected in the spotty history of OPEC. In 1985, the average price of oil reached $34 a barrel. By 1998, because of competition among the world's oil producers, the price dropped to less than half that. Many of the 11 OPEC members are poor countries that rely on oil as a major source of revenue, so they argue over the price and their market share. OPEC members also cheat on the cartel.

Like other cartels, OPEC has experienced difficulty with new entrants. The high prices resulting from OPEC's early success back in the 1970s attracted new oil suppliers from the North Sea, Mexico, and elsewhere. Nearly two-thirds of the world's oil supply now comes from non-OPEC countries. Most observers doubt that OPEC will ever regain its former power. Efforts to cartelize the world supply of a number of products, including bauxite, copper, and coffee, have failed so far.

Price Leadership

Price leader A firm whose price is adopted by the rest of the industry

An informal, or *tacit,* type of collusion occurs in industries that contain **price leaders,** who set the price for the rest of the industry. A dominant firm or a few firms establish the market price, and other firms in the industry follow that lead, thereby avoiding price competition. The price leader also initiates any change in the price, and others follow.

Historically, the steel industry has been an example of the price-leadership form of oligopoly. Typically, U.S. Steel, the largest firm in the industry, would set the price for various products, and other firms would follow. Congressional investigations into the pricing policy in this industry indicate that smaller steel producers relied on the price schedules of U.S. Steel. Public pressure on U.S.

Steel not to raise the price shifted the price-leadership role onto smaller producers, resulting in a rotation of the leadership function among firms. Although the rotating price leadership did reduce price conformity among firms in the industry, particularly during the 1970s, prices in the steel industry were still higher than they would have been with no price leadership.

Like other forms of collusion, price leadership is subject to a variety of obstacles. First, the practice usually violates U.S. antitrust laws. Second, the greater the product differentiation among sellers, the less effective price leadership will be as a means of collusion. Third, there is no guarantee that other firms will follow the leader. If other firms in the industry do not follow a price increase, the leading firm must either roll back prices or risk losing sales to lower-priced competitors. Fourth, as with formal cartels, some firms will try to cheat on the agreement by cutting the price to increase sales and profits. And finally, unless there are barriers to entry, a profitable price will attract entrants into the market, which could destabilize the price leadership agreement.

Game Theory

How will firms act when they recognize their interdependence but either cannot or do not collude? Because oligopoly involves interdependence among a few firms, we can think of interacting firms as like players in a poker game. **Game theory** examines oligopolistic behavior as a series of strategic moves and counter-moves among rival firms. It analyzes the behavior of decision makers, or players, whose choices affect one another. The focus is on the players' incentives either to cooperate or to compete.

As an example, consider the market for gasoline in a rural community with only two gas stations, Mobil and Exxon. Here we focus on an oligopoly consisting of two firms, or a **duopoly.** Suppose customers are indifferent between the two brands and consider only the price when choosing between stations. To keep the analysis manageable, suppose only two prices are possible: a high price or a low price. If both gas stations charge the high price, they split the total quantity demanded and each gas station earns a profit of $700 per day. If they both charge the low price, they also split the market, but profit drops to only $400 per day. If one charges the high price but the other charges the low price, the low-price station earns a profit of $500 per day. But the high-price station has virtually no customers and loses $200 per day.

What price will each gas station charge? The answer depends on the assumptions about firm behavior—that is, what *strategy* each player pursues. A **strategy** reflects a player's operational plan. Exhibit 6 shows the *payoff matrix* for the two gas stations, with the price strategy that Mobil pursues shown along the left-hand margin and the price strategy that Exxon pursues shown along the top. A **payoff matrix** is a table listing the profits, or payoff, that each of the two rival firms can expect based on the strategy that each firm adopts. As we have seen already, each firm can charge either a "high price" or a "low price." Each cell of the matrix reports each firm's earnings, depending on the combination of strategies pursued by each seller. For example, the upper left-hand cell indicates that if both firms charge the high price, then each will earn $700 per day.

Given this payoff matrix, what does each firm do? Again, the answer depends on each firm's strategy. Suppose you are running the Mobil station and are trying to decide what to do. If you charge a high price, you will earn $700

Game theory A model that analyzes oligopolistic behavior as a series of strategic moves and counter-moves by rival firms

Duopoly A market with only two producers, who compete with each other; a type of oligopoly market structure

Strategy In game theory, the operational plan pursued by a player; for example, one strategy is to avoid the worst outcome

Payoff matrix In game theory, a table listing the payoffs that each player can expect based on the strategy that each player pursues

EXHIBIT 6

A Payoff Matrix

Exxon's Strategy

		High Price		Low Price	
Mobil's Strategy	**High Price**	Mobil's profit = $700	Exxon's profit = $700	Mobil's loss = $200	Exxon's profit = $500
	Low Price	Mobil's profit = $500	Exxon's loss = $200	Mobil's profit = $400	Exxon's profit = $400

per day as long as the Exxon station charges a high price as well, but you will lose $200 a day if your rival charges a low price. If you charge a low price and your rival does too, you both earn $400 per day. If you charge a low price and your rival charges a high price, you really clean up, earn $500 per day. What to do, what to do?

One common game-theory strategy is to avoid the worst outcome. The worst outcome is to lose $200 per day by being the only gas station charging the high price. You avoid that outcome by charging the low price. If each gas station tries to avoid the worst outcome, both will charge the low price and each will earn $400 per day, as is reflected by the cell in the lower right-hand corner. Both would be better off if they each agreed to charge a high price.

Avoiding the worst outcome is only one of several strategies we could consider in analyzing oligopoly markets in terms of game theory. Outcomes can be as volatile as the personalities involved. Some players are more conservative, and some are more willing to take risks. Price wars sometimes break out among oligopolists. For example, in the summer of 1997, auto makers aggressively matched and exceeded one another's price cuts, leaving cars more affordable relative to consumers' average income than they had been in a decade.[4] And just before a recent Thanksgiving weekend, a price war erupted in airfares. American Airlines first announced holiday discounts. TWA quickly cut fares even more, then Delta topped them both with cuts of up to 50 percent. Within hours, American, United, and other major carriers said they would match Delta's reductions. So go sporadic price wars.

The Kinked Demand Curve

Prices in some oligopolistic industries appear to be stable even during periods when altered cost conditions suggest that a price change would be appropriate. An often-cited case of price stability occurred in the sulfur industry, where the price remained at $18 per ton for a dozen consecutive years, despite major changes in the cost of production. One oligopoly model that sheds light on this

---

4 Keith Bradsher, "Price War Leaves Cars Positively Affordable," *New York Times* (3 July 1997).

EXHIBIT 7

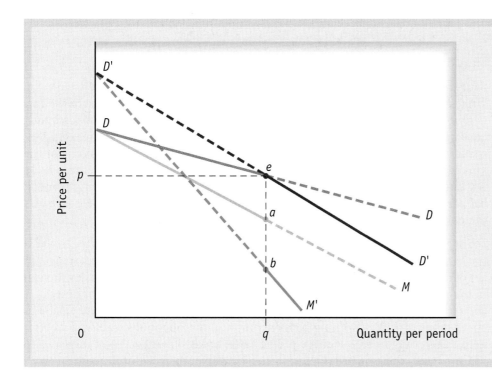

The Kinked Demand Model of Oligopoly

In the initial situation, an oligopolist is at point *e*, selling *q* units at price *p*. The firm's demand curve is *DD* if its competitors do not match its price changes; its demand curve is *D'D'* if competitors do match price changes. Assuming that the firm's rivals match price cuts but not price increases, the relevant demand curve is *DeD'* , with a kink at quantity *q*. *DabM'* is the associated marginal revenue curve, with a gap at quantity *q*.

apparent price stability relies on the simple idea that if a firm cuts its price, other firms will cut theirs as well to avoid losing customers to the price cutter. But if a firm raises its price, other firms will stand pat, hoping to attract customers away from the price raiser. If an oligopolist expects such responses from competitors, the **kinked demand curve** describes the oligopolist's pricing strategy. Firms in the tire industry have been said to have a kinked demand curve.[5]

To develop the kinked demand curve model, we start at point *e* in Exhibit 7, with the firm producing *q* units at price *p*. The firm's demand curve will depend on whether other firms follow price moves or ignore them. Demand curve *DD* assumes that rivals will not follow a change in price. Alternatively, demand curve *D'D'* assumes that rivals will match any change in price. Notice that *DD* is flatter than *D'D'*. To see why, suppose that Michelin raises its prices, but other tire makers do not. In this situation, Michelin will lose far more sales than if other producers also raised their prices. Likewise, if Michelin cuts prices but others do not, Michelin will pick up more sales than if other producers also cut prices. Thus, if rivals do not follow price changes, any price increase will drive away more customers and any price decrease will attract more customers than if rivals matched price changes. Therefore, Michelin's demand curve is flatter when rivals do not follow price changes than when they do.

If rivals follow a price decrease but do not follow a price increase, the oligopolist's demand curve consists of the two solid segments shown in Exhibit 7 by *DeD'*. That solid portion of the demand curve reflecting a price increase, *De,*

Kinked demand curve A demand curve that illustrates price stickiness; if one firm cuts its prices, other firms in the industry will cut theirs as well, but if the firm raises its prices, other firms will not change theirs

---

5 See the remarks of economist Dennis Byrne in Miles Moore's "Tire Oligopoly Leaves Dealers in Tough Spot," *Tire Business* (17 March 1997).

is flatter than that solid portion of the demand curve reflecting a price decrease, *eD'*. Because rivals match a price decrease but not a price increase, this oligopolist's demand curve, *DeD'*, has a *kink* at the firm's current price-quantity combination, point *e*.

Marginal Revenue. To find the marginal revenue curve associated with the kinked demand curve, we simply piece together the relevant portions of the underlying marginal revenue curves. The solid segment *Da* is the marginal revenue curve applicable to portion *De* of the kinked demand curve. And the solid segment *bM'* is the marginal revenue curve associated with the portion *eD'* of the kinked demand curve. The marginal revenue curve is thus *DabM'*. Because there is a kink in the demand curve, the marginal revenue curve is not a single line; it has a gap at the currently produced quantity, *q*. The kinked demand curve and the corresponding marginal revenue curve appear in Exhibit 8.

Price Rigidity. Within the gap in the marginal revenue curve, *ab*, the firm will not respond to small shifts in the marginal cost curve. Suppose that curve *MC* in Exhibit 8 is the initial marginal cost curve. The point where *MC* crosses the gap in the marginal revenue curve identifies the profit-maximizing rate of output, *q*, and price, *p*. What happens to equilibrium price and quantity if the marginal cost curve drops to *MC'*? Nothing happens, because the oligopolist can do no better than to offer quantity *q* at price *p*. The same holds if marginal cost increases to *MC"*—again, there is no change in the equilibrium price and quantity. *Since changes in the marginal cost curve do not necessarily affect the price, the price tends to be rigid, or stable, in oligopolistic industries if firms behave in the manner described by the kinked demand curve.* It takes a greater shift in the marginal cost curve to produce a change in equilibrium price and quantity. Specifically, to change the equilibrium price and quantity, the marginal cost curve must change enough to intersect the marginal revenue curve above point *a* or below point *b* in Exhibit 8.

EXHIBIT   8

Demand and Marginal Revenue Curves for the Kinked Demand Model

If *MC* is the initial marginal cost curve, the firm will produce quantity *q* (where marginal cost equals marginal revenue) at price *p*. Marginal cost could fall to *MC'* or increase to *MC"* without affecting the quantity produced. Likewise, price *p* will be rigid if marginal cost for output *q* varies between *a* and *b*.

Although the kinked demand model offers a possible explanation for the price stickiness observed over the years, it says nothing about how the equilibrium price and quantity are initially determined. That's a major weakness of the model. What's more, not all prices in oligopolies are rigid. For example, during the inflationary periods of the 1970s and early 1980s, some oligopolies increased prices frequently. In fact, some oligopolies change prices more often than some monopolies, even though the kinked demand model predicts just the opposite.

Summary of Oligopoly Models

Each of the oligopoly models we have considered helps explain certain phenomena observed in oligopolistic markets. Interdependence, which these models explain, gives rise to all kinds of behavior, so many models exist. The *cartel,* or *collusion,* model shows why oligopolists might want to cooperate to determine market price and output; that model also explains why cartels are hard to establish and maintain. The *price-leadership* model explains why and how firms may act in unison on prices without actually establishing a formal cartel. *Game theory* models show that, because of firm interdependence, market strategies can range from cooperation to price wars. Finally, the *kinked demand curve* explains why some oligopoly prices tend to remain unchanged for long periods even while costs are changing.

Comparison of Oligopoly and Perfect Competition

As we have seen, each oligopoly model explains a piece of the oligopoly puzzle. Each model has limitations, however, and none provides a complete depiction of all oligopoly behavior. Consequently, since there is no typical, or representative, model of oligopoly, "the" oligopoly model cannot be compared with the competitive model. We might, however, imagine an experiment in which we took the hundreds of firms that populate a competitive industry and, through a series of giant mergers, combined them to form, say, four firms. We would thereby transform the industry from perfect competition to oligopoly. How would the behavior of firms in this industry differ before and after the massive merger?

Price Is Usually Higher Under Oligopoly. With fewer competitors after the merger, remaining firms would become more interdependent. Oligopoly models presented in this chapter suggest that the firms may act in concert in their pricing policies. *If the oligopolists engaged in some sort of implicit or explicit collusion, industry output would be smaller and the price would be higher than under perfect competition.* Even if oligopolists did not collude but simply operated with excess capacity, the long-run average cost of production would be higher with oligopoly than with perfect competition. The price could become temporarily lower under oligopoly compared to perfect competition only if a price war broke out among oligopolists.

Higher Profits Under Oligopoly. In the long run, easy entry prevents perfect competitors from earning more than a normal profit. With oligopoly, however, there are presumably barriers to entry, such as economies of scale or brand names, that allow firms in the industry to earn long-run economic profits. Such barriers could be insurmountable for a new entrant. Therefore, *we should expect profit rates in the long run to be higher under oligopoly than under perfect competition.*

Profit rates do in fact appear to be higher in industries where a few firms account for a high proportion of industry sales. Some economists view these higher profit rates as troubling evidence of market power. But not all economists share this view. Some note that the largest firms in oligopolistic industries tend to earn the highest rate of profit. Hence, the higher profit rates observed in oligopolistic industries stem not necessarily from market power per se. Rather, these higher profit rates stem from the greater efficiency arising from economies of scale in these large firms.[6] Many of these issues will be examined later, when we explore the government's role in regulating markets.

CONCLUSION

This chapter moves us from the extremes of perfect competition and pure monopoly to the gray area inhabited by most firms. Firms in monopolistic competition and firms in oligopoly face a downward-sloping demand curve for their products. In choosing the profit-maximizing price-output combination, a monopolistically competitive firm is not concerned much about the effects of this choice on the behavior of competitors. There are so many firms in the market that each individual firm tends to get lost in the crowd. But oligopolistic firms are interdependent and therefore must consider the effects their pricing and output decisions will have on other firms. This interdependence complicates the analysis of oligopoly, leaving open a wide array of possible models.

The analytical results derived in this chapter are not as neat as those derived for the polar cases of perfect competition and pure monopoly, but we can still point to general conclusions, using perfect competition as our benchmark. In the long run, perfect competitors operate at minimum average cost, while the other types of firms usually operate with some excess capacity. Therefore, given identical cost curves, monopolistic competitors and oligopolists tend to charge higher prices than perfect competitors, especially in the long run. In the long run, monopolistic competitors, like perfect competitors, earn only a normal profit because entry barriers are low. But oligopolists can earn economic profit in the long run if new entry is somehow restricted. In a later chapter, we will examine how government policy is often aimed at making industries more competitive. *Regardless of the market structure, however, profit maximization prompts firms to produce the output rate at which marginal cost equals marginal revenue.*

SUMMARY

1. Whereas the pure monopolist produces a product that has no close substitutes, a monopolistic competitor must contend with many rivals offering close substitutes. Because there are some differences among the products offered by different firms, even if the difference stems just from the location of the seller, each monopolistic competitor faces a downward-sloping demand curve.

2. Sellers in monopolistic competition differentiate their products through (1) physical qualities, (2) sales locations,

---

6 For this argument, see Harold Demsetz, "Industry Structure, Market Rivalry, and Public Policy," *Journal of Law and Economics* 16 (April 1973): 1–10.

(3) services provided with the product, and (4) the image of the product established in the consumer's mind.

3. In the short run, monopolistic competitors that can at least cover their average variable costs will maximize profits or minimize losses by producing where marginal cost equals marginal revenue. In the long run, free entry and exit of firms ensure that monopolistic competitors earn only a normal profit, which occurs where the average total cost curve is tangent to the firm's downward-sloping demand curve.

4. An oligopoly is an industry dominated by a few sellers, some of which are large enough relative to the entire market to influence price. In some oligopolistic industries, such as steel or oil, the product is homogeneous; in other oligopolistic industries, such as automobiles or breakfast cereal, the product differs.

5. Because an oligopolistic industry consists of just a few firms, each firm may react to another firm's changes in quality, price, output, services, or advertising policy. Because of this interdependence, the behavior of oligopolists is difficult to analyze. No single model of behavior characterizes oligopolistic markets.

6. In this chapter, we considered four models of oligopoly behavior: (1) the cartel, through which firms collude to behave like a monopolist; (2) price leadership, whereby one or a few firms set the price for the industry and other firms follow the leaders; (3) game theory, which focuses on each firm's strategy, based on the expected response of rivals; and (4) the kinked demand curve, which assumes that a firm's rivals follow price decreases but do not follow price increases.

QUESTIONS FOR REVIEW

1. *(Characteristics of Monopolistic Competition)* Why does the demand curve facing a monopolistically competitive firm slope downward in the long run, even after the entry of new firms?

2. *(Product Differentiation)* What are four ways in which a firm can differentiate its product? What role can advertising play in product differentiation? How can advertising become a barrier to entry?

3. *(Zero Economic Profit in the Long Run)* In the long run, a monopolistically competitive firm earns zero economic profit, which is exactly what would occur if the industry were perfectly competitive. Assuming that the cost curves for each firm are the same whether the industry is perfectly or monopolistically competitive, answer the following questions.
   a. Why don't perfectly and monopolistically competitive industries produce the same equilibrium quantity in the long run?
   b. Why is a monopolistically competitive industry said to be economically inefficient?
   c. What benefits might cause us to prefer the monopolistically competitive result to the perfectly competitive result?

4. *(Varieties of Oligopoly)* Do the firms in an oligopoly act independently or interdependently? Explain your answer.

5. *(CaseStudy: The Unfriendly Skies)* One complaint frequently heard about airfares is that flying from an airline's hub city airport is more expensive than flying from a nearby city that is not a hub. How may this reflect a different level of competition in hub city airports?

6. *(Collusion and Cartels)* Why would each of the following induce some members of OPEC to cheat on their cartel agreement?
   a. Newly joined cartel members are less-developed countries.
   b. The number of cartel members doubles from 10 to 20.
   c. International debts of some members grow.
   d. Expectations grow that some members will cheat.

7. *(Price Leadership)* Why might a price-leadership model of oligopoly not be an effective means of collusion in an oligopoly?

8. *(The Kinked Demand Curve)* If a firm believes that it is facing a kinked demand curve, what assumptions is it making about its rivals' reactions to its own price changes? How would the firm react to changes in its production costs?

9. *(Market Structures)* Determine whether each of the following is a characteristic of perfect competition, monopolistic competition, oligopoly, and/or monopoly:
   a. A large number of sellers
   b. A homogeneous product
   c. Advertising by firms
   d. Barriers to entry
   e. Firms that are price searchers

PROBLEMS AND EXERCISES

10. *(Short-Run Profit Maximization)* A monopolistically competitive firm has the following demand and cost structure in the short run:

Output	Price	FC	VC	TC	TR	Profit/Loss
0	$100	$100	$ 0	___	___	___
1	90	___	50	___	___	___
2	80	___	90	___	___	___
3	70	___	150	___	___	___
4	60	___	230	___	___	___
5	50	___	330	___	___	___
6	40	___	450	___	___	___
7	30	___	590	___	___	___

   a. Complete the table.
   b. What is the best profit or loss available to this firm?
   c. Should the firm operate or shut down in the short run? Why?
   d. What is the relationship between marginal revenue and marginal cost as the firm increases output?

11. *(Case**Study:** Fast Forward)* Use a cost-and-revenue graph to illustrate and explain the short-run profits in the video rental business. Then use a second graph to illustrate the long-run situation. Explain fully.

12. *(Monopolistic Competition Versus Perfect Competition)* Illustrated below are the marginal cost and long-run average total cost curves for a small firm.
   a. Locate the long-run equilibrium price and quantity if the firm is perfectly competitive.
   b. Label the price and quantity P_1 and Q_1.
   c. Draw in a demand and marginal revenue curve to illustrate long-run equilibrium if the firm is monopolistically competitive. Label the price and quantity P_2 and Q_2.

   d. How do the monopolistically competitive firm's price and output compare to those of the perfectly competitive firm?
   e. How do long-run profits compare for the two types of firms?

13. *(Collusion and Cartels)* Use revenue and cost curves to illustrate and explain the sense in which a cartel behaves like a monopolist.

14. *(Game Theory)* Suppose there are only two automobile companies, Ford and Chevrolet. Ford believes that Chevrolet will match any price it sets. Use the following price and profit data to answer the following questions.

If Ford sells for	and Chevrolet sells for	Ford's profits (millions)	Chevrolet's profits (millions)
$ 4,000	$ 4,000	$ 8	$ 8
4,000	8,000	12	6
4,000	12,000	14	2
8,000	4,000	6	12
8,000	8,000	10	10
8,000	12,000	12	6
12,000	4,000	2	14
12,000	8,000	6	12
12,000	12,000	7	7

   a. What price will Ford charge?
   b. What price will Chevrolet charge?
   c. What is Ford's profit after Chevrolet's response?
   d. If the two firms collaborated to maximize joint profits, what prices would they set?
   e. Given your answer to part (d), how could undetected cheating on price cause the cheating firm's profit to rise?

EXPERIENTIAL EXERCISES

15. *(Product Differentiation)* One important way monopolistic competitors differentiate their products is by location. Review John Campbell's article, "Time to Shop: The Geography of Retailing," from the Federal Reserve Bank of Boston's *The Region* at http://www.bos.frb.org/economic/nerr/camp96_3.htm. What locational strategies are retailers using? What does the theory of monopolistic competition predict about the success of such strategies in the short run and in the long run?

16. *(OPEC)* OPEC is the economist's favorite cartel to study. That is partly because it had such a spectacular short-run success and partly because oligopoly theory could be used to predict how OPEC pricing actually evolved. Take a look at the U.S. Department of Energy's OPEC Fact Sheet at http://www.eia.doe.gov/emeu/cabs/opec.html. What are some recent developments in petroleum pricing? How relevant are the factors listed in this chapter as affecting the difficulty of maintaining a cartel?

17. *(Wall Street Journal)* If you look carefully, you can often find evidence of price leadership. For example, the *Wall Street Journal* frequently runs stories about airfares. Typically, one airline will raise its fares—on certain routes or across the board—and other airlines match those changes within a day or two. As you read through the *Wall Street Journal* this week, be on the lookout for such stories. They are typically reported on the front page—in the What's News column. When you find such a story, check back over the next few days. Did other airlines match the leader, or was the leader forced to back off its price changes?

Resource Markets

Why does Charles Schulz, the cartoonist, earn $25 million a year for drawing *Peanuts,* while Charles Schultze, the economist, earns peanuts, relatively speaking, for drawing conclusions about the economy? Why do surgeons earn twice as much as general practitioners? Why do tractor-trailer drivers earn more than rickshaw drivers? Why did a 30-second ad on the final episode of *Seinfeld* cost $2 million, when the prime-time average was only $120,000? Why does prime Iowa corn acreage sell for more than scrubland in the Texas panhandle? Why are the buildings in downtown Chicago taller than those in the farm towns of southern Illinois? To answer these and other questions, we turn in this chapter to the supply and demand for resources.

You say you've been through demand and supply already? True. But the earlier discussion focused on the product market—that is, the market for final goods and services. Goods and services, however, are produced by resources—labor, capital, land, and entrepreneurial ability. Demand and supply in resource markets determine the price and employment of resources. The distribution of resource ownership determines the distribution of income throughout the economy.

Because your earnings depend on the market value of your resources, you should find resource markets particularly interesting. Certainly one key element in your career decision is the expected income associated with various careers. The next three chapters will examine how demand and supply interact to establish market prices for various resources. Topics discussed in this chapter include:

- Demand and supply of resources
- Opportunity cost and economic rent

- Marginal revenue product
- Marginal resource cost
- Shifts in resource demand
- Distribution of resource earnings

THE ONCE OVER

Just to prove you already know a lot more about resource markets than you may think, try answering the questions in the following paragraphs.

Resource Demand

We begin with the demand for labor. The manager of Wal-Mart estimates that hiring one more sales clerk would increase total cost by $400 per week but would increase total revenue by $500 per week. Should an additional sales clerk be hired? Sure. The additional clerk would increase Wal-Mart's profit by $100 per week. *As long as the additional revenue from employing another worker exceeds the additional cost, the firm should hire that worker.*

How about capital? Suppose that you operate a lawn-and-garden service during the summer, earning an average of $20 per lawn. You mow about 15 lawns a week, for a total revenue of $300. You are considering upgrading to a larger, faster mower called the Lawn Monster, which would cost an extra $200 per week. The bigger mower would cut your time per lawn in half, enabling you to mow 30 lawns per week, so your total revenue would double to $600. Should you make the switch? Since the additional revenue of $300 exceeds the additional cost of $200, you should move up to the Monster.

What about land? A neighbor offers Farmer Jones the opportunity to lease 100 acres of farmland. Jones figures that farming the extra land would cost $70 per acre but would yield $60 per acre in additional revenue. Should he lease the extra land? What do you think? Since the additional cost of farming that land would exceed the additional revenue, the answer is no.

These examples show that *a firm demands an additional unit of a resource as long as the marginal revenue generated by that additional unit exceeds its marginal cost.*

Derived demand The demand for a resource derived from the demand for the product the resource produces

Resource Supply

You likely also understand the economic logic behind resource supply. Suppose you are deciding between two jobs that are identical except that one pays more than the other. Is there any question which job you will take? If the working conditions of both jobs are equally attractive, you will choose the higher-paying job. Now consider your choice between two jobs that pay the same; one has normal nine-to-five hours, but the other starts at 5:00 A.M., an hour when your body tends to reject conscious activity. Which would you choose? You would select the job more in accord with your natural body rhythms.

Resource owners will supply their resources to the highest-paying alternative, other things equal. Since other things are not always equal, resource owners must often be paid more to supply their resources to certain uses. In the case of labor, the worker's utility depends on both monetary and nonmonetary aspects of the job. People must be paid more to work in jobs that are dirty, dangerous, dull, exhausting, of low status, that have no future, and that involve inconvenient hours than to work in jobs that are clean, safe, stimulating, of high status, have bright prospects, and involve convenient hours.

THE DEMAND AND SUPPLY OF RESOURCES

In the market for goods and services—that is, in the product market—households are the demanders and firms are suppliers. Households demand the goods and services that maximize utility, and firms supply the goods and services that maximize profit. In the resource market, the roles of demander and supplier are reversed: Firms are demanders and households are suppliers. Firms demand resources so as to maximize profit and households supply resources so as to maximize utility. *Any differences between the profit-maximizing goals of firms and the utility-maximizing goals of households are reconciled through voluntary exchange in markets.*

Exhibit 1 presents the market for a particular resource—in this case, carpenters. As you can see, the demand curve slopes downward and the supply curve slopes upward. *Like the demand and supply for final goods and services, the demand and supply for resources depend on the willingness and the ability of buyers and sellers to participate in market exchange.* This market will converge to the equilibrium wage rate, or the market price, for this type of labor.

The Market Demand for Resources

Why does a firm employ resources? Resources are used to produce goods and services, which the firm tries to sell for a profit. The firm does not value any resource itself but rather that resource's ability to produce goods and services that can be sold for a profit. Because the value of any resource depends on the value of what it produces, the demand for a resource is said to be a **derived demand**—derived from the demand for the final product. For example, a carpenter's pay derives from the market demand for the carpenter's output, such as a cabinet or a new deck; a professional baseball player's pay derives from the market demand for ball games; a truck driver's pay derives from the market demand for transporting goods. The derived nature of resource demand helps explain why professional

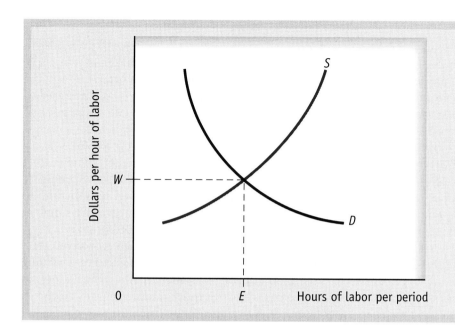

EXHIBIT 1

Resource Market for Carpenters

The intersection of the upward-sloping supply curve of carpenters with the downward-sloping demand curve determines the equilibrium wage rate, *W*, and the level of employment, *E*.

baseball players usually earn more than professional hockey players, why brain surgeons earn more than tree surgeons, why drivers of big rigs earn more than drivers of delivery vans, and why a 30-second TV ad during the Superbowl costs more than one during a typical game.

The market demand for a particular resource is the sum of demands for that resource in all its different uses. For example, the market demand for carpenters adds together the demands for carpenters in residential and commercial construction, remodeling, cabinet making, and so on. Similarly, the market demand for the resource, timber, sums the demand for timber as lumber, railway ties, firewood, furniture, pencils, toothpicks, paper products, and so on. The demand curve for a resource, like the demand curves for the goods produced by that resource, slopes downward, as depicted in Exhibit 1.

As the price of a resource falls, producers are more willing and able to employ that resource. Consider first the producer's greater *willingness* to hire resources as the resource price falls. In developing the demand curve for a particular resource, we assume the prices of other resources remain constant. So if the price of a particular resource falls, it becomes relatively cheaper compared to other resources the firm could use to produce the same output. Firms therefore are more willing to hire this resource rather than hire other, now relatively more costly, resources. Thus, we observe *substitution in production*—coal for oil, security alarms for security guards, and backhoes for grave diggers, as the relative prices of coal, security alarms, and backhoes fall.

A lower price for a resource also increases a producer's *ability* to hire that resource. For example, if the resource price falls, a firm can hire more of the resource for the same total cost. The lower resource price means the firm is *more able* to buy the resource.

The Market Supply for Resources

The market supply curve of a resource sums all the individual supply curves for that resource. Resource suppliers tend to be both more *willing* and more *able* to supply the resource as the resource price increases, so the market supply curve slopes upward, as the supply curve for carpenters does in Exhibit 1. Resource suppliers are more *willing* because the higher the market price of a particular resource, other things constant, the more goods and services can be purchased with the earnings obtained from supplying the resource.

Resource prices are signals about the rewards for supplying resources to alternative activities. A high resource price tells the resource owner, "The market really values your resource and is willing to pay you well for what you supply." Higher resource prices will draw resources from lower-valued uses, including leisure. For example, as the wage for carpenters increases, the quantity supplied will increase; some carpenters will give up leisure to work more hours.

The second reason a resource supply curve slopes upward is that resource owners are *able* to supply more of the resource at a higher price. For example, higher paper prices increase the market price of timber used to make paper, so logging companies can afford to harvest trees in more remote regions. A higher resource price *enables* resource suppliers to increase their quantity supplied.

Temporary and Permanent Resource Price Differences

Resource owners have a strong interest in selling their resources where they are most valued. *Resources tend to flow to their highest-valued use.* If carpenters, for example, can earn more by building homes than making furniture, then carpenters will shift from making furniture to building homes until wages in the two activities are equal. Because resource owners seek the highest pay, *other things constant,* the prices paid for identical resources should tend toward equality.

For example, suppose the wage paid to carpenters engaged in home building is $25 per hour, which is $5 more than the wage paid to carpenters who work as furniture makers. This difference is shown in Exhibit 2 by a wage of $25 per hour in panel (a) and a wage of $20 per hour in panel (b). This wage difference will encourage some carpenters to move from furniture making to home building. This shift will decrease the wage in home building and increase the wage in furniture making. Carpenters will move into home building until wages equalize. In Exhibit 2, supply shifts until the wage is $24 in both markets. Note that in the adjustment process, 2,000 hours of labor per week move from furniture making to home building. *As long as the nonmonetary benefits of supplying resources to alternative uses are identical and as long as resources are freely mobile, resources will adjust across uses until they earn the same in their alternative uses.*

Sometimes earnings appear to differ between seemingly similar resources. For example, corporate economists on average earn more than academic economists, and land in the city sells for more than land in the country. As you will now see, these differences reflect the workings of demand and supply.

Temporary Differences in Resource Prices. Resource prices sometimes differ temporarily across markets because market adjustment takes time. For example, there are sometimes wage differentials among workers who appear equally qualified. As we have seen, however, a difference between the prices of similar resources prompts resource owners and firms to make adjustments that drive

EXHIBIT 2

Market for Carpenters in Alternative Uses: Home Building and Furniture Making

(a) Home building

(b) Furniture making

Suppose the wage offered carpenters is $25 per hour in home building but only $20 per hour in furniture making. As a result of the wage differential, some carpenters will shift from furniture making to home building, and this will continue until the wage offered carpenters is identical in both alternative uses. In panel (b), the reduction in the supply of carpenters to furniture making increases the equilibrium wage from $20 per hour to $24 per hour. In panel (a), the increase in the supply of carpenters to home building decreases the equilibrium wage from $25 per hour to $24 per hour. A total of 2,000 carpenter hours per week are shifted from furniture making to home building.

resource prices toward equality, as with the carpenters in the previous exhibit. The process may take years, but when resource markets are free to adjust, price differences trigger the reallocation of resources, which equalizes payments for similar resources.

Permanent Differences in Resource Prices. Not all resource price differences cause a reallocation of resources. For example, land along New York's Fifth Avenue sells for as much as $36,000 a *square yard!* For that amount, you could buy several acres of land in upstate New York. Yet such a differential does not prompt land owners in upstate New York to supply their land to New York City—obviously that's impossible. The price per acre of farmland varies widely, reflecting differences in the land's productivity and location. Such differences do not trigger actions that result in price equality. Similarly, certain wage differentials stem in part from the different costs of acquiring the education and training required to perform particular tasks. This difference explains why brain surgeons earn more than tree surgeons, why ophthalmologists earn more than optometrists, and why airline pilots earn more than truck drivers.

Other earning differentials reflect differences in the nonmonetary aspects of similar jobs. For example, other things constant, most people require higher pay to work in a grimy factory than in a pleasant office. Similarly, corporate economists earn more than academic economists in part because corporate economists typically have less freedom in their daily schedules, their attire, their choices of research topics, or even their public statements.

Temporary price differentials are just that, for they spark the movement of resources away from lower-paid uses toward higher-paid uses. Permanent price differentials cause no such reallocations. Permanent price differentials are explained by *a lack of resource mobility* (rural land versus urban land), *differences in the inherent quality of the resource* (scrubland versus fertile land), *differences in the time and money involved in developing the necessary skills* (file clerk versus certified public accountant), and *differences in nonmonetary aspects of the job* (prison guard at San Quentin versus lifeguard at Malibu Beach).

Opportunity Cost and Economic Rent

Shaquille O'Neal reportedly earned over $25 million in 1998, mostly from product endorsements. But he would likely be willing to play basketball and to endorse products for less money. The question is, how much less? What is his best alternative? Suppose his best alternative is to devote his energy full time to becoming a rap artist, something he now pursues in his spare time. Suppose as a full-time rap artist he could earn $2 million per year, including endorsements. Assume too that, if it weren't for the pay difference, he would be indifferent between rap and basketball, so the nonmonetary aspects of the two jobs balance out. Thus he must earn at least $2 million to remain a basketball player. This amount represents his *opportunity cost*—the amount he must be paid to prevent him from supplying his time to rap. *The opportunity cost of a resource is what that resource could earn in its best alternative use.*

The amount O'Neal earns in excess of his opportunity cost is called *economic rent*. **Economic rent** is that portion of a resource's total earnings that is not necessary to keep the resource in its present use; it is, as the saying goes, "pure gravy." In O'Neal's case, economic rent is $25 million minus $2 million, or $23 million. Economic rent is a form of producer surplus earned by resource suppliers. The *division* of earnings between opportunity cost and economic rent depends on the resource owner's elasticity of supply. *In general, the less elastic the resource supply, the greater the economic rent as a proportion of total earnings.* To develop a feel for the difference between opportunity cost and economic rent, consider the following three cases.

Case A: All Earnings Are Economic Rent. If the supply of a resource to a particular market is perfectly inelastic, that resource has no alternative uses. Hence, there is no opportunity cost, and all returns are economic rent. For example, scrubland in the high plains of Montana has no use other than for cattle graz-

Economic rent The portion of a resource's total earnings above its opportunity cost; earnings above the amount necessary to keep the resource in its present use ing. The supply of this grazing land is depicted by the vertical line in panel (a) of Exhibit 3, which indicates that the 10 million acres have no alternative use. Since the supply is fixed, the amount paid to rent this land for grazing has no effect on the quantity supplied. The land has no alternative use, so the opportunity cost is zero and all earnings are economic rent, shown by the blue shaded area. Here, *fixed supply determines the equilibrium quantity of the resource, but demand determines the equilibrium price.*

Case B: All Earnings Are Opportunity Costs. At the other extreme is the case in which a resource can earn as much in its best alternative use as in its present use. This situation is illustrated by the perfectly elastic supply curve in panel (b) of Exhibit 3. Suppose this figure depicts the market for janitors in the local school system. The school system can employ as many janitors as it wants at the market wage of $10 per hour; here, schools demand 1,000 hours of labor per week. If the wage offered janitors falls below $10 per hour, they will find jobs elsewhere, perhaps in nearby factories, where the wage is $10 per hour. In this case, all earnings equal opportunity costs because any reduction in the wage reduces the quantity of labor supplied to this particular use to zero. In this case, *the horizontal supply curve determines the equilibrium wage, but demand determines the equilibrium quantity.*

Case C: Earnings Include Both Economic Rent and Opportunity Costs. If the resource supply curve slopes upward, most resource suppliers will earn economic rent in addition to their opportunity cost. For example, if the wage for unskilled work in your college community increases from $5 to $10 per hour, the quantity of labor supplied will increase, as will the economic rent earned by resource suppliers. This situation occurs in panel (c) of Exhibit 3, where the pink area identifies opportunity costs and the blue area identifies economic rent. If the wage increases from $5 to $10, the quantity supplied per week will increase by 5,000 hours. For those resource suppliers who had been offering their services at a wage of $5 per hour, the difference between $5 and $10 is economic rent. These workers did not require the higher price to supply their services, but they certainly are not going to turn it down. *In the case of an upward-sloping supply curve and a downward-sloping demand curve, both demand and supply determine the equilibrium price and quantity.*

Note that specialized resources tend to earn a higher proportion of economic rent than do resources with many alternative uses. Thus, Shaquille O'Neal earns a greater *proportion* of his income as economic rent than does the janitor who cleans the Los Angeles Lakers' locker room. O'Neal would take a huge pay cut if he didn't play professional basketball, but the Lakers' janitor could find another unskilled job that would pay nearly as much.

To review: Given a resource demand curve that slopes downward, when the resource supply curve is vertical (perfectly inelastic), all earnings are economic rent; when that supply curve is horizontal (perfectly elastic), all earnings reflect opportunity cost; and when that supply curve slopes upward (an elasticity greater than zero but less than infinity), earnings divide between opportunity cost and economic rent. Remember, *the opportunity cost of a resource is what that resource could earn in its best alternative use. Economic rent is earnings in excess of opportunity cost.*

EXHIBIT 3

Opportunity Cost and Economic Rent

(a) All resource returns are economic rent

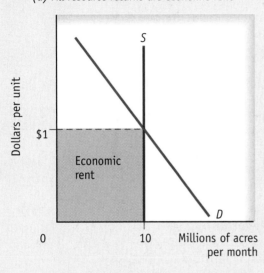

(b) All resource returns are opportunity costs

(c) Resource returns are divided between economic rent and opportunity cost

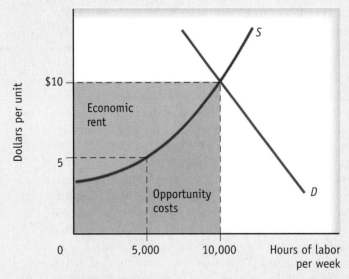

In panel (a), the resource supply curve is vertical, indicating that the resource has no alternative use. The price is demand-determined, and all earnings are in the form of economic rent. In panel (b), the supply curve is horizontal, indicating that the resource can earn $10 in its best alternative use. Employment is demand-determined, and all earnings are opportunity costs. Panel (c) shows an upward-sloping supply curve. At the equilibrium wage of $10, resource earnings are partly opportunity costs and partly economic rent. Both supply and demand determine the equilibrium price and quantity.

This completes our introduction to resource supply. In the balance of this chapter, we take a closer look at the demand side of resource markets. The determinants of the demand for a resource are largely the same whether we are talking about labor, capital, or land. The supply of different resources, however, has certain peculiarities depending on the resource, so the supply of specific resources will be taken up in the next two chapters.

A CLOSER LOOK AT RESOURCE DEMAND

Although production usually involves many inputs, we will cut the analysis down to size by focusing on a single resource, assuming that the quantities of other resources are constant. As usual, we assume that firms try to maximize profit and households try to maximize utility.

The Firm's Demand for a Resource

You may recall that when the firm's costs were first introduced, we considered a moving company, where labor was the only variable resource in the short run. By varying the amount of labor employed, we examined the relationship between the quantity of labor employed and the amount of furniture moved per day. We use the same approach in Exhibit 4, where all but one of the firm's inputs remain constant. The first column in the table lists possible employment levels of the variable resource, in this case measured as workers per day. The second column presents the total output, or total product, and the third column

EXHIBIT 4

The Marginal Revenue Product When a Firm Sells in a Competitive Market

Workers Per Day (1)	Total Product (2)	Marginal Product (3)	Product Price (4)	Total Revenue (5) = (2) × (4)	Marginal Revenue Product (6)
0	0	—	$20	$ 0	—
1	10	10	20	200	$200
2	19	9	20	380	180
3	27	8	20	540	160
4	34	7	20	680	140
5	40	6	20	800	120
6	45	5	20	900	100
7	49	4	20	980	80
8	52	3	20	1040	60
9	54	2	20	1080	40
10	55	1	20	1100	20
11	55	0	20	1100	0
12	53	−2	20	1060	−40

presents the marginal product. The *marginal product* of labor indicates how much additional output each additional unit of labor produces.

When one worker is employed, total product is 10 units and so is the marginal product. The marginal product of adding the second worker is 9 units. As the firm hires more workers, the marginal product of labor declines, reflecting the law of diminishing marginal returns. In Exhibit 4, diminishing marginal returns set in immediately—that is, right after the first worker is employed.

Although labor is the variable resource here, we could examine the marginal product of any resource. For example, we could consider how many lawns could be cut per week by varying the quantity of capital employed. We might start off with very little capital—imagine cutting grass with a pair of scissors—then moving up to a push mower, a power mower, and the Lawn Monster. By holding labor constant and varying the quantity of capital employed, we could compute the marginal product of capital. Likewise, we could compute the marginal product of land by examining crop production for varying amounts of land, holding other inputs, such as the amount of farm labor and capital, constant.

Marginal Revenue Product

Marginal revenue product
The change in total revenue when an additional unit of a resource is hired, other things constant

The important question is, what happens to the firm's *revenue* as a result of hiring additional workers? The first three columns of Exhibit 4 show what happens to output as the firm hires more workers. The *marginal revenue product* of labor indicates how total revenue changes as more labor is employed, other things constant. The **marginal revenue product** of any resource is the change in the firm's total revenue resulting from employing an additional unit of the resource, other things constant. You could think of the marginal revenue product as the firm's "marginal benefit" from hiring one more unit of the resource. A resource's marginal revenue product depends on (1) how much additional output the resource produces and (2) the price at which output is sold.

Selling Output as a Price Taker. The calculation of marginal revenue product is simplest when the firm sells output in a perfectly competitive market, which is the assumption underlying Exhibit 4. Since an individual firm in perfect competition can sell as much as it wants without affecting the product's price, a perfectly competitive firm is said to be a *price taker.* That firm must accept, or "take," the market price for its product. The marginal revenue product, listed in column (6), is the change in total revenue that results from changing input usage by one unit. For the perfectly competitive firm, the marginal revenue product is simply the marginal product of the resource multiplied by the product price of $20. Note that because of diminishing returns, the marginal revenue product falls steadily as the firm employs additional units of the resource.

Selling Output as a Price Searcher. If the firm has some market power in the product market—that is, some ability to set the price—the demand curve for that firm's output slopes downward. To sell more output, the firm must lower its price. The firm, consequently, must search for the price that maximizes profit. Such a firm is called a *price searcher.* Exhibit 5 reproduces the first two columns of Exhibit 4; the remaining columns reflect the revenue of a firm selling as a price searcher. Total output multiplied by the price at which that output sells yields the firm's total revenue, which appears in column (4).

EXHIBIT 5

Workers Per Day (1)	Total Product (2)	Product Price (3)	Total Revenue (4) = (2) × (3)	Marginal Revenue Product (5)	The Marginal Revenue Product When a Firm Sells as a Price Searcher
0	0	—	—	—	
1	10	$40.00	$400.00	$400.00	
2	19	35.20	668.80	268.80	
3	27	31.40	847.80	179.00	
4	34	27.80	945.20	97.40	
5	40	25.00	1000.00	54.80	
6	45	22.50	1012.50	12.50	
7	49	20.50	1004.50	−8.00	
8	52	19.00	988.00	−16.50	
9	54	18.00	972.00	−16.00	
10	55	17.50	962.50	−9.50	
11	55	17.50	962.50	0.00	

The marginal revenue product of labor, which is the change in total revenue resulting from a 1-unit change in the quantity of labor employed, appears in column (5). For example, the first worker produced 10 units per day, which sell for $40 each, yielding total revenue of $400. Hiring the second worker adds 9 more units to the total product, but to sell 9 more units, the firm must lower the price of all units from $40 to $35.20. Total revenue increases to $668.80, which means the marginal revenue product from hiring a second worker is $268.80.

Again, *the marginal revenue product is the additional revenue that results from employing each additional worker.* The profit-maximizing firm should be willing and able to pay as much as the marginal revenue product for an additional unit of the resource, hence *the marginal revenue product curve can be thought of as the firm's demand curve for that resource.* You could think of the marginal revenue product curve as the marginal benefit to the firm of hiring each additional unit of the resource.

To review, whether a firm is a price taker or a price searcher, the marginal revenue product of a resource is the change in total revenue resulting from a 1-unit change in that resource, other things held constant. The marginal revenue product curve of a resource is the demand curve for that resource— it shows the most a firm would be willing and able to pay for each successive unit of the resource. *For a price taker, the marginal revenue product curve declines only because of diminishing marginal returns. For a price searcher, the marginal revenue product curve declines both because of diminishing returns and because additional output can be sold only if the price declines.* For both price takers and price searchers, the marginal revenue product is the change in total revenue resulting from hiring an additional unit of the resource.

Marginal Resource Cost

Marginal resource cost
The change in total cost when an additional unit of a resource is hired, other things constant

Given the firm's marginal revenue product, can we determine how much labor the firm should employ to maximize profit? Not yet, because we must also know how much labor costs the firm. Specifically, what is the **marginal resource cost**—that is, what is the additional cost to the firm of employing one more unit of labor? The typical firm hires such a tiny fraction of the available resource that its employment decision has no effect on the market price of the resource. Thus, each firm usually faces a given market price for the resource and decides only on how much to hire at that price.

For example, panel (a) in Exhibit 6 shows the market for factory workers, measured in workers per day. The intersection of market demand and supply determines the equilibrium wage of $100 dollars per day. Panel (b) shows the situation for the individual firm. The market-determined wage for factory workers of $100 per day becomes the marginal resource cost of labor to the firm regardless of how many workers the firm employs. The *marginal resource cost* curve appears as the horizontal line drawn at the $100 level in panel (b); this is the labor supply curve to the firm. Panel (b) also shows the marginal revenue product curve, or resource demand curve, based on the schedule presented in Exhibit 4. The marginal revenue product curve indicates the additional revenue the firm receives as a result of employing each additional unit of labor.

EXHIBIT 6

Market Equilibrium for a Resource and the Firm's Employment Decision

Market demand and supply determine the equilibrium price and quantity. Given the market price of the resource, the individual firm employs as much as it wants at the market price, so the market price is the firm's marginal resource cost. The firm's demand curve for the resource is based on that resource's marginal revenue product. The firm maximizes profit by hiring up to the point where the marginal revenue product equals the marginal resource cost.

Given a marginal resource cost of $100 per worker per day, how much labor will the firm employ to maximize profit? *The firm will hire more labor as long as doing so adds more to revenue than to cost—that is, as long as the marginal revenue product exceeds the marginal resource cost. The firm will stop hiring labor only when the two are equal.* If marginal resource cost is a constant $100 per worker, the firm will hire 6 workers per day because the marginal revenue product from hiring a sixth worker equals $100. Thus, the firm should hire additional inputs up to the level at which

$$\text{marginal resource cost} = \text{marginal revenue product}$$

or MRC = MRP. This equality holds for all resources employed, whether the firms sells output as a price taker or a price searcher. The profit-maximizing employment occurs where the market wage, or the market-determined resource price, equals the marginal revenue product. Based on data presented thus far, we cannot determine the firm's actual profit because we don't yet know about the firm's other costs. We do know, however, that in Exhibit 6 a seventh worker would add $100 to cost but would add less than that to revenue, so hiring a seventh worker would reduce the firm's profit (or increase its loss).

Whether the firm sells output as a price taker or as a price searcher, the profit-maximizing level of employment occurs where the marginal revenue product of labor equals its marginal resource cost. Similarly, the profit-maximizing employment of other resources, such as land and capital, occurs where their respective marginal revenue products equal their marginal resource costs. Each resource must "pull its own weight"—it must yield a marginal revenue at least equal to its marginal cost.

In an earlier chapter, we developed a rule for determining the profit-maximizing level of output. Maximum profit (or minimum loss) occurs at the output level where the marginal cost of producing *output* equals the marginal revenue from selling that *output*. Likewise, maximum profit (or minimum loss) occurs at the resource level where the marginal cost of employing a *resource* equals the marginal revenue that *resource* yields. Although the first rule focuses on output and the second on input, the two approaches are equivalent ways of deriving the same principle of profit maximization. For example, in Exhibit 6, the firm maximizes profit by hiring 6 workers when the wage is $100 per day. The details of production were provided in Exhibit 4: Employing a sixth worker adds 5 more units to output, which sell for $20 per unit, for a marginal revenue product of $100. The marginal cost of that output is the change in total cost, $100, divided by the change in output, 5 units; so the marginal cost of output is $100/5, or $20. The marginal revenue of that output is simply its price of $20. Thus, *in equilibrium, the marginal cost of output equals its marginal revenue.*

Now that you have some idea of how to derive the demand for a resource, let's determine what could shift resource demand.

Shifts in the Demand for Resources

As we have seen, a resource's marginal revenue product consists of two components: the resource's marginal product and the price at which that product is sold. A resource's marginal product will change following a change in the amount of other resources employed or a change in technology. The output's selling price will change due to a change in demand for that output. Let's first consider changes that could affect marginal product, then changes that could affect the demand for the final product.

Other Inputs Employed. Although our analysis thus far has focused on a single input, in practice the marginal product of any resource depends on the quantity and quality of other resources used in the production process. Sometimes resources are *substitutes.* For example, coal substitutes for oil in generating electricity. And automatic teller machines substitute for tellers in handling bank transactions. If two resources are substitutes, an increase in the price of one will increase the demand for the other. An increase in the price of oil will increase the demand for coal, and an increase in the wage of tellers will increase the demand for ATMs.

Sometimes resources are *complements,*—trucks and truck drivers, for example. If the relationship is complementary, an increase in the price of one reduces the demand for the other. If the price of tractor-trailer trucks increases, the quantity demanded decreases, which will reduce the demand for truck drivers.

One reason why U.S. truck drivers earn about $20 an hour and why rickshaw drivers in the Far East earn less than $1 per hour is the *truck.* The rickshaw driver pulls a cart worth maybe $100; the cart can carry relatively little and can move only as fast and as far as the driver's legs will take it. The truck driver is behind the wheel of a $200,000 machine that can haul huge amounts great distances at high speeds. The truck makes the driver more productive.

A valuable resource is one that helps other resources become more productive. In sports, the "most valuable player" is typically the team member who not only contributes directly but makes other players on the team more productive as well. For example, Michael Jordan scored so easily that opponents typically "double-teamed" him—that is, had two players try to prevent him from scoring. This allowed Jordan to "assist" other team members left open for a shot. More generally, *the greater the quantity and quality of complementary resources used in production, the greater the marginal productivity of the resource in question and the greater the demand for that resource.*

Changes in Technology. *Technological improvements can enhance the productivity of some resources and can make others obsolete.* The development of computer-controlled machines increased the demand for computer-trained machinists, but decreased the demand for machinists without computer skills. The development of synthetic fibers, such as rayon and orlon, increased the demand for these synthetic fibers, but reduced the demand for natural fibers, such as cotton and wool. Breakthroughs in fiber-optic and satellite communication increased the demand for fiberglass and satellites and reduced the demand for copper wire.

New computer programs are changing job prospects in the fields of law, medicine, accounting, architecture, computer programming, banking, and insurance, to name a few. For example, the computer program *WillMaker* has written more wills than any lawyer alive. In medicine, a program called *Iliad* can, in response to a series of questions, help diagnose about 1,000 diseases plus another 1,500 intermediate conditions in a chain of diagnostic deductions. Web page construction is now as easy as other forms of desktop publishing with programs such as *Fusion, Texture,* and *FrontPage.* And in accounting, programs like *TurboTax* and *Quicken* reduce the demand for CPAs. As the software gets cheaper and better, the demand for some professional skills will diminish, although the demand for those who write new software will increase.

Changes in the Demand for the Final Product. Because the demand for a resource *derives* from the demand for the final output, any change in the demand for output will affect resource demand. For example, an increase in the demand for automobiles will increase their market price and thereby increase the marginal revenue product of auto workers. Let's look at the derived demand for architects in the following case study.

The Derived Demand for Architects

CaseStudy

The World of Business

What is the current demand for architects? The American Institute of Architects maintains a career center with a job board at http://www. e-architect.com/career/ jobboard/job_SearchP.asp. How many architect positions are available in your part of the country? What is the employment outlook for future professional architects? You can find analysis and forecasts of future employment trends for many jobs in the Bureau of Labor Statistics' *Occupational Outlook Handbook*. The prospectus for architects is at http://www. bls.gov/oco/ocos038.htm. What is the typical size of a firm that hires architects? What does this tell you about search costs for both job seekers and employers?

The big drop in real estate prices, particularly commercial real estate prices, that occurred in the late 1980s and early 1990s cut demand for new construction, and in so doing reduced the demand for resources used in construction, such as builders and architects. Consider what happened to the demand for architects. In New York City, the number of classified ads for architectural positions declined from 5,000 in 1987 to 500 in 1991. Similar drops took place in other major cities. Employment at one national architectural firm shrank from 1,600 to 700 between 1988 and 1992.

Among entry-level architects, job losses were compounded because of improved technology. Drafting jobs long represented the traditional entry-level positions for new architects, but computer-assisted design programs coupled with more powerful and cheaper computers reduced the demand for new architects. Programs such as *Auto-Architect* and *3D Manager* help configure all aspects of a structure and create plans that can be manipulated in three-dimensional space, something impossible with traditional drawings. Programs also help estimate the cost of structures. Design software such as *Design Your Own Home*, *Planix Home Design Kit*, and *This Old House Kitchen & Home Architect* even help amateurs with designs and may have an accompanying Web site and on-line help desk. Whereas construction-grade blueprints drafted by an architect cost about $550 a set, do-it-yourself design CDs sell for $40 to $70. Thus new software substitutes for entry-level architectural positions.

The declining demand for architects had an interesting impact on the demand for higher education, which itself is a derived demand. Enrollment in undergraduate classes in architecture declined as entry-level positions disappeared. Enrollment in graduate courses, however, remained relatively stable. Apparently many out-of-work architects decided to pursue graduate study, since the poor job market reduced their opportunity cost of time. The exception that proves the rule about derived demand is that those architectural firms that specialize in the health-care industry flourished, because health care became the fastest-growing sector of the economy.

Sources: Tracie Rozhou, "At Hospitals, Construction Is Regaining Its Health," *New York Times* (7 July 1997); D. W. Dunlap, "Recession Is Ravaging Architects' Firms," *New York Times* (17 May 1992); Paul Stern, "Remodel Your House with Your Home Computer: Click to Fix," *Hartford Courant* (3 December 1998); Steven Ross, "Will Amateur CAD Put Residential Architects Out of Business?" *Architectural Record* (April 1994); and Internet site http:// www.softdesk.com/index.html.

In summary, the demand for a resource depends on its marginal revenue product. Any change that increases a resource's marginal revenue product will increase resource demand.

Optimal Use of More than One Resource

As long as the marginal revenue product exceeds the marginal resource cost, the firm can increase profit by employing more of a resource. The firm will increase resource use until the marginal revenue product just equals the marginal resource cost, or

$$\text{marginal revenue product} = \text{marginal resource cost}$$

Rearranging terms yields:

$$\frac{\text{marginal revenue product}}{\text{marginal resource cost}} = 1$$

This holds for each resource employed. Profit-maximizing employers will hire each resource up to the point at which the last unit hired adds as much to revenue as it does to cost.

Recall that at the outset of the chapter, you were asked why the buildings at the center of Chicago are taller than those farther out. Land and capital, to a large extent, substitute in the production of building space. Since land is more expensive at the center of the city, builders there substitute additional capital for land, building up instead of out. Hence, buildings are taller when they are closer to the center of the city and are tallest in cities where the land is most expensive. Buildings in Chicago and New York City are taller than buildings in Salt Lake City and Tucson, for example.

The high price of land in metropolitan areas has other implications for the efficient employment of resources. For example, in New York City, as in many large cities, vending carts on street corners specialize in everything from hot dogs to ice cream. Why are there about 4,100 licensed pushcarts in New York City? Consider the resources used to supply hot dogs: land, labor, capital, entrepreneurial ability, plus intermediate goods such as hot dogs, buns, and other ingredients. Which of these do you suppose is most expensive in New York City? Retail space along Madison Avenue rents for an average of $550 a year per square foot.[1] Since operating a hot dog cart requires about four square yards, it could cost up to $20,000 a year to rent the required commercial space. Aside from the necessary public permits, however, space on the public sidewalk is free to vendors. Profit-maximizing street vendors substitute public sidewalk space, which is free to them, for costly commercial rental space.

Government policy can affect resource allocation in other ways, as is discussed in the following case study.

---

1 As reported by Leslie Eaton in "Madison Ave. Strip Now Has Highest Store Rents," *New York Times* (27 November 1998).

The McMinimum Wage

CaseStudy

Public Policy

In March 1998, President Clinton proposed raising the minimum wage by $1.00 to $6.15 over two years. Ever since a federal minimum wage of 25 cents was established in 1938, economists have debated the benefits and costs of the law. The federal law initially covered only 43 percent of the work force—primarily workers in large firms involved in interstate commerce. Over the years, the minimum wage has been raised and the coverage has been broadened, so that by 1998 the law covered 86 percent of the work force (groups still not covered include domestic workers and those in small retail establishments and small restaurants).

At the time of Clinton's proposed increase, about 12 million workers earned between $5.15 and $6.15 an hour, and thus could potentially be affected by an increase. This group included many young workers, the majority working part time, primarily in service and sales occupations. Advocates of minimum-wage legislation argue that an appropriately applied minimum wage can increase the income of the poorest workers at little or no cost to overall employment. Critics argue that a minimum wage set above the market-clearing level causes employers either to cut nonwage compensation or to scale back employment.

There have been over 40 U.S. studies published since 1970 looking at the effect of changes in the minimum wage on employment. A few found a small positive effect of the minimum wage on employment, but most found either no effect or a negative effect, particularly among teenage workers. One reason an increase in the minimum wage may not always have the expected negative effect on total employment is that employers often react to a wage increase by substituting part-time jobs for full-time jobs, by substituting more-qualified minimum-wage workers (such as college students) for less-qualified workers (such as high-school dropouts), and by adjusting some nonwage features of the job to reduce costs or increase productivity.

Here are some of the nonwage job features that an employer could alter in response to a higher minimum wage: the convenience of work hours, expected work effort, on-the-job training, time allowed for lunch and for breaks, vacation days, paid holidays, sick leave policy, health-care benefits, tolerance for tardiness, parking provisions, air conditioning, dress code, and so on. Of most concern to economists is a possible reduction in the provision of on-the-job training to young workers, particularly those with little education.

A higher minimum wage also raises the opportunity cost of staying in school. For example, one study found that an increase in the minimum wage encouraged some 16- to 19-year-olds to quit school to seek work, although many failed to find a job. And those who had already left school were more likely to become unemployed because of a higher minimum wage. Thus there may be a significant enrollment effect associated with an increase in the minimum wage.

The US Department of Labor maintains a Minimum Wage page at http://www.dol.gov/dol/esa/public/minwage/main.htm with questions and answers about the legal aspects and history of the minimum wage. Be sure to view the chart showing the real value of the minimum wage. In what year was it greatest? A link to Questions and Answers about the economic impact of the minimum wage is provided by the Employment Policies Institute at http://www.epionline.org/minimum_frame.htm. There are also links to several research reports on the impacts of minimum wage laws. The liberal view can be found at the Economic Policy Institute's Web page on labor markets at http://epinet.org/subjectpages/labor.html. In particular, look for the report on Making Work Pay. What percent of those receiving the minimum wage are supporting families?

In one survey of 193 labor economists, 87 percent believed "a minimum wage increases unemployment among young and unskilled workers." Minimum-wage increases, however, have broad public support. According to one recent poll, the highest support, 81 percent, came from those aged 18 to 29, the group most likely to be affected by a hike in the minimum wage. The typical college student has a part-time job that pays the minimum wage or close to it. The unemployment rate is usually twice as high for high-school dropouts as for college students. An increase in the minimum wage would benefit college students more than high-school dropouts.

Sources: Louis Uchitelle, "Better Pay vs. Job Stability in Wage Debate," *New York Times* (20 March 1998); "$6.15 Minimum Wage Approved in Hartford," *New York Times* (24 April 1998); Jane Blotzer, "Closing the Gap: A How-To Guide," *Pittsburgh Post-Gazette* (3 May 1998); "Review Symposium: Myth and Measurement: The New Economics of the Minimum Wage," *Industrial and Labor Relations Review* 48 (July 1995): 827–849; and Robert Whaples, "Is There Consensus Among American Labor Economists? Survey Results of Forty Propositions," *Journal of Labor Research* 27 (Fall 1996): 725–734.

DISTRIBUTION OF U.S. RESOURCE EARNINGS

This chapter showed that firms increase resource employment as long as a resource's marginal revenue product exceeds its marginal resource cost. This employment rule results in an allocation of earnings based on each resource's marginal productivity. So *earnings in a market economy are based on the marginal productivity of resources.* Resources that are more productive earn more, sometimes much more, than resources that are less productive. Not everyone is happy with the market outcome, especially those whose resources are not highly valued in the market. In this final section, we examine the distribution of earnings across different kinds of resources in the United States.

Exhibit 7 shows the percentage share of national income that goes to (1) wages and salaries, (2) proprietors' income, (3) corporate profits, (4) interest, and (5) rent. Proprietors' income consists of incomes of farmers, doctors, lawyers, small-business owners, and other unincorporated business owners. Over time, wages and salaries have claimed by far the largest share of national income, accounting most recently for 71.8 percent of the total during the 1990s. But this understates the proportion going to labor, because a large portion of proprietors' income consists of labor income as well. During the 1990s, labor's share declined slightly and profit's share increased.

Exhibit 7 also shows the decline over time in the share of national income received by proprietors. A generation ago, the income from the corner store was proprietors' income; these stores were named after the owner-operator, such as "Phil's Market" and "Pam's Pantry." Today these corner stores are more likely to be called "7-Eleven" or "Circle K," and the cashier who rings up your Pepsi and Cheetos typically earns a wage paid by the corporate chain. Note that wages and salaries combined with proprietors' income have remained relatively constant at about 80 percent for the entire century.

The column headings "Corporate Profits," "Interest," and "Rent" do not correspond exactly to the terms *profit, interest,* and *economic rent* used by economists, but the definitions in Exhibit 7 are similar enough to make the table useful. *The most important conclusion to draw from Exhibit 7 is that labor's share of total*

EXHIBIT 7

Functional Distribution of Income: Percentage Share of Each Source of National Income by Decade

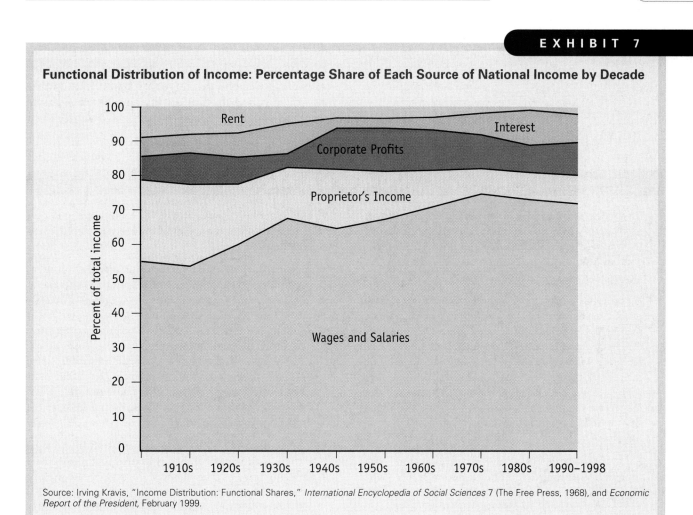

Source: Irving Kravis, "Income Distribution: Functional Shares," *International Encyclopedia of Social Sciences* 7 (The Free Press, 1968), and *Economic Report of the President*, February 1999.

income is relatively large and has grown during this century. This conclusion still holds even if the definitions of some other income categories do not exactly match our economic definitions. Labor's share has grown primarily because proprietors' income has decreased, as reflected, for example, by the shift from owner-operators to corporate chains.

CONCLUSION

The framework we have developed focuses on the marginal analysis of resource use to determine equilibrium price and quantity. The firm uses each resource up to the point where the marginal revenue product of that resource equals its marginal cost. The objective of profit maximization ensures that to produce any given level of output, firms will employ the least-cost combination of resources and will thereby use the economy's resources most efficiently. If this were not so, firms could produce the same output at a lower cost by adjusting the resource mix.

Although our focus has been on the marginal productivity of each resource, we should keep in mind that resources combine to produce output, so the marginal productivity of a particular resource will depend in part on what other resources are employed. For example, a baseball player whose teammates get on base more frequently will have more runs batted in during the season and will thereby be considered more productive.

SUMMARY

1. Firms demand resources to maximize profits. Households supply resources to maximize utility. The profit-maximizing goals of firms and the utility-maximizing goals of households are harmonized through voluntary exchange in resource markets.

2. Because the value of any resource depends on what it produces, the demand for a resource is a derived demand—derived from the demand for the final product. Resource demand curves slope downward because firms are more willing and able to increase their quantity demanded as the price of a resource declines. Resource supply curves tend to slope upward because resource owners are more willing and able to increase their quantity supplied as their reward for supplying the resource increases.

3. Some differentials in the market prices of similar resources trigger the reallocation of resources to equalize those prices. Other price differentials do not cause a shift in resources among uses because of a lack of resource mobility, differences in the inherent quality of the resources, differences in the time and money involved in developing necessary skills, and differences in nonmonetary aspects of jobs.

4. Resource earnings divide between (1) earnings that reflect the resource's opportunity cost, the amount that must be paid to get a resource owner to supply that resource to a particular use, and (2) economic rent, that portion of a resource's total earnings that exceeds the resource's opportunity cost. If a resource has no alternative uses, earnings consist entirely of economic rent; if a resource has other uses of similar value, opportunity cost predominates.

5. A firm's demand curve for a resource is the resource's marginal revenue product curve, which shows the change in total revenue that results from each one-unit increase in the amount of the resource employed, other things constant. If a firm sells output in a perfectly competitive market, the marginal revenue product curve slopes downward because of diminishing marginal returns. If a firm has some market power in the product market, the marginal revenue product curve slopes downward both because of diminishing marginal returns and because the product price must fall to sell more output.

6. The demand curve for a resource will shift to the right if there is an increase either in its marginal productivity or in the price of the output. An increase in the use of a complementary resource or a decrease in the use of a substitute resource will increase a resource's marginal productivity.

7. Marginal resource cost is the change in total cost resulting from employing one more unit of a resource. A firm maximizes profit by employing each resource up to the point where the marginal revenue product equals its marginal resource cost.

8. Wages and salaries have grown as a percentage of total resource income this century and proprietors' income has fallen.

QUESTIONS FOR REVIEW

1. *(Resource Demand and Supply)* Answer each of the following questions about the labor market:
   a. Which economic decision makers determine the demand for labor? What is their goal and what decision criteria do they use in trying to reach that goal?
   b. Which economic decision makers determine the supply of labor? What is their goal and what decision criteria do they use in trying to reach that goal?
   c. In what sense is the demand for labor a derived demand?

2. *(Market Supply of a Resource)* Explain why the market supply curve of a resource slopes upward.

3. *(Resource Price Differences)* Distinguish between the market reaction to a temporary difference in prices for the same resource and the market reaction to a permanent difference. Why do the reactions differ?

4. *(Opportunity Cost and Economic Rent)* On-the-job experience typically enhances a person's productivity in that particular job. If the person's salary increases to reflect increased experience but if the additional experience has no relevance for other jobs, does this higher salary reflect an increase in opportunity cost or in economic rent?

5. *(Firm's Demand for a Resource)* How does the law of diminishing marginal productivity affect a firm's demand for labor?

6. *(Shifts in Resource Demand)* Many countries are predominantly agrarian. How would changes in the supply of fertilizer affect the marginal product, and thus the income, of farmers in such countries?

7. *(Optimal Use of More Than One Resource)* Explain the rule for determining optimal resource use when a firm employs more than one resource.

8. *(Distribution of Resource Earnings)* What resource employment rule determines the allocation of earnings in a market economy? In the United States, which resource receives the largest share of national income? What has happened to this resource's share of income during the 20th century?

PROBLEMS AND EXERCISES

9. *(Opportunity Cost and Economic Rent)* Define economic rent. In the graph below, assume that the market demand curve for labor is initially D_1.

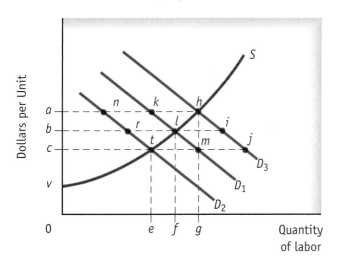

a. What are the equilibrium wage rate and level of employment? What is the amount of economic rent?
b. Next assume that the price of a substitute resource increases, other things constant. What happens to demand for labor? What are the new equilibrium wage rate and level of employment? What happens to the amount of economic rent?
c. Suppose instead that demand for the final product drops, other things constant. Using labor demand curve D_1 as your starting point, what happens to

demand for labor? What are the new equilibrium wage rate and level of employment? Does the amount of economic rent change?

10. *(Firm's Demand for a Resource)* Use the following data to answer the questions below. Assume a perfectly competitive output market.

Units of Labor	Units of Output
0	0
1	7
2	13
3	18
4	22
5	25

a. Calculate the marginal revenue product for each additional unit of labor if output sells for $3 per unit.
b. Draw the demand curve for labor based on the above data and the $3 per unit output price.
c. If the wage rate is $15 per hour, how much labor will be hired?
d. Using your answer to part (c), compare the firm's total revenue to the total amount paid for labor. Who gets the difference?
e. What would happen to your answers to parts (b) and (c) if the price of output increased to $5 per unit, other things constant?

11. *(Selling Output as a Price Taker)* If a competitive firm hires another full-time worker, total output will increase from 100 units to 110 units per week. Suppose the market price of output is $25 per unit. What is the maximum weekly wage at which the firm would hire that additional worker?

12. *(Shifts in Resource Demand)* A local pizzeria hires college students to prepare pizza, wait on tables, take telephone orders, and deliver pizzas. For each situation described, determine whether the demand for student employees by the restaurant would increase, decrease, or remain unchanged. Explain each answer.

a. The demand for pizza increases.
b. Another pizzeria opens up next door.
c. An increase in the minimum wage raises the cost of hiring student employees.
d. The restaurant buys a computer system for taking telephone orders.

13. *(Case**Study**: The Derived Demand for Architects)* Use a supply-and-demand diagram to illustrate the change in the market for entry-level architects as described in the case study. Explain your conclusions.

EXPERIENTIAL EXERCISES

14. *(A Closer Look at Resource Demand)* The *Occupational Outlook Handbook* (OOH) is a U.S. Department of Labor publication that projects employment trends. Using the search feature available at the OOH Web site at http://stats.bls.gov/ocohome.htm, search several occupations. What factors seem to be affecting employment prospects in those fields? What role does derived demand play? How about technological change?

15. *(Case**Study**: The McMinimum Wage)* In the absence of legislated changes, the federal minimum wage decreases in real terms whenever the economy experiences inflation. Go to the Department of Labor's Minimum Wage page at http://dol.gov/dol/esa/public/minwage/chart2.htm and look at Chart 2. How

would these changes in the inflation-adjusted minimum wage affect the market for low-skilled workers? Use a labor supply and demand diagram to illustrate your conclusions.

16. *(Wall Street Journal)* Review the Work Week column on the front page of Tuesday's *Wall Street Journal*. Choose an interesting article, read it, then try to interpret it using the tools developed in this chapter. Did labor supply, labor demand, or both change? Was only a single labor market affected, or were the effects felt in several markets simultaneously? Be sure that your explanation accounts for what happened to both the wage rate and the level of employment.

Labor Markets and Labor Unions

H ow do we allocate our time among different possible uses, especially
between work and leisure? What factors other than the wage rate are
important in the decision to supply labor? Why do some people choose to
work *less* if the wage rate increases sharply? For example, why do unknown
rock groups perform for hours for hardly anything, while famous ones perform
much less for much more. More generally, what determines the wage structure
in the economy?

You don't need a course in economics to figure out why corporate presidents earn more than file clerks, or why heart surgeons earn more than
registered nurses. But why do lawyers earn more than accountants, and school-
teachers more than truck drivers? Will we observe similar patterns ten years

from now? You can be sure of one thing: Demand and supply play a central role in the wage structure. In this chapter, we focus on labor markets to dig more deeply into wage determination.

You have already examined the demand for resources. Demand depends on a resource's marginal productivity. In the first half of this chapter, we focus on the supply of labor, then bring demand and supply together to arrive at the market wage. In the latter part of the chapter, we consider the role that labor unions play in labor markets. We examine the economic effects of unions and review recent trends in union membership. Topics discussed in this chapter include:

- Theory of time allocation
- Backward-bending supply curve for labor
- Nonwage factors and labor supply

- Why wages differ
- Unions and collective bargaining
- Union wages and employment
- Recent trends in union membership

LABOR SUPPLY

As a resource supplier, you have a labor supply curve for each of the many possible uses of your labor. To some markets, your quantity supplied is zero over the realistic range of wages. The qualifier "over the realistic range" is added because, for a high enough wage (say, $1 million per hour), you might supply labor to just about *any* activity. In most labor markets, your quantity supplied may be zero either because you are *willing* but *unable* to perform the job (for example: airline pilot, professional golfer, novelist) or because you are *able* but *unwilling* to do so (for example: soldier of fortune, prison guard, gym teacher).

So you have as many supply curves as there are labor markets, just as you have as many demand curves as there are markets for goods and services. Your labor supply to each market depends, among other things, on your ability, your taste for the job in question, and the opportunity cost of your time—how much you could earn in other activities. Your supply to a particular labor market assumes that wages in other markets are constant, just as your demand for a particular product assumes that other prices are constant.

Labor Supply and Utility Maximization

Recall the definition of economics: *the study of how people use their scarce resources in an attempt to satisfy their unlimited wants.* That is, individuals attempt to use their scarce resources so as to maximize their utility. Two sources of utility are of special interest to us in this chapter: the consumption of goods and services and the enjoyment of leisure. The utility derived from consuming goods and services is obvious and serves as the foundation for consumer demand. Another valuable source of utility is leisure—time spent relaxing, sleeping, eating, and in recreational activities. Leisure is a normal good that, like other goods, is subject to the law of diminishing marginal utility. Thus, the more leisure time you have, the less you value each additional unit of leisure. Sometimes you may have so much leisure that you "have time on your hands" and are "just killing time." As that sage of the comic page Garfield the cat once lamented, "Spare time would be more fun if I had less to spare." Or as Shakespeare wrote, "If all the year were playing holidays, to sport would be as tedious as to work." Leisure's diminishing marginal utility explains why some of the so-called idle rich grow bored in their idleness.

Three Uses of Time. Some of you are at a point in your career when you have few resources other than time. Time is the raw material of life. You can use your time in three ways. First, you can undertake **market work**—selling your time in the labor market in return for income. When you supply labor, you usually surrender control of your time to the employer in return for a wage. Second, you can undertake what we will call **nonmarket work**—using time to produce your own goods and services. Nonmarket work includes the time you spend doing your laundry, preparing your meals, or typing your term paper. Nonmarket work also includes the time spent acquiring skills and education that enhance your future productivity. Although the time spent studying and attending class provides little immediate payoff, you are betting that the knowledge and perspective you gain will pay off in the future. Third, you can convert time directly into **leisure**—nonwork uses of your time.

Market work Time sold as labor in return for a money wage

Nonmarket work Time spent producing goods and services in the home or acquiring an education

Leisure Time spent on non-work activities

Work and Utility. Unless you are one of the fortunate few, work is not a pure source of utility, as it often generates some boredom, discomfort, or aggravation. In short, time spent working can be "a real pain," a source of *disutility*—the opposite of utility. And work is subject to increasing marginal disutility—the more you work, the greater the marginal disutility of working another hour. You work nonetheless, because your earnings buy goods and services. You expect the utility from these goods and services to more than offset the disutility of work. Thus, the *net utility of work*—the utility of the consumption made possible through work minus the disutility of the work itself—usually makes some amount of work an attractive use of your time. In the case of market work, your income buys goods and services. In the case of nonmarket work, either you produce goods and services directly, as in making yourself a tuna sandwich, or you invest your time in education with an expectation of higher future earnings and higher future consumption. The additional utility you expect from the tuna sandwich and higher future consumption resulting from education are the marginal benefits of nonmarket work.

Utility Maximization. Within the limits of a 24-hour day, seven days a week, you balance your time among market work, nonmarket work, and leisure so as to maximize utility. As a rational consumer, *you attempt to maximize utility by allocating your time so that the expected marginal utility of the last unit of time spent in each activity is identical.* Thus, in the course of a week or a month, the marginal utility of the last hour of leisure equals the net marginal utility of the last hour of market work, which equals the net marginal utility of the last hour of nonmarket work. In the case of time devoted to acquiring skills, you must consider the marginal utility expected from the future increase in earnings that will result from your enhanced productivity.

Perhaps at this point you are saying, "Wait a minute. I don't allocate my time with that sort of precision or logic. I just sort of go along, doing what feels good." Economists do not claim that you are even aware of making such marginal calculations. But as a rational decision maker, you allocate your scarce time to satisfy your wants, or to maximize utility. And utility maximization, or "doing what feels good," implies that you act *as if* you allocated your time to derive the same expected net marginal utility from the last unit of time spent in each alternative use.

You probably have settled into a rough plan (for meals, work, entertainment, study, sleep, and so on) that fits your overall objectives and seems reasonable. This plan is probably in constant flux as you make expected and unexpected adjustments in the use of your time. For example, this morning you may have slept later than you planned because you were up late last night; last weekend you may have failed to crack a book, despite good intentions. Over a week or a month, however, your use of time is roughly in line with an allocation that maximizes utility as you perceive it. Put another way, given the various constraints on your time, money, energy, and other resources, if you could change your use of time to increase your utility, you would do so. Nobody is stopping you! You may emphasize immediate gratification over long-term goals, but that's your choice and you bear the consequences. *This time-allocation process ensures that at the margin, the expected net utilities from the last unit of time spent in each activity are equal.*

Because information is costly and because the future is uncertain, you sometimes make mistakes in allocating time; you do not always get what you expect. Some mistakes are minor, such as going to a movie that proves to be a waste of time. But other mistakes can be costly. For example, you may now be studying for a field that will grow crowded by the time you graduate, or you may be acquiring skills that will become obsolete because of new computer software.

Implications. The model of time allocation described thus far has several implications for individual choice. First, consider the choice among market work, nonmarket work, and leisure. The higher your market wage, other things constant, the higher your opportunity cost of leisure and nonmarket work. For example, individuals with a high market wage will spend less time on nonmarket work, other things constant. Surgeons are less likely to mow their own lawns than are butchers. And among those earning the same market wage, people who are handy around the house and are good cooks will tend to do more for themselves and hire fewer household services. Conversely, those who are all thumbs around the house and who have difficulty boiling water will hire more household services and will eat out more frequently. In short, *utility maximization implies that individuals will spend time in nonmarket work if they can produce goods and services more cheaply than the market can.* By the same logic, the higher the expected earnings right out of high school, other things constant, the higher the opportunity cost of attending college.

Most young, successful movie stars do not go to college. Some, such as Tom Cruise, are high-school dropouts. And the most promising athletes "turn pro" right after high school or before completing college. Top players who never attended college include Ken Griffey, Jr., and Mark McGwire in baseball; Kobe Bryant and Kevin Garnett in basketball; Mario Lemieux and Wayne Gretsky in hockey; and most top tennis players. But the vast majority of people do not face such a high opportunity cost of higher education. As one fellow explained, "Since my wife left me, my kids joined a cult, and my dog died, now would be a good time to go back and get my MBA."

Wages and Individual Labor Supply

To breathe life into the time-allocation problem, consider your choices for the summer. If you can afford to, you can take the summer off, spending it entirely on leisure, perhaps as a fitting reward for a rough academic year. Or you can supply your time to market work. Or you can undertake nonmarket work, such as cleaning the basement or attending summer school. As a rational decision maker, you will select that combination of leisure, market work, and nonmarket work that you expect will maximize your utility. And the optimal combination is likely to involve allocating some time to each activity. For example, even if you work during the summer, you might still consider taking one or two summer courses.

Suppose the only summer job available is some form of unskilled labor, such as working in a fast-food restaurant or for the town parks department. For simplicity, let's assume that you view all such jobs as equally attractive (or unattractive) in terms of their nonmonetary aspects, such as working conditions, working hours, and so on. (These nonmonetary aspects are discussed in the next section.) If there is no difference among these unskilled jobs, the most important question for you in deciding how much market labor to supply is: What is the market wage for unskilled labor?

Suppose the wage is $6 per hour. At a wage that low, you might decide to work around the house, attend summer school full-time, take a really long nap, travel across the country to find yourself, or perhaps do some combination of these. In any case, you supply no market labor at such a low wage. The market wage must rise to $7 per hour before you supply any market labor. Suppose that at a wage of $7 per hour, you supply 20 hours per week, perhaps taking fewer summer courses and shorter naps.

As the wage increases, this raises your opportunity cost of time spent in other activities, so you substitute market work for other uses of your time. You decide to work 30 hours per week at a wage of $8 per hour, 40 hours at $9 per hour, 48 hours at $10 per hour, and 55 hours at $11 per hour. At a wage of $12 you go to 60 hours per week; you are starting to earn serious money—$720 per week.

If the wage hits $13 per hour, a wage you consider to be very attractive indeed, you decide to cut back to 58 hours per week, so you earn $754 per week—more than when the wage was $12 per hour. Finally, if the wage hits $14 per hour, you cut back to 55 per week and earn $770. To explain why you may eventually reduce the quantity of labor supplied, let's consider the impact of wage increases on your allocation of time.

Substitution and Income Effects. An increase in the wage rate affects your choice between market work and other uses of your time in two ways. First, a higher wage provides you with an incentive to work more, since each hour of work now buys more goods and services. As the wage increases, the opportunity cost of other uses of your time, such as leisure, also increases. Thus, as the wage increases, you substitute market work for other activities; this is the **substitution effect of a wage increase.** But a higher wage means a higher income for the same number of hours, and a higher income means that you demand more of all normal goods. Since leisure is a normal good, a higher income increases your demand for leisure, thereby reducing your allocation of

Substitution effect of a wage rate increase When the wage increases, workers substitute market work for other activities, which now have a higher opportunity cost

Income effect of a wage increase A higher wage rate increases workers' real income, increasing their demand for all normal goods, including leisure, so the quantity of labor supplied decreases

time to market work. This **income effect of a wage increase** tends to reduce the quantity of market labor supplied.

As the wage rate increases, the substitution effect causes you to supply more time to market work, but the income effect causes you to demand more leisure and, hence, to supply less time to market work. In our example, the substitution effect exceeds the income effect for wage rates up to $12 per hour, resulting in a greater quantity of market labor supplied as the wage increases. When the wage rises above $12 per hour, however, the income effect exceeds the substitution effect, causing a net reduction in the quantity of labor supplied to market work.

Backward-Bending Labor Supply Curve. The labor supply curve just described appears in Exhibit 1. As you can see, this supply curve slopes upward until a wage of $12 per hour is reached, then it begins to bend backward. The **backward-bending supply curve** gets its shape as the income effect of a higher wage eventually exceeds the substitution effect, reducing the quantity of labor supplied as the wage increases. We see evidence of a backward-bending supply curve, particularly among high-wage individuals, who reduce their work and consume more leisure as the wage increases. For example, doctors often play golf on a weekday afternoon. Entertainers typically perform less as they become more successful. Unknown bands play hours for hardly anything; famous bands play much less for much more. Despite top pay, the cast from *Seinfeld* decided to call it quits in 1998, in part to take more leisure. The income effect of rising real wages helps explain the decline in the U.S. work week from an average of 60 hours in 1900 to less than 40 hours today.

Backward-bending supply curve of labor Occurs if the income effect of a higher wage dominates the substitution effect

---

EXHIBIT 1

Individual Labor Supply Curve for Market Work

When the substitution effect of a wage increase outweighs the income effect, the quantity of labor supplied increases with the wage rate. Above some wage (here, $12), the income effect dominates. Above that wage, the supply curve bends backward; further increases in the wage rate reduce the quantity of labor supplied.

Flexibility of Hours Worked. The model we have been discussing assumes that workers have some control over the number of hours they work per week. Opportunities for part-time work and overtime allow workers to put together their preferred quantity of hours (for instance, 30 hours in a restaurant and 15 hours at the college bookstore). Workers also have some control over the timing and length of their vacations. More generally, individuals can control the length of time they stay in school, when and to what extent they enter the workforce, and when they choose to retire. Thus, they actually have more control over the number of hours worked than you might think if you focused on the benchmark of, say, 40 hours per week.

Nonwage Determinants of Labor Supply

The supply of labor to a particular market depends on a variety of factors other than the wage rate, just as the demand for a particular good depends on factors other than the price. As we have already seen, the supply of labor to a particular market depends on wage rates in other labor markets. So what are the nonwage factors that shape a college student's labor supply for the summer?

Other Sources of Income. Although some jobs are rewarding in a variety of nonmonetary ways, the primary reason people work is to earn money to buy goods and services. Thus the willingness to supply time to a labor market depends on income from other sources, including savings, borrowing, family support, and scholarships. A student who receives a generous scholarship, for example, may feel less pressure to earn additional income. More generally, wealthy people have less incentive to work. For example, multimillion-dollar lottery winners often quit their jobs after hitting the jackpot.

Nonmonetary Factors. Labor is a special kind of resource. Unlike capital and land, which can be supplied regardless of the whereabouts of the resource owners, time supplied to market work usually requires the seller of that time to be on the job. Because the individual must be physically present to supply labor, such *nonmonetary factors* as the difficulty of the job and the quality of the work environment have important effects on the labor supply. For example, deckhands on fishing boats in the winter waters of the Bering Sea off Alaska earn over $3,000 for five days' work, but the temperature seldom gets above zero and daily shifts are 21 hours long, allowing only three hours for sleep. Consider the different working conditions you might encounter. If you are a college student, a library job that allows you to study much of the time is more attractive than a job that affords no study time. Some jobs have flexible hours; others impose rigid work schedules. Is the workplace air-conditioned or do you have to sweat it out? The more attractive the working conditions, the more labor you will supply to that particular market, other things constant.

The Value of Job Experience. All else equal, you are more inclined to take a job that provides valuable experience. Serving as the assistant treasurer for a local business provides better job experience and looks better on a résumé than serving hash at the college cafeteria. Some people are willing to accept relatively low wages now because of the promise of higher wages later. For example, new lawyers are eager to fill clerkships for judges, although the pay is low and the hours long, because these positions provide experience and contacts valued by future employers. Likewise, athletes who play in the minor leagues do so because they hope the experience so gained will move them up to the major leagues. Thus *the more a job enhances future earning possibilities, the greater the supply of labor to that occupation, other things constant.* Because of the greater supply of labor to such positions, other things constant, the pay is usually lower than for similar jobs that impart less experience.

Taste for Work. Just as the tastes for goods and services differ, tastes for work also differ among labor suppliers. Some people prefer physical labor and would avoid a desk job. Some become surgeons; others can't stand the sight of blood. Some become airline pilots; others are afraid to fly. Many struggling writers, artists, actors, and dancers could earn more elsewhere, but apparently the satisfaction of the creative process and the chance, albeit slim, of hitting it big more than offset the low pay. Some people evidently have such a strong preference for certain jobs that they do them for free, such as auxiliary police officers or volunteer fire fighters.

As with the taste for goods and services, economists do not attempt to explain the origin of taste for work. They simply argue that your supply of labor will be greater to those jobs that are more in accord with your tastes. Voluntary sorting based on tastes allocates workers among different jobs in a way that tends to minimize the disutility of work. This is not to say that everyone will end up in his or her most preferred occupation. The cost of acquiring information about jobs and the cost of changing jobs may prevent some matchups that might otherwise seem desirable. But in the long run, people tend to find jobs that suit them. We are not likely to find tour directors who hate to travel, zoo keepers who are allergic to animals, or garage mechanics who can't stand getting their hands dirty.

Market Supply of Labor

In the previous section we considered those factors, both monetary and nonmonetary, that influence individual labor supply. *The supply of labor to a particular market is the horizontal sum of all the individual supply curves.* The horizontal sum is found by adding the quantities supplied by each individual supplier at each particular wage rate. If an individual supply curve of labor bends backward, does this mean that the market supply curve for labor also bends backward? Not necessarily. Since different individuals have different opportunity costs and different tastes for work, the bend in the supply curve occurs at different wages for different individuals. And, for some individuals, the labor supply curve may not bend backward over the realistic range of wages. Exhibit 2 shows how just three individual labor supply curves sum to yield a market supply curve that slopes upward.

Why Wages Differ

Just as both blades of a pair of scissors contribute equally to cutting cloth, both demand and supply determine the market wage. Therefore, wage differences across markets can be traced to differences in labor demand, in labor supply, or in both. In the previous chapter we discussed the elements that influence the demand for resources, and we examined labor in particular. In brief, *a profit-maximizing firm*

EXHIBIT 2

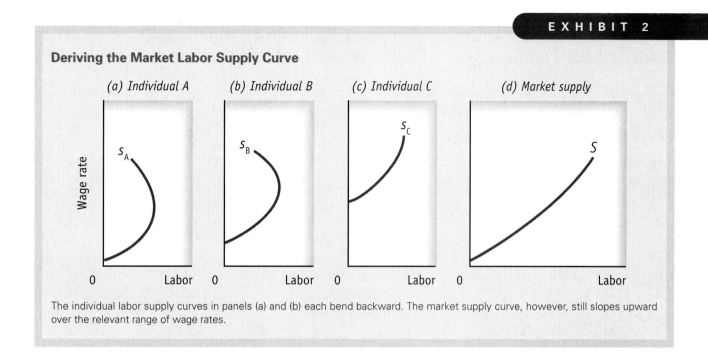

Deriving the Market Labor Supply Curve

(a) Individual A   (b) Individual B   (c) Individual C   (d) Market supply

The individual labor supply curves in panels (a) and (b) each bend backward. The market supply curve, however, still slopes upward over the relevant range of wage rates.

hires labor up to the point where labor's marginal revenue product equals its marginal resource cost—that is, where the last unit employed earns the firm just enough to cover its cost (MRP = MRC). Since we have already discussed the forces that affect the demand for labor, let's focus here primarily on market supply.

Differences in Training, Education, Age, and Experience. Some jobs pay more than others because they require a long and costly training period. Costly training reduces market supply because fewer individuals are willing to incur the time and expense. But the training increases the productivity of labor, thereby increasing the demand for these skills. Reduced supply and increased demand both have a positive effect on the market wage. Certified public accountants earn more than file clerks both because the extensive training of CPAs limits the supply to this field and because this training increases the productivity of CPAs compared to file clerks.

Exhibit 3 shows how education and experience affect average earnings based on education and age. Age groups are indicated on the horizontal axis and average annual earnings on the vertical axis. The lines are labeled to reflect the highest level of education achieved and range from no high school degree at the bottom to a doctorate at the top.

The relationship between income and education is clear. At every age, those with more education earn more. For example, among the 45-to-54 age group, those with a doctorate earn on average three times as much as high school graduates and more than four times as much as those with no high school degree. Age itself also has an important effect on income. For most of their careers, earnings increase as workers acquire valuable job experience, get promoted, and assume added responsibility. Average earnings rise more sharply with age for more educated workers. Earnings begin to fall as workers reach retirement age,

E X H I B I T   3

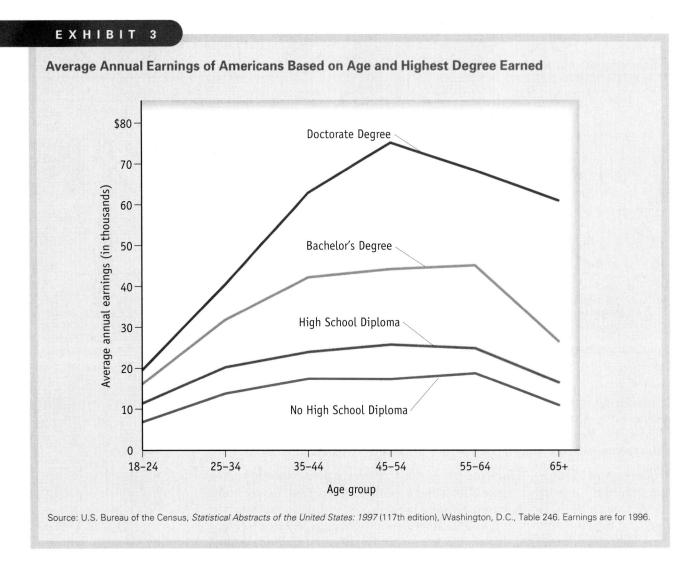

Average Annual Earnings of Americans Based on Age and Highest Degree Earned

Source: U.S. Bureau of the Census, *Statistical Abstracts of the United States: 1997* (117th edition), Washington, D.C., Table 246. Earnings are for 1996.

although even among those 65 and over, those with a doctorate degree earn twice as much as those with bachelor's degrees, nearly five times as much as those with high school diplomas, and six times as much as those without a high school diploma. Differences in earnings reflect the normal workings of resource markets, whereby workers are rewarded according to their marginal productivity.

Differences in Ability. Because they are more able and talented, some individuals earn more than others with the same training and education. Two lawyers may have an identical education, but one earns more because of differences in underlying ability. Most executives have extensive training and business experience, but only a few become chief executives of large corporations. In major-league sports, some players earn up to 50 times more than others. From lawyers to executives to professional athletes, pay differences often reflect differing abilities. The following case study examines why the premium awarded greater ability has grown in the last two decades.

Winner-Take-All Labor Markets

CaseStudy

The World of Business

Each year *Forbes* magazine reports on the multimillion-dollar pay of top entertainers and professional athletes. Entertainment and sports have come to be called "winner-take-all" labor markets because a few key people critical to the overall success of an enterprise are rewarded substantially. For example, the credits at the end of a movie list the dozens of people directly involved in the production. Hundreds, sometimes thousands, more are employed behind the scenes. Despite a cast and crew of thousands, the difference between a movie's financial success and failure depends primarily on the performance of just a few people in crucial roles—the leads, the director, and the screenwriters. Competition for these top few people bids up their pay to extremely high levels, such as the $20 million per movie garnered by top stars. The same happens in sports. Even though thousands of players compete each year in professional tennis, the value of television time, ticket sales, and endorsements is based on the drawing power of just the top players. In professional basketball, attendance and TV ratings were significantly higher for games in which Michael Jordan played. Thus, top performers generate a high marginal revenue product.

But high marginal productivity alone is not enough. To be paid the value of that marginal product, there must be an open competition for the talents of the top people. Before the free-agency rule was introduced in professional sports (which allows players to go to the highest bidder), top players could not move on their own from team to team. They were, in a sense, trapped with their team and, consequently, earned only a fraction of today's pay, despite their huge economic value to a team.

So relatively high pay in entertainment and sports is not that new. What is new is the proliferation of winner-take-all pay structures to other markets in the United States. The "star" treatment has spread to such fields as management, law, banking, finance, even academia. Consider, for example, what has happened to the pay of top U.S. executives in the last two decades. In 1974 the chief executive officers (CEOs) of the 200 largest U.S. corporations earned on average about $310,000, or about 35 times the $8,820 earned by the average U.S. production worker. By 1997, average pay for this top group had increased twelvefold to about $4 million, versus a mere tripling of production-worker pay to $26,600, so CEO pay in 1997 averaged 150 times production worker pay. Comparable multiples were only 21 in Germany and 16 in Japan. Why the big jump in the U.S. multiple?

Robert Frank and Philip Cook argue in their book *The Winner-Take-All Society* that the relatively higher pay for top U.S. performers resulted from three developments. First, breakthroughs in communications, production, and transportation allowed talented performers to serve wider markets, thereby increasing the value of their services. For example, a well-run U.S. company supplying a valued product can now sell that product around the world.

Second, greater market freedom has enhanced competition for the top performers, so these top people earn closer to their marginal productivity. For

For current news stories about executive compensation, visit *Forbes* magazine's subsection about trends in this area at http://www.forbes.com/forbes/SubSect/Executiv.htm. What is the latest explanation for the pay differential? Who are the highest-paid CEOs? For a union's view on the executive pay differential, read the United Auto Workers' article on unionization and executive compensation at http://www.uaw.org/publications/jobs_pay/1098/jpe_02.html. How does having a unionized work force affect executive pay, according to the UAW?

example, in the 1970s, U.S. businesses usually selected their CEOs from company ranks, promoting mainly from within (a practice still alive today in Germany and Japan). Because other firms were not trying to bid away the most talented executives, companies were able to retain executives for just a fraction of the pay that now prevails in a more competitive market. Today top executives are attracted from outside the firm and even outside the industry. This wider competition for the top people has ratcheted up the average pay. A final reason cited by Frank and Cook is that large salaries have become more socially acceptable in the United States than they once were. High salaries are still frowned upon in some countries.

Sources: Robert Frank, "Talent and the Winner-Take-All Society," *American Prospect* 17 (Spring 1994): 97–107 http://epn.org/prosect/17/17fran.html; Robert H. Frank and Philip J. Cook, *The Winner-Take-All Society*, The Free Press, 1995; "Who Gets Paid What," *Forbes* (18 May 1998): 234–266; "The Forbes 500s," *Forbes* (20 April 1998): 246–342; and *Economic Report of the President*, February 1999.

Differences in Risk. Research indicates that jobs with a higher probability of injury or death, such as coal mining, pay more, other things constant. Workers also earn more, other things constant, in fields such as construction, where the risks of unemployment are greater.

Geographic Differences. People have a strong incentive to sell their resources in the market where they earn the most, other things constant. For example, place kickers come to the United States from around the world for the attractive salaries available in the National Football League. Likewise, because physicians earn more in the United States than elsewhere, thousands of foreign-trained physicians migrate here each year. The flow of labor is not all one way: Some Americans seek their fortune abroad. Basketball players not quite talented enough to excel in the NBA head for the high pay in Europe; likewise, baseball players go to Japan. Most workers face migration hurdles if they seek higher pay in another country. Any reduction in these hurdles would reduce wage differentials across countries.

Job Discrimination. Sometimes individuals earn different wages because of racial or gender discrimination in the job market. Although such discrimination is illegal, history shows that certain groups—including blacks, Hispanics, and women—have systematically earned less than others of apparently equal ability.

Union Membership. Other things equal, members of organized labor tend to earn more than nonmembers. The balance of this chapter discusses the effects of unions on the market for labor.

UNIONS AND COLLECTIVE BARGAINING

Few aspects of the labor market make the news more often than the activities of labor unions. Labor negotiations, strikes, picket lines, confrontations between workers and employers—all fit neatly into TV's "action news" format. Despite media attention, only about one out of seven workers belongs to a union and well over 95 percent of union agreements are reached without a strike. For the balance of this chapter, we will study the tools that unions employ to seek higher pay and other benefits for their members.

Kinds of Unions

A **labor union** is a group of workers who join together to improve their terms of employment. Labor unions in the United States date back to the early days of national independence, when employees in various crafts, such as carpenters, shoemakers, and printers, formed local groups to seek higher wages and shorter hours. Such **craft unions** confined their membership to workers with a particular skill, or craft. These craft unions eventually formed their own national organization, the *American Federation of Labor (AFL)*. The AFL, founded in 1886 under the direction of Samuel Gompers, was not a union itself but rather an organization of national unions, with each retaining its autonomy.

By the beginning of World War I, the AFL, still under Gompers, was viewed as the voice of labor. The Clayton Act of 1914 exempted labor unions from antitrust laws, meaning that *unions at competing companies could join forces in an attempt to raise wages.* Unions were also tax exempt. Union membership jumped during World War I but dropped after the war as the government retreated from its support of union efforts. Membership dropped by half between 1920 and 1933.

The *Congress of Industrial Organizations (CIO)* was established in 1935 to serve as a national organization of unions in mass-production industries, such as autos and steel. Whereas the AFL had organized workers in particular crafts, such as plumbers and carpenters, the CIO was made up of unions whose membership embraced all workers in a particular industry. These **industrial unions** included unskilled, semiskilled, and skilled workers in an industry, such as all autoworkers or all steelworkers.

Collective Bargaining

Collective bargaining is the process by which representatives from the union and management negotiate a mutually agreeable contract specifying wages, employee benefits, and working conditions. Once a tentative agreement has been reached, union representatives must present it to the membership for a vote. If the agreement is rejected, the union can strike or continue negotiations.

Mediation and Arbitration. If negotiations over a contract reach an impasse and the public interest is involved, government officials may ask an independent mediator to step in. A **mediator** is an impartial observer who listens to both sides separately then suggests how each side could adjust its position to resolve differences. If a resolution appears possible, the mediator brings the parties together to iron out a contract. The mediator has no power to impose a settlement on the parties.

In certain critical sectors, such as police and fire protection, where a strike could seriously harm the public interest, an impasse in negotiations is sometimes settled through **binding arbitration,** whereby a neutral third party evaluates both sides of the dispute and issues a ruling that the parties are committed to accept. Some disputes skip the mediation and arbitration steps and go directly from impasse to strike.

The Strike

A major source of union power in the bargaining relationship is the threat of a **strike,** which is the union's attempt to withhold labor from the firm. The purpose of a strike is to stop production, thereby forcing the firm to accept the

---

Labor union A group of employees who join together to improve their terms of employment

Craft union A union whose members have a particular skill or work at a particular craft, such as plumbers or carpenters

Industrial union A union of both skilled and unskilled workers from a particular industry, such as autoworkers or steelworkers

Collective bargaining The process by which union and management negotiate a labor agreement

Mediator An impartial observer who helps resolve differences between union and management

Binding arbitration Negotiation in which both parties in a union-management dispute agree to accept an impartial observer's resolution of the dispute

Strike A union's attempt to withhold labor from a firm

union's position. But strikes can also impose significant costs on union members, who forgo pay and benefits for the duration of the strike and risk losing their jobs. Union funds and other sources, such as unemployment benefits in some states, may provide support during a strike, but the typical striker's income falls substantially. The threat of a strike hangs over labor negotiations and can serve as a real spur to reach an accord. *Although neither party usually wants a strike, both sides, rather than concede on key points, typically act as if they could and would endure a strike.*

The strike's success depends on blocking the supply of labor. Unions usually picket the targeted employer to prevent or discourage so-called strikebreakers, or "scabs," from crossing the picket lines to work. But the firm, by hiring temporary workers and nonstriking union workers, can sometimes continue production.

UNION WAGES AND EMPLOYMENT

Union members, like everyone else, have unlimited wants, but no union can regularly get everything it desires. Because resources are scarce, choices must be made. A menu of union desires includes higher wages, more benefits, greater job security, better working conditions, and so on. To keep the analysis manageable, let's focus on a single objective: higher wages. We will examine three possible ways unions might increase wages: (1) by forming an inclusive, or industrial, union; (2) by forming an exclusive, or craft, union; and (3) by increasing the demand for union labor.

Inclusive, or Industrial, Unions

With the *inclusive, or industrial,* approach, the union tries to negotiate an industry-wide wage for each class of labor. In panel (a) of Exhibit 4, the market demand and supply for a particular type of labor are presented as D and S. In the absence of a union, the equilibrium wage is W and the equilibrium employment level is E. At the market wage, each individual employer faces a horizontal, or perfectly elastic, supply of labor, as reflected by s in panel (b) of Exhibit 4. Thus, each firm, as a labor price taker, can hire as much labor as it wants at the market wage of W. The firm hires labor up to the point where the marginal revenue product equals the marginal resource cost; this amount is represented by quantity e in panel (b). As we saw earlier, in equilibrium each worker hired is paid a wage just equal to the marginal revenue product.

Now suppose that the union is able to negotiate a wage above the market-clearing wage. Specifically, suppose the wage negotiated is W', meaning that no labor will be supplied at a lower wage, but any amount desired by the firms, up to the quantity identified at point a in panel (a) of Exhibit 4, will be supplied at the wage floor. In effect, the supply of union labor is perfectly elastic at the union wage up to point a. If more than E'' workers are demanded, however, the wage floor no longer applies; the upward-sloping portion, aS, becomes the relevant part of the labor supply curve. For an industry facing a wage floor of W', the entire labor supply curve is $W'aS$, which has a kink where the wage floor joins the upward-sloping portion of the original supply curve.

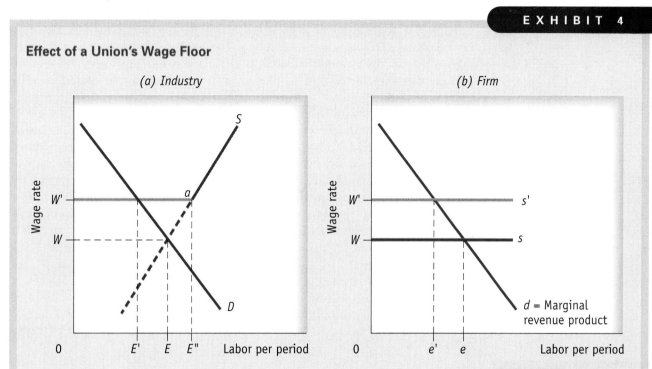

EXHIBIT 4

Effect of a Union's Wage Floor

(a) Industry

(b) Firm

In panel (a), the equilibrium wage rate in the absence of a labor union is W. At that wage, the individual firm of panel (b) hires labor up to the point where the marginal revenue product equals W. Each firm hires quantity e; total employment is E. If a union can negotiate a wage W' above the equilibrium level, the supply curve facing the firm shifts up to s'. The firm hires fewer workers, e', and total employment falls to E'. At wage W' there is an excess supply of labor equal to $E' - E''$.

Once this wage floor has been established, each firm faces a horizontal supply curve of labor at the collectively bargained wage, W'. Since the wage is now higher, the quantity of labor demanded by each employer declines, as reflected by the reduction in employment from e to e' in panel (b) of Exhibit 4. Consequently, the higher wage leads to a reduction in total employment; the quantity demanded by the industry drops from E to E' in panel (a). Notice that since the wage is set above the market-clearing wage, the demand curve dictates the quantity of labor employed.

At wage W', the amount of labor workers would like to supply, E'', exceeds the amount demanded, E'. In the absence of a union, this excess quantity of labor supplied would cause unemployed workers to lower their asking wage. But union members agree *collectively* to a wage, so individual workers cannot offer to work for less, nor can employers hire them at a lower wage. Because the number of union members willing and able to work exceeds the number of jobs available, the union must develop some mechanism for rationing available jobs, such as awarding jobs based on worker seniority or connections within the union. *With the inclusive, or industrial, union, which negotiates with the entire industry, the wage rate is higher and total employment lower than they would be in the absence of a union.*

Those who cannot find union employment will look for jobs in the nonunion sector. *This increased supply of labor in the nonunion sector drives down the nonunion wage.* So wages are relatively higher in the union sector: first, because unions bargain for a wage that exceeds the market-clearing wage, and second, because those unable to find employment in the union sector crowd into the nonunion sector. A survey of more than 200 studies concluded that unions increased members' wages by an average of about 15 percent above the wages of similarly skilled nonunion workers.[1] Unions tend to be less successful at raising wages in competitive industries and more successful in less-competitive industries. For example, unions have little impact on the wages in the garment and textile industries, which are competitive industries, but have greater impact on the wages in airline, auto, steel, mining, and transportation industries, which historically have been less-competitive industries. Competitive firms cannot easily pass along higher union wages as higher product prices. New firms can enter the competitive industry, pay nonunion wages, and sell the product for less.

Exclusive, or Craft, Unions

One way to increase wages while avoiding an excess quantity of labor supplied is for the union to somehow shift the supply curve of labor to the left, as is shown in panel (a) of Exhibit 5. Successful supply restrictions of this type

EXHIBIT 5

Effect of Reducing Supply or Increasing Labor Demand

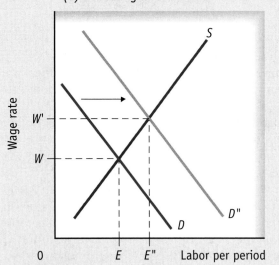

If a union can restrict labor supply to an industry, the supply curve shifts to the left from S to S', as in panel (a). The wage rate rises from W to W', but at the cost of a reduction in employment from E to E'. In panel (b), an increase in labor demand from D to D" raises both the wage and the level of employment.

---

1 See H. Gregg Lewis, *Union Relative Wage Effects: A Survey* (Chicago: University of Chicago Press, 1986).

require that the union first limit its membership and second force all employers in the industry to hire only union members. The union can restrict membership with high initiation fees, long apprenticeship periods, difficult qualification exams, restrictive licensing requirements, and other devices aimed at slowing down or discouraging new membership. But even if unions can restrict membership, unions have difficulty requiring all firms in the industry to hire only union workers.

Whereas wage setting is more typical of the industrial unions, restricting supply (and employment) is more characteristic of the craft unions, such as unions of carpenters, plumbers, and bricklayers. Groups of professionals such as doctors, lawyers, and accountants also impose entry restrictions through education and examination standards. Such restrictions, usually defended on the grounds that they protect the public, are often no more than self-serving attempts to increase wages by restricting supply.

Increasing Demand for Union Labor

A third way to increase the wage is to increase the demand for union labor by somehow shifting the labor demand curve outward as from D to D'' in panel (b) of Exhibit 5. This approach is an attractive alternative *because it increases both the wage rate and employment,* so there is no need to ration jobs. Here are some ways unions try to increase the demand for union labor.

Increase Demand for Union-Made Goods. The demand for union labor may be increased through a direct appeal to consumers to buy only union-made products. Because the demand for labor is a derived demand, an increase in the demand for union-made products will increase the demand for union labor.

Restrict Supply of Nonunion-Made Goods. Another way to increase the demand for union labor is to restrict the supply of products that compete with union-made products. Again, this approach relies on the derived nature of labor demand. The United Auto Workers (UAW) have, for example, supported restrictions on imported cars. Fewer imported cars means a greater demand for cars produced by U.S. workers, who are mostly union members. Now that Japanese and German automakers also build cars in the United States, the UAW has a trickier problem trying to limit imports.

Increase Productivity of Union Labor. Some observers claim that the efficiency with which unions organize and monitor the labor-management relationship increases the demand for union labor. According to this theory, unions increase worker productivity by minimizing conflicts, resolving differences, and at times even straightening out workers who are goofing off. In the absence of a union, a dissatisfied worker may simply look for another job, thereby causing job turnover, which is costly to the firm. With a union, however, workers usually have grievance and arbitration channels through which they can complain, and the negotiated responses they receive may reduce their urge to leave the firm. Quit rates are in fact significantly lower among union workers (although this could be due to the higher pay). If unions increase the productivity of workers in this way, the demand for union labor will increase.

Featherbedding. Still another way unions attempt to increase the demand for union labor is by **featherbedding,** which is an attempt to ensure that more

Featherbedding Union efforts to force employers to hire more workers than demanded for the task union labor is hired than producers would prefer. For example, union rules require that each Broadway theater have a permanent "house" carpenter, electrician, and property manager. Once the show run begins, these workers appear only on payday. The box office must be staffed by three people. And the musicians' union requires that from 9 to 22 musicians be employed at each theater staging a musical, even if the show calls for fewer musicians.

Featherbedding does not create a true increase in demand, in the sense of shifting the demand curve to the right; instead, it forces firms to hire more labor than they really want, thus moving the firm to a point to the right of its true labor demand curve. The union tries to limit a firm to an all-or-none choice: either hire the number the union requires, or a strike will halt production. Thus, with featherbedding, *the union attempts to dictate not only the wage but also the quantity that must be hired at that wage, thereby moving employers to the right of their labor demand curve.*

We have examined three ways in which unions can try to raise members' wages: (1) by negotiating a wage floor above the equilibrium wage for the industry and somehow rationing the limited jobs among union members, (2) by restricting the supply of labor, and (3) by increasing the demand for union labor. Unions try to increase the demand for union labor in several ways: (1) through a direct public appeal to buy only union-made products, (2) by restricting the supply of products made by nonunion labor, (3) by reducing labor turnover and thereby increasing productivity, and (4) through featherbedding, which forces employers to hire more union workers than they would prefer.

Recent Trends in Union Membership

In 1955, about one-third of nonfarm wage and salary workers belonged to unions. Union membership as a fraction of the work force has declined since then; now only one in seven workers belongs to a union. The decline in union membership in recent decades is due partly to an increase in product market competition, particularly from imports. Increased competition from nonunion employers, both foreign and domestic, has also reduced the ability of unionized firms to pass on higher labor costs as higher prices.

Another factor in the decline of the union movement is structural changes in the economy. Unions have long been more important in the industrial sector than in the service and agricultural sectors. But employment in the industrial sector, including manufacturing, mining, and construction, has declined from 37 percent of the nonfarm work force in 1960 to 20 percent today. Over the same period, service-sector employment increased from 63 percent to 80 percent. These days, membership rates are highest among government employees, over one-third of whom are unionized, compared to only one-eighth of the private sector. Union workers are now more likely brain-workers than brawn-workers. A typical union member now is a schoolteacher.

The bar graph in Exhibit 6 indicates recent U.S. union membership rates by age and gender. The rates for men, shown by the dark shaded bars, are higher than the rates for women, in part because men tend to be employed more in manufacturing and women more in the service sector, where union membership historically has been lower. The highest membership rates are for middle-

EXHIBIT 6

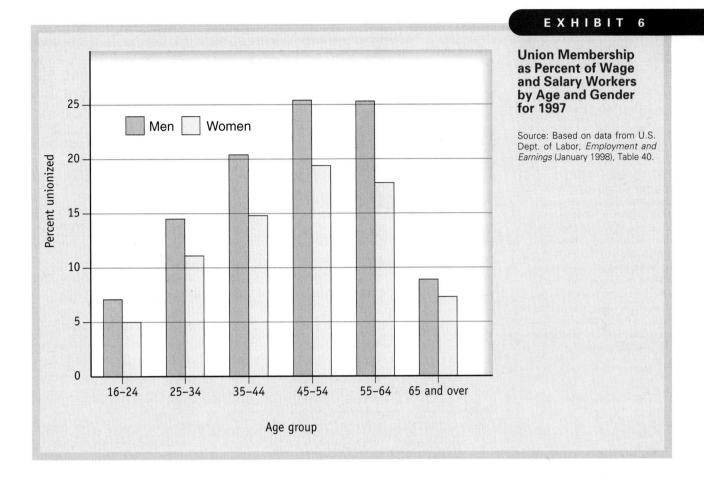

Union Membership as Percent of Wage and Salary Workers by Age and Gender for 1997

Source: Based on data from U.S. Dept. of Labor, *Employment and Earnings* (January 1998), Table 40.

aged males. Although the exhibit does not show it, blacks have a higher union membership rate than whites (20 percent versus 15 percent), in part because blacks are more often employed by government and by heavy industries such as autos and steel, where union membership rates tend to be higher. In fact, black women have a higher union membership rate (18 percent) than white men (17 percent). Union membership among those of Hispanic origin, who can be of any race, is only 14 percent.

Union membership rates also vary greatly across states. Rates in 1998 were 20 percent or more in the industrial states of the North and 8 percent or less in the South. The highest rate was 29 percent in New York; the lowest was 4 percent in South Carolina. Compared with those of other industrialized countries, the union participation rate in the United States ranks relatively low.

During the 1970s, there were nearly 300 strikes a year in the United States involving 1,000 or more workers. But there were only 29 such strikes in 1997, or only about 10 percent of strike levels of two decades ago. Let's close this section with the following case study, which helps explain why unions have grown more reluctant to strike.

CaseStudy

The World of Business

In the Fall 1998 issue of the US Department of Labor's online magazine *Compensation and Working Conditions,* Michael Cimini documents the history and conclusion of the strike in "Caterpillar's Prolonged Dispute Ends" at http://www.bls.gov/opub/cwc/1998/Fall/art1full.pdf. What contract changes were favorable to the union? What concessions did the union make? How many union members crossed the picket lines? How were they to be treated under the new agreement?

Hardball at Caterpillar

Labor troubles began for Caterpillar in November 1991, when the company refused to accept the job-security provisions that the United Auto Workers (UAW) negotiated with Deere & Co., a rival firm in the heavy equipment industry. In a system called *pattern bargaining,* a union reaching a settlement with one firm in an industry could expect that contract to serve as a model for agreements with other firms in the industry.

Caterpillar's refusal to go along with the Deere settlement prompted the UAW to strike. Five months after the strike began, management threatened to replace permanently any union member who failed to return to work. Faced with the prospect of lost jobs, union members went back to work without a contract. After two years of wrangling with the company, the UAW struck again in June 1994.

The UAW showed its commitment to the 13,000 strikers by tripling the usual level of monthly strike pay to $1,200. This sweetened strike pay, which would ultimately cost the union over $200 million, was aimed in part at keeping strikers from crossing picket lines. Strikers believed their skills made them irreplaceable, but as the strike dragged on, Caterpillar introduced more labor-saving techniques. Skilled workers also came from across the country for a chance at these high-paying jobs. By employing a combination of 5,600 temporary workers, plus thousands of nonunion salaried workers and UAW members who crossed picket lines, Caterpillar's production rate during the strike exceeded prestrike levels.

In December 1995, some 17 months after the walkout began and with no evidence that the company was about to give in, union officials decided that the 8,700 members still on strike were "available immediately and unconditionally for return to work." This unconditional surrender by the union was a crushing defeat for a union movement badly in need of a victory. Each striking worker had lost on average about $37,000 in wages during the strike. Union members worked without a contract until March 1998, when they ratified a contract that provided pay increases but allowed the company to introduce greater flexibility in scheduling and to pay new workers 30 percent less.

During the long labor dispute, Caterpillar restructured its manufacturing process to utilize all resources more efficiently, particularly labor. Profits increased to record levels, boosting Caterpillar's share price fourfold. The company's performance apparently refuted the conventional wisdom that both sides suffer during a long strike.

Sources: Robert Rose and Carl Quintanilla, "Caterpillar Touts Its Gains as UAW Battle Ends," *Wall Street Journal* (24 March 1998); "UAW Members Back Contract with Caterpillar, First Since '91," *New York Times* (23 March 1998); and Carl Quintanilla, "Caterpillar Posts Record Earnings," *Wall Street Journal* (20 April 1998).

The experience at Caterpillar underscores two reasons why unions have grown more reluctant to strike: (1) the increased willingness of employers to hire strikebreakers and (2) the increased willingness of workers—both union and nonunion—to cross picket lines. With fewer voters belonging to labor unions, the political climate is also less supportive of unions. Similar strike scenarios have played out at Phelps–Dodge Copper, Continental Airlines, and Hormel Meatpacking—all companies that successfully broke strikes by hiring replacement workers. Thus the strike and the threat of a strike has become less important, and this has diminished the power of unions.

CONCLUSION

The first half of this chapter focused on the supply of labor and explained why wages differ both across occupations and among individuals within occupations. The interaction of the demand and supply for labor determines wage rates and the level of employment. The second half of the chapter explored the effect of unions on the labor market. At one time unions dominated some key industries. But as global competition intensifies, employers have a harder time passing higher union labor costs along to consumers. What's more, the decline of production workers relative to service workers and the growing reluctance to strike have eroded union strength. Both in the United States and in other industrial economies, union members represent a dwindling segment of the labor force.

SUMMARY

1. The demand for labor is the relationship between the wage rate and the quantity of labor producers are willing and able to hire, other things constant. The supply of labor is the relationship between the wage rate and the quantity of labor workers are willing and able to supply, other things constant. The intersection of demand and supply curves determines the equilibrium wage rate.

2. There are three uses of time: market work, nonmarket work, and leisure. People allocate their time so as to maximize utility. The higher the market wage, other things constant, the more goods and services can be purchased with that wage, so a higher wage encourages labor suppliers to substitute market work for other uses of time. But the higher the wage, the higher the income, and as income increases, people consume more of all normal goods, including leisure. The net effect of a higher wage on an individual's quantity of market labor supplied depends on both the substitution effect and the income effect.

3. The supply of labor depends on factors other than the wage, including (1) other sources of income, (2) job amenities, (3) the value of job experience, and (4) worker tastes.

4. Market wages differ because of (1) differences in training and education requirements, (2) differences in the skill and ability of workers, (3) differences in the riskiness of the work, both in terms of the workers' safety and the chances of getting laid off, (4) geographic differences, (5) racial and gender discrimination, and (6) union membership.

5. Unions and employers attempt to negotiate a mutually agreeable labor contract through collective bargaining. A major source of union power has been the threat of a strike, which is an attempt to withhold labor from the firm.

6. Inclusive, or industrial, unions attempt to establish a wage floor that exceeds the competitive market wage. But a wage above the market-clearing level creates an excess quantity of labor supplied, so the union must somehow ration jobs among its members. Exclusive, or craft, unions try to raise the wage by restricting the supply of labor. Another way to raise union wages is to increase the demand for union labor.

7. Union membership as a percentage of the labor force has been decreasing for decades. Today, only one-seventh of the nonfarm labor force is unionized, compared to

one-third in 1955. Unions' problems have included a shift in employment from goods production to service production, more intense global competition, a greater willingness of firms to hire replacements for striking workers, a greater willingness of union members and others to cross picket lines, and less political support for the labor movement.

QUESTIONS FOR REVIEW

1. *(Uses of Time)* Describe the three possible uses of an individual's time, and give an example of each.

2. *(Work and Utility)* Explain the concept of the "net utility of work." How is it useful in developing the labor supply curve?

3. *(Utility Maximization)* How does a rational consumer allocate time among competing uses?

4. *(Substitution and Income Effects)* Suppose that the substitution effect of an increase in the wage rate exactly offsets the income effect as the hourly wage increases from $12 to $13. What would the supply of labor curve look like over this range of wages? Why?

5. *(Substitution and Income Effects)* Suppose that the cost of living increases, thereby reducing the purchasing power of your income. If your money wage doesn't increase, you may work *more* hours because of this cost-of-living increase. Is this an income or substitution effect response? Explain.

6. *(Nonwage Determinants of Labor Supply)* Suppose that two jobs are exactly the same except that one is performed in an air-conditioned workplace. How could you measure the value workers attach to such a job amenity?

7. *(Why Wages Differ)* Why might permanent wage differences occur between different markets for labor or within the same labor market?

8. *(Mediation and Arbitration)* Distinguish between mediation and binding arbitration. Under what circumstances do firms and unions use these tools? What is the role of strikes in the bargaining process?

9. *(The Strike)* Why might firms in industries with high fixed costs be inclined to prevent strikes or end strikes quickly?

10. *(Industrial Unions)* Why are unions more effective in oligopolistic industries than in competitive industries?

11. *(Craft Unions)* Both industrial unions and craft unions attempt to raise their members' wages, but each goes about it differently. Explain the difference in approaches and describe the impact these differences have on excess quantity of labor supplied.

12. *(CaseStudy: Hardball at Caterpillar)* What is *pattern bargaining?* What were the consequences of the decision by Caterpillar to "break the pattern"?

PROBLEMS AND EXERCISES

13. *(Market Supply of Labor)* The following table shows the number of hours per week supplied to a particular market by three individuals at various wage rates. Calculate the total hours per week (Q_T) supplied to the market.

Hourly Wage	Hours per Week			
	Q_1	Q_2	Q_3	Q_T
$ 5	20	0	0	____
$ 6	25	0	0	____
$ 7	35	10	0	____
$ 8	45	25	10	____
$ 9	42	40	30	____
$10	38	37	45	____

Which individuals, if any, have backward-bending supply curves in the wage range shown? Does the market supply curve bend backward in this wage range?

14. *(Inclusive Unions)* Review the logic underlying Exhibit 4. Then determine the effect, on the industry and a typical firm, of an increase in the demand for industry output. Show your conclusions on a graph. Does the magnitude of the increase in demand make a difference?

EXPERIENTIAL EXERCISES

15. *(Wages and Labor Supply)* Interview five of your classmates to determine the nature of their labor supply curves for a summer job. Ask each of them how many hours of work he or she would be willing to supply at wage rates of $10, $15, $20, $25, and $30 per hour. Plot the results on a labor supply diagram. Do any of these individuals exhibit a backward-bending labor supply curve? Is the market supply curve for these five individuals backward bending?

16. *(**CaseStudy:** Winner-Take-All Labor Markets)* Robert Frank's "Talent and the Winner-Take-All-Society" appeared in *The American Prospect* (Spring, 1994) at http://epn.org/prospect/17/17fran.html. Read this nontechnical article. What are some of the problems that Frank identifies?

17. *(Unions and Collective Bargaining)* Visit the AFL-CIO home page at http://www.aflcio.org/publ/estatements/index.htm and look at some recent Executive Council actions. Choose one such action and depict its intended effects, using the models developed in this chapter.

18. *(Wall Street Journal)* It shouldn't be too hard to find a *Wall Street Journal* story dealing with labor unions. Check the Economy page in the First Section, the Work Week report on the front page of the Tuesday *Journal*, or the Legal Beat column inside the Marketplace section. What's going on in the world of organized labor? Is the example you found consistent with the trends described in this chapter?

Capital, Interest, and Corporate Finance

Visit the McEachern
Interactive Study Center
for this chapter at
http://mcisc.swcollege.com

Why do first-run movie theaters charge more for admission than other theaters? Why do you burn your mouth eating pizza? What determines the interest rate a bank charges you? Why would that bank charge IBM less? These and other questions are answered in this chapter, which concerns investment.

So far, our discussion of resource markets has focused primarily on labor. This emphasis is appropriate because labor claims most resource income. The rewards to labor, however, depend in part on the amount and quality of the other resources employed, particularly capital. A farmer plowing a field with a tractor is more productive than one scraping the soil with a stick. A CPA using spreadsheet software is more productive balancing the company books than a high-school–trained bookkeeper using pencil and paper. In this chapter, you will examine the role of capital in production—its cost and its expected return. You will learn about optimal employment of capital and how firms finance that investment.

First a note of caution. Earlier we distinguished between opportunity cost (the payment necessary to attract a resource to a particular use) and economic rent (a payment in excess of opportunity cost). Often economists refer to the return on land as rent, because land is typically thought to be in fixed supply; and the return on a resource in fixed supply consists entirely of economic rent. Describing the earnings on land as rent is quite appropriate, but land as a resource will not receive special treatment in this book. Topics discussed in this chapter include:

- Consumption, saving, and time
- Production, saving, and time
- Optimal investment

- Loanable funds market
- Present value and discounting
- Corporate finance
- Corporate ownership and control

THE ROLE OF TIME IN CONSUMPTION AND PRODUCTION

Time plays an important role in both production and consumption. In this section, we first consider the effect of time on the production decision and show why firms are willing to pay for the use of household savings. Next we consider time in the consumption decision and show why households must be rewarded for saving, or for deferring consumption. Then, bringing together the desires of borrowers and the desires of savers, we examine the market rate of interest.

Production, Saving, and Time

Suppose Jones is a primitive farmer in a simple economy. Isolated from any neighbors or markets, he literally scratches out a living on a plot of land, using only crude sticks as farm implements. While a crop is growing, none of it is available for current consumption. Since production takes time, Jones must rely on food saved from prior production to support himself while the new crop grows. The longer the growing season, the more saving is required. Thus even in this simple example, it is clear that *production cannot occur without saving*.

Suppose that with his current resources, consisting of land, labor, seed corn, fertilizer, and some crude sticks, Jones grows about 500 bushels of corn per year. He soon realizes that if he had a plow—a type of investment good, or capital— his productivity would increase. Making a plow in such a crude setting, however, would be time-consuming, keeping him away from the fields for a year. Thus the plow has an opportunity cost of 500 bushels of corn. Jones will be unable to sustain such a temporary drop in production unless he has saved enough food from previous harvests.

The question is, should he invest his time in making the plow? The answer depends on the costs and benefits of the plow. We already know that the cost is 500 bushels—the forgone output. The benefit depends on how much the plow will increase crop production and how long it will last. Jones figures that the plow will increase production by 200 bushels per year and will last his lifetime. In making the investment decision, he compares current costs to future benefits.

Suppose he decides the benefit of increasing corn production by 200 bushels per year exceeds the one-time cost of 500 bushels sacrificed to make the plow.

In making the plow, he engages in *roundabout production.* Rather than working the soil with his crude sticks, the farmer produces capital, which will increase his future productivity. An increased amount of roundabout production in an economy means that more capital accumulates, so more consumer goods (and more capital goods) can be produced in the future. Advanced industrial economies are characterized by much roundabout production and abundant capital accumulation.

You can see why production cannot occur without saving. *Production requires saving because both direct and roundabout production require time—time during which goods and services are not available from current production.* Now let's modernize the example by introducing the ability to borrow. Many farmers visit the bank each spring to borrow enough "seed money" to finance production until their crop is grown and sold. Likewise, other businesses often borrow at least a portion of the start-up funds they need to get going. Thus, in a modern economy, producers do not rely exclusively on their own prior saving. Banks and other financial institutions serve as *intermediaries* between savers and borrowers. As you will see later, financial markets for trading stocks and bonds also help channel savings to producers. Let's take a look at saving incentives.

Consumption, Saving, and Time

Did you ever burn the roof of your mouth by biting into a slice of pizza that hadn't cooled sufficiently? Have you done this more than once? Why do you persist in such self-mutilation? You persist because that bite of pizza is worth more to you now than the same bite five minutes from now. In fact, you are willing to risk burning your mouth rather than wait until the pizza has lost its destructive properties. In a small way, this phenomenon reflects the fact that you and other consumers value *present* consumption more than *future* consumption. You and other consumers have a **positive rate of time preference.**

Positive rate of time preference A characteristic of consumers, who value present consumption more highly than future consumption

Because present consumption is more valuable than future consumption, you are willing to pay more to consume something now rather than later. And prices often reflect this greater willingness to pay. Consider the movies. You pay more to see a movie at a first-run theater rather than wait until it appears at other theaters. If you are patient, you can wait until it comes out on video or appears on TV. The same is true for books. By waiting for a new book to come out in paperback, you can save more than half the hardback price. Photo developers, dry cleaners, fast-food restaurants, convenience stores, and other producers tout the speed of their services, knowing that consumers are willing to pay more for earlier availability, other things constant.

Thus *impatience* is one explanation for a positive rate of time preference. Another explanation is *uncertainty.* If you wait, something may intervene to prevent your consumption of the good. There is a T-shirt slogan that perhaps captures this point best: "Life is uncertain. Eat dessert first."

Because present consumption is valued more than future consumption, households must be rewarded to postpone consumption. In other words, saving must be rewarded. Saving equals income minus consumption. By saving a portion of their income in financial institutions such as banks, households refrain from spending on present consumption in return for the promise of a greater ability to consume in the future. Interest is the reward offered households for forgoing present consumption. The **interest rate** is the interest per year as a percentage of the amount saved. For example, if the interest rate is 5 percent, the interest is $5 per year for each $100 saved. The higher the interest rate, other things constant, the more consumers are rewarded for saving, so the greater the amount they are willing to save. You will read more on this later in the chapter.

Interest rate The amount of money paid per year to savers as a percentage of the amount saved

Optimal Investment

In a market economy characterized by specialization and exchange, Farmer Jones no longer needs to produce his own capital, nor does he need to rely on his own savings. He can purchase capital using borrowed funds.

Suppose he is interested in buying farm equipment and he estimates its expected productivity. Column (1) in panel (a) of Exhibit 1 identifies six pieces of farm equipment, ranked from most productive, a Tractor-Tiller, to least productive, a Post-Hole Digger. The total product of each piece of farm equipment is listed in column (2) and its marginal product is listed in column (3). Note that other resources are assumed to be constant (in this case, the farmer's labor, land, seeds, and fertilizer).

With no equipment, Jones can grow 1,000 bushels of corn per year. Jones figures that the purchase of a Tractor-Tiller would allow him to increase production to 2,000 bushels per year. Thus the Tractor-Tiller would yield a marginal product of 1,000 bushels per year. The addition of a Combine would increase total output to 2,800 bushels a year, thus yielding a marginal product of 800 bushels. Note that in this example, diminishing marginal returns set in immediately. Marginal product continues to decrease as more capital is added, dropping to zero for a Post-Hole Digger.

Suppose Jones sells corn in a perfectly competitive market, so he is a price taker in the market for corn. He can sell all he wants at the market price of $4 per bushel. This price is multiplied by the marginal product from column (3) to yield capital's *marginal revenue product* in column (4). The marginal revenue product in this example is the marginal product times the price, or the change in total revenue resulting from adding another piece of farm equipment

Suppose each piece of farm equipment costs $10,000. Thus, the marginal resource cost is $10,000, as listed in column (5). Suppose also that the equipment is so durable that it lasts indefinitely, that operating expenses are negligible, and that the price of corn is expected to remain at $4 per bushel in the future. This farm equipment will increase revenue not only in the first year but in every year into the future. Since the equipment costs a sum of money now but yields a stream of revenue this year and in the future, the optimal investment solution requires Jones to take *time* into account. He can't simply equate marginal resource cost with marginal revenue product, because the marginal cost is for capital expected to last indefinitely, whereas the marginal product is an annual amount this year and each year in the future. As we will see, *markets bridge time by use of the interest rate.*

Jones must decide how much to invest in farm equipment. The first task in determining the optimal investment is to compute the *marginal rate of return* that could be earned each year by investing in equipment. Given the scenario described thus far, the **marginal rate of return on investment** is capital's marginal revenue product as a percentage of its marginal resource cost.

Marginal rate of return on investment The marginal revenue product of capital expressed as a percentage of its marginal cost

Marginal Rate of Return on Investment in Farm Equipment

The marginal rate of return shown in column (6) of panel (a) equals the marginal revenue product of each additional piece of farm equipment divided by its marginal resource cost. The marginal rate of return curve in panel (b) consists of line segments showing the relationship between the market rate of interest and the amount invested in farm equipment. This curve is the demand for investment.

(a)

Farm Equipment (1)	Total Product (bushels) (2)	Marginal Product (bushels) (3)	Marginal Revenue Product (4) = (3) × $4	Marginal Resource Cost (5)	Marginal Rate of Return (6) = (4)/(5)
No equipment	1,000	—	—	—	—
Tractor-Tiller	2,000	1,000	$4,000	$10,000	40%
Combine	2,800	800	3,200	10,000	32
Irrigator	3,400	600	2,400	10,000	24
Harrow	3,800	400	1,600	10,000	16
Crop Sprayer	4,000	200	800	10,000	8
Post-Hole Digger	4,000	0	0	10,000	0

(b)

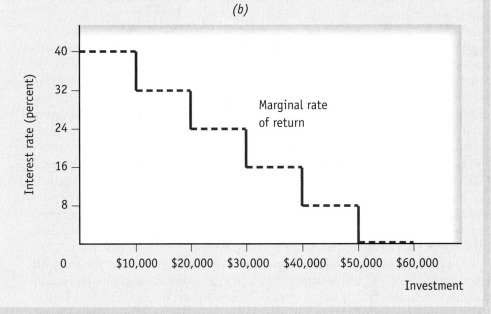

The Tractor-Tiller yields a marginal revenue product of $4,000 per year and has a marginal resource cost of $10,000. As long as Jones has that $10,000 invested in the Tractor-Tiller, the rate of return earned on that investment is $4,000/$10,000, or 40 percent per year. Thus this investment yields a *marginal rate of return* of 40 percent per year, as shown in column (6). The Combine yields a marginal revenue product of $3,200 per year and has a marginal cost of $10,000, so its marginal rate of return equals $3,200/$10,000, or 32 percent per year. Dividing the marginal revenue product of capital in column (4) by the marginal resource cost of that capital in column (5) yields the marginal rate of return in column (6) for each piece of equipment.

Given the marginal rate of return, how much should Jones invest in order to maximize profit? Suppose he borrows the money, paying the *market rate of interest*. Jones will invest in more equipment as long as its marginal rate of return exceeds the market rate of interest. He will not buy an additional piece of equipment if its marginal rate of return falls below the market rate of interest.

For example, if the market interest rate is 20 percent, Jones will invest $30,000 buying three pieces of equipment. The marginal rate of return on the last item purchased, an Irrigator, is 24 percent. Investing another $10,000 to buy a Harrow would yield a marginal return of only 16 percent, a rate below his cost of borrowing. If the market interest rate were 10 percent, Jones would invest in the Harrow as well. If the interest rate were 6 percent, Jones would buy the Crop Sprayer.

Farmer Jones should increase his investment as long as the marginal rate of return on that investment exceeds the market rate of interest. The marginal rate of return reflects the marginal benefit of the investment and the market rate of interest reflects the marginal cost of that investment, so Jones is simply maximizing profit (or minimizing the loss) by investing up to the point where the marginal benefit equals the marginal cost. The data in column (6) are depicted in panel (b) of Exhibit 1 as a step-like curve, where the solid lines reflect the amount that should be invested based on the market interest rate. The curve steps down to reflect the diminishing marginal productivity of additional farm equipment. For example, if the market interest rate is between 32 percent and 40 percent, a Tractor-Tiller should be purchased. If the interest rate is between 24 percent and 32 percent, a Combine should be added. Since the marginal rate of return curve shows how much should be invested at each interest rate, this step-like curve represents the farmer's *demand for investment*. This demand is a derived demand, based on each additional piece of equipment's marginal productivity.

Would the example change if Jones already had the money saved and did not need to borrow? Not as long as he can save at the market rate of interest. For example, suppose Jones has $50,000 in savings that is earning a market rate of interest of 10 percent. In that case, Jones should invest $40,000 in capital, with the Harrow, which earns a marginal rate of return of 16 percent, the last piece purchased. The 10 percent Jones earns on his remaining $10,000 in savings exceeds the 8 percent he could have earned if he had invested that money in the Crop Sprayer. Thus as long as he can borrow and save at the same interest rate, Jones ends up with the same equipment whether he borrows funds or draws on his own savings. *Whether Jones borrows the money or uses savings on hand, the market rate of interest represents his opportunity cost of funds.*

Let's review the procedure used to determine the optimal amount of investment. First, compute the marginal revenue product of capital. Next, divide the marginal revenue product by the marginal resource cost to determine the marginal rate of return. A firm should invest more in capital as long as the marginal rate of return on capital exceeds the market interest rate. The market interest rate reflects the opportunity cost of investing either borrowed funds or savings. Finally, the marginal rate of return curve is a firm's demand curve for capital— that is, it shows the amount a firm is willing and able to invest at each alternative interest rate.

The Market for Loanable Funds

We have now examined why producers are willing to pay interest to borrow money: *money provides a command over resources that makes roundabout production possible.* The simple principles developed for Farmer Jones can be generalized to other producers. The major demanders of loans are firms that borrow to invest in capital goods, such as computers, machines, trucks, and buildings. At any time, each firm has a variety of possible investment opportunities. Each firm ranks its opportunities from highest to lowest, based on the expected marginal rates of return on the investments. Firms will increase their investment until their expected marginal rate of return just equals the market rate of interest. With other inputs held constant, as they were on the farm, the demand curve for investment slopes downward.

But firms are not the only demanders of loans. As we have seen, households value present consumption more than future consumption; they are often willing to pay extra to consume now rather than later. One way to ensure that goods and services are available now is to borrow money for present consumption. Mortgages, car loans, college loans, and credit-card purchases are examples of household borrowing. The household's demand curve for loans, like the firm's, slopes downward, reflecting consumers' greater ability and greater willingness to borrow at lower interest rates, other things constant. The government sector and the rest of the world are also demanders of loans.

Banks are willing to pay interest on consumer savings because the banks can, in turn, lend these savings to those who need credit, such as farmers, home buyers, and entrepreneurs looking to start a new business. Banks play the role of *financial intermediaries* in what is known as the market for loanable funds. The **loanable funds market** brings together savers, or suppliers of loanable funds, and borrowers, or demanders of loanable funds, to determine the market rate of interest. The **supply of loanable funds** curve reflects the positive relationship between the market rate of interest and the quantity of savings, other things constant, as reflected by the usual upward-sloping supply curve. This upward-sloping supply curve is shown as *S* in Exhibit 2.

For the economy as a whole, if the amount of other resources and the level of technology are fixed, diminishing marginal productivity causes the marginal rate of return curve, which is the demand curve for investment, to slope downward. The **demand for loanable funds** curve is based on the expected marginal rate of return these borrowed funds yield when invested in capital. Each firm has a downward-sloping demand curve for loanable funds, reflecting a declining marginal rate of return on investment. With some qualifications, the demand for loanable funds by each firm can be summed horizontally to yield the demand for loanable funds by all firms, as shown by *D* in Exhibit 2. Factors assumed constant along this demand curve include the prices of other resources, the level of technology, and the tax laws.

By bringing the demand and supply for loanable funds together, as in Exhibit 2, we can determine the market interest rate. In this case, the equilibrium interest rate of 8 percent is the only rate that will exactly match the wishes of borrowers and savers. The equilibrium quantity of loanable funds is $100 billion per year. Any change in the supply or demand for loanable funds will change the equilibrium interest rate. For example, a major technological breakthrough that increases the productivity of capital will increase its marginal rate of return

Loanable funds market
The market in which savers (suppliers of funds) and borrowers (demanders of funds) come together to determine the market rate of interest

Supply of loanable funds
The relationship between the market interest rate and the quantity of loanable funds supplied to the economy, other things constant

Demand for loanable funds The relationship between the market interest rate and the quantity of loanable funds demanded, other things constant

EXHIBIT 2

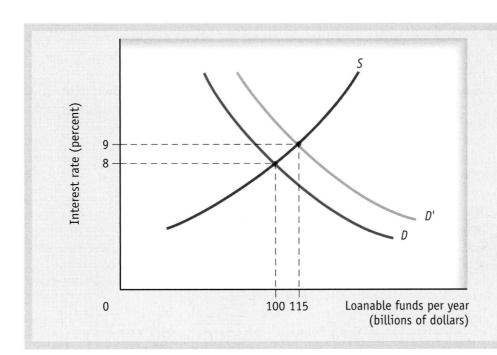

Market for Loanable Funds

Because of the declining marginal rate of return on capital, the quantity of loanable funds demanded is inversely related to the rate of interest. The equilibrium rate of interest, 8 percent, is determined at the intersection of the demand and supply curves for loans. An increase in the demand for loans from D to D' leads to an increase in the equilibrium rate of interest from 8 percent to 9 percent.

and shift out the demand curve for loanable funds, as shown in the movement from D to D' in Exhibit 2. Such an increase in the demand for loanable funds would raise the equilibrium interest rate to 9 percent and increase the quantity of loanable funds to $115 billion per year.

Why Interest Rates Differ

So far, we have been talking about *the* market rate of interest, implying that only one interest rate prevails in the loanable funds market. At any particular time, however, a range of interest rates can be found in the economy. For example, there are different interest rates on home mortgages, car loans, student loans, and credit cards, as well as the so-called *prime rate,* which is offered to the most trustworthy borrowers. Let's see why interest rates differ.

Risk. Some borrowers are more likely than others to repay their loans. Differences in the risk associated with various borrowers are reflected in differences in the interest rate negotiated. As loans become more risky, lenders are less willing to supply loanable funds, so the market interest rate on these loans rises, reflecting the higher risk. For example, the interest rate charged on a home mortgage is lower than on a car loan in part because a home serves as better collateral for the loan than does a car, which depreciates faster and can be driven away.

Duration of the Loan. The future is uncertain, and the further into the future a loan is to be repaid, the more uncertain that repayment becomes. Thus as the duration of a loan increases, lenders are less willing to supply funds. Hence loans extended for longer periods usually involve a higher interest rate to compensate the lender for this greater risk. The **term structure of interest rates** is the relationship between the duration of a loan and the interest rate charged. This

Term structure of interest rates The relationship between the duration of a loan and the interest rate charged term structure usually indicates that the interest rate increases as the duration of loans increases.

Cost of Administration. The costs of executing the loan agreement, monitoring the conditions of the loan, and collecting the payments on the loan are called the *administration costs* of the loan. These costs, as a proportion of the total amount of the loan, decrease as the size of the loan increases. For example, the cost of administering a $100,000 loan will be less than 10 times the cost of administering a $10,000 loan. Consequently, that portion of the interest charge reflecting the cost of administering the loan will be smaller for large loans than for small loans.

Tax Treatment. Differences in the tax treatment of different types of loans will also affect the market rate of interest. For example, the interest earned on funds loaned to state and local governments is not subject to federal income taxes. Since lenders are interested in their after-tax rate of interest, state and local governments can pay lower interest rates than those paid by other borrowers.

We have now discussed investing in capital. We close this section with a case study on a special form of capital—intellectual property.

CaseStudy

The Information Economy

For a comprehensive Internet resource on technology law, containing pages on patent, copyright, trademark, and Internet legal issues, visit http://www.bitlaw.com/. Also visit the Web site of *The Industry Standard,* an on-line magazine about the Internet economy, at http://www. industrystandard.net/ on. What are the current issues in these fields? What can you learn about protecting music copyright with the advent of MP3 and other music digitizing technologies?

The Value of a Good Idea—Intellectual Property

One potentially valuable capital asset is information, or so-called *intellectual property.* But information is an unusual commodity. On the demand side, consumers are uncertain about the value of information until they acquire it. But they can't acquire it until they pay for it. So there is a circularity problem. There is also a problem on the supply side. Information is costly to produce, but it can be transmitted at relatively low cost. For example, the first copy of a new software program may cost $100 million to develop. But each additional copy may cost only $1 to produce.

Because of these demand and supply problems, producers of information may have difficulty appropriating its value through the sale of information. As soon as the producer sells information, that first customer, because of the low cost of transmitting information, becomes a potential supplier of the information. For example, a producer could invest millions developing a new software application, then sell a single copy. The buyer could, in turn, make copies and give or sell the software to others (are you using any "pirated" software?). The original producer has difficulty preventing nonpaying beneficiaries from consuming the good. As a result of these problems in the market for information, creators have less incentive to invest time and money to develop new ideas and new inventions.

To address these problems, the law grants property rights to the creators of new ideas and new inventions. By conferring monopoly power on such creators, those originators are better able to appropriate the value of their creations and thus have more incentive to develop new ideas and new inventions. The *patent system* establishes ownership rights to inventions and other technical advances. The *copyright system* confers ownership rights to the original expression of an idea by an author, artist, or composer. And the *trademark system* establishes property in unique commercial marks and symbols, such as the Nike swoosh or McDonald's golden arches.

Granting copyright protection is one thing, but enforcing it is quite another. Many of the CDs, movie videos, and software programs sold in other countries, especially China, are pirated editions of products originally developed in the United States. In fact, some movie videos are sold on the black market before the movie is released in theaters. So enforcement of these property rights is costly, and this diminishes the incentive to create new ideas.

Revisions have adapted copyright laws to a changing world. For example, computer software is now protected by copyright laws. The courts have also granted copyright protection for the wiring and circuitry design that make up a computer chip. The Internet has given rise to some special problems of intellectual property, since someone can download the contents of a site, change the headings, and derive commercial benefit from that content. Some digital gurus have argued that the ease of duplicating data on the Internet spells an end to copyright benefits. They say that anything that can be reduced to bits can be copied. But several companies are now developing software and hardware that, through the use of encryption and passwords, allow producers of information to specify how digital works can be used. Each new generation of technology has created new ways of communicating ideas and thus has called for new ways to help protect the rights of the creators of those ideas.

Sources: *Journal of Intellectual Property Law* (http://www.lawsch.uga.edu/~jipl/); "World Wide Web Link Creation, Intellectual Property, Copyrights and Trademarks," *Computerworld* (www.computerworld.com/links/970505linklinks.html); Mark Stefik, "Trusted Systems," *Scientific American* (March 1997) (www.sciam.com/0397issue/0397stefik.html); and Peter Burrows, "A Nest of Software Spies," *Business Week*, (19 May 1997) (www.businessweek.com/1997/20/b352792.htm).

PRESENT VALUE AND DISCOUNTING

Because present consumption is valued more than future consumption, present and future consumption cannot be directly compared. What we need is a yardstick to compare present and future amounts. A way of standardizing the discussion is to measure all consumption in terms of its present value. **Present value** is the current value of a payment or payments that will be received in the future. For example, how much would you pay now for the right to receive $100 one year from now? Put another way, what is the *present value* to you of receiving $100 one year from now?

Present value The value today of income or an income stream to be received in the future

Present Value of Payment One Year Hence

Suppose that the market interest rate is 10 percent, so you can either lend or borrow money at that rate. One way to determine how much you would pay for the opportunity to receive $100 one year from now is to ask how much you would have to save now, at the market interest rate, to end up with $100 one year from now. Here is the problem we are trying to solve: What amount of money, if saved at a rate of 10 percent, will accumulate to $100 one year from now? We can calculate the answer with a simple formula. We can say

$$\text{present value} \times 1.10 = \$100$$

or

$$\text{present value} = \frac{\$100}{1.10} = \$90.91$$

Thus if the interest rate is 10 percent, $90.91 is the present value of receiving $100 one year from now; it is the most you would be willing to pay today to receive $100 one year from now. Rather than pay more than $90.91, you could simply deposit your $90.91 at the market rate of interest and end up with $100 a year from now. The procedure of dividing the future payment by 1 plus the prevailing interest rate in order to express it in today's dollars is called **discounting.** The interest rate used to discount future payments is called the **discount rate.**

Discounting Determining the present value of income to be received in the future

Discount rate The interest rate used to convert income to be received in the future into present value

The present value of $100 to be received one year from now depends on the interest rate, or discount rate. The more that present consumption is preferred to future consumption, the higher the interest rate that must be offered savers to defer consumption. *The higher the interest rate, or discount rate, the more the future payment is discounted and the lower its present value.* Put another way, the higher the interest rate, the less you need to save now to yield a given amount in the future. For example, if the interest rate is 15 percent, the present value of receiving $100 one year from now is $100/1.15, which equals $86.96.

Conversely, the less present consumption is preferred to future consumption, the less savers need be paid to defer consumption and the lower the interest rate. The lower the interest rate, or discount rate, the less the future income is discounted and the greater its present value. A lower interest rate means that you must save more now to yield a given amount in the future. As a general rule, the present value of receiving an amount one year from now is

$$\text{present value} = \frac{\text{amount received one year from now}}{1 + \text{interest rate}}$$

For example, when the interest rate is 5 percent, the present value of receiving $100 one year from now is

$$\text{present value} = \frac{\$100}{1 + 0.05} = \frac{\$100}{1.05} = \$95.24$$

Present Value for Payments in Later Years

Now consider the present value of receiving $100 two years from now. What amount of money, if deposited at the market rate of interest of 5 percent, would yield $100 two years from now? At the end of the first year, the value would be the present value $\times$ 1.05, which would then earn the market rate of interest during the second year. At the end of the second year, the deposit would have accumulated to the present value $\times$ 1.05, $\times$ 1.05. Thus, we have the equation

$$\text{present value} \times 1.05 \times 1.05 = \text{present value} \times (1.05)^2 = \$100$$

Solving for the present value yields

$$\text{present value} = \frac{\$100}{(1.05)^2} = \frac{\$100}{1.1025} = \$90.70$$

If the $100 were to be received three years from now, we would discount the payment over three years:

$$\text{present value} = \frac{\$100}{(1.05)^3} = \$86.38$$

If the interest rate is i, the present value formula of a payment of M dollars t years from now is

$$\text{present value} = \frac{M}{(1 + i)^t}$$

Because $(1 + i)$ is greater than 1, the more times it is multiplied by itself (as determined by t), the greater the denominator will be and the smaller the present value will be. Thus *the present value of a given payment will be smaller the further in the future that payment is to be received.*

Present Value of an Income Stream

The previous method is used to compute the present value of a single sum to be paid at some point in the future. Most investments, however, yield a stream of income over time. In cases where the income is received over a period of years, the present value of each receipt can be computed individually, and the results summed to yield the present value of the entire income stream. For example, the present value of receiving $100 next year and $150 the year after is simply the present value of the first year's receipt plus the present value of the second year's receipt. If the interest rate is 5 percent,

$$\text{present value} = \frac{\$100}{1.05} + \frac{\$150}{(1.05)^2} = \$231.29$$

Present Value of an Annuity

A given sum of money received each year for a specified number of years is called an **annuity.** Such an income stream is called a *perpetuity* if it continues indefinitely into the future, as it would in our earlier example of the productivity gain stemming from the purchase of indestructible farm equipment. The present value of receiving a certain amount forever seems like it should be a very large sum indeed. But because future income is valued less the more distant into the future it is to be received, the present value of receiving a particular amount forever is not much more than that of receiving it for, say, 20 years.

To determine the present value of receiving $100 each year forever, we need only ask how much money must be deposited in a savings account to yield $100 in interest each year. When the interest rate is 10 percent, a deposit of $1,000 will earn $100 per year. Thus, the present value of receiving $100 a year indefinitely when the interest rate is 10 percent is $1,000. More generally, the present value equals the amount received each year divided by the interest rate, or discount rate.

The concept of present value is useful in making investment decisions. Farmer Jones, by investing $10,000 in the Crop Sprayer, expected to earn $800

Annuity A given sum of money received each year for a specified number of years more per year. Thus, his marginal rate of return was 8 percent. At a market interest rate of 8 percent, the present value of a cash flow of $800 per year discounted at that rate would be $800/0.08, which equals $10,000. Thus, *Jones was willing to invest in capital an amount that, at the margin, would yield a cash stream with a present value just equal to the marginal amount invested.*

What about your decision to invest in human capital—to go to college? In the previous chapter you learned that individuals with at least a college degree earn about twice as much throughout their working life as those with only a high school education. We could compute the present value of each level of education by discounting earnings based on that level of education, then summing the total earnings over your working life. Even without carrying out those calculations, we can say with reasonable certainty that the present value of at least a college education will be about twice that of just a high school education. You also learned way back in Chapter 1 that some college majors earn more than others. For example, based on a survey of those 35 to 44 years of age with a college degree as their highest degree, males who majored in economics had median earnings that were 55 percent higher than those who majored in philosophy. Among females, that advantage was 91 percent for the same majors. If such an advantage prevailed throughout all working years, the present value of a degree in economics would be 55 percent higher than the present value of a degree in philosophy for males and 91 percent higher for females.

To develop a hands-on appreciation for present value and discounting, consider the following case study.

CaseStudy

Public Policy

Lottery winners in Virginia can receive either a series of annual payments over 25 years or a lump sum in cash (cash option). For details, visit the Virginia Lottery Web site at http://www.valottery.com/cashopt.htm. How does the Virginia Lottery determine the value of the jackpot? What interest rate does it use?

The Million-Dollar Lottery

Since New Hampshire introduced the first modern state-run lottery, 36 states and the District of Columbia have followed suit, generating profits of $12 billion in 1997. Multi-million-dollar prizes are now ho-hum. Some winners expect to be handed a check for the prize. Instead, they are usually paid in installments. For example, a million-dollar prize-winner gets $50,000 a year for 20 years. You now know that such a payment stream has a present value of less than the advertised million.

To put this payment schedule in perspective, keep in mind that at a discount rate of 10 percent, the $50,000 received in the twentieth year has a present value of only $7,432. If today you deposited $7,432 in an account earning 10 percent interest, you would wind up with $50,000 in 20 years.

If the discount rate is 10 percent, the present value of a $50,000 annuity for the next 20 years is $425,700. Thus the present value of the actual payment stream is less than half of the promised million, which is why lottery officials pay it out in installments (the multi-state Powerball lottery pays out over 25 years, but offers winners the choice of a much smaller lump-sum payment).

Incidentally, we might consider the present value of receiving $50,000 per year forever. Using the formula for an annuity discussed earlier, the present value when the interest rate is 10 percent is $50,000/0.10 = $500,000. Since the present value of receiving $50,000 for 20 years is $425,700, continuing the $50,000 annual payment forever adds only $74,300 to the present value. This shows the dramatic effect of discounting on the present value of payments beyond year 20.

In some states, lottery winners are allowed to sell their jackpots. Winners typically receive only 40 cents on the dollar for the 20-year annuity. So a million-dollar pot, if sold by the winner, would fetch only $400,000. At tax rates prevailing in 1998, federal income taxes on $400,000 for a single tax filer amount to at least $140,000. State and local income taxes could add an additional $50,000. All told, because of time and taxes, the much-touted million could shrink to about $200,000 in after-tax income—only one-fifth the amount advertised.

Sources: Adam Wolfson, "Life Is a Gamble," *Wall Street Journal* (14 August 1998); Lin Bixby, "A Ticket to Paradise? Don't Bet on It," *Hartford Courant* (28 June 1998); and Michelle Malkin, "The State's Lottery Ads Are Hazardous to Your Health," *Seattle Times* (6 May 1997). Internet links to lottery sites can be found at www.state.wv.us/lottery/links.htm.

This discussion of present value and discounting concludes our treatment of capital and interest. We now have the tools to consider how firms, especially corporations, are financed.

CORPORATE FINANCE

During the Industrial Revolution, labor-saving machinery made large-scale production more profitable, so construction of the huge factories to house this heavy machinery began to require large capital investments. The corporate structure became the easiest way to finance these large investments, and by 1920 corporations accounted for most employment and output in the U.S. economy. Way back in Chapter 4, you learned about the pros and cons of the corporate form of business organization, but thus far little has been said about corporate finance.

As was noted in Chapter 4, a corporation is a legal entity, distinct from its shareholders. The corporation may own property, earn a profit, sue or be sued, and incur debt. Stockholders, the owners of the corporation, are liable only to the extent of their investment in the firm. Use of the abbreviation "Inc." or "Corp." in the company name serves as a warning to potential creditors that stockholders will not accept unlimited personal liability for the debts the company incurs.

Corporate Stock and Retained Earnings
Corporations acquire funds for investment in three ways: by issuing stock, by retaining part of their profit, and by borrowing. Corporations *issue and sell stock* to raise money for operations and for new plant and equipment. Suppose you have developed a recipe for a hot, spicy chili that your friends have convinced you will be a

best-seller. You decide to incorporate and raise $1 million by issuing stock in the company, which you call the Six-Alarm Chili Corporation. To do this, you sell 10,000 shares for $100 per share. This initial sale of stock to the public is called an **initial public offering,** or an **IPO.** A *share* of **stock** represents a claim on the net income and assets of a corporation, as well as the right to vote on corporate directors and on other important matters. A person who buys 1 percent of the shares issued thereby owns 1 percent of the corporation, is entitled to 1 percent of any profit, and gets to cast 1 percent of the votes.

Initial public offering (IPO) The initial sale of stock to the public

Stock A certificate reflecting part ownership of a corporation

Dividends After-tax corporate profits that are paid to stockholders rather than reinvested in the firm

Retained earnings After-tax corporate profits that are reinvested in the firm rather than paid to stockholders as dividends

Corporations must pay corporate income taxes on any profits. After-tax profits are either paid as **dividends** to shareholders or reinvested in the corporation. Reinvested profits, or **retained earnings,** allow the firm to finance expansion. Stockholders expect dividends, but the corporation is not bound by contract to pay dividends. Once shares are issued, their price tends to fluctuate directly with the firm's profit prospects. People buy stock because of the dividends and because they usually expect the value of the stock to increase in the future.

Corporate Bonds

Bond A certificate reflecting a firm's promise to pay the holder periodic interest until the date of maturity, then to pay a fixed sum of money on the designated maturity date

Again, your corporation can acquire funds by issuing stock, by retaining earnings, or by borrowing. The corporation can go to a bank for a loan or can issue and sell bonds. A **bond** is the corporation's promise to pay back the holder a fixed sum of money on the designated *maturity date* plus make annual interest payments until that date of maturity. For example, a corporation might sell for $1,000 a bond that promises to make an annual interest payment of, say, $100 and to repay the $1,000 at the end of 20 years.

The payment stream for bonds is more predictable than that for stocks. Unless this corporation goes bankrupt, it is obliged to pay bondholders the promised amounts. In contrast, stockholders are last in line when resource holders get paid, so bondholders get paid before stockholders. Investors usually consider bonds less risky than stocks, although bonds involve risk as well.

Securities Exchanges

Once stocks and bonds have been issued and sold, owners of these securities are free to resell them on *security exchanges*. In the United States, there are seven security exchanges registered with the *Securities and Exchange Commission,* or *SEC,* the federal body that regulates securities markets. The New York Stock Exchange is the largest, trading the securities of over 2,000 major companies and accounting for well over half of U.S. securities trades. Nearly all the securities traded each day are *secondhand securities* in the sense that they have already been sold by the issuing company. So the bulk of the daily transactions do not provide funds to firms in need of investment capital. Most money goes from a securities seller to a securities buyer. *Institutional investors,* such as banks, insurance companies, and mutual funds, account for over half the trading volume on the New York Stock Exchange. By providing a *secondary market* for securities, exchanges enhance the *liquidity* of these securities—that is, the exchanges make the securities more readily exchangeable for cash and thus more attractive to investors.

The secondary markets for stocks also determine the current market value of the corporation. The market value of a firm at any given time can be found by multiplying the share price times the number of shares outstanding. For example, if your chili company's stock price increases from $100 to $150 per share, the market value of the firm, or *market capitalization*, would equal $150 times the 10,000 outstanding shares, or $1.5 million. The share price reflects the present value of the discounted stream of expected profits. Just to give you some idea, the market capitalization of the top-valued U.S. firm, Microsoft, exceeded $400 billion in May 1999, and the total market capitalization of all firms on U.S. exchanges exceeded $14 trillion.

Securities prices give the firm's management some indication of the wisdom of raising new capital through retained earnings, new stock issues, or new bond issues. The more profitable the company is expected to be, other things constant, the higher the value of shares on the stock market and the lower the interest rate that would have to be paid on new bond issues. *Thus, securities markets allocate funds more readily to successful firms than to firms in financial difficulty.* Some firms may be in such poor financial shape that they cannot sell new securities. Securities markets usually promote the survival of the fittest.

So one function of securities markets is to allocate investment funds to those firms that appear capable of making the most profitable use of those funds. Securities markets also help determine the ownership and control of corporations. We examine this function next.

CORPORATE OWNERSHIP AND CONTROL

As the founder of the Six-Alarm Chili Corporation, you are that firm's entrepreneur. An **entrepreneur** is a profit-seeking decision maker who organizes an enterprise and assumes the risk of operation. An entrepreneur pays resource owners for the opportunity to use those resources in the firm. The entrepreneur need not actually manage the firm's resources as long as he or she has the power to hire and fire the manager—that is, as long as the entrepreneur controls the manager.

Entrepreneur A profit-seeking decision maker who organizes an enterprise and assumes the risk of its operation

Managerial Behavior in Large Corporations

Up to this point, we have assumed that firms attempt to maximize profits. In a small firm, there is usually little danger that the hired manager will not follow the wishes of the owner; the manager and owner are often the same person. As the modern corporation has evolved, however, its ownership has become widely distributed among many stockholders, often leaving no single stockholder with either the incentive or the ability to control the manager.

Ownership has become widely distributed in part because individual stockholders prefer to diversify their portfolios across different types of assets rather invest in just a single company. A **portfolio** is an individual's collection of stocks, bonds, and other financial assets. The exact composition of the portfolio depends on the individual's financial needs and attitude toward risk. For example, a young family may prefer a portfolio that yields no current income but will grow to finance college costs. An older couple, on the other hand, would prefer a portfolio that provides a reliable stream of retirement income. Even an individual who is wealthy enough to purchase a large fraction of a particular firm usually prefers to buy a small fraction of many firms instead. That way, if a particular firm performs poorly and its share price drops, the portfolio

Portfolio A collection of stocks, bonds, and other financial assets still retains most of its value. Simply put, investors choose diversified portfolios to avoid putting all their eggs in one basket. The upshot is that the ownership of most firms is spread across many stockholders.

Economists since the days of Adam Smith have been concerned with what is known as the **separation of ownership from control** in the large corporation. Various economists have formulated theoretical models suggesting that, when freed from the control of a dominant stockholding influence, managers might attempt to pursue their own selfish goals rather than those of the firm's owners. The alternatives vary from model to model, but emphasis has focused on such goals as maximizing the firm's size or increasing the discretionary resources available to the managers, such as attractive surroundings, private dining rooms, corporate jets, and other amenities. A manager may try to increase the firm's size, by, for example, acquiring other firms, even if profits suffer in the process, because managers want the power, security, and status associated with a larger firm. They want to appear on the cover of *Business Week*. As goals other than profit are pursued, so the argument goes, the firm's resources are used less efficiently, resulting in a lower level of profit. Thus, stockholders—the owners of the firm—suffer because managers are not pursuing the owners' best interests.

Separation of ownership from control The situation that exists when no single stockholder or unified group of stockholders owns enough shares to control the management of a corporation

Constraints on Managerial Discretion

Analysts have identified a variety of constraints that can serve as checks on wayward managers. The nature and effectiveness of each constraint will be examined next.

Economics of Natural Selection. Some economists argue that even if managers are freed from the control of a dominant stockholder, the rigors of competition in the product market will force them to maximize profits. This "economics of natural selection" theoretically ensures that only the most efficient firms will survive; inefficient firms will not earn enough profit to attract and retain resources and so will eventually go out of business.

The problem with this argument is that although pressure to pursue profits may arise when firms sell their products in competitive markets, many large corporations are at least partially insulated from intense product competition. Either because government regulations protect their firms from competition or because their firms enjoy some degree of market power, many managers have a certain amount of discretion in how they use their firms' resources. Such managers could divert corporate resources into activities reflecting their own interests, yet still earn enough profit to ensure their firms' survival.

Managerial Incentives. Other economists have examined the manager's incentive structure. If executive pay is linked closely to the firm's profit, the compensation scheme may encourage the manager to pursue profit even in the absence of a dominant stockholder or competition in the product market. Evidence suggests that at least a portion of the typical manager's compensation is tied to the firm's profitability through some type of bonus pay scheme or stock option plan. But even if the manager's income is tied to profit, the manager will not necessarily attempt to maximize profit. The manager in a large corporation who diverts profit to other ends will simply forgo some income. This profit diversion may be "cheap" in view of the small fraction of the firm's shares typically owned by management. For example, if a manager who owns 1 percent of the firm's shares diverts $50,000 of potential profit to buy an antique desk for the executive suite, this diversion will cost the manager only $500 in forgone pretax profit. After corporate taxes and personal income taxes are figured in, the cost is less than half that. Thus, the existence of a link between executive pay and firm profit is not necessarily evidence that managers will attempt to maximize profit; it is only evidence that profit diversion will involve some personal cost, but that cost may be quite small.

Stockholder Voting. Each year stockholders have an opportunity to attend the company meeting and elect the board of directors. Couldn't stockholders join forces to oust an inefficient manager? Chances of an effective stockholder revolt are slim. The average stockholder does not have the information, the resources, or the incentive to challenge management. Most shareholders either ignore the election or dutifully pass their proxy votes to the managers. Dissatisfied stockholders, however, do have one very important alternative. They can "fire" the manager and the firm simply by selling their shares in the corporation. As dissatisfied stockholders sell their holdings, the share price drops and the firm becomes more attractive as a target for a reform-minded entrepreneur. An outside individual or another firm can buy a controlling interest in the firm at a relatively low price, reform or replace the management, and then benefit as the firm's rising profits lead to an increase in the value of shares. Some firms specialize in acquiring, then shaping up, other firms that do not appear to be performing up to their potential.

Institutional Investors. A growing fraction of corporate shares are purchased not by individual investors but by institutional investors such as mutual funds, who purchase these shares as part of a portfolio. Large institutional investors can exercise corporate control either directly through the election of the board of directors or indirectly through buying and selling corporate shares. Some top executives have been ousted by institutional investors.

CONCLUSION

This chapter introduced you to capital, interest, and corporate finance. Capital is a more complicated resource than this chapter has conveyed. For example, the demand curve for investment is a moving target, not the stable relationship drawn in Exhibit 1. An accurate depiction of the investment demand curve calls for knowledge of the marginal product of capital and the price of output in the future. But capital's marginal productivity changes with breakthroughs in technology and with changes in the employment of other resources. And the future price of the product can also vary widely. Consider, for example, the dilemma of a firm contemplating an investment in drilling rigs in recent years, when oil prices fluctuated between $10 and $36 per barrel.

One final point. When economists talk about investing they have in mind purchases of new capital, such as new machines and new buildings. When business journalists talk about investing, they usually mean buying stocks and bonds. To an economist, Farmer Jones is investing only when he purchases new capital, not when he buys corporate stocks and bonds.

SUMMARY

1. Production cannot occur without savings because both direct production and roundabout production require time—time during which the resources required for production must be paid. Because present consumption is valued more than future consumption, consumers must be rewarded to defer consumption. Interest is the reward paid to savers for forgoing present consumption and is the cost paid by borrowers to increase present consumption.

2. Choosing the profit-maximizing level of capital is complicated because capital purchased today yields a stream of benefit for years into the future. The marginal rate of return on a capital investment equals the marginal revenue product of capital as a percentage of the marginal resource cost of capital. The profit-maximizing firm invests up to the point where its marginal rate of return on capital equals the market rate of interest, which is the opportunity cost of investing savings or borrowed funds.

3. The demand and supply for loanable funds determine the market rate of interest. At any given time, market rates of interest may differ because of differences in risk, maturity, administrative costs, and tax treatment.

4. Corporations secure investment funding from three sources: new stock issues, retained earnings, and borrowing (either directly from a lender or by issuing bonds). Once new stocks and bonds are issued, these securities are then bought and sold on securities exchanges. Securities prices tend to vary directly with the firm's expected profitability.

5. The ownership of a large corporation is typically fragmented among many stockholders, with no stockholder owning a dominant share. The fact that a poorly performing firm can be bought at a bargain price, shaped up, and sold for a profit is said to keep management behavior in accord with stockholders' interests.

QUESTIONS FOR REVIEW

1. *(Role of Time)* Complete the following sentences:
   a. If Bryan values current consumption more than future consumption, he has a _____.
   b. The reward to households for forgoing current consumption is _____.
   c. Producing capital goods rather than producing final goods is known as _____ .

2. *(Consumption, Saving, and Time)* Explain why the supply of loanable funds curve slopes upward to the right.

3. *(Why Interest Rates Differ)* At any given time, a range of interest rates prevails in the economy. What are some factors that contribute to differences among interest rates?

4. *(Present Value of an Annuity)* Why is $10,000 a close approximation of the price of an annuity that pays $1,000 each year for 30 years at 10 percent annual interest?

5. *(Present Value of an Annuity)* Suppose you are hired by your state government to determine the profitability of a lottery offering a grand prize of $10 million paid out in equal annual installments over 20 years. Show *how* to calculate the cost to the state of paying out such a prize. Assume payments are made at the end of each year.

6. *(CaseStudy: The Million-Dollar Lottery)* In many states with lotteries, people can take their winnings in a single, discounted, lump-sum payment or in a series of annual payments for 20 years. What factors should a winner consider in determining how to take the money?

7. *(Corporate Finance)* Describe the three ways in which corporations acquire funds for investment.

8. *(Securities Exchanges)* What role do securities exchanges play in financing corporations?

9. *(Managerial Behavior in Large Corporations)* How could the separation of ownership from control lead to lower profits for a firm?

10. *(Constraints on Managerial Discretion)* The separation of ownership from control in a large corporation can allow managers to follow goals other than profit maximization. Discuss reasons why managers may continue to maximize profits. Why might these reasons be insufficient to ensure profit maximization?

PROBLEMS AND EXERCISES

11. *(Optimal Investment)* Look back at Exhibit 1 in this chapter. If the marginal resource cost rose to $24,000 what would be the optimal investment at a market interest rate of 10 percent? If the interest rate then rose to 16.6 percent, what would be the optimal level of investment?

12. *(Market for Loanable Funds)* Using a supply-demand for loanable funds diagram, show the effect on the market interest rate of each of the following:
    a. An increase in the marginal resource cost of capital
    b. An increase in the marginal productivity of capital
    c. A shift in preferences toward present consumption and away from future consumption

13. *(Present Value)* Calculate the present value of each of the following future payments. **(For some of these problems you may wish to use the on-line calculator available at** http://www.datachimp.com/articles/finworks/fmpresval.htm.
    a. A $10,000 lump sum received 1 year from now if the market interest rate is 8 percent

    b. A $10,000 lump sum received 2 years from now if the market interest rate is 10 percent
    c. A $1,000 lump sum received 3 years from now if the market interest rate is 5 percent
    d. A $25,000 lump sum received one year from now if the market interest rate is 12 percent
    e. A $25,000 lump sum received one year from now if the market interest rate is 10 percent
    f. A perpetuity of $500 per year if the market interest rate is 6 percent

14. *(Present Value of an Income Stream)* Suppose the market interest rate is 10 percent. Would you be willing to lend $10,000 if you were guaranteed to receive $1,000 at the end of each of the next 12 years plus a $5,000 payment 15 years from now? Why or why not?

EXPERIENTIAL EXERCISES

15. *(CaseStudy: The Value of a Good Idea)* MIT's Michael Kremer has suggested an interesting way to encourage innovation in drug development. The basic idea is explained in a nontechnical article in the June 15, 1996 issue of *The Economist* at http://rider.wharton. upenn.edu/~faulhabe/790/patent_cure-all.html. Take a look at the article and determine how Kremer places a value on an innovation.

16. *(Corporate Ownership and Control)* Read Jane Katz, "Who Should Be in Charge," in the Federal Reserve Bank of Boston's *Regional Review* at http:// www.bos.frb.org/economic/nerr/katz97_4.htm. What are some of the current issues in corporate finance outlined by Katz?

17. *(Wall Street Journal)* The *Wall Street Journal* is the quintessential source for information about U.S. financial markets. Most of the Money & Investing section is devoted to reporting on individual firms' financial activities and on the stock and bond markets generally. This section is worth scanning every day, but today try to find an article related to corporate ownership and control. Are there any examples of takeover attempts in which a firm or a group of institutional investors is trying to buy up shares of another firm? What factors are motivating this behavior?

Transaction Costs, Imperfect Information, and Market Behavior

Visit the McEachern
Interactive Study Center
for this chapter at
http://mcisc.swcollege.com

General Motors offers car loans and issues credit cards, so why don't some banks make automobiles? Why do some firms, such as Domino's Pizza, specialize in a single product, while other firms, such as General Electric, make hundreds of different products? Why stop at hundreds of different products? Why not thousands? In fact, why isn't there one giant firm that produces everything? Why does buying a used car make us nervous? Why is proper spelling so important on your résumé? Answers to these and other seemingly unrelated questions are addressed in this chapter, which digs deeper into some assumptions made about firms, households, and the role that information plays in market interaction.

Little has been said so far about the internal structure of the firm. We have ignored the internal workings of the firm because our objective has been to understand how the price system coordinates resource allocation. In the first half of this chapter, we will step inside the factory gates to reconsider some assumptions made about the firm.

We have also assumed thus far that consumers have all the information they need to make informed choices, including knowledge of the price, availability, and quality of the goods and services they demand. As you will see in the second half of the chapter, participants in most markets do not operate with complete information about the variables that matter most, such as price and quality. To further complicate matters, at times sellers know more than do buyers about the quality of the product; at times it's the other way around. The second half of this chapter examines how a lack of information affects the behavior of market participants and shapes market outcomes. Overall, this chapter should help you develop a better understanding of market behavior. Topics discussed in this chapter include:

- Transaction costs and the firm
- Vertical integration
- Economies of scope
- Optimal search
- Winner's curse

- Asymmetric information
- Adverse selection
- Signaling and screening
- Principal-agent problems

RATIONALE FOR THE FIRM AND ITS SCOPE OF OPERATION

The competitive model assumes that all participants in the market know everything they need to know about the price and availability of all inputs, outputs, and production processes. Perfect competition assumes that the firm is headed by a decision maker with a computer-like ability to calculate all the relevant marginal productivities. This individual knows everything necessary to solve complex production and pricing problems.

The irony is that if the marginal products of all inputs could be measured easily and if prices for all inputs could be determined without cost, there would be little reason for production to take place in firms. In a world characterized by perfect competition, perfect information, constant returns to scale, and costless exchange, the consumer could bypass the firm to deal directly with resource suppliers, purchasing inputs in the appropriate amounts. Someone who wanted a table could buy timber, have it milled, contract with a carpenter, contract with a painter, and end up with a finished product. The consumer could carry out transactions directly with each resource supplier.

Firms Reduce Transaction Costs

This section explores why production is carried out within firms. More than 60 years ago, in a classic article entitled "The Nature of the Firm," Nobel prize winner Ronald Coase asked the fundamental question, "Why do firms exist?"[1]

---

1 *Economica* 4 (November 1937): 386–405.

Why do people organize in the hierarchical structure of the firm and coordinate their decisions through a manager rather than simply relying on market exchange? His answer would not surprise today's students of economics: *Organizing activities through the hierarchy of the firm is often more efficient than market exchange, because production requires the coordination of many transactions among many resource owners. The firm is the favored means of production when the transaction costs involved in using the price system exceed the costs of organizing those same activities through direct managerial controls within a firm.*

Consider again the example of purchasing a table by contracting directly with all the different resource suppliers, from the grower of timber to the individual who paints the table. Using resource markets directly involves (1) the cost of determining what inputs are needed and how they should be combined and (2) the cost of negotiating a separate agreement with each resource owner for each specific contribution to production *over and above* the direct costs of the timber, nails, machinery, paint, and labor required to make the table. Where inputs are easily identified, measured, priced, and hired, production can be carried out through a price-guided "do-it-yourself" approach using the market. For example, getting your house painted is a relatively simple production task: You can buy the paint and brushes and hire painters by the hour. In this case you, the consumer, become your own painting contractor, hiring inputs in the market and combining these inputs to do the job.

Where the costs of identifying the appropriate inputs and negotiating a contract for each specific contribution are high, the consumer minimizes transaction costs by purchasing the finished product from a firm rather than hiring all the inputs directly through markets. For example, although some people serve as their own contractor to get their house painted, few do so when building a house; most hire general contractors. The more complicated the task, the greater the ability to economize on transaction costs through specialization and centralized control. For example, attempting to buy a car by contracting with the hundreds of resource suppliers required to assemble one would be time-consuming and costly. What type of skilled labor should be hired and at what wages? How much steel, aluminum, plastic, glass, paint, and other materials should be purchased? How should the resources be combined and in what proportions? The task is impossible for someone who lacks specialized engineering knowledge of auto production. Consequently, it is more efficient for a consumer to buy a car produced by a firm than to contract separately with each resource supplier.

At the margin there will be some activities that could go either way, with some consumers using firms and some hiring resources directly in the markets. The choice will depend on each consumer's skill and opportunity cost of time. For example, some people may not want to be troubled with hiring all the inputs to get their house painted; instead, they will simply contract with a firm to do the entire job for an agreed-upon price—they will hire a contractor. As you will see later in the chapter, however, hiring a contractor may give rise to other problems of quality control.

The Bounds of the Firm

So far, the chapter has explained why firms exist: *Firms minimize both the transaction costs and the production costs of economic activity.* The next question is, What are the efficient bounds of the firm? The theory of the firm described in earlier chapters is largely silent on questions concerning the boundaries of the firm—that is, on the appropriate degree of vertical integration. **Vertical integration** is the expansion of a firm into stages of production earlier or later than those in which it has previously specialized. For example, a steel company may decide (1) to integrate backward by mining its own iron ore or even mining the coal used to smelt ore (e.g., U.S. Steel owns coal mines in Kentucky) or (2) to integrate forward by forming raw steel into various components. A large manufacturer employs an amazing variety of production processes, but on average about half of the cost of production goes to purchasing inputs from other firms. For example, General Motors spends well over $60 billion a year on parts and raw materials, an amount that exceeds the annual output of some countries.

How does the firm determine which activities to undertake and which to purchase from other firms? Should IBM manufacture its own computer chips or buy them from another firm? The answer depends on a comparison of the costs and benefits of internal production versus market purchases. The point bears repeating: *Internal production and markets are alternative ways of organizing transactions.* The choice will depend on which form of organization is the more efficient way to carry out the transaction in question. Keep in mind that market prices coordinate transactions *between* firms, whereas managers coordinate activities *within* firms. The market coordinates resources by harmonizing the independent plans of separate decision makers, but a firm coordinates resources through the conscious direction of managers.

The usual assumption is that transactions will be organized by market exchange unless markets pose problems. Market exchange allows each firm to benefit from specialization and comparative advantage. For example, IBM can specialize in making computers and buy from chip makers who specialize in what they do best. But sometimes the item to be purchased in the market is not standardized or the exact performance requirements are hard to specify. For example, suppose one firm wants another firm to supply research and development services. The uncertainty involved in the purchase of such a nonspecific service makes it difficult to write, execute, and enforce a purchase agreement covering all possible contingencies that could arise. What if the R&D supplier, in the course of fulfilling the agreement, makes a valuable discovery for an application in an unrelated field? Who has the right to that new application—the firm that purchased the R&D service or the firm that supplied it? And who determines if the field is unrelated? Since incomplete contracts create potentially troublesome situations, conducting research and development *within the firm* often involves a lower transaction cost than purchasing it in the market.

At this point, it might be useful to discuss specific criteria the firm considers when deciding whether to purchase a particular input from the market, thereby benefiting from another producer's comparative advantage, or to produce the input internally.

Bounded Rationality of Managers. To direct and coordinate activity in a conscious way in the firm, a manager must understand how all the pieces of the puzzle fit together. As the firm takes on more and more activities, however, the manager starts losing track of things and the quality of managerial decisions suffers. The more production tasks the firm takes on, the longer the lines of

Vertical integration The expansion of a firm into stages of production earlier or later than those in which it has specialized, such as a steel producer that buys a coal mine communication between the manager and production workers who must implement the decision. One constraint on vertical integration is the manager's **bounded rationality,** which limits the amount of information the manager can comprehend about the firm's operation. When the firm takes on additional functions, coordination and communication become more difficult. The firm can experience diseconomies similar to those it experiences when it expands output beyond the efficient scale of production. The solution is for the firm to reduce its functions to those it does best. Such cutbacks occurred when automakers increased the proportion of parts they purchased from other firms.

Minimum Efficient Scale. As noted when firm costs were first discussed, the *minimum efficient scale* is the minimum level of output at which economies of scale have been fully exploited. For example, suppose that minimum efficient scale in the production of personal computers is achieved when output reaches 1 million computers per year, as shown by the long-run average cost curve in panel (a) of Exhibit 1. Suppose also that this output rate turns out to be the amount the firm wants to produce to maximize profit. Since the computer chip is an important component in the personal computer, should the PC maker integrate backward into chip production? Suppose that the minimum efficient scale in chip production is not achieved until production reaches a rate of 5 million chips per year, so a PC manufacturer needs only 20 percent of the chips produced at the minimum efficient scale. As you can see in panel (b) of Exhibit 1, if only 1 million chips were produced per year, the cost per chip would be high relative to the cost that could be achieved at minimum efficient scale in chip production. The PC manufacturer therefore minimizes production costs by buying chips from a chip firm of optimal size. More generally, *other things constant, a firm should buy an input if the price is below what it would cost the firm to make.*

Easily Observable Quality. If an input is well defined and its quality is easily determined at the time of purchase, that input is more likely to be purchased in the market than produced internally, other things equal. For example, a flour mill will typically buy wheat in the market rather than grow its own, as the quality of the wheat can be easily assessed by inspection. In contrast, the quality of certain inputs can be determined only during the production process. Firms whose reputations depend on the operation of a key component are likely to produce that component, especially if the quality of that component varies widely across producers over time and cannot be easily observed by inspection. For example, suppose that the manufacturer of a sensitive measuring instrument requires a crucial gauge, the quality of which can be observed only as the gauge is assembled. If the firm produces the gauge itself, it can closely monitor quality.

Producers sometimes integrate backward so they can offer consumers a guarantee about the quality of the components or ingredients in a product. For example, Frank Perdue can talk about the health and quality of the chickens he sells because he raises his own. Kentucky Fried Chicken, however, does not discuss the family background of its chickens because the company makes no claim about raising them. Instead, KFC ads focus on such aspects as the secret ingredients used to fry the chicken and the fact that, by specializing in chicken preparation, the company does a better job than other fast-food franchises that sell much more than chicken.

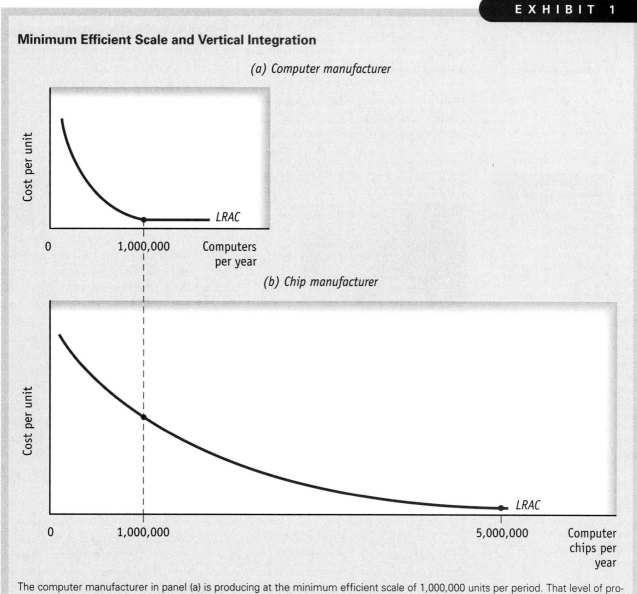

Minimum Efficient Scale and Vertical Integration

(a) Computer manufacturer

(b) Chip manufacturer

The computer manufacturer in panel (a) is producing at the minimum efficient scale of 1,000,000 units per period. That level of production requires 1,000,000 computer chips. If the manufacturer produced its own chips, the cost would be much higher than if it purchased them from a chip manufacturer operating on a much larger scale. As panel (b) shows, at 1,000,000 chips, economies of scale in chip production are far from exhausted.

Number of Suppliers. A firm wants an uninterrupted source of component parts. When there are many interchangeable suppliers of a particular input, a firm is more likely to purchase that input in the market than produce it internally, other things constant. Not only does the existence of many suppliers ensure a dependable source of components, but competition among these suppliers keeps the component price down. If the resource market is so unstable that the firm cannot rely on a consistent supply of components, the firm may produce the item to insulate itself from the vagaries of that market.

In summary, if a firm relies on market purchases of inputs rather than vertical integration, it can benefit from the specialization and comparative advantage of individual suppliers. Other things constant, the firm is more likely to buy a component part rather than produce it if (1) the item can be purchased for less than it could be if produced by the firm, (2) the item is well defined and its quality easily observable, or (3) there are many possible suppliers. These issues are discussed further in the following case study.

The Trend Toward Outsourcing

CaseStudy
The World of Business

Should a firm hire an outside consulting firm to help manage its outsourcing? There are now firms that specialize in helping other firms with outsourcing. For example, Everest provides outsourcing management services. Visit its site at http://www.outsourcing-mgnt.com/index.html. Look under Outsourcing and browse through some of its reports, such as "How to Avoid a Multi-Million Dollar Mistake?" The Outsourcing Institute provides information on the hows and whys of outsourcing at http://www.outsourcing.com/howandwhy/. What do these reports say about how outsourcing is defined and why firms might outsource?

Outsourcing A firm sticks to its core competency, while buying inputs such as auto parts from outside suppliers

Outsourcing occurs when a firm buys products, such as auto parts, or services, such as data processing, from outside suppliers. The firm relies on the division of labor and the law of comparative advantage to focus on what it does best, while depending on other firms to supply component parts, payroll services, data processing, building security, and other inputs that are beyond that firm's "core competency." Firms, particularly manufacturing firms, have long purchased some components from other firms, but the outsourcing movement extended these purchases to a broader range of products and activities that typically had been produced internally. Japanese firms pioneered outsourcing to reduce production costs and enhance quality. In the United States, outsourcing blossomed in manufacturing during the 1980s and spread to virtually every industry. The boom in outsourcing has created many new firms that specialize in supplying what some firms no longer want to do for themselves.

For example, faced with outdated computer hardware and software, Bethlehem Steel executives realized they could no longer hire and retain enough skilled people to keep up with the changes in such a dynamic field. So Bethlehem outsourced its management information system. Dell Computer, a large mail-order personal computer vendor, turned over all shipping responsibility to an outside firm. Du Pont outsourced responsibility for shipping all imports and exports. And a growing number of computer makers are outsourcing computer assembly.

Amazon.com offers more than a million book titles plus CDs and videos, but it has no inventory and no real store—its bookstore being a virtual one on the Internet. Many Internet companies are just order-takers that pass these orders along to a local retailer. TopsyTail sells millions of its simple hair-styling gadgets, but the company has only a few employees. Nearly everything the company does—design, production, marketing, forecasting, packaging, and distribution—is carried out by subcontractors. The founder says the company could not have grown so fast any other way.

What are the limits to outsourcing? One cost of outsourcing can be a loss of control. For example, when Compaq Computer outsourced some laptop-computer production to a Japanese producer, problems mushroomed in design, production, cost, and quality. Compaq now has a separate management team to oversee outsourced activities. Some companies fear that outsourcing can weaken ties with customers. For example, several auto manufacturers had to recall a total of 8 million vehicles because of faulty seat belts from a Japanese supplier. Customers blamed the auto companies for the recall, not the subcontractor.

Recently, there has been a modest move back to more in-house production. For example, because of better software and cheaper computers, some companies are now "insourcing" many of the data processing activities once supplied by other firms. Insourcing reduces the number of times that records must be handled, improving data quality and reducing errors. Chrysler, before it merged with Daimler-Benz, considered outsourcing its data processing, but its own division was the low bidder. Because computer software has made Harley-Davidson more efficient, the company now makes more of its own motorcycle components. By taking back or keeping key production steps in house, some managers think they can respond more flexibly to custom orders and changing market conditions.

Sources: Julia King, "Farming Out Everything: TopsyTail Focus," *Computerworld* (23 March 1998); Saul Hansell, "On the Internet Clock, Middlemen Are Turning into Manufacturers," *New York Times* (26 July 1998); and Loise Lee, "Hiring Outside Firms to Run Computers Isn't Always a Bargain," *Wall Street Journal* (18 May 1995). Amazon Books can be found at www.amazon.com.

Economies of Scope

Thus far we have considered issues affecting the optimal degree of vertical integration in producing a particular product. Even with outsourcing, the focus is on how best to produce a particular product, such as an automobile or a computer. But sometimes firms branch out into product lines that do not have a vertical relationship. **Economies of scope** exist when it is cheaper to combine two or more product lines in one firm than to produce them in separate firms. For example, General Electric produces hundreds of different products ranging from light bulbs to jet engines, because outlays for research and development and marketing can be minimized when spread over different products. Ford Motor Company owns Hertz Rent-A-Car. Travelers Insurance and Citibank merged to offer consumers a worldwide smorgasbord of financial services. Or consider economies of scope on the farm. A farmer often grows a variety of crops and raises different kinds of farm animals—animals that recycle damaged crops and food scraps into useful fertilizer. With economies of *scale,* the average cost per unit of output falls as the *scale* of the firm increases; *with economies of scope, average costs per unit fall as the scope of the firm increases—that is, as the firm produces more types of products.* The cost of some fixed resources, such as specialized knowledge, can be spread across product lines.

Economies of scope Forces that make it cheaper for a firm to produce two or more different products rather than just one

Some combinations of production don't work out. For example, in 1994 The Quaker Oats Company paid $1.7 billion for the Snapple drink business. Over the next three years, Snapple sales dropped. Quaker sold its Snapple division in 1997 for $300 million, or less than one-fifth the purchase price. Likewise, AT&T bought NCR for $7.5 billion in 1991 and spent another $2 billion trying to make the marriage work. In 1997, NCR was sold for $3.4 billion—a huge loss. In short, many mergers of firms in different business lines do not yield the expected economies of scope.

Our focus thus far has been on why firms exist, why they often integrate vertically, why they outsource, and why they often produce a whole range of products. These steps toward greater realism move us beyond the simple depiction of the firm employed earlier. The rest of the chapter challenges some simplifying assumptions about how much information is available to market participants.

MARKET BEHAVIOR WITH IMPERFECT INFORMATION

For the most part, our analysis of market behavior has assumed that market participants have full information about products and resources. For consumers, full information involves knowledge about a product's price, quality, and availability. For firms, full information includes knowledge about the marginal productivity of various resources, about the appropriate technology for combining them, and about the demand for the firm's product. In reality, *reliable information is costly for both consumers and producers.* What's more, in some markets, one side of a transaction has better information than does the other side of the transaction. This section examines the impact of less-than-perfect information on market behavior.

Optimal Search with Imperfect Information

Suppose you want to buy a new computer. You need information about the quality and features of each model and the prices of each model at various retail outlets, mail-order firms, and Internet sites. To learn more about your choices, you may read promotional brochures and computer publications and visit the Web. You may also talk with experts.

Once you narrow your choice to one or two models, you may price-shop by going from store to store or by letting your fingers do the walking through the *Yellow Pages,* computer catalogs, Internet search engines, newspaper ads, and the like. Searching for the lowest price involves a cost, primary the opportunity cost of your time. This cost will obviously vary from individual to individual and from item to item. Some people actually enjoy shopping, but this "shop-'til-you-drop" attitude does not necessarily carry over to all items. *For most of us, the process of gathering consumer information can be considered nonmarket work.*

Marginal Cost of Search. In your quest for product information, you gather the easy and obvious information first, such as the range of products on the market and where these products are sold. For example, you may check on the price and availability at the few computer stores at the mall. But as your search widens, the *marginal cost* of acquiring additional information increases, both because you may have to travel greater distances to check prices and services and because the opportunity cost of your time increases as you spend more time acquiring information. Consequently, the marginal cost curve for additional information slopes upward, as is shown in Exhibit 2. Note the assumption in Exhibit 2 is that some amount of information, as shown by I_f, is common knowledge and is freely available.

Marginal Benefit of Search. The *marginal benefit* from acquiring additional information is any improvement you uncover in the quality of the product of a given price or any reduction in the price of a product of given quality. The marginal benefit is relatively large at first, but as you gather more information and

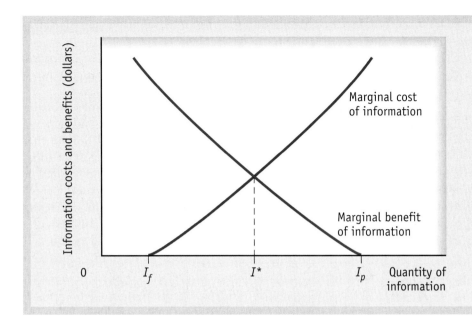

EXHIBIT 2

Optimal Search with Imperfect Information

When information is costly, additional information is acquired as along as its marginal benefit exceeds its marginal cost. Equilibrium, or optimal search, occurs where marginal benefit equals marginal cost.

grow more acquainted with the market, additional information yields less and less additional benefit. For example, the likelihood of uncovering valuable information, such as an attractive feature or a lower price, at the second store visited is greater than finding this information at the twentieth store visited. Thus the marginal benefit curve for additional information slopes downward, as is shown in Exhibit 2.

Optimal Search. Market participants will continue to gather information as long as the marginal benefit of additional information exceeds its marginal cost. *Optimal search occurs where the marginal benefit just equals the marginal cost,* which in Exhibit 2 occurs where the two curves intersect. Note that at search levels exceeding the equilibrium amount, the marginal benefit of additional information is still positive, but it's below the marginal cost. Note also that at some point the value of additional information reaches zero, as identified by I_p on the horizontal axis. This level of information could be identified as complete information or *perfect information*. The high marginal cost of acquiring I_p, however, makes it impractical to become perfectly informed. Thus firms and consumers, by gathering the optimal amount of information, I^*, have less-than-perfect information about the price, availability, and quality of products and resources.

Implications. The search model we have presented was developed by George Stigler, winner of the Nobel prize in 1982. Nearly four decades ago, he showed that the price of a product can differ among sellers because some consumers are unaware of lower prices offered by some sellers.[2] Thus, *search costs result in price dispersion, or different prices, for the same product.* Some sellers call attention to price dispersions by claiming to have the lowest prices around and by promising to

---

2 George Stigler, "The Economics of Information," *Journal of Political Economy* (June 1961): 213-225.

match any competitor's price. *Search costs also lead to quality differences across sellers, even for identically priced products, because consumers find it too costly to shop for a higher-quality product.*

There are other implications of Stigler's search model. The more expensive the commodity, the greater the price dispersion in dollar terms. Thus, the more expensive the item, the greater the incentive to shop around. Also, as the consumer's wage rises, the opportunity cost of time increases. This increases the marginal cost of additional information, resulting in less search and more price dispersion in the market. On the other hand, any change in technology that lowers the marginal cost of information will reduce the marginal cost of additional information, resulting in more information and less price dispersion. For example, some Internet search engines identify the lowest price for products offered by booksellers, airlines, computers, and dozens of other products. Some Internet sellers, such as Buycomp, maintain the lowest prices on the Web as a way of attracting customers carrying out such searches.

The Winner's Curse

In 1996 the federal government auctioned off leases to valuable space on the scarce radio spectrum. The space can be used for newly invented personal communications services, such as pocket telephones, portable fax machines, and wireless computer networks. The bidding was carried out in the face of much uncertainty about future competition in the industry, the potential size of the market, and future technological change. Thus bidders had little experience with the potential value of such leases. At the time, 89 companies made winning bids for 493 licenses, totaling $10.2 billion. But by 1998 it became clear that many of the winning bidders could not pay, and dozens of licenses were tied up in bankruptcy proceedings.[3] The auction eventually raised only half the amount of the winning bids. In auctions for products of uncertain value, such as wireless communications licenses or drilling rights in the Gulf of Mexico, why do many "winners" end up losers?

The actual value of space on the radio spectrum was unknown and could only be estimated. For example, suppose the average bid price was $10 million, with some companies bidding more and others bidding less. Suppose also that the winning bid was $20 million. The winning bid was not the average bid, which may have been the most reliable estimate of the true value, but the highest bid, which was the most optimistic estimate. Winners of such bids are said to experience the **winner's curse** because they often lose money after winning the bid. The winner's curse applies to all cases of bidding in which the true value is unknown at the outset. For example, movie companies often bid up the price of screenplays to what many argue are unrealistic values. Likewise, publishers get into bidding wars over book manuscripts and even book proposals that are little more than titles. Sports team owners bid for free agents and often overpay. CBS lost money on the 1998 Winter Olympics, and NBC may have overbid by offering $2.3 billion for the rights to broadcast the Olympics in the years 2002, 2006, and 2008; at the time of the bid, Olympic cities had not yet been selected. If there were perfect information about the market value of a resource, potential buyers would never bid more than the market value. But when

Winner's curse The plight of the winning bidder for an asset of uncertain value who has overestimated the asset's true value

---

3 See Scott Ritter, "FCC Says Several Bidders to Return Wireless Licenses," *Wall Street Journal* (18 June 1998).

competitive bidding is coupled with imperfect information, the winning bidder often loses money on the deal.

ASYMMETRIC INFORMATION IN PRODUCT MARKETS

Thus far we have considered the effects of costly information and limited information on market behavior. The issue becomes more complicated when one side of the market has more reliable information than does the other side, a situation in which there is **asymmetric information.** This section examines several examples of asymmetric information in the product market and the effect on market efficiency.

There are two types of information that a market participant may want but lack. First, one side of the market may know more about *characteristics* of the product for sale than the other side knows. For example, the seller of a used car knows more about that car's record of reliability than does the buyer. Likewise, the buyer of a health insurance policy knows more about his or her general state of health than does the insurance company. When one side of the market knows more than the other side about product characteristics that are important in the transaction, the asymmetric information problem involves **hidden characteristics.**

A second type of asymmetric information problem occurs when one side of a transaction can pursue an *action* that affects the other side but that cannot be observed by the other side. For example, the mechanic you hire to check out that strange noise in your car engine may undertake unneeded repairs, charging three hours' work for a job that should have taken only 10 minutes. Whenever one side of an economic relationship can take a relevant action that the other side cannot observe, the situation is described as one of **hidden actions.**

Hidden Characteristics: Adverse Selection

One type of hidden-characteristic situation occurs when sellers know more about the quality of the product than do buyers, such as with the market for used cars. The seller of a used car normally has abundant experience with important *characteristics* of that car: breakdowns, accidents, gas mileage, record of maintenance, performance in bad weather, and so on. A prospective buyer can only guess at these based on the car's appearance and perhaps a test drive. The buyer cannot really know how good the car is without driving it for several months under varying traffic and weather conditions. So buyers of used cars have less information than sellers do.

To simplify the problem, suppose there are only two types of used cars for sale: good ones and bad ones, or "lemons." Again, only the seller knows which type is for sale. Suppose that a buyer who is certain about a car's type would be willing to pay $10,000 for a good used car but only $4,000 for a lemon. A buyer who believes that half the used cars on the market are good ones and half are lemons would be willing to pay, say, $7,000 for a car of unknown type (the average perceived value of cars on the market). Would $7,000 be the equilibrium price of used cars?

So far, the analysis has ignored the actions of potential sellers, who know which type of cars they have. Since sellers of good cars can get only $7,000 for

Asymmetric information A situation in which one side of the market has more reliable information than the other side does

Hidden characteristics A type of asymmetric information problem in which one side of the market knows more than the other side about product characteristics that are important to the other side of the market

Hidden actions A type of asymmetric information when one side of an economic relationship can take a relevant action that the other side cannot observe cars they know to be worth $10,000 on average, many will choose not to sell their cars or will sell them to friends or relatives. But sellers of lemons will find $7,000 an attractive price, since they know their cars are worth only $4,000 on average. As a result, the proportion of good cars on the market will fall and the proportion of lemons will increase, reducing the average value of available used cars.

As buyers come to realize that the mix has shifted toward lemons, they will reduce the amount they are willing to pay for a car of unknown quality. As the market price of used cars falls, potential sellers of good cars become even more reluctant to sell at such a low price, so the proportion of lemons increases still more, leading to lower prices still. The process could continue until there were very few good cars sold on the open market. More generally, *when sellers have better information about a product's quality than buyers do, lower-quality products tend to dominate the market.*

When those on the informed side of the market self-select in a way that harms the uninformed side of the market, the problem is one of **adverse selection.** In our example, car sellers, the informed parties, self-select—that is, decide whether to offer their cars for sale—in a way that increases the percentage of lemons for sale. Because of this adverse selection, car buyers, the uninformed side of the market, end up trading primarily with owners of lemons—exactly the group buyers do not want to deal with.

Hidden Actions: Principal-Agent Problem

In this age of specialization, there are many tasks we do not do for ourselves because others do them better and because others have a lower opportunity cost of time. Suppose your objective is to get your car repaired, but you don't know how to repair it yourself. The mechanic you hire may have other objectives, such as maximizing on-the-job leisure or maximizing the garage's revenue. But the mechanic's actions are hidden from you. Even though your car may have only a loose electrical wire, the mechanic could inflate the bill by charging you for "repairs" that were not really needed or that were not performed. This asymmetric information problem occurs because one side of a transaction can pursue *hidden actions* that affect the other side. When buyers have difficulty monitoring and evaluating the quality of goods or services purchased, some suppliers may substitute poor-quality resources or exercise less diligence in providing the service.

The problem that arises from hidden actions is called the **principal-agent problem,** which describes a relationship in which one party, known as the **principal,** makes a contractual agreement with another party, known as the **agent,** in the expectation that the agent will act on behalf of the principal. *The problem arises when the goals of the agent are incompatible with those of the principal and when the agent can pursue hidden actions.* You could confront a principal-agent problem when you deal with a doctor, lawyer, auto mechanic, or financial advisor, to name a few. Any employer-employee relationship could potentially be a source of a principal-agent problem. The owners of a corporation are the principals and the managers are the agents. Again, the problem arises because the agent's objectives are not the same as the principal's *and* because the agent's actions are hidden. Not all principal-agent relationships pose a problem. For

---

Adverse selection A situation in which those on the informed side of the market self-select in a way that harms the uninformed side of the market

Principal-agent problem A situation in which the agent's objectives differ from those of the principal's objectives and the agent can pursue hidden actions

Principal A person who enters into a contractual agreement with an agent in the expectation that the agent will act on behalf of the principal

Agent A person who performs work or provides a service on behalf of another person, the principal example, when you hire someone to mow your lawn or cut your hair, there are no hidden actions and you are able to judge the results.

Asymmetric Information in Insurance Markets

Asymmetric information also creates problems in insurance markets. For example, from an insurance company's point of view, ideal candidates for health insurance are those who will lead long, healthy lives, then die peacefully in their sleep. But many people are poor risks for health insurers because of hidden characteristics (bad genes) or hidden actions (smoking and drinking excessively, getting exercise only on trips to the refrigerator, and thinking a seven-course meal consists of beef jerky and a six-pack of beer). In the insurance market, it is the buyers, not the sellers, who have more information about the characteristics and actions that predict their likely need for insurance in the future.

If the insurance company has no way of distinguishing among applicants, it must charge those who are poor health risks the same premiums as those who are good health risks. This rate is attractive to poor health risks, but will seem too high to good health risks, some of whom will choose to self-insure. As the number of healthy people who self-insure increases, the insurance pool becomes less healthy on average, so rates must rise, making insurance even less attractive to healthy people. Because of adverse selection, insurance buyers tend to be less healthy than the population as a whole. Adverse selection has been used as an argument for a universal national health insurance program.

The insurance problem is compounded by the fact that once people buy insurance, their behavior may change in a way that increases the probability that a claim will be made. For example, after buying theft insurance, people may take less care of their valuables. This incentive problem is referred to as *moral hazard*. **Moral hazard** occurs when an individual's behavior changes in a way that increases the likelihood of an unfavorable outcome.

More generally, *moral hazard is a principal-agent problem since it occurs when those on one side of a transaction have an incentive to shirk their responsibilities because the other side is unable to observe them.* The responsibility could be to repair a car or to safeguard valuables. In the car-repair example, the mechanic is the agent; in the insurance example, the policy buyer is the principal. Both the mechanic and the policy buyer may take advantage of the ignorant party. Thus moral hazard arises on the part of the party that can undertake hidden action; this could be either the agent or the principal, depending on the circumstance.

Moral hazard A situation in which one party to a contract has an incentive after the contract is made to alter behavior in a way that harms the other party to the contract

Coping with Asymmetric Information

There are ways of reducing the consequences of asymmetric information. An incentive structure or an information-revealing system can be developed to reduce the problems associated with the lopsided availability of information. For example, some states have passed "lemon laws" that offer compensation to buyers of new or used cars that turn out to be lemons. Used-car dealers also usually offer warranties to reduce the buyer's risk of getting stuck with a lemon. Some auto-repair garages provide written estimates before a job is done and return the defective parts to the customer as evidence that the repair was necessary and was carried out. Consumers often get multiple estimates for major expenditures and may seek second and third opinions on medical procedures.

Health insurance companies deal with adverse selection and moral hazard in a variety of ways. Most require applicants to take a physical exam and to answer questions about their medical histories. A policy often covers all those in a group, such as all company employees, not just those who would otherwise self-select. Such group policies avoid the problem of adverse selection. Insurers reduce moral hazard by making the policyholder pay, say, the first $250 of a claim as a "deductible" or by requiring the policyholder to pay a certain percentage of a claim. Also, the premiums on some automobile and theft policies go up, and policies may be canceled as more claims are filed.

ASYMMETRIC INFORMATION IN LABOR MARKETS

Our market analysis for particular kinds of labor typically assumed that workers are identical. In equilibrium, each worker in a particular labor market is assumed to be paid the same wage, a wage that is equal to the marginal revenue product of the last unit of labor hired. But what if ability differs across workers?

Differences in worker ability present no particular problem as long as these differences can be readily observed by the employer. If the productivity of each particular worker is easily quantified through a measure such as the quantity of oranges picked, the number of garments sewed, or the number of cars sold, that measure itself can and does serve as the basis for pay. But because production often takes place through the coordinated efforts of several workers, the employer may not be able to attribute specific outputs to each particular worker. Because information about each worker's marginal productivity is hard to come by, employers usually pay workers by the hour rather than keep track of each worker's contribution to total output.

Often the pay is some combination of an hourly rate and incentive pay linked to a measure of productivity. For example, a sales representative typically receives a base salary plus a commission tied to the amount sold. At times, the task of evaluating performance is left to the consumer rather than to the firm. Workers who provide personal services, such as waiters and waitresses, barbers and beauticians, pizza deliverers, and bellhops, are paid partly in tips. Since these services are by definition "personal," customers are in the best position to judge the quality and timeliness of service and to tip accordingly.

Adverse-Selection Problems in Labor Markets

An adverse-selection problem arises in the labor market when labor suppliers have better information about their own productivities than do employers, because a worker's ability is not easily observed prior to employment. Before the individual is hired, a worker's true abilities—motivation, work habits, skills, ability to get along with others, and the like—are, to a large extent, *hidden characteristics*.

Suppose an employer wants to hire a program coordinator for a new project, a job that calls for imagination, organizational skills, and the ability to work independently. The employer would like to attract the most qualified person in the market, but the qualities demanded are not directly observable. The employer offers a market wage for such a position. Individual workers have a good idea of their own intelligence and creativity and are able to evaluate this wage in view of their own abilities and opportunities. Talented people will find that wage to be below the true value of their abilities and will be less inclined to apply for the job. Less-talented individuals, however, will find that the offered wage exceeds their marginal productivity, so they will be more likely to seek the job. Because of adverse selection, the employer ends up with a pool of applicants of below-average ability. In a labor market with hidden characteristics, employers might be better off offering a higher wage. The higher the wage, the more attractive the job is to more-qualified workers. Paying a higher wage also encourages workers not to goof off or otherwise do anything that would risk losing an attractive job. So paying a high wage gets at the problem of hidden actions by workers. Paying a higher wage to attract and retain more-productive workers is called paying **efficiency wages,** a theory also discussed in macroeconomics.

> **Efficiency wage theory** The idea that offering high wages attracts a more talented labor pool, making it easier for firms to hire more productive workers; also a higher wage that encourages those more productive workers to do a good job

Signaling and Screening
The side of the market with hidden characteristics and hidden actions has an incentive to say the right thing. For example, a job applicant might say, "Hire me because I am hard-working, reliable, prompt, highly motivated, and just an all-around great employee." Or a producer might say, "At Ford, quality is job one." But such direct claims of quality appear self-serving and therefore are not necessarily believable. So both sides of the market have an incentive to develop credible ways of communicating reliable information.

Therefore, adverse selection may give rise to **signaling,** which is the attempt by the informed side of the market to communicate information that the other side would find valuable. Consider signaling in the job market. Because the true requirements for many jobs are qualities that are unobservable on a résumé or in an interview, job applicants offer evidence of the unobservable features by relying on proxy measures, such as years of education, college grades, and letters of recommendation. A proxy measure is called a *signal,* which is an observable indicator of some hidden characteristic. A signal is sent by the informed side of the market to the uninformed side and will serve as a useful way of sorting out applicants as long as less qualified applicants have more difficulty sending the signal.

> **Signaling** Using a proxy measure to communicate information about unobservable characteristics; the signal is more effective if more productive workers find it easier to send the signal than do less productive workers

In order to identify the best workers, employers try to *screen* applicants. **Screening** is the attempt by the uninformed side of the market to uncover the relevant but hidden characteristics of the informed party. An initial screen might be to check each résumé for spelling and typographical errors. Although not important in themselves, such errors indicate a lack of attention to detail—attention to detail that could prove important on the job. The uninformed party must find signals that less-productive individuals will have more difficulty sending. A signal that can be sent with equal ease or difficulty by all workers, regardless of their productivity, does not provide a useful way of screening applicants. But if, for example, more productive workers find it easier to succeed in college than do less-productive workers, a good college record is a measure worth using to screen workers. In this case, education may be valuable, not so much because of its effects on a worker's productivity, but because it enables employers to distinguish among types of workers. To summarize, an employer often cannot directly measure the potential productivity of job applicants, so the employer must rely

> **Screening** The process used by employers to select the most qualified workers based on readily observable characteristics, such as level of education and course grades

on some proxy to screen applicants. The most valuable proxy is one that best reflects future productivity.

The problems of adverse selection, signaling, and screening are discussed in the following case study of McDonald's.

The Reputation of a Big Mac

McDonald's has over 15,000 restaurants and is opening more than 500 a year. The secret to their success is that customers can count on product consistency whether they are buying a Big Mac in Anchorage, Moscow, or Singapore. McDonald's has grown because it has attracted competent and reliable franchise owners and has provided these owners with appropriate incentives and constraints.

To avoid adverse selection, McDonald's seldom advertises for franchisees, but it still averages more than 10 applicants for each new franchise. To be granted an interview, applicants must show sufficient financial resources and adequate business experience. Those who pass an initial screening must come up with a security deposit and must complete the 12- to 18-month training program. During this period, the individual is paid nothing, not even expenses. Some who complete the training are rejected for a franchise. Those accepted may wait up to three years for their own restaurants. Once the restaurant opens, a franchisee is required to work full-time in its daily operation and is also encouraged to become involved in community service.

Franchisees make a huge commitment of time and money. Forty percent of the $400,000 to $675,000 cost of a new restaurant must come from the franchisee's own savings, not from borrowed funds. Thus the franchisee has a clear financial stake in the success of the operation. And the fact that the potential franchisee saved so much reflects some financial competence.

The franchisee cannot sell the restaurant without prior approval and the company retains the right to better any offer for the restaurant. Any buyer must have company approval and must complete the same training program as all other franchisees.

Because each franchisee gets a large share of the restaurant's operating profit, there is a strong incentive to be efficient. As a further reward, successful operators may get additional restaurants. If all goes well, the franchise is valid for 20 years and renewable after that, but it can be canceled *at any time* if the restaurant fails the company's standards of quality, pricing, cleanliness, hours of operation, and so on. Thus, the franchisee is bound to the company by highly specific investments of money and time, such as the time required to learn McDonald's operating system. The loss of a franchise could represent the loss of the individual's life savings. In selecting and monitoring franchisees, McDonald's has successfully addressed problems stemming from hidden characteristics and hidden actions.

Source: D. L. Noren, "The Economics of the Golden Arches," *American Economist* (Fall 1990): 60–64; Richard Gibson, "McDonald's Sales Fail to Meet Projected Plans and Ad Outlays, *Wall Street Journal Interactive Edition* (10 April 1998); Dana Canedy, "McDonald's Alters System for Kitchens," *New York Times* (27 March 1998); and McDonald's home page at http://www.mcdonalds.com/.

CONCLUSION

The firm has evolved through a natural selection process as the form of organization that minimizes both transaction and production costs. According to this theory of natural selection, those forms of organization that are most efficient will be selected by the economic system for survival. Attributes that yield an economic profit will thrive, and those that do not will fall by the wayside. The form of organization selected may not be optimal in the sense that it cannot be improved upon, but it will be the most efficient of those that have been tried. If there is a way to organize production that is more efficient than the firm, some entrepreneur will stumble upon it one day and will be rewarded with greater profit. Thus the improvement may not be the result of any conscious design. Once a more efficient way of organizing production is uncovered, others will imitate the successful innovation.

Problems created by asymmetric information are not reflected in the simple account of how markets work. In conventional demand-and-supply analysis, trades occur in impersonal markets, and the buyer has no special concern about who is on the selling side. But with asymmetric information, the mix and characteristics of the other side of the market become important. When the problem of adverse selection is severe enough, some markets may cease to function. Market participants try to overcome the limitations of asymmetric information by signaling, screening, and trying to be quite explicit and transparent about the terms of the transaction.

SUMMARY

1. According to Ronald Coase, firms exist because production often can be accomplished more efficiently through the hierarchy of the firm than through a series of market transactions. Because production requires the extensive coordination of transactions among many resource owners, all this activity can usually be carried out more efficiently under the direction of a manager in a firm than by consumers specifying detailed performance contracts with many separate suppliers.

2. The extent to which a firm integrates vertically will depend on both the transaction and the production costs of economic activity. Other things constant, the firm is more likely to buy a component part than to produce it if (1) the item can be purchased for less than the firm would spend to make it, (2) the item is well defined and its quality is easily observable, and (3) there are many suppliers of the item. Economies of scope exist when it is cheaper to produce two or more types of products in one firm than to produce them in separate firms.

3. A buyer acquires additional information as long as the marginal benefit exceeds the marginal cost of searching for that information. In equilibrium, the marginal cost of information equals the marginal benefit. Because information is costly, the same good may be offered for different prices by different sellers.

4. Asymmetric information occurs when one side of the market is better informed about the quality of a product than the other side. The uninformed party may not know about hidden characteristics or about hidden actions. Because of adverse selection, those on the uninformed side of the market may find they are dealing with exactly the wrong people.

5. When the productivity of potential employees is not directly observable, employers sometimes try to screen workers based on some signal that more productive workers can send more easily than less productive workers can.

QUESTIONS FOR REVIEW

1. *(Rationale for the Firm)* Explain Ronald Coase's theory of why firms exist. Why isn't all production consolidated in one large firm?

2. *(Bounds of the Firm)* Define vertical integration. What factors should a firm consider when determining the degree of vertical integration to undertake?

3. *(Bounds of the Firm)* Ashland Oil, Inc., is an oil refiner that buys its crude oil in the market. Larger oil companies, such as Texaco, have their own crude oil production facilities. Why do some oil companies drill for their own crude oil and others buy crude oil in the market?

4. *(CaseStudy: The Trend Toward Outsourcing)* In the movement to downsize government, advocates often recommend turning over some government services to private firms hired by the government. What are the potential benefits and costs of such outsourcing? Prepare your answer by reviewing The Outsourcing Institute's "Top 10 Reasons Companies Outsource" at http://www.outsourcing.com/howandwhy/top10.

5. *(Economies of Scope)* Distinguish between economies of scale and economies of scope. Why do some firms produce multiple product lines, while others produce only one?

6. *(Search with Imperfect Information)* Fifty years ago, people shopped by mail using catalogs from large mail-order houses. In the last few years, catalog shopping has again become a widely used method of buying. On-line shopping is also growing. What reasons can you suggest for the growth in these forms of shopping?

7. *(Asymmetric Information)* Define asymmetric information. Distinguish between hidden characteristics and hidden actions. Which type of asymmetric information contributes to the principal-agent problem?

8. *(The Principal-Agent Problem)* Discuss the nature of the principal-agent problem. Determine which is the principal and which is the agent in each of the following relationships:
   a. A firm that produces export goods and the export management company that helps market its goods
   b. The management of a firm and its stockholders
   c. A homeowner and the plumber hired to make repairs
   d. A dentist and a patient
   e. An employee-pension management firm and the company using its services

9. *(Adverse Selection and Moral Hazard)* Describe the problems faced by health insurance companies as a result of adverse selection and moral hazard. How do insurance companies try to reduce these problems?

10. *(Signaling)* Give an example of signaling in each of the following situations:
   a. Choosing a doctor
   b. Applying to graduate school
   c. Filling out a form for a dating service

11. *(Signaling and Screening)* What roles do signaling and screening play in a labor market with asymmetric information?

12. *(CaseStudy: The Reputation of a Big Mac)* Explain how the time and financial requirements involved in obtaining a McDonald's franchise relate to the hidden-characteristics problem. Why would each franchise owner have an interest in the maintenance of high application standards for new franchise owners?

PROBLEMS AND EXERCISES

13. *(Search with Imperfect Information)* The following questions concern the accompanying graph.
   a. Identify the two curves shown on the graph, and explain their upward or downward slopes.
   b. Why does curve A intersect the horizontal axis?
   c. What is the significance of quantity *d*?
   d. What does point *e* represent?
   e. How would the optimal quantity of information change if the marginal benefit of information increased; that is, if the marginal benefit curve shifted upward?

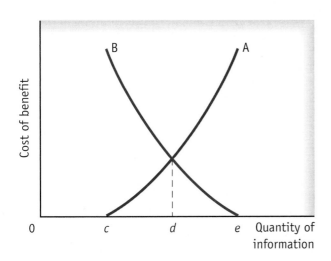

14. *(Search with Imperfect Information)* Determine the effect of each of the following on the optimal level of search.
    a. The consumer's income increases.
    b. One seller guarantees to offer the lowest price on the market.
    c. The technology of gathering and transmitting information improves.

EXPERIENTIAL EXERCISES

15. *(Market Behavior with Imperfect Information)* Kenneth Arrow, a Nobel laureate, has contributed many important ideas in the economics of information. Read the interview with Arrow in *The Region* at http://woodrow.mpls.frb.fed.us/pubs/region/int9512.html. What does he think are the policy implications that arise because of imperfect information?

16. *(Adverse Selection)* Adverse selection is a serious problem for health insurers. As an example, read the brief analysis in "Medical Savings Accounts for Medicare" at http://www.public-policy.org/~ncpa/ba/bal183.html. What is the mechanism by which adverse selection can make health insurance unprofitable for private insurers to provide?

17. *(Wall Street Journal)* Once you learn about the economics of asymmetric information, you begin to see examples all around you. To demonstrate this point, check today's *Wall Street Journal*. It should not be too hard to find a story that describes some new development that is a response to an asymmetric information problem. Look on the Economy page in the First Section or in the Marketplace section. When you've found an article, try to analyze it using the ideas developed in this chapter.

Economic Regulation and Antitrust Activity

Visit the McEachern
Interactive Study Center
for this chapter at
http://mcisc.swcollege.com

I f the invisible hand of competition yields such desirable results for the economy, why does the government need to stick its nose into people's business? When is monopoly good for the economy and when is it harmful? Who benefits most when government tries to regulate monopoly? Why is government so interested in Microsoft? Is the U.S. economy more competitive now than it used to be? Answers to these and other questions are addressed in this chapter, which discusses government regulation of business.

It has been said that business people praise competition but love monopoly. They praise competition because it harnesses the diverse and often conflicting objectives of various market participants and channels them into the efficient production of goods and services. And competition does this "as if by an invisible hand." Business people love monopoly because it provides the surest path to economic profit in the long run—and, after all, profit is the name of the game. The fruits of monopoly are so tempting that firms sometimes try to eliminate the competition or to conspire with them. As Adam Smith remarked more than 200 years ago, "People of the same trade seldom meet together, even for merriment or diversion, but the conversation ends in a conspiracy against the public, or in some contrivance to raise prices."

The tendency of firms to seek monopolistic advantage is understandable, but the pursuit of monopoly often harms the economy. Public policy can play a role by promoting competition in those markets where competition seems desirable and by reducing the harmful consequences of monopolistic behavior in those markets where the output can be most efficiently produced by one or a few firms. Topics discussed in this chapter include:

- Market power
- Regulating natural monopolies
- Theories of economic regulation
- Deregulation
- Antitrust activity
- Per-se illegality
- Rule of reason
- Merger movements
- Competitive trends

BUSINESS BEHAVIOR AND PUBLIC POLICY

You'll recall that a monopolist supplies a product with no close substitutes and so can charge a higher price than would prevail with more competition. When a few firms account for most of the sales in a market, those firms are sometimes able to coordinate their actions, either explicitly or implicitly, to approximate the behavior of a monopolist. This ability of one or more firms to maintain a price above the competitive level is termed **market power.** The presumption is that a monopoly or firms acting together as a monopoly will restrict output and charge a higher price than a competitive firm would. With output restricted, the marginal benefit of the final unit produced exceeds its marginal cost, so social welfare could be increased by expanding output. By failing to expand output to the point where marginal benefit equals marginal cost, monopoly misallocates resources.

Other distortions have also been associated with monopolies. For example, because monopolies are insulated from competition, many critics argue that they are not as innovative as aggressive competitors would be. Worse yet, because of their size and economic importance, monopolies have been said to exert a disproportionate influence on the political system, which they use to protect and enhance their monopoly power.

Government Regulation of Business

There are three kinds of government policies designed to alter or control firm behavior: social regulation, economic regulation, and antitrust activity. **Social regulation** consists of government measures designed to improve health and safety, such as control over unsafe working conditions and dangerous products. **Economic regulation** is concerned with controlling the price, the output, the entry of new firms, and the quality of service *in industries in which monopoly appears inevitable or even desirable.* The regulation of *natural monopolies,* such as local

Market power The ability of one or a few firms to maintain a price above the competitive level

Social regulation Government regulations aimed at improving health and safety

Economic regulation Government regulations aimed at controlling prices, output, market entry and exit, and product quality in situations in which, because of economies of scale, average production costs are lowest when the market is served by only one or a few firms electricity transmission and local phone service, is an example of this type of regulation. Several other industries, such as land and air transportation, have also been regulated, for reasons that will be discussed later in this chapter. Economic regulation is carried out by various regulatory bodies at the federal, state, and local levels.

Antitrust activity attempts to prohibit firm behavior aimed at monopolizing, or cartelizing, markets where competition is desirable. Antitrust activity is pursued in the courts by government attorneys and by individual firms that charge other firms with violating antitrust laws

Both economic regulation and antitrust activity will be examined in this chapter. The first type of economic regulation we consider is the regulation of natural monopolies.

Antitrust activity Government activity aimed at preventing monopoly and fostering competition in markets where competition is desirable

REGULATING NATURAL MONOPOLIES

Because of economies of scale, natural monopolies have a downward-sloping long-run average-cost curve over the entire range of market demand. This means that the lowest average cost is achieved when one firm serves the entire market. Local electricity transmission is an example of a good provided by a natural monopoly. If two competing electric transmission companies both strung their own wires throughout the community, the average cost per household would be higher than if a single provider wired the community.

Unregulated Profit Maximization

Exhibit 1 shows the demand and cost conditions for a natural monopoly. A natural monopoly usually faces large capital costs, such as those associated with laying the tracks for a railroad, putting a satellite in orbit, installing a natural gas pipeline, or stringing the wires to transmit electricity, local phone service, or cable TV signals. Because of heavy capital outlays, average cost tends to fall as production increases, so the average-cost curve slopes downward over a broad range of output. In this situation, the average cost of production is minimized when a single firm produces the market output.

We know that a monopolist, if unregulated, will choose the price-quantity combination that maximizes profit. In Exhibit 1, the monopolist maximizes profit by producing where marginal cost equals marginal revenue, which occurs at output level Q. The monopolist will charge price p and earn the economic profit identified by the purple-shaded rectangle. The problem is that the monopolist's choice of price and output is inefficient in terms of social welfare: Consumers pay a price that exceeds the marginal cost of producing the good. Economic welfare would improve if output were to expand, because the marginal value of additional output exceeds the marginal cost of that output.

Government has four options when dealing with a natural monopoly. First, government can do nothing. If left alone, a monopolist will maximize profits, as at price p in Exhibit 1, so inefficiency results. Second, government can sell the monopoly right to this market, such as the right to run concession stands at the municipal stadium. The winning bidder would still maximize profit at price p in Exhibit 1, but at least the winning monopolist would pay for the privilege, in the process increasing government revenue, which can be used to fund public goods or reduce taxes. Third, the government can own and operate the monopoly, as with the Tennessee Valley Authority, many urban electricity and transit systems, and state-run lotteries and liquor stores. And fourth, government can *regulate* a privately operated monopoly, as it does with local phone services. Government-owned or -regulated industries are called *public utilities*. The focus in this chapter will be on government regulation rather than government ownership, although the issues discussed are similar whether the government operates as a monopoly or regulates the monopoly. Many facets of a natural monopoly have been regulated, but the object of regulation that captures the most attention is the monopolist's price-output combination.

Setting Price Equal to Marginal Cost

Let's assume that government regulators decide to make the monopolist produce at the level of output that is allocatively efficient—that is, where price, or marginal value, equals marginal cost. Such a price-output combination is depicted as point *e* in Exhibit 1, where price equals marginal cost, yielding a price *p'* and quantity *Q'*. Consumers will clearly prefer this outcome because the

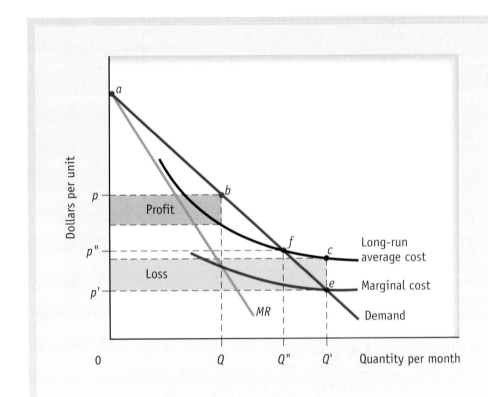

EXHIBIT 1

Regulating the Natural Monopoly

In a natural monopoly, the long-run average-cost curve slopes downward at its point of intersection with the market-demand curve. The unregulated firm produces output *Q* (where marginal cost equals marginal revenue) and charges price *p*. This situation is inefficient because price, or marginal benefit, exceeds marginal cost. To obtain the efficient level of output, government could regulate the monopolist's price. At price *p'*, the monopoly would produce output *Q'*—an efficient solution. However, at that price and quantity, the firm would suffer a loss and require a subsidy. As an alternative, the government could set a price of *p"*. The monopoly would produce output *Q"*—an inefficient level. Since *p"* equals the average cost, the firm would earn a normal profit and no subsidy would be required.

price is lower than when the monopolist is free to maximize profit. The consumer surplus, a measure of consumers' net gain from consuming this good, increases from triangle *abp* with profit maximization to *aep'* with regulation.

Notice, however, that the monopolist now has a problem. At output level Q', the regulated price, p', is below the firm's average total cost, identified as point c. Rather than earning a profit, the monopolist now suffers a loss, identified by the red-shaded rectangle. *Forcing the natural monopolist to produce where marginal cost equals price results in an economic loss.* In the long run, the monopolist would go out of business rather than continue suffering such a loss.

Subsidizing the Natural Monopolist

How can regulators encourage the monopolist to stay in business and yet produce where marginal cost equals price? One way is for the government to compensate the monopolist for the losses—to *subsidize* the firm so that it earns a normal profit. Bus and subway fares are typically set below the average cost of providing the service; the difference is made up through a government subsidy. For example, in 1996 the Washington, D.C., subway system received over $200 million in subsidies from the federal government; Amtrak also receives substantial federal subsidies. One problem with the subsidy solution is that, to provide the subsidy, the government must raise taxes, borrow more, or forgo spending in some other area.

Setting Price Equal to Average Cost

Although some public utilities are subsidized, most are not. Instead, the regulators attempt to establish a price that will provide the monopolist with a "fair return." Recall that the average-total-cost curve includes a normal profit. Thus, *setting price equal to average total cost* provides a normal, or "fair," profit for the monopolist. In Exhibit 1, the demand curve and the average cost curve intersect at point f, yielding a price of p'' and a quantity of Q''. Such a price will allow the monopolist to stay in business without a subsidy.

Setting price equal to average total cost enhances economic welfare relative to the unregulated situation, but the regulated monopolist would rather earn an economic profit. If given no other choice, however, the monopolist will continue to operate with a normal profit, since that is what could be earned if the resources were redirected to their most profitable alternative uses. Also, the marginal value that consumers attach to output level Q'' exceeds the marginal cost of that output level. Therefore social welfare could be enhanced by expanding output until consumers' marginal value equals the marginal cost of production at e.

The Regulatory Dilemma

Setting price equal to marginal cost yields the *socially optimal* allocation of resources because *the marginal cost of producing the last unit sold equals the consumers' marginal value of that last unit.* For example, suppose the price of subway tokens is 50 cents, which is the marginal cost per rider on the subway system. With this pricing policy, however, the monopolist will face recurring losses unless a subsidy is provided. These losses disappear if price is set equal to average cost, which for the subway system is, say, $1.50. That higher price ensures that the monopolist earns a normal profit, but ridership is much lower than would be socially optimal. Thus the dilemma facing regulators is whether to require a price equal to marginal cost, which is socially optimal but which would require a subsidy, or to allow the monopolist to break even by setting price equal to average cost but thereby restrict ridership well below the socially optimal level. There is no right answer. Compared to point *b*, the outcome without regulation, either point *f* or point *e* reduces price, increases output, increases consumer surplus, eliminates economic profit, and increases social welfare.

Although Exhibit 1 neatly lays out the options, regulators usually face an unclear picture of things. Demand and costs can only be estimated, and the regulated firm may not always be completely forthcoming about cost information. For example, a utility may overstate its costs so it can charge a higher price and earn more profit.

ALTERNATIVE THEORIES OF ECONOMIC REGULATION

Why does government regulate certain markets? Why not let market forces allocate resources? There are two views of government regulation. The first view has been implicit in the discussion thus far—namely, that economic regulation is in the *public interest*. Economic regulation is designed to promote social welfare by controlling the price and output when a market is most efficiently served by one or just a few firms. A second view of economic regulation is that it is not in the public's, or consumers', best interest, but rather is in the *special interest* of producers. According to this view, *well-organized producer groups expect to profit from economic regulation and are able to persuade public officials to impose the restrictions existing producers find attractive, such as limiting entry into the industry or preventing competition among existing firms.* Individual producers have more to gain or lose from regulation than do individual consumers; producers typically are also better organized and more focused than consumers and therefore better able to bring about regulations that are favorable to them.

Producers Have a Special Interest in Economic Regulation

To understand how producer interests could influence public regulation, think back to the last time you got your hair cut. Most states regulate the training and licensing of hair professionals. If any new regulations affecting the profession are proposed, such as higher entry restrictions or longer training requirements, who do you suppose has more interest in the outcome of that legislation, you or a person who cuts hair for a living? *Producers have a strong interest in matters that affect their source of income, so they play a disproportionately large role in trying to influence such legislation.* If there are public hearings on haircut regulations, the industry will provide expert witnesses, while consumers will largely ignore the proceedings.

As a consumer, you do not specialize in getting haircuts. You purchase haircuts, socks, soft drinks, software, underwear, and thousands of other goods and services. You have no *special interest* in legislation affecting hair cutting. Some critics argue that because of this asymmetry between the interests of producers and consumers, business regulations often favor producer interests rather than consumer interests. Well-organized producer groups, as squeaky wheels in the legislative system, receive the most grease in the form of favorable regulations.

Legislation favoring producer groups is usually introduced under the guise of advancing consumer interests. Producer groups may argue that unbridled competition in their industry would lead to results that are undesirable for consumers. For example, the alleged problem of "cutthroat" competition among taxi drivers has led to regulations that eliminate price competition and limit the number of taxis in most large metropolitan areas. Or regulation may appear under the guise of quality control, as in the case of state control of professional groups such as barbers, doctors, and lawyers, in which case regulations are viewed as necessary to keep unlicensed "quacks" out of these professions.

The special-interest theory may be valid even when the initial intent of the legislation is in the consumer interest. Over time, the regulatory machinery may begin to act more in accord with the special interests of producers, because producers' political power and strong stake in the regulatory outcome lead them, in effect, to "capture" the regulating agency and prevail upon it to serve producers. This *capture theory* of regulation was best explained by George Stigler, the Nobel prize winner mentioned in the previous chapter, who argued that "as a general rule, regulation is acquired by the industry and is designed and operated for its benefit."[1]

Perhaps it would be useful at this point to discuss in some detail the direction that economic regulation and, more recently, deregulation has taken in a particular industry—airlines.

Airline Regulation and Deregulation

CaseStudy

Public Policy

A review of the history of airline deregulation from a conservative viewpoint is available online from the Heritage Foundation's magazine at http://www.heritage.org/library/backgrounder/bg1173es.html. What actions was the Department of Transportation considering at the time this review was written? What non-regulatory alternatives does the author suggest? The concerns of airline pilots about employment security and getting what they see as their fair share of industry revenues are presented through the Airline Pilots' Association Web site at http://www.alpa.org/. What particular issues related to industry structure are of current concern to the pilots?

The interstate airline business was once closely regulated by the Civil Aeronautics Board (CAB), established in 1938. Any potential entrant interested in serving an interstate route had to persuade the CAB that the route needed another airline, a task that proved impossible. During the 40 years prior to deregulation, more than 150 applications for long-distance routes were submitted by potential entrants, *but not a single new interstate airline was allowed.* The CAB also forced strict compliance with regulated prices. A request to lower prices on any route would result in a rate hearing, during which the request was scrutinized by both the CAB and competitors. In effect, the CAB had created a cartel that fixed prices among the 10 existing major airlines.

Although the CAB prohibited price competition in the industry, *nonprice competition flourished.* Airlines competed on the basis of the frequency of flights, the quality of meals, the width of the seats, even the friendliness of the staff. For example, American Airlines put Wurlitzer pianos in its jumbo jet lounges. United Airlines countered with wine tastings and guitarists. Such competition

---

1 George Stigler, "The Theory of Economic Regulation," *Bell Journal of Economics and Management Science* (Spring 1971):3.

increased operating costs. Costs rose until firms in the industry earned only a normal rate of return. Thus, *air fares set above competitive levels, coupled with entry restrictions, were no guarantee of economic profit as long as airlines were free to compete in other ways, such as in the frequency of flights.*

The CAB did not regulate airlines that flew *intrastate* routes. The record shows that fares on intrastate airlines were about 50 percent below fares on identical routes flown by regulated airlines. So regulated airlines were more costly to consumers.

Airline Deregulation. In 1978, despite opposition from the major airlines and relevant labor unions, Congress passed the Airline Deregulation Act, which reduced restrictions on price competition and on new entry. By 1990, airline fares in inflation-adjusted dollars were about 10 to 18 percent lower because of deregulation. The fall in fares contributed to a doubling of passenger miles flown. The savings to travelers are estimated to exceed $12 billion per year. The airlines could afford to lower fares because they became more productive by adding more seats to planes and by filling a greater percentage of seats. The hub-and-spoke system developed under deregulation also allowed airlines to route planes more efficiently. Airline routes used to be straight lines from one city to another. Now they radiate like the spokes of a wagon wheel from a "hub" city. From 29 hub airports across the country, airlines send out planes along the spokes to the 400 commercial airports, then quickly bring them back to the hubs.

The insulation from price competition provided by regulation allowed firms to pay higher wages than they would have in a more competitive industry. The Air Line Pilots Association, the union that represented pilots for all the major airlines prior to deregulation, had been able to negotiate extremely attractive wages for its members, annual wages that reached into six digits for working less than two weeks a month (many pilots had so much free time, they pursued second careers). Just how attractive a pilot's position was became apparent after deregulation. America West Airlines, a nonunion firm that sprouted from deregulation, paid its pilots only $32,000 a year and required them to work 40 hours a week, performing dispatch and marketing tasks when they were not flying. Yet America West received more than 4,000 applications for its 29 pilot openings.

Some critics of deregulation were concerned that the government would lose the control it had, under regulation, over the quality and safety of airline service. Despite the demise of the CAB, however, the Federal Aviation Administration (FAA) still regulates the safety and quality of air service. And the Department of Transportation has the authority to stop any unfair practices. Research indicates that between 1979 and 1990, accident rates declined by anywhere from 10 to 45 percent, depending on the specific measure used. What's more, the lower fares encouraged more people to fly rather than drive, thereby saving lives that would have been lost driving (per passenger mile, flying is about twenty times safer than driving).

Another concern was that smaller communities would no longer be served by a deregulated industry. This has not been a problem; commuter airlines have replaced major airlines in servicing smaller communities. Because of the hub-and-spoke system, the number of scheduled departures from smaller cities and rural communities has actually increased by 35 percent.

Airport Capacity Has Restricted Competition. But competitive trends in the airline industry in recent years raise some troubling questions. Although airline traffic nearly doubled in the 1980s, no new airports were opened during that decade (Denver has since opened a new airport) and the air traffic control system did not expand. Airports and air traffic controllers are provided by the government. Thus, *the government did not follow up deregulation with an expansion of airport capacity.* Consequently, departure gates and landing rights became the scarce resources in the industry. Those airlines unable to secure such facilities at major airports went out of business. Some argue that the major airlines have not pushed for an expansion of airport facilities because additional capacity could encourage new entry and greater competition. Deregulation initially promoted a wave of new entry by such upstarts as People Express and New York Air. By the early 1990s, however, most of the new entrants had disappeared or had been absorbed by larger airlines. *New entrants could not acquire the necessary departure gates and landing slots at key airports.* A landing slot can sell for hundreds of thousands of dollars. The market share of the five largest airlines climbed from 63 percent before deregulation to 70 percent during the 1990s, and most key airports came to be dominated by a one or two airlines. For example, United and American control 82 percent of the landing slots at Chicago's O'Hare Airport, up from 66 percent in 1986. American and Delta control 83 percent of the slots at New York's Kennedy Airport, up from 43 percent in 1986. This concentration at certain hubs gives airlines some market power to raise prices; prices average about 5 percent more for trips involving concentrated hubs than more competitive airports

Foreign airlines can fly to and from U.S. cities from abroad, but cannot operate between U.S. cities. British-owned Virgin Atlantic, for example, would like to launch a low-cost airline in the United States but so far is prevented by law from doing so.

The federal government is concerned that some airlines may have acquired more landing slots and more long-term gate leases than they need simply as a way to block possible competitors from entering that market. In 1998 several major airlines announced plans to form alliances. Northwest bought a controlling interest in Continental. United planned an alliance with Delta. And American planned to tie its networks to Delta's. These airlines control 85 percent of the U.S. market.

Despite concerns about recent anticompetitive trends in the industry, deregulation has been quite beneficial for consumers. Few economists are calling for reregulation of the industry.

Sources: Steven Morrison and Clifford Winston, *The Evolution of the Airline Industry* (Washington, D.C.: Brookings Institution, 1995); "Come Fly with Me," *Economist* (20 June 1998); Bruce Ingersoll, "Administration's Plan for Hubs Is Target of Airlines' Media Blitz," *Wall Street Journal* (19 June 1998); and Matthew L. Wald, "U.S. Seeks to Curb Unfair Practices of Major Airlines," *New York Times* (7 April 1998).

The course of regulation and deregulation raises some interesting questions about the true objective of regulation. Recall the competing views of regulation: one holds that regulation is in the public, or consumer, interest; the other holds that regulation is in the special, or producer, interest. In the airline industry, regulation appeared more in accord with producer interests, and producer groups fought deregulation.

This concludes our discussion of economic regulation, which tries to reduce the harmful consequences of monopolistic behavior in those markets where the output can be most efficiently produced by one or a few firms. We now turn to antitrust activity, which aims to promote competition in those markets where competition seems desirable.

ANTITRUST LAW AND ENFORCEMENT

Although competition typically ensures the most efficient use of the nation's resources, an individual firm would prefer to operate as a monopoly. If left alone, some competing firms might try to create a monopolistic environment by driving competitors out of business, by merging with competitors, or by colluding with competitors. In the United States, *antitrust policy* is an attempt to curb these anticompetitive tendencies by (1) promoting the sort of market structure that will lead to greater competition and (2) reducing anticompetitive behavior. *Antitrust laws attempt to promote socially desirable market performance.*

Origins of Antitrust Policy

A variety of economic developments that occurred in the last half of the 19th century created a political climate supportive of antitrust legislation. Perhaps the two most important developments were (1) technological breakthroughs that led to more extensive use of capital and a larger optimal plant size in manufacturing industries and (2) reduced transportation cost as railroads increased from 9,000 miles of track in 1850 to 167,000 miles by 1890. *Economies of scale in production and the cheaper cost of transporting goods extended the geographical reach of markets.* So firms grew larger and reached wider markets.

Declines in the national economy in 1873 and in 1883, however, caused panics among these large manufacturers, who were now committed to large-scale production with heavy fixed costs. Their defensive reaction was to lower prices in an attempt to stimulate sales. Price wars erupted, creating economic turmoil. Firms desperately sought ways to stabilize their markets. One solution was for competing firms to form a *trust* by transferring their voting stock to a single board of trustees, which would vote in the interest of the entire group. Early trusts were formed in the sugar, tobacco, and oil industries. Although the activity of these early trusts is still a matter of debate today, they allegedly pursued anticompetitive practices to develop and maintain a dominant market position. Gradually the word "trust" came to represent any firm or group of firms that tried to monopolize a market.

These practices provoked widespread criticism and earned creators of trusts the derisive title of "robber barons." Public sentiment lay on the side of the smaller competitors. Farmers, especially, resented the higher prices of manufactured goods, which resulted from the trusts' activities, particularly since farm prices were declining through the latter part of the 19th century. At the time, agriculture accounted for 40 percent of the U.S. workforce and thus had political clout. Eighteen states, primarily agricultural, enacted *antitrust* laws in the 1880s, prohibiting the formation of trusts. But these laws were largely ineffective because the trusts could simply move across state lines to avoid them.

Sherman Antitrust Act of 1890. In 1888, the major political parties put antitrust planks in their platforms. This consensus culminated in the passage of the *Sherman Antitrust Act* of 1890, the first national legislation in the world against monopoly. The law prohibited the creation of trusts, restraint of trade, and monopolization, although it failed to define what constituted such activities. Enforcement of the law was hampered by its vague language.

Clayton Act of 1914. Ambiguous language in the Sherman Act let much anticompetitive activity slip by. The *Clayton Act* of 1914 was passed to outlaw certain practices not prohibited by the Sherman Act and to help government stop a potential monopoly before it developed. For example, the Clayton Act prohibits *price discrimination* when this practice tends to create a monopoly. You'll recall that price discrimination is charging different customers different prices for the same good or charging the same customer different prices for different quantities of a good. The Clayton Act also prohibits *tying contracts* and *exclusive dealing* if they substantially lessened competition. **Tying contracts** require the buyer of one good to purchase another good as well. For example, a seller of a patented machine might require customers to purchase other supplies from the seller as part of the deal. **Exclusive dealing** occurs when a producer will sell a product only if the buyer agrees not to purchase from other manufacturers. For example, a computer-chip maker might sell chips to a computer maker only if the computer maker agrees not to purchase chips elsewhere. The law also prohibited **interlocking directorates,** whereby the same individual serves on the boards of directors of competing firms. Finally, mergers through the acquisition of the stock of a competing firm were outlawed in cases in which the merger would substantially lessen competition. More on mergers later.

Federal Trade Commission Act of 1914. The *Federal Trade Commission (FTC)* was established in 1914 to help enforce antitrust laws. The commission consists of five full-time commissioners appointed by the president for seven-year terms and assisted by a staff of mostly lawyers and economists.

The Sherman, Clayton, and FTC acts provided the antitrust framework, a framework that has been clarified and embellished by subsequent amendments. A loophole in the Clayton Act was closed in 1950 with the passage of the *Celler-Kefauver Anti-Merger Act,* which prevents one firm from buying the assets of another firm if the effect is to reduce competition. This law can block both **horizontal mergers**, or the merging of firms that produce the same product, such as a merger between Coke and Pepsi, and **vertical mergers**, or the merging of firms where one supplies inputs to the other or demands output from the other, such as a merger between Microsoft and Dell Computer.

Antitrust Law Enforcement

Any law's effectiveness depends on the vigor and vigilance of enforcement. The pattern of antitrust enforcement goes something like this. Either the Antitrust Division of the Justice Department or the Federal Trade Commission charges a firm or group of firms with breaking the law. These government agencies are often acting on a complaint by a customer or a competitor. At that point, those charged with the wrongdoing may be able, without admitting guilt, to sign a **consent decree** whereby they agree not to continue doing what they had been charged with. If the charges are contested, evidence from both sides is pre-

---

Tying contract An arrangement in which a seller of one good requires buyers to purchase other goods as well

Exclusive dealing The situation that occurs when a producer prohibits customers from purchasing from other sellers

Interlocking directorate An arrangement whereby one individual serves on the boards of directors of competing firms

Horizontal merger A merger in which one firm combines with another firm that produces the same product

Vertical merger A merger in which one firm combines with another from which it purchases inputs or to which it sells output

Consent decree A legal agreement through which the accused party, without admitting guilt, agrees to refrain in the future from certain illegal activity if the government drops the charges sented in a court trial, and a decision is rendered by a judge. Certain decisions may be appealed all the way to the Supreme Court, and in such cases the Court may render new interpretations of existing law.

Per-Se Illegality and the Rule of Reason

The courts have interpreted antitrust laws in essentially two ways. One set of practices has been declared **per se illegal**—that is, without regard to economic rationale or consequences. For example, under the Sherman Act, all formal agreements among competing firms to fix prices, restrict output, or otherwise restrain the forces of competition are viewed as illegal *per se*. In order for the defendant to be found guilty under a per-se rule, the government need only show that the offending practice took place; thus, the government need only examine the firm's *behavior*.

Another set of practices falls under the **rule of reason.** Here the courts engage in a broader inquiry into the facts surrounding the particular offense—namely, the reasons why the offending practices were adopted and the effect of these practices on competition. The rule of reason was first set forth in 1911, when the Supreme Court held that Standard Oil had illegally monopolized the petroleum refining industry. Standard Oil allegedly had come to dominate 90 percent of the market by acquiring more than 120 former rivals and by implementing **predatory pricing** tactics to drive remaining rivals out of business, such as by temporarily selling below cost or dropping the price only in certain markets. In finding Standard Oil guilty, the Court focused on both the company's *behavior* and the *market structure* that resulted from that behavior. Based on this approach, the Court found that the company had behaved *unreasonably*.

But in 1920 the rule of reason led the Supreme Court to find U.S. Steel not guilty of monopolization. In that case, the Court ruled that not every contract or combination in restraint of trade was illegal—only those that "unreasonably" restrained trade violated antitrust laws. The Court said that *mere size was not an offense*. Although U.S. Steel clearly possessed market power, the company was not in violation of antitrust laws because, in the Court's view, it had not unreasonably used that power. The Court switched positions again 25 years later in reviewing the charges against the Aluminum Company of America (Alcoa). In a 1945 decision, the Supreme Court held that although a firm's conduct might be reasonable and legal, the mere possession of market power—Alcoa controlled 90 percent of the aluminum ingot market—violated the antitrust laws. Here the Court was using *market structure* rather than firm *behavior* as the test of legality.

Mergers and Public Policy

Some firms have pursued rapid growth by merging with other firms. In some industries, the *merging,* or joining together, of two firms has created oligopolies. Much of what the Antitrust Division does is approve or deny proposed mergers and acquisitions. In determining the possible detrimental effects a merger might have on competition, one important consideration is its impact on the share of sales accounted for by the largest firms. If a few firms account for a relatively large share of sales, the industry is considered to be *concentrated*. As a measure of sales concentration, the Justice Department uses the **Herfindahl index,** which is calculated by squaring the percent market share of each firm in the market and then adding those squares. For example, if the industry consists of 100 firms of

Per se illegal A category of illegality in antitrust law, applied to business practices that are deemed illegal regardless of their economic rationale or their consequences

Rule of reason A principle used by a court to examine the reasons for certain business practices and their effects on competition before ruling on their legality

Predatory pricing Pricing tactics employed by a dominant firm to drive competitors out of business, such as temporarily selling below cost or dropping the price only in certain markets

Herfindahl index The sum of the squared percentages of market share of all firms in an industry; a measure of the level of market concentration in that industry equal size, the Herfindahl index is 100 [$= 100 \times (1)^2$]. If the industry is a pure monopoly, the index is 10,000 [$= (100)^2$], the largest possible value. The more firms there are in the industry and the more equal in size the firms are, the smaller the Herfindahl index. This index gives greater weight to firms with larger market shares, as can be seen for the three examples presented in Exhibit 2. Note that the index for Industry III is nearly triple that for the two other industries.

The Justice Department's guidelines also sort all mergers into two types: *horizontal mergers*, which involve firms in the same market, and *nonhorizontal mergers*, which include all others. Of greatest interest for antitrust purposes are horizontal mergers, such as a merger between competing oil companies like Mobil and Exxon. The Justice Department generally challenges any merger in an industry where two conditions are met: (1) the post-merger Herfindahl index would exceed 1,800 and (2) the merger would increase the index by more than 100 points. Mergers in an industry that would have a post-merger index of less than 1,000 are seldom challenged. Other factors such as the ease of entry into the market are considered for intermediate cases.

Merger Movements

Over the last century there have been four major merger waves in this country. These merger waves are outlined in Exhibit 3. The first occurred between 1887 and 1904. Some of today's largest firms, including U.S. Steel and Standard Oil, were formed during this first merger movement. These tended to be horizontal mergers. For example, the firm that is today U.S. Steel was created in 1901 through a billion-dollar merger that involved dozens of individual steel producers and two-thirds of the industry's productive capacity. During this first wave, similar mergers occurred in Canada, Great Britain, and elsewhere, creating dominant firms, some of which still exist today.

EXHIBIT 2

Computation of the Herfindahl Index Based on Market Share in Three Industries

Firm	Industry I		Industry II		Industry III	
	Market Share (percent)	Market Share Squared	Market Share (percent)	Market Share Squared	Market Share (percent)	Market Share Squared
A	23	529	15	225	57	3,249
B	18	324	15	225	1	1
C	13	169	15	225	1	1
D	6	36	15	225	1	1
Remaining 40 firms (at 1 percent each)	1 each	40	1 each	40	1 each	40
Herfindahl Index		1,098		940		3,292

EXHIBIT 3

Merger Waves in the
Past Century

Wave	Years	Dominant Type of Merger	Examples
First	1887–1904	Horizontal	U.S. Steel, Standard Oil
Second	1916–1929	Vertical	Copper refiners with fabricators
Third	1948–1969	Conglomerate	Litton Industries
Fourth	1982–present	Horizontal & Vertical	Banking, telecommunications, health services, insurance

The second merger wave took place between 1916 and 1929, when vertical mergers were more common. A vertical merger, recall, is the merging of one firm with a firm that either supplies its inputs or demands its outputs: it is the merging of firms at different stages of the production process. For example, a steel firm might merge with a firm that mines iron ore or a copper refiner might merge with a firm that fabricates copper parts.

The third merger wave was from 1948 to 1969. More than 200 of the 1,000 largest firms in 1950 had disappeared by the early 1960s as a result of mergers. In that period, many large firms were absorbed by other, usually larger, firms. The third merger wave culminated in the peak merger activity of 1964 to 1969, when **conglomerate mergers,** which join firms in different industries, accounted for four-fifths of all mergers. For example, Litton Industries combined firms that made calculators, appliances, electrical equipment, and machine tools.

Conglomerate merger A merger involving the combination of firms in different industries

The fourth merger wave, which is still underway today, began with the "deal decade" of the 1980s. This wave involves both horizontal and vertical mergers. Some of the big conglomerate mergers that occurred during the 1960s were dissolved in the 1980s as the core firm sold off unrelated operations. About one-third of mergers in the 1980s resulted from *hostile takeovers*, where one firm would buy control of another against the wishes of the target firm's management. Hostile takeovers dwindled to less than 10 percent of all mergers during the 1990s. Most mergers of the 1990s were financed by the exchange of corporate stock and were fueled by a booming stock market (just like mergers during the 1920s).

Merger activity gained momentum during the latter half of the 1990s. The $1 trillion in mergers in 1997 exceeded the 1996 level by 50 percent. The five largest mergers in U.S. history were proposed between April and December 1998. Sectors with heavy merger activity during the 1990s included banking, radio and television, insurance, telecommunications, and health services.

During the 1990s there was little objection to mergers on antitrust grounds either from academics or regulatory officials. The government shifted from rules that restrict big mergers to a more flexible economic approach that allows big companies to merge. Notable exceptions include the $4-billion merger proposed in 1997 between Staples and Office Depot, the nation's two largest office-supply retailers. Evidence showed that consumers in areas with only one office superstore paid higher prices than consumers in areas with more competition. On the other hand, the government approved Boeing's $15 billion acquisition of McDonnell Douglas, the commercial aircraft manufacturer, because the key customers of the airplanes, the airlines, said it made no difference to them whether or not the two combined. As one Justice Department official said, "We have very flexible guidelines. Bigness in and of itself doesn't tell me much. I want to know about the market, the players and what competition exists to judge."[2] The Chairman of the Federal Trade Commission said in 1998 that "the mergers we see these days make more sense" than earlier mergers.[3] He also said, "I do not believe that size alone is a basis to challenge a merger transaction."[4] Only 2 percent of all proposed mergers in the 1990s were ultimately challenged by regulators.

Mergers during the 1990s were for strategic concerns, where companies often merged to achieve a stronger competitive position in global markets. The end of the Cold War stabilized world markets and expanded capitalism around the world. The combination of a surging stock market and relatively low interest rates reduced the cost of funding mergers through stock swaps.

One industry where mergers seem to be having anticompetitive effects is local phone service. In 1996 Congress enacted a law designed to reduce the monopoly power of local phone companies by allowing long-distance carriers, cable operators, and other telecommunications providers to enter the local market. But rather than enhancing more competition, the 1996 act spawned a wave of mergers among local providers as they raced to span the country. For example, in May 1998 SBC Communications offered $62 billion for Ameritech. The proposed merger, if approved by regulators, would give the resulting company control over one-third of the 178 million local phone lines.[5]

COMPETITIVE TRENDS IN THE U.S. ECONOMY

For years there has been concern about the sheer size of some firms because of the real or potential power these firms might exercise in both the economic and the political arenas. One way to measure the power of the largest corporations is to calculate the share of the nation's corporate assets controlled by the 100 largest firms. What percentage of the nation's manufacturing assets do the top 100 manufacturing companies own, and how has this share changed over time?

The largest 100 manufacturers now control about half of all production assets in the United States, up from a 40 percent share after World War II. We should recognize, however, that size alone is not synonymous with market power. A very big firm, such as a large oil company, may face stiff competition from other very big oil companies both foreign and domestic; on the other hand, the only movie theater in an isolated community may be able to raise its price with less concern about competition.

---

2 As quoted by Leslie Wayne in "Wave of Mergers Recasts the Face of Business," *New York Times* (19 January 1998).

3 As quoted by John R. Wilke in "Greenspan Questions Governments Antitrust-Enforcement Campaigns," *Wall Street Journal,* (17 June 1998).

4 As quoted by Leslie Wayne in "Wave of Mergers Recasts the Face of Business," *New York Times* (19 January 1998).

5 See Stephanie N. Mehta, "SBC-Ameritech Deal, Formally Unveiled, Draws Criticism from Rival Carriers," *Wall Street Journal* (12 May 1998).

Market Competition over Time

More important than the size of the largest firms in the nation is the market structure in each industry. Various studies have examined the level of competition and change in industry structure over the years. All have used some measure of market share, such as the Herfindahl index, as a point of departure, sometimes supplementing these measures with data from each industry. Among the most comprehensive of these studies is the research of William Shepherd, of the University of Massachusetts, who relied on many sources to determine the competitiveness of each industry in the U.S. economy.[6]

Shepherd sorted industries into four groups: (1) pure monopoly, in which a single firm controlled the entire market and was able to block entry; (2) dominant firm, in which a single firm had over half the market share and had no close rival; (3) tight oligopoly, in which the top four firms supplied more than 60 percent of market output, with stable market shares and evidence of cooperation; and (4) effective competition, in which firms in the industry exhibited low concentration, low entry barriers, and little or no collusion.

Exhibit 4 presents Shepherd's breakdown of all U.S. industries into the four categories for the years 1939, 1958, and 1988. The table shows a modest trend toward greater competition between 1939 and 1958, with the percentage of those industries rated as "effectively competitive" growing from 52.4 percent to 56.3 percent of all industries. Between 1958 and 1988, however, there was a sharp rise in competitiveness in the economy, with the percentage of effectively competitive industries jumping from 56.3 to 76.7 percent.

According to Shepherd, the growth in competition from 1958 to 1988 can be traced to three primary causes: *competition from imports, deregulation, and antitrust activity.* Foreign imports between 1958 and 1988 resulted in increased competition in 13 major industries, including autos, tires, and steel. According to Shepherd, the growth in imports accounted for one-sixth of the overall increase in competition. Imports were attractive to consumers because of their superior quality and lower price. Because they were competing with U.S. producers that often had been tightly knit domestic oligopolies, foreign competitors found these U.S. markets relatively easy to penetrate. Finding themselves at a cost and technological disadvantage, domestic producers initially responded by seeking protection from foreign competitors through trade barriers, such as quotas and tariffs.

According to Shepherd, deregulation accounted for one-fifth of the increase in competition. Trucking, airlines, and telecommunications were among the industries deregulated between 1958 and 1988. We have already discussed some of the effects of this deregulation in airlines, particularly in reducing barriers to entry and in eliminating uniform pricing schedules. With regard to telecommunications, in 1982 AT&T was forced to divest itself of 22 companies that provided most of the country's local phone service. Between 1984 and 1996, AT&T's share of the long-distance market declined from 88 to 54 percent. This enhanced competition reduced long-distance rates. But, as noted

---

6 William G. Shepherd, "Causes of Increased Competition in the U.S. Economy, 1939–1980," *Review of Economics and Statistics* 64 (November 1982); and William G. Shepherd, *The Economics of Industrial Organization*, 3rd ed. (Englewood Cliffs, NJ: Prentice Hall, 1990): 15.

E X H I B I T   4

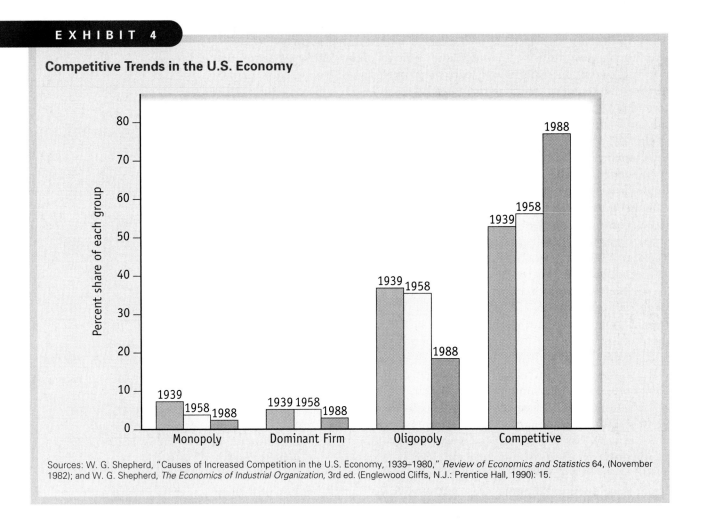

Competitive Trends in the U.S. Economy

Sources: W. G. Shepherd, "Causes of Increased Competition in the U.S. Economy, 1939–1980," *Review of Economics and Statistics* 64, (November 1982); and W. G. Shepherd, *The Economics of Industrial Organization*, 3rd ed. (Englewood Cliffs, N.J.: Prentice Hall, 1990): 15.

earlier, local service providers are starting to join forces again. Deregulation has also occurred in securities trading and banking.

Although it is difficult to attribute an increase in competition to specific antitrust cases, Shepherd concludes that about two-fifths of the increase in competition between 1958 and 1988 could be credited to the effects of antitrust activity.

Recent Competitive Trends

What has been the recent trend in competition? Growing world trade has increased competition in the U.S. economy. Until the 1970s, for example, the so-called big three auto makers—General Motors, Ford, and Daimler-Chrysler—controlled 80 percent of the U.S. auto market. By 1997 their market share had dropped to about 60 percent. And federal action to deregulate international phone service should force down the average price of international phone calls from 88 cents a minute in 1997 to 20 cents a minute by 2002.

Other major markets are also growing more competitive in part as a result of technological change. In the last two decades, the prime-time audience share controlled by the three major television networks (NBC, CBS, and ABC) dropped from 91 percent to 46 percent, as satellite and cable technology brought in many more networks. Despite Microsoft's dominance in operating systems, the packaged software market for personal computers barely existed in 1980 but has flourished in a technology-rich environment now populated by more than 7,800 producers with sales in 1997 of $30 billion. And the Internet has opened possibilities for enhanced competition in a number of industries, from on-line stock trading to all kinds of electronic commerce.

But some deregulation has hit bumps in the road. Airlines are now more concentrated than they were before deregulation, although plane service is still cheaper and safer than during the regulation era. The bankruptcy of many savings institutions has been blamed in part on deregulation. And the recent federal measure to promote competition in local phone service seems to have backfired, as local providers merge with other local providers across the country. Despite these setbacks, the trend toward deregulation continues, both here and abroad, with the deregulation of electricity generation being the most recent development.

Problems with Antitrust Legislation

There is growing doubt about the economic value of some of the lengthy antitrust cases pursued in the past. One case against Exxon was in the courts for 17 years before the company was cleared of charges in 1992. Another case began in 1969 when IBM, with nearly 70 percent of domestic sales of electronic data-processing equipment, was accused of monopolizing that market. IBM responded that its large market share was based on its innovative products and on its economies of scale. The trial began in 1975, and the government took nearly three years to present its case. Litigation dragged on for years. In the meantime, many other computer manufacturers emerged both in this country and abroad to challenge IBM's dominance. In 1982, the government dropped the case, noting that the threat of monopoly had diminished enough that the case was "without merit."

Too Much Emphasis on the Competitive Model. Joseph Schumpeter argued half a century ago that competition should be viewed as a dynamic process, one of "creative destruction." Firms are continually in flux—introducing new products, phasing out old products, trying to compete for the consumer's dollar in a variety of ways. In light of this, antitrust policy should not necessarily be aimed at increasing the number of firms in each industry. In some cases, firms will grow large because they are more efficient than rivals at offering what consumers want. Accordingly, firm size should not be the primary concern. Moreover, as noted in the case study in the chapter on perfect competition, economists have shown through market experiments that most of the desirable properties of perfect competition can be achieved with a relatively small number of firms.[7]

---

7 See, for example, Vernon Smith, "Markets as Economizers of Information: Experimental Examinations of the 'Hayek Hypothesis'," *Economic Inquiry* 20 (1982); and Douglas Davis and Charles Holt, *Experimental Economics* (Princeton, N.J.: Princeton University Press, 1993).

Abuse of Antitrust. Parties that can show injury from firms that have violated antitrust laws can sue the offending company and recover three times the amount of the damages sustained. These so-called *treble damage* suits increased after World War II; more than 1,000 cases are initiated each year. Courts have been relatively generous to those claiming to have been wronged. But studies show that such suits can be used to intimidate an aggressive competitor or to convert a contract dispute between, say, a firm and its supplier into treble damage payoffs. The result can have a chilling effect on competition. Many economists now believe that the anticompetitive costs from this abuse of treble damage suits may exceed the procompetitive benefits of these laws.

Growing Importance of International Markets. Finally, a standard approach to measuring the market power of a firm is its share of the market. With the growth of international trade, however, the local or even the national market share becomes less relevant. General Motors may dominate U.S. auto manufacturing, accounting for half of sales in the United States by domestically owned firms. But when auto sales by Japanese and European producers are included, GM's share of the U.S. auto market falls to less than one-third. GM's share of world production has declined steadily since the mid-1950s. *Where markets are open to foreign competition, antitrust enforcement that focuses on domestic producers makes less economic sense.*

We close this chapter by looking at the most visible antitrust case of the decade

Windows 98 Sold With Microsoft Browser

CaseStudy

The Information Economy

Microsoft released its long-awaited Windows 98 operating system in June 1998 under a cloud. The U.S. Justice Department and 20 state attorneys general had filed lawsuits a month earlier alleging that Microsoft engaged in a pattern of predatory conduct to protect its operating-system monopoly and to extend that monopoly into Internet software. Windows software is used on 90 percent of the nation's desktop computers. The plaintiffs charged that Microsoft's integration of its browser, Internet Explorer, into Windows 98 was not, as the company claimed, solely to make life easier for customers, but was aimed at boosting the browser's market share. A dominance in browser software is important, because controlling the gateway to the Internet is a big step in directing traffic and commerce in cyberspace. Government officials wanted Microsoft customers to be free to choose a browser. Microsoft disputed the charges and said the government was interfering with its right to create new products that benefit consumers.

Prior to any judicial ruling on the suit, Microsoft's choices were (a) to separate its Internet browser from Windows 98, a task the company claimed would take "months if not years;" (b) ship their major rival's browser, Netscape, as well as their own browser, with Windows 98—a task Bill Gates likened to "requiring Coca-Cola to include three cans of Pepsi in every six-pack it sells;" or (c) release Windows 98 with Microsoft's browser bundled in the software. Microsoft chose (c), which involved some risk, since if the practice was ultimately found to be anticompetitive, other companies could try to sue Microsoft for treble damages.

The trial began in October 1998, with 24 witnesses scheduled. Frederick Warren-Boulton, an economist hired by the government, testified that Microsoft holds monopoly power because it has the ability to set prices for its products in a way that excludes competitors: "I believe Microsoft has raised prices over the competitive level" because of its lack of rivals. He said that Microsoft had engaged in predatory practices aimed at harming competitors (the company's actions would be considered illegal only if it is found to possess monopoly power). Warren-Boulton argued that Microsoft's actions were "predatory" because they were aimed not at adding revenue but at winning the browser war. For example, Microsoft's decision to give away its Internet Explorer browser sacrificed revenue but was viewed as a way of beating Netscape. With Microsoft's browser on more than 60 percent of new Internet users' computers, the company may become dominant in the browser market, he said.

Microsoft, for its part, characterized itself as an aggressive but legal player in a fiercely competitive industry. Lawyers detailed Microsoft's frequent efforts to improve its operating system software all the way from MS-DOS to Windows 98. They said that the product would not have such a huge share of the market if it failed to improve quality and value with each new version. They argued that the high market share "does not begin to reflect the intense competitive dynamic in the software industry." Even such a lead is "susceptible to rapid deterioration should the market leader fail to innovate at a rapid and competitive pace." The company said it planned to invest $3 billion in fiscal year 1999 on research and development.

Bill Gates was not among the 24 witnesses scheduled to testify live. But he was interrogated by government lawyers for 20 hours during a videotaped deposition, parts of which were show during the trial to support the government's case. The federal judge presiding at the trial said "I think it is evident to every spectator that, for whatever reasons, in many respects, Mr. Gates has not been particularly responsive to his deposition."

A report by the Software and Information Industry Association, the nation's largest software-industry trade group, recommended to the Justice Department that Microsoft be restructured. As a cure for what the report says is a lack of competition in the software industry, the report argued that Microsoft should be broken into three companies. The first company would be Microsoft's operating systems business, including Windows. The second would get Microsoft's software applications such as Word, Excel, and PowerPoint. The third would get their Internet-related business. According to the report, the problem is that companies now competing with Microsoft in the applications business very much need the company's cooperation in sharing its operating system technology. Software not compatible with Microsoft's operating system simply doesn't survive. As a consequence, competition in the applications business is blunted by the dominance of Microsoft's operating system.

For the latest developments in the case, check the Web sites mentioned in the margin at the beginning of this case study.

Sources: Bryan Gruley and Keith Perine, "U.S. Witness Criticizes Microsoft for Operating System Monopoly," *Wall Street Journal* (19 November, 1998); John R. Wilke, "Witness Cites Microsoft Monopoly Power," *Wall Street Journal* (2 December 1998); "Judge Finds Gates Unresponsive," *New York Times* (20 November 1998); and Steve Lohr, "On Breaking Up Microsoft Into 'Baby Bills,'" *New York Times* (5 March 1999). For a library of *Wall Street Journal* articles about the case and for a discussion forum on the case, see http://interactive.wsj.com/pages/microsft.htm.

CONCLUSION

Competition has been growing in recent decades because of changing technology, greater international trade, industry deregulation, and antitrust activity. The current merger wave could ultimately diminish competition, but the jury is still out on that question.

Federal Reserve Chairman Alan Greenspan, testifying in 1998 before Congress about antitrust policy, expressed skepticism about the need for antitrust intervention, arguing that changes in market conditions and technologies tend to undermine monopolies over time. He called for "a higher degree of humility when enforcers make . . . projections" about the lasting effects of monopoly power. But, at the same hearing, Joel Klein, the antitrust chief for the Justice Department, said "we reject categorically the notion that markets will self-correct and we should sit back and watch."[8] So goes the public policy debate.

SUMMARY

1. In this chapter, we examined two forms of government regulation of business: (1) economic regulation, such as the regulation of natural monopolies, and (2) antitrust activity, which promotes competition and prohibits efforts to monopolize, or to cartelize, an industry.

2. Natural monopolies are regulated by government so that output is greater and prices lower than they would be if the monopolist were allowed to maximize profits. One problem with regulation is that the price that maximizes social welfare results in an economic loss, whereas the price that allows the firm to earn a normal profit does not maximize social welfare.

3. There are two views of economic regulation. The first is that economic regulation is in the public interest because it controls natural monopolies where production by one or a few firms is most efficient. A second view is that regulation is not in the public's, or consumer's, best interest, but is more in the special interest of regulated producers as a means of fixing the price and blocking entry.

4. The airline industry was regulated for much of this century. Regulation had the effect of restricting entry and fixing prices. Deregulation in 1978 stimulated new entry and reduced prices overall, though the industry once again is growing more concentrated because new entrants have difficulty securing landing rights at the nation's major airports.

5. Antitrust laws are aimed at promoting competition and prohibiting efforts to cartelize, or monopolize, an industry. The Sherman, Clayton, and FTC acts provided the basic framework for antitrust enforcement, a framework that has been clarified and embellished by subsequent amendments and judicial decisions.

6. Research indicates that competition in U.S. industries has been increasing since World War II. Four reasons for the growth in competition are foreign trade, deregulation, antitrust activity, and technological change.

---

8 As quoted in John R. Wilke, "Greenspan Questions Government's Antitrust-Enforcement Campaigns," *Wall Street Journal* (17 June 1998).

QUESTIONS FOR REVIEW

1. (*Business Behavior and Public Policy*) Define market power, then discuss the rationale for government regulation of firms with market power.

2. (*Government Regulation of Business*) What three types of government policies are used to alter or control firm behavior? Determine which type of regulation is used for each of the following:
   a. Preventing a merger that the government believes would lessen competition.
   b. The activities of the Food and Drug Administration.
   c. Regulation of fares charged by a municipal bus company.
   d. Occupational safety and health regulations that affect working conditions.

3. (*Regulating Natural Monopolies*) What is the "regulatory dilemma?" That is, what tradeoffs do regulators have to consider when deciding how to control a natural monopoly?

4. (*Theories of Regulation*) Compare and contrast the public-interest and special-interest theories of economic regulation. Which better describes the case of airline

deregulation? Which better explains the U.S. government's case against Microsoft?

5. (*Case Study: Airline Regulation and Deregulation*) Since the Airline Deregulation Act of 1978, has concentration in the airline industry increased or decreased? Explain why.

6. (*Antitrust Law and Enforcement*) Discuss the difference between *per se* illegality and the rule of reason.

7. (*Antitrust Activity*) "The existence of only three or four big U.S. auto manufacturers is evidence that the market structure is anticompetitive and that antitrust laws are being broken." Evaluate this assertion.

8. (*Mergers and Public Policy*) Under what circumstances, and why, would the government be opposed to a merger of two firms? How does the Justice Department decide which mergers to challenge?

9. (*Competitive Trends in the U.S. Economy*) William Shepherd's study of U.S. industries showed a clear increase in competition in the U.S. economy between 1958 and 1988. How did Shepherd explain this trend?

PROBLEMS AND EXERCISES

10. (*Regulating Natural Monopolies*) The following graph represents a natural monopoly.
    a. Why is this firm considered a natural monopoly?
    b. If the firm is unregulated, what price and output would maximize its profit? What would be its profit or loss?

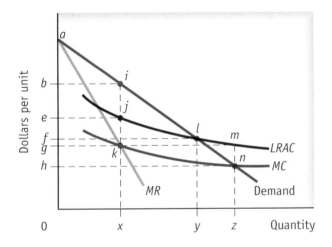

c. If a regulatory commission establishes a price with the goal of achieving allocative efficiency, what would be the price and output? What would be the firm's profit or loss?
d. If a regulatory commission establishes a price with the goal of allowing the firm a "fair return," what would be the price and output? What would be the firm's profit or loss?
e. Which of the prices in parts b, c, and d maximizes consumer surplus? What problem, if any, occurs at this price?

11. (*Origins of Antitrust Policy*) Identify the type of anticompetitive behavior illustrated by each of the following:
    a. A university requires buyers of season tickets for its basketball games to buy season tickets for its football games as well.
    b. Dairies that bid on contracts collude to artificially inflate the price of milk sold to school districts.
    c. The same individual serves on the boards of directors of General Motors and Ford.

d. A large retailer sells merchandise below cost in certain regions in order to drive competitors out of business.

e. A producer of carbonated soft drinks sells to a retailer only if the retailer agrees not to buy from the producer's major competitor.

12. (*Mergers and Public Policy*) Calculate the Herfindahl index for each of the following industries. Which of the industries is the most concentrated?

a. An industry with five firms that have the following market shares: 50 percent, 30 percent, 10 percent, 5 percent, and 5 percent

b. An industry with five firms that have the following market shares: 60 percent, 20 percent, 10 percent, 5 percent, and 5 percent

c. An industry with five firms, each of which has a 20 percent market share.

EXPERIENTIAL EXERCISES

13. (*Mergers and Public Policy*) Find the Department of Justice and Federal Trade Commission merger guidelines at http://www.antitrust.org/law/mg.html. How does the government use the Herfindahl index to determine which proposed mergers to allow and which to challenge? Do these guidelines indicate that the Justice Department is using the *per se* illegality or rule of reason approach to antitrust enforcement?

14. (*CaseStudy: Windows 98 Sold with Microsoft Browser*) The latest information on the Justice Department's case against Microsoft is available at http://www.usdoj.gov/atr/cases/ms_index.htm. To get the other side of the story, check Microsoft's PressPass page at http://microsoft.com/presspass/. What has happened in this case since this textbook went to press?

15. (*Wall Street Journal*) The best place for finding late breaking information about antitrust activity is in the Legal Beat column of the *Wall Street Journal*. You can find it inside the Marketplace section. Try to find at least one relevant article and determine the basis for the antitrust action. Were the Justice Department guidelines and the Herfindahl index mentioned in the article?

Public Goods and Public Choice

Visit the McEachern
Interactive Study Center
for this chapter at
http://mcisc.swcollege.com

Ⴖow do public goods differ from private goods? Why do most people remain largely ignorant about what's happening in the public sector? Why is voter turnout so low? Why do politicians cater to special interests? Why are elected officials more likely than challengers to support campaign spending limits? Answers to these and related questions are discussed in this chapter, which focuses on the public sector—both the rationale for public goods and public choices about those goods.

The effects of government are all around us. Stitched into the clothes you put on this morning are government-regulated labels providing washing instructions. The prices of the milk and sugar you put on your cereal were propped up by government price supports. The condition of the vehicle in which you rode to campus was regulated by the government, as were the speed and sobriety of the driver. Your education has been subsidized by the public sector in a variety of ways. Government has a pervasive influence on all aspects of your life and on the economy. Yes, government is big business. The federal government alone spends over $1,800,000,000,000.00 a year—over $1.8 *trillion*—more than $1 million on paper clips alone. State and local governments raise and spend another $1 trillion on their own.

The role of government has been discussed throughout this book. For the most part, the discussion has assumed that government makes optimal decisions in response to the shortcomings of the private sector—that is, when confronted with a market failure, government adopts and implements the appropriate program to address the problem. But there are limits to the effectiveness of government activity, just as there are limits to the effectiveness of market activity. In this chapter, we look at the pros and cons of government activity. We begin with public goods, discuss the decision-making process, then examine the limitations of that process. Topics discussed in this chapter include:

- Private versus public goods
- Representative democracy
- Rational ignorance
- Special-interest legislation
- Rent seeking
- Underground economy
- Bureaucratic behavior
- Private versus public production

OPTIMAL PROVISION OF PUBLIC GOODS

Throughout most of this book, we have been talking about *private goods*. As noted in Chapter 4, private goods have two important features. First, private goods are *rival* in consumption, meaning that the amount consumed by one person is unavailable for others to consume. For example, when you and a friend share a pizza, each slice your friend eats is one less available for you. A second key feature of private goods is that suppliers can easily *exclude* those who don't pay. Only paying customers get pizzas from Domino's. Thus private goods are said to be *exclusive*.

Private Goods, Public Goods, and In Between

In contrast to private goods, public goods, such as national defense, a lighthouse, or a neighborhood mosquito-control program, are *nonrival* in consumption. One person's consumption does not diminish the amount available to others. Once produced, such goods are available to all in equal amount; the marginal cost of providing the good to an additional consumer is zero. But once a public good is produced, suppliers cannot easily deny the good to those who fail to pay for it. For example, if a company sprays a community for mosquitoes, all households in the community benefit from having fewer mosquitoes. But the firm would be unable to exclude those households that failed to pay for the service. The mosquito spraying is *nonexclusive*—it is available to all households, regardless of who pays and who doesn't. Producers find it difficult or impossible to charge people for nonexclusive goods. So recipients figure, "Why bother paying if you can enjoy the benefits without paying?"

In short, public goods are both *nonrival* and *nonexclusive*. Once produced, public goods are available for all to consume, regardless of who pays and who doesn't. As a consequence, private firms cannot profitably sell public goods. There are no vending machines for public goods. In this case of market failure, government comes to the rescue by providing public goods and paying for them through enforced taxation.

But the economy consists of more than just private goods and public goods. Some goods are *nonrival* but *exclusive*. For example, additional households can watch a TV show without affecting the TV reception of other viewers. It's not as if there's only a limited amount of TV signal to go around. Television signals are nonrival in consumption. Yet the program's producers, should they choose to, could use cable boxes to charge each household for the show, as with pay-per-view. Along the same lines, short of the point of congestion, additional people can benefit from a golf course, swimming pool, rock concert, or bridge crossing without diminishing the benefit to other users. These goods, when not congested, are nonrival. Yet producers can, with relative ease, exclude those who don't pay the green fee, pool admission, ticket price, or bridge toll. A good that is nonrival but exclusive is called a **quasi-public good**. If congestion sets in, however, these goods become rival—space is scarce on a backed-up golf course, in a crowded swimming pool, at a jam-packed rock concert, or on a traffic-laden bridge. Essentially, once congestion sets in these quasi-public goods become private goods—both rival and exclusive.

Some other goods are *rival* but *nonexclusive*. The fish in the ocean are rival, in the sense that every fish caught is not available for others to catch; the same goes for migrating birds. But fish and game are nonexclusive, in that it would be costly or impossible for a private firm to prevent access to these goods. A good that is rival but nonexclusive is called an **open-access good** since it would be difficult and costly to prevent individuals from using the good. Problems that arise with open-access goods are examined in the next chapter.

Exhibit 1 offers a matrix that sorts out the four types of goods discussed. Across the top, goods are categorized as either *rival* or *nonrival*, and along the

Quasi-public good A good that is nonrival but exclusive, such as cable TV

Open-access good A good that is rival but nonexclusive, such as fish in the sea

EXHIBIT 1

Categories of Private and Public Goods

	Rival	**Nonrival**
Exclusive	1. Private Goods —pizza —crowded swimming pool	2. Quasi-Public Goods —Cable TV —uncrowded swimming pool
Nonexclusive	3. Open-Access Goods —ocean fish —migratory birds	4. Public Goods —national defense —mosquito control

left-hand margin, goods are categorized as either *exclusive* or *nonexclusive*. Box 1 shows *private goods*, such as a pizza or a crowded swimming pool. These goods, by definition, are both rival and exclusive. Box 2 shows *quasi-public goods*, such as cable TV or an uncrowded swimming pool; these goods are nonrival but exclusive. Box 3 shows *open-access goods*, such as fish in the ocean or migrating birds, which are rival but nonexclusive. And Box 4 shows public goods, such as national defense or mosquito control, which are both nonrival and nonexclusive. Private goods are usually provided by the private sector. Quasi-public goods are sometimes provided by government, as with a municipal golf course, and sometimes provided by the private sector, as with a private golf course. Open-access goods are usually regulated by government, as you will see in the next chapter. And public goods are usually provided by government.

Optimal Provision of Public Goods

Because private goods are rival in consumption, the market demand for a private good is the sum of the quantities demanded by each consumer. For example, the market quantity of pizza demanded when the price is $5 is the quantity demanded by Alan plus the quantity demanded by Maria plus the quantity demanded by all other consumers in the market. The market demand curve for a private good is the *horizontal* sum of individual demand curves. The efficient quantity of a private good occurs where the market demand curve intersects the market supply curve.

But since a public good is nonrival in consumption, that good, once produced, is available to all consumers in an identical amount. For example, the market demand for a given level of mosquito control reflects the marginal benefit that Alan gets from the good plus the marginal benefit that Maria gets plus the marginal benefit that all others in the community get from the good. Therefore, the market demand curve for a public good is the *vertical* sum of each consumer's demand for the public good. To arrive at the efficient level of provision of the public good, we find where the market demand curve intersects the marginal cost curve—that is, where the sum of the marginal valuations equals the marginal cost.

Suppose the public good in question is mosquito control in a neighborhood, which, for simplicity consists of only two houses, one headed by Alan and the other by Maria. Alan spends a lot of time in the yard and thus values a mosquito-free environment more than does Maria, who spends more time away from home. Their demand curves are shown in Exhibit 2 as D_a and D_m, reflecting the marginal benefits that Alan and Maria get, respectively, at each rate of output. Quantity is measured here as hours of mosquito spraying per week.

For example, when the town sprays two hours a week, Maria is willing to pay $5 for the second hour and Alan is willing to pay $10 for the second hour. To derive the sum of the marginal benefits for the neighborhood, we simply add each resident's marginal benefit to get $15, as identified by point *e*. By vertically summing marginal valuations at each rate of output, we derive the neighborhood demand curve, *D*, for mosquito spraying.

How much of this public good should be produced? Suppose the marginal cost of spraying is a constant $15 an hour, as shown in Exhibit 2. The efficient level of output is found where the marginal benefit to the neighborhood equals the marginal cost, which occurs where the neighborhood demand curve inter-

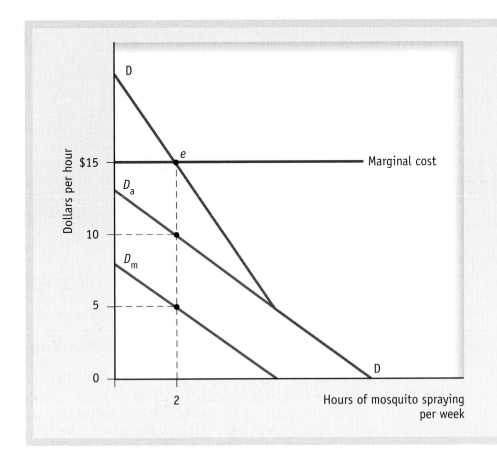

EXHIBIT 2

**Market for
Public Goods**

Because public goods, once
produced, are available to all
in identical amounts, the demand for a public good is the
vertical sum of each individual's demand. Thus, the market demand for mosquito
spraying is the vertical sum
of Maria's demand, D_m, and
Alan's demand, D_a. The efficient level of provision is
found where the marginal
cost of mosquito spraying
equals its marginal benefit.
This occurs where the marginal cost curve intersects
the market demand curve, D,
resulting in point e.

sects the marginal cost curve. In our example, these curves intersect where output is two hours per week.

The government pays for the mosquito spray through taxes, user fees, or
some combination of the two. The most straightforward approach might be to
impose a tax on each resident equal to his or her marginal valuation. Simple
enough, but there are at least two problems with this. First, once people realize
their taxes are based on how much the government thinks they value the good,
they tend to understate their true valuation. Why admit you really value the
good if, as a result, you get smacked with a higher tax bill? Thus taxpayers are
reluctant to offer information about their true valuation of public goods. But
even if the government had accurate information about marginal valuations,
some households earn much higher incomes than other households and thus
have a greater ability to pay taxes. In our example, Alan valued mosquito control more because he spent more time around the house than did Maria. What
if Alan was around the house more because he couldn't find a job. Should his
taxes be double those of Maria, who, say, has a good job?

Once the public good is produced, only that rate of output is available.
Since only one quantity is produced, each individual's consumption is limited
to that particular quantity. In contrast, with private goods, each consumer is free
to purchase any quantity he or she prefers. Thus public goods are much more

complicated than private goods in terms of what goods should be provided, in what quantities, and who should pay. These decisions are thrashed out through public choices, which are examined in the balance of this chapter.

PUBLIC CHOICE IN A REPRESENTATIVE DEMOCRACY

Government decisions about the provision of public goods and the collection of tax revenues are *public choices*. In a democracy, public choices usually require approval by a majority of voters. As it turns out, we can frequently explain the choice of the electorate by focusing on the preferences of the median voter. The *median voter* is the voter whose preferences lie in the middle of the set of all voters' preferences. For example, if the issue is the size of the government, half the voters prefer a larger government and half prefer a smaller one.

Median Voter Model

Median voter model Under certain conditions, the preference of the median, or middle, voter will dominate other public choices

The **median voter model** predicts that under certain conditions, the preference of the median, or middle, voter will dominate other choices. Here is the logic behind the model. Suppose you and two roommates have just moved into an apartment, and the three of you must decide on furnishings. You all agree that the common costs will be shared equally by the three of you and that majority rule will prevail, with one vote per person. The issue at hand is whether to buy a TV and, if so, of what size. The problem is that you each have different preferences. Your studious roommate considers a TV an annoying distraction and would rather go without; otherwise, the smaller the TV, the better. Your other roommate, a real TV fan, prefers a 48-inch screen but would settle for a smaller size rather than go without. Although you are by no means a TV addict, you enjoy watching TV as a relief from the rigors of academe; a 26-inch screen is your first choice, but you prefer the 48-inch screen to no TV. What to do, what to do?

You all agree to make the decision by voting on two alternatives at a time, then pairing the winning alternative against the remaining alternative until one choice dominates the others. When the 26-inch set is paired with the no-TV option, the 26-inch set wins because this option gets both your vote and the TV fan's vote. When the 26-inch screen is then paired with the 48-inch screen, the 26-inch screen wins a majority again, this time because your studious roommate sides with you rather than voting for the super screen.

Majority voting in effect delegates the public choice to the person whose preference is the median for the group. You, as the median voter in this case, can have your way; if you preferred a 12-inch screen or a 36-inch screen, you could have received majority support for either. Similarly, *the median voter in an electorate often determines public choices. Political candidates try to get elected by appealing to the median voter.* This is one reason why candidates often seem so much alike.

Note that under majority rule, only the median voter gets his or her way. Other voters are required to go along with what the median voter wants. Thus other voters usually end up paying for what they consider to be either too much or too little of the public good.

People vote directly on issues at New England town meetings and on the occasional referendum, but direct democracy is not the most common means of public choice. When you consider the thousands of public choices made on behalf of individual voters, it becomes clear that direct democracy through referenda would be unwieldy and impractical. Rather than make decisions by direct referenda, voters elect *representatives*, who, at least in theory, make public choices that reflect their constituents' views. Under certain conditions, the resulting public choices reflect the preferences of the median voter. Some complications of making public choices through representative democracy will be explored next.

Goals of the Participants

We assume that consumers maximize utility and firms maximize profit, but what about governments? As noted in Chapter 4, there is no common agreement about what governments maximize or, more precisely, what elected officials maximize, if anything. One theory that parallels the rational self-interest assumption employed in private choices is that elected officials attempt to *maximize their political support*.

It is possible that elected representatives will cater to special interests rather than serve the interests of the majority. The problem arises because of the asymmetry between special interests and the public interest, an idea introduced in the previous chapter. Consider only one of the thousands of decisions that are made each year by elected representatives: funding an obscure federal program that subsidized U.S. wool production. Under the wool-subsidy program, the federal government guarantees that a floor price is paid to sheep farmers for each pound of wool they produced, a subsidy that costs taxpayers over $75 million per year. During deliberations to renew the program, the only person to testify before Congress was a representative of the National Wool Growers Association, who claimed that the subsidy was vital to the nation's economic welfare. Why didn't a single taxpayer challenge the subsidy? Why were sheep farmers able to pull the wool over the taxpayers' eyes?

Rational Ignorance

Households consume so many different public and private goods and services that they have neither the time nor the incentive to understand the effects of public choices on every one of these products. What's more, voters realize that each of them has only a tiny possibility of influencing the outcome of public choices. And even if an individual voter is somehow able to affect the outcome, the impact on that voter is likely to be small. For example, even if a taxpayer could successfully stage a grass-roots campaign to eliminate the wool subsidy, the taxpayer would save, on average, less than $1 per year in federal income taxes. Therefore, unless voters have a special interest in the legislation, they adopt a stance of **rational ignorance**, which means that they remain largely oblivious to the costs and benefits of the thousands of proposals considered by elected officials. The cost to the typical voter of acquiring and acting on such information is typically greater than any expected benefit.

In contrast, consumers have a greater incentive to gather and act on information about decisions they make in private markets because they benefit directly from the knowledge so acquired. *Since information and the time required to acquire and digest it are scarce, consumers concentrate on private choices rather than public choices because the payoff in making wise private choices is usually more immediate, more*

Rational ignorance A stance adopted by voters when they find that the cost of understanding and voting on a particular issue exceeds the benefit expected from doing so *direct, and more substantial.* For example, a consumer in the market for a new car has an incentive to examine the performance records of different models, test-drive a few, and check prices at dealerships and on the Internet. That same individual has less incentive to examine the performance records of candidates for public office because that single voter has virtually no chance of deciding the election. What's more, political candidates, who aim to please the median voter, will often take positions that are quite similar anyway.

Distribution of Costs and Benefits

Let's turn now to how the costs and benefits of public choices are spread across the population. The costs imposed by a particular legislative measure may be either narrowly or widely distributed over the population, depending on the issue. Likewise, the benefits may be conferred on only a small group or on much of the population. The possible combinations of costs and benefits yield four alternative types of distributions: (1) widespread costs and widespread benefits, (2) widespread costs and concentrated benefits, (3) concentrated costs and concentrated benefits, and (4) concentrated costs and widespread benefits.

Traditional public goods, such as national defense and a system of justice, have widespread costs and widespread benefits—nearly everyone pays and nearly everyone benefits from this category of distribution. Traditional public goods usually have a positive impact on the economy because the sum of the benefits outweighs the costs.

Special-interest legislation Legislation that generates concentrated benefits but imposes widespread costs

With **special-interest legislation**, benefits are concentrated but costs are widespread. For example, as you'll see shortly, price supports for dairy products mean consumers pay a higher price for milk than would result from normal market forces. The program benefits are concentrated on dairy farmers. The costs are widespread across consumers and taxpayers. And the total cost far exceeds the total benefit. Legislation that caters to special interest groups usually harms the economy, on net, because total costs exceed total benefits.

Competing-interest legislation Legislation that imposes concentrated costs on one group and provides concentrated benefits to another group

Competing-interest legislation involves both concentrated costs and concentrated benefits. For example, restrictions on sugar imports boost the price of U.S. sugar to twice the world price,[1] thereby benefiting growers of sugarcane and sugar refiners. But major sugar-using manufacturers such as Hershey and M&M Mars must pay these higher sugar prices, which cut into their profits. The issue pits sugar growers against sugar buyers—two special interests.

The fourth possible combination of costs and benefits involves concentrated costs but widespread benefits. If legislators try to impose costs in a concentrated way so as to confer benefits widely, the group getting hit with the concentrated costs will object strenuously. Meanwhile, those who benefit usually remain rationally ignorant of the proposed legislation, so they provide little political support. For example, whenever Congress considers imposing a tax on a particular industry, that industry floods Washington with lobbyists, phone calls, faxes, e-mail, snail mail, and telegrams, usually claiming that the tax will lead to economic ruin, not to mention the decline of Western civilization as we know it. Here, for example, is a recent account from The *New York Times*:

---

1 See "Sugar Battle Brews in Congress," *New York Times* (13 June 1998).

A lobbying blitz by some of the biggest names in corporate America has succeeded in maintaining a lucrative tax break for multinational corporations—one that allows them to avoid U.S. taxes and reduce their foreign tax bill, too. . . . Business succeeded through a combination of arm-twisting, letter-writing, and hiring some of the best tax-lobbying talent in Washington, including many who helped create the tax law.[2]

Thus legislation that imposes costs on a small group but confers benefits widely has less chance of approval than do measures that confer benefits narrowly but spread costs widely.

In the following case study, we consider the redistributive and efficiency effects of a particular special-interest program—supports for milk prices.

Farm Subsidies

The Agricultural Marketing Agreement Act became law in 1937 to prevent what was viewed as "ruinous competition" among farmers. In the years since, the government introduced a variety of policies to set floor prices for a wide range of farm products. Until the federal government began scaling back farm subsidies in 1996, direct costs exceeded $10 billion a year for dozens of agricultural products. Support programs for milk and sugar persist.

In most parts of the country, milk prices are the most heavily regulated of farm products. Explaining the intricacies of the complicated milk-price support program takes up three volumes of the *Code of Federal Regulations*, and administering the regulations employs 500 people at the U.S. Department of Agriculture—as many as oversee the entire federal budget in the Office of Management and Budget. These rules cost consumers an estimated $1.7 billion a year, according to Agriculture Department studies.

Let's see how price supports worked in the dairy industry using a hypothetical example. Exhibit 3 depicts a simplified view of the market for milk. Suppose that, in the absence of government intervention, the market price of milk would average $1.50 per gallon and the equilibrium quantity would average 100 million gallons per week. In long-run equilibrium, dairy farmers would earn a normal rate of return. Consumers as a group would capture the consumer surplus shown by the blue shaded area. Recall that consumer surplus is the difference between the most that consumers would have been willing to pay and the amount actually paid.

But suppose that dairy farmers persuade Congress that the free-market price is too low, so legislation establishes a price floor for milk of, say, $2.50 per gallon. The higher price floor provides farmers with an incentive to increase the quantity supplied to 150 million gallons per week. In response to the higher price, however, consumers reduce their quantity demanded to 75 million gallons per week. To make the higher price stick, the government must buy the 75 million

CaseStudy

Public Policy

Provisions of the Federal Agriculture Improvement and Reform Act of 1996, available at http://www.econ.ag.gov/ epubs/pdf/aib729/, describes new legislation aimed at reducing farmer reliance on price support programs. You can learn about its impact on the dairy sector by reading the summary of *The Structure of Dairy Markets: Past, Present and Future* at http:// www.econ.ag.gov/epubs/html sum/aer757.htm. Which type of firm buys most of the fluid milk produced by dairy farmers? What does the future hold for dairy markets? More reports on the marketing of dairy products are at http:// www.inform.umd.edu/EdRes/ Topic/AgrEnv/ndd/marketin/ from the U.S. National Dairy Database maintained by the University of Maryland.

---

2 This is the lead paragraph in a story by Leslie Wayne, "Tax Break Intact for Now After Fight By Business," *New York Times* (12 July 1998).

gallons of "surplus" milk generated by the floor price or somehow get dairy farmers to restrict their output to 75 million gallons per week. For example, the government could pay dairy farmers not to produce or could buy cows from farmers to reduce production (as was done in the 1980s).

Consumers end up paying dearly to subsidize the farmers. First, the price per gallon increases by $1. Second, consumers, as taxpayers, must pay for the surplus milk or otherwise pay farmers not to produce that milk. And third, if the government buys the surplus milk, taxpayers must then pay for storage. So the consumer pays $2.50 per gallon for milk purchased on the market; the consumer as an average taxpayer also pays another $2.50 for each gallon the government buys, plus, say, an extra $0.50 per gallon to convert surplus milk into powder and to store it. Instead of paying just $1.50 for a gallon of milk, which is the price in the absence of government price supports, the typical consumer-taxpayer in our example pays $5.50 per gallon, or an extra outlay of $4.00 per gallon of milk actually consumed.

How do the farmers make out? Each farmer receives an extra $1 per gallon in additional revenue over the price that would have prevailed in a free market. As farmers increase their output, however, the marginal cost of production increases; at the margin, the higher price the farmer receives is just offset by higher production costs. Still, farmers gain an increase in producer surplus because of the subsidy program, identified in Exhibit 3 by the area above the supply curve that is between the market price of $1.50 and the floor price of $2.50.

EXHIBIT 3

Effects of Milk Price Supports

In the absence of government intervention, the market price of milk is $1.50 per gallon and 100 million gallons are sold per week. If Congress establishes a floor price of $2.50 per gallon, then the quantity supplied will increase and the quantity demanded will decrease. To maintain the higher price, the government must buy up the excess quantity at $2.50 per gallon.

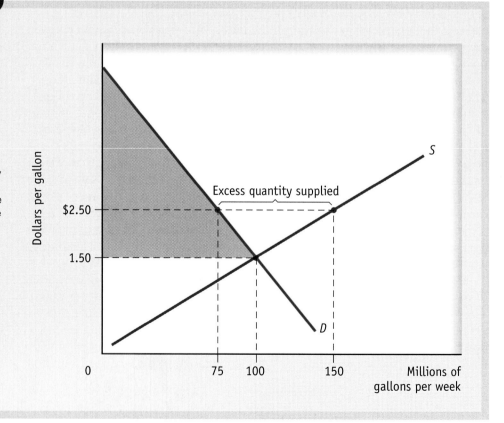

The subsidy will increase the value of resources specialized to dairy farming, such as cows and grazing land, and farmers who own these resources when the subsidy program goes into effect will benefit. Farmers who purchase these resources after the subsidy has been introduced will pay more and will end up earning just a normal rate of return on that investment. So with free entry into the dairy industry, most farmers in the long run earn just a normal rate of return, despite the billions spent on farm subsidies.

If the extra $1 per gallon that farmers receive for milk were pure profit, farm profits would increase by $150 million per week. But consumer-taxpayer costs would increase by $300 million per week ($75 million for the higher price of each of the 75 million gallons consumers purchase, plus $187.5 million in higher taxes for the 75 million surplus gallons purchased by the government, plus $37.5 million to store the 75 million surplus gallons). Thus, consumer-taxpayer costs are double the farmers' maximum possible gain of $150 million. The government subsidy therefore has a negative impact on the economy, as the losses outweigh the gains. This does not mean nobody gains—those who owned specialized resources gained when the subsidy was first introduced. But once the price of farm resources increases, new farmers must pay more to get in a position to reap the subsidies. Ironically, subsidies aimed at preserving the family farm raise the costs of a young person entering the industry.

Over the years, federal price support programs bought up the surplus, paid dairy farmers not to produce, and bought cows from farmers. By the mid-1980s, dairy herds had expanded so much that the government spent more than $1 billion to reduce herd size (herds are now growing again). Since 1980, U.S. milk prices have averaged twice the price on world markets, yet imports are restricted. Federal regulations also limit farmers in one part of the country from selling their milk in another part of the country. For decades minimum milk prices in each region around the country were determined by a complicated formula based on the distance from Eau Claire, Wisconsin.

The dairy industry is supported in other ways. Some state programs support even higher prices. Other laws promote the consumption of dairy products. For example, laws in many states prohibit restaurants from serving margarine unless customers specifically request it instead of butter. Margarine has faced a long history of discrimination dating back a century.

In November 1997 a federal judge threw out the federal regulations on milk pricing, but the battle to deregulate milk prices is not over. The U.S. Department of Agriculture is appealing the judge's ruling, and dairy farmers in some parts of the country are trying to bypass the ruling by forming their own interstate pricing agreements. For example, the New England states approved a milk-price compact that establishes minimum prices to farmers, prices that average 5 percent to 22 percent above the mandated minimum prices under existing federal legislation. Dairy farmers in other states are looking to follow New England's example.

The profound long-run problem for dairy farmers is that technological breakthroughs, such as genetically engineered hormones that stimulate milk production, have made dairies far more productive. Yet milk consumption remains flat (despite the widely advertised "Got milk?" and milk-mustache campaigns). The combination of increased supply and stagnant demand is a recipe for excess quantity supplied.

Everyone would be better off if the government made a direct transfer payment to farmers, a payment not tied to milk production or price. Although a direct transfer payment to dairy farmers would be more efficient, such a transparent special-interest proposal could attract the public's attention and be doomed. Special-interest legislation is often promoted under the cover of some greater good. The ostensible goal of farm subsidies, for example, is to save the family farm, but farm households on average earn more than nonfarm households and are wealthier. And business failure rates are lower in agriculture than the average for all industries.

Sources: Bruce L. Gardner, "Changing Economic Perspectives on the Farm Problem," *Journal of Economic Literature* 30 (March 1992): 62–101; Scott Kilman, "Byzantine Method of Pricing Milk Won't Be Simplified Anytime Soon," *Wall Street Journal* (25 November 1997); "Consumer Prices Vary Widely," *New York Times* (18 April 1998); and Kim Archer, "U.S. House Defeats Sugar, Milk Amendments in Ag Debate," *Dow Jones Newswire* (24 June 1998).

Rent Seeking

An important feature of representative democracy is the incentive and political power it offers participants to employ legislation that increases their wealth, either through direct transfers or through favorable public expenditures and regulations. Special-interest groups, such as sugarcane growers, dairy farmers, or trial lawyers, try to persuade elected officials to approve measures that provide the special interest with some market advantage or some outright transfer or subsidy. Such benefits are sometimes called *rents*. The term in this context implies that the government transfer or subsidy constitutes a payment to the resource owner that exceeds the earnings necessary to call forth that resource—*a payment exceeding opportunity cost*. The activity that interest groups undertake to elicit these special favors from government is called *rent seeking*.

The government frequently bestows some special advantage on a producer or group of producers, and abundant resources are expended to secure these rights. For example, *political action committees,* known more popularly as *PACs,* contribute millions to congressional campaigns. More than 4,000 PACs try to shape federal legislation; the top contributors recently included the tobacco lobby and the American Trial Lawyers Association. Tobacco interests would like to influence cigarette legislation and lawyers fear legal reforms that would limit liability lawsuits.

To the extent that special-interest groups engage in rent-seeking activities, they shift resources from productive endeavors that create income to activities that focus more on transferring income. *Resources employed in an attempt to get government to redistribute income or wealth are unproductive because they do nothing to increase output and usually end up reducing it.* Often many firms compete for the same government advantage, thereby wasting still more resources. If the advantage conferred by government on some special-interest group requires higher income taxes, the net return individuals expect from working and investing will fall, so less work and less investment may occur. If this happens, productive activity will decline.

As a firm's profitability becomes more and more dependent on decisions made in Washington, resources are diverted from productive activity to rent seeking, or lobbying efforts to gain special advantage. One firm may thrive because it secured some special advantage at a critical time; another firm may fail because its managers were more concerned with productive efficiency than with rent seeking.

Special-interest groups have little incentive to make the economy more efficient. In fact, special-interest groups will usually support legislation that transfers wealth to them even if the measure reduces the economy's overall efficiency. For example, suppose that the American Trial Lawyers Association is able to push through product-liability legislation that has the effect of increasing lawyers' incomes by a total of $1 billion per year, or about $1,900 for each lawyer in private practice. Suppose, too, that this measure drives up insurance premiums, raising the total cost of production by, say, $5 billion per year. Lawyers themselves will have to bear part of this higher cost, but since they account for only about 1 percent of the spending in the economy, they will bear only about 1 percent of the $5 billion in higher costs, or a total of $50 million, which amounts to about $100 per lawyer per year. Thus, the legislation is a bargain for lawyers because it increases the income of each by an average of about $1,900 per year but increases the cost each faces by an average of only about $100 a year.

Think of the economy's output in a particular period as depicted by a pie. The pie is the total value of goods and services produced. In deciding on answers to the "what," "how," and "for whom" questions introduced in Chapter 2, policy makers have three alternatives: (1) they can introduce changes that will yield a bigger pie (that is, positive-sum changes), (2) they can decide simply to carve up the existing pie differently (redistribution of income), or (3) they can start fighting over the pie, causing some of it to end up on the floor (negative-sum changes). Much special-interest legislation leads to a net reduction in social welfare. Some of the nation's best minds are occupied with devising schemes to avoid taxes or divert income to favored groups at the expense of market efficiency. For example, the pursuit of tax loopholes fills the days of some of the brightest lawyers and accountants.

There are hundreds of special-interest groups representing farmers, physicians, lawyers, teachers, manufacturers, barbers, and so on. One way special interests try to gain access to the political process is through campaign contributions. The elusive issue of campaign-finance reform is discussed in the following case study.

Campaign Finance Reform

Critics of the current campaign finance system have argued that American politics is awash in special-interest money. Most Americans seem to agree. In one poll, two-thirds of those surveyed said they would be willing to have their tax dollars used for campaigns if this meant the elimination of financing by large private donations and organized interest groups. Since the 1970s, presidential campaigns have been publicly funded, but not Congressional races (the Clinton and Dole campaigns each received $62 million during the 1996 presidential election).

A campaign finance reform measure proposed recently in the House of Representatives would establish a $600,000 voluntary spending limit for House candidates and sharply reduce special-interest influence by restricting PAC

CaseStudy

Public Policy

You can find a comprehensive list of Web sites on campaign reform compiled by the Electronic Policy Network at http://epn.org/camfinre.html. Among these you will find the Brookings Institution, a Washington, DC thinktank at http://www.brook.edu/gs/campaign/cfr_hp.htm and Common Cause, a nonpartisan lobbying group promoting accountable government at http://www.commoncause.org/issue_agenda/campaign_finance.htm. What bills are pending?

contributions, large individual contributions, and contributions from lobbyists. Proposed legislation would also restrict individual contributions that exceed $200 (since 1974, contributions to candidates have been limited to $1,000 per person.) If candidates voluntarily agree to limit their spending, they would get public money and cut-rate television time.

Limits on special-interest contributions may help reduce their influence in the political process, but such limits would heighten the current advantage of incumbency. The overwhelming majority of congressional incumbents are re-elected. For example, 380 of the 405 Congress members who ran for reelection in 1996 won, yielding a reelection rate of 94 percent. Observers claim that this results from the unfair advantages that incumbents have in the electoral process, especially because of taxpayer-funded staff and free mailing privileges (campaign literature masquerading as official communications).

Limits on campaign spending would magnify the advantages of incumbency by reducing a challenger's ability to appeal directly to voters. Some liberal *and* conservative thinkers agree that the supply of political money should be increased, not decreased. As Curtis Gans of the Committee for the Study of the American Electorate argues, "The overwhelming body of scholarly research . . . indicates that low spending limits will undermine political competition by enhancing the existing advantages of incumbency." *Money matters more to challengers than to incumbents* since the public knows less about challengers than about incumbents. Challengers must be able to spend enough to get their message out. One study found a positive relationship between spending by challengers and election success but found no relationship between spending by incumbents and their reelection success. So a limit on spending favors incumbents.

Although many decry the amount spent on campaigns, spending is a relative concept. For example, total direct campaign spending for all congressional races in 1994 averaged about $3 per eligible voter. All 1993–1994 PAC contributions for all federal races would not cover the cost of the movie *Titanic*.

The U.S. Supreme Court has struck down mandatory campaign spending limits. According to the Constitution, "Congress shall make no law . . . abridging freedom of speech." The Supreme Court ruled that "dollars are not stuffed in ballot boxes . . . The mediating factor that turns money into votes is speech. . . . Advocacy cannot be proscribed because it's effective."

The point is that legislation often has unintended consequences. Efforts to limit campaign spending may or may not reduce the influence of special-interest groups, but a limit would reduce a challenger's ability to reach the voters and thereby increase the advantage of incumbency.

Sources: Jill Abramson, "When $10 Million Is in Trough, Few Want to Overturn It," *New York Times* (15 June 1998); Stanley Brubaker, "The Limits of Campaign Spending Limits," *Public Interest* (Fall 1998): 33–54; Edward Crane, "Testimony before the Committee on House Oversight, U.S. House of Representatives," 16 November 1995; Alison Mitchell, "House Votes to Consider 258 Amendments to Campaign Bill," *New York Times* (19 June 1998); and James Dao, "Shay Leads Battle in House for Campaign Finance Bill," *New York Times* (22 June 1998).

The Underground Economy

A government subsidy promotes production, as we saw in the case study on milk price supports. Conversely, a tax discourages production. Perhaps it would be more accurate to say that when government taxes productive activity, less production is *reported*. If you have worked as a waitress or waiter, did you faithfully report all your tips to the Internal Revenue Service? To the extent that you did not, your income became part of the underground economy. The **underground economy** is a term used for all market activity that goes unreported to the government either to avoid taxes or because the activity itself is illegal. Thus income arising in the underground economy ranges from unreported tips to the earnings of a drug dealer.

The introduction of a tax on productive activity has two effects. First, resource owners may supply less of the taxed resource because the tax reduces the net return from supplying the resource. Second, in an attempt to evade taxes, some people will divert their economic activity from the formal, reported economy to an underground, "off-the-books" economy. Thus, when the government taxes market exchange or the income it generates, less market activity is reported.

We should take care to distinguish between tax *avoidance* and tax *evasion*. Tax avoidance is a legal attempt to arrange one's economic affairs so as to pay the least tax possible, such as buying municipal bonds because they yield tax-free interest. Tax evasion is illegal; it takes the form of either failing to file a tax return or filing a fraudulent return by understating income or overstating deductions. Research around the world indicates that the underground economy grows (1) when government regulations increase, (2) when the tax burden increases, and (3) where government corruption is more widespread.[3]

Although there are no official figures on the size of the underground economy, federal agencies try to make estimates based on other data. The Commerce Department estimates that official figures capture only 90 percent of U.S. income. An Internal Revenue Service survey estimated that only 87 percent of tax liabilities are paid. These studies suggest an underground economy amounting to between $675 billion and $900 billion in 1999.

Those who pursue rent-seeking activity and those involved in the underground economy view government from opposite perspectives. Rent seekers want government to become actively involved in transferring wealth to them, but those in the underground economy want to avoid government contact. *Subsidies and other advantages bestowed by government draw some groups closer to government; taxes drive others underground.*

BUREAUCRACY AND REPRESENTATIVE DEMOCRACY

Elected representatives approve legislation, but the task of implementing that legislation is typically left to various government departments and agencies. The organizations charged with implementing legislation are usually referred to as **bureaus,** which are government agencies whose activities are financed by appropriations from legislative bodies.

Ownership and Funding of Bureaus

We can get a better feel for government bureaus by comparing them to corporations. Ownership of a corporation is based on the shares owned by stockhold-

---

3 For a summary of these studies, see Simon Johnson, et al., "Regulatory Discretion and the Unofficial Economy," *American Economic Review* 88 (May 1988): 387–392.

ers. Stockholders are the residual claimants of any profits or losses arising from the firm's operations. Ownership in a corporation is *transferable:* the shares can be sold in the stock market. In contrast, taxpayers are in a sense the "owners" of government bureaus in the jurisdiction in which they live. If the bureau earns a "profit," taxes will be reduced; if the bureau operates at a "loss," as most do, this loss must be covered by taxes. Each taxpayer has just one vote, regardless of the taxes paid. Ownership in the bureau is surrendered only if the taxpayer dies or moves out of the jurisdiction; ownership is not transferable—it cannot be bought and sold directly.

Whereas firms receive their revenue when customers voluntarily purchase their products, bureaus are typically financed by a budget appropriation from the legislature. Most of this budget comes from taxpayers. On occasion, bureaus earn revenue through user charges, such as admission fees to state parks or tuition at state colleges, but supplementary funds for these activities often come from budget appropriations. Because of these differences in the forms of ownership and in the sources of revenue, bureaus have different incentives than do profit-making firms, so they are likely to behave differently as well.

Ownership and Organizational Behavior

A central assumption of economics is that people behave rationally and respond to economic incentives. The more tightly compensation is linked to individual incentives, the more people will behave in accordance with those incentives. If a letter carrier's pay is based on the customers' satisfaction, the carrier will make a greater effort to deliver mail promptly and intact.

The private firm receives a steady stream of consumer feedback. If the price is too high or too low to clear the market, the firm will see surpluses or shortages develop. Not only is consumer feedback abundant, but the firm's owners have a profit incentive to act on that information in an attempt to satisfy consumer wants. The promise of profits also creates incentives to produce output at minimum cost. Thus, the firm's owners stand to gain from any improvement in customer satisfaction or in production efficiency.

Since public goods and services are not sold in markets, government bureaus receive less consumer feedback and are less sensitive to the feedback they do receive. There are no prices and no obvious shortages or surpluses. For example, how would you know whether there was a shortage or a surplus of police protection in your community? (Would gangs of police officers hanging around the doughnut shop indicate a surplus?) Not only do bureaus receive less consumer feedback than do firms, they also have less incentive to act on the information available. Because any "profits" or "losses" arising in the bureau are spread among all taxpayers, and because there is no transferability of ownership, bureaus have less incentive to satisfy customers or to produce their output using the least-cost combination of resources. (Laws prevent bureaucrats from taking home any "profit.")

Some pressure for customer satisfaction and cost minimization may be communicated by voters to their elected representatives and thereby to the bureaus. But this discipline is not very precise, particularly since any gains or losses in efficiency are diffused among all taxpayers. For example, suppose that you are one of a million taxpayers in a jurisdiction and you know about an inefficiency that wastes a million dollars a year. If you undertake measures that succeed in correcting the shortcoming, you save yourself about a dollar per year in taxes.

Voters can also leave a jurisdiction if they believe government is inefficient. Yet this mechanism, whereby people "vote with their feet" by moving to a more responsive jurisdiction, is a rather crude way to approximate voter satisfaction. Moreover, voters dissatisfied with the national government cannot easily vote with their feet.

Because of differences between public and private organizations—in the owners' ability both to transfer ownership and to appropriate profits—we expect bureaus to be less concerned with satisfying consumer demand and minimizing costs than private firms are. A variety of empirical studies has attempted to compare costs for products that are provided by both public bureaus and private firms, such as garbage collection. Of those studies that show a difference, some find public bureaus to be more efficient, but the majority find private firms to be more efficient.

Bureaucratic Objectives

Assuming that bureaus are not simply at the beck and call of the legislature—that is, assuming that bureaucrats have some autonomy—what sort of objectives will they pursue? The traditional view is that bureaucrats are "public servants," who try to serve the public as best they can. No doubt many public employees do just that, but is this a realistic assumption for bureaucrats more generally? Why should we assume self-sacrificing behavior by public-sector employees when we make no such assumption about private-sector employees?

One widely discussed theory of bureaucratic behavior has been proposed by William Niskanen. He argues that bureaus attempt to *maximize their budgets,* for along with a bigger budget comes size, prestige, amenities, staff, and pay—all features that are valued by bureaucrats.[4] How do bureaucrats maximize the bureau's budget? According to Niskanen, bureaus are monopoly suppliers of their output to the legislature. Rather than charge a price per unit, bureaus offer the legislature the entire amount as a package deal in return for the requested appropriation. According to this theory, the legislature has little ability to dig into the budget and cut particular items (no line-item veto). If the legislature proposes cuts in the bureau's budget, the bureau may threaten to make those cuts as painful to the legislature and constituents as possible. For example, if city officials attempt to reduce the school budget, school bureaucrats, rather than increase teaching loads, may threaten to eliminate kindergarten, abolish the high-school football team, or cut textbook purchases. If such threats are effective in forcing the legislature to back off from any cuts, the government budget turns out to be larger than most taxpayers would prefer. *Budget maximization results in a budget larger than that desired by the median voter.* The key to this argument is that bureaus are monopoly suppliers. If taxpayers have alternatives in the private sector, the monopoly power of the bureau is diminished.

Private Versus Public Production

Simply because some goods and services are financed by the government does not mean that they must be produced by the government. Elected officials may contract directly with private firms to produce public output. For example, a city council may contract with a firm to handle garbage collection for the city.

---

4 William A. Niskanen, Jr., *Bureaucracy and Representative Government* (Chicago: Aldine-Atherton, 1971).

Profit-making firms now provide everything from fire protection to prisons to local education. Elected officials may also use some combination of bureaus and firms to produce the desired output. For example, the Pentagon, a giant bureau, hires and trains military personnel, yet contracts with private firms to develop and produce various weapon systems. State governments typically hire private contractors to build roads but employ state workers to maintain roads. The mix of firms and bureaus varies over time and across jurisdictions, but the trend is toward increased *privatization,* or production by the private sector, of government goods and services. For example, among a sample of a dozen services provided by local governments, the share of services privatized increased from 24 percent in 1987 to 34 percent in 1992.[5]

When governments produce public goods and services, they are using *the internal organization of the government*—the bureaucracy—to supply the product. When governments contract with private firms to produce public goods and services, they are using *the market* to supply the product. Legislators might prefer dealing with bureaus rather than with firms for two reasons. First, in situations where it is difficult to specify a contract that clearly spells out all the possible contingencies, the internal organization of the bureau may be more responsive to the legislature's concerns than the manager of a firm would be. Second, to the extent that bureaus are vehicles for political patronage, legislators may prefer bureaus because bureaus provide opportunities to reward friends and supporters with jobs.

Using market competition to supply services that are not well defined, such as the guidance provided by a social worker, may lead to poor service. A private firm that wins the contract might be tempted to skimp on quality, particularly if the quality of the service can be determined only by direct observation when the service is provided. For example, suppose that government puts social work out for bid, selects the lowest bidder, then attempts to monitor the quality of the service through direct observation. The government would find direct monitoring quite costly. These services thus might best be provided by a government bureau. Because the bureau is less concerned with minimizing costs, it has less reason to lower the quality to reduce cost.

CONCLUSION

This chapter examined public goods and how preferences are reflected in public choices. After examining public goods, we discussed the problems arising from representative democracy and then examined bureaus, the organizations that usually implement public choices. We also considered indirect income transfers, or rent seeking, which arise because of changes in the rules governing economic activity in the private sector. Price supports, import restrictions, and other indirect transfers are not reflected fully in the government budget but often have profound effects on the economy. Whenever governments become involved in the workings of the economy to favor one group over another, some resources are shifted from productive activity to rent-seeking activity—that is, efforts to persuade the government to confer benefits on certain groups.

---

5 Robert Barro, "The Imperative to Privatize," *Wall Street Journal* (29 June 1995).

Individual incentives may also be distorted in a way that reduces the economy's output.

Governments attempt to address market failures in the private economy. But simply turning problems of perceived market failure over to government may not always be the best solution, because government has failings of its own. Participation in markets is based on voluntary exchange. Governments, however, have the legal power to enforce public choices. We should employ at least as high a standard in judging the performance of government, where allocations have the force of law, as we do in judging the private market, where allocations are decided by voluntary exchange between consenting parties.

SUMMARY

1. Private goods are rival and exclusive, such as a pizza. Public goods are nonrival and nonexclusive such as national defense. Goods that are in between include quasi-public goods, which are nonrival but exclusive, such as cable TV, and open-access goods, which are rival but nonexclusive, such as fish in the sea. Since private-sector producers cannot easily exclude nonpayers from consuming a public good, such goods are typically provided by government, which has the power to impose taxes.

2. Public choice based on majority rule usually reflects the preferences of the median voter. Other voters often must "buy" either more or less of the public good than they would prefer.

3. Producers have an abiding interest in any legislation that affects their livelihood. Consumers, however, purchase thousands of different goods and services and have no special interest in legislation affecting any particular product. Most consumers adopt a posture of rational ignorance about producer-oriented legislation, because the costs of keeping up with special-interest issues usually outweigh the expected benefits.

4. The intense interest that producer groups express in relevant legislation, coupled with the rational ignorance of voters on most issues, leaves government officials vulnerable to rent seeking by special interests. Elected officials interested in maximizing their political support may tend to serve producer interests rather than consumer interests—that is, to serve special interests at the expense of the public interest.

5. Bureaus differ from firms in the amount of consumer feedback they receive, in their incentive to minimize costs, and in the transferability of their ownership. Because of these differences, bureaus may not be as efficient or as sensitive to consumer preferences as private firms are.

QUESTIONS FOR REVIEW

1. *(Private and Public Goods)* Distinguish among private goods, quasi-public goods, open-access goods, and public goods. Provide examples of each.

2. *(Median Voter Model)* In a single-issue majority vote, such as the TV example in this chapter, will the median voter always get his or her most preferred outcome?

3. *(Representative Democracy)* Major political parties typically produce "middle-of-the-road" platforms rather than take extreme positions. Is this consistent with the concepts of the median voter and rational ignorance discussed in this chapter?

4. *(Distribution of Costs and Benefits)* Why are consumer interest groups usually less effective than producer lobbies in influencing legislation?

5. *(Distribution of Costs and Benefits)* Which groups typically bear the costs and which groups enjoy the benefits of (a) traditional public goods, (b) special-interest legislation, and (c) competing-interest legislation?

6. *(CaseStudy: Farm Subsidies)* "Subsidizing the price of milk or other agricultural products is not very expensive considering how many consumers there are in the

United States. Therefore, there is little harmful effect from such subsidies." Evaluate this statement.

7. (*CaseStudy: Farm Subsidies*) Subsidy programs are likely to have a number of secondary effects in addition to the direct effect on dairy prices. What impact do you suppose such subsidies are likely to have on the following?
    a. Housing prices
    b. Technological change in the dairy industry
    c. The price of dairy product substitutes

8. (*Rent Seeking*) Explain how rent seeking can lead to a drop in production. What role might the underground economy play in lessening the drop in productive activities?

9. (*The Underground Economy*) What is the underground economy? What is the impact on the underground economy of instituting a tax on a certain productive activity?

10. (*Bureaucracy and Representative Democracy*) How do the incentives and feedback for government bureaus differ from those for profit-making firms?

11. (*Bureaucracy and Representative Government*) Earlier in the text, the firm was described as combining managerial coordination with market exchange in order to produce its good or service. Does similar behavior occur in government bureaus? Explain.

PROBLEMS AND EXERCISES

12. (*Optimal Provision of Public Goods*) Using at least two individual consumers, show how the market demand curve is derived from individual demand curves (1) for a private goods and (2) for a public good. Once you have derived the market demand curve in each case, introduce a market supply curve and then show the optimal level of production.

13. (*Median Voter Model*) Suppose that the voters on a school property tax issue can be divided into three groups: A, B, and C. The graph at the right illustrates the preferences of these groups for the size of the school budget. If the budget decision is made by voting on two alternatives at a time, what is the most likely result of the vote?

14. (*Distribution of Costs and Benefits*) Suppose that the government decides to guarantee an above-market price for a good by buying up any surplus at that above-market price. Using a conventional supply-demand diagram, illustrate the following gains and losses from such a price support:

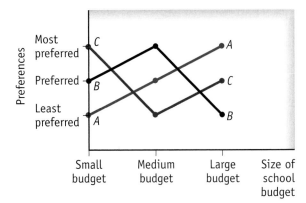

a. The loss of consumer surplus
b. The gain of producer surplus in the short run
c. The cost of running the government program (assuming no storage costs)
d. What is the total cost of the program to consumers?
e. Are the costs and benefits of the support program widespread or concentrated?

EXPERIENTIAL EXERCISES

15. (*CaseStudy: Campaign Finance Reform*) The Economic Policy Network's briefing book on campaign finance reform at http://epn.org/camfinre.html provides numerous links to information on the issues. Try to determine which individuals, firms, and PACs have been the major contributors in your local congressional district. Based on your knowledge of these groups, what specifically are they trying to accomplish by contributing to a congressional campaign?

16. (*Rational Ignorance*) Loren Lomasky, in "The Booth and Consequences" at http://www.magnolia.

net/~leonf/sc/tbac.html wrestles with the question of why people bother to vote. Read the article and decide for yourself: Is voting rational?

17. (*Wall Street Journal*) The Politics & Policy column in the First Section of the Wall Street Journal is a good source for articles on politics at every level. Choose one such article and decide whether it describes special-interest or general-interest legislation. Then, classify the benefits and the costs as either concentrated or widespread.

Externalities and the Environment

Visit the McEachern
Interactive Study Center
for this chapter at
http://mcisc.swcollege.com

What do the following have to do with economics? The rivers in Jakarta, Indonesia, are dead—killed by acid, alcohol, and oil. Coral reefs in the South Pacific have been ripped apart by dynamite fishing. Breathing the air in Bombay, India, is reportedly equivalent to smoking 10 cigarettes a day. In Mexico City some people buy oxygen tanks for use in their homes. The air in Paris has more lead and carbon monoxide than the air in any other major city in the world. Five of the world's 10 most polluted cities are in China, where air pollution levels are two to five times the guidelines for safe exposure. The air in some U.S. cities does not meet health standards, and some U.S. soil has been poisoned with toxic waste. And certain streams in Colorado are still considered toxic from gold mining that ended more than a century ago.

What does all that have to do with economics? Plenty! Market prices can efficiently allocate resources only as long as property rights are well defined and can be easily enforced. But property rights to clean water, air, and soil, to fish in the ocean, to peace and quiet, and to scenic vistas are hard to establish and enforce. *This chapter examines the difficulty of assigning property rights to some key resources, and why the lack of property rights results in inefficient use.*

As you learned in Chapter 4, externalities, which are unpriced byproducts of production or consumption, may be either negative (for example, air pollution) or positive (for example, the general improvement in the civic climate that results from better education). This chapter concentrates mostly on negative externalities. The focus is on how externalities affect resource allocation and on how well-designed public policies can promote greater efficiency. Topics discussed in this chapter include:

- Exhaustible resources
- Renewable resources
- The common-pool problem
- Private property rights
- Optimal pollution

- Marginal social cost
- Marginal social benefit
- The market for pollution permits
- The Coase theorem
- Environmental protection

EXTERNALITIES AND THE COMMON-POOL PROBLEM

Exhaustible resource A resource available in fixed supply, such as crude oil or copper ore

Let's begin our discussion by distinguishing between *exhaustible* resources and *renewable* resources. An **exhaustible resource,** such as oil, coal, or copper ore, does not renew itself, and so is available in a finite amount. Each gallon of oil burned is gone forever. Sooner or later, all oil wells will run dry. The world's oil reserves are exhaustible.

Renewable Resources

Renewable resource A resource that can regenerate itself and so can be used periodically for an indefinite period of time if used conservatively, such as a properly managed forest

A resource is **renewable** if, when used conservatively, the resource can be drawn on indefinitely. Thus timber is a renewable resource if felled trees can be replaced at rates that provide a steady supply. The atmosphere and rivers are renewable resources to the extent that they can absorb and neutralize a certain level of pollutants. More generally, biological resources such fish, game, forests, rivers, grasslands, and agricultural soil are renewable if managed appropriately.

Some renewable resources are also *open-access goods*, an idea introduced in the previous chapter, meaning that the good is rival in consumption but exclusion is costly. For example, fish caught in the ocean are not available for others to catch, yet it would be costly for an individual to own the fish in the sea and prevent someone from catching them. An open-access good is often subject to the **common-pool problem,** which results because such a good will be used until the marginal value of additional use drops to zero. Consequently, open-access goods are often overused or overharvested.

Common-pool problem Unrestricted access to a resource that results in overuse until the marginal value of additional use drops to zero

Because the atmosphere is an open-access resource, we use the air as a dump for unwanted gases. Air pollution is a negative externality imposed by polluters on society. As noted already, *negative externalities* are unpriced byproducts of production or consumption that impose costs on other consumers or other firms. For example, some spray cans release fluorocarbons into the atmosphere; these gases are said to cause a thinning of the ozone layer that protects us from the sun's ultraviolet rays.

In a market system, specific individuals usually own the rights to resources and therefore have a strong interest in using those resources efficiently. **Private property rights** allow individuals to control the use of certain resources and to charge others for their use. Private property rights are defined and enforced by government, by informal social actions, and by ethical norms. But because specifying and enforcing property rights to certain resources is quite costly, not all resources are owned as private property. For example, how could specific individuals claim and enforce a right to the air, to the fish in the ocean, or to migrating birds? There are usually no individual property rights to such resources because no individual can (1) easily exclude others from using the resource and (2) easily capture the value of the resource by "consuming" it all or selling it all. Thus we say that some resources are both *nonexclusive* (preventing someone from using the resource is costly if not impossible) and *nonappropriable* (no individual can easily capture the entire value of the resource).

Pollution and other negative externalities arise because there are no practical, enforceable, private property rights to open-access resources, such as the air. Market prices usually fail to include the costs that negative externalities impose on society. For example, the cost of a can of hair spray powered by fluorocarbons does not reflect the effect of gas emissions on the atmosphere's ozone layer. The price you pay for a gallon of gasoline does not reflect the costs imposed by the dirtier air and the traffic congestion your driving creates. And electric rates in the Midwest do not reflect the negative externalities, or *external* costs, that sulfur-dioxide emissions impose on people living downwind from power plants. Note that externalities are unintended side effects of actions that are themselves useful and purposeful. Electricity producers, for example, did not go into business to pollute.

Private property rights
The right of an owner to use, rent, or sell, property

Resolving the Common-Pool Problem

Because property rights are not attached to open-access resources, individual users of fresh air, clean water, wildlife, or other open-access goods tend to ignore the effects of their activities on the resource's renewal ability. As stocks diminish from overuse or overharvesting, the resource grows more scarce. A lack of regulation in the fishing industry allowed decades of massive harvesting of the ocean's bounty, which depleted the stock of fish. For example, Georges Bank, off New England, long one of the world's most productive fishing grounds, has been so depleted by overfishing that by the 1990s the catch was down 85 percent from peak years.[1] The United Nations says 11 of the world's 15 primary fishing grounds are seriously depleted.

The common-pool problem of resource exploitation can be reduced if some central authority imposes restrictions on resource use. By restricting output or by imposing an appropriate depletion tax, a regulatory authority can force competitive firms to use the resource at a rate that is socially optimal. For example, in the face of the tendency to overfish and to catch fish before they are sufficiently mature, the government has imposed a variety of restrictions on the fishing industry. There are limits on the total amount of the catch, on the

---

1 See Deborah Cramer, "Troubled Waters," *Atlantic Monthly* (June 1995): 22-26.

size of fish caught, on the length of the fishing season, on the equipment used, and on other aspects of the business.

More generally, *when imposing and enforcing private property rights would be too costly, government regulations may improve allocative efficiency.* For example, stop signs and traffic lights allocate the scarce road space at an intersection, minimum-size restrictions control lobster fishing, hunting seasons control the stock of game, and official study hours may calm the din in the dormitory.

But not all regulations are equally efficient. For example, fishing authorities sometimes limit the *total* industry catch and allow all firms to fish until that total is reached. Consequently, when the fishing season opens, there is a mad scramble to catch as much as possible before the industry limit is reached. Since time is of the essence, firms make no effort to fish selectively. And the catch reaches fish processors all at once, creating a problem for all segments of the industry. Also, each firm has an incentive to expand its fishing fleet to catch more in those precious few weeks. Thus, large fleets of technologically efficient fishing vessels sit in port for most of the year, except during the beginning of the fishing season. *Each firm is acting rationally, but the collective effect of the regulation is grossly inefficient in terms of social welfare.* Consider the complicated and sometimes confounding nature of fishing regulations in Iceland:

> The Icelandic government realized that it would have to curb the capacity of its own fleet. But the fishermen compensated by buying more trawlers. Then the government restricted the size of the fleet and the number of days at sea; the fishermen responded by buying larger, more efficient gear. The cod stocks continued to decline. In 1984, the government introduced quotas on species per vessel per season. This was a controversial and often wasteful system. A groundfish hauled up from fifty fathoms [300 feet] is killed by the change in pressure. But if it is a cod and the cod quota has been used up, it is thrown overboard. Or if the price of cod is low that week and cod happens to come in the haddock or plaice net, the fishermen will throw them overboard because they do not want to use up their cod quota when they are not getting a good price.[2]

Fish remain a common-pool good because the technology has not yet been developed to establish and enforce rights to particular schools of fish. But advances in technology may some day allow the creation of private property rights to ocean fish, migrating birds, and even the air we breathe. At one time, establishing property rights to cattle on the Great Plains seemed impossible, but the invention of barbed wire allowed ranchers to fence the range. In a sense, barbed wire tamed the "wild West."

OPTIMAL LEVEL OF POLLUTION

Research suggests (though the issue is far from resolved) that the sulfur dioxide emitted by coal-fired power plants during electricity production mixes with moisture in the air to form sulfuric acid, which is carried by the prevailing winds and falls as acid rain. Many argue that acid rain has killed lakes and forests and has corroded buildings, bridges, and other structures. Electricity produc-

---

2 Quoted from Mark Kurlansky, *Cod: A Biography of the Fish that Changed the World,* Walker & Co., 1997, p. 172.

tion, therefore, involves the external cost of using the atmosphere as a gas dump. In this section we show how to analyze this externality problem.

External Costs with Fixed Technology

Suppose the demand curve for electricity in the Midwest is depicted by *D* in Exhibit 1. Recall that the demand curve reflects consumers' marginal benefit for each level of consumption. The lower horizontal line reflects the *marginal private cost* of production incurred by electricity producers. If producers base their pricing and output decisions on their private marginal costs, the equilibrium quantity of electricity used per month is 50 million kilowatt hours and the equilibrium price is $0.10 per kilowatt hour. At that price and output level, the marginal private cost of production just equals the marginal benefit enjoyed by consumers of electricity.

Electricity production involves not only the private marginal cost of the resources employed but also the external cost of using the atmosphere as a gas dump. Suppose that the marginal external cost imposed on the environment by the generation of electricity is $0.04 per kilowatt hour. If the only way of reducing the emission of sulfur is by reducing the generation of electricity, then the relationship between the production of electricity and the production of pollution is a fixed one. Thus we say that pollution in this case occurs with **fixed-production technology.**

The marginal external cost of $0.04 per kilowatt hour is shown by the vertical distance between the marginal private cost curve and the marginal social

Fixed-production technology The relationship between output rate and the generation of an externality is a fixed one; the only way to the reduce the externality is to reduce the output rate.

EXHIBIT 1

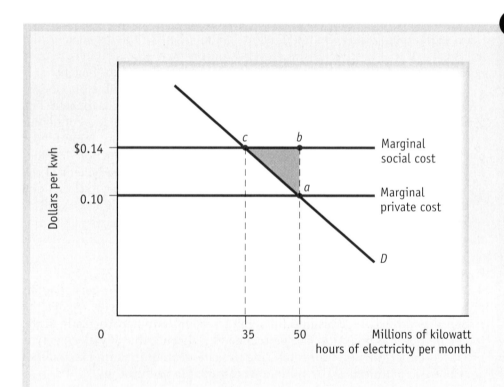

Negative Externalities: The Market for Electricity in the Midwest

If producers base their output on marginal private cost, 50 million kilowatt hours of electricity are produced per month. The marginal external cost of electricity production reflects the cost of pollution imposed on society. The marginal social cost curve includes both the marginal private cost and the marginal external cost. If producers base their output decisions on marginal social cost, only 35 million kilowatt hours are produced, which is the optimal level of output. The total social gain from basing production on marginal social cost is reflected by the blue triangle.

Marginal social cost
The sum of the marginal private cost and the marginal external cost of production or consumption

cost curve in Exhibit 1. The **marginal social cost** includes both the marginal private cost and the *marginal external cost* that production imposes on society. Because the marginal external cost is assumed to be constant, the two cost curves are parallel. Notice that at the private-sector equilibrium output level of 50 million kilowatt hours, the marginal social cost, identified at point *b*, exceeds society's marginal benefit from that unit of electricity, identified at point *a* on the demand curve. The last kilowatt hour of electricity produced costs society $0.14 to produce but has a marginal benefit of only $0.10. Because the marginal cost to society exceeds the marginal benefit, the firm's choice of output results in a *market failure*. Too much electricity is generated, and too much pollution is produced in the process. What's more, the price of electricity is too low because it fails to reflect the social cost.

The efficient level of output from society's point of view is where the demand, or marginal benefit, curve intersects the marginal social cost curve—a point identified as *c* in Exhibit 1. How could output be restricted to the socially efficient level of 35 million kilowatts per month? If government policy makers knew the demand curve and the marginal cost curves, they could simply require electric utilities to produce no more than the optimal level. Or they could impose on each unit of output a *pollution tax* equal to the marginal external cost of generating electricity. If correctly determined, such a tax would raise the industry supply curve up to the marginal social cost curve, so the marginal private cost of electricity would equal the marginal social cost. The externality would, in effect, be internalized.

With the appropriate tax, the equilibrium combination of price and output moves from point *a* to point *c*. The price rises from $0.10 to $0.14 per kilowatt hour, and output falls to 35 million kilowatt hours. Setting the tax equal to the marginal external cost results in a level of output that is socially efficient; at point *c*, the marginal social cost of production equals the marginal benefit.

Notice that pollution is not eliminated at point *c*, but the utilities no longer generate electricity whose marginal social cost exceeds its marginal benefit. The total social gain from reducing production to the socially optimal level of output is shown by the blue shaded triangle in Exhibit 1. This triangle also measures the total social cost of ignoring the negative externalities in the production decision; it reflects the total amount by which the social cost exceeds the benefit of the good if 50 million kilowatt hours are produced. Although Exhibit 1 offers a tidy solution, the external costs of pollution often cannot be easily calculated or taxed. At times, government intervention may result in more or less production than the optimal solution calls for.

External Cost with Variable Technology

The preceding example assumes that the only way to reduce the total amount of pollution is to reduce output. But power companies can usually change the resource mix to reduce emissions for a given level of output, particularly in the long run. Because pollution can be reduced by altering the way electricity is produced rather than by simply altering the rate of output, these externalities are said to be produced under conditions of **variable technology**.

To examine the optimal amount of pollution under variable technology, consider Exhibit 2. The horizontal axis measures air quality. If all firms made their production decisions based simply on their private cost—that is, if the cost

Variable technology The amount of externality generated at a given rate of output can be reduced by altering the production process rather than by simply reducing the rate of output.

EXHIBIT 2

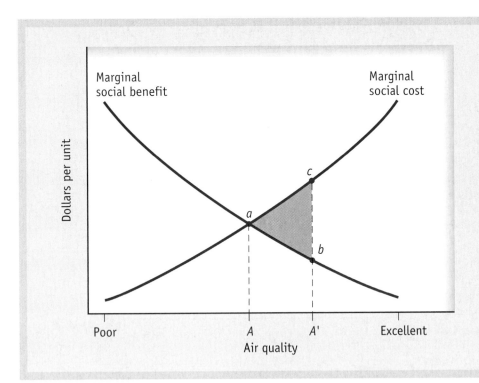

The Optimal Level of Air Quality

The optimal level of air quality is found at point *a*, where the marginal social cost of cleaner air equals its marginal social benefit. If some higher level of air quality were dictated by the government, the marginal social cost would exceed the marginal social benefit, and social waste would result. The total social waste resulting from a higher-than-optimal air quality is indicated by the red shaded triangle.

of pollution is external to the firm—then the firm would have no incentive to search for production methods that would reduce pollution, so too much pollution as a by-product of production would occur.

But air quality can be improved by adopting cleaner production technology. For example, coal-burning plants can be fitted with smoke "scrubbers" to reduce toxic emissions. Yet the production of cleaner air, like the production of other goods, is subject to diminishing returns. Cutting emissions of the largest particles may involve simply putting a screen over the smokestack, but eliminating successively finer particles requires more sophisticated and more expensive processes. Thus, the marginal social cost curve of cleaning the air slopes upward, as shown in Exhibit 2.

The **marginal social benefit** curve reflects the additional benefit society derives from improving air quality. When air quality is poor, an improvement can save lives and will be valued by society more than when air quality is excellent. Cleaner and cleaner air, like other goods, has a declining marginal benefit to society (though the total benefit still increases). The marginal social benefit curve from cleaner air therefore slopes downward, as shown in Exhibit 2.

The optimal level of air quality is found at point *a,* where the marginal social cost of cleaner air equals the marginal social benefit. In this example, the optimal level of air quality is *A*. What if the government decreed that the level of air quality should exceed *A*? For example, suppose a law were passed setting *A'* as the minimum acceptable level. The marginal social cost, identified as *c*, of achieving that improved level of air quality exceeds the marginal social benefit, identified as *b*. The total social waste associated with imposing a greater-than-optimal

Marginal social benefit
The sum of the marginal private benefit and the marginal external benefit of production or consumption

EXHIBIT 3

Effect of Changes in Costs and Benefits on the Optimal Level of Air Quality

Either a reduction in the marginal social cost of cleaner air, as shown in panel (a), or an increase in the marginal social benefit of cleaner air, as shown in panel (b), will increase the optimal level of air quality.

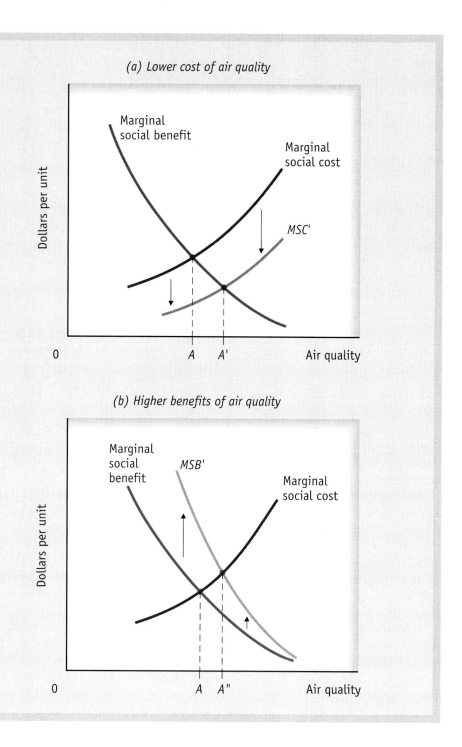

(a) Lower cost of air quality

Marginal social benefit

Marginal social cost

MSC'

Dollars per unit

0   A   A'   Air quality

(b) Higher benefits of air quality

Marginal social benefit

MSB'

Marginal social cost

Dollars per unit

0   A   A"   Air quality

level of air quality is represented by the red shaded triangle, *abc.* This is the total amount by which the additional social costs of cleaner air (associated with a move from *A* to *A'*) exceed the additional social benefits.

The idea that all pollution should be eliminated is a popular misconception. Usually some pollution is consistent with efficiency. *Improving air quality benefits society as a whole as long as the marginal benefit of cleaner air exceeds its marginal cost.*

What would happen to the optimal level of air quality if either the marginal cost or the marginal benefit of cleaner air changed? Suppose, for example, that some technological breakthrough reduces the marginal cost of cleaning the air. As shown in panel (a) of Exhibit 3, the marginal social cost curve of reducing pollution would shift down to *MSC'*, thereby increasing the optimal level of air quality from *A* to *A'*. The simple logic is that the *lower the marginal cost of reducing pollution, other things constant, the greater the optimal level of air quality.*

An increase in the marginal benefit of air quality would have a similar effect. For example, what if we discovered that bad air quality increases the incidence of certain types of cancer? The perceived marginal benefit of cleaner air would increase, as reflected in panel (b) of Exhibit 3 by a shift upward in the marginal social benefit curve to *MSB'*. As a result, the optimal level of air quality would increase. *The greater the marginal benefit of air quality, other things constant, the greater the optimal level of air quality.*

The atmosphere has the ability to cleanse itself of some emissions, but the destruction of the tropical rain forest has reduced this ability, as discussed in the following case study.

Destruction of the Tropical Rain Forest

The tropical rain forests have been called "the lungs of the world" because they naturally recycle carbon dioxide by transforming it into oxygen and wood, thus helping to maintain the world's atmospheric balance. The Amazon rain forest contains the largest collection of plant and animal life on Earth, along with 20 percent of the world's water supply. But the high world demand for timber has caused loggers to cut down much of the tropical forest. Worse yet, farmers burn down these forests to create farmland and pastures. Burning the world's forests has a triple-barreled effect. The loss of trees reduces the atmosphere's ability to cleanse itself, the burning adds yet more harmful gases to the atmosphere, and the forest subsoil usually contains huge quantities of carbon subject to oxidization when the trees are removed. Since the world's atmosphere is a common pool, the costs of deforestation are imposed on people around the globe.

Forest acreage throughout the world has declined by 15 percent over the last decade. The Amazon has lost 260,000 square miles of rain forest, an area the size of Texas. The north coast of South America contains one of the world's largest unspoiled tropical rain forests, but the governments of Guyana and Suriname have opened huge tracts of forest for logging by companies from Korea, Indonesia, and Malaysia. In Central America, the forests have been cleared for cattle ranches. Commercial logging has been so extensive in the African countries of Ghana and the Ivory Coast that the business is already winding down, leaving behind poverty and devastation. According to the World Bank, two-thirds of the countries that export tropical forest products are running out of trees.

The Rainforest Alliance at http://www.rainforest-alliance.org/ is an international nonprofit organization dedicated to the conservation of tropical forests. Its goal is to promote economically viable alternatives to the destruction of this endangered natural resource. Look through this site to find examples of the role economics plays in the projects and research the group supports. The Rainforest Action Network is another group devoted to rainforest conservation but focuses more on citizen activism. Visit its site at http://www.ran.org/ran/ and compare and contrast the approaches of these two groups.

The loss of the tropical forests causes other negative externalities as well. As long as the tropical forest has its canopy of trees, it remains a rich, genetically diverse ecosystem. Tropical forests cover only 6 percent of the Earth's land surface (down from 12 percent 50 years ago), but they contain *half* of the world's species of plants and animals, and thus represent an abundant source of fruits, crops, and medicines. One-fourth of the prescription drugs used in the United States are derived from tropical plants, such as seeds that may help cure some types of cancer. Biologists estimate that 50,000 species are condemned to extinction each year because of deforestation. Yet most tropical plants have not been tested for their medicinal properties.

Small farmers and wood gatherers and big lumber companies are stripping the tropical forests. Once the forests are cut down, the tropical soil is eroded by rains and baked by the sun and soon runs out of nutrients. When the nutrients are lost, the system is not very resilient. It takes a century for a clear-cut forest to return to its original state. The policy of cutting down everything in sight is of benefit only to loggers, who usually do not own the land and thus have little interest in its future.

The world's rain forests are located in countries that are relatively poor: Brazil, Peru, Indonesia, Zaire, and the Philippines. Environmental quality is a normal good, meaning that as incomes rise, the demand for it increases. In poor countries, however, the priority is not environmental quality but food and shelter. Brazil and other developing countries are destroying their forests to provide jobs. But since the soil quickly loses its nutrients to erosion and the sun, few settlers have become successful farmers.

The tropical rain forests, by serving as the lungs of the world, confer benefits around the globe. But the positive effects that the trees have on the atmosphere tend to be ignored in the decision to clear the land. Worse yet, the taking of timber is often "first come, first served," and government investment programs frequently subsidize the harvesting of timber. *It is not the greed of peasants and timber companies that leads to inefficient, or wasteful, uses of resource, but the fact that the atmosphere, and, indeed, the rain forests are open-access resources that can be degraded with little immediate personal cost to those who clear the forests.*

What to do? Those who benefit from the tropical rain forest should be willing to pay for the benefits. Government programs that encourage selective cutting and replanting would allow the forest to remain an air filter and a renewable source of forest products. For example, with help from the World Bank and the World Wildlife Fund, Brazil announced plans in 1998 to protect an area of rain forest the size of Colorado. Other ideas are on the drawing board, but a systematic solution is still a long way off.

Sources: Edmund Andrews, "For Europeans, Greenhouse-Gas Issue Is How Much to Cut," *New York Times* (4 December 1997); "Brazil to Set Aside 62 Million Acres of Forest Lands," *Minneapolis Star Tribune* (30 April 1998); Thomas C. Schelling, "Some Economics of Global Warming," *American Economic Review* 82 (March 1992): 1–14; "Argentina Makes Plans to Aid Reduction of Global Warming," *Hartford Courant* (12 November 1998); and "Saving Rain Forests," *San Francisco Examiner* (24 April 1998)

The Coase Analysis of Externalities

The traditional analysis of externalities assumes that market failures arise because people ignore the external effects of their actions. Suppose a research laboratory that tests delicate equipment is located next to a manufacturer of heavy machinery. The vibrations caused by the manufacturing process throw off the delicate machinery in the lab next door. Professor Ronald Coase, who won the Nobel prize in 1991, would point out that the negative externality in this case is not necessarily imposed by the machinery producer on the testing lab—rather, *it arises from the incompatible activities of the two parties.* The externality is the result both of vibrations created by the factory *and* of the location of the testing lab next door. One efficient solution to this externality problem might be to modify the machines in the factory; others might be to make the equipment in the testing lab more shock resistant or to move the lab elsewhere.

According to Coase, the efficient solution to an externality problem depends on which party can avoid the problem at the lower cost. Suppose the factory has determined that it would cost $2 million to reduce vibrations enough to allow the lab to function normally. For its part, the testing lab has concluded that it cannot easily alter its equipment to reduce the effects of the vibrations, so its only recourse would be to move the lab elsewhere at a cost of $1 million. Based on these costs, the least-cost, or most efficient, resolution to the externality problem is for the testing lab to relocate.

Coase argues that when property rights are assigned to one party or another, the two parties will agree on the efficient solution to an externality problem as long as transaction costs are low. This efficient solution will be achieved regardless of which party is assigned the property right. Suppose the testing lab is granted the right to operate free of vibrations from next door, so the testing lab has the right to ask the factory to reduce its vibration. Rather than cut vibrations at a cost of $2 million, the factory can offer to pay the lab to relocate. Any payment by the factory owners that is greater than $1 million but less than $2 million will make both firms better off, since the lab will receive more than its moving cost and the factory will pay less than its cost of reducing vibrations. Thus the lab will move, which is the efficient outcome.

Alternatively, suppose the factory is granted the right to generate vibrations in its production process. For the factory, this means business as usual. The lab may consider paying the factory to alter its production method, but since the minimum payment the factory would accept is $2 million, the lab would rather move at a cost of $1 million. Thus whether property rights are granted to the lab or to the factory, the lab will move, which is the most efficient, or least-cost, solution. The **Coase theorem** says that as long as bargaining costs are small, the assignment of property rights will generate an efficient solution to an externality problem regardless of which party is assigned the property rights. A particular assignment of property rights determines only who incurs the externality costs, not the efficient outcome.

Inefficient outcomes do occur, however, when the transaction costs of arriving at a solution are high. For example, an airport located in a populated area would have difficulty negotiating with all the surrounding residents about noise levels. Or a power plant emitting sulfur dioxide would have trouble negotiating with the millions of people scattered across the downwind states. Or a would-be farmer contemplating clearing a portion of the tropical rain forest cannot negotiate with the millions, and perhaps, billions, of people ultimately affected by that decision. When the number of parties involved in the transaction is large, the chance for a voluntary agreement is small.

Coase theorem As long as bargaining costs are small, an efficient solution to the problem of externalities will be achieved by assigning property rights.

A Market for Pollution Rights

According to Coase, the assignment of property rights is often sufficient to re-solve the market failure typically associated with externalities. Additional gov-ernment intervention is not necessary. If pollution can be easily monitored and polluters easily identified, the government may be able to achieve an efficient solution to the problem of pollution simply by assigning the right to pollute. For example, firms that dump waste into a river evidently value the ability to discharge their waste matter in this way. For them, the river provides an inex-pensive outlet for pollutants that otherwise would have to be disposed of at greater cost. The river provides disposal services, and the demand curve for this pollutant transportation system slopes downward just like the demand for other resources.

The demand for the river as a discharge system is presented as *D* in Exhibit 4. The horizontal axis measures the amount of pollutants dumped into the river per day, and the vertical axis measures firms' marginal benefits of disposing of their waste in this way. The demand curve thus measures the marginal value to firms of using the river as a resource for discharging pollutants. With no restrictions on river pollution—that is, if all are free to discharge their wastes into the river—the daily discharge rate would occur where the private marginal value of discharging wastes falls to zero, which is at output level *Q* in Exhibit 4. Dumping will con-tinue as long as it yields some private marginal benefit. If dumping remains unregulated, the river must carry away whatever polluters choose to dump there.

The river, like the atmosphere and the soil, can absorb and neutralize a certain amount of pollution per day without deteriorating in quality. Suppose

EXHIBIT 4

Optimal Allocation of Pollution Rights

Suppose the demand for a river as an outlet for pollution is *D*. In the absence of any environmental controls, pol-lution will occur up to point *Q*, where the marginal bene-fit of further pollution equals zero. If regulatory authorities establish *Q** as the maxi-mum allowable level of pollu-tion and then sell the rights to pollution, the market for these pollution rights will clear at price *p*. If the de-mand for pollution rights in-creases to *D'*, the market-clearing price will rise to *p'*.

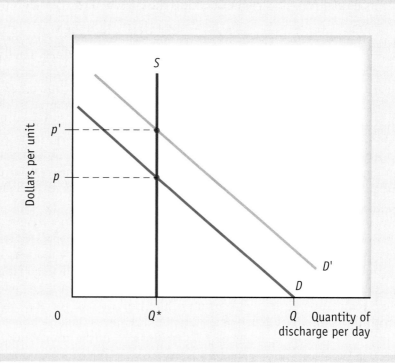

voters in the jurisdiction that encompasses the river make the public choice that the river should be clean enough for swimming and fishing. The maximum level of waste discharge that is consistent with this quality is Q^* in Exhibit 4. Hence, if the river is to be preserved at the specified level of quality, the "supply" of the river available as a discharge resource must be fixed at S.

If government regulators can easily identify polluters and monitor their behavior, authorities can allocate an amount of pollution permitted equal to Q^*. If polluters are simply given these permits (that is, if the price of permits is zero), there will be an excess demand for them, since the quantity supplied is Q^* but the quantity demanded at a price of zero would be Q. An alternative is to *sell* the specified quantity of pollution permits at the market-clearing price. The intersection of the supply curve, S, and the demand curve, D, yields a permit price, p, which is the marginal value of dumping quantity Q^* into the river each day. To most purchasers, the marginal value of a permit will exceed p.

The beauty of this system is that those producers that value the discharge rights the most will ultimately end up with them. Producers that attach a lower marginal value to river dumping obviously have cheaper ways of resolving their waste problems, including changing production techniques. And if conservation groups wish to maintain a higher river quality than the government's standard, they can purchase pollution permits but not exercise them.

What if additional firms locate along the river and want to discharge wastes? This added demand for discharge rights is reflected in Exhibit 4 by the higher level of demand, D'. This greater demand would bid up the market price of pollution permits to p', so some existing permit owners will sell to those who value the permits more. Regardless of the comings and goings of would-be polluters, the total quantity of discharge rights is restricted to Q^*, so the river's quality will be maintained. Thus the value of pollution permits, but not the total amount of pollution, may fluctuate over time.

If the right to pollute could be granted, monitored, and enforced, then what had been a negative externality problem could be solved through market allocation. Historically, the U.S. government has relied on setting discharge standards and fining offenders, and has used pollution rights only in some metropolitan areas. But in 1989, a pollution-rights market for fluorocarbon emissions was established and was followed in 1990 by a market for sulfur dioxide. The price for the right to emit a ton of sulfur dioxide was recently $140. So the market for pollution rights is alive and growing.[3]

Unfortunately, legislation dealing with pollution is affected by the same problems of representative democracy that trouble other public policy questions. Polluters have a special interest in government proposals relating to pollution, and they fight measures to limit pollution. But members of the public remain rationally ignorant about pollution legislation. So pollution regulations may be less in accord with the public interest than with the special interests of polluters. This is why pollution permits are often given free to existing firms. For example, under the sulfur-dioxide program, the nation's 101 dirtiest power plants receive credits equal to between 30 and 50 percent of the pollution they

---

3 For a discussion of the market for sulfur dioxide emissions, see Paul Joskow, Richard Schmalensee, and Elizabeth Bailey, "The Market for Sulfur-Dioxide Emissions," *American Economic Review* 88 (September 1998): 669–685.

emitted prior to the program. Because they receive something of value, polluters are less inclined to fight the institution of the program. Once the permits are granted, some recipients find it profitable to sell their permits to other firms that value them more. Thus a market emerges that leads to an efficient allocation of pollution permits. According to some analysts, the sulfur program saves up to $3 billion annually compared to the old system.[4] More generally, a system of marketable pollution rights can reduce the cost of pollution abatement by as much as 75 percent.

Now that you know something about the theory of externalities, let's turn to the primary application of the theory—environmental protection.

ENVIRONMENTAL PROTECTION

Federal efforts to address the common-pool problem of air, water, and soil are coordinated by the *Environmental Protection Agency (EPA)*. Four federal laws and subsequent amendments underpin U.S. efforts to protect the environment: the Clean Air Act of 1970, the Clean Water Act of 1972, the Resource Conservation and Recovery Act of 1976 (which governs solid waste disposal), and the *Superfund* law of 1980, legislation focusing on toxic waste dumps. In 1970, the EPA had about 4,000 employees and a budget of $200 million. By the 1990s, the EPA had about 18,000 employees and a budget of $5 billion.

According to EPA estimates, compliance with pollution-control regulations costs U.S. producers and consumers an amount equivalent to 2 percent of gross domestic product,[5] the market value of all final goods and services produced in the economy in a given year. We can divide pollution-abatement spending into three main categories: spending for air-pollution abatement, spending for water-pollution abatement, and spending for solid-waste disposal. About 40 percent of the pollution-abatement expenditures in the United States goes toward cleaner air, another 40 percent goes toward cleaner water, and 20 percent goes toward disposing of solid waste. In this section we will consider, in turn, air pollution, water pollution, Superfund activities, and disposing of solid waste.

Air Pollution

In the Clean Air Act of 1970 and in subsequent amendments, Congress set national standards for the amount of pollution that could be emitted into the atmosphere. Congress thereby recognized the atmosphere as an economic resource, which, like other resources, has alternative uses. The air can be used as a source of life-giving oxygen, as a prism for viewing breathtaking vistas, or as a dump for carrying away unwanted soot and gases. The 1970 act gave Americans the right to breathe air of a certain quality and at the same time gave producers the right to emit certain specified pollutants.

---

4 This saving was estimated by Paul R. Portney, "Air Pollution Policy," in P. R. Portney, Ed., *Public Policies for Environmental Protection* (Washington, D.C.: Resources for the Future 1990): 27–96.

5 Other researchers estimate that clean-air and clean-water regulations reduced GDP in 1990 to be about 6 percent less than what it would have been in the absence of such regulations. See Michael Hazilla and Raymond Kopp, "Social Cost of Environmental Quality Regulations: A General Equilibrium Analysis," *Journal of Political Economy* 98 (August 1990): 544–551.

Smog is the most visible form of air pollution. Automobile emissions account for 40 percent of smog. Another 40 percent comes from consumer products, such as paint thinner, fluorocarbon sprays, dry-cleaning solvents, and baker's yeast by-products. Surprisingly, only 15 percent of smog comes from manufacturing. The 1970 Clean Air Act mandated a reduction of 90 percent in auto emissions, leaving it to the auto industry to achieve this target. At the time, auto makers complained that the objective was impossible. Between 1970 and 1990, however, average emissions of lead fell 97 percent, carbon monoxide emissions fell 41 percent, and sulfur oxide emissions fell 25 percent. In fact, a recent EPA study concluded that because auto emissions and industrial smoke have been reduced, air pollution now runs two to five times higher indoors than outdoors. U.S. air quality is good compared to the air quality in some parts of the world.

Efforts are underway to improve air quality on a global scale. A tentative accord reached in Kyoto, Japan, in December 1997, would require the 38 industrial countries to reduce emissions of carbon dioxide and other so-called greenhouse gases by one-third over ten years. The measure would impose a carbon tax on coal, natural gas and oil. The cost to the U.S. economy could reach $300 billion a year, according to one study. Only industrial economies would be required to reduce emissions; developing countries need not participate. Thus even if industrial nations meet their Kyoto targets, carbon dioxide emissions would continue to rise since most of the projected global increase would come from exempted countries. The treaty requires approval by legislative bodies in the United States and in the other countries, which appears doubtful at this point.

Critics of the treaty argue that cleaner air requires a greater commitment from the developing world, such as China and India, which are major polluters. Argentina is the first developing nation offering to voluntarily cut back greenhouse emissions. The following case study examines the problem of cleaning up the polluted air in one developing country.

City in the Clouds

CaseStudy

Other Times, Other Places

GAIA, a collaborative effort of European research centers and universities, builds multimedia tools for environmental education and management. It presents an interesting case study, "Urban Air Pollution in Mexico City," at http://www.ess. co.at/GAIA/CASES/MEX/ index.html. What are the major sources of air pollutants in Mexico City, and what are their primary effects? What plans are there to control emissions? A photographic essay illustrating the problem is archived by the National Geographic Society at //www. nationalgeographic.com/features/96/mexico/a011.html.

Mexico City has a metropolitan population of 24 million, ranking it the second-largest city in the world. There are 41,000 people per square mile, about four times the density of New York City. More than half of Mexico's industrial output is produced in or near Mexico City. Millions of vehicles and tens of thousands of small, poorly regulated businesses spew a soup of pollution into the atmosphere. For example, brickmakers fire their kilns with old rubber tires and with sawdust soaked in kerosene—fuels that generate black, acrid smoke. A recent study suggests that leaks from tanks of liquefied gas used widely for cooking and heating are the primary source of smog over the city. In all, an estimated 12,000 tons of pollutants are released into the atmosphere each day.

Pollution problems are compounded by the city's geography and altitude. Mexico City is surrounded on three sides by mountains, so the wind that blows in from the north (the open side) traps pollution over the city. Worse yet, the city's high altitude reduces the oxygen content of the atmosphere by about one-quarter. The combination of high pollution and low oxygen makes for unhealthy air. In the last decade, the number of days when the city's air quality fell below acceptable levels has doubled. Winter smog sends thousands to the city's hospitals with respiratory problems. Some medical specialists claim that living in Mexico City is equivalent to smoking a pack of cigarettes a day. Pollution also contributes to a high infant death rate. Foreign countries advise their diplomats not to have babies while stationed there. Some foreigners who are stationed in Mexico City earn a 10-percent premium as hardship pay.

City officials have taken steps to address the common-pool problem, but their efforts have been halfhearted. The price of gasoline in Mexico City is among the lowest in the world, so price is not much of a check on fuel consumption. Unleaded gas has been introduced but accounts for less than half of the total used. New regulations prohibit half of the city's three million cars from traveling the streets during weekdays, yet fuel consumption has actually increased. And, although stricter regulations have been imposed on business activity, enforcement has been lax.

Part of the problem is that low income levels in Mexico make environmental protection there costly luxury. After adjusting for differences in the cost of living, per capita income there was less than 30 percent of the U.S. level in 1997.

Sources: "Pollution Costs Mexico Millions, Official Says," *St. Louis Post-Dispatch* (30 May 1998); Sam Howe Verhovek, "Pollution Problems Fester South of the Border," *New York Times* (4 July 1998); "Mexico City Pollution Link to Infant Deaths Is Studied," *Chicago Tribune* (7 May 1998); and *World Development Report: Knowledge for Development 1998/99* (World Bank, Oxford University Press, 1999).

Water Pollution

Two major sources of water pollution are sewage and chemicals. For decades, U.S. cities had an economic incentive to dump their sewage directly into waterways rather than incur the expense of cleaning it up first. Frequently, the current or tides would carry the waste away to become someone else's problem. Although each community found it rational, based on a narrow view of the situation, to dump into the river or sea, the combined effect of these individual choices was polluted waterways. Water pollution is a negative externality imposed by one community on other communities.

Most federal money over the years has funded sewage treatment plants, and real progress has been made in lessening sewage-related water pollution. Hundreds of once-polluted waterways have been cleaned up enough to permit swimming and fishing. The majority of U.S. cities now have modern sewage control. Notable exceptions include Boston, which still dumps sewage directly into Boston Harbor, and New York City, which teams up with New Jersey to dump raw sewage into the Atlantic Ocean, using a discharge point 106 miles off Cape May, New Jersey. At a huge cost, Boston is in the process of cleaning up its harbor. By the year 2000, the typical Boston resident's water and sewer bill is expected to be more than four times higher than it was in 1990.

Chemicals are another source of water pollution. Chemical pollution may conjure up an image of a chemical company dumping in a river, but only about

10 percent of water pollution comes from *point* pollution, which means pollution from factories and other fixed industrial sites. About two-thirds of chemical pollutants in water come from what is called *nonpoint* pollution, derived mostly from runoff of agricultural pesticides and fertilizer. Congress has been reluctant to limit the use of pesticides, although pesticides pollute water and contaminate food. Industrial America seems an easier target than Old MacDonald's farm.

In 1970, Congress shifted control of pesticides from the U.S. Department of Agriculture to the newly formed Environmental Protection Agency (EPA). But the EPA already had its hands full administering the Clean Water Act, so it turned pesticide regulation over to the states. Most states handed the job to their departments of agriculture. But these state agencies often *promote* the interests of farmers, not *restrict* what farmers can do. The EPA now reports that in most states pesticides have fouled some groundwater. The EPA also argues that pesticide residues on food pose more health problems than do toxic waste dumps or air pollution. The EPA's Inspector General said in 1998 that federal and state officials failed to enforce the nation's clean air and water laws. For example, for three quarters of the streams in Missouri, the state failed to adopt the Clean Water Act's central goal of making the water clean enough for swimming.[6]

Hazardous Waste and the Superfund

The U.S. synthetic chemical industry has flourished in the last 40 years, and about 55,000 chemicals are now in common use. Some have harmful effects on humans and other living creatures. These chemicals can pose risks at every stage of their production, use, and disposal. New Jersey manufactures more toxic chemicals than any other state and, not surprisingly, has the worst toxic waste burden. Prior to 1980, the disposal of toxic waste created get-rich-quick opportunities for anyone who could rent or buy a few acres of land to open a toxic waste dump. One site in New Jersey took in 71 million gallons of hazardous chemicals during a three-year period.[7]

Prior to 1980, once a company paid someone to haul away its hazardous waste, the company was no longer responsible. The Comprehensive Environmental Response, Compensation, and Liability Act of 1980, known more popularly as the *Superfund* law, now requires any company that generates, stores, *or* transports hazardous wastes to pay to clean up any wastes that are improperly disposed of. A producer or hauler that is the source of even one barrel of pollution dumped at a site can be held liable for cleaning up the entire site.

The Superfund law gives the federal government authority over sites contaminated with toxins. But to get an offending company to comply with its edicts, the EPA frequently must sue the company. The process is slow, and nearly half the budget goes to lawyers, consultants and administrators rather than to site cleanups. As of 1997, fewer than 200 of the 1400 sites identified under the Superfund law had actually been cleaned up. The law does not require that benefits exceed costs or even that such comparisons be attempted.[8] A General

---

6 As reported by John Cushman in "E.P.A. and States Found to Be Lax on Pollution Law," *New York Times* (7 June 1998).

7 See Jason Zweig, "Real-Life Horror Story," *Forbes* (12 December 1988).

8 For a fuller discussion of the costs and benefits of environmental protection, see Maureen L. Cropper and Wallace E. Oates, "Environmental Economics: A Survey," *Journal of Economic Literature* 30 (June 1992): 675–740.

Accounting Office study says that the number of cleanup sites could reach 4,000 and the cost could reach $40 billion. An Office of Technology Assessment study says the site total could reach 10,000 and the cost could climb to $100 billion.

But a recent EPA study concluded that the health hazards of Superfund sites have been vastly exaggerated. Chemicals in the ground often move slowly, sometimes taking years to travel a few feet, so any possible health threat may be confined to the site itself. In contrast, air pollution represents a more widespread threat because the air is so mobile and polluted air is drawn directly into the lungs. Those who are neighbors of toxic waste sites know it and can exert political pressure to get something done. But those who may in the future develop some disease from air- or water-borne pollution do not know it now. Thus most people see no reason to press public officials for legislation that mandates clean air and clean water. *Because of their greater media appeal and political urgency, toxic waste dumps tend to receive more attention than air or water pollution.*

Solid Waste: "Paper or Plastic?"

Throughout most of history, households tossed their trash outside as fodder for pigs and goats. New York City, like other cities, had no trash collection, so domestic waste was thrown into the street, where it mixed with mud and horse manure; decades of such behavior explains why the oldest Manhattan streets are anywhere from 3 to 15 feet above their original levels. About 200 years ago, people began to bury their trash near their homes or take it to the town dump. Now U.S. households generate about 4.3 pounds of garbage per resident per day—more than twice the quantity produced in 1960 and the largest amount per capita in the world. Much of our solid waste consist of packaging material. The question is how to dispose of the more than 200 million tons of household garbage generated in this country each year.

Advanced economies produce and buy more than less-developed economies, so there is more to throw away. And because of higher incomes in advanced economies, the opportunity cost of time is higher, so there is a tendency to discard items rather than repair or recycle them. A broken toaster, for example, is more likely to be sent to the dump than to the repair shop. It's cheaper to buy a new toaster for $25 than to pay up to $40 an hour to have it repaired, assuming you can find a repair shop. (Look up "Appliance Repair, Small" in the *Yellow Pages* on the Internet's BigBook and see if you can find even one such repair shop in your area.)

About 70 percent of the nation's garbage is bulldozed and covered with soil in landfills. Although a well-managed landfill poses few environmental concerns, at one time communities dumped all kinds of toxic materials in them, materials that could leach into the soil, contaminating wells and aquifers. So landfills developed a bad reputation. The prevailing attitude with landfills is *Nimby* (Not in my back yard!). Everybody wants the garbage picked up but nobody wants it put down anywhere nearby.

As the cost of solid-waste disposal increases, state and local governments are instituting economizing measures, such as requiring households to sort their trash, charging households by the pound for trash pickups, and requiring returnable bottles. A little over one third of U.S. households participate in curbside recycling programs. **Recycling** is the process of converting waste products into reusable material. Still, according to the EPA, only about 15 percent of the

Recycling The process of converting waste products into reusable material

200 million tons of garbage generated annually in the United States gets recycled. About 15 percent is incinerated and the remaining 70 percent goes into landfills. Of the recycled material, three quarters consists of corrugated boxes, newspapers, and office paper. Some of the paper product is shipped to Korea and Taiwan, where it becomes packaging material for U.S. imports such as VCRs, CD players, and computer components.

Most of the 15 percent of garbage that is incinerated each year is burned in trash-to-energy plants, which generate electricity using the heat from incineration. Until recently, such plants looked like the wave of the future, but a decline in energy prices, less favorable tax treatment, and environmental concerns over the siting of incinerators (Nimby) have taken the steam out of the trash-to-energy movement.

So about 70 percent of our garbage goes to landfills, and only 30 percent is incinerated or recycled. In contrast, the Japanese recycle 40 percent of their waste and incinerate 33 percent, leaving only 27 percent to be deposited in landfills. Japanese households sort their trash into as many as 21 categories. Because land is more scarce in Japan—we know this because it costs relatively more—it is not surprising that the Japanese deposit a smaller share of their garbage in landfills.

Some recycling is clearly economical—such as aluminum cans, which are a cheap source of aluminum compared to producing new aluminum. About two out of three aluminum cans now get recycled. Recycling paper and cardboard is also economical and occurred long before the environmental movement. Still, despite promotional efforts, curbside programs account for only one-seventh of U.S. recycling. Such old standbys as paper drives, drop-off bins, and redemption centers still collect more tonnage than curbside programs. Most recycling results from salvaging scrap material from business and industry, a practice that goes back decades.

Governments have tried to stimulate demand for recycled material—for example, by requiring newspapers to use a certain amount of recycled newsprint. Other recycled products are not in such demand. In fact, some recycled products have become worthless and must be hauled to the dump.[9] Plastic containers, for example, have limited recycling potential.

Recycling imposes its own cost on the environment. Curbside recycling requires fleets of trucks that pollute the air. Newsprint must first be de-inked, creating a sludge that must be disposed of. But greater environmental awareness has made consumers more receptive to more efficient packaging material. For example, liquid laundry detergent is now available in a more concentrated "ultra" form, which cuts volume in half. And labels for all kinds of products proudly identify the recycled content of the packaging.

POSITIVE EXTERNALITIES

Until now, we have considered only negative externalities. Externalities can sometimes be positive, or beneficial. *Positive externalities* occur when the unpriced by-product of consumption or production benefits other consumers or other firms.

---

9 For example, see the discussion by Jeff Bailey, "Curbside Recycling Comforts the Soul, But Benefits Are Scant," *Wall Street Journal* (19 January 1995).

For example, people who get inoculated against a disease reduce their own likelihood of contracting the disease, but in the process they also reduce the chances of transmitting the disease to others. Inoculations thus provide *external benefits* to others. Education also confers external benefits on society as a whole because those who acquire more education become better citizens, can read road signs, are better able to support themselves and their families, and are less likely to require public assistance or to resort to crime for income. Education confers private benefits but it also confers additional social benefits to others.

The effect of external benefits on the optimal level of consumption is illustrated in Exhibit 5, which presents the supply and demand for education. The demand curve, *D*, represents the private demand for education, which reflects the *marginal private benefit* for those who acquire the education. More education is demanded at a lower price than at a higher price.

The benefit of education, however, spills over to others in society. If we add this positive externality, or *marginal external benefit,* to the marginal private benefit of education, we get the marginal social benefit of education. The *marginal social benefit* includes all the benefit society derives from education, both private and public. The marginal-social-benefit curve is above the private demand curve in Exhibit 5. At each level of education, the marginal social benefit exceeds the marginal private benefit by the amount of marginal external benefit generated by that particular unit of education.

If education were a strictly private decision, the amount purchased would be determined by the intersection of the private demand curve, *D*, with the

EXHIBIT 5

Education and Positive Externalities

In the absence of government intervention, the quantity of education demanded is *E,* at which the marginal cost equals the marginal private benefit of education. However, education also confers a positive externality on the rest of society, so the marginal social benefit exceeds the private benefit. At quantity *E,* the marginal social benefit exceeds the marginal cost, so more education is in society's best interest. In such a situation, government will try to encourage an increase in the quantity of education to *E',* at which point the marginal cost equals the marginal social benefit.

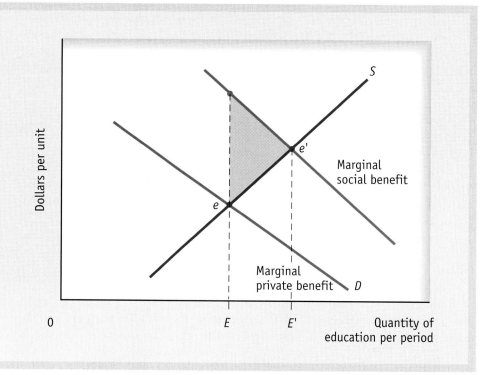

supply curve, *S*. The supply curve reflects the marginal cost of producing each unit of the good. This intersection, identified as point *e*, yields education level *E*, where the marginal cost of education equals the marginal private benefit.

But at level *E* the marginal social benefit of education exceeds its marginal cost. Net social welfare will increase if education is expanded beyond *E*. *As long as the marginal social benefit of education exceeds its marginal cost, social welfare is increased by expanding education.* Social welfare is maximized at point *e'* in Exhibit 5, where *E'* units of education are provided—that is, where the marginal social benefit equals the marginal cost, as reflected by the supply curve. The blue-shaded triangle identifies the net increase in social welfare that results from increasing the quantity of education to *E'*.

Thus, society is better off if the amount of education provided exceeds the private equilibrium. *When positive externalities are present, decisions based on private marginal benefits result in less than the socially optimal quantity of the good.* Hence, like negative externalities, positive externalities typically point to *market failure,* which is why government often gets into the act. When there are external benefits, public policy tries to increase the level of output beyond the private optimum. For example, government attempts to encourage education by providing free primary and secondary education, by requiring students to stay in school until they reach 16 years of age, and by subsidizing public higher education.

CONCLUSION

Six billion people inhabit the globe, whose population increases by about 90 million each year. World population is projected to increase 50 percent by the middle of the 21st century, with most of this growth occurring in less-developed countries, where most people barely eke out a living. Growing population pressure coupled with a lack of incentives to preserve open-access resources results in deforestation, dwindling fish stocks, and polluted air, land, and water.

Ironically, because of tighter pollution controls, industrial countries tend to be less polluted than developing countries, where there is more pollution per capita from what little industry there is. Most developing countries have such profound economic problems that environmental quality is not high on their list of priorities. The air in places such as Mexico City and Lagos, Nigeria, is dangerous. Residents of China's cities cover their mouths with masks when the smog is especially thick. The average Chinese car produces 10 to 15 times more emissions than the average U.S. car.[10] Farmers in Central America douse their crops with pesticides long banned in the United States.

Market prices can direct the allocation of resources only as long as property rights are well defined and can be enforced at a reasonable cost. Pollution of air, land, and water arises not so much from the greed of producers and consumers as from the fact that these open-access resources are subject to the common-pool problem.

---

10 As noted by Elisabeth Rosenthal, "China Finally Confronts Its Air-Pollution Crisis," *New York Times* (14 June 1998).

SUMMARY

1. Private choices will result in too little output when positive externalities exist and too much output when negative externalities exist. Public policy should subsidize or otherwise promote production that generates positive externalities and should tax or otherwise discourage production that generates negative externalities.

2. The optimal amount of environmental quality occurs where the marginal social cost of higher quality equals its marginal social benefit. A decrease in the marginal cost or an increase in the marginal benefit of environmental quality increases the optimal level of environmental quality.

3. The world's tropical rain forests have served to recycle noxious gases and convert them into oxygen and wood. The destruction of these forests reduces the environment's ability to cleanse itself.

4. The Coase theorem argues that as long as bargaining costs are small, assigning property rights to one party leads to an efficient solution to the problem of externalities. An example of the Coase theorem in action is the market for pollution permits.

5. In the last two decades, progress has been made in cleaning up the nation's air and waterways. The air is cleaner because of stricter emissions standards for motor vehicles; the water is cleaner because of billions spent on sewage treatment facilities. Although much of the federal attention and federal budget goes toward cleaning up toxic waste dumps, this pollution source does not pose as great a health threat to the population as a whole as do other forms of pollution, such as smog and pesticides.

QUESTIONS FOR REVIEW

1. *(Types of Resources)* Complete each of the following sentences:
   a. Resources that are available only in a finite amount are _____ resources.
   b. The possibility that a nonexcludable resource will be used until the net marginal value of additional use equals zero is known as the _____.
   c. Resources for which periodic use can be continued indefinitely are known as _____ resources.
   d. If no individual can easily capture the value of a resource, it is termed_____.

2. *(Resolving the Common-Pool Problem)* Why have authorities found it so difficult to regulate the fishing catch to allow for a sustainable yield?

3. *(Optimal Level of Pollution)* Explain the difference between fixed-technology production and variable-technology production. Should the government set a goal of reducing the marginal social cost of pollution to zero in industries with fixed technology? Should they do so in industries with variable technology?

4. *(**Case**Study: Tropical Rain Forests)* Why does a solution to the overharvesting of timber in the tropical rain forests require some form of international cooperation? Would this be a sufficient solution to the deforestation problem?

5. *(Coase Analysis of Externalities)* Suppose a firm pollutes a stream that has a recreational value only when pollution is below a certain level. If transaction costs are low, why does the assignment of property rights to the stream lead to the same (efficient) level of pollution whether the firm or the recreational users own the stream?

6. *(Coase Analysis of Externalities)* Ronald Coase points out that a market failure does not arise simply because people ignore the external cost of their actions. What other condition is necessary? What did Coase consider to be efficient solution to a negative externality?

7. *(Positive Externalities)* The value of a home depends in part on how attractive other homes and yards in the neighborhood are. How do local zoning ordinances try to promote land uses that generate external benefits for neighbors?

P R O B L E M S   A N D   E X E R C I S E S

8. *(External Costs with Fixed Technology)* Review the situation illustrated in Exhibit 1 in this chapter. If the government sets the price of electricity at the socially optimal level, why is the net gain equal to triangle *abc* even though consumers now pay a higher price for electricity? What would the net gain be if the government set the price above the optimal level?

9. *(Negative Externalities)* Suppose you wish to reduce a negative externally by imposing a tax on the activity that creates that externality. If the amount of the externality produced per unit of output increases as output increases, show the correct tax can be determined by using a supply-demand diagram. Assume that the marginal-private-cost curve slopes upward.

10. *(External Costs)* Use this data to answer the following questions.

Quantity	Marginal Private Benefit (Demand)	Marginal Private Cost (Supply)	Marginal Social Cost
0	—	$ 0	$ 0
1	$10	2	4
2	9	3	5
3	8	4	6
4	7	5	7
5	6	6	8
6	5	7	9
7	4	8	10
8	3	9	11
9	2	10	12
10	1	11	13

a. What is the external cost per unit of production?
b. What level will be produced if there is no regulation of the externality?
c. What level should be produced to achieve economic efficiency?
d. Calculate the dollar value of the net gain to society from correcting the externality.

11. *(External Costs with Variable Technology)* Think of an industry that pollutes the water and has access to variable technology for reducing that water pollution. Graphically illustrate and explain the impact of each of the following, other things constant, on the optimal level of water quality:
a. New evidence is discovered of a greater risk of cancer from water pollution.
b. The cost of pollution-abatement equipment increases.
c. A technological improvement reduces the cost of pollution abatement.

12. *(Market for Pollution Rights)* The following graph shows the market for pollution rights.
a. If there are no restrictions on pollution, what will be the amount of discharge?
b. What will be the quantity supplied and the quantity demanded if the government restricts the amount of discharge to Q★ but gives the permits away?
c. Where is market equilibrium if the government sells the permits? Illustrate this on the graph.
d. What happens to market equilibrium if the government reduces the amount of permitted discharged to Q★★? Illustrate this on the graph.

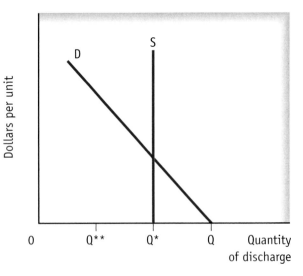

EXPERIENTIAL EXERCISES

13. *(CaseStudy: City in the Clouds)* Suppose you are the mayor on Mexico City. How can you use some of the techniques outlined in this chapter to control pollution there? (For background information check http:cesimo.ing.ul.ve/GAIA/CASES/MEX)

14. *(The Common-Pool Problem)* Garret Hardin's 1968 article," The Tragedy of the Commons," is available on-line at http://www.aloha.net/~jhanson/ page95.htm. Download and read this clearly written article. Then describe some examples of the common-pool problem or, as he calls it, the tragedy of the commons.

15. *(External Costs with Fixed Technology)* Download Betty Joyce Nash, "Pollution Allowances Help Clear the Air" at http://www.rich.frb.org/cross/cross134/ 2.html. Based on what you've learned in this chapter, evaluate Nash's case for pollution allowances as a way of controlling negative exteranlities.

16. *(Wall Street Journal)* The Marketplace section of the *Wall Street Journal* is a good place to look for information related to externalities. On a given day, see how many stories you can find that deal with externalities—positive or negative. Are businesses taking steps to "internalize" externalities? What role does technology play in controlling negative externalities?

Income Distribution and Poverty

hy are some families poor even in the most productive nation on Earth? Who are the poor and how did they get that way? What has been the trend in poverty rates over time? What has been the impact of the changing family structure on that trend? What programs are aimed at reducing poverty and how have they changed over time? Answers to these and related questions are addressed in this chapter, which examines poverty in the United States.

To establish a reference point, we first examine the distribution of income in the United States, paying special attention to poverty in recent years. We then discuss and evaluate the "social safety net"—government programs aimed at helping the poor. We also consider the impact of the changing family structure on the incidence of poverty, focusing in particular on the increase in female householders. We will explore the effects of discrimination on the distribution of income and close the chapter by examining recent welfare reforms. Topics discussed in this chapter include:

- Distribution of income
- The official poverty level
- Public policy and poverty
- The feminization of poverty
- Poverty and discrimination
- Recent welfare reforms

THE DISTRIBUTION OF HOUSEHOLD INCOME

In a market economy, income depends primarily on earnings, which depend on the productivity of one's resources. The problem with allocating income according to productivity is that some people have difficulty earning income. Those born with mental or physical disabilities tend to be less productive and may be unable to earn a living. Others may face limited job choices and reduced wages because of advanced age, poor education, discrimination, or the demands of caring for small children.

Income Distribution by Quintiles

As a starting point, let's consider the distribution of income in the economy and see how it has changed over time, focusing on the household as the economic unit. After dividing the total number of households into five groups of equal size, or *quintiles*, ranked according to income, we can examine what percentage of income is received by each group. Such a division is presented in Exhibit 1 by decade since 1967. Take a moment to look over this exhibit. Notice that households in the lowest, or poorest, fifth of the population received only 4.0 percent of the income in 1967, whereas households in the highest, or richest, fifth received 43.8 percent of the income. Income here is measured after cash transfer payments have been received but before taxes have been paid.

In recent years, the share of income going to the top fifth has increased and the share going to the bottom fifth has declined slightly. The richest group's share of income increased from 43.8 percent in 1967 to 49.4 percent in 1997. So most recently, the top fifth received over 13 times as much income as the bottom fifth. A primary contributor to the growing share of income going to highest group has been the growth of two-earner households in the top group and the growth of single-parent households in the bottom group.

Also shown in Exhibit 1 is the share of income going to the top 5 percent of households; that share jumped between 1987 and 1997, and accounts for the jump in income going to the top 20 percent of households.

A College Education Pays Relatively More

Also contributing the dominance of the top group is a growing pay premium for individuals with a college education. Between 1980 and 1996, for example, the median wage (adjusted for inflation) for those with only a high school diploma declined 6 percent, while the median wage of college graduates rose 12 percent. Why have more educated workers done better? First, new computer-based information technologies have increased the demand for skilled labor—for knowledge workers—relative to unskilled labor. Second, trends such as industry deregulation, declining unionization, and freer international trade have reduced the demand for

EXHIBIT 1

Share of Aggregate Household Income by Quintile: 1967, 1977, 1987, and 1997

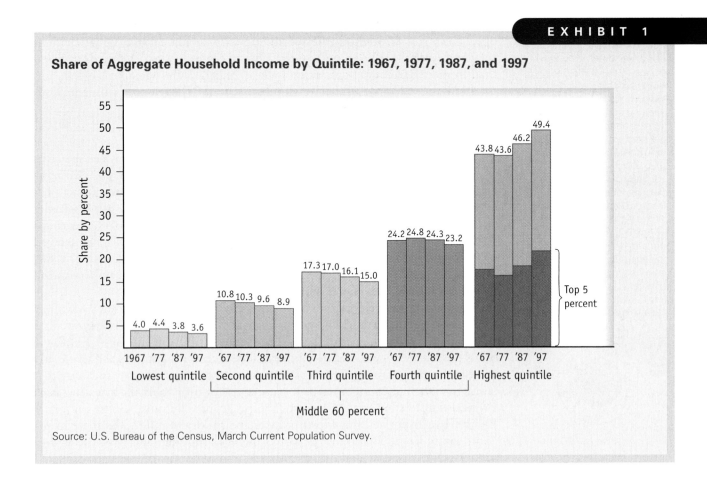

Source: U.S. Bureau of the Census, March Current Population Survey.

workers with less education. Labor unions, for example, help to increase the wages of many workers who would otherwise end up in the bottom half of the income distribution. The share of the labor force that is unionized declined from 26 percent in 1973 to only 15 percent in 1998.

Third, recent U.S. immigrants have tended to be less well-educated than existing residents, thus increasing the supply of relatively poorly educated workers and depressing their wages. For example, the U.S. Hispanic population roughly doubled in size between 1980 and 1996, and during that time the percentage of Hispanics who are foreign-born has grown. Only 62 percent of Hispanics aged 25 to 29 had at least a high school education in 1996, compared to 88 percent of whites and 86 percent of blacks.[1]

So economic developments in recent years have benefited the better educated, and this helps explain the growing disparity in household income. Note that it is not necessarily the same households who remain rich or poor over time. Some households drop out of high-income ranks and are replaced by others. Likewise, some households work their way out of poverty to be replaced, for example, by families headed by young unmarried women who become mothers. So we are not talking about the same households getting richer or poorer over time.

1 As reported by Rick Green in "Education Gap Closes for Blacks and Whites," *Hartford Courant* (29 June 1998).

Median income The middle income in a series of incomes ranked from smallest to largest

Income in the United States is less evenly distributed than in other developed countries throughout the world, such as Canada, France, Great Britain, Italy, and Australia. But income in the United States is more evenly distributed than in most developing countries, such as Brazil, Chile, Mexico, Nigeria, and the Philippines. More than half of all income in most developing countries goes to the richest 20 percent of the population.

Problems with Distributional Benchmarks

One problem with examining income distributions is that there is no objective standard for evaluating them. The usual assumption is that a more equal distribution of income is more desirable, but is a perfectly even distribution most preferred? If not, then how uneven should the distribution be? For example, among major league baseball players, about 54 percent of the pay goes to 20 percent of the players. Earnings in professional basketball are even more skewed toward the top players. So income among baseball and basketball players is less evenly distributed than household income in the economy. Does this mean the economy as a whole is "fairer" than these professional sports?

Households receive income from two primary sources: resource earnings and transfer payments from the government. Exhibit 1 measures money income after cash transfers but before taxes. Thus the distribution shown in Exhibit 1 omits the effects of taxes and in-kind transfers, such as food stamps and free medical care for poor families. The tax system as a whole is progressive, meaning that families with higher incomes pay a larger fraction of their incomes in taxes. In-kind transfers benefit the lowest-income groups the most. Consequently, if Exhibit 1 incorporated the effects of taxes and in-kind transfers, the share of income going to the lower groups would increase, the share going to the higher groups would decrease, and income would be more evenly distributed.

Finally, the income distribution estimates include only reported sources of income. If people receive payment "under the table" to evade taxes, or if they earn money through illegal activities, their actual income will exceed their reported income. The omission of unreported income will distort the data in Exhibit 1 only if unreported income as a percentage of total family income differs across income levels.

Why Do Household Incomes Differ?

The **median income** of all households is the middle income when incomes are ranked from lowest to highest. In any given year, half the households are above the median income and half are below it. We have already seen one reason why incomes differ across households, namely that some workers are better educated than others. Income differences across households also stem from differences in the *number* of workers in each household. Thus *another reason household incomes differ is that the number of household members who are working differs.* For example, among households in the bottom 20 percent based on income, only one household in five has a full-time, year-round worker. Over two-thirds of households in the bottom 20 percent are headed by unmarried females.

The median income for households with two earners is about 82 percent higher than for households with only one earner and nearly *four times* higher than for households with no earners. Incomes also differ for all the reasons labor incomes differ, such as differences in education, ability, job experience, and so on. At every age, those with more education earn more, on average. For example, according to the U.S. Census Bureau, males with a professional degree had average earnings of $109,206 in 1997, or about four times the average of $28,307 earned by males with only a high school education. Age itself also has an important effect on income. As workers mature, they acquire valuable job experience, get promoted, and earn more.

Differences in earnings based on age and education reflect the normal *life-cycle* pattern of income. In fact, most income differences across households reflect the normal workings of resource markets, whereby workers are rewarded according to their productivity. A high-income household usually consists of a well-educated couple who are both employed. A low-income household is usually headed by single parent who is young, female, poorly educated, and not employed. Low incomes are a matter of public concern, especially when children are involved, as we will see in the next section.

POVERTY AND THE POOR

Since poverty is such a relative concept, how do we measure it objectively and how do we ensure that our measure can be applied with equal relevance over time? The federal government has developed a method for calculating an official poverty level; this level has become the benchmark for poverty analysis in the United States.

Official Poverty Level

To derive the **U.S. official poverty level**, the U.S. Department of Agriculture first estimates the cost of a nutritionally adequate diet. Then, based on the assumption that the poor spend about one-third of their income on food, the official poverty level is calculated by multiplying these food costs by three. Adjustments are made for family size and for inflation over time. The official poverty threshold of money income for a family of four was $16,400 in 1997; a family of four at or below that income threshold was regarded as living in poverty. Poverty thresholds in 1997 ranged from $8,350 for a person living alone to $32,566 for a family with nine or more members. The poverty definition is based on pretax money income, including cash transfers, but it excludes the value of noncash transfers such as food stamps, Medicaid, subsidized housing, or employer-provided health insurance.

Each year since 1959, the Census Bureau has conducted a survey comparing individual families' annual cash incomes to the annual poverty threshold applicable to that family. Results of this survey are presented in Exhibit 2, which indicates both the millions of people living below the official poverty level and the percentage of the U.S. population below that level. Periods of U.S. recession are also shown (a recession is defined as two or more successive quarters of declining gross domestic product). Note that beginning in the early 1970s, poverty increased during recessions.

The biggest decline in poverty occurred prior to 1970; *the poverty rate dropped from 22.4 percent in 1959 to 12.1 percent in 1969.* During that period, the number of poor people dropped from about 40 million to 24 million. The poverty rate bottomed out during the 1970s, then rose between 1979 and 1983. After a modest decline between 1983 and 1989, the rate turned up in 1990 and

U.S. official poverty level Benchmark level of income computed by the federal government to track poverty over time, based on three times the cost of a nutritionally adequate diet

EXHIBIT 2

Number and Percent of U.S. Population in Poverty: 1959–1997

Source: Census Bureau, March 1998 Current Population Survey, http://census.gov/hhes/poverty/poverty/pov.97.html

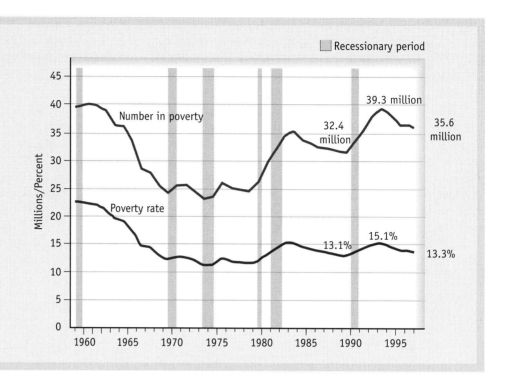

topped out in 1993 at 15.1 percent before falling to 13.3 percent in 1997. The 35.6 million people in poverty in 1997 is down from 39.3 million in 1993.

Poverty is a relative term. If we examined the distribution of income across countries, we would find huge gaps between rich and poor nations. The official U.S. poverty level of income is many times greater than the average income for three-fourths of the world's population.[2] For example, the U.S. minimum wage in 1998 was $5.15 per hour; in Mexico the minimum wage was the equivalent of $3.40 *per day!*

An income at the U.S. poverty level today provides a standard of living that would have been considered attractive by most people who lived in the United States in 1900, when only 15 percent of families had flush toilets, only 3 percent had electricity, and only 1 percent had central heating. Finally, the official definition of poverty ignores a household's other assets, such as owner-occupied housing or automobiles. According to one study carried out in the 1980s, three in ten households identified as poor owned their own home and half owned a motor vehicle.

Programs to Help the Poor

What should society's response to poverty be? *Families with a full-time worker are nine times more likely to escape poverty than are families with no workers.* Thus the government's first line of defense in fighting poverty is to promote a healthy economy. Yet even when the unemployment rate is relatively low, some people may remain poor because they lack marketable skills, must care for small children, or face discrimination in the labor market.

---

2 See World Bank, *World Development Report 1998/99* (New York: Oxford University Press, 1998), Table 30.

Although some government programs to help the poor involve direct market intervention, such as minimum-wage laws, the most visible programs redistribute income after the market has provided an initial distribution. Since the mid-1960s, social welfare expenditures at all levels of government have increased significantly. We can divide social welfare programs into two major categories: social insurance and income assistance.

Social Insurance. Social insurance programs are designed to replace the lost income of those who worked but are now retired, temporarily unemployed, or unable to work because of disability or work-related injury. The major social insurance program is **Social Security**, established during the Great Depression of the 1930s to supplement retirement income to those with a work history and a record of contributing to the program. **Medicare**, another social insurance program, provides health insurance for short-term medical care to about 37 million Americans mostly aged 65 and older, regardless of income. Other social insurance programs include *unemployment insurance* and *worker's compensation*, which supports workers injured on the job; both programs require that beneficiaries have a prior record of employment.

The social insurance system deducts "insurance premiums" from workers' pay to provide benefits to other retired, disabled, and unemployed individuals. These programs protect some families from poverty, particularly the elderly receiving Social Security, but they are aimed more at those with a work history. Still, the social insurance system tends to redistribute income from rich to poor and from young to old. Most current Social Security beneficiaries receive far more in benefits than they paid into the program, especially those with a brief work history or a record of low wages.

Income Assistance. **Income assistance programs**—what we usually call "welfare"—provide money and in-kind assistance to the poor. Unlike social insurance programs, income assistance programs do not require the recipient to have a work history or to have contributed to the program. Income assistance programs are means tested. In a **means-tested program,** a household's income and assets must lie below a certain level to qualify for benefits. The federal government funds two-thirds of welfare spending, and state and local governments fund one-third. Nearly half of all welfare spending pays for medical care for the poor.

The two primary *cash transfer* programs are **Temporary Assistance for Needy Families (TANF)**, which provides cash to poor families with dependent children, and **Supplemental Security Income (SSI)**, which provides cash to the elderly poor and the disabled. Cash transfers vary inversely with family income from other sources. In July 1997, TANF replaced Aid for Families with Dependent Children (AFDC), which began during the Great Depression and was originally aimed at providing support for widows with young children. Whereas AFDC was a federal *entitlement* program, meaning that anyone who met the criteria was *entitled* to benefits, TANF is under the control of each state government and carries no federal entitlement. The federal government provides each state a fixed grant to help fund TANF programs.

The Supplemental Security Income program provides support for the elderly and disabled poor. SSI is the fastest-growing cash transfer program, with outlays increasing from $8 billion in 1980 to nearly $30 billion in 1998. SSI coverage has been broadened to include those addicted to drugs and alcohol,

Social Security By far the largest social insurance program; supplements retirement income to those with a record of contributing to the program during their working years

Medicare Social insurance program providing health insurance for short-term medical care to older Americans, regardless of income

Income assistance programs Welfare programs that provide money and in-kind assistance to the poor; benefits do not depend on prior contributions.

Means-tested program To be eligible for such a program, an individual's income and assets must not exceed specified levels.

Temporary Assistance for Needy Families (TANF) An income assistance program run by the states that provides cash transfer payments to poor families with dependent children.

Supplemental Security Income (SSI) An income assistance program that provides cash transfer payments to the elderly poor and the disabled; a uniform federal payment is supplemented by transfers that vary across states.

children with learning disabilities, and, in some cases, the homeless. The federal portion of this program is uniform across states, but states can supplement federal aid. Benefit levels in California average nearly twice those in Alabama. Most states also offer modest *General Assistance* aid to those who are poor but do not qualify for TANF or SSI.

The federal government also provides an *earned income tax credit* to the working poor. For example, a family with two children and earnings of $13,000 in 1998 would not only pay no federal income tax but would also receive a cash transfer of $3,600. More than 12 million workers received transfers under the program.

In addition to cash transfer programs, a variety of *in-kind transfer* programs provide health care, food stamps, and housing assistance to the poor. **Medicaid** pays for medical care for those with incomes below a certain level who are aged, blind, disabled, or are living in families with dependent children. Medicaid is by far the largest welfare program, costing nearly twice as much as all cash transfer programs combined. It has grown more than any other poverty program, quadrupling in the last decade and accounting for one-fifth of the typical state's budget (though states receive federal grants covering half or more of their Medicaid budget). The qualifying level of income is set by each state, and some states are quite strict. Therefore, the proportion of poor covered by Medicaid varies greatly across states. In 1998, about 36 million individuals received Medicaid; outlays averaged about $4,200 per recipient. Spending on the 3.5 million beneficiaries aged 65 and older averaged about $8,000 per year. For many elderly, Medicaid pays for long-term nursing care (Medicaid pays half the nation's nursing home costs). Although half the nation's welfare budget goes for health care, nearly 40 million U.S. residents still have no health insurance.

Food stamps are vouchers that can be redeemed for food. The program is aimed at reducing hunger and providing nutrition to poor families. The cost is paid by the federal government, and benefits are uniform across states. About 1 in 10 Americans received food stamps in 1998, with an average monthly benefit per recipient of about $80.

Housing assistance programs include direct assistance for rental payments and subsidized low-income housing. Spending for housing assistance has doubled since 1990. About 10 million people receive some form of housing assistance.[3] Other in-kind programs include the *school lunch program* for poor children; supplemental food vouchers for pregnant women, infants, and children; *energy assistance* to help pay the energy bills of poor families; and *education and training assistance* for poor families, such as Head Start and the Job Training Partnership Act. In all, there are about 75 means-tested federal welfare programs.

Medicaid In-kind transfer program that provides medical care for poor people; by far the most costly welfare program

Food stamps An in-kind transfer program that offers low-income households vouchers redeemable for food; benefit levels vary inversely with household income.

WHO ARE THE POOR?

Who are the poor, and how has the composition of this group changed over time? We will slice poverty statistics in several ways to examine the makeup of the group. Keep in mind that we are relying on official poverty estimates, which ignore the value of in-kind transfers and to that extent overstate poverty.

---

3 This is an increase of about 50 percent over the number receiving benefits in 1980. About 60 percent of the families in public housing in 1990 had incomes below the poverty level.

Poverty and Age

Earlier we looked at the poverty rate among the entire population. Now we focus on poverty and age. Exhibit 3 presents the poverty rates for three age groups since 1959: those less than 18 years old, those between 18 and 64, and those 65 and older. The poverty rates for each group declined between 1959 and 1968. Between the mid-1970s and the early 1980s, the rate among those under 18 years of age trended upward. In 1997, the poverty rate among people under 18 years of age was 19.9 percent—nearly twice the rate of those 18 and over.

In 1959, the elderly were the poorest group, with a poverty rate about 35 percent. Since then, poverty among the elderly has fallen steadily; in 1997, the rate was 10.5 percent, slightly below the rate of 10.9 percent for those 18 to 64 years of age. This reduction in poverty among the elderly can be attributed to a tremendous growth in Social Security and Medicare spending, which in real terms grew tenfold from $60 billion in 1959 to about $600 billion in 1998 (measured in 1998 dollars). Social Security and Medicare spending is now *triple* what the federal government spends on income assistance, or welfare, programs. *Although not welfare programs in a strict sense, Social Security and Medicare have been extremely successful in reducing poverty among the elderly.*

Poverty and Public Choice

In a democratic country such as ours, public policies depend very much on the political power of the interest groups involved. In recent years, the elderly have become a strong political force. Unlike most interest groups, the elderly are a group we all expect to join one day. The elderly actually are represented by four constituencies: (1) the elderly themselves, (2) those under 65 who are concerned about the current benefits to their parents or other elderly relatives, (3) those

EXHIBIT 3

Poverty Rates by Age: 1959–1997

Source: Census Bureau, March Current Population Survey: http://www.census.gov/hhes/poverty/poverty97/povage97.html

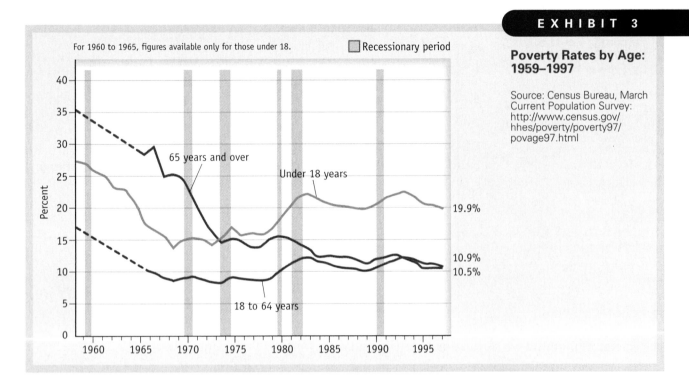

under 65 who are concerned about their own benefits in the future, and (4) those who earn their living by caring for the elderly, such as doctors and nursing home operators. So the elderly have a broad constituency.

Moreover, the voter participation rate of those 65 and over is higher than that of other age groups. For example, voter participation of those 65 years of age and older is typically triple that of those between 18 and 24 and four times that of welfare recipients. The political muscle of the elderly has been flexed whenever a question of Social Security benefits has come up for a vote.

The Feminization of Poverty

One way of classifying the incidence of poverty is by age. Another way is based on the marital status and race of the household head. Exhibit 4 compares, for white, black, and Hispanic families, the poverty rates for married couples with the rates among families headed by females. Three trends are unmistakable. First, married couples have poverty rates only about one-third the rates of female householders. Second, Hispanic families have the highest poverty rates (individuals of Hispanic origin may be of any race) followed by black families, then white families. And third, since the early 1980s, rates have remained relatively unchanged among white and Hispanic families, but have fallen among black families. Specifically, among black married couples the poverty rate declined from about 15 percent in the early 1980s to 8 percent in 1997. Among black female householders, poverty rates declined from about 54 percent to 40 percent.

Not shown in the exhibit are poverty rates among male householders, which are higher than among married couples but still only about half the rates of female householders. The findings show that regardless of race or Hispanic

EXHIBIT 4

Percentage of U.S. Families in Poverty by Type of Household

Developed from data found in U.S. Bureau of the Census Home Page, Income and Poverty, Table 4, 1998, at http://www.census.gov/hhes/poverty/histpov/hstpov4.html

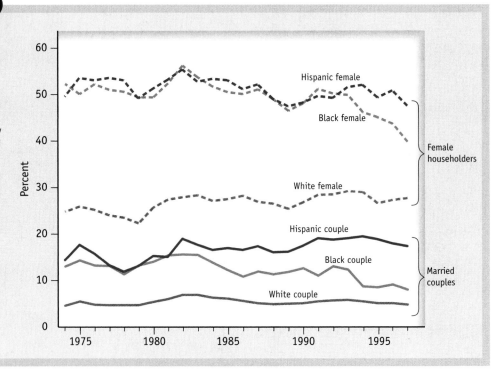

origin, people living in two-parent families are much less likely to be poor than those living in one-parent families.

Though poverty rates among female householders are high, *these rates have increased little since 1969.* What has increased is the *number* of female householders in the economy. The percentage of births to unmarried mothers is five times greater today than in 1960. In 1960, only one in 200 children lived with a single parent who had never married. Today, one in ten children lives with a single parent who has never married.

The United States has the highest teenage pregnancy rate in the developed world—twice the rate of Great Britain and 15 times that of Japan. Since the father in such cases typically assumes little responsibility for child support, children born outside marriage are likely to be poorer than other children. The divorce rate has also increased since 1960. Because of the higher divorce rate, even children born to married couples now face a greater likelihood of living in a one-parent household before they grow up. Divorce usually reduces the resources available to the children. *Children of female householders are five times more likely to live in poverty than are other children.*

Increases in the number of unwed mothers and in the divorce rate increased the number of female householders by 126 percent between 1969 and 1997. With this came a similar increase in the number of poor people from such families. Thus, even though the poverty *rate* among female householder has remained relatively constant at about 32 percent since 1969, the *number* of poor female householders has increased because the *number* of female householders has increased. Whereas the number of female householders jumped 126 percent between 1969 and 1998, the number of other families grew only 27 percent and their poverty rate *declined* from 6.9 percent to 5.7 percent.

Between 1969 and 1997, the number of poor families in the United States increased by 2.3 million, or 46 percent. Poverty among families with female householders increased 2.2 million, or 119 percent. Poverty in other families increased only 0.1 million, or 5 percent. Thus female householders accounted for nearly all of the increase in poor families since 1969. *The growth in the number of poor families since 1969 resulted overwhelmingly from the growth in the number of female householders.* Since 1969, the U.S. economy has generated 50 million new jobs. Families with a female householder were in the worst position to take advantage of this job growth.

Young, single motherhood is a recipe for instant poverty. Often the young mother drops out of school, which reduces her future earning possibilities when and if she seeks work outside the home. Even a strong economy is little aid to households with nobody in the labor force. Worse yet, young, single mothers-to-be are less likely to seek adequate medical care; the result is a higher proportion of premature, underweight babies. This is one reason why the U.S. infant mortality rate exceeds many other industrialized countries. Compared to two-parent families, children in one-parent families are twice as likely to drop out of school, and girls from one-parent families are twice as likely to become single mothers themselves.

Each year, about 1.2 million children in the United States are born to single mothers. There is a clear link between unwed parenthood and welfare dependency. Two-thirds of all out-of-wedlock births are to 15- to 24-year olds. Only 57 percent of these mothers have a high-school diploma, and only 28 percent ever worked full time (another 9 percent worked part time). Because of a lack of education and limited job skills, most unwed mothers go on welfare. Prior to recently imposed lifetime limits on welfare, the average never-married mother was on welfare for a decade, twice as long as divorced mothers on welfare. Of all births to teenage girls, the proportion who were unmarried was 13 percent in 1950, 30 percent in 1970, 67 percent in 1990 and 76 percent in 1994.[4]

Poverty has therefore become increasingly feminized, mostly because female householders have become more common. Children from mothers who finished high school, married before having a child, and gave birth after age twenty are ten times less likely to be poor than children from mothers who fail to do these things.[5] Because the number of female householders has grown more rapidly among blacks, the feminization of poverty has been more dramatic in black households. Seventy percent of all black births in 1994 were to unmarried women, compared to 43 percent of all births among those of Hispanic origin and 25 percent of births among whites.[6]

Poverty and Discrimination

Is the lower family income and greater incidence of poverty among minorities the result of discrimination in job markets, or are there other explanations? We should note that discrimination can occur in many ways: in school funding, in housing, in employment, in career advancement. Also, discrimination in one area can affect opportunities in another. For example, housing discrimination may reduce job opportunities if a black family cannot move within commuting distance of the best employers. Moreover, the legacy of discrimination can affect career choices long after discrimination has ceased. Someone whose father and grandfather found job avenues blocked may be less inclined to pursue an education or to accept a job that requires a long training program. Thus discrimination is a complex topic, and we cannot do it justice in this brief section.

Job-market discrimination can take many forms. An employer may fail to hire a black job applicant because the applicant lacks training. But this lack of training may arise from discrimination in the schools, in union apprenticeship programs, or in training programs run by other employers. For example, evidence suggests that black workers receive less on-the-job training than otherwise similar white workers.

Let's first consider the difference between the earnings of nonwhite and white workers. After adjusting for a variety of factors that could affect the wage, such as education and work experience, research shows that whites earn more than blacks, but the wage gap between the two narrowed between 1940 and 1976 to the point where blacks earned only 7 percent less than white workers. The gap then widened a bit,[7] but has narrowed since 1993.

Could explanations besides job discrimination account for the wage gap? Though the data adjust for *years* of schooling, some research suggests that black

4   As noted by James Q. Wilson, "Human Remedies for Social Disorder," *Public Interest* (Spring 1998): 27.

5   As noted by James Q. Wilson, p. 28.

6   These figures are from *Statistical Abstracts of the United States: 1997,* U.S. Bureau of the Census (Austin, Texas: Hoover's Business Press, 1997), Table 89.

7   See the evidence in M. Boozer, A. Krueger, and S. Wolken, "Race and School Quality Since Brown v. Board of Education," *Brookings Papers on Economic Activity: Microeconomics,* 1992: 269–326.

workers received a lower *quality* of schooling than white workers. For example, black students are less likely to use computers in school. Inner-city schools often have more problems with classroom discipline, which takes time and attention away from instruction. Such quality differences could account for at least a portion of the remaining gap in standardized wages. Although any differences attributable to a poorer-quality education would not necessarily reflect job discrimination, they might well reflect discrimination in the funding of schools.

Evidence of discrimination comes from audit studies, where otherwise similar white and minority candidates are sent to the same source to seek jobs, rent apartments, or apply for mortgage loans. For example, a white and a black job applicant with similar qualifications and résumés applied for the same job. These studies find that employers are less likely to interview or offer a job to minority applicants. Minority applicants also tend to be treated less favorably by real estate agents and lenders. The President's Council of Economic Advisers concluded in 1998 that discrimination against members of racial and ethnic minorities, while "far less pervasive and overt" than it was, still persists.[8]

Affirmative Action

The Equal Employment Opportunity Commission, established by the Civil Rights Act of 1964, monitors cases involving unequal pay for equal work and unequal access to promotion. Executive Order 11246, signed by President Lyndon Johnson, required all companies doing business with the federal government to set numerical hiring, promotion, and training goals to ensure that these firms did not discriminate in hiring on the basis of race, sex, religion, or national origin. For three decades, the order governed employment practices in firms that accounted for one-third of all jobs. Black employment increased in those firms required to file affirmative-action plans.[9] The fraction of the black labor force employed in white-collar jobs increased from 16.5 percent in 1960 to 40.5 percent in 1981—an increase that greatly exceeded the growth of white-collar jobs in the labor force as a whole. Research also suggests that civil-rights legislation played a role in narrowing the black-white earnings gap between 1960 and the mid-1970s.[10]

Attention focused on hiring practices and equality of opportunity at the state and local levels as well, as governments introduced so-called set-aside programs to guarantee minorities a share of contracts. But in 1989, the U.S. Supreme Court rejected Richmond, Virginia's, set-aside program, which had reserved 30 percent of construction work for minorities. Within a year of the ruling, many local affirmative action programs, including Richmond's, had been suspended or eliminated.

A 1995 U.S. Supreme Court decision challenged affirmative-action programs more broadly, ruling that Congress must meet a rigorous legal standard in order to justify any contracting or hiring practice based on race, especially programs that reserve job slots for minorities and women. Programs must be shown to be in response to injustices created by past discrimination, said the

---

8 See the *Economic Report of the President,* February 1998, p. 152.

9 See the evidence provided in James Smith and Finis Welch, "Black Economic Progress After Myrdal," *Journal of Economic Literature* 27 (June 1989): 519–563.

10 See David Card and Alan Krueger, "Trends in Relative Black-White Earnings Revisited," *American Economic Review* 83 (May 1993): 85–91.

Court. The ruling could affect the 200,000 federal contractors operating under Executive Order 11246.

In summary, evidence suggests that blacks earn less than whites after adjustment for other factors that could affect wages, such as education and job experience. Part of this wage gap may reflect differences in the quality of education, differences that could themselves be the result of discrimination. Keep in mind that unemployment rates are twice as high among blacks as among whites and are higher still among black teenagers, the group most in need of job skills and job experience. *But we should also note that black families are not a homogeneous group. In fact, the distribution of income is more uneven among black families than it is among the population as a whole.*

On the upside, according to the 1998 *Economic Report of the President*, the median income of black families has risen faster since 1993 than that of whites. The proportion of black families living below the poverty line fell to a record low by 1997. And the ratio of black-to-white average income for married couples increased from 0.71 in 1967 to 0.80 in 1997; for female-headed families, that ratio increased from 0.63 to 0.73.

There is also a growing middle class among black households. The number of black-owned businesses increased by 46 percent between 1987 and 1992, according to the Census Bureau. Some of the progress among blacks stems from their steady advances in education. In 1975, the percentage of young blacks without a high school diploma was 12.3 percentage points above that of whites (27.0 percent versus 14.7 percent). By 1995, the percentage of young blacks without diplomas had fallen to within 2 percentage points of whites (15.8 percent versus 13.8 percent). In 1960, the average black adult had only a junior high school education; by 1990, a high school education was the average. In 1980, only 7 percent of middle-aged blacks had a college degree; by 1990, that figure had jumped to 17 percent. More generally, since 1970, the number of black doctors, nurses, college teachers, and newspaper reporters has more than doubled; the number of black engineers, computer programmers, accountants, managers, and administrators has more than tripled; the number of black elected officials has quadrupled; and the number of black lawyers has increased sixfold.

UNINTENDED CONSEQUENCES OF INCOME ASSISTANCE

On the plus side, antipoverty programs increase the consumption possibilities of poor families, and this is significant, especially since children are the largest poverty group. But programs to assist the poor may have secondary effects that limit their ability to reduce poverty. Here we consider some unintended consequences.

Work Disincentives

Society, through government, tries to provide families with an adequate standard of living, but society also wants to ensure that only those in need receive benefits. As we have seen, income assistance consists of a bundle of cash and in-kind transfer programs. Because these programs are designed to help the poor and only the poor, the level of benefits is inversely related to income from other sources. This has resulted in a system in which transfers decline sharply as earned income increases, in effect imposing a high marginal tax rate on that earned income. An increase in earnings may cause a decline in benefits received from TANF, Medicaid, food stamps, housing assistance, energy assistance, and other programs. If a bite is taken from each transfer program as earned income increases, working may result in little or no increase in total income. In fact, over certain income ranges, the welfare recipient may lose well over $1 in transfer benefits for each $1 increase in earnings. The *marginal tax rate* on earned income could exceed 100 percent.

Since holding even a part-time job involves additional expenses, such as transportation and child-care costs, not to mention the loss of free time, such a system of perverse incentives can frustrate those trying to work their way off welfare. *This high marginal tax rate discourages employment and self-sufficiency.* In many cases, the value of welfare benefits exceeds the disposable income resulting from full-time employment. For example, according to one study, the value of welfare benefits in most states exceeded the full-time earning of a janitor or the starting salary for a secretary.[11]

Just how much the higher marginal tax rates reduced the incentive to work remains unclear. We do know that prior to recent welfare reforms only about one of every 20 persons receiving welfare was employed. Twice as many welfare recipients worked in the mid-1970s. These high marginal tax rates also encouraged welfare recipients to conceal earned income; some worked "off the books" for cash or became involved in illegal activities.

The longer people are out of the labor force, the more their job skills deteriorate, so when they do seek employment, their productivity and their pay are lower than when they were last employed. This lowers their expected wage and makes work less attractive. Some economists argue that in this way, welfare benefits can lead to long-term dependency. While welfare seems to be a rational choice in the short run, it has an unfavorable long-term outcome both for the family and for society.

Does Welfare Cause Dependency?

Does the system of incentives created by high marginal tax rates create dependency among welfare recipients? How could we examine such a question? A relatively brief average stay on welfare would be evidence of little dependency. If, however, the same families were found to be poor year after year, this would be a matter of concern.

To explore the possibility of welfare dependency in the United States, a University of Michigan study tracked 5,000 families over a number of years, paying particular attention to economic mobility both from year to year and from one generation to the next.[12] The study first examined poverty from year to year, or dependency within a generation. It found that most recipients received welfare for less than a year, but about 30 percent of all welfare recipients remained on welfare for at least eight years. Thus there was a core of long-term recipients.

---

11 See Michael Tanner and Stephen Moore, "Why Welfare Pays," *Wall Street Journal* (28 September 1995).
12 Greg J. Duncan, Richard D. Coe, et al., *Years of Poverty, Years of Plenty* (Ann Arbor: University of Michigan Press, 1984).

A second and more serious concern is whether the children of the poor end up in poverty as well. Is there a cycle of poverty? Why might we expect such a transmission mechanism? Children in welfare households may learn the ropes about the welfare system and may come to view welfare as a normal way of life rather than as a temporary bridge over a rough patch. Research indicates that daughters from welfare families are more likely than daughters in families not on welfare to participate in the welfare system themselves and are more likely to have premarital births.[13] The evidence is weaker when it comes to sons from welfare families. What's difficult to say is whether welfare "caused" the link between mother and daughter, since the same factors that contributed to a mother's welfare status could also have contributed to her daughter's welfare status.

WELFARE REFORM

There has been much dissatisfaction with the welfare system, both among those who pay for the programs and among direct beneficiaries. A variety of welfare reforms has been introduced in recent years aimed mostly at reducing long-term dependence on poverty.

Recent Reforms

Some analysts believe that one way to reduce poverty is to provide welfare recipients with job skills and make them find jobs. Even before the 1996 federal reform of welfare, to be discussed shortly, some sort of "workfare" component for welfare recipients operated in over 35 states. In such states, as a condition of receiving welfare, the head of the household had to participate in education and training programs, search for work, or take some paid or unpaid position. The idea was to acquaint those on welfare with the job market. Evidence from various states indicates that programs involving mandatory job searches, short-term unpaid work, and training could operate at low cost and increase employment. The government saved money because those in welfare-to-work programs left welfare rolls sooner.

Reforms at the state level set the stage for federal reform. By far the biggest reform in the welfare system in the last 60 years came with the 1996 Personal Responsibility and Work Reconciliation Act, which replaced the Aid to Families with Dependent Children (AFDC) entitlement program with Temporary Assistance for Needy Families (TANF). Whereas the AFDC program set eligibility rules and left federal costs open-ended through a matching grant to the state, TANF offers a block grant called the Family Assistance Grant to the states to run their welfare programs. States ended AFDC and began TANF by July 1, 1997. The total Family Assistance Grant is fixed at $16.4 billion per year from 1997 to 2002, though supplementary grants will go to the states with the highest population growth.

Under the new system, states are granted wide latitude to run their own welfare programs. But concerns about welfare dependency fostered some special provisions. The act imposes a lifetime limit of five years that a recipient can

---

13   See Robert Moffit, "Incentive Effects of the U.S. Welfare System: A Review," *Journal of Economic Literature* 30 (March 1992): 37.

be on welfare. All able-bodied recipients on welfare for two years must participate in welfare-to-work programs. When fully implemented, states must have half their welfare recipients working at least 30 hours per week.

Provisions of the act limit benefits for noncitizens and for teenage mothers not living at home. States must also be more aggressive in enforcing child support from fathers of children on welfare. Finally the act tightens eligibility requirements for disabled children receiving Supplemental Security Income, extending aid only to those who suffer from "marked or severe" disabilities. Food Stamps, Supplemental Security Income, and Medicaid continue as federal entitlement programs.

Given the structure of the new program, states now have an incentive to constrain the growth of welfare rolls. Under the old system the federal government helped fund each dollar of spending, with the state paying from 22 to 50 cents per dollar, depending on its per capita income. For example, Mississippi spent 22 cents per dollar of welfare and Connecticut spent 50 cents per dollar. Under the new system, each state must pay 100 percent of any welfare costs above its Family Assistance Grant.

Aside from the time limits and work participation rates imposed by the federal government, states are free to set benefit levels and experiment however they choose. About half the states imposed time limits shorter than five years; 10 states have a two-year limit. In 33 states, all cash benefits are lost if recipients fail to comply with work requirements. Some observers fear that states now have a strong incentive to keep welfare costs down by cutting benefits. To avoid becoming destinations for poor people—that is, to avoid becoming "welfare magnets"—states may be tempted to offer relatively low levels of benefits.

The fear is that states will undercut benefit levels in what has been called a "race to the bottom." Another concern with ending federal entitlements and capping grants to states is what will happen should the economy enter a recession. One economist estimates that a 1-percent increase in unemployment will increase the welfare rolls by 2.5 percent and increase public spending on welfare by 3 percent.[14] Since state tax revenue drops during a recession, budgeters may be forced to cut welfare benefits, causing hardship for poor families.

The following case study surveys some results of welfare reform so far.

Is Welfare-to-Work Working?

Here are some preliminary conclusions based on the course of welfare reform as of 1998. Work requirements *do* seem to yield substantial declines in caseloads. In 1994 the number of welfare recipients peaked at 14 million, mostly single women with children. By 1998 the rolls had dropped by nearly one-third. Exhibit 5 shows the percentage of the U.S. population on welfare since 1960, where welfare includes Aid to Families with Dependent Children and, more recently, Temporary Assistance to Needy

CaseStudy

Public Policy

The Urban Institute is a policy research organization working to increase citizens' awareness of important public choices. According to its report "Does Work Pay?," at http://newfederalism.urban.org/html/anf28.html, going to work improves the standard of living for low-income single mothers on welfare, so long as other benefit programs continue to provide assistance. What are some of these other assistance programs and policies? What happens to income when wages increase but benefits decrease? For more reports about welfare to work, visit the following Web sites: Idea Central's recommended links on Welfare and Families at http://epn.org/idea/welf-bkm.html#2.

---

14 See the analysis by Elizabeth Powers, "Welfare Reform and the Cyclicality of Welfare Programs," *Economic Commentary* (June 1996).

Families. Notice the sharp decline in recent years. The percentage of the population on welfare in 1998 was lower than at any time since 1968. Fortunately the reforms occurred during an expanding economy, with jobs plentiful, and the unemployment rate the lowest it had been in three decades. But welfare rolls declined both in good economies, such as in Wisconsin, and in lagging economies, such as in New York City, where the unemployment rate was more than twice the national average.

Many of those on welfare had other ways to support themselves. One expert who counted everything from food stamps to income from unreported jobs said cash transfers accounted for about 34 percent of the average welfare recipient's income, food stamps provided about 25 percent, and 36 percent came from unreported sources such as secret jobs, boyfriends, contributions from relatives, or private charities. (Medicaid was not counted as income although it costs taxpayers more than any other welfare program).

Despite the "welfare-to-work" slogan, only about half those leaving welfare found jobs. In Massachusetts, 50 percent of former recipients said they had jobs. Job rates were 52 percent in Idaho, 56 percent in New Mexico, 50 percent in Tennessee, and 66 percent in Maryland. This is not much of an improvement compared to employment rates prior to the reforms. Remember that even before the recent reforms, most beneficiaries remained on welfare only temporarily.

Since most people on welfare are poorly educated and have few job skills, wage levels for those who find jobs remain low. For example, annual earnings for individuals who found jobs in Maryland averaged $8,300 (the poverty level for a family of three in 1997 was $12,800). Part-time work is also common, as is job loss among those who initially found jobs. Tennessee surveyed 205 welfare recipients who had found jobs. Three months later, one-quarter had lost their jobs and only about half were working full time. On the plus side, the earned income tax credit adds up to $3,650 a year in additional income to low-income workers. Most of those working can also receive food stamps, child care, and Medicaid.

Because the welfare rolls declined but the federal grant to the states remained constant, there has been a significant increase in welfare spending per recipient. Most states are combining tough new rules with an expanded menu of welfare services. States have made large investments in work-related services such as job placement, transportation, and especially child care. Because of the increase in state outlays for child care, expected day-care shortages never materialized.

Finally, one effect of the work requirements of welfare reform has been to raise the "price" of welfare to the recipients. Raising the price of going on welfare reduced the amount of welfare demanded. As one welfare director noted, a lot of people who are leaving welfare are saying, "It's not worth the hassle." We might say that the demand curve for welfare is downward sloping, with "hassle" measured on the vertical axis. The greater the "hassle," the less welfare is demanded. What's more, welfare rolls declined more in states where efforts to get people to work are the greatest. For example, Wisconsin and Minnesota had similar economies as reflected by identical unemployment rates, but Wisconsin's much more aggressive work requirements cut welfare rolls there three times faster than in Minnesota.

Sources: Jason DeParle, "U.S. Welfare System Dies as State Programs Emerge," *New York Times* (30 June 1997); Michael Grunwald, "Welfare-to-Work: The Challenge Grows Harder," *Boston Globe* (20 April 1998); Joe Sexton, "In a Part of Brooklyn, the New Welfare Rules Change Everything," *New York Times* (10 March 1997); and Joe Sexton, "Only Severely Troubled Children Need Apply," *New York Times* (22 December 1997).

EXHIBIT 5

Welfare Recipients Since 1960 as Percentage of U.S. Population by Year

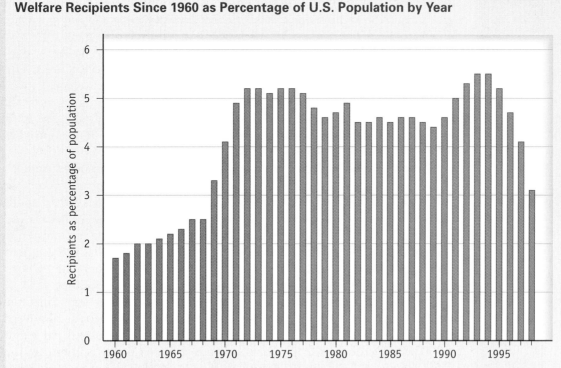

Source: U.S. Department of Health and Human Services, August 1998, at http://www.acf.dfhhs.gov/news/6097rf.htm. Figure for 1998 is as of June 1998.

Perhaps the most successful welfare reform in the country is taking place in Oregon, which is discussed in this final case study.

Oregon's Program of "Tough Love"

Oregon's welfare caseload fell from 43,600 in March 1994 to 18,000 by February 1999. The drop came not as a result of strict time limits or tougher eligibility standards, but by providing strong work incentives and working more closely with clients. TANF in Oregon provided $460 a month in 1998 for a family of three, a benefit level in the upper third for all states. The typical family on welfare and food stamps was living at about 75 percent of the poverty level in 1998.

After leaving TANF for work, people in Oregon continue to qualify for health benefits for at least a year, for day care until

CaseStudy

Public Policy

Visit Oregon's Healthcare, Human Services and Labor Policy Web site at http://www. governor.state.or.us/ governor/hhslp/index.html for progress reports on welfare reform policy. Notice that the policy is referred to as "social support." The site includes a link to a quarterly newsletter. Read the report, "The Oregon Strategy for Social Support," for details about how the policy is being implemented. What is the difference between support and services? In what ways is the state considering changing how services are delivered?

income reaches 200 percent of the federal poverty level, for food stamps for those who are income-eligible, and for the federal earned income tax credit, which in effect raises the wage by about $1 an hour. By working at even the state's minimum wage of $6 an hour, the family's living standard increases to 130 percent of the poverty level. The average starting wage in the first job placement off welfare in fact exceeded $7 an hour. Thus work is attractive compared to welfare.

One federal study tracked 5,500 welfare applicants and recipients in Oregon over a two-year period. Half the group participated in the welfare-to-work program and half did not. Taking part in the welfare-to-work program increased employment by 18 percent, raised average earnings over the two years by 35 percent, and boosted the proportion of individuals with employer-provided health insurance by 71 percent.

Oregon became the first state to require drug addicts to attend treatment as a condition of receiving welfare. An evaluation of that program found that clients who completed drug treatment earned 65 percent more than similar clients in a comparison group. Those completing treatment for addiction were 45 percent less likely to be arrested and only half as likely to be investigated for child abuse or neglect. The study also found that for every dollar Oregon spent on drug treatment it saved at least $5.60 on other social services. The approach in most other states is simply to ban recent drug felons from receiving aid.

The Oregon program offers abundant services, but welfare applicants must first spend a month looking for work before getting help. The federal government requires states to enroll 50 percent of their recipients in job-related activity by 2002. By October of 1997, Oregon had 89 percent of its recipients in job-related activity, including unpaid workfare jobs to develop experience and wage-subsidized jobs for those who could not otherwise find work. Perhaps the most persuasive evidence that Oregon's approach of tough love is working is that after 18 months, only 8 percent of those who left welfare returned to the rolls.

Sources: Jason DeParle, "Newest Challenge for Welfare: Helping the Hard-Core Jobless," *New York Times* (20 November 1997); "Oregon Welfare Reform Fact Sheet," Oregon Department of Human Resources (June 1998); Gary Weeks, "Oregon a Success Story in Welfare Reform," *Business Journal of Portland* (1 July 1996); and "Oregon's Welfare-to-Work Efforts Bring National Recognition," Oregon Department of Human Services (23 June 1998).

CONCLUSION

Government redistribution programs have been most successful at reducing poverty among the elderly. But poverty rates among children have increased since 1970 because of the growth in the number of female householders. We might ask why transfer programs have reduced poverty rates among the elderly but not among female householders. Transfer programs do not encourage people to get old; that process occurs naturally and is independent of the level of transfers. But the level and availability of transfer programs at the margin influences some young unmarried women as they are deciding whether to have a child and may, at the margin, influence a married mother's decision to get divorced.

Most transfers in the economy are not from the government but rather are in-kind transfers within the family, from parents to children. Thus any change in a family's capacity to earn income has serious consequences for dependent

EXHIBIT 5

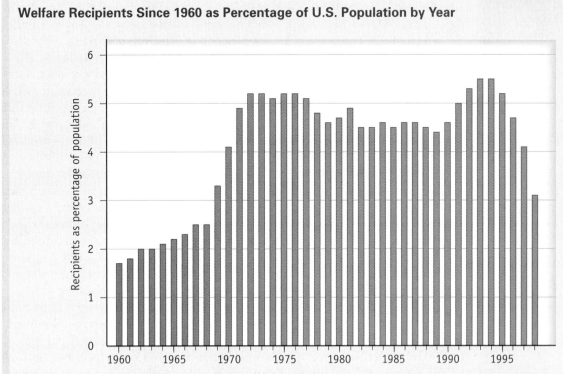

Welfare Recipients Since 1960 as Percentage of U.S. Population by Year

Source: U.S. Department of Health and Human Services, August 1998, at http://www.acf.dfhhs.gov/news/6097rf.htm. Figure for 1998 is as of June 1998.

Perhaps the most successful welfare reform in the country is taking place in Oregon, which is discussed in this final case study.

Oregon's Program of "Tough Love"

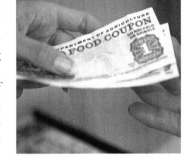

Oregon's welfare caseload fell from 43,600 in March 1994 to 18,000 by February 1999. The drop came not as a result of strict time limits or tougher eligibility standards, but by providing strong work incentives and working more closely with clients. TANF in Oregon provided $460 a month in 1998 for a family of three, a benefit level in the upper third for all states. The typical family on welfare and food stamps was living at about 75 percent of the poverty level in 1998.

After leaving TANF for work, people in Oregon continue to qualify for health benefits for at least a year, for day care until

CaseStudy

Public Policy

Visit Oregon's Healthcare, Human Services and Labor Policy Web site at http://www.governor.state.or.us/governor/hhslp/index.html for progress reports on welfare reform policy. Notice that the policy is referred to as "social support." The site includes a link to a quarterly newsletter. Read the report, "The Oregon Strategy for Social Support," for details about how the policy is being implemented. What is the difference between support and services? In what ways is the state considering changing how services are delivered?

income reaches 200 percent of the federal poverty level, for food stamps for those who are income-eligible, and for the federal earned income tax credit, which in effect raises the wage by about $1 an hour. By working at even the state's minimum wage of $6 an hour, the family's living standard increases to 130 percent of the poverty level. The average starting wage in the first job placement off welfare in fact exceeded $7 an hour. Thus work is attractive compared to welfare.

One federal study tracked 5,500 welfare applicants and recipients in Oregon over a two-year period. Half the group participated in the welfare-to-work program and half did not. Taking part in the welfare-to-work program increased employment by 18 percent, raised average earnings over the two years by 35 percent, and boosted the proportion of individuals with employer-provided health insurance by 71 percent.

Oregon became the first state to require drug addicts to attend treatment as a condition of receiving welfare. An evaluation of that program found that clients who completed drug treatment earned 65 percent more than similar clients in a comparison group. Those completing treatment for addiction were 45 percent less likely to be arrested and only half as likely to be investigated for child abuse or neglect. The study also found that for every dollar Oregon spent on drug treatment it saved at least $5.60 on other social services. The approach in most other states is simply to ban recent drug felons from receiving aid.

The Oregon program offers abundant services, but welfare applicants must first spend a month looking for work before getting help. The federal government requires states to enroll 50 percent of their recipients in job-related activity by 2002. By October of 1997, Oregon had 89 percent of its recipients in job-related activity, including unpaid workfare jobs to develop experience and wage-subsidized jobs for those who could not otherwise find work. Perhaps the most persuasive evidence that Oregon's approach of tough love is working is that after 18 months, only 8 percent of those who left welfare returned to the rolls.

Sources: Jason DeParle, "Newest Challenge for Welfare: Helping the Hard-Core Jobless," *New York Times* (20 November 1997); "Oregon Welfare Reform Fact Sheet," Oregon Department of Human Resources (June 1998); Gary Weeks, "Oregon a Success Story in Welfare Reform," *Business Journal of Portland* (1 July 1996); and "Oregon's Welfare-to-Work Efforts Bring National Recognition," Oregon Department of Human Services (23 June 1998).

CONCLUSION

Government redistribution programs have been most successful at reducing poverty among the elderly. But poverty rates among children have increased since 1970 because of the growth in the number of female householders. We might ask why transfer programs have reduced poverty rates among the elderly but not among female householders. Transfer programs do not encourage people to get old; that process occurs naturally and is independent of the level of transfers. But the level and availability of transfer programs at the margin influences some young unmarried women as they are deciding whether to have a child and may, at the margin, influence a married mother's decision to get divorced.

Most transfers in the economy are not from the government but rather are in-kind transfers within the family, from parents to children. Thus any change in a family's capacity to earn income has serious consequences for dependent children. Family structure appears to be a primary determinant of family income. One-fifth of the children in the United States live in poverty. Children are the innocent victims of the changing family structure.

SUMMARY

1. Money income (before taxes but after cash transfers) in the United States became somewhat less evenly distributed between 1967 and 1997. Since 1959, poverty rates have dropped most among the elderly.

2. Young, single motherhood is a recipe for instant poverty. Often the young mother drops out of school, which reduces her future earning possibilities when and if she seeks work outside the home. Growth in the number of female householders has increased poverty among children.

3. The wage gap between blacks and whites narrowed between 1940 and 1975, widened until the early 1990s, and has been narrowing again since 1993. Affirmative-action programs seem to have increased employment opportunities among blacks.

4. Among the undesirable effects of income assistance is a high marginal tax rate on earned income, which discourages employment and encourages welfare dependency. According to one survey, about 30 percent of families on welfare remain there for eight years or more.

5. Welfare reforms introduced by the states set the stage for federal welfare reforms aimed at promoting the transition from welfare to work. The states have been experimenting with different systems aimed at promoting greater personal responsibility. The welfare rolls dropped by about one-third between 1994 and 1998.

QUESTIONS FOR REVIEW

1. *(Distribution of Household Income)* Look back at Exhibit 1 in this chapter. How would you explain the shift in the U.S. income distribution in the last two decades?

2. *(Official Poverty Level)* Although the poverty rate among single mothers has remained constant at 32 percent for the last three decades, the number of poor children from such families has more than doubled. Explain.

3. *(Official Poverty Level)* How does the U.S. Department of Agriculture calculate the official poverty level? What government assistance programs does the Census Bureau consider when calculating a household's income? What programs are ignored?

4. *(Income Differences)* List some reasons why household incomes differ. Which factors are the most important?

5. *(Programs to Help the Poor)* Distinguish between social insurance programs and income assistance programs. Identify the key examples of each.

6. *(Poverty and Age)* Poverty among the elderly fell dramatically between 1959 and 1974 and has continued to decline since then. However, poverty among that portion of the U.S. population that is less than 18 years old is higher today that in the mid-1970s. Why have the experiences of these two age groups differed?

7. *(Poverty and Public Choice)* Why is it difficult to pass legislation to reduce Social Security or Medicare benefits?

8. *(Poverty and Discrimination)* Which types of discrimination can drive a wedge between what whites earn and what nonwhites earn? Consider discrimination in schooling, for example. How could you detect such discrimination?

9. *(Work Disincentives)* How does the implicit tax on earned income (in the form of lost benefits from government assistance programs) affect work incentives? How do some people avoid the implicit tax?

10. *(Welfare Reform)* What has happened to the welfare caseload in recent years? Discuss some differences in results across states.

11. *(CaseStudy: Is Welfare-to-Work Working?)* Discuss the key features of welfare reforms introduced by the federal government in 1996. Why were policy makers worried that turning welfare over to the states would result in a "race to the bottom"?

EXPERIENTIAL EXERCISES

12. *(Poverty and the Poor)* Visit the Census Bureau's page on poverty statistics at www.census.gov/ hhes/www/poverty.html. Look at the Small Area Income and Poverty Estimates and find the latest poverty estimate for your county. How does the poverty rate there compare to the overall rate in your state and in the United States as a whole?

13. *(CaseStudy: Oregon's Program of "Tough Love")* The National Governors' Association maintains a page on state-level welfare reform efforts at http://www. nga.org/Welfare/WelfareDocs/WelfareStateWebLinks.htm. Look up Oregon and see how the state's program is evolving. Has it been a success?

14. *(Wall Street Journal)* The front page of the Marketplace section of the *Wall Street Journal* often carries articles on income distribution and the personal impact of poverty. Pay particular attention to the Work & Family and Business and Race columns in the Wednesday paper. How are the actions of U.S. businesses affecting income distribution and poverty?

International Trade

This morning you pulled up your Levi jeans from Mexico, pulled over your Benetton sweater from Italy, and laced up your Nikes from Indonesia. After a breakfast that included bananas from Honduras and coffee from Brazil, you climbed into your Volvo from Sweden fueled by Saudi Arabian oil and headed for a lecture by a visiting professor from Hungary. If the United States is such a rich and productive nation, why do we import so many goods and services? Why don't we produce everything ourselves? And why do some groups try to restrict foreign trade? Answers to these and other questions are addressed in this chapter.

The world is a giant shopping mall, and Americans are big spenders. Americans buy Japanese cars, French wine, Swiss clocks, European vacations, and thousands of other goods and services from around the globe. But foreigners spend a lot on American products too—grain, personal computers, aircraft, movies, trips to Disney World, and thousands of other goods and services. In this chapter, we examine the gains from international trade and the effects of trade restrictions on the allocation of resources. The analysis is based on the familiar tools of supply and demand. Topics discussed in this chapter include:

- Gains from trade
- Absolute and comparative advantage revisited
- Tariffs

- Import quotas
- Welfare loss from trade restrictions
- Arguments for trade restrictions

THE GAINS FROM TRADE

A family from Virginia that sits down for a meal of Kansas prime rib, Idaho potatoes, and California string beans, with Georgia peach cobbler for desert is benefiting from interstate trade. You already understand why the residents of one state trade with those of another. Back in Chapter 2, you learned about the gains arising from specialization and exchange. You may recall the discussion of how you and your roommate could maximize output by specializing in typing or ironing. The law of comparative advantage says that the individual with the lowest opportunity cost of producing a particular output should specialize in producing that output. Just as individuals benefit from specialization and exchange, so do states and, indeed, nations. To reap the gains that arise from specialized production, countries engage in international trade. *With trade, each country can concentrate on producing those goods and services that involve the least opportunity cost.*

A Profile of Imports and Exports

Some nations are more involved in international trade than others, just as some states are more involved in interstate trade than others. For example, exports account for about half of the gross domestic product (GDP) in Holland; about one-third of the GDP in Germany, Sweden, and Switzerland; and about one-quarter of the GDP in Canada and the United Kingdom. Despite the perception that Japan has a giant export sector, only about 13 percent of Japanese production is exported.

In the United States, exports of goods and services amounted to about 11 percent of GDP in 1998. Although small relative to GDP, exports play a growing role in the U.S. economy. The four main U.S. exports are (1) high-technology manufactured products, such as computer software and hardware, aircraft, telecommunication equipment, and military equipment; (2) industrial supplies and materials; (3) agricultural products, especially corn and soybeans; and (4) entertainment products, such as movies and recorded music.

The United States depends on imports for some key inputs. For example, our position as the world's largest producer of aluminum depends on our importing vast amounts of bauxite. Most of our platinum and chromium and all of our manganese, mica, diamonds, and nickel are imported. Two-thirds of U.S. imports are (1) manufactured consumer goods, such as automobiles from Japan and Germany and electronic equipment from Taiwan, and (2) capital goods, such as high-tech printing presses from Germany. *U.S. imports of goods and services amounted to about 13 percent relative to GDP in 1998.*

The big change in U.S. exports over the last 25 years has been a growth in the dollar value of machinery exports; nearly half of the capital goods produced in the United States are exported. The primary change in U.S. imports over the last 25 years has been the increase in spending on foreign oil. Canada is our largest trading partner, followed by Japan and Mexico. Other important trading partners include Germany, Great Britain, South Korea, France, Hong Kong, Italy, and Brazil.

Production Possibilities Without Trade

The rationale behind some international trade is obvious. The United States grows no coffee beans because our climate is not suited to coffee. It is more revealing, however, to examine the gains from trade where the cost advantage is not so obvious. Suppose that just two goods—food and clothing—are produced and consumed and that there are only two countries in the world—the United States, with a labor force of 100 million workers, and the mythical country of Izodia, with 200 million workers. The conclusions we derive from this simple model will have general relevance to the pattern of international trade.

Exhibit 1 presents each country's production possibilities table, based on the size of the labor force and the productivity of workers in each country. We assume a given technology and that labor is fully and efficiently employed. Since no trade occurs between countries, Exhibit 1 presents each country's *consumption possibilities* table as well, reflecting each country's consumption alternatives.

The production numbers imply that each worker in the United States can produce either 6 units of food or 3 units of clothing per day. If all 100 million U.S. workers produce food, 600 million units can be produced per day, as reflected by combination U_1 in part (a) of Exhibit 1. If all U.S. workers produce clothing, U.S. output would be 300 million units per day, as reflected by combination U_6.

EXHIBIT 1

Production Possibilities Schedules for the United States and Izodia

(a) United States

	Units Produced (per worker per day)	Production Possibilities with 100 Million Workers (millions of units per day)					
		U_1	U_2	U_3	U_4	U_5	U_6
Food	6	600	480	360	240	120	0
Clothing	3	0	60	120	180	240	300

(b) Izodia

	Units Produced (per worker per day)	Production Possibilities with 200 Million Workers (millions of units per day)					
		I_1	I_2	I_3	I_4	I_5	I_6
Food	1	200	160	120	80	40	0
Clothing	2	0	80	160	240	320	400

Combinations in between represent alternatives if some workers produce food and some produce clothing. Because a U.S. worker can produce either 6 units of food or 3 units of clothing, *his opportunity cost of 1 more unit of food is ½ unit of clothing*.

Suppose Izodian workers are less educated, work with less capital, and farm less fertile land than U.S. workers. So each Izodian can produce only 1 unit of food or 2 units of clothing per day. If all 200 million Izodian workers specialize in food, they can produce 200 million units of food per day, as reflected by combination I_1 in part (b) of Exhibit 1. If all Izodian workers produce clothing, total output is 400 million units of clothing per day, as reflected by combination I_6. Some intermediate production possibilities are also listed in the exhibit. Because an Izodian worker can produce either 1 unit of food or 2 units of clothing, *her opportunity cost of 1 more unit of food is 2 units of clothing*.

We can convert the data in Exhibit 1 to a production possibilities frontier for each country, as is shown in Exhibit 2. In each diagram, the amount of food produced is measured on the vertical axis and the amount of clothing is measured on the horizontal axis. U.S. combinations are shown in panel (a) by U_1, U_2, and so on; Izodian combinations are designated in panel (b) by I_1, I_2, and so on. Because we assume that resources are perfectly adaptable to the production of each commodity, each production possibilities curve is a straight line reflecting constant opportunity cost.

Exhibit 2 illustrates—in red—the possible combinations of food and clothing that residents of each country can produce and consume if all resources are fully and efficiently employed and there is no trade between the two countries. **Autarky** is the situation of national self-sufficiency, in which there is no economic interaction with foreigners. Suppose that U.S. producers maximize profit

Autarky A situation of national self-sufficiency in which there is no economic interaction with foreigners

---

EXHIBIT 2

Production Possibilities Frontiers for the United States and Izodia Without Trade (in millions of units per day)

Panel (a) shows the U.S. production possibilities curve; its slope indicates that the opportunity cost of an additional unit of food is 1/2 unit of clothing. Panel (b) shows production possibilities in Izodia; an additional unit of food costs 2 units of clothing. Food is relatively cheaper to produce in the United States.

and U.S. consumers maximize utility with the combination of 240 million units of food and 180 million units of clothing—combination U_4. This combination will be called the *autarky equilibrium*. Suppose also that Izodians have an autarky equilibrium, identified as combination I_3, of 120 million units of food and 160 million units of clothing.

Consumption Possibilities Based on Comparative Advantage

In our example, each U.S. worker can produce both more clothing and more food per day than can each Izodian worker. U.S. workers therefore have an *absolute advantage* in the production of both goods because a U.S. worker can produce each good in less time than can an Izodian worker. With an absolute advantage in the production of both commodities, should the U.S. economy remain in autarky—that is, self-sufficient in both food and clothing productions—or could there be gains from trade?

As long as the opportunity cost of the two goods differs between the two countries, there are gains from specialization and trade. The opportunity cost of producing 1 more unit of food in the United States is ½ unit of clothing, compared to 2 units of clothing in Izodia. *According to the law of comparative advantage, each country should specialize in producing the good with the lower opportunity cost.* Since the opportunity cost of producing food is lower in the United States than in Izodia, both countries will gain if the United States specializes in producing food and exports some to Izodia, and Izodia specializes in producing clothing and exports some to the United States.

Before countries can trade, they must somehow determine how much of one good will be exchanged for another—that is, they must establish the **terms of trade.** Suppose that market forces shape terms of trade whereby 1 unit of clothing exchanges for 1 unit of food. Based on those terms of trade, Americans trade 1 unit of food to Izodians for 1 unit of clothing. To produce 1 unit of clothing Americans would have to sacrifice 2 units of food. Likewise, Izodians sacrifice 1 unit of clothing by trading clothing to Americans for 1 unit of food, which is only half what Izodians would sacrifice to produce 1 unit of food themselves.

Terms of trade How much of one good exchanges for a unit of another good

Exhibit 3 shows that with 1 unit of food trading for 1 unit of clothing, Americans and Izodians can consume anywhere along or below their blue consumption possibilities frontiers. *The consumption possibilities frontier* shows a nation's alternative combinations of goods available as a result of production and foreign trade. (Note that the U.S. consumption possibilities curve does not extend to the right of 400 million units of clothing, since that is the most the Izodians can produce.) The amount each country actually consumes will depend on its relative preferences for food and clothing. Suppose Americans select point U in panel (a) and Izodians select point I in panel (b).

Without trade, the United States produced and consumed 240 million units of food and 180 million units of clothing. With trade, the United States specializes in food by producing 600 million units; Americans eat 400 million units and exchange the remaining 200 million for 200 million units of Izodian clothing. This consumption combination is reflected by point U in panel (a). Through exchange, Americans increase their consumption of both food and clothing.

EXHIBIT 3

Production (and Consumption) Possibilities Frontiers with Trade (in millions of units per day)

If Izodia and the United States can trade at the rate of 1 unit of clothing for 1 unit of food, both can benefit. Consumption possibilities at those terms of trade are shown by the blue lines. The United States was previously producing and consuming combination U_4. By trading with Izodia, it can produce only food and still consume combination U—a combination that contains more food and more clothing than combination U_4 does. Likewise, Izodia can attain the preferred combination I by trading its clothing for U.S. food. Both countries are better off as a result of international trade.

Without trade, Izodians produced and consumed 120 million units of food and 160 million units of clothing. With trade, Izodians specialize in clothing to produce 400 million units; Izodians wear 200 million units of clothing and exchange the remaining 200 million units for 200 million units of food. This consumption combination is shown by point I in panel (b). Izodians, like Americans, are able to increase their consumption of both food and clothing through trade. How is this possible?

Since Izodians are relatively more efficient in the production of clothing and Americans relatively more efficient in the production of food, total output increases when each country specializes. Specifically, without specialization, total world production was 360 million units of food and 340 million units of clothing. With specialization, food production increases to 600 million units and clothing production increases to 400 million units. The only constraint on trade is that, for each good, *total world production must equal total world consumption.* In our two-country world, this means that the amount of food the United States exports must equal the amount of food Izodia imports. The same goes for Izodia's exports of clothing.

Thus, both countries have more goods and services after trade. *Although the United States has an absolute advantage in both goods, differences in the opportunity cost of production between the two nations ensure that specialization and exchange will result in mutual gains.* Remember that comparative advantage, not absolute advantage, is the source of gains from trade.

We simplified trade relations in our example to highlight the gains from specialization and exchange. We assumed that each country would completely specialize in producing a particular good, that resources were equally adaptable to the production of either good, that the costs of transporting the goods from one country to another were inconsequential, and that there were no problems in arriving at the terms of trade. The world is not that simple (for example, we don't expect a country to produce just one good), but the law of comparative advantage still points to gains from trade.

Reasons for International Specialization

Countries trade with one another—or, more precisely, people and firms in one country trade with those in another—because each side expects to gain from the exchange. How do we know what each country should produce and what goods should be traded?

Differences in Resource Endowments. Trade is often prompted by differences in resource endowments. Two key resources are labor and capital. Countries differ not only in their amounts of labor and capital but in the qualities of those resources. A well-educated and well-trained labor force is more productive than an uneducated and unskilled one. Similarly, capital that reflects the most recent technological developments is more productive than nonexistent or obsolete capital. Some countries, such as the United States and Japan, have an educated labor force and an abundant stock of modern capital. Both resources result in greater productivity per worker, making each nation quite competitive in producing goods that require skilled labor and sophisticated capital.

Some countries are blessed with an abundance of fertile land and favorable growing seasons. The United States, for example, has been called the "breadbasket of the world" because of its rich farmland. Honduras has the ideal climate for growing bananas. Coffee is grown best in the climate and elevation of Colombia, Brazil, and Jamaica. Thus, the United States exports corn and imports coffee and bananas. Differences in the seasons across countries also serve as a basis for trade. For example, during the winter months, Americans import fruit from Chile and Canadian tourists travel to Florida for sun and fun. During the summer months, Americans export fruit to Chile and American tourists travel to Canada for fishing and camping.

Mineral resources are often concentrated in particular countries: oil in Saudi Arabia, bauxite in Jamaica, diamonds in South Africa. The United States has abundant coal supplies, but not enough oil to satisfy domestic demand. Thus the United States exports coal and imports oil. More generally, *countries export those products that they can produce more cheaply in return for those that are unavailable domestically or are more costly to produce than to buy from other countries.*

Economies of Scale. If production is subject to *economies of scale*—that is, if the average cost falls as the rate of production increases—countries can gain from trade if each nation specializes. Such specialization allows each nation to produce at a greater output rate, which reduces average production costs. The primary reason for establishing the single integrated market in Western Europe is to offer European producers a large, open market of over 320 million consumers so that producers can increase production, experience economies of scale, and in the process become more competitive in international markets.

Differences in Tastes. Even if all countries had identical resource endowments and combined those resources with equal efficiency, each country would still gain from trade as long as tastes and preferences differed among countries. Consumption patterns differ. For example, the per-capita consumption of beer in Germany is more than double that in Portugal or Sweden. The French drink three times as much wine as Danes do. The Danes consume twice as much pork as Americans do. Americans consume twice as much chicken as Hungarians do. Soft drinks are four times more popular in the United States than in Western Europe. The English like tea; Americans coffee. Algeria has an ideal climate for growing grapes, but its large Muslim population abstains from alcohol. Thus Algeria exports wine.

TRADE RESTRICTIONS

Despite the benefits of international trade, nearly all countries at one time or another erect barriers to impede or block free trade among nations. Trade restrictions usually benefit domestic producers but harm domestic consumers. In this section, we will consider the effects of restrictions and the reasons they are imposed.

Consumer and Producer Surplus

Before we consider the net effect of world trade on social welfare, let's develop a framework for describing the benefits that consumers and producers derive from exchange. To do this, let's consider a hypothetical market for chicken shown in Exhibit 4. The height of the demand curve reflects the amount that consumers are willing and able to pay for each additional pound of chicken. In effect, the height of the demand curve shows the *marginal benefit* consumers expect from each pound of chicken. For example, the demand curve indicates that some consumers are willing to pay $1.50 or more per pound for the first few pounds of chicken. But all consumers get to buy chicken at the market-clearing price, which in Exhibit 4 is only $0.50 per pound. The blue shaded triangle below the demand curve and above the market price reflects the *consumer surplus,* which is the difference between the maximum sum of money consumers would pay for 60 pounds of chicken per day and the actual sum they do pay. Consumers thus get a bonus, or a surplus, from market exchange. We all enjoy a consumer surplus from most products we consume.

There is a similar surplus on the producer side. The height of the supply curve reflects the minimum amount of money that producers are willing and able to accept for each additional pound of chicken. That is, the height of the supply curve shows the *marginal cost* producers incur in supplying each additional pound of chicken. For example, the supply curve indicates that some producers incur a marginal cost of $0.25 or less per pound for supplying the first few pounds of chicken. But all producers get to sell chicken for the market-clearing price—in this case, $0.50 per pound. The gold shaded triangle above the supply curve and below the market price reflects the *producer surplus,* which is the difference between the actual sum of money producers receive for 60 pounds of chicken and the minimum sum they would accept for that quantity.

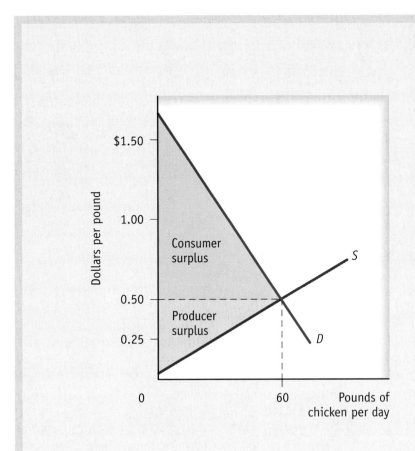

EXHIBIT 4

Consumer Surplus and Producer Surplus

Consumer surplus, shown by the blue shaded triangle, shows the net benefits consumers reap by being able to purchase 60 pounds of chicken at $0.50 per pound. Some consumers would have been willing to pay $1.50 or more per pound for the first few pounds. Consumer surplus measures the difference between the maximum sum of money consumers would pay for 60 pounds of chicken and the actual sum they pay. Producer surplus, shown by the gold shaded triangle, shows the net benefits producers reap by being able to sell 60 pounds of chicken at $0.50 per pound. Some producers would have been willing to supply chicken for $0.25 per pound or less. Producer surplus measures the difference between the actual sum of money producers receive for 60 pounds of chicken and the minimum amount they would accept for this amount of chicken.

The point is that market exchange usually yields a surplus, or a bonus, to both producers and consumers. In the balance of the chapter, we focus on how restrictions on international trade affect consumer surplus and producer surplus.

Tariffs

A *tariff*, a term first introduced in Chapter 4, is a tax on imports. (Tariffs can also be applied to exports, but we will focus on import tariffs.) A tariff can be either *specific*, such as a tariff of $5 per barrel of oil, or *ad valorem*, a percentage of the price of imports at the port of entry. Consider the effects of a specific tariff on a particular good. In Exhibit 5, *D* is the domestic demand for sugar and *S* is the supply provided by domestic producers. Suppose that the world price of sugar is $0.10 per pound, as it was in 1998. The **world price** is the price determined by the world supply and world demand for a product. It is the price at which any supplier can sell output on the world market and at which any demander can purchase output on the world market.

World price The price at which a good is traded internationally; determined by the world supply and demand for the good

EXHIBIT 5

Effect of a Tariff

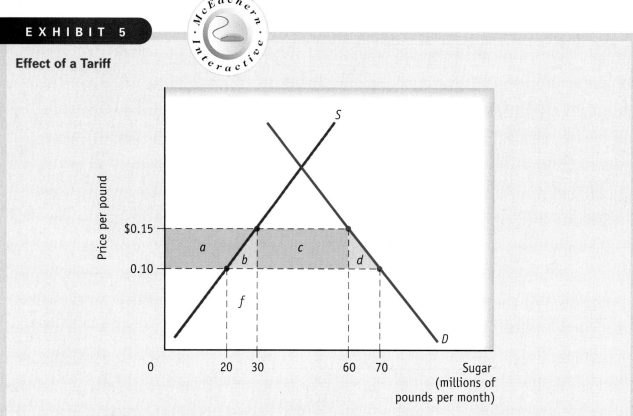

At a world price of $0.10 per pound, domestic consumers demand 70 million pounds per month and domestic producers supply 20 million pounds per month; the difference is imported. With the imposition of a $0.05 per pound tariff, the domestic price rises to $0.15 per pound, domestic producers increase production to 30 million pounds, and domestic consumers cut back to 60 million pounds. Imports fall to 30 million pounds. At the higher domestic price, consumers are worse off; their loss of consumer surplus is the sum of areas *a, b, c,* and *d.* Area *a* represents an increase in producer surplus: a transfer from consumers to producers. Areas *b* and *f* reflect the portion of additional revenues to producers that is just offset by the higher production costs of expanding domestic output by 10 million pounds. Area *c* shows government revenue from the tariff. The net welfare loss to society is the sum of area *d,* which reflects the loss of consumer surplus resulting from the drop in consumption, and area *b,* which reflects the higher marginal cost of domestically producing output that could have been produced more cheaply abroad.

With free trade, domestic consumers can buy any amount desired at the world price, so the quantity demanded is 70 million pounds per month, of which 20 million pounds are supplied by domestic producers and 50 million pounds are imported. Domestic producers cannot charge more than the world price, since domestic buyers can purchase as much sugar as they want at $0.10 per pound in the world market.

Now suppose that a specific tariff of $0.05 is imposed on each pound of sugar imported, raising the price of imported sugar from $0.10 to $0.15 per pound. Domestic producers can therefore raise their price to $0.15 per pound as well without losing sales to imports. At the higher price, the quantity supplied by domestic producers increases to 30 million pounds per month, but the quantity demanded by domestic consumers declines to 60 million pounds per month. Because the quantity demanded has declined and the quantity supplied by domestic producers has increased, imports decline from 50 million to 30 million pounds per month.

Since the price is higher after the tariff, consumers are worse off. The loss in consumer surplus is identified in Exhibit 5 by the blue and red shaded areas. Because both the domestic price and the quantity of sugar supplied by domestic producers have increased, the total revenue received by domestic producers increases by the areas *a* plus *b* plus *f.* But only the light-blue shaded area, *a,* represents an increase in producer surplus. The increase in revenue represented by the areas *b* plus *f* merely offsets the higher marginal cost of expanding domestic production from 20 million to 30 million pounds. The red shaded triangle, *b,* represents part of the net welfare loss to the domestic economy, because those 10 million pounds could have been purchased from abroad for $0.10 per pound rather than produced domestically at a higher marginal cost.

Government revenue from the tariff is identified by the light-blue shaded area, *c,* which equals the tariff of $0.05 per pound multiplied by the 30 million pounds that are imported, or $1.5 million per month. Tariff revenue represents a loss to consumers, but since the tariff is revenue to the government, this loss can potentially be offset by a reduction in taxes or an increase in public services. The red-shaded triangle, *d,* shows a loss in consumer surplus resulting from the fact that less sugar is consumed at the higher price. This loss in consumer surplus is not redistributed as a gain to anyone else, so area *d* reflects part of the net welfare loss of the tariff. Therefore, the two red-shaded triangles, *b* and *d,* show the domestic economy's net welfare loss of the tariff; the *two triangles measure a net loss in consumer surplus that is not offset by a net gain to anyone else.*

Of the total loss in consumer surplus (areas *a, b, c,* and *d*) resulting from the tariff, area *a* is redistributed from consumers to domestic producers, area *c* becomes tariff revenue for the government, and the two red-shaded triangles, *b* and *d,* reflect a net loss in social welfare because of the tariff.

Import Quotas

An *import quota* is a legal limit on the quantity of a particular commodity that can be imported. Quotas often target exports from certain countries. For example, a quota may limit automobile imports from Japan or shoe imports from Brazil. To have an impact on the market, or to be *effective,* a quota must restrict imports to less than the amount imported with free trade.

Let's consider the impact of a quota on the domestic market for sugar. In panel (a) of Exhibit 6, the domestic supply curve of sugar is *S* and the domestic demand curve is *D.* Suppose again that the world price of sugar is $0.10 per pound. With free trade, that price would prevail in the domestic market, and a total of 70 million pounds per month would be demanded. Domestic producers would supply 20 million pounds and importers would supply 50 million pounds. With a quota of 50 million pounds or more per month, the domestic price would remain the same as the world price of $0.10 per pound, and domestic sales would be 70 million pounds per month. In short, a quota of at least 50 million pounds would have no effect. A more stringent quota, however, would reduce the supply of imports, which, as we will see, would raise the domestic price.

Suppose that a quota of 30 million pounds per month is established. As long as the price in the U.S. market is at or above the world price of $0.10 per pound, foreign producers supply 30 million pounds to the U.S. market. So at

EXHIBIT 6

Effect of a Quota

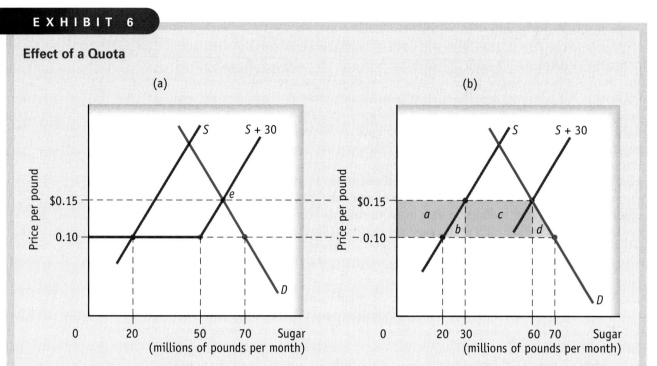

In panel (a), *D* is the domestic demand curve and *S* is the domestic supply curve. When the government establishes a sugar quota of 30 million pounds per year, the supply curve from both domestic production and imports becomes horizontal at the world price of $0.10 per pound and remains horizontal until the supply reaches 50 million pounds. For higher prices, the supply curve equals the horizontal sum of the domestic supply curve, *S*, and the quota. The new domestic price, $0.15 per pound, is determined by the intersection of the new supply curve, *S* + 30, with the domestic demand curve, *D*. Panel (b) shows the welfare effect of the quota. As a result of the higher domestic price, consumer surplus is reduced by the amount of shaded area. Area *a* represents a transfer from domestic consumers to domestic producers. Rectangular area *c* shows the gain to those who can import sugar at the world price and sell it at the higher domestic price. Triangular area *b* reflects a net loss; it represents the amount by which the cost of producing an extra 10 million pounds of sugar in the United States exceeds the cost of buying it from abroad. Area *d* also reflects a net loss—a reduction in consumer surplus as consumption falls. Thus, the blue-shaded areas illustrate the loss in consumer surplus that is captured by domestic producers and those who are permitted to fulfill the quota, and the red-shaded triangles illustrate the minimum net welfare cost.

prices at or above $0.10 per pound, the total supply of sugar to the domestic market is found by adding 30 million pounds of sugar to the amount supplied by domestic producers. At the world price of $0.10 per pound, domestic producers supply 20 million pounds, and importers supply the quota of 30 million pounds, for a total quantity supplied of 50 million pounds. At prices above $0.10, domestic producers can and do expand their quantity supplied in the U.S. market, but imports are restricted to the quota of 30 million pounds.

Domestic and foreign producers will never sell their output for less than $0.10 per pound in the U.S. market because they can always sell for that price on the world market. Thus the supply curve that sums both domestic production and imports becomes horizontal at the world price of $0.10 per pound and remains horizontal until the quantity supplied reaches 50 million pounds. For prices above $0.10 per pound, the supply curve equals the horizontal sum of the supply curve of domestic producers, *S*, and the quota of 30 million pounds. The domestic price is found where this new supply curve intersects the domestic demand curve, which in panel (a) of Exhibit 6 occurs at point *e. An effective quota, by limiting imports, raises the domestic price of sugar above the world price and reduces quantity below the free-trade level.* (Note that to compare more readily the effects of tariffs and quotas, this quota was designed to yield the same equilibrium price and quantity as the tariff we examined earlier.)

Panel (b) of Exhibit 6 focuses on the distributional and efficiency effects of the quota. The decline in consumer surplus after the imposition of the quota is depicted by the blue-and red-shaded areas. The loss in consumer surplus represented by the blue-shaded area *a* is converted into the gain in producer surplus resulting from the higher price. Because the value of area *a* is simply transferred from domestic consumers to domestic producers, area *a* involves no loss in domestic welfare. The blue-shaded rectangle *c* shows the gain to those permitted by the quota to sell 30 million pounds per month at the domestic price of $0.15 per pound. To the extent that the gains from the quota go to foreign exporters rather than to domestic importers, area *c* reflects a net loss in domestic welfare.

The red-shaded triangle *b* shows the amount by which the marginal cost of producing another 10 million pounds in the United States exceeds the world price of the good. This triangular area represents a welfare loss to the domestic economy, because sugar could have been purchased abroad for $0.10 per pound, and the domestic resources employed to increase sugar production could have been used more efficiently in the production of other goods. The red-shaded triangle *d* also represents a welfare loss, because it reflects a reduction in consumer surplus (resulting from the fact that less sugar is consumed at the higher price) with no offsetting gain to anyone. Thus, the two red-shaded triangles in panel (b) of Exhibit 6 measure the minimum welfare cost imposed on the domestic economy by an effective quota. To the extent that the profit from quota rights (area *c*) accrues to foreigners, the welfare loss imposed on the domestic economy includes area *c*.

Quotas in Practice

The United States has granted quotas to specific countries. These countries, in turn, award these rights to their exporters through a variety of means. *By rewarding domestic producers with higher prices and foreign producers with the right to sell goods to the United States, the quota system creates two groups intent on securing and perpetuating these quotas.* Lobbyists for foreign producers work the halls of Congress seeking the right to export to the United States. This strong support from producers, coupled with a lack of opposition from consumers (who remain largely unaware of all this), has resulted in quotas that have lasted for decades. Apparel quotas have been in effect for over 30 years, and sugar quotas for over 50 years.

Some economists have argued that if quotas are to be used, the United States should auction off quota allocations to foreign producers, thereby capturing the difference between the world price and the U.S. price. Auctioning off quotas would not only increase federal revenue but also reduce the attractiveness of quotas to foreign sellers, thereby reducing pressure on Washington to perpetuate quotas.

Consider the similarities and differences between a quota and a tariff, which in our example were designed to increase the domestic price of sugar by the same amount. Since the tariff and the quota in our example had identical effects on the price, they reflect the same change in quantity demanded. In both cases, domestic consumers suffer the same loss in consumer surplus and domestic producers reap the same gain in producer surplus. The net welfare loss of both restrictions is the loss in consumer surplus. The primary difference between the two restrictive policies is that the revenue resulting from the tariff goes to the domestic government, whereas the revenue resulting from the quota goes to whoever secures the right to sell foreign goods in the domestic market. *If quota rights accrue to foreigners, then the domestic economy is worse off with a quota than with a tariff.* But even if quota rights go to domestic importers, quotas, like tariffs, still increase the domestic price, restrict quantity, and thereby reduce consumer surplus.

Other Trade Restrictions

Besides tariffs and quotas, a variety of other measures affect free trade. A country may provide *export subsidies* to encourage firms to export, or *low-interest loans* to foreign buyers to promote exports of large capital goods. Some countries impose *domestic content requirements* specifying that a certain percentage of a final good's value must be produced domestically. Other requirements concerning health, safety, or technical standards often discriminate against foreign goods. For example, European countries prohibit imports of beef from hormone-fed cattle, a measure aimed at U.S. beef producers. Purity laws in Germany bar importing many non-German beers. Until uniform standards were adopted by members of the European Community, differing technical standards forced manufacturers to make as many as seven different models of the same TV for that market. Even though the U.S. and Mexico have a free trade agreement, Mexican customs agents usually inspect every package crossing the border. For example, if a shipment contains 20 VCRs, all in identical boxes, customs officials open every box rather than sample them. This inconveniences shippers and slows down free trade. Sometimes exporters will voluntarily agree to limit exports, as when Japanese auto makers agreed to restrain auto exports to the United States. *The point is that tariffs and quotas are only two of many devices that restrict foreign trade.*

Recent research on the cost of protectionism points to the fact that international trade barriers prevent new goods and new technologies from being introduced into an economy. So rather than simply raising the cost of goods that are currently available, the cost of protection is much higher and helps explain why highly protected developing economies remain poor.

Freer Trade by Multilateral Agreement

Mindful of the welfare loss from trade restrictions, the United States, after World War II, invited its trading partners to negotiate less stringent restrictions. The result was the **General Agreement on Tariffs and Trade (GATT),** an international trade treaty adopted in 1947 by 23 countries, including the United States. Each member of GATT agreed to (1) treat all member nations equally with respect to trade, (2) reduce tariff rates through multinational negotiations, and (3) reduce import quotas. The agreement resulted in thousands of tariff reductions.

The greatest improvements in trade liberalization have come through trade negotiations among many countries, or "trade rounds," under the auspices of GATT. Trade rounds offer a package approach rather than an issue-by-issue

GeneralAgreement on Tariffs and Trade(GATT) An international tariff-reduction treaty adopted in 1947 that resulted in a series of negotiated "rounds" aimed at freer trade; the Uruguay Round created GATT's successor, the World Trade Organization (WTO).

approach to trade negotiations. Concessions that are necessary but otherwise difficult to defend in domestic political terms can be made more acceptable in the context of a package that also contains politically and economically attractive benefits. Most early GATT trade rounds aimed at reducing tariffs. The Kennedy Round in the mid-1960s included new provisions against **dumping,** which is selling a commodity abroad at a price that is below its cost of production or below the price charged in the home market. The Tokyo Round of the 1970s was a more sweeping attempt to extend and improve the system.

The most recent round of negotiations was launched in Uruguay in September 1986 and ratified by 123 participating countries in April 1994 with 550 pages of legal text spelling out the results of the negotiations. This so-called Uruguay Round, the most comprehensive of the eight postwar multilateral trade negotiations, called for a phased reduction in tariffs on 85 percent of world trade and eventual elimination of quotas. The Uruguay Round also created the World Trade Organization to take over from GATT. The new organization is discussed in the following case study.

The World Trade Organization

The **World Trade Organization (WTO)** now provides the legal and institutional foundation for the multilateral trading system. The WTO offers the platform on which trade relations among member countries can evolve through collective debate. Whereas GATT was a multilateral agreement with no institutional foundation, the WTO is a permanent institution with its own secretariat, located in Geneva, Switzerland. With a staff of 450 headed by a director general and four deputies, the secretariat's responsibilities include supporting WTO delegate bodies, providing trade policy analysis, and assisting in the resolution of trade disputes involving the interpretation of WTO rules and precedents. The staff has a special responsibility of providing technical support to the member countries that are least developed.

Whereas GATT involved only merchandise trade, the WTO includes services and trade-related aspects of intellectual property, such as books, movies, and computer programs. For example, the agreement ensures that computer programs will be protected as literary works and specifies which databases should be protected by copyright. The agreement also requires that a 20-year patent protection be available for all inventions in almost all fields of technology, whether of products or processes (developing-country members that do not currently provide patent protection have up to 10 years to introduce such protection).

Under the *most-favored-nation* clause, each WTO member must offer all other member countries the same trade concessions offered to any member country. While quotas will eventually be outlawed by the WTO, tariffs and customs duties remain legal. Tariff reductions made by the Uruguay Round are contained in some 22,500 pages of national tariff schedules that are considered

Dumping Selling a commodity abroad at a price that is below its cost of production or below the price charged in the domestic market

World Trade Organization (WTO) The legal and institutional foundation of the multilateral trading system that succeeded GATT in 1995

CaseStudy

Other Times, Other Places

The World Trade Organization's Web site describes its role and functions and explains the value of reducing trade barriers. The basic principles underlying the most recent trade agreement can be found at http://www.wto.org/wto/about/facts2.htm#mfn. What policies support the goal of nondiscriminatory trade? For an example of how one industry has been affected, read the case study on agriculture at http://www.wto.org/wto/about/agmnts3.htm. How is the concept of distortion defined, and why is it important in this case? What will happen to agricultural quotas under the new agreement?

an integral part of the WTO. Tariff reductions, in most cases phased in over five years, will result in a drop in the average tariff level from 6.3 percent to 3.8 percent (when GATT began in 1947, the average tariff was 40 percent). If the negotiated reforms are implemented by all 123 participating countries, by the year 2005 (the target date for full implementation) world income is projected to be $510 billion a year higher because of the Uruguay Round.

Dispute settlements under WTO are expected to be faster, more automatic, and less susceptible to blockage than under the GATT system. The WTO extends and clarifies previous GATT rules regarding two forms of "unfair" competition: dumping and export subsidies. Whereas GATT relied on voluntary cooperation, the WTO has a permanent dispute settlement body.

Countries that were not parties to the Uruguay Round must negotiate conditions of entry if they want to join the WTO. For example, China is trying to join the WTO as a developing country (thereby getting a longer grace period to comply with provisions such as patent laws). But the U.S. government would like China admitted only as a developed country, because of concern about China's violations of human rights, the widespread pirating of American products there, and restrictions imposed on the entry of U.S. firms into China's markets. As a developed country, China would have less time to comply with WTO standards.

So far, the United States is the major user of the WTO's dispute settlement system. Charges brought by the United States include accusing Japan of unfair liquor taxes, Canada of discrimination against magazine publishers, Pakistan of violating pharmaceutical copyrights, and Turkey of excessive taxation of U.S. movies. In all, the United States filed about one-third of the cases brought in the first two years of the WTO and was successful in nearly all of them.

Sources: Boris Aliabyev, "Gabunia Key to Russia's WTO Bid," *Moscow Times* (14 May 1998): Paul Meller, "E.U. Requests WTO Panel on U.S. Export Subsidies," *Dow Jones Newswire* (1 July 1998); Paul Meller, "Clinton: U.S. Demands for China WTO Entry Won't Soften," *Dow Jones Newswire* (30 June 1998); and Anne Swardson, "Trial for the Trade Police," *Washington Post* (16 October 1996.)

Common Markets

Some countries have looked to the success of the U.S. economy, which is essentially a free-trade zone across 50 states, and have developed free-trade pacts of their own. The largest and best known is the European Union, which began in 1958 with a half-dozen countries and has now expanded to more than a dozen. The idea was to create a barrier-free European market like the United States in which goods, services, people, and capital are free to flow to their highest-valued use without restrictions. Eleven members of the European Union introduced a common currency, the euro, in 1999; the euro will replace national currencies by 2002.

Another trading bloc has formed among the newly industrialized nations of East Asia. The United States, Canada, and Mexico have developed a free-trade pact called the North American Free Trade Agreement, (NAFTA). And South Africa and its four neighboring countries have formed the Southern African Customs Union. Regional trading bloc agreements such as NAFTA and the European Union require an exception to World Trade Organization rules because bloc members can make special deals among themselves and can then discriminate against outsiders. Recall that under the WTO's most-favored nation clause, any trade concession granted one country must be given to *all other* WTO members.

Through NAFTA, Mexico hopes to increase U.S. investment in Mexico by guaranteeing to those who build manufacturing plants in Mexico duty-free access to U.S. markets, which is where over two-thirds of Mexico's exports go. The United States is interested in NAFTA because Mexico's 100 million people represent an attractive export market for U.S. producers, and because Mexico's huge oil reserves could ease U.S. energy problems. The United States would also like to bolster Mexico's move toward a more market-oriented economy, as is reflected, for example, by Mexico's privatization of its phone system and banks.

ARGUMENTS FOR TRADE RESTRICTIONS

Trade restrictions often appear to be little more than welfare programs for the domestic industries they protect. Given the welfare loss that results from these restrictions, it would be more efficient simply to transfer money from domestic consumers to domestic producers. But such a blatant transfer would be politically unpopular. Arguments for trade restrictions avoid mention of transfers to domestic producers and instead cite loftier concerns. As we shall now see, some of these arguments are more valid than others.

National Defense Argument

Certain industries are said to be in need of protection from import competition because their production is vital in time of war. Products such as strategic metals and weapons of war are sometimes insulated from foreign competition by trade restrictions. Thus national defense considerations outweigh concerns about efficiency and equity.

How valid is this argument? Trade restrictions may shelter the defense industry, but other methods of sheltering it, such as government subsidies to U.S. producers, might be more efficient. Or the government could stockpile basic military hardware so that maintaining an ongoing productive capacity would become less essential, though technological change soon makes many weapons obsolete. Since most industries can make some claim to being vital to national defense, instituting trade restrictions on this basis can get out of hand. For example, one reason U.S. wool producers benefited from protective policies is that wool was said to be critical for military uniforms.

Infant Industry Argument

The infant industry argument was formulated as a rationale for protecting emerging domestic industry from foreign competition. According to this argument, in industries where a firm's average cost per unit falls as production expands, new domestic firms may need protection from foreign competitors until those domestic firms reach sufficient size to be competitive. Trade restrictions are thus defended as temporary devices for allowing domestic firms to achieve sufficient economies of scale needed to compete with established foreign producers.

One problem is how to identify which industries merit protection. And when do domestic firms become old enough to look after themselves? The very existence of protection may foster inefficiencies that firms may not be able to outgrow. The immediate cost of such restrictions is the net welfare loss from higher domestic prices. These costs may become permanent if the industry never realizes the expected economies of scale and thus never becomes competitive. As with the national defense argument, policy makers should be careful in adopting trade restrictions based on the infant industry argument. Here again, production subsidies may be more efficient than import restrictions.

Antidumping Argument

As we have noted already, *dumping* is selling a commodity abroad at a price that is below its cost of production or below the price charged in the home market. Exporters may be able to sell the good for less overseas because of export subsidies, or firms may simply find it profitable to charge lower prices in foreign markets, where there are more competitors. Critics of dumping recommend imposing a tariff to raise the price of dumped goods.

Why should U.S. consumers be prevented from buying products for as little as possible even if these low prices are the result of a foreign subsidy? If the dumping is *persistent,* the lower price may increase consumer surplus by an amount that will more than offset losses to domestic producers. *There is no good reason why consumers should not be allowed to buy imports for a persistently lower price.*

An alternative form of dumping, termed *predatory dumping,* is the *temporary* sale of an export at a lower price in order to drive out competing producers in that foreign market. Once the competition has been eliminated, so the story goes, the exporting firm can raise the price in the foreign market. Predatory dumping may also be a way to discourage production in the country that buys these goods for less. Firms in this importing country would not find entry into this industry attractive because they would not be able to sell at the low price that results from dumping. By driving out established firms or by discouraging domestic entry, the dumpers try to monopolize the market. The trouble with this argument is that if dumpers try to take advantage of their monopoly position by sharply increasing the price, then other firms, either domestic or foreign, may enter the market and sell for less. There are few documented cases of predatory dumping.

Sometimes dumping may be *sporadic,* as firms occasionally sell at a discount to unload excess inventories; retailers hold periodic "sales" for the same reason. Sporadic dumping can be unsettling for domestic industry, but the economic impact is not a matter of great public concern. Regardless, all dumping is prohibited in the United States by the Trade Agreements Act of 1979, which calls for the imposition of tariffs when a good is sold for less in the United States than in its home market. In addition, WTO rules allow for the imposition of offsetting tariffs when products are sold for "less than fair value" and when there is "material injury" to domestic producers. U.S. producers of lumber and beer have accused their Canadian counterparts of dumping.

Jobs and Income Argument

One rationale for trade restrictions that is commonly heard in the United States today is that they protect U.S. jobs and wage levels. Using trade restrictions to protect domestic jobs is a strategy that dates back centuries. One problem with such a policy is that other countries will likely retaliate by restricting *their* imports to save *their* jobs, so international trade is reduced, jobs are lost in export industries, and potential gains from trade fail to materialize.

Wage rates in other countries, especially developing countries, are often a small fraction of wages in the United States. Looking simply at differences in wage rates, however, narrows the focus too much. Wages represent just one component of the total production cost and may not necessarily be the most important. Employers are interested in the labor cost per unit of output, which depends on both the wage rate and labor productivity.

Wage rates are high in the United States partly because U.S. labor productivity remains the highest in the world. This high productivity can be traced to education and training and to the abundant computers, machines, and other physical capital that make workers more productive. Workers in the United States also benefit from a business climate that is relatively stable and that offers appropriate incentives to produce.

But how about the lower wages in many competing countries? These low wages can often be linked to workers' lack of education and training, the meager amount of physical capital available to each worker, and a business climate that is less stable and less attractive. In industries where higher U.S. wages are supported by higher U.S. output per worker, the labor cost per unit of output may be as low, or lower, in the United States as in many countries with low wages and low productivity. For example, although total hourly compensation is more than twice as high at Birmingham Steel, a U.S. corporation, as at South Korean steel plants, Birmingham's labor productivity is four times greater, so the labor cost per ton of steel is lower for Birmingham.

Once multinational firms build plants and provide technological know-how in developing countries, however, U.S. workers lose some of their competitive edge, and their relatively high wages could price some U.S. products out of the world market. This has already happened in the stereo and consumer electronics industries, and General Motors is planning to make more cars in Mexico.

Over time, as labor productivity in developing countries increases, wage differentials among countries will narrow, much as wage differentials between northern and southern U.S. states have narrowed. As technology and capital spread, U.S. workers, particularly unskilled workers, cannot expect to maintain wage levels that are far above those in other countries. The U.S. government may promote research and development to keep U.S. producers on the cutting edge of technological developments, but staying ahead in the technological game is a constant battle.

Domestic producers do not like to compete with foreign producers whose costs are lower, so they often push for trade restrictions. But if restrictions negate any cost advantage a foreign producer might have, the law of comparative advantage becomes inoperative, and domestic consumers are denied access to the lower-priced goods.

Declining Industries Argument

Where an established domestic industry is in jeopardy of being displaced by lower-priced imports, there could be a rationale for *temporary* import restrictions to allow the orderly adjustment of the domestic industry. After all, domestic producers employ many industry-specific resources—both specialized machines and specialized labor. This physical and human capital is worth less in its best alternative use. If the extinction of the domestic industry is forestalled through trade restrictions, specialized machines can be allowed to wear out naturally and specialized workers can retire voluntarily or can gradually pursue more promising careers.

Thus in the case of declining domestic industries, trade protection can be a temporary measure that helps lessen shocks to the economy and allows for an orderly transition to a new industrial mix. But the protection offered should not be so generous as to encourage continued investment in the industry. Protection should be of specific duration and should be phased out over that period.

The clothing industry is an example of a declining U.S. industry. The 22,000 U.S. jobs saved as a result of trade restrictions paid an average of about $23,000 per year. But a Congressional Budget Office study estimated that because of higher domestic prices, U.S. consumers paid between $39,000 and $74,000 per year for each textile and apparel job saved. Trade restrictions in the U.S. clothing and textile industry are scheduled to be phased out under the Uruguay Round of trade agreements.

Free trade may displace some U.S. jobs through imports, but it also creates U.S. jobs through exports. And even where foreign competition appears to have displaced U.S. workers, many foreign companies have built plants in the United States and employ U.S. workers. For example, a dozen foreign television manufacturers and all major Japanese automobile manufacturers now have plants in the United States.

The number of jobs in the United States has more than doubled since 1960. To recognize this job growth is not to deny the problems facing workers who are displaced by imports. Some displaced workers, particularly those in blue-collar jobs in steel and other unionized industries, are not likely to find jobs that will pay as well as the jobs they lost. As with infant industries, however, the problems posed by declining industries need not be solved by trade restrictions. To support the affected industry, the government could offer wage subsidies or special tax breaks that decline over time. The government could also fund programs to retrain workers for jobs that are in greater demand.

Problems with Protection

Trade restrictions raise a number of problems in addition to the ones already mentioned. First, protecting one stage of production often requires protecting downstream stages of production. Protecting the U.S. textile industry from foreign competition, for example, may raise the cost of cloth to U.S. clothing manufacturers, reducing their competitiveness. Thus if the government protects domestic textile manufacturers, it should also protect the domestic garment industry. Otherwise, foreign manufacturers will fashion lower-priced foreign textiles into garments for export to the United States, where they will sell for less than U.S.-made garments fashioned from higher-priced U.S. textiles.

Second, the cost of protection includes not only the welfare loss arising from the higher domestic price, but also the cost of the resources used by domestic producers and groups to secure the favored protection. The cost of *rent seeking*—lobbying fees, propaganda, legal actions—can equal or exceed the direct welfare loss from restrictions. A third problem with imposing trade restrictions is that other countries often retaliate, thus shrinking the gains from trade. Retaliation can set off still greater trade restrictions, leading to an outright trade war. A final problem with trade restrictions is the costs of enforcing the myriad quotas, tariffs, and other restrictions. These policing and enforcement costs are discussed in the following case study.

Enforcing Trade Restrictions

The United States is the richest, most attractive market in the world. Trade restrictions often make U.S. markets even more appealing to foreign producers because U.S. prices exceed world prices. With thousands of different quota and tariff classifications and with tariffs ranging from zero to over 100 percent, the U.S. Customs Service has difficulty keeping things straight. Customs operates 24 hours a day, 365 days a year and must also process the 435 million people who enter the country each year. From Mexico alone, some 300,000 rail cars enter the United States each year through eight border crossings.

We should not be surprised that some importers try to skirt trade restrictions, either evading restrictions by redefining the product slightly or illegally importing goods that are restricted by quotas. For example, lumber from Canada is subject to quota restrictions. But take a 2-by-4, which is considered lumber, and drill a few small holes in it for electrical wiring, and that 2-by-4 is no longer classified as lumber but as "carpentry," which is not subject to quotas. A diverse array of goods is imported in violation of quotas, including clothing, sugar, coffee, gems, and steel pipes. It has been estimated that more than 10 percent of all imports are illegal.

Restrictions affect not only the quantity of imports but also the quality. Nearly all schemes to import clothing illegally involve fraudulent documents intended to misrepresent the clothing so that it fits into some quota or qualifies for a lower tariff. Sometimes the garments are altered to evade detection. For example, because imports of men's running shorts were controlled by a quota, manufacturers often added a flimsy inner lining so the shorts could pass for swimming trunks, which faced no quotas.

Because the United States allows some countries more generous quotas than others, exporters in a country under tight control sometimes ship their goods through a country with a liberal ceiling. For example, Japan makes so little clothing for export that the United States imposes no clothing quota for imports from Japan. As a result, clothing made in Korea is often shipped through Japan to evade U.S. quotas on Korean goods. Similarly, because Nepal is not subject to a clothing quota but India is, India ships clothing to the United States through Nepal. And China ships clothing through Macau, a tiny island next to Hong Kong.

Some foreign producers and U.S. importers engage in "port shopping," or testing various ports to see where inspections are most lax. Documents are often forged. U.S. Customs inspectors are responsible for policing all this activity.

CaseStudy

Other Times, Other Places

The U.S. Customs Service maintains a Web page devoted to its enforcement activities at http://www. customs.treas.gov/enforce/ index.htm. What enforcement topics are currently listed? Information about protecting copyrighted material can be found under the Importing and Exporting category of the Customs Service's main Web page.

These inspectors must remain alert because of the thousands of tariffs, quotas, and other trade restrictions in effect and the myriad ways to get around them. Add to this the problem of keeping out illegal drugs and counterfeit copies of brand-name products, and you can see why Customs inspectors have their hands full.

Sources: "U.S. Customs Service Hearing of the Trade Subcommittee of the House Ways and Means Committee," *Federal News Service* (30 April 1998); Richard Lawrence, "US, EU Smooth Over Differences on Country-of-Origin Regulations," *Journal of Commerce* (15 April 1998); and David Parkinson, "U.S. Formally Imposes Quotas on Canadian Pre-drilled Studs," *Dow Jones Newswire* (29 June 1998).

CONCLUSION

Comparative advantage, specialization, and trade allow people to use their scarce resources most efficiently to satisfy their unlimited wants. International trade arises from voluntary exchange among buyers and sellers pursuing their self-interest. Since 1950 the volume of world output has risen 7-fold, while the volume of world trade has increased 17-fold.

World trade offers many advantages to the trading countries: the chance to take advantage of economies of scale, the opportunity to utilize abundant resources, the improvements that come with competitive pressure, more ready access to information about markets and technology, and lower prices for consumers.

Despite the clear gains from free trade, restrictions on international trade date back hundreds of years, and pressure to impose trade restrictions continues today. For example, in 1997 Congress refused to grant President Clinton so-called fast-track negotiating authority on trade agreements, a privilege that had been granted to previous presidents. And China restricts imports with high tariffs, taxes, and non-tariff measures such as limitations on which enterprises can import goods. Billions of dollars have been lost to Americans because of Chinese pirating of CDs and software.

Those who benefit from trade restrictions are the domestic producers (and their resource suppliers) who are able to sell their output for a higher price because of the restrictions. Protection insulates an industry from the rigors of global competition, in the process stifling innovation and leaving the industry vulnerable to technological change in other countries. Under a system of quotas, the winners also include those who have secured the right to import goods at the world prices and sell them at the domestic prices.

Consumers who must pay higher prices for protected goods suffer from trade restrictions, as do the domestic producers who use imported resources. Other losers are U.S. exporters, who face higher trade barriers if foreigners retaliate. Even if other countries do not retaliate, U.S. trade restrictions reduce the gains from comparative advantage and thereby reduce world income. With world income lower, U.S. exporters find that their foreign markets have shrunk. Some of these exporters may go out of business; others may never even start producing.

Trade restrictions are often imposed gradually over a period of years. Because the domestic adjustments to restrictions are slow and because those who lose out are scattered throughout the economy, the losers frequently do not know that they are losers or they fail to connect their troubles with trade policy. On the other hand, those who benefit from trade restrictions are usually a well-defined group of producers who can clearly identify the source of their gains. *One reason trade restrictions get introduced is that most of those harmed by restrictions do not know they are losers, whereas beneficiaries know what's at stake.*

Producers have an interest in trade legislation, but consumers remain largely ignorant. Consumers purchase thousands of different goods and thus have no special interest in the effects of trade policy on any particular good. Congress tends to support the group that makes the most noise, so trade restrictions persist, despite the clear gains from free trade.

SUMMARY

1. Even if a country has an absolute advantage in producing all goods, that country should specialize in producing the goods in which it has a comparative advantage. If each country specializes and trades according to the law of comparative advantage, all countries will have greater consumption possibilities.

2. Tariff revenues go to the government and could be used to lower taxes. Quotas confer benefits on those with the right to buy the good at the world price and sell it at the higher domestic price. Both restrictions harm domestic consumers more than they help domestic producers, although tariffs at least yield domestic government revenue.

3. Despite the gains from free trade and the net welfare losses arising from tariffs and quotas, trade restrictions

have been a part of trade policy for hundreds of years. The General Agreement on Tariffs and Trade (GATT) was an international treaty ratified in 1947 to reduce tariffs. Subsequent rounds of negotiations promoted lower tariffs and discouraged trade restrictions. The Uruguay Round, ratified by 123 countries in 1994, created the World Trade Organization (WTO) to succeed GATT.

4. Reasons given for instituting trade restrictions include promoting national defense, giving infant industries time to grow, preventing foreign producers from dumping goods in domestic markets, protecting domestic jobs, and allowing declining industries time to phase out.

QUESTIONS FOR REVIEW

1. *(Profile of Imports and Exports)* What are the major U.S. exports and imports? How does international trade affect consumption possibilities?

2. *(Gains from Trade)* Complete each of the following sentences:
   a. When a nation has no economic interaction with foreigners and produces everything it consumes, the nation is in a state of _____.
   b. According to the law of comparative advantage, each nation should specialize in producing the goods in which it has the lowest _____.
   c. The amount of one good that a nation can exchange for one unit of another good is known as the _____.
   d. Specializing according to comparative advantage and trading with other nations results in _____.

3. *(Reasons for International Specialization)* What determines which goods a country should produce and export?

4. *(Tariffs)* High tariffs usually lead to black markets and smuggling. How is government revenue reduced by such activity? Relate your answer to the graph in Exhibit 5 in this chapter. Does smuggling have any social benefits?

5. *(Trade Restrictions)* Exhibits 5 and 6 show net losses to the economy of a country that imposes tariffs or quotas on imported sugar. What kinds of gains and losses would occur in the economies of countries that export sugar?

6. *(CaseStudy: The World Trade Organization)* What is the World Trade Organization (WTO) and how does it help foster multilateral trade? (Check the WTO website at http://www.wto.org/).

7. *(Arguments for Trade Restrictions)* Explain the national defense, declining industries, and infant industry arguments for protecting a domestic industry from international competition.

8. *(Arguments for Trade Restrictions)* Firms hurt by cheap imports typically argue that restricting trade will save U.S. jobs. What's wrong with this argument? Are there ever any reasons to support such trade restrictions?

9. *(Case**Study:** Enforcing Trade Restrictions)* Increasingly, goods are manufactured using a variety of domestic and imported parts or resources. What problem does this create in enforcing such trade restrictions?

PROBLEMS AND EXERCISES

10. *(Comparative Advantage)* Suppose that each U.S. worker can produce 8 units of food or 2 units of clothing daily. in Fredonia, which has the same number of workers, each worker can produce 7 units of food or 1 unit of clothing daily. Why does the United States have an absolute advantage in both goods? Which country enjoys a comparative advantage in food? Why?

11. *(Comparative Advantage)* The consumption possibilities frontiers shown in Exhibit 3 assume terms of trade of 1 unit of clothing for 1 unit of food. What would the consumption possibilities frontiers look like if the terms of trade were 1 unit of clothing for 2 units of food?

12. *(Import Quotas)* What is an effective import quota? Using a supply-and-demand diagram, illustrate and explain the net welfare loss from imposing such a quota. Under what circumstances would the net welfare loss from an import quota exceed the net welfare loss from an equivalent tariff (one that results in the same price and import level as the quota)?

13. *(Trade Restrictions)* Suppose that the world price for steel is below the U.S. domestic price, but the government requires that all steel used in the United States be domestically produced.
    a. Use a diagram like the one in Exhibit 5 to show the gains and loses from such a policy.
    b. How could you estimate the net welfare loss (deadweight loss) from such a diagram?
    c. What response to such a policy would you expect from industries (like automobile producers) that use U.S. steel?
    d. What government revenues are generated by this policy.

EXPERIENTIAL EXERCISES

14. *(Arguments for Trade Restrictions)* Visit the Office of the U.S. Trade representative at http://www.ustr.gov/. The U.S. Trade Representative is a Cabinet member who acts as the principal trade advisor, negotiator, and spokesperson for the president on trade and related investment matters. Look at some of the most recent press releases. What are some of the trade-related issues the United States is currently facing?

15. *(Antidumping Argument)* Thomas Klitgaard and Karen Schiele have analyzed dumping in their article "Free Trade or Fair Trade: The Dumping Issue." Current Issues in Economics and Finance, (August 1998). Download this article at http://www.ny.frb.org/rmaghome/curr-iss/ci4-8.htm. How can we tell whether foreign firms are selling products in the U.S. at a price below the cost of production?

16. *(Wall Street Journal)* The *Wall Street Journal* is one of the world's best sources of information regarding international trade. A good place to look is the International page inside the First Section of each day's *Journal*. Look at today's issue and find an article dealing with trade barriers—tariffs, quotas, and so on. Model the trade barrier using a graph, and try to determine who are the beneficiaries and who bears the costs. If you are lucky, the article will provide sufficient information to allow you to actually estimate costs and benefits in dollar terms.

International Finance

What do we mean when we talk about a "strong dollar"? How come U.S. consumers favor a strong dollar more than U.S. producers? Should we worry when we hear about a rising U.S. trade deficit? And what about the new European currency, the euro? Answers to these and other questions are explored in this chapter, which focuses on international finance.

A U.S. firm that plans to buy a German printing press will be quoted a price in euros. Suppose that machine costs one million euros. How many dollars is that? The cost in dollars will depend on the current exchange rate. When buyers and sellers from two countries trade, two currencies are usually involved. Supporting the flows of goods and services are flows of currencies that connect all international transactions.

The *exchange rate* between two currencies—the price of one in terms of the other—is the means by which the price of a good produced in one country gets translated into the price to the buyer in another country. The willingness of buyers and sellers to strike deals, therefore, depends on the rate of exchange between currencies. In this chapter we examine the international transactions that determine the relative value of one currency in terms of another. Topics discussed in this chapter include:

- Balance of payments
- Trade deficits and surpluses
- Foreign exchange markets
- Floating exchange rates
- Purchasing power parity

- Fixed exchange rates
- The international monetary system
- Managed float
- Bretton Woods agreement

BALANCE OF PAYMENTS

A country's gross domestic product measures the flow of economic activity that occurs within that country during a given period. To account for dealings abroad, countries also keep track of their international transactions. A country's *balance of payments,* as introduced in Chapter 4, summarizes all economic transactions that occur during a given time period between residents of that country and residents of other countries. *Residents* include individuals, firms, and governments.

International Economic Transactions

Balance-of-payments statements measure economic transactions that occur between countries, whether they involve goods and services, real or financial assets, or transfer payments. Because it reflects the volume of transactions that occur during a particular time period, usually a year, the balance of payments measures a *flow.*

Some transactions included in the balance-of-payments account do not involve payments of money. For example, if *Time* magazine ships a new printing press to its Australian subsidiary, no payment occurs, yet an economic transaction involving another country has taken place and must be included in the balance-of-payments account. Similarly, if CARE sends food to Africa, or if the Pentagon sends military assistance to Israel, these transactions must be captured in the balance of payments. So remember, although we speak of the *balance of payments,* a more descriptive phrase would be the *balance of economic transactions.*

Balance-of-payments accounts are maintained according to the principles of *double-entry bookkeeping,* in which entries on one side of the ledger are called *debits,* and entries on the other side are called *credits.* As we will see, the balance-of-payments accounts are made up of several individual accounts; a deficit in one or more accounts must be offset by a surplus in the other accounts. Thus the total debits must be in balance with, or equal to, the total credits—hence the expression *balance* of payments. The balance of payments involves a comparison during a given time period, such as a year, between the outflow of payments to the rest of the world, which are entered as debits, and the inflow of receipts from the rest of the world, which are entered as credits. The next few sections describe the major accounts in the balance of payments.

Merchandise Trade Balance

The *merchandise trade balance,* a term first introduced in Chapter 4, equals the value of merchandise exported minus the value of merchandise imported. The merchandise account reflects trade in tangible products (stuff you can drop on your toe), such as French wine and U.S. computers, and is often referred to simply as the *trade balance.* The value of U.S. merchandise exports is listed as a credit in the U.S. balance-of-payments account because U.S. residents must *be paid* for the exported goods. The value of U.S. merchandise imports is listed as a debit in the balance-of-payments account because U.S. residents must *pay* for the imported goods.

If the value of merchandise exports exceeds the value of merchandise imports, there is a *surplus* in the merchandise trade balance, or, more simply, a *trade surplus.* If the value of merchandise imports exceeds the value of merchandise exports, there is a *deficit* in the merchandise trade balance, or a *trade deficit.* The merchandise trade balance, which is reported monthly, influences foreign exchange markets, the stock market, and other financial markets. The trade balance depends on a variety of factors, including the relative strength and competitiveness of the domestic economy compared to other economies and the relative value of the domestic currency compared to other currencies.

The U.S. merchandise trade balance since 1979 is presented in Exhibit 1. Because imports have exceeded exports every year, the balance has been in deficit, as is reflected by the bottom line. Note that during recessions, which are indicated by shading, imports growth are relatively flat, as is the trade deficit. Between 1983 and 1990, and since 1991, the U.S. economy has expanded. *When the domestic economy expands, spending on all goods increases, so imports have increased.* In 1998 the merchandise trade deficit exceeded $300 billion, a record level.

Balance on Goods and Services

The merchandise trade balance focuses on the flow of goods, but services are also traded internationally. *Services* are intangibles, such as transportation, insurance, banking, consulting, and tourist expenditures. Services also include the income earned from foreign investments less the income earned by foreigners from their investment in the U.S. economy. Services are often called "invisibles," because they are not tangible—not something you can drop on your toe. The value of U.S. service exports, such as when an Irish tourist visits New York City, is listed as a credit in the U.S. balance-of-payments account because U.S. residents receive payments for these services. The value of U.S. service imports, such as when a computer specialist in Ireland enters policy information for a Connecticut insurer, is listed as a debit in the balance of payments account because U.S. residents must pay for the imported services.

The **balance on goods and services** is the difference between the value of exports of goods and services and the value of imports of goods and services. Currently-produced goods and services that are sold or otherwise provided to foreigners form part of U.S. output. The production of these goods and services generates income during the current period. Conversely, imports of goods and services form part of the nation's current expenditures—part of consumption, investment, and government expenditures. Allocating imports to each of the

Balance on goods and services The section of a country's balance of payments account that measures the difference in value between a country's exports of goods and services and its imports of goods and services

EXHIBIT 1

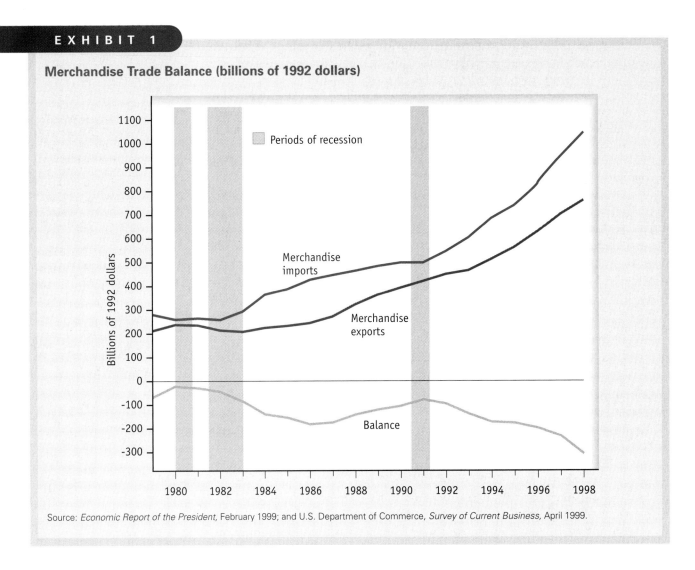

Merchandise Trade Balance (billions of 1992 dollars)

Source: *Economic Report of the President*, February 1999; and U.S. Department of Commerce, *Survey of Current Business*, April 1999.

major expenditure components is an accounting nightmare, so we usually just subtract imports from exports to yield *net exports.* Thus the U.S. gross domestic product in a given year equals total expenditures for consumption, investment, government purchases, and net exports.

Unilateral Transfers

Unilateral transfers consist of government transfers to foreign residents, foreign aid, personal gifts to friends and relatives abroad, personal and institutional charitable donations, and the like. For example, money sent abroad by a U.S. resident to friends or relatives would be included in U.S. unilateral transfers and would be a debit in the balance of payments account. U.S. **net unilateral transfers** equal the unilateral transfers received from abroad by U.S. residents minus the unilateral transfers sent to foreign residents. U.S. net unilateral transfers have been negative each year since World War II, except for 1991, when the U.S. government received sizable transfers from foreign governments to support the Persian Gulf war.

Net unilateral transfers
The unilateral transfers (gifts and grants) received from abroad by residents of a country minus the unilateral transfers residents send abroad

The United States places no restrictions on money sent out of the country.[1] Other countries, particularly developing countries, strictly limit the amount of money that may be sent abroad. More generally, developing countries often restrict the convertibility of their currency into other currencies.

When we add net unilateral transfers to the exports of goods and services minus the imports of goods and services, we get the **balance on current account,** which is reported quarterly. Thus, *the current account includes all transactions in currently produced goods and services plus net unilateral transfers.* It can be negative, reflecting a current account deficit; positive, reflecting a current account surplus; or zero.

Balance on current account The section of a country's balance-of-payments account that measures the sum of the country's net unilateral transfers and its balance on goods and services

Capital Account

Whereas the current account records international transactions involving the flows of goods, services, and unilateral transfers, the **capital account** records international transactions involving the flow of financial assets, such as borrowing, lending, and investments. For example, U.S. investors purchase foreign assets in order to earn a higher rate of return and to diversify their portfolios. When economists talk about capital, they usually mean the physical and human resources employed to produce goods and services. But sometimes *capital* is used as another word for *money*—money used to acquire financial assets, such as stocks, bonds, bank balances, and money used to make direct investments in foreign plants and equipment. U.S. capital outflows result when Americans purchase foreign assets. U.S. capital inflows result from foreign purchases of U.S. assets.

Capital account The record of a country's international transactions involving purchases or sales of financial and real assets

Between 1917 and 1982, the United States was a net capital exporter, and the net return on all this foreign investment over the years improved our balance on current account. In 1983, high real interest rates in the United States (relative to those in the rest of the world) resulted in a net inflow of capital for the first time in 65 years. A net inflow of capital shows up as a surplus in the capital account. Since then, U.S. imports of capital have exceeded exports of capital nearly every year, meaning that Americans owe foreigners more and more. *The United States is now the world's largest net debtor nation.* This is not as bad as it sounds, since foreign investment in the United States adds to America's productive capacity and promotes employment. But the return on foreign investment in the United States flows to foreigners, not to Americans.

The **official reserve transactions account** indicates the net amount of international reserves that shift among central banks to settle international transactions. (Many government publications show this not as a separate account but as part of the capital account.) International reserves consist of gold, dollars, euros, other major currencies, and a special-purpose reserve currency called *Special Drawing Rights*, or *SDRs*.

Official reserve transactions account The section of a country's balance-of-payments account that reflects the flow of gold, Special Drawing Rights, and currencies among central banks

Statistical Discrepancy

As we have seen, the U.S. balance of payments is a record of all transactions between U.S. residents and foreign residents over a specified period. It is easier to

---

1 Federal authorities do, however, require reporting the source of cash exports of $10,000 or more. This measure is aimed at reducing money laundering overseas.

describe this record than to compile it. Despite efforts to capture all international transactions, some go unreported. Yet as the name *balance of payments* suggests, debits must equal credits—the entire balance of payments account must by definition be in balance. This idea that debits equal credits is expressed in a double-entry bookkeeping system in which debits are recorded on one side of the ledger and credits are recorded on the other side. To ensure that the two sides of the ledger balance, a residual account called the *statistical discrepancy* was created. An excess of credits in all other accounts is offset by an equivalent debit in the statistical discrepancy account, or an excess of debits in all other accounts is offset by an equivalent credit in the discrepancy account. So you might think of the statistical discrepancy as the "fudge factor." The statistical discrepancy provides analysts with both a measure of the net error in the balance of payments data and a means of satisfying the double-entry bookkeeping requirement that total debits must equal total credits.

Deficits and Surpluses

Nations, like households, operate under a cash-flow constraint. Expenditures cannot exceed income plus cash on hand and borrowed funds. We have distinguished between *current* transactions, which are the income and expenditures from exports, imports, and unilateral transfers, and *capital* transactions, which reflect international investments and borrowing. Any surplus or deficit in one account must be balanced by other changes in the balance of payments accounts. The current account has been in deficit since 1982, meaning that the sum of U.S. imports and unilateral transfers to foreigners has exceeded the sum spent by foreigners on our exports and sent as unilateral transfers to us.

Exhibit 2 presents the U.S. balance of payments statement for 1998. All transactions requiring payments from foreigners to U.S. residents are entered as credits, indicated by a plus sign (+), because they result in a flow of funds from foreign residents to U.S. residents. All transactions requiring payments to foreigners from U.S. residents are entered as debits, indicated by a minus sign (−), because they result in a flow of funds from U.S. residents to foreign residents. As you can see, a surplus in the capital account offsets deficits in the current account, in the official reserve transactions account, and in the statistical discrepancy.

Foreign exchange is the currency of another country that is needed to carry out international transactions. A country runs a deficit in its current account when the amount of foreign exchange that country gets from exporting goods and services and from receipts of unilateral transfers falls short of the amount needed to pay for its imports and to make unilateral transfers. The additional foreign exchange required must come from either a net capital inflow (international borrowing, foreign purchases of domestic stocks and bonds, and so forth) or through official government transactions in foreign currency. If a country runs a current account surplus, the foreign exchange received from selling exports and from unilateral transfers exceeds the amount required to pay for imports and to make unilateral transfers. This excess foreign exchange could be held in a bank account, converted to the domestic currency, or used to purchase foreign stocks, bonds, or other foreign investments.

When all transactions are considered, the balance of payments must always balance, though specific accounts may not. A deficit in a particular account

EXHIBIT 2

U.S. Balance of Payments: 1998 (billions of dollars)

Item	
Current Account	
1. Merchandise exports	+671.0
2. Merchandise imports	−919.0
3. Trade balance (1 + 2)	−248.0
4. Service exports	+503.0
5. Service imports	−446.6
6. Goods and services balance (3 + 4 + 5)	−191.6
7. Net unilateral transfers	−41.9
8. Current account balance (6 + 7)	−233.5
Capital Account	
9. Outflow of U. S. capital	−297.8
10. Inflow of foreign capital	+564.6
11. Capital account balance (9 + 10)	+266.8
Official Reserve Transactions Account	
12. Change in U. S. official assets abroad	−7.6
13. Change in foreign official assets in U. S.	−22.1
14. Official reserve balance (12 + 13)	−29.7
15. Statistical discrepancy	−3.6
TOTAL (8 + 11 + 14 + 15)	**0.0**

Source: *Survey of Current Business*, U. S. Department of Commerce, April 1999.

should not necessarily be viewed as a source of concern, nor should a surplus be a source of satisfaction. The deficit in the U.S. current account in recent years has been offset by a net inflow of capital from abroad. As a result of the net inflow of capital, foreigners are acquiring more claims on U.S. assets.

FOREIGN EXCHANGE RATES AND MARKETS

Now that you have some idea about the international flow of products and investment funds, we can take a closer look at the forces that determine the underlying value of the currencies involved in these transactions. We begin by looking at exchange rates and the market for foreign exchange.

Foreign Exchange

Foreign exchange, recall, is foreign currency needed to carry out international transactions. The **exchange rate** is the price of one currency measured in terms of another currency. Exchange rates are determined by the interaction of the households, firms, private financial institutions, governments, and central banks that buy and sell foreign exchange. The exchange rate fluctuates to equate

Exchange rate The price of one country's currency measured in terms of another country's currency the quantity of foreign exchange demanded with the quantity supplied. Typically, foreign exchange is made up of bank deposits denominated in the foreign currency. When foreign travel is involved, foreign exchange may consist of foreign paper money.

The foreign exchange market incorporates all the arrangements used to buy and sell foreign exchange. This market is not so much a physical place as it is a network of telephones and computers connecting large banks all over the world. Perhaps you have seen pictures of foreign exchange traders in New York, Frankfurt, London, or Tokyo amid a tangle of phone lines. The foreign exchange market is like an all-night diner—it never closes. Some trading center is always open somewhere in the world.

We will consider the market for the euro in terms of the dollar. But first a bit about the euro, since it may be new to you. In January 1999, the euro became the official common currency of eleven European countries, now known collectively as the euro zone or *Euroland*. By 2002, the national currencies of Germany, France, Italy, Austria, Spain, Portugal, Finland, Ireland, Belgium, Luxembourg, and the Netherlands are scheduled to disappear. In the mean time, the euro will be interchangeable with the local currency at a fixed rate.

The price, or exchange rate, of the euro in terms of the dollar is the number of dollars required to purchase one euro. An increase in the number of dollars needed to purchase a euro indicates a weakening, or a **depreciation,** of the dollar. A decrease in the number of dollars needed to purchase a euro indicates a strengthening, or an **appreciation,** of the dollar. Put another way, a decrease in the number of euros needed to purchase a dollar is a depreciation of the dollar, and an increase in the number of euros needed to purchase a dollar is an appreciation of the dollar.

Since the exchange rate is a price, it can be determined using the conventional tools of supply and demand: the equilibrium price of foreign exchange is the one that equates quantity demanded with quantity supplied. To simplify the analysis, let's suppose that the United States and Euroland make up the entire world, so the supply and demand for euros is the supply and demand for foreign exchange from the U.S. perspective.

Currency depreciation
With respect to the dollar, an increase in the number of dollars needed to purchase 1 unit of foreign exchange

Currency appreciation
With respect to the dollar, a decrease in the number of dollars needed to purchase 1 unit of foreign exchange

Demand for Foreign Exchange

U.S. residents need euros to pay for goods and services produced in Euroland, to invest in assets there, to make loans to Euroland, or simply to send cash gifts to friends or relatives there. Whenever U.S. residents need euros, they must buy them in the foreign exchange market, which could be their local bank, paying for them with dollars.

Exhibit 3 depicts a market for foreign exchange—in this case, for euros. The horizontal axis identifies the quantity of foreign exchange, measured here in millions of euros. The vertical axis identifies the price per unit of foreign exchange, measured here as the number of dollars required to purchase each euro. The demand curve for foreign exchange, identified as *D,* shows the inverse relationship between the dollar price of the euro and the quantity of euros demanded, other things constant. Some of the factors held constant along the demand curve are the incomes and preferences of U.S. consumers, the expected inflation rates in the United States and Euroland, the euro price of goods in Euroland, and interest rates in the United States and Euroland. People have many

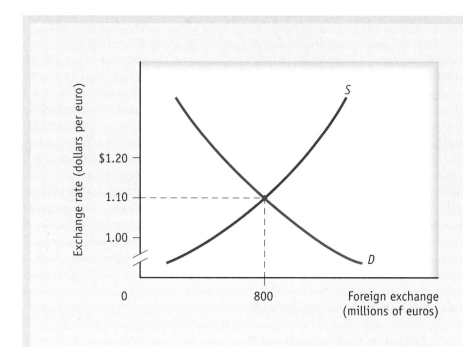

The Foreign Exchange Market

The fewer dollars needed to purchase 1 unit of foreign exchange, the lower the price of foreign goods and the greater the quantity of foreign goods demanded. The greater the demand for foreign goods, the greater the amount of foreign exchange demanded. The demand curve for foreign exchange slopes downward. An increase in the exchange rate makes U.S. products cheaper for foreigners. The increased demand for U.S. goods implies an increase in the quantity of foreign exchange supplied. The supply curve of foreign exchange slopes upward.

different reasons for demanding foreign exchange, but in the aggregate, the lower the dollar price of foreign exchange, other things constant, the greater the quantity demanded.

A drop in the dollar price of foreign exchange, in this case the euro, means that fewer dollars are needed to purchase each euro, so the dollar prices of Euroland products (such as German cars, Italian shoes, French wine, along with investments in Euroland), which have price tags listed in euros, become cheaper. The cheaper it is to buy euros, the lower the dollar price of Euroland products to U.S. residents, so the greater the quantity of euros demanded by U.S. residents, other things constant. For example, a cheap enough euro might persuade you to tour Rome, climb the Austrian Alps, wander the museums of Paris, or crawl the pubs of Dublin.

Supply of Foreign Exchange

The supply of foreign exchange is generated by the desire of foreign residents to acquire dollars—that is, to exchange euros for dollars. Foreign residents want dollars to buy U.S. goods and services, to buy U.S. assets, to make loans in dollars, or to make cash gifts in dollars to their U.S. friends and relatives. Also, citizens of countries suffering from economic and political turmoil, such as Malaysia, Indonesia, and South Korea, may want to buy dollars as a hedge against the depreciation and instability of their own currencies. The dollar has long been accepted as an international medium of exchange. It is also the currency of choice in the world markets for oil and for illegal drugs. But the euro may challenge that dominance, in part because the largest euro denomination, the 500 euro note, is worth about five times more than the top dollar note, the

$100 bill (hence, with euro notes, it would be five times easier to smuggle, say, a million dollars).

Europeans supply euros in the foreign exchange market to acquire the dollars they need. An increase in the dollar-per-euro exchange rate, other things constant, makes U.S. products cheaper for foreigners, since foreign residents need fewer euros to get the same number of dollars. For example, suppose a Dell computer sells for $1,100. If the exchange rate is $1.10 per euro, that computer costs 1,000 euros; if the exchange rate is $1.25 per euro, it costs only 880 euros. The number of Dell computers demanded in Euroland increases as the dollar-per-euro exchange rate increases, other things constant, so more euros will be supplied on the foreign exchange market to buy dollars.

More generally, the higher the dollar-per-euro exchange rate, other things constant, the greater the quantity of euros supplied to the foreign exchange market. The positive relationship between the dollar-per-euro exchange rate and the quantity of euros supplied on the foreign exchange market is expressed in Exhibit 3 by the upward-sloping supply curve for foreign exchange (again, euros in our example).[2] The supply curve is drawn holding other things constant, including Euroland incomes and preferences, expectations about the rates of inflation in Euroland and the United States, and interest rates in Euroland and the United States.

Determining the Exchange Rate

Exhibit 3 brings together the supply and demand for foreign exchange to determine the exchange rate. At an exchange rate of $1.10 per euro, the quantity of euros demanded equals the quantity of euros supplied—in our example, 800 million euros. Once achieved, this equilibrium exchange rate will remain constant until a change occurs in one of the factors that affect supply or demand. If the exchange rate is allowed to adjust freely, or to *float,* in response to market forces, the market will clear continually, as the quantities of foreign exchange demanded and supplied are equated.

What if the initial equilibrium is upset by a change in one of the underlying forces that affect supply or demand? For example, suppose an increase in U.S. income causes Americans to increase their demand for all normal goods, including Euroland goods and services. Such an increase in income will shift the U.S. demand curve for foreign exchange to the right, as Americans seek more euros to buy more Italian marble, Dutch chocolate, French couture, German machines, and euro securities.

This increased demand for euros is shown in Exhibit 4 by a shift to the right in the demand curve for foreign exchange. The supply curve does not change. The shift of the demand curve from D to D' leads to an increase in the exchange rate from $1.10 per euro to $1.15 per euro. Thus the euro increases in value, or appreciates, while the dollar falls in value, or depreciates. The higher exchange value of the euro prompts some Euroland residents to purchase more American products, which are now cheaper in terms of the euro. In our

---

2 As the exchange rate rises, Europeans have a greater incentive to buy more U.S. goods and services because their prices in terms of euros have decreased. As more is bought at lower prices, however, the total expenditure of euros rises only if the percentage increase in quantities of U.S. products demanded by the Europeans exceeds the percentage decrease in the prices in terms of euros. If the percentage increase in quantities demanded is less than the percentage decrease in the price in terms of euros, the supply curve of euros will slope downward.

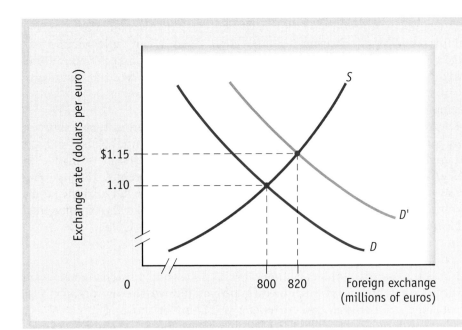

EXHIBIT 4

Effect on the Foreign Exchange Market of an Increase in Demand for Euros

The intersection of supply curve *S* and demand curve *D* determines the exchange rate. At an exchange rate of $1.10 per euro, the quantity of euros demanded equals the quantity supplied. An increase in the demand for euros from *D* to *D'* leads to an increase in the exchange rate from $1.10 to $1.15 per euro.

example, the equilibrium quantity of euros increases from 800 million to 820 million.

Any increase in the demand for foreign exchange or any decrease in its supply, other things constant, causes an increase in the number of dollars required to purchase one unit of foreign exchange, which is a depreciation of the dollar. On the other hand, any decrease in the demand for foreign exchange or any increase in its supply, other things constant, causes a reduction in the number of dollars required to purchase one unit of foreign exchange, which is an appreciation of the dollar.

Arbitrageurs and Speculators

Exchange rates between specific currencies are nearly identical at any given time in the different markets around the world. For example, the price of a dollar in terms of the euro is the same in New York, Frankfurt, Tokyo, London, Zurich, Istanbul, and other financial centers. This equality is ensured by **arbitrageurs**—dealers who take advantage of any temporary difference in exchange rates between markets by buying low and selling high. Their actions help to equalize exchange rates across markets. For example, if one euro costs $1.09 in New York and $1.10 in Frankfurt, an arbitrageur could buy, say, $10,000,000 worth of euros in New York and at the same time sell them in Frankfurt for $10,091,743, thereby earning $91,743 minus the transaction costs of executing the trades. Because exchange rate differences tend to be very small and because of transaction costs, an arbitrageur has to trade huge amounts to make enough profit to survive.

Because an arbitrageur buys and sells simultaneously, relatively little risk is involved. In our example, the arbitrageur increased the demand for euros in

Arbitrageur A person who takes advantage of temporary geographic differences in the exchange rate by simultaneously purchasing a currency in one market and selling it in another market

New York and increased the supply of euros in Frankfurt. Therefore, the actions of arbitrageurs increase the dollar price of euros in New York and decrease it in Frankfurt, thereby eliminating the differential. Even a tiny difference in exchange rates across markets will prompt arbitrageurs to act, and this action will quickly eliminate discrepancies in exchange rates across markets. Exchange rates may still change because of market forces, but they tend to change in all markets simultaneously.

Speculator A person who buys or sells foreign exchange in hopes of profiting from fluctuations in the exchange rate over time

The demand and supply of foreign exchange arises from many sources: from importers and exporters, investors in foreign assets, central banks, tourists, arbitrageurs, and speculators. **Speculators** buy or sell foreign exchange in hopes of profiting by trading the currency at a more favorable exchange rate later. By taking risks, speculators aim to profit from market fluctuations—they try to buy low and sell high. In contrast, arbitrageurs take little risk, since they *simultaneously* buy and sell a currency in different markets.

Purchasing Power Parity

Purchasing power parity (PPP) theory The theory that exchange rates between two countries will adjust in the long run to reflect price level differences between the countries

As long as trade across borders is unrestricted and as long as exchange rates are allowed to adjust freely, the **purchasing power parity theory** predicts that the exchange rate between two currencies will adjust in the long run to reflect price-level differences between the two currency regions. *A given basket of internationally traded goods should therefore sell for similar amounts around the world (except for differences reflecting transportation costs and the like).* Suppose a basket of internationally traded commodities that sells for $11,000 in the United States sells for 10,000 euro in Euroland. According to the purchasing power parity theory, the equilibrium exchange rate between the dollar and the euro should be $1.10. If this were not the case—if the exchange rate were, say, $1.00 per euro—then the basket of goods could be purchased in Euroland for 10,000 euro and sold in the United States for $11,000. The $11,000 could then be exchanged for 11,000 euro, yielding a profit of 1,000 euro (minus any transaction costs). Selling dollars and buying euros drives up the dollar price of euros.

The purchasing power parity theory is more of a long-run predictor than a day-to-day predictor of the relationship between changes in the price level and the exchange rate. For example, a country's currency generally appreciates when its inflation rate is lower than the rest of the world's and depreciates when its inflation rate is higher. Likewise, a country's currency generally appreciates when its real interest rates are higher than the rest of the world, since foreigners are more willing to buy and hold investments denominated in that currency. As a case in point, the dollar appreciated during the first half of the 1980s, when real U.S. interest rates were relatively high, and depreciated in the early 1990s, when real U.S. interest rates were relatively low.

Because of trade barriers, central bank intervention in exchange markets, and the fact that many products are not traded or are not comparable across countries, the purchasing power parity theory usually does not explain exchange rates at a particular point in time. For example, if you went shopping in Zurich, you would soon notice that one dollar's worth of Swiss francs buys less than that dollar will buy in the United States. The following case study considers the theory in light of the price of Big Macs around the globe.

The Big Mac Price Index

As you have already learned, the purchasing power parity (PPP) theory says that, in the long run, the exchange rate between two currencies should move toward the rate that equalizes the prices, in each country, of an identical basket of internationally traded goods. A light-hearted test of the theory has been developed by the *Economist* magazine, which each year compares prices across countries of a "market basket" consisting simply of one McDonald's Big Mac—a product that, although not internationally traded, is made using the same recipe in more than 100 countries. The *Economist* begins with the price of a Big Mac in the local currency, then converts that price into dollars based on the actual exchange rate prevailing at the time. A comparison of the dollar price of Big Macs across countries offers a crude test of the PPP theory, which predicts that these prices should move toward equality in the long run.

Exhibit 5 lists the dollar price of a Big Mac on March 30, 1999, in each of 31 countries plus an average for the 11 countries in Euroland. By comparing the price of a Big Mac in the United States with prices in other countries, we can derive a crude measure of whether particular currencies are undervalued or overvalued relative to the dollar. For example, because the price of a Big Mac in Switzerland, at $3.97, was 51 percent higher than the U.S. price of $2.43, the Swiss franc seemed overvalued by 63 percent compared to the dollar. The same approach suggests that the Danish krona was 47 percent overvalued, the Israeli shekel 42 percent overvalued, and the British pound 26 percent overvalued. The cheapest Big Mac was in Malaysia, where recent devaluations because of the "Asian contagion" cut the price to $1.19, or 51 percent below the U.S. level.

Big Mac prices around the world have been converging in recent years. In 1995 the price of a Big Mac in Switzerland was tops in the world, 124 percent above the U.S. price. By 1999, the Swiss price was still tops but only 63 percent above the U.S. price. At the bottom end, the lowest price in 1995 was 55 percent below the U.S. price. By 1999 the lowest price was only 51 percent below the U.S. price. Finally, in 1995 the price of a Big Mac in Japan was double the U.S. price. In 1999, the Japanese price was about the same as the U.S. price. So prices around the world have converged since 1995 in a way consistent with the PPP theory.

Still, prices in 1999 ranged from 63 percent above to 51 percent below the U.S. price. Some may view this misalignment as a rejection of the PPP theory, but that theory relates only to traded goods. The Big Mac is not traded internationally. A large share of the total cost of a Big Mac is rent, which varies substantially across countries. Local prices may also be distorted by taxes and trade barriers, such as a tariff on beef. Furthermore, prices for similar goods vary across the United States even though we all use dollars here. For example, housing prices are higher in the Northeast and the West Coast than in the Midwest and the South. Still, the Big Mac index offers a crude test of the PPP theory.

CaseStudy

*Other Times,
Other Places*

The *Economist* has published a focus article titled "Ten Years of the Big Mac Index." It is available at http://www. economist.com/editorial/ freeforall/focus/bigmac_ webonly.html. From there you can also access the latest edition of the index. Which currencies have had the largest changes in value? Which currencies went from being overvalued to undervalued between 1989 and 1998? Compare the index numbers among countries that are adopting the new euro as their currency. How close are they to one another?

EXHIBIT 5

Big Mac Prices Around the World on March 30,1999

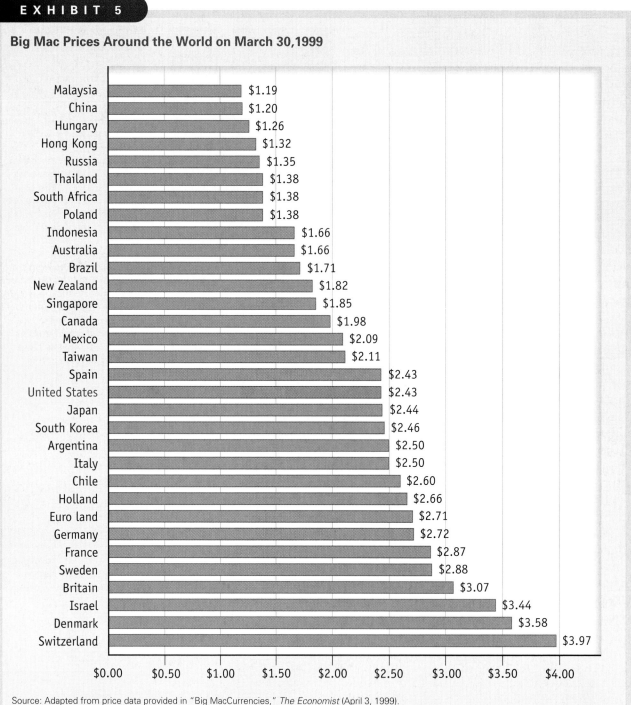

Country	Price
Malaysia	$1.19
China	$1.20
Hungary	$1.26
Hong Kong	$1.32
Russia	$1.35
Thailand	$1.38
South Africa	$1.38
Poland	$1.38
Indonesia	$1.66
Australia	$1.66
Brazil	$1.71
New Zealand	$1.82
Singapore	$1.85
Canada	$1.98
Mexico	$2.09
Taiwan	$2.11
Spain	$2.43
United States	$2.43
Japan	$2.44
South Korea	$2.46
Argentina	$2.50
Italy	$2.50
Chile	$2.60
Holland	$2.66
Euro land	$2.71
Germany	$2.72
France	$2.87
Sweden	$2.88
Britain	$3.07
Israel	$3.44
Denmark	$3.58
Switzerland	$3.97

Source: Adapted from price data provided in "Big MacCurrencies," *The Economist* (April 3, 1999).

Sources: "Big MacCurrencies," *Economist* (3 April 1999); "Big MacCurrencies," *Economist* (15 April 1995); and Peter Liu and Paul Burkett, "Instability in Short-Run Adjustments to Purchasing Power Parity: Results for Selected Latin American Countries," *Applied Economics* (October 1995): 973–83.

Flexible Exchange Rates

For the most part, we have been discussing a system of **flexible exchange rates,** in which each exchange rate is determined by the forces of supply and demand. Flexible, or *floating,* exchange rates adjust continually to the myriad forces that buffet the foreign exchange market. Consider how the exchange rate is linked to the balance of payments accounts. Debit entries in the current and capital accounts increase the demand for foreign exchange, resulting in a depreciation of the dollar. Credit entries in these accounts increase the supply of foreign exchange, resulting in an appreciation of the dollar.

Flexible exchange rates Rates determined by the forces of supply and demand without government intervention

Fixed Exchange Rates

When exchange rates are flexible, government officials usually have little direct role in foreign exchange markets. But if government officials try to set exchange rates, active and ongoing central bank intervention is necessary to establish and maintain these **fixed exchange rates.** Suppose the European Central Bank selects what it thinks is an appropriate rate of exchange between the dollar and the euro. It attempts to *fix,* or to "peg," the exchange rate within a narrow band around the particular value selected. If the value of the euro threatens to drop below the minimum acceptable exchange rate, monetary authorities will sell dollars and buy euros in foreign exchange markets. This increased demand for the euro will keep its value up relative to the dollar. Conversely, if the value of the euro threatens to climb above the maximum acceptable exchange rate, monetary authorities will sell euros and buy dollars, thereby keeping the dollar price of the euro down. Through such intervention in the foreign exchange market, monetary authorities can stabilize the exchange rate, keeping it within the specified band.

Fixed exchange rates Rates pegged within a narrow range of values by central banks' ongoing purchases and sales of currencies

If monetary officials must keep selling foreign exchange to maintain the pegged rate, they risk running out of foreign exchange reserves. When this threat occurs, the government has several options for eliminating the exchange rate disequilibrium. First, the pegged exchange rate can be increased, which is a **devaluation** of the domestic currency. (A decrease in the pegged exchange rate is called a **revaluation.**) Second, the government can attempt to reduce the domestic demand for foreign exchange directly by imposing restrictions on imports or on capital outflows. China and many other developing countries do this. Third, the government can adopt contractionary fiscal or monetary policies to reduce the country's income level, increase interest rates, or reduce inflation relative to that of the country's trading partners, thereby indirectly decreasing the demand for foreign exchange. Several Asian economies, such as Korea and Indonesia, pursued such policies to stabilize their currencies in 1998. Finally, the government can allow the disequilibrium to persist and ration the available foreign currency through some form of foreign exchange control.

Currency devaluation An increase in the official pegged price of foreign exchange in terms of the domestic currency

Currency revaluation A reduction in the official pegged price of foreign exchange in terms of the domestic currency

We have now concluded our introduction to international finance in theory. Let's examine how international finance works in practice.

DEVELOPMENT OF THE INTERNATIONAL MONETARY SYSTEM

From 1879 to 1914, the international financial system operated under a **gold standard,** whereby the major currencies were convertible into gold at a fixed

Gold standard An arrangement whereby the currencies of most countries are convertible into gold at a fixed rate

rate. For example, the U.S. dollar could be redeemed at the U.S. Treasury for one-twentieth of an ounce of gold. The British pound could be redeemed at the British Exchequer, or treasury, for one-fourth of an ounce of gold. Since each pound could buy five times as much gold as each dollar, one pound exchanged for $5.

The gold standard provided a predictable exchange rate, one that did not vary as long as currencies could be redeemed for gold at the announced rate. But the money supply in each country was determined in part by the flow of gold between countries, so each country's monetary policy was influenced by the supply of gold. A balance-of-payments deficit resulted in a loss of gold, which theoretically caused a country's money supply to drop. A balance-of-payments surplus resulted in an increase in gold, which theoretically caused a country's money supply to rise. The supply of money throughout the world also depended to some extent on the vagaries of gold discoveries. When gold production was so slow that the money supply did not keep pace with the growth in economic activity, the result was a drop in the price level, or *deflation*. When gold production grew so much that the growth of the money supply exceeded the growth in economic activity, the result was a rise in the price level, or *inflation*. For example, gold discoveries in Alaska and South Africa in the late 1890s expanded the U.S. money supply, leading to inflation.

The Bretton Woods Agreement

During World War I, many countries could no longer convert their currencies into gold, and the gold standard eventually collapsed, disrupting international trade during the 1920s and 1930s. Once an Allied victory in World War II appeared certain, the Allies met in Bretton Woods, New Hampshire, in July of 1944, to formulate a new international monetary system. Because the United States was not ravaged by World War II and had a strong economy, the dollar was selected as the key reserve currency in the new international monetary system. All exchange rates were fixed in terms of the dollar, and the United States, which held most of the world's gold reserves, stood ready to convert foreign holdings of dollars into gold at a rate of $35 per ounce. Even though exchange rates were fixed by the Bretton Woods accord, *other* countries could adjust *their* exchange rates relative to the U.S. dollar if they found a fundamental disequilibrium in their balance of payments—that is, if a country faced a large and persistent deficit or surplus.

International Monetary Fund (IMF) An international organization that establishes rules for maintaining the international monetary system and makes loans to countries with temporary balance of payments problems

The Bretton Woods agreement also created the **International Monetary Fund (IMF)** to set rules for maintaining the international monetary system and to make loans to countries with temporary balance of payments problems. IMF loans to Russia, to Brazil, and to struggling Asian economies, such as Indonesia and South Korea, have been in the news lately. The IMF, which today has more than 150 member countries, also standardized financial reporting for international trade and finance.

Demise of the Bretton Woods System

During the latter part of the 1960s, inflation began heating up in the United States, and the higher U.S. prices meant that those exchanging foreign currencies for dollars at the official exchange rates found these dollars bought less in U.S. goods and services. Because of U.S. inflation, the dollar had become *over-*

valued at the official exchange rate, meaning that the gold value of the dollar exceeded the exchange value of the dollar. With the dollar overvalued, foreigners redeemed more dollars for gold. To stop this outflow of gold, something had to give. On August 15, 1971, President Richard Nixon closed the "gold window," refusing to exchange gold for dollars. In December 1971, the 10 richest countries of the world met in Washington and devalued the dollar by 8 percent. The hope at the time was that this devaluation would put the dollar on firmer footing and would save the "dollar standard." With prices rising at different rates around the world, however, an international monetary system based on fixed exchange rates was doomed.

In 1971, U.S. merchandise imports exceeded merchandise exports for the first time since World War II. When the trade deficit tripled in 1972, it became clear that the dollar was still overvalued. In early 1973, the dollar was devalued another 10 percent, but this did not quiet foreign exchange markets. The dollar, for three decades the anchor of the international monetary system, suddenly looked vulnerable, and speculators began betting the dollar would fall even more. Dollars were exchanged for German marks because the mark appeared to be the most stable currency. Monetary officials at the Bundesbank, Germany's central bank, exchanged marks for dollars in an attempt to defend the official exchange rate and to prevent an appreciation of the mark. Why didn't Germany want the mark to appreciate? Appreciation of the mark would make German goods more expensive abroad and foreign goods cheaper in Germany, thereby reducing German exports and increasing German imports. This would reduce German output and employment. But after selling $10 billion worth of marks, the German central bank gave up defending the dollar. As soon as the value of the dollar was allowed to float against the mark, the Bretton Woods system, already on shaky ground, collapsed.

The Current System: Managed Float

The Bretton Woods system has been replaced by a **managed float system,** which combines features of a freely floating exchange rate with sporadic intervention by central banks as a way of moderating exchange rate fluctuations among the world's major currencies. Most smaller countries, particularly developing countries, peg their currencies to one of the major currencies (such as the U.S. dollar) or to a "basket" of major currencies. What's more, in developing countries, private international borrowing and lending are severely restricted; governments may allow residents to purchase foreign exchange only for certain purposes. In some countries, different exchange rates apply to different categories of transactions.

The exchange rate between the Japanese yen and the U.S. dollar has been relatively unstable, particularly because of international speculation about official efforts to stabilize that exchange rate. Major criticisms of flexible exchange rates are that (1) they are inflationary, since they free monetary authorities to pursue expansionary policies, and (2) they have often been volatile, especially since the late 1970s. This volatility creates uncertainty and risk for importers and exporters, increasing the transaction costs of international trade and thus reducing its volume. Furthermore, exchange rate volatility can lead to wrenching changes in the competitiveness of a country's export sector and of those domestic producers who must compete with imports. These changes in

Managed float system An exchange rate system that combines features of freely floating rates with intervention by central banks competitiveness cause swings in employment, resulting in louder calls for import restrictions.

Policy makers are always on the lookout for an international monetary system that will perform better than the current managed float system, with its fluctuating currency values. *Their ideal is a system that will foster international trade, lower inflation, and promote a more stable world economy.* International finance ministers have acknowledged that the world must find an international standard and establish greater exchange rate stability.

The wild swings in exchange rates that sometimes occur with flexible exchange rates have caused policy makers to intervene to reduce undesirable fluctuations, as discussed in the following case study about financial troubles in Asia.

The Asian Contagion

CaseStudy

**Other Times,
Other Places**

The Institute for International Economics Policy Brief, "The Depressing News from Asia" at http://www.iie.com/ NEWSLETR/news98-5.htm, predicts the impact of the Asian financial crisis on other countries. Notice how it uses various scenarios involving different potential changes in key variables. How is the crisis expected to affect industrialized economies, and the United States in particular? Other economists' views and analyses were published in the Summer 1998 edition of the Brookings Institution magazine accessible through http://www.brook.edu/pub/ review/oldtoc.htm.

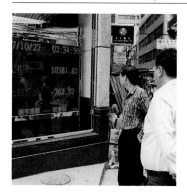

It started in Thailand in early 1997, when a booming economy ran into trouble because of a decline in exports and over-lending in the property sector. Speculators began betting that the Thai currency, the baht, was in for a fall. The Thai central bank attempted to defend the baht's value, which at the time was tied to the U.S. dollar, by buying baht and selling foreign reserves. As the central bank's foreign reserves dwindled, the government decided in July 1997 to let the baht float. It immediately went into free-fall, losing 40 percent of its value against the dollar in a matter of weeks. With the baht worth so much less, Thai businesses and the government had difficulty paying foreign loans, most of which were denominated in dollars.

The crisis prompted a $17-billion bailout supervised by the International Monetary Fund (IMF) aimed at helping Thailand pay back some foreign debts. But problems in Thailand deepened, as outside credit agencies continued to downgrade Thai debt. Trouble soon spread to neighboring Indonesia, Malaysia, South Korea, Hong Kong, Singapore, and even mighty Japan, as the so-called Asian Contagion ripped through the region. South Korea and Indonesia were forced to seek IMF assistance; Indonesia was promised $40 billion in loans and South Korea, $58 billion, the most costly rescue package in history. In exchange for the aid, both countries agreed to cut government spending and open up their markets to foreign goods and foreign investors.

In Japan, where the economy had been struggling since 1990, matters worsened. In November 1997, four large financial institutions went bankrupt, the yen suffered its biggest drop against the dollar in years, and the stock market continued its eight-year slide. In June 1998, Japanese officials confirmed that national output had declined two quarters in a row and thus the country was officially in recession. For the full fiscal year, Japan's GDP declined, the first officially acknowledged annual drop since the oil shocks of the mid-1970s.

A big problem overhanging the Japanese economy was a trillion dollars worth of bad debts in the banking system. Banks had extended real estate loans during the booming 1980s. But when property values crashed, the loans could not be repaid, so the banks were in big trouble. Japan, the second-largest economy in the world (after the United States), is by far the largest economy in Asia. A weakened Japan threatened the fragile economies of Asia as they tried to recover from financial chaos. A weakened economy meant Japan would buy less from its Asian neighbors, and a weakened yen meant Japanese exports would be cheaper on world markets, thus competing with exports from elsewhere in Asia.

Faced with growing problems in Asia, the U.S. government joined forces with the Japanese government on June 17, 1998 to intervene in currency markets and spent $2 billion buying yen. In return for help from the United States, Japan agreed to allow more companies to fail by abandoning the system whereby the government forced stronger companies to bail out weaker ones.

By increasing the demand for yen, the U.S. intervention reversed the slide in the yen's value. In one day the yen-per-dollar exchange rate appreciated from 143.3 yen to 136.6, or by 4.7 percent. This was the first U.S. intervention in world currency markets in nearly three years. As the yen appreciated against the dollar, other currencies in Asia also stabilized. By the end of April 1999, the yen had appreciated to 118 yen to the dollar, and Asia was showing preliminary signs of recovery.

Sources: David Wessel, "Wealthy Nations Are Trying to Save Japan from Itself," *Wall Street Journal* (18 June 1998); "Stocks Stumble Across Asia as Yen Hits Lowest Since '90," *Wall Street Journal* (11 June 1998); "Asia's Symptoms," *Economist* (13 June 1998): 14; "Will Tokyo Finally Clean House?" *Economist* (27 June 1998): 71–72; and Fareed Zakaria, "Will Asia Turn Against the West?" *New York Times* (10 July 1998).

CONCLUSION

At one time the United States was largely self-sufficient. A technological lead over the rest of the world, an abundance of natural resources, a well-trained work force, a modern and extensive capital stock, and a currency as good as gold made the United States the envy of the world, with an economy that produced 40 percent of the world's output in the 1950s.

The situation has changed. The United States is now very much a part of the world economy, not only as the largest exporter but also as the largest importer. Although the dollar remains the unit of transaction in many international settlements—OPEC, for example, still states oil prices in dollars—the wild gyrations of exchange rates have made those involved in international finance wary of putting all their eggs in one basket. The euro could replace the dollar as the currency of choice on world markets.

The international monetary system is now going through a difficult adjustment period as it continues to grope for a new source of stability nearly three decades after the collapse of the Bretton Woods agreement.

SUMMARY

1. The balance of payments reflects all economic transactions across national borders. The current account measures the flows of (1) merchandise; (2) services, including investment income, military transactions, and tourism; and (3) unilateral transfers, or public and private transfer payments to foreign residents. The capital account measures international flows involving purchases or sales of financial and real assets.

2. Currencies support the flow of goods and services across international borders. The interaction of the supply and demand for foreign exchange determines the equilibrium exchange rate.

3. Under a system of floating exchange rates, the value of the dollar relative to foreign exchange varies over time. An increase in the demand for foreign exchange or a reduction in its supply, other things constant, will cause an increase in the value of foreign exchange relative to the dollar, which is a depreciation of the dollar. Conversely, a reduction in the demand for foreign exchange or an increase in its supply will cause a decrease in the value of foreign exchange relative to the dollar, which is an appreciation of the dollar.

4. Under a system of fixed exchange rates, monetary authorities usually try to stabilize the exchange rate, keeping it between a specified ceiling and floor.

5. For much of this century, the international monetary system was based on fixed exchange rates. A managed float system has been in effect for the major currencies since the demise of the Bretton Woods system in the early 1970s. Although central banks have often tried to stabilize exchange rates, recent swings in exchange rates have troubled policy maker.

QUESTIONS FOR REVIEW

1. *(Balance of Payments)* Suppose the United States ran a balance on goods and services surplus by exporting goods and services while importing nothing.
   a. How would such a surplus be offset elsewhere in the balance-of-payments accounts?
   b. If the level of U.S. production does not depend on the balance on goods and services, how would running this surplus affect our *current* standard of living?
   c. What is the relationship between total debits and total credits in the goods and services balance?
   d. When all international economic transactions are considered, what must be true about the sum of debits and credits?
   e. What is the role of the statistical discrepancy account?

2. *(Foreign Exchange)* What is the difference between a depreciation of the dollar and a devaluation of the dollar?

3. *(Purchasing Power Parity)* According to the theory of purchasing power parity, what will happen to the value of the dollar (against foreign currencies) if the U.S. price level doubles and price levels in other countries remain constant? Why is the theory more suitable to analyzing events in the long run?

4. *(Case**Study:** The Big Mac Index)* The Big Mac Index computed by the *Economist* has found the U.S. dollar to be undervalued against some other major currencies, which seems to call for a rejection of the purchasing power parity theory. Explain why this index may not be a valid test of the theory.

5. *(The Current System: Managed Float)* What is a managed float? What are the disadvantages of freely floating exchange rates that led countries to the managed float system?

6. *(Merchandise Trade Balance)* Explain why U.S. recessions (which are not at the same time world recessions) tend to reduce the U.S. trade deficit.

PROBLEMS AND EXERCISES

7. *(Balance of Payments)* The following are hypothetical data for the U.S. balance of payments. Use the data to calculate each of the following:
   a. Merchandise trade balance
   b. Balance on goods and services
   c. Balance on current account
   d. Capital account balance
   e. Official reserve transactions account balance
   f. Statistical discrepancy

	Billions of Dollars
Merchandise exports	350.0
Merchandise imports	-425.0
Service exports	170.0
Service imports	-145.0
Net unilateral transfers	-21.5
Outflow of U.S. capital	-45.0
Inflow of foreign capital	70.0

Decrease in U.S. official assets abroad	2.5
Increase in foreign official assets in U.S.	35.0

8. *(Balance of Payments)* Explain where in the U.S. balance of payments an entry would be made for each of the following:
    a. A Hong Kong financier buys some U.S. corporate stock
    b. A U.S. tourist in Paris buys some perfume to take home
    c. A Japanese company sells machinery to a pineapple company in Hawaii
    d. U.S. farmers make a gift of food to starving children in Ethiopia
    e. The U.S. Treasury sells a thirty-year bond to a Saudi Arabian prince
    f. A U.S. tourist flies to France on Air France
    g. A U.S. company sells insurance to a foreign firm

9. *(Determining the Exchange Rate)* Use these data to answer the following questions about the market for British pounds:

Price of pounds (in $)	Quantity Demanded (of pounds)	Quantity Supplied (of pounds)
$4.00	50	100
3.00	75	75
2.00	100	50

a. Draw the supply and demand curves for pounds, and determine the equilibrium exchange rate (dollars per pound).
b. Suppose that the supply of pounds doubles. Draw the new supply curve.
c. What is the new equilibrium exchange rate?
d. Has the dollar appreciated or depreciated?
e. What happens to U.S. imports of British goods?

EXPERIENTIAL EXERCISES

10. *(Foreign Exchange Rates and Markets)* Trade among European nations will be bolstered by the introduction of a common European currency called the euro. Not surprisingly, there is a special Web page devoted to the introduction of the euro—EmuNet at http://www.euro-emu.co.uk/. Go to the EmuNet home page to review the latest developments in the introduction of the euro.

11. *(CaseStudy: The Asian Contagion)* Yahoo, an online search engine, maintains a page devoted to the Asian financial crisis. Visit this page at http://headlines.yahoo.com/Full_Coverage/World/Asian_ Economic_Woes/ and determine whether the crisis seems to be easing or getting worse.

12. *(Wall Street Journal)* The latest data on exchange rates appear in the Currency Trading column in the daily *Wall Street Journal*. You can find it in the Money & Investing section. Try tracking a particular foreign currency over the course of several weeks. Has the dollar been appreciating or depreciating relative to that currency? Try to explain why it has been appreciating or depreciating.

Developing and Transitional Economies

People around the world face the day under very different circumstances. Many Americans rise from a comfortable bed in a nice home, select the day's clothing from a wardrobe, choose from a variety of breakfast foods, and drive to school or to work in one of the family's personal automobiles. But most of the world's nearly six billion people have little housing, clothing, or food. They own no automobile, and many have no formal job. Their health is poor, as is their education. Many cannot read or write. An estimated one billion people need glasses but can't afford them. Why are some countries so poor while others are so rich? What determines the wealth of nations?

In this chapter, we sort out rich nations from poor ones and try to explain the difference. Although there is no widely accepted theory of economic development, one approach that seems to be gaining favor lately is the introduction of market forces, especially in formerly socialist countries. Around the world, the demise of central planning has been stunning and pervasive. We close the chapter with a discussion of these rich experiments—these works in progress. Topics discussed in this chapter include:

- Developing countries
- Obstacles to development
- Import substitution
- Export promotion
- Foreign aid
- Transitional economies
- Big bang versus gradualism
- Privatization

WORLDS APART

Differences in economic activity among countries are profound. For example, the United States, with its 270 million people, has a gross domestic product that exceeds the *combined* output of 2.7 billion people living in poor countries. The United States, with only 5 percent of the world's population, produces more than does the poorer half of the world's population.

Countries are classified in a variety of ways based on their level of economic development. The yardstick most often used to compare living standards across nations is *output per capita*. The World Bank, an economic development institution affiliated with the United Nations, attempts to estimate comparable output per capita figures and then uses these figures to classify economies. The World Bank divides countries into three major groups based on their per capita output: low-income economies, middle-income economies, and high-income economies.

Developing and Industrial Economies

The low- and middle-income economies are usually referred to as **developing countries**, and the high-income economies are usually referred to as **industrial market countries** (though some of the high-income countries have incomes based primarily on oil and are viewed as still developing). A few primarily socialist countries, such as Cuba, North Korea, and Libya, do not report data on their economic status and consequently are classified by the World Bank as *nonreporting countries*.

Developing countries usually have a high rate of illiteracy, high unemployment, extensive underemployment, rapid population growth, and exports consisting primarily of agricultural products and raw materials. On average, about two-thirds of the labor force in developing countries is in agriculture. Because farming methods are relatively primitive, farm productivity is low and most people barely subsist. Industrial market countries or *developed countries* are the economically advanced capitalist countries of Western Europe, North America, Australia, New Zealand, and Japan. They were the first to experience long-term economic growth during the 19th century.

The measure of output used by the World Bank to classify countries is gross national product (GNP) per capita. GNP measures the market value of all goods and services produced by resources supplied by the countries' residents and firms, regardless of the location of the resource. For example, U.S. GNP includes profit earned by a Ford factory in Great Britain but excludes profits earned by a Toyota factory in the United States.

Developing countries Nations typified by high rates of illiteracy, high unemployment, high fertility rates, and exports of primary products

Industrial market countries Economically advanced capitalist countries of Western Europe, North America, Australia, New Zealand, and Japan; also known as developed countries

Data on total population, GNP per capita, and growth in private consumption per capita are summarized in Exhibit 1 for all reporting countries with a population of 1 million or more. GNP per capita figures have been adjusted to reflect the actual purchasing power of the native currency in its respective economy. The idea is to measure the actual GNP per capita for each country. Low-income countries made up about one-third of the 5.8 billion people on Earth in 1997, middle-income countries accounted for half, and high-income countries accounted for only one-sixth.

India and China are two population giants shown separately in Exhibit 1. Together they account for more than one-third of the world's population, but produce only about one-twentieth of the world's output. India's GNP per capita of $1,650 in 1997 was slightly above the average of $1,400 for all low-income economies. India's 1.6 percent average growth rate in private consumption per capita between 1980 and 1996 was above the 1.0 percent average for all low-income economies. China's GNP per capita of $3,570 was below the average of $4,550 for all middle-income economies, but its growth rate in private consumption exceeded that of all middle-income economies. High-income economies averaged $22,770 per capita in 1997, or about 16 times the average for low-income economies—quite a difference.

Exhibit 2 presents GNP per capita in 1997 for selected countries, arranged from top to bottom in descending order. Again, figures have been adjusted by the United Nations to reflect the actual purchasing power of the native currency in its respective economy. The United States, the top-ranked country, had a GNP per capita that was 7.5 times that of Paraguay. But GNP per capita in Paraguay, in turn, was 7.5 times that of Sierra Leone, the poorest country in the world. Residents of Paraguay likely feel poor relative to industrialized nations, but they appear well off compared to the poorest developing nations. Per capita GNP in the United States was 56 times greater than in Sierra Leone. Thus there is a tremendous range in productive performance around the world.

Health and Nutrition

Differences in stages of development among countries are reflected in a number of ways besides per capita income levels. For example, many people in

---

EXHIBIT 1

Population, GNP per Capita, and Annual Growth Rate in Private Consumption per Capita

Source: Based on data presented by the World Bank in *World Development Report 1998/99* (New York: Oxford University Press, 1998), Tables 1 and 2. Data are for countries with populations of 1 million or more.

Classification	Population, 1997 (millions)	GNP per Capita 1997 Dollars	Annual Growth Rate, in Private Consumption per Capita, 1980–1996 (percent)
1. Low–income economies	2,048	1,400	1.0
India	961	1,650	1.6
2. Middle-income economies	2,855	4,550	2.8
China	1,227	3,570	4.5
3. High-income economies	926	22,770	1.4

EXHIBIT 2

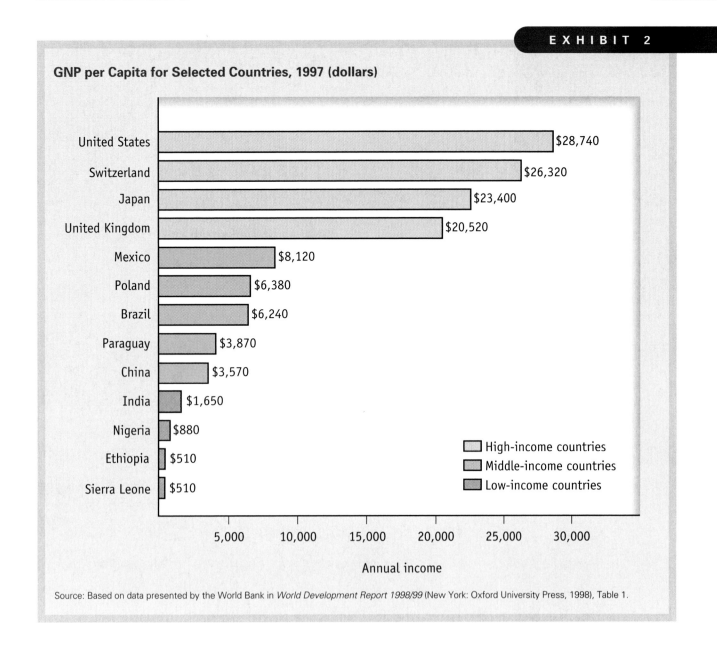

GNP per Capita for Selected Countries, 1997 (dollars)

Country	GNP per Capita
United States	$28,740
Switzerland	$26,320
Japan	$23,400
United Kingdom	$20,520
Mexico	$8,120
Poland	$6,380
Brazil	$6,240
Paraguay	$3,870
China	$3,570
India	$1,650
Nigeria	$880
Ethiopia	$510
Sierra Leone	$510

Legend:
- High-income countries
- Middle-income countries
- Low-income countries

x-axis: Annual income — 5,000 · 10,000 · 15,000 · 20,000 · 25,000 · 30,000

Source: Based on data presented by the World Bank in *World Development Report 1998/99* (New York: Oxford University Press, 1998), Table 1.

developing countries suffer from poor health as a result of malnutrition and disease. AIDS is devastating some developing countries, particularly those in central and east Africa. Life expectancy at birth in 1996 averaged 59 years in low-income economies, 68 years in middle-income economies, and 77 years in high-income economies. Average life expectancy ranged from 37 years in Sierra Leone to 80 years in Japan.

Infant Mortality. Health differences among countries are reflected in infant mortality rates. Mortality rates for selected countries are presented as Exhibit 3.

EXHIBIT 3

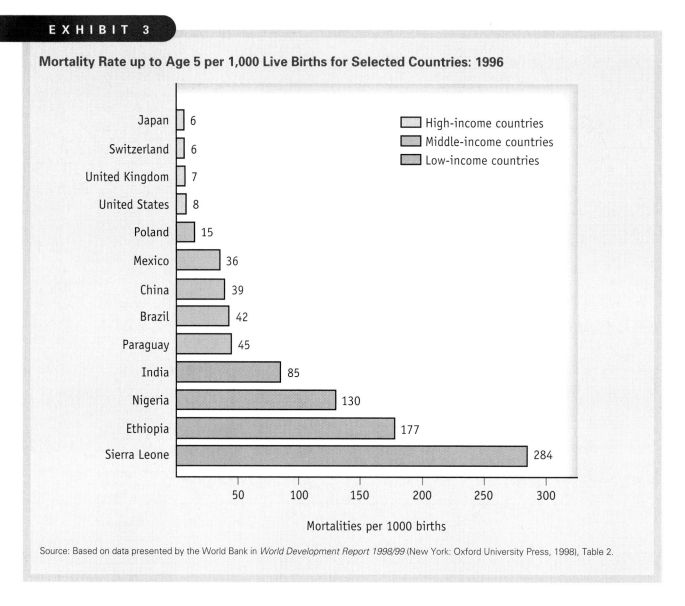

Mortality Rate up to Age 5 per 1,000 Live Births for Selected Countries: 1996

Legend:
- High-income countries
- Middle-income countries
- Low-income countries

Country	Mortalities per 1000 births
Japan	6
Switzerland	6
United Kingdom	7
United States	8
Poland	15
Mexico	36
China	39
Brazil	42
Paraguay	45
India	85
Nigeria	130
Ethiopia	177
Sierra Leone	284

Mortalities per 1000 births

Source: Based on data presented by the World Bank in *World Development Report 1998/99* (New York: Oxford University Press, 1998), Table 2.

As might be expected, countries with the longest life expectancies also have the lowest infant mortality rates. Similarly, the countries with the shortest life expectancies have the highest infant mortality rates. The infant mortality rate in Sierra Leone is at least 35 times the rates in Japan, Switzerland, the United Kingdom, and the United States.

Malnutrition. Many people living in Africa, South Asia, and the Indian subcontinent often do not have enough food to maintain good nutrition. Those in the very poorest countries consume only half the calories of those in high-income countries. Even if an infant survives the first year, malnutrition can turn normal childhood diseases, such as measles, into life-threatening events. Malnutrition is a primary or contributing factor in more than half of all deaths among children under five in low-income countries. Diseases that are well controlled in the industrial countries—malaria, whooping cough, polio, dysentery, typhoid, and cholera—become epidemics in poor countries. Many of these diseases are water borne, because residents of urban areas in less-developed countries are often unable to obtain safe drinking water.

High Birth Rates

Developing countries are identified not only by their low incomes and high mortality rates but also by their high birth rates. This year, about 80 million of the 90 million people added to the world's population will be born in developing countries. In fact, the birth rate is one of the clearest ways of distinguishing between industrial and developing countries. Few developing countries have a total fertility rate per woman of less than 2.2 births, but no industrial country has a fertility rate above that level.

Exhibit 4 presents total fertility rates per woman for 1980 and 1996. Note that fertility rates for all groups declined between the two years. Note also that fertility rates are highest in the low-income economies and lowest in the high-income economies. The fertility rate dropped most in India, where it went from 5.0 in 1980 to 3.1 in 1996. Fertility rates dropped the least in high-income economies, where they were already relatively low in 1980.

Families tend to be larger in developing countries because children are viewed as a source of farm labor and as economic and social security as the parents age. Most developing countries have no pension or social security system for the aged. The higher infant mortality rates in poorer countries also engender higher birth rates, as parents strive to ensure a sufficiently large family.

Sub-Saharan African countries are the poorest in the world and have the fastest-growing populations. Because of high fertility rates in developing countries, children under 15 make up almost half their total population. In industrial countries, children make up only about a quarter of the population. Italy recently became the first country in history to have more people over the age of 60 than under the age of 20. Germany, Greece, and Spain will soon join Italy.[1]

EXHIBIT 4

Total Fertility Rates: Births per Woman

The total fertility rate is the number of children that would be born to a woman if she were to live to the end of her childbearing years and to bear children in accordance with current age-specific fertility rates.

Classification	1980	1996
1. Low-income economies	5.6	4.1
India	5.0	3.1
Sub-Saharan Africa	6.6	5.6
2. Middle-income economies	3.2	2.3
China	2.5	1.4
3. High-income economies	1.9	1.7

Source: Based on data presented by the World Bank in *World Development Report 1998/99* (New York: Oxford University Press, 1998), Table 7.

---

1 As reported in Michael Specter, "Population Implosion Worries a Graying Europe," *New York Times* (10 July 1998).

In some developing countries, the population growth rate has exceeded the real GNP growth rate, so the standard of living as measured by per capita GNP has declined. Still, even in the poorest of countries, attitudes about family size are changing. According the United Nations, the birth rate during a typical woman's lifetime in a developing country has fallen since 1965 from six children to three children. Evidence from developing countries more generally indicates that when women have better employment opportunities outside the home, fertility rates decline. And as women become better educated, they tend to earn more and have fewer children.

Women in Developing Countries

Throughout the world, poverty is greater among women than men, particularly women who head households. The percentage of households headed by women varies from country to country, but exceeds 40 percent in some areas of the Caribbean and Africa. Because women often must work in the home as well as in the labor market, poverty can impose a special hardship on them. In many cultures, women's responsibilities include gathering firewood and carrying water, tasks that are especially burdensome if firewood is scarce and water is far from home.

Women in developing countries tend to be less educated than men. In the countries of sub-Saharan Africa and South Asia, for example, only half as many women as men complete high school. And in Indonesia, girls are six times more likely than boys to drop out of school before the fourth grade. Women have fewer employment opportunities and earn lower wages than men do. For example, Sudan's Muslim fundamentalist government bans women from working in public places after 5:00 P.M. In Algeria, Egypt, Jordan, Libya, and Saudi Arabia, women account for only about one-quarter of the labor force. Women are often on the fringes of the labor market, working long hours in agriculture. They also have less access to other resources, such as land, capital, and technology. Worse yet, according to social workers and press reports, during the recent economic crisis in Asia, some peasant girls were sold to traders who in turn sold them to brothels in places like Bangkok, Thailand.[2]

PRODUCTIVITY: KEY TO DEVELOPMENT

We have examined some symptoms of poverty in developing countries, but not why poor countries are poor. At the risk of appearing simplistic, we might say that poor countries are poor because they do not produce many goods and services. In this section, we will examine why some developing countries experience such low productivity.

Low Labor Productivity

Labor productivity, measured in terms of output per worker, is low in low-income countries. Why? Labor productivity depends on the quality of the labor and on the amount of capital, land, and other resources that combine with labor. For example, one certified public accountant with a computer and specialized

---

2   As reported in Nicholas D. Kristof, "Asian Crisis Deals Setbacks to Women," *New York Times* (11 June 1998). This story tells of a 15-year-old sold by her grandmother for $40.

software can sort out a company's finances more quickly and more accurately than can a thousand high-school–educated file clerks with pencils and paper.

One way a country raises its productivity is by investing more in human and physical capital. This investment must be financed by either domestic savings or foreign funds. Income per capita is often too low in developing countries to permit extensive investments to be financed with internal funds. In poor countries with unstable governments, the wealthy minority frequently invests in more stable foreign economies. Thus there are few domestic funds available for investment in either human or physical capital; without sufficient capital, workers are less productive.

Technology and Education

What exactly is the contribution of education to the process of economic development? Education makes people more receptive to new ideas and methods. Countries with the most advanced educational systems were also the first to develop. In this century, the leader in schooling and economic development has been the United States. In Latin America, Argentina was the most educationally advanced nation 100 years ago, and it is one of the most developed Latin American nations today. The growth of education in Japan during the 19th century contributed to a ready acceptance of technology and thus to Japan's remarkable economic growth in the 20th century.

If knowledge is insufficient, other resources may not be used efficiently. For example, a country may be endowed with fertile land, but farmers may lack knowledge of irrigation and fertilization techniques. Or farmers may not know how to rotate crops and avoid soil depletion. In low-income countries, about 60 percent of adults were illiterate in 1995, compared to less than 5 percent in high-income countries.

Child labor in developing countries reduces educational opportunities. In Pakistan, for example, the education system can accommodate only one-third of the country's school-age children. More than 10 million Pakistani children work full-time—half of whom are less than 10 years old.[3] Worldwide, more than 200 million children under 14 years of age work full-time.

Inefficient Use of Labor

Another feature of developing countries is that they use labor less efficiently than developed nations. Unemployment and underemployment reflect inefficient uses of labor. *Underemployment* occurs when skilled workers are employed in low-skill jobs or when people are working less than they would like—a worker seeking full-time employment may find only a part-time job. *Unemployment* occurs when those willing and able to work cannot find jobs.

Unemployment is measured primarily in urban areas, because in rural areas farm work is usually an outlet for labor even if many workers are underemployed there. The unemployment rate in developing nations on average is about 10 to 15 percent of the urban labor force. Unemployment among young workers—those aged 15 to 24—is typically twice that of older workers. In developing nations, about 30 percent of the combined urban and rural work forces is either unemployed or underemployed.

---

3 Pakistani children in the lowest castes become laborers almost as soon as they can walk. See Jonathan Silvers, "Child Labor in Pakistan," *Atlantic Monthly* (February 1996).

In some developing countries, the average farm is as small as two acres. Productivity is also low because few other inputs, such as capital and fertilizer, are used. Even where more land is available, the absence of capital limits the amount of land that can be farmed. *Although about two-thirds of the labor force in developing countries works in agriculture, only about one-third of GNP in these countries stems from agriculture.* In the United States, where farmers account for only 2.5 percent of the labor force, a farmer with modern equipment can farm hundreds of acres. In developing countries a farmer with a hand plow or an ox-drawn plow can farm maybe 10 to 20 acres. As you would expect, U.S. farmers, though one-fortieth of the workforce, grow enough to feed a nation and to lead the world in farm exports.

Low productivity obviously results in low income, but low income can, in turn, affect worker productivity. Low income means less saving and less saving means less investment in human and physical capital. Low income can also mean poor nutrition during the formative years, which can retard mental and physical development. These difficult beginnings may be aggravated by poor diet and insufficient health care in later life, making workers poorly suited for regular employment. Thus, *low income and low productivity may reinforce each other in a vicious cycle.* Poverty can result in less saving, less capital formation, an inadequate diet, and insufficient attention to health care—all of which can reduce a worker's productive ability.

Natural Resources

Some countries are richer than others because they are blessed with natural resources. The difference is most striking when we compare countries with oil reserves and those without. Some developing countries of the Middle East are classified as high-income economies because they are lucky enough to be sitting atop major oil reserves. But oil-rich countries are the exception. Many developing countries, such as Chad and Ethiopia, have little in the way of natural resources. Most developing countries without oil reserves were in trouble when oil prices rose. Oil had to be imported, and these imports drained the oil-poor countries of precious foreign exchange.

Financial Institutions

Another requirement for development is an adequate and trusted system of financial institutions. An important source of funds for investment is the savings of households and firms. People in developing countries often have little confidence in their currency because some governments finance a large fraction of public outlays by printing money. This practice results in high inflation and sometimes very high inflation, or hyperinflation, as occurred recently in Russia. High and unpredictable inflation discourages saving and hurts development.

Developing countries have special problems because banks are often not held in high regard. At the first sign of economic problems, many depositors withdraw their funds. Since banks cannot rely on a continuous supply of deposits, they cannot make loans for extended periods. Also governments often impose ceilings on the interest rates that lenders can charge, forcing lenders to ration credit among borrowers. If financial institutions fail to serve as intermediaries between borrowers and lenders, the resulting lack of funds for investment becomes an obstacle to growth.

Capital Infrastructure

Some development economists believe that the most important ingredient in economic development is the administrative competence of the government. Production and exchange rely on an infrastructure of communication and transportation networks provided by the public sector. Roads, bridges, airports, harbors, and other transportation facilities are vital to commercial activity. Reliable mail service, telephone communication, clean water, and electricity are also essential for advanced production techniques. Imagine how difficult it would be to run even a personal computer if the supply of electricity and phone service were continually interrupted, as is often the case in developing countries. Many developing countries have serious deficiencies in their infrastructures. And some of the poorest countries in Africa have been ravaged by internal strife. For example, Ethiopia, one of the poorest countries in the world, has been caught up in a war with the break-away province of Eritrea. Both sides have spent millions on jet fighters, even though neither has any qualified pilots to fly the new planes.

Entrepreneurial Ability

An economy can have abundant supplies of land, labor, and capital, but without entrepreneurial ability, the other resources will not be combined efficiently to produce goods and services. Unless a country has a class of entrepreneurs who are able to bring together resources and take the risk of profit or loss, development may never begin. Many developing countries were once under colonial rule, a system of government that offered the local population little opportunity to develop entrepreneurial skills.

Government Monopolies

Government officials often decide that local private-sector entrepreneurs are unable to generate the kind of economic growth the country needs. State enterprises are therefore created to do what government believes the free market cannot do. State-owned enterprises may have objectives other than producing goods efficiently—objectives that could include maximizing employment and providing jobs for friends and relatives of government officials, as discussed in the following case study.

Crony Capitalism in Indonesia—All in the Family

Indonesia is a country of more than 200 million people spread across some 13,000 islands in the Indian Ocean. The country is rich in natural resources, including oil, yet economic development has been hampered by bureaucratic red tape and corruption. At the center was President Suharto, who ruled the nation as a virtual dictator between 1965 and his forced resignation in 1998. Over the years, he conferred monopoly privileges on family and friends.

Based on the strength of government-granted monopolies, President Suharto and his

CaseStudy

*Other Times,
Other Places*

Is crony capitalism an example of market failure or government failure? "TRB From Washington: Super Markets," by Charles Lane in the *New Republic,* takes the latter view, citing Indonesia and Russia as examples. See http://www. thenewrepublic.com/ magazines/tnr/archive/1198/ 110298/trb110298.html. What else does he blame for the financial crisis? What good does he think might follow from it?

six children were able to build an economic empire valued at more than $4 billion, spanning over 2,000 Indonesian companies. Because of government-imposed monopolies, the prices of products in Indonesia were higher than those prevailing on the world market. For example, friends and relatives held the exclusive rights to import steel, plastic, tin, cotton, industrial machinery, cement, and other key resources. In 1990 one of Suharto's sons and some business partners were awarded an exclusive license to import, buy, and sell cloves, a spice used in cooking and to flavor tobacco in Indonesian cigarettes. To finance the monopoly, the central Bank of Indonesia advanced the group $325 million in loans and credits, or half the Bank's annual budget for agricultural subsidies. At the time the son claimed, "We're doing it for the good of the farmers." The monopoly purchased cloves from farmers for less than the world price and sold the cloves to cigarette manufacturers for twice the world price. The monopoly was a hugely profitable.

These monopolies reduced competition, increased costs to consumers, and hindered the development of an export sector that could compete on the world market. In this environment, a combination of "crony capitalism" and nepotism, political connections become more important than ability or expertise; free enterprise was thereby discouraged. Businesses were better off developing political contacts than producing goods and services more efficiently.

By the time Suharto resigned in 1998, the Indonesian economy was in shambles. Economic output declined 12 percent in the first half of 1998. The government had taken over 70 percent of the nation's banks. The national currency, the rupiah, had fallen 80 percent against the dollar. And half the population was living below the poverty level. Some of this was caused, no doubt, by the economic malaise sweeping through Asia, but Indonesia was hit hardest because its economy had been distorted for so long.

Sources: Maggie Farley, "A Familiar Scent of Monopoly," *Los Angeles Times* (21 March 1998); Steven Erlanger, "Suharto's Cling to Power Undermines His Legacy," *New York Times* (22 May 1998); Peter Waldman, "Hand in Glove: How Suharto's Circle, Mining Firm Did So Well Together," *Wall Street Journal* (29 September 1998); and "The World's Working Rich," *Forbes* (6 July 1998): 198–199.

INTERNATIONAL TRADE AND DEVELOPMENT

Developing countries need to trade with developed countries in order to acquire the capital and technology that will increase labor productivity on the farm, in the factory, in the office, and in the home. To import capital and technology, developing countries must first acquire the funds, or foreign exchange, needed to pay for imports. Exports usually generate more than half of the annual flow of foreign exchange in developing countries. Foreign aid and private investment make up the rest.

Primary products, such as agricultural goods and other raw materials, make up the bulk of exports from developing countries, just as manufactured goods make up the bulk of exports from developed countries. Developing countries must export a large amount of raw materials in order to buy back the finished products made from these same materials. Another problem is that the prices of primary products, such as coffee, cocoa, sugar, and rubber, fluctuate more widely than do the prices of finished goods, because crop production fluctuates with the weather.

A third problem of developing countries has been their deteriorating trade position. In recent years, the prices of raw materials have fallen as demand has softened (in part because of the troubles in Asia) and as substitutes have been developed for products such as rubber. Since the prices of manufactured imported goods have not dropped as much, developing countries receive less money from exports than they spend on imports, resulting in trade deficits. To reduce these deficits, developing countries have tried to restrict imports. Because imported food often is critical to survival, developing countries are more likely to cut imports of capital goods—the very items needed to promote long-term growth and productivity. Thus many developing countries cannot afford the modern machinery that will help them become more productive. Developing countries must also confront industrial countries' trade restrictions, such as tariffs and quotas, which often discriminate against primary products. For example, the United States strictly limits sugar imports. *Developing countries' share of world trade has fallen since 1950.*

Import Substitution Versus Export Promotion

Economic development frequently involves a shift from the production of raw materials and agricultural products to manufacturing. If a country is fortunate, this transformation occurs gradually through natural market forces. Sometimes the shift is pushed along by government. Many developing countries, including Argentina and India, pursued a policy called **import substitution**, whereby the country manufactures products that until then had been imported. To insulate domestic producers from foreign competition, the government imposes tariffs and import quotas. This development strategy became popular for several reasons. First, demand already existed for these products, so the "what to produce" question was readily answered. Second, by reducing imports, the approach addressed the lack of foreign exchange so common among developing countries. Third, import substitution nurtured infant industries, providing them a protected market. Finally, import substitution was popular with those who supplied capital, labor, and other resources to the favored domestic industries.

Import substitution A development strategy that emphasizes domestic manufacturing of products that are currently imported

Like all protection measures, however, import substitution erases the gains from specialization and comparative advantage among countries. Often the developing country replaced relatively low-cost foreign goods with high-cost domestic goods. And domestic producers, insulated from foreign competition, usually fail to grow efficient. Even the balance-of-payments picture did not improve, because other countries often retaliated with their own trade restrictions.

Critics of the import-substitution approach claim that export promotion is a surer path to economic development. **Export promotion** is a development strategy that concentrates on producing for the export market. This approach begins with relatively simple products, such as textiles. As a developing country builds its technological and educational base—that is, as the developing economy learns by doing—producers can then export more complex products. Economists tend to favor export promotion over import substitution because the emphasis is on comparative advantage and trade expansion rather than trade restriction. Export promotion also forces producers to grow more efficient in order to compete

Export promotion A development strategy that concentrates on producing for the export market on world markets. Recent research shows that global competition has a profound effect on domestic efficiency.[4] What's more, export promotion requires less government intervention in the market than does import substitution.

Export promotion has been the more successful development strategy, as reflected for example by the newly industrialized countries of East Asia, which in recent decades have grown much more quickly than import-substituting countries such as Argentina, India, and Peru. Since 1965 the four Asian newly industrialized economies raised their average real income from 20 percent of the high income countries' level to 70 percent. Most Latin American nations, which for decades had favored import substitution, are now pursuing free trade agreements with the United States. Even India is in the process of dismantling trade barriers, although the emphasis has been on importing high-technology capital goods. One slogan of Indian trade officials is "Microchips, yes! Potato chips, no!"

Migration and the Brain Drain

Migration plays an important role in the economies of developing countries. A major source of foreign exchange in some countries is the money sent home by migrants who find jobs in industrial countries. Thus migration provides a valuable safety valve for poor countries. But there is a downside. Often the best and the brightest professionals, such as doctors, nurses, and engineers, migrate to developed countries. Since human capital is such a key resource, this "brain drain" hurts the developing economy.

Trade Liberalization and Special Interests

Although most people would benefit from freer international trade, some would be worse off. Consequently, governments in some developing countries have difficulty pursuing policies conducive to development. Often the gains from economic development are widespread, but the beneficiaries, such as consumers, do not recognize their potential gains. On the other hand, the losers tend to be concentrated, such as producers in an industry that had been sheltered from foreign competition, and they know quite well the source of their losses. So the government often lacks the political backing to remove impediments to development, because the potential losers fight reforms that might harm their livelihood while the potential winners remain largely unaware of what's at stake. What's more, consumers have difficulty organizing even if they become aware of what's going on. A recent study by the World Bank suggests a strong link in Africa between governments that cater to special-interest groups and low rates of economic growth.

Nonetheless, many developing countries have been opening their borders to freer trade. People around the world have been exposed to information about the opportunities and goods available on world markets. So consumers want the goods and firms want the technology and capital that are available abroad. Both groups want government to ease trade restrictions. Studies by the World Bank and others have underscored the successes of countries that have adopted trade liberalization policies.

---

4 See Martin Baily and Hans Gersbach, "Efficiency in Manufacturing and the Need for Global Competition," in *Brookings Papers on Economic Activity: Microeconomics,* M. Baily, P. Reiss, and C. Winston, eds. (Washington D.C.: Brookings Institution, 1995): 307–347.

FOREIGN AID AND ECONOMIC DEVELOPMENT

We have already seen that because poor countries do not generate enough savings to fund an adequate level of investment, these countries often rely on foreign financing. Private international borrowing and lending are heavily restricted by the governments of developing countries. Governments may allow residents to purchase foreign exchange only for certain purposes. In some developing countries, different exchange rates apply to different categories of transactions. Thus the local currency is not easily convertible into other currencies. Some developing countries also require foreign investors to find a local partner who must be granted controlling interest. All these restrictions discourage foreign investment. In this section, we will look primarily at foreign aid and its link to economic development.

Foreign Aid

Foreign aid is any international transfer made on *concessional* (i.e., especially favorable) terms for the purposes of promoting economic development. Foreign aid includes grants, which need not be repaid, and loans extended on more favorable repayment terms than the recipient could normally secure. Concessional loans have lower interest rates, longer repayment periods, or grace periods during which repayments are reduced or waived (similar to some student loans). Foreign aid can take the form of money, capital goods, technical assistance, food, and so forth.

Some foreign aid is granted by a specific country, such as the United States, to another specific country, such as the Philippines. Country-to-country aid is called *bilateral* assistance. Other foreign aid goes through international bodies such as the World Bank. Assistance provided by organizations that use funds from a number of countries is called *multilateral*. For example, the World Bank provides loans and grants to support activities that are viewed as prerequisites for development, such as health and education programs or basic development projects like dams, roads, and communications networks. And the International Monetary Fund extends loans to countries that have trouble with their balance of payments, with recent loans to Indonesia, Korea, and Brazil.

During the last four decades, the United States has provided the developing world with over $400 billion in aid. Since 1961, most U.S. aid has been coordinated by the U.S. Agency for International Development (AID), which is part of the U.S. Department of State. This agency concentrates primarily on health, education, and agriculture, providing both technical assistance and loans. AID emphasizes long-range plans to meet the basic needs of the poor and to promote self-sufficiency. Foreign aid is a controversial, though relatively small, part of the federal budget. Since 1993, official U.S. aid has been less than 0.2 percent of U.S. GDP, compared to an average of 0.3 percent from 21 other industrialized nations.

Does Foreign Aid Promote Economic Development?

In general, foreign aid provides additional purchasing power and thus the possibility of increased investment, capital imports, and consumption. But it remains unclear whether foreign aid *supplements* domestic saving, thus increasing investment, or simply *substitutes* for domestic saving, thereby increasing consumption

Foreign aid An international transfer made on especially favorable terms for the purpose of promoting economic development rather than investment. What is clear is that foreign aid often becomes a source of discretionary funds that benefit not the poor but their leaders. More than 90 percent of the funds distributed by AID go to governments, whose leaders assume responsibility for distributing these funds.

Much bilateral funding is tied to purchases of goods and services from the donor nation, and such programs can sometimes be counterproductive. For example, in the 1950s, the United States began the Food for Peace program, which helped sell U.S. farm products abroad, but some governments sold that food to finance poorly conceived projects. Worse yet, the availability of low-priced food drove down farm prices in the developing countries, hurting farmers there.

Foreign aid may have raised the standard of living in some developing countries, but it has not necessarily increased their ability to become self-supporting at that higher standard of living. Many countries that receive aid are doing less of what they had done well. Their agricultural sectors have suffered. For example, though we should be careful when drawing conclusions about causality, per capita food production in Africa has fallen since 1960. Outside aid has often insulated government officials from the fundamental troubles of their own economies. No country receiving U.S. aid in the past 20 years has moved up in status from developing to industrial. And most countries today that have achieved industrial status did so without foreign aid.

Because of disappointment with the results of government aid, the trend is toward channeling funds through private nonprofit agencies such as CARE. More than half of the flow of aid now goes through private channels.

The privatization of foreign aid follows a larger trend toward privatization around the world. We discuss that important development in the balance of this chapter.

TRANSITIONAL ECONOMIES

As we have seen, there is no widely accepted theory of economic development, but around the world markets are replacing central plans in once-socialist countries. Economic developments in these emerging market economies have tremendous significance for those who study economics. Like geologists, economists must rely primarily on natural experiments to figure out how things work. *The attempt to replace central planning with markets is one of the greatest economic experiments in history.* In the study of geology, this would be comparable to a huge earthquake. In this section, we take a look at these so-called transitional economies.

Types of Economic Systems

First, let's briefly review economic systems. In Chapter 2, we considered the three questions that every economic system must answer: what to produce, how to produce it, and for whom to produce it. Laws regarding resource ownership and the role of government in resource allocation determine the "rules of the game"—the incentives and constraints that guide the behavior of individual decision makers. Economic systems can be classified based on the ownership of resources, the way resources are allocated to produce goods and services, and the incentives used to motivate people.

As we discussed in Chapter 2, resources in *capitalist* systems are owned mostly by individuals and are allocated through market coordination. In socialist economies, resources other than labor are owned by the state. For example, a country such as Cuba or North Korea carefully limits the private ownership of resources such as land and capital. Each country employs a slightly different system of resource ownership, resource allocation, and individual incentives to answer the three economic questions.

So under capitalism, the rules of the game include private ownership of most resources and the coordination of economic activity by price signals generated by market forces; market coordination answers the three questions. Under socialism, the rules of the game include government ownership of most resources and the allocation of resources through central plans.

Enterprises and Soft Budget Constraints

In the socialist system, enterprises that earn a "profit" see that profit appropriated by the state. Firms that end up with a loss find that loss covered by a state subsidy. Thus socialist enterprises face what has been called a **soft budget constraint**. This can lead to inefficiency, a lack of response to changes in supply or demand, and poor investment decisions. Quality has also been a problem under central planning, because plant managers would rather meet production quotas than satisfy consumer demand. For example, plant managers do not score extra bureaucratic points by producing garments that are in style and in popular sizes. Tales of shoddy products in socialist systems abound.

> **Soft budget constraint** The budget condition faced by socialist enterprises that are subsidized if they lose money

Most prices in centrally planned economies are established not by market forces but by central planners. As a result, consumers have little to say about what to produce. Once set, prices tend to be inflexible. For example, in the former Soviet Union, the price of a cabbage slicer was stamped on the metal at the factory. In the spirit of equity, Soviet planners priced most consumer goods below the market-clearing level, so shortages (or "interruptions in supply," as they were called) were common. As of 1990, the price of bread had not changed since 1954, and that price in 1990 amounted to only 7 percent of bread's production cost. Meat prices had not changed since 1962. Some rents had not changed in 60 years.

Capitalist economies equate quantity supplied with quantity demanded through the *invisible hand* of market coordination; centrally planned economies use the *visible hand* of bureaucratic coordination assisted by taxes and subsidies. If quantity supplied and quantity demanded are not in balance, something has to give. In a capitalist system, what gives is the price. In a centrally planned economy, what usually gives is the central plan itself. A common problem in the Soviet system was that the amount produced often fell short of planned production. When the quantity supplied fell below the planned amount, central planners reduced the amount supplied to each sector, cutting critical sectors such as heavy industry and the military the least and cutting lower-priority sectors such as consumer products the most. Evidence of shortages of consumer goods included long waiting lines at retail stores; empty store shelves; the "tips," or bribes, shop operators expected for supplying scarce consumer goods; and higher prices for goods on the black market. Shoppers would sometimes wait in line all night and into the next day. Consumers often relied on "connections" through acquaintances to obtain most goods and services. Scarce goods were frequently diverted to the black market.

CaseStudy

Other Times, Other Places

Médecins Sans Frontières is an international medical relief agency aiding victims of armed conflict, epidemics, and natural and man-made disasters. The ecological catastrophe that resulted from Soviet mismanagement of the Aral Sea has gained this group's attention. Their Web site contains a special section, at http://www.msf.org/aralsea/index.html, that gives you some feel for magnitude of the disaster. An .mpeg animation file showing the shrinking of the sea can be found at http://www.dfd.dlr.de/app/land/aralsee/index.html.

Another distinction between socialist economies and capitalist economies involves the ownership of resources. The following case study considers the effect of ownership on the efficient use of resources.

Ownership and Resource Use

Because most property is owned by the state in a socialist economy, nobody in particular owns it. Because there are no individual owners, resources are often wasted. For example, in the former Soviet Union, about one-third of the harvest reportedly deteriorated before it reached retailers. Likewise, to meet Soviet planning goals, oil producers often pumped large pools of oil reserves so quickly that the remaining oil became inaccessible. Soviet workers usually had little regard for equipment that belonged to the state. New trucks or tractors might be dismantled for parts, or working equipment might be sent to a scrap plant. Pilfering of state-owned property, though officially a serious crime, was a high art and a favorite sport. As an old Soviet saying goes, "If you don't steal from the State, you are stealing from your family."

A narrow focus on meeting the objectives of the central plan also imposed a heavy cost on the environment. The Aral Sea, which is about the size of Lake Michigan, has been called "a salinated cesspool." Thousands of barrels of nuclear waste were dumped into Soviet rivers and seas. The 1986 Chernobyl reactor meltdown still poses a threat of nuclear contamination; similar reactors continue to supply energy to Russia, Ukraine, and Lithuania. In a drive for military supremacy, the Soviet government set off 125 nuclear explosions *above* ground. The resulting bomb craters later filled with water, forming contaminated lakes.

In contrast to the treatment of state property, Soviet citizens took extremely good care of their personal property. For example, personal cars were so well maintained that they lasted 20 years or more on average—twice the official projected automobile life. The incentives of private ownership were also evident in agriculture, where farmers typically worked as a group on a *collective*. But each farmer on the collective was also allowed a small plot of land on which to cultivate crops for personal consumption or for sale at prices determined in unregulated markets. Despite the small size of the plots and high taxes on earnings from these plots, farmers produced a disproportionate share of output on private plots. Privately farmed plots constituted only 3 percent of the Soviet Union's farmland, but they supplied 30 percent of all meat, milk, and vegetables and 60 percent of all potatoes.

Perhaps the benefits of privately held resources are no better illustrated than where countries were divided by ideology: West and East Germany before unification, South and North Korea, and Taiwan and mainland China. In each case the economies began with similar human and physical resources, but income per capita diverged sharply, with the market economies outperforming the centrally planned markets. For example, despite recent turmoil in Asia, per capita income in South Korea was still at least five times greater than in North Korea, a communist country.

Recognizing the incentive power of private property, even the most die-hard socialist economies now allow some free-market activity. For example, Cuba allows foreigners to buy Cuban companies and repatriate profits earned in Cuba. On a more down-to-earth level, hundreds of farmers' markets have been established in Cuba to sell everything from live goats to tropical fruit. And for the first time in fifty years, in 1998 China announced plans to allow urban residents the ability to buy homes. But sale prices will still be dictated by the government. The point is that the personal incentives provided by private property usually promote a more efficient use of that property than does state, or common, ownership.

Sources: "Stuck in a Rut," *Wall Street Journal* (23 June 1998); Esther Dyson, *Release 2.0 : A Design for Living in the Digital Age* (New York: Broadway Books, 1997); Erik Eckholm, "China Spells Out Rules On New National Housing Policy," *New York Times* (19 June 1998); Vito Echevarria, "Capitalism Grows in Cuba," *New American News Service* (30 April 1998); and "Viewing Cuba's Market Culture," *Times-Picayune* (29 April 1998).

MARKETS AND INSTITUTIONS

A study of economic systems underscores the importance of institutions in the course of development. *Institutions*, or "rules of the game," are the incentives and constraints that structure political, economic, and social interaction. They consist of (1) formal rules of behavior, such as a constitution, laws, and property rights, and (2) informal constraints on behavior, such as sanctions, manners, customs, traditions, and codes of conduct. Throughout history, institutions have been devised by people to create order and reduce uncertainty in exchange. Thus underlying the surface of economic behavior is a grid of informal, often unconscious, habits, customs, and norms that make the functioning of markets possible. *A reliable system of property rights and enforceable contracts are prerequisites for creating incentives that support a healthy market economy.*

Together with the standard constraints of economics, such as income, resource availability, and prices, institutions shape the incentive structure of an economy. As the incentive structure evolves, it can direct economic change toward growth, stagnation, or decline. Economic history is largely a story of economies that have failed to produce a set of economic rules of the game that lead to sustained economic growth. After all, more than three-quarters of the world's economies are still trying to develop—still trying to get their act together.

Customs and conventions can sometimes be obstacles to development. In developed market economies, resource owners tend to supply their resources where they are most valued; but in developing countries, links to the family or clan may be the most important consideration. For example, in some cultures, children are expected to remain in their father's occupation even though some are better suited to other lines of work. Family businesses may resist growth because such growth would involve hiring people from outside the family.

Institutions and Economic Development

Institutions shape the incentive structure of an economy, but, as we have already noted, most countries in the world have failed to produce a set of economic rules of the game that lead to sustained economic growth. Although political and judicial decisions may change formal rules overnight, informal constraints embodied in customs, traditions, and codes of conduct are more immune to deliberate policies. For example, respect for the law cannot be legislated.

Prior to the market reforms in the former Soviet Union, widespread corruption and a lack of faith in formal institutions were woven into the social fabric. Workers bribed officials to get good jobs and consumers bribed clerks to get desired products. Bribery became a way of life, a way of dealing with the distortions that arise when prices are not allowed to allocate resources efficiently.

In centrally planned economies, the exchange relationship was typically personal, based as it was on bureaucratic ties on the production side and inside connections on the consumption side. But in the United States and other market economies, successful institutional evolution permits the *impersonal* exchange necessary to capture the potential economic benefits of specialization and modern technology. Impersonal exchange allows for a far greater division of labor, but it requires a richer and more stable institutional setting.

The Big Bang Versus Gradualism

The Hungarian economist Janos Kornai believes that a market order should be grown from the bottom up. First, small-scale capitalism in farming, trade, light manufacturing, and services thrives. These grass-roots markets can serve as a foundation for the privatization of larger industrial sectors. Large industrial enterprises should quickly find the market-clearing price so that input and output decisions are consistent with market preferences. In the meantime, state-owned enterprises should be run more like businesses in which state directors attempt to maximize profit. Money-losing enterprises should be phased out. This "bottom-up" approach proposed by Kornai could be termed **gradualism**, which can be contrasted with a **big-bang** approach, whereby the transition from central planning to a market economy would take place in a matter of months.

One example of gradualism is taking place in China. In 1978, the government began dismantling agricultural communes in favor of a "household-responsibility" system of small-farm agriculture. Land was assigned to individual families, which could keep any excess production after meeting specific state-imposed goals. Initially the system was to be applied only to the poorest 20 percent of rural areas. Once the positive effects became apparent, however, the system spread on its own. Eventually farmers established their own wholesale and retail marketing systems and were allowed to sell directly to urban areas at market-clearing prices. This gave rise to a market for truckers to buy, transport, and resell farm products. Over the next seven years, agricultural output increased by an impressive 8 to 10 percent per year.

In structuring the transition from central planning to a market system, economists are feeling their way. Nobel prize-winner Friedrich von Hayek argued that competitive markets provide instant information about the price and quantity resulting from the interaction of supply and demand. But central planning provides no way to discover what the equilibrium price and quantity should be. And the more rigid prices become, the less information they convey. According to Hayek, not only is finding equilibrium price and quantity a discovery process, but developing appropriate rules of the game to nurture market activity is also a discovery process. Both discovery processes are especially

Gradualism A "bottom-up" approach to moving from a centrally planned to a market economy emphasizing established markets at the most decentralized level first, such as on small farms or in light industry

Big-bang theory The argument that the transition from a centrally planned to a market economy should be broad and swift, taking place in a matter of months difficult for transitional economies, which usually have no history of market interaction and no established record of codified law or rules of conduct for market participants. For example, based on China's success with privately run farms, Russia's 1993 constitution guaranteed the right to buy and sell land. But that guarantee was never fleshed out with supporting legislation. Thus farm cooperatives in Russia today operate much as they did in the Soviet days. Hayek believed that *government's role should be to help establish competitive markets by identifying and codifying the conventions of trade and by protecting property rights.*

Privatization

Privatization is the process of turning public enterprises into private enterprises. It is the opposite of *nationalization*. For example, Russian privatization began in April 1992 with the sale of municipally owned shops. Although most property in countries of the former Soviet Union is nominally owned by the state, it often remains unclear who has the authority to sell the property and who should receive the proceeds. This ambiguity results in cases in which the same property has been purchased from different officials by different buyers. Yet *there is no clear legal process for resolving title disputes.* Worse still, some enterprises have been stripped of their assets by self-serving managers, a process that derisively came to be called "spontaneous" privatization. The necessarily complex process of privatization will be undermined if the general population perceives it to be unfair.

Privatization The process of turning public enterprises into private enterprises

Transparent Finances

Privatization requires modern accounting and other information systems, the training of competent managers, and the installation of adequate facilities for telecommunication, computing, travel, and transportation. This transformation cannot be accomplished overnight. Consider just the accounting problem. A market economy depends on financial accounting rules as well as on an independent system for auditing financial reports. The needed information must show up in a company's balance sheet and income statement. Prospective buyers of enterprises need such information, as do banks and other lenders. Thus, a firm's finances should be **transparent**, meaning someone should be able to look at the books and the balance sheet and tell exactly what's going on.

Transparent finances A firm's financial records that clearly indicate the economic health of the company

By all reports, the accounting systems of most formerly socialist firms are almost worthless. For decades, data had been aimed more at central planners, who wanted to know about *physical* flows, than at someone who wanted to know about the efficiency and financial promise of the firm. So there is much information, but little that is relevant. Incidentally, the major advantage of the market economy is that it minimizes the need for the kind of resource-flow data that had been reported under central planning. Prices convey most of the information necessary to coordinate economic activity among firms.

Institutional Requirements of Efficient Markets

Some may look at the initial instability that resulted from the dismantling of socialist states and argue that the move toward markets has been a failure. But in the former Soviet Union the state dismantled central controls before institutions such as property rights, customs, codes of conduct, and a legal system were in place. For example, more than half of the 17-year-olds surveyed in Russia saw nothing wrong with looking for a job that offered opportunities to collect bribes and nearly half believed it acceptable to take what they wanted by force.[5]

Tax laws are applied unevenly and the rates change frequently. For example, the personal income tax in Russia jumped from a graduated rate topping at 13 percent to a flat rate of 60 percent and then to a graduated rate topping at 40 percent. Most Russians evade taxes—only one million people filed income tax returns in 1997, a tiny fraction of the 147 million population.[6] Corporate taxes appear just as arbitrary in Russia, with politically connected companies paying little or no taxes. The head of Russia's Statistics Service was fired in 1998 after his arrest for helping big companies evade taxes.[7] Harvard economist and Russian expert Marshall Goldman argues that "tax evasion by both enterprises and individuals is a source of pride dating back to czarist times."[8] Millions of Russians carry out their business in the underground economy.

The shift from central planning to a market economy is easier said than done. Simply loosening constraints to create private property may not be enough for successful reform. The development of supporting institutions is essential, but *there is no unified economic theory of how to construct the institutions that are central to the success of capitalism.* Most so-called economists employed in Soviet-type systems did not understand even the basics of how markets work. They had been trained to regard the alleged "anarchy" of the market as a primary defect of capitalism.

A more fundamental problem is that, although Western economic theory focuses on the operation of efficient markets, *even market economists usually do not understand the institutional requirements of efficient markets.* Market economists often take the necessary institutions for granted. Those involved in the transition must develop a deeper appreciation for the institutions that nurture and support impersonal market activity.

So the jury is still out on the transition to markets. Exhibit 5 presents, for some key transitional economies, the GNP per capita in 1997 based on the purchasing power of the domestic currency. Notice the dramatic differences across these economies, with per capita GNP in the Czech Republic more than five times greater than that of the Ukraine. By way of comparison, U.S. GNP per capita in 1997 was $28,740, or about 150 percent above the Czech Republic, the most successful transitional economy.

Lessons about the nature of economic processes will likely emerge from the analysis of these transitional economies. The course of economic reform will provide insights into both the potential and the limits of economics itself.

---

5 As reported by James Meek, "For Youth, Bribery a Matter of 'Maybe' Rather than 'Nyet,'" *Sydney Morning Herald* (21 March 1998).
6 Michael R. Gordon, "Russia's New Enforcer of Taxes Is Taking On a Land of Evaders," *New York Times* (4 July 1998).
7 "Russia's Finance: Taxman in a Tank," *Economist* (13 June 1998): 72.
8 Marshall Goldman, "Russian Tax Evasion Is Source of Pride," letter to the editor, *New York Times* (9 August 1998).

E X H I B I T   5

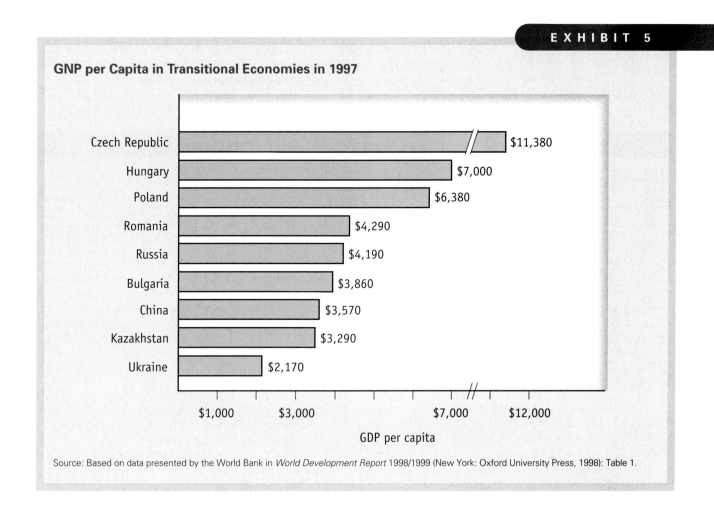

GNP per Capita in Transitional Economies in 1997

Czech Republic — $11,380
Hungary — $7,000
Poland — $6,380
Romania — $4,290
Russia — $4,190
Bulgaria — $3,860
China — $3,570
Kazakhstan — $3,290
Ukraine — $2,170

GDP per capita

Source: Based on data presented by the World Bank in *World Development Report* 1998/1999 (New York: Oxford University Press, 1998): Table 1.

CONCLUSION

Because no single theory of economic development has become widely accepted, this chapter has been more descriptive than theoretical. We can readily define the features that distinguish developing from industrial economies, but we are less sure how to foster growth and development. Economic history is largely a story of economies that have failed to produce a set of economic rules of the game that lead to sustained economic growth.

Perhaps the most elusive ingredients for development are the formal and informal institutions that promote economic activity: the laws, customs, conventions, and other institutional elements that encourage people to undertake productive activity. A stable political environment with well-defined property rights is important. Little private sector investment will occur if potential investors believe their capital might be appropriated by government, destroyed by civil unrest, or stolen by thieves. Education is also key to development, both because of its direct effect on productivity and because those who are more educated tend to be more receptive to new ideas. A physical infrastructure of transportation and communication systems and utilities is needed to link economic participants. And trusted financial institutions help link savers and borrowers. Finally, a country needs entrepreneurs with the vision to move the economy forward. Some newly emerging industrial countries prove that economic development is achievable, though not necessarily easy.

SUMMARY

1. Developing countries are distinguished by low levels of output per capita, poor health and nutrition, high fertility rates, low levels of education, and saving rates that are too low to finance sufficient investment.

2. Worker productivity is low in developing countries because the stocks of physical and human capital are low, technological advances are not widely diffused throughout the economy, natural resources and entrepreneurial ability are scarce, financial markets are not well developed, some talented professionals migrate to high-income countries, formal and informal institutions do not provide sufficient incentives for market activity, and governments may serve the interests of the group in power rather than the public interest.

3. The key to growth and a rising standard of living is increased productivity. To foster productivity, developing nations must stimulate investment, support education and training programs, and provide the infrastructure necessary to promote economic development.

4. Increases in productivity do not occur without prior saving, but most people in developing countries have such low incomes that there is little opportunity to save. Even if some higher-income people have the money to save, financial institutions in developing countries are not well developed, and savings are often sent abroad, where there is a more stable investment climate.

5. Foreign aid has been a mixed blessing for most developing countries. In some cases, that aid has helped countries build the roads, bridges, schools, and other capital infrastructure necessary for development. In other cases, foreign aid has simply increased consumption and insulated government from painful but necessary reforms. Worse still, subsidized food from abroad has undermined domestic agriculture.

6. Major reforms have been introduced in recent years in formerly socialist economies to decentralize decision making, to provide greater production incentives to workers, and to introduce competitive markets. But in many cases, central controls were dismantled before the institutional framework had developed to support a market economy.

QUESTIONS FOR REVIEW

1. *(Worlds Apart)* Compare developing and industrial market economies on the basis of each of the following general economic characteristics, and relate the differences to the process of development:
   a. Diversity of the industrial base
   b. Distribution of resource ownership
   c. Educational level of the labor force

2. *(Developing Countries)* How would you explain why agricultural productivity in developing countries is usually low?

3. *(Classification of Economies)* What are the arguments for using real per capita GNP to compare living standards between countries? What weakness does this measure have?

4. *(Productivity and Development)* Among the problems that hinder growth in developing economies are poor infrastructure, lack of financial institutions and a sound money supply, a low saving rate, poor capital base, and lack of foreign exchange. Explain how these problems are interconnected.

5. *(CaseStudy: Crony Capitalism in Indonesia)* How did President Suharto and his family undermine the economy of Indonesia? Did the Indonesian economy have any special features that made it vulnerable to crony capitalism?

6. *(International Trade and Development)* From the perspective of citizens in a developing country, what are some of the benefits and drawbacks of international trade?

7. *(Foreign Aid and Economic Development)* Foreign aid, if it is to be successful in enhancing economic development, must lead to a more productive economy. Describe some of the problems in achieving such an objective through foreign aid.

8. *(Foreign Aid and Economic Development)* It is widely recognized that foreign aid that promotes productivity in developing economies is superior to merely shipping products like food to these countries. Yet the latter is the approach frequently taken. Why do you think this is the case?

9. *(Types of Economic Systems)* One of the questions every economic system must answer is for whom products are produced. How is the answer determined in a market system? How is it answered in a centrally planned system?

10. *(Transitional Economies)* What special problems are being faced by Eastern European economies as they make the transition from central planning to free markets?

11. *(CaseStudy: Ownership and Resource Use)* In what ways were the incentives of private ownership evident even in the Soviet Union?

12. *(Markets and Institutions)* Why is a system of well-defined and enforceable property rights crucial when a country is converting to a market-based system of resource allocation?

13. *(Big Bang Versus Gradualism)* Explain the difference between the big bang and gradualism approaches to moving from central planning to market coordination.

PROBLEMS AND EXERCISES

14. *(Worlds Apart)* Per capita GNP most recently is about 56 times greater in the richest country on Earth than in the poorest country. Suppose per capita GNP grows an average of 2 percent per year in the richest country and 4 percent per year in the poorest country. Assuming such growth rates continue indefinitely into the future, how many years would it take before the per capita GNP in the poorest country reaches that of the richest country?

15. *(Import Substitution versus Export Promotion)* Using supply and demand curves for a particular good, show why domestic producers who supply a good that competes with imports would prefer an import-substitution approach to trade policy rather than an export-promotion approach. Which policy would domestic consumers prefer and why?

EXPERIENTIAL EXERCISES

16. *(Foreign Aid)* Review the most recent *World Bank News,* a weekly publication of events, activities, and initiatives involving the World Bank at http://www.world.bank.org/html/extdr/extcs/news.html. Review one report specific to a developing country. What is the World Bank doing to help this country? In return for assistance, what has the developing country done, or what does it plan to do?

17. *(Transitional Economies)* The World Bank's *Transition Newsletter* at http://www.worldbank.org/html/prddr/trans/WEB/trans.htm is a good source for the latest information on economies in transition. Review the latest issue of the *Newsletter.* What are some of the special problems currently faced by transitional economies?

18. *(Wall Street Journal)* Go to the Money & Investing section of today's *Wall Street Journal* and find an article relating to a developing or transitional economy. What kinds of changes are described there? What are the implications of those changes for investors in the United States?

Glossary

Glossary

A

Ability-to-pay-tax principle Those with a greater ability to pay should pay more tax

Absolute advantage The ability to produce something using fewer resources than other producers use

Accounting profit A firm's total revenue minus its explicit cost

Adverse selection A situation in which those on the informed side of the market self-select in a way that harms the uninformed side of the market

Agent A person who performs work or provides a service on behalf of another person, the principal

Allocative efficiency The condition that exists when firms produce the output that is most preferred by consumers; the marginal cost of each good just equals the marginal benefit that consumers derive from that good.

Alternative goods Other goods that use some of the same resources as used to produce the good in question

Annuity A given sum of money received each year for a specified number of years

Antitrust activity Government activity aimed at preventing monopoly and fostering competition in markets where competition is desirable

Arbitrageur A person who takes advantage of temporary geographic differences in the exchange rate by simultaneously purchasing a currency in one market and selling it in another market

Association-is-causation fallacy The incorrect idea that if two variables are associated in time, one must necessarily cause the other

Autarky A situation of national self-sufficiency in which there is no economic interaction with foreigners

Average revenue Total revenue divided by output; in all market structures, average revenue equals the market price.

Average total cost Total cost divided by output

Average variable cost Variable cost divided by output

B

Backward-bending supply curve of labor Occurs if the income effect of a higher wage dominates the substitution effect of a higher wage

Balance of payments A record of all economic transactions between residents of one country and residents of the rest of the world during a given time period

Balance on current account The section of a country's balance-of-payments account that measures the sum of the country's net unilateral transfers and its balance on goods and services

Balance on goods and services The section of a country's balance-of-payments account that measures the difference in value between a country's exports of goods and services and its imports of goods and services

Barrier to entry Any impediment that prevents new firms from competing on an equal basis with existing firms in an industry

Barter The direct exchange of one good for another without the use of money

Behavioral assumption An assumption that describes the expected behavior of economic decision makers

Benefits-received tax principle Those who receive more benefits from the government program funded by a tax should pay more tax

Big-bang theory The argument that the transition from a centrally planned to a market economy should be broad and swift, taking place in a matter of months

Binding arbitration Negotiation in which both parties in a union-management dispute agree to accept an impartial observer's resolution of the dispute

Bond A certificate reflecting a firm's promise to pay the holder periodic interest until the date of maturity, then to pay a fixed sum of money on the designated maturity date

Bounded rationality The notion that there is a limit to the amount of information an economic agent, such as a manager, can comprehend

Budget line A line showing all combinations of two goods that can be purchased at given prices with a given amount of income

Bureaus Government agencies charged with implementing legislation and financed by appropriations from legislative bodies

C

Capital All buildings, equipment, and human skill used to produce goods and services

Capital account The record of a country's international transactions involving purchases or sales of financial and real assets

Cartel A group of firms that agree to coordinate their production and pricing decisions to maximize cartel profits, thereby behaving as a monopolist

Change in demand A shift in a given demand curve caused by a change in any of the determinants of demand for the good other than its price

Change in quantity demanded A movement along the demand curve in response to a change in the price, other things constant

Change in quantity supplied A movement along the supply curve in response to a change in the price, other things constant

Change in supply A shift in a given supply curve caused by a change in one of the determinants of the supply of the good other than its price

Circular flow model A diagram that outlines the flow of resources, products, income, and revenue among households, firms, governments, and the rest of the world

Coase theorem a As long as bargaining costs are small, an efficient solution to the problem of externalities will be achieved by assigning property rights.

Collective bargaining The process by which union and management negotiate a labor agreement

Collusion An agreement among firms to divide the market or to fix the market price to maximize economic profit.

Common-pool problem aUnrestricted access to a resource that results in overuse until the marginal value of additional use drops to zero

Comparative advantage The ability to produce something at a lower opportunity cost than other producers face

Competing-interest legislation Legislation that imposes concentrated costs on one group and provides concentrated benefits to another group

Complements Goods that are related in such a way that an increase in the price of one leads to a decrease in the demand for the other

Conglomerate merger A merger involving the combination of firms in different industries

Consent decree A legal agreement through which the accused party, without admitting guilt, agrees to refrain in the future from certain illegal activity if the government drops the charges

Constant elasticity demand curve The type of demand that exists when price elasticity is the same everywhere along the curve; the elasticity value is constant

Constant-cost industry An industry that can expand or contract without affecting the long-run, per-unit cost of production; the long-run industry supply curve is horizontal.

Consumer equilibrium The condition in which an individual consumer's budget is completely spent and the last dollar spent on each good yields the same marginal utility; therefore, utility is maximized

Consumer surplus The difference between the maximum amount that a consumer is willing to pay for a given quantity of a good and what the consumer actually pays

Corporation A legal entity owned by stockholders whose liability is limited to the value of their stock

Craft union A union whose members have a particular skill or work at a particular craft, such as plumbers or carpenters

Cross-price elasticity of demand The percent change in the demand of one good as a result of the percent change in the price of another good

Currency appreciation A decrease in the number of dollars needed to purchase 1 unit of foreign exchange

Currency depreciation An increase in the number of dollars needed to purchase 1 unit of foreign exchange

Currency devaluation An increase in the official pegged price of foreign exchange in terms of the domestic currency

Currency revaluation A reduction in the official pegged price of foreign exchange in terms of the domestic currency

D

Deadweight loss A loss of consumer surplus and producer surplus that is not transferred to anyone else; it can result from monopolization of an industry

Decreasing-cost industry The rare case in which an industry faces lower per-unit production costs as industry output expands in the long run; the long-run industry supply curve slopes downward.

Demand A relation showing the quantities of a good that consumers are willing and able to buy at various prices during a given period of time, other things constant

Demand curve A curve showing the quantities of a particular good demanded at various possible prices during a given time period, other things constant

Demand for loanable funds The relationship between the market interest rate and the quantity of loanable funds demanded, other things constant

Derived demand The demand for a resource derived from the demand for the product the resource produces

Developing countries Nations typified by high rates of illiteracy, high unemployment, high fertility rates, and exports of primary products

Discount rate The interest rate used to convert income to be received in the future into present value

Discounting Determining the present value of income to be received in the future

Diseconomies of scale Forces that cause a firm's average cost to increase as the scale of operation increases in the long run

Disequilibrium A mismatch between quantity supplied and quantity demanded as the market seeks equilibrium

Dividends After-tax corporate profits that are paid to stockholders rather than reinvested in the firm

Division of labor The organization of production of a product into separate tasks in which people specialize

Dumping Selling a commodity abroad at a price that is below its cost of production or below the price charged in the domestic market

Duopoly A market with only two producers, who compete with each other; a type of oligopoly market structure

E

Economic growth A shift outward in the production possibilities frontier; an increase in the economy's ability to produce goods and services

Economic profit A firm's total revenue minus its explicit and implicit costs

Economic regulation Government regulations aimed at controlling prices, output, market entry and exit, and product quality in situations in which, because of economies of scale, average production costs are lowest when the market is served by only one or a few firms

Economic rent The portion of a resource's total earnings above its opportunity cost; earnings above the amount necessary to keep the resource in its present use

Economic system The set of mechanisms and institutions that resolve the what, how, and for whom questions

Economic theory, **economic model** A simplification of reality used to make predictions about the real world

Economics The study of how people use their scarce resources in an attempt to satisfy their unlimited wants

Economies of scale Forces that cause a reduction in a firm's average cost as the scale of operation increases in the long run

Economies of scope Forces that make it cheaper for a firm to produce two or more different products rather than just one

Efficiency The condition that exists when there is no way resources can be reallocated to increase the production of one good without decreasing the production of another

Efficiency wage theory The idea that offering high wages attracts a more talented labor pool, making it easier for firms to hire more productive workers; also a higher wage that encourages those more productive workers to do a good job

Elastic demand The type of demand that exists when a change in price has a relatively large effect on quantity demanded; the percent change in quantity demanded exceeds the percent change in price

Entrepreneur A profit-seeking decision maker who organizes an enterprise and assumes the risk of its operation

Entrepreneurial ability Managerial and organizational skills combined with the willingness to take risks

Equilibrium The condition that exists in a market when the plans of the buyers match the plans of the sellers; the market clears

Excess capacity The difference between the rate of output at a firm's minimum average cost and the profit-maximizing rate of output

Exchange rate The price of one country's currency measured in terms of another country's currency

Exclusive dealing The situation that occurs when a producer prohibits customers from purchasing from other sellers

Exhaustible resource aA resource available in fixed supply, such as crude oil or copper ore

Expansion path A line connecting points of tangency that identify the least-cost input combinations for producing alternative output rates; the expansion path need not be a straight line, though it will generally slope upward

Explicit cost Opportunity cost of a firm's resources that takes the form of cash payments

Export promotion A development strategy that concentrates on producing for the export market

Externality A cost or a benefit that falls on third parties and is therefore ignored by the two parties to the market transaction

F

Fallacy of composition The incorrect belief that what is true for the individual, or part, must necessarily be true for the group, or whole

Featherbedding Union efforts to force employers to hire more workers than demanded for the task

Firms Economic units formed by profit-seeking entrepreneurs who employ resources to produce goods and services for sale

Fiscal policy The use of government purchases, transfer payments, taxes, and borrowing to influence aggregate economic activity

Fixed cost Any production cost that is independent of the firm's rate of output

Fixed exchange rates Rates pegged within a narrow range of values by central banks' ongoing purchases and sales of currencies

Fixed resource Any resource that cannot be varied in the short run

Fixed production technology The relationship between output rate and the generation of an externality is a fixed one; the only way to the reduce the externality is to reduce the output rate

Flexible exchange rates Rates determined by the forces of supply and demand without government intervention

Food stamps An in-kind transfer program that offers low-income households vouchers redeemable for food; benefit levels vary inversely with household income

Foreign aid An international transfer made on especially favorable terms for the purpose of promoting economic development

Foreign exchange Foreign currency needed to carry out international transactions

G

Game theory A model that analyzes oligopolistic behavior as a series of strategic moves and counter-moves by rival firms

GeneralAgreement on Tariffs and Trade (GATT) An international tariff-reduction treaty adopted in 1947 that resulted in a series of negotiated "rounds" aimed at freer trade; the Uruguay Round created GATT's successor, the World Trade Organization (WTO)

Gold standard An arrangement whereby the currencies of most countries are convertible into gold at a fixed rate

Golden rule of profit maximization To maximize profit or minimize loss, a firm should produce at the rate of output at which marginal cost equals marginal revenue; this rule holds for all market structures.

Good A tangible item that is used to satisfy wants

Gradualism A "bottom-up" approach to moving from a centrally planned to a market economy emphasizing established markets at the most decentralized level first, such as on small farms or in light industry

H

Herfindahl index The sum of the squared percentages of market share of all firms in an industry; a measure of the level of market concentration in that industry

Hidden actions A type of asymmetric information when one side of an economic relationship can take a relevant action that the other side cannot observe

Hidden characteristics A type of asymmetric information problem in which one side of the market knows more than the other side about product characteristics that are important to the other side of the market

Horizontal merger A merger in which one firm combines with another firm that produces the same product

Householder The key decision maker in the household

Hypothesis A statement about relationships among key variables

I

Implicit cost A firm's opportunity cost of using its own resources or those provided by its owners without a corresponding cash payment

Import substitution A development strategy that emphasizes domestic manufacturing of products that are currently imported

Income assistance programs Welfare programs that provide money and in-kind assistance to the poor; benefits do not depend on prior contributions

Income effect A fall in the price of a good increases consumers' real income, making the consumers more able to purchase all goods; for normal goods, the quantity demanded increases

Income effect of a wage increase A higher wage increases workers' real income, increasing their demand for all normal goods including leisure, so the quantity of labor supplied decreases

Income elasticity of demand The percent change in demand (at a given price) divided by the percent change in income

Increasing marginal returns Marginal product increases experienced by a firm when another unit of a particular resource is employed, all other resources constant

Increasing-cost industry An industry that faces higher per-unit production costs as industry output expands in the long run; the long-run industry supply curve slopes upward.

Indifference curve A curve showing all combinations of goods that provide the consumer with the same satisfaction, or the same utility

Indifference map A set of indifference curves representing each possible level of total utility that can be derived by a particular consumer from consumption of the two goods

Industrial market countries Economically advanced capitalist countries of Western Europe, North America, Australia, New Zealand, and Japan; also known as developed countries

Industrial Revolution Development of large-scale factory production that began in Great Britain around 1750 and spread to the rest of Europe, North America, and Australia

Industrial union A union of both skilled and unskilled workers from a particular industry, such as auto workers or steelworkers

Inelastic demand The type of demand that exists when a change in price has relatively little effect on quantity demanded; the percent change in quantity demanded is smaller than the percent change in price

Inferior good A good for which demand decreases as consumer incomes rise

Initial public offering (IPO) The initial sale of stock to the public

Innovation The process of turning an invention into a marketable product

Interest rate Interest per year as a percentage of the amount loaned, or as a percentage of the amount saved

Interest The dollar amount paid by borrowers to lenders to forgo present consumption; the payment resource owners receive for the use of their capital

Interlocking directorate An arrangement whereby one individual serves on the boards of directors of competing firms

International Monetary Fund (IMF) An international organization that establishes rules for maintaining the international monetary system and makes loans to countries with temporary balance of payments problem.

Isocost line Line identifying all combinations of capital and labor the firm can hire for a given total cost

Isoquant A curve that shows all the technologically efficient combinations of two resources, such as labor and capital, that produce a certain amount of output

K

Kinked demand curve A demand curve that illustrates price stickiness; if one firm cuts its prices, other firms in the industry will cut theirs as well, but if the firm raises its prices, other firms will not change theirs.

L

Labor The physical and mental effort of humans used to produce goods and services

Labor union A group of employees who join together to improve their terms of employment

Land Plots of ground and other natural resources used to produce goods and services

Law of comparative advantage The individual, firm, region, or country with the lowest opportunity cost of producing a particular good should specialize in producing that good.

Law of demand The quantity of a good demanded during a given time period is inversely related to its price, other things constant

Law of diminishing marginal rate of substitution The amount of good A a consumer is willing to give up to get one more unit of good B declines as the consumption of B increases.

Law of diminishing marginal returns As more and more of a variable resource is added to a given amount of a fixed resource, the resulting change in output will eventually diminish and could become negative

Law of diminishing marginal utility The more of a good consumed per period, the smaller the increase in total utility from consuming one more unit, other things constant

Law of increasing opportunity cost To produce each additional increment of a particular good, a successively larger increment of an alternative good must be sacrificed if the economy's resources are already being used efficiently

Law of supply The quantity of a product supplied in a given time period is usually directly related to its price, other things constant

Leisure Time spent on nonwork activities

Linear demand curve A straight-line demand curve; such a demand curve has a constant slope.

Loanable funds market The market in which savers (suppliers of funds) and borrowers (demanders of funds) come together to determine the market rate of interest

Long run A period during which all resources under the firm's control are variable

Long-run average cost curve A curve that indicates the lowest average cost of production at each rate of output when the firm's size is allowed to vary; also called the planning curve and the envelope curve

Long-run industry supply curve A curve that shows the relationship between price and quantity supplied by the industry once firms fully adjust to any change in market demand

M

Macroeconomics The study of the economic behavior of entire economies

Managed float system An exchange rate system that combines features of freely floating rates with intervention by central banks

Marginal cost The change in total cost resulting from a one-unit change in output; the change in total cost divided by the change in output

Marginal product The change in total product that occurs when the use of a particular resource increases by one unit, all other resources constant

Marginal rate of return on investment The marginal revenue product of capital expressed as a percentage of its marginal cost

Marginal rate of substitution (MRS) A measure of how much of one good a consumer would give up to get one more unit of another good, while remaining equally satisfied

Marginal rate of technical substitution (MRTS) The rate at which one resource, such as labor, can be substituted for another, such as capital, without affecting total output

Marginal resource cost The change in total cost when an additional unit of a resource is hired, other things constant

Marginal revenue The change in total revenue resulting from a one-unit change in sales; in perfect competition, marginal revenue equals the market price.

Marginal revenue product The change in total revenue when an additional unit of a resource is hired, other things constant

Marginal social benefit aThe sum of the marginal private benefit and the marginal external benefit of production or consumption

Marginal social cost aThe sum of the marginal private cost and the marginal external cost of production or consumption

Marginal tax rate The percentage of each additional dollar of income that goes to taxes

Marginal utility The change in total utility derived from a one-unit change in consumption of a good

Marginal valuation The dollar value of the marginal utility derived from consuming each additional unit of a good

Marginal A term meaning incremental, additional, or extra; used to describe the result of a change in an economic variable

Market A set of arrangements through which buyers and sellers carry out exchange at mutually agreeable terms

Market failure A condition that arises when unrestrained operation of markets yields socially undesirable results

Market power The ability of one or a few firms to maintain a price above the competitive level

Market structure Important features of a market, such as the number of firms, uniformity of product among firms, ease of entry and exit, and forms of competition

Market work Time sold as labor in return for a money wage

Means-tested program To be eligible for such a program, an individual's income and/or assets must not exceed specified levels

Median income The middle income in a series of incomes ranked from smallest to largest

Median voter model Under certain conditions, the preference of the median, or middle, voter will dominate other public choices

Mediator An impartial observer who helps resolve differences between union and management

Medicaid In-kind transfer program that provides medical care for poor people; by far the most costly welfare program

Medicare Social insurance program providing health insurance for short-term medical care to older Americans regardless of income

Merchandise trade balance The value of a country's exported goods minus the value of its imported goods during a given time period

Microeconomics The study of the economic behavior in particular markets, such as the market for computers or for unskilled labor

Minimum efficient scale The lowest rate of output at which a firm takes full advantage of economies of scale

Mixed system An economic system characterized by private ownership of some resources and public ownership of other resources; some markets are unregulated and others are regulated.

Monetary policy Regulation of the money supply in order to influence aggregate economic activity

Monopolistic competition A market structure characterized by a large number of firms selling products that are close substitutes, yet different enough that each firm's demand curve slopes downward

Monopoly A sole producer of a product for which there are no close substitutes

Moral hazard A situation in which one party to a contract has an incentive after the contract is made to alter behavior in a way that harms the other party to the contract

N

Natural monopoly One firm that can serve the entire market at a lower per-unit cost than can two or more firms

Net unilateral transfers The unilateral transfers (gifts and grants) received from abroad by residents of a country minus the unilateral transfers residents send abroad

Nonmarket work Time spent producing goods and services in the home or acquiring an education

Normal good A good for which demand increases as consumer incomes rise

Normal profit The accounting profit required to persuade a firm's owners to employ their resources in the firm; the accounting profit earned when all resources used by the firm earn their opportunity cost

Normative economic statement A statement that represents an opinion, which cannot be proved or disproved

O

Official reserve transactions account The section of a country's balance-of-payments account that reflects the flow of gold, Special Drawing Rights, and currencies among central banks

Oligopoly A market structure characterized by a small number of firms whose behavior is interdependent

Open-access good A good that is rival but nonexclusive, such as fish in the sea

Opportunity cost The value of the best alternative forgone when an item or activity is chosen

Other-things-constant assumption The assumption, when focusing on key economic variables, that other variables remain unchanged

Outsourcing A firm sticks to its core competency, while buying inputs such as auto parts from outside suppliers

P

Partnership A firm with multiple owners who share the firm's profits and each of whom bears unlimited liability for the firm's debts

Patent A legal barrier to entry that conveys to its holder the exclusive right to supply a product for a certain period of time

Payoff matrix In game theory, a table listing the payoffs that each player can expect based on the strategy that each player pursues

Per se illegal A category of illegality in antitrust law, applied to business practices that are deemed illegal regardless of their economic rationale or their consequences

Perfect competition A market structure in which there are large numbers of fully informed buyers and sellers of a homogeneous product, with no obstacles to entry or exit of firms in the long run

Perfectly discriminating monopolist A monopolist who charges a different price for each unit of a good

Perfectly elastic demand curve A horizontal line reflecting a situation in which any price increase reduces quantity demanded to zero; the elasticity value is minus infinity

Perfectly elastic supply curve A horizontal line reflecting a situation in which any price decrease reduces the quantity supplied to zero; the elasticity value is infinity

Perfectly inelastic demand curve A vertical line reflecting a situation in which a price change has no effect on the quantity demanded; the elasticity value is zero

Perfectly inelastic supply curve A vertical line reflecting a situation in which a price change has no effect on the quantity supplied; the elasticity value is zero

Portfolio An collection of stocks, bonds, and other financial assets.

Positive economic statement A statement that can be proved or disproved by reference to facts

Positive rate of time preference A characteristic of consumers, who value present consumption more highly than future consumption

Predatory pricing Pricing tactics employed by a dominant firm to drive competitors out of business, such as temporarily selling below cost or dropping the price only in certain markets

Present value The value today of income or an income stream to be received in the future

Price ceiling A maximum legal price above which a good or service cannot be sold; to be effective, a price ceiling must be set below the equilibrium price

Price discrimination Increasing profit by selling the same good for different prices to different consumers for reasons unrelated to cost

Price elasticity formula Percent change in quantity divided by the percent change in price; the average quantity and the average price are used as bases for computing percent changes in quantity and in price

Price elasticity of demand A measure of the responsiveness of quantity demanded to a price change; the percent change in quantity demanded divided by the percent change in price

Price elasticity of supply A measure of the responsiveness of quantity supplied to a price change; the percent change in quantity supplied divided by the percent change in price

Price floor A minimum legal price below which a good or service cannot be sold; to be effective, a price floor must be set above the equilibrium price

Price leader A firm whose price is adopted by the rest of the industry

Price searcher A firm that has some control over the price it charges because its demand curve slopes downward

Price taker A firm that faces a given market price and whose actions have no effect on that market price

Principal A person who enters into a contractual agreement with an agent in the expectation that the agent will act on behalf of the principal

Principal-agent problem A situation in which the agent's objectives differ from those of the principal's objectives and the agent can pursue hidden actions

Private property rights aThe right of an owner to use, rent, or sell, property

Privatization The process of turning public enterprises into private enterprises

Producer surplus The amount by which total revenue from production exceeds total variable cost

Product market A market in which goods and services are bought and sold

Production possibilities frontier (PPF) A curve showing alternative combinations of goods that can be produced when available resources are used efficiently

Productive efficiency The condition that exists when output is produced with the least-cost combination of inputs, given the level of technology

Profit The payment resource owners receive for their entrepreneurial ability; the total revenue from sales minus the total cost of resources employed by the entrepreneur

Progressive taxation The tax as a percentage of income increases as income increases.

Proportional taxation The tax as a percentage of income remains constant as income increases; also called a flat-rate tax

Public good A good that, once produced, is available for all to consume, regardless of who pays and who does not

Purchasing power parity (PPP) theory The theory that exchange rates between two countries will adjust in the long run to reflect price level differences between the countries

Pure command system An economic system characterized by public ownership of resources and centralized economic planning

Pure market system An economic system characterized by private ownership of resources and the use of prices to coordinate economic activity in unregulated markets

Q

Quasi-public good A good that is nonrival but exclusive, such as cable TV

Quota A legal limit on the quantity of a particular product that can be imported or exported

R

Rational ignorance A stance adopted by voters when they find that the cost of understanding and voting on a particular issue exceeds the benefit expected from doing so

Real income Income measured in terms of the goods and services it can buy

Recycling The process of converting waste products into reusable material

Regressive taxation The tax as a percentage of income decreases as income increases

Relevant resources Resources used to produce the good in question

Renewable resource aA resource that can regenerate itself and so can be used periodically for an indefinite period of time if used conservatively, such as a properly managed forest

Rent The payment resource owners receive for the use of their land

Rent seeking Activities undertaken by individuals or firms to influence public policy in a way that will directly or indirectly redistribute income to them

Resource market A market in which resources are bought and sold

Resources The inputs, or factors of production, used to produce the goods and services that humans want; resources consist of labor, capital, land, and entrepreneurial ability

Retained earnings After-tax corporate profits that are reinvested in the firm rather than paid to stockholders as dividends

Rule of reason A principle used by a court to examine the reasons for certain business practices and their effects on competition before ruling on their legality

S

Scarcity When the amount people desire exceeds the amount available at a zero price

Screening The process used by employers to select the most qualified workers based on readily observable characteristics, such as level of education and course grades

Secondary effects Unintended consequences of economic actions that develop slowly over time as people react to events

Separation of ownership from control The situation that exists when no single stockholder or unified group of stockholders owns enough shares to control the management of a corporation

Service An activity that is used to satisfy wants

Short-run firm supply curve A curve that indicates the quantity a firm supplies at each price in the short run; that portion of a firm's marginal cost curve that intersects and rises above the low point on its average variable cost curve

Short-run industry supply curve A curve that indicates the quantity supplied by the industry at each price in the short run; the horizontal sum of each firm's short-run supply curve

Shortage An excess of quantity demanded compared to quantity supplied at a given price; a shortage puts upward pressure on price

Signaling Using a proxy measure to communicate information about unobservable characteristics; the signal is more effective if more productive workers find it easier to send the signal than do less productive workers.

Social insurance programs Programs that replace lost income of those who contributed to the programs while working but who are now retired, temporarily unemployed, or unable to work because of total disability or work-related injury

Social regulation Government regulations aimed at improving health and safety

Social Security By far the largest social insurance program; supplements retirement income to those with a record of contributing to the program during their working years

Soft budget constraint The budget condition faced by socialist enterprises that are subsidized if they lose money

Sole proprietorship A firm with a single owner who has the right to all profits and who bears unlimited liability for the firm's debts

Special-interest legislation Legislation that generates concentrated benefits but imposes widespread costs

Specialization of labor Focusing an individual's efforts on a particular product or a single task

Speculator A person who buys or sells foreign exchange in hopes of profiting from fluctuations in the exchange rate over time

Stock A certificate reflecting part ownership of a corporation

Strategy In game theory, the operational plan pursued by a player; for example, one strategy is to avoid the worst outcome

Strike A union's attempt to withhold labor from a firm

Substitutes Goods Goods that are related in such a way that an increase in the price of one leads to an increase in the demand for the other

Substitution effect of a wage increase When the wage increases, workers substitute market work for other activities, which now have a higher opportunity cost

Substitution effect When the price of a good falls, consumers will substitute that good for other goods, which are now relatively more expensive

Sunk Cost A cost that has already been incurred in the past and, hence, a cost that is irrelevant to present and future economic decisions

Supplemental Security Income (SSI) An income assistance program that provides cash transfer payments to the elderly poor and the disabled; a uniform federal payment is supplemented by transfers that vary across states

Supply A relation showing the quantities of a good producers are willing and able to sell at various prices during a given time period, other things constant

Supply curve A curve showing the quantities of a good supplied at various prices, other things constant

Supply of loanable funds The relationship between the market interest rate and the quantity of loanable funds supplied to the economy, other things constant

Surplus An excess of quantity supplied compared to quantity demanded at a given price; a surplus puts downward pressure on the price

T

Tariff A tax on imports or exports

Tastes A consumer's preferences for different goods and services

Tax incidence The distribution of tax burden among taxpayers

Technologically efficient Produces the maximum possible output given the combination of resources employed; that same output could not be produced with fewer resources.

Temporary Assistance for Needy Families (TANF) An income assistance program run by the states that provides cash transfer payments to poor families with dependent children

Term structure of interest rates The relationship between the duration of a loan and the interest rate charged

Terms of trade How much of one good exchanges for a unit of another good

Total cost The sum of fixed cost and variable cost; the opportunity cost of all resources employed by the firm

Total product The total output produced by a firm

Total revenue Price multiplied by the quantity sold at that price

Total utility The total satisfaction a consumer derives from consumption; it could refer either to the total utility of consuming a particular good or the total utility from all consumption

Transaction costs The costs of time and information required to carry out market exchange

Transfer payments Cash or in-kind benefits given to individuals as outright grants from the government

Transparent finances A firm's financial records that clearly indicate the economic health of the company

Tying contract An arrangement in which a seller of one good requires buyers to purchase other goods as well

U

U.S. official poverty level Benchmark level of income computed by the federal government to track poverty over time; based on three times the cost of a nutritionally adequate diet

Underground economy An expression used to describe all market exchange that does unreported either because it is illegal or because those involved want to evade taxes

Unit-elastic demand The type of demand that exists when a given percent change in price causes an equal (but of opposite sign) percent change in quantity demanded; the elasticity value is −1.0

Unit-elastic supply curve A percent change in price causes an identical percent change in quantity supplied; depicted by a supply curve that is a straight line through the origin; the elasticity value is 1.0

Utility The satisfaction received from consumption; satisfaction, sense of well-being

V

Variable A measure, such as price or quantity, that can take on different possible values

Variable cost Any production cost that changes as output changes

Variable resource Any resource that can be varied in the short run to increase or decrease the rate of output

Variable technology The amount of externality generated at a given rate of output can be reduced by altering the production process rather than by simply reducing the rate of output.

Vertical integration The expansion of a firm into stages of production earlier or later than those in which it has specialized, such as a steel producer that buys a coal mine

Vertical merger A merger in which one firm combines with another from which it purchases inputs or to which it sells output

W

Wages The payment resource owners receive for their labor

Winner's curse The plight of the winning bidder for an asset of uncertain value who has overestimated the asset's true value

World price The price at which a good is traded internationally; determined by the world supply and demand for the good

World Trade Organization (WTO) The legal and institutional foundation of the multilateral trading system that succeeded GATT in 1995

Index

Note: The letter *d* after an entry indicates marginal *definition; e* indicates *exhibit; i* indicates *Internet address.*

A

Ability, and labor supply, 274
Ability-to-pay tax principle, 80*d*
Absolute advantage, 30*d*, 30–31
Accounting profit, 142*d*
Acid Rain program (EPA), 374*i*
Adverse selection, 320*d*
AFDC. *See* Aid for Families with Dependent Children
Affirmative Action
  and poverty, 407–408
AFL-CIO, 27*i*, 28*i*
Age, and labor supply, 273–274, 274*e*
Agent, 320*d*
Agricultural Marketing Agreement Act (1937), 359
AID. *See* United States Agency for International Development
Aid for Families with Dependent Children (AFDC), 401, 410
Airline Deregulation Act (1978), 335
Airline industry, 227
  Case Study: *Airline Regulation and Deregulation,* 334–336
  Case Study: *The Unfriendly Skies,* 227–228
  competition, 336
  deregulation, 335
Airline Pilots' Association, 334*i*, 335
Air pollution, 384–385
Air Transport Association, 227*i*
Allocative efficiency, 188*d*
Alternative goods, 55*d*
Amazon Books, 315*i*
AMC Theatres, 155*i*
American Institute of Architects, 257*i*
American Prospect, 276*i*, 286*i*
American Trial Lawyers Association, 363
Annuity, 299*d*
  present value of, 299–300
Antidumping
  and international trade, 434
Antitrust activity, 330*d*
  abuse of, 346
  Case Study: *Windows 98 Sold With Microsoft Browser,* 346–347
  competitive model, emphasis on, 345
  and international markets, 346
  and law enforcement, 338–339
  legislation, problems with, 345–346
  mergers
    movements, 340–342, 341*e*
    and public policy, 339–340, 340*e*
  origins of policy, 337–338
  per-se illegality and the rule of reason, 339
Antitrust issues, 337*i*
Appreciation
  currency, 448*d*
Arbitrageur, 451*d*
Arbitration, binding, 277*d*
Arrow, Kenneth, 327*i*
Asia
  Case Study: *The Asia Contagion,* 458–459
  financial crisis information, 461*i*
Association-is-causation fallacy, 11*d*
Asymmetric information, 319*d*
  adverse selection of, 319–320, 322–323
  Case Study: *The Reputation of a Big Mac,* 324
  coping with, 321–322
  in insurance markets, 321
  in labor markets, 322–324
  principal-agent problem, 320–321
  signaling, and screening, 323–324
Autarky, 420*d*
Automobile industry
  Case Study: *Wheel of Fortune,* 83–84
Average revenue, 172*d*
Average total cost, 149–150, 150*d*, 150*e*
  and marginal cost, 150–151, 151*e*
Average variable cost, 149–150, 150*d*, 150*e*

B

Backward-bending supply curve of labor, 270*d*
Balance on current account, 445*d*
Balance on goods and services, 443*d*, 443–444
Balance of payments, 83*d*
  international transactions and, 442, 447*e*
Bank of Sweden, 17*i*
Banking
  in developing countries, 470
Bargaining
  collective, 277*d*
  pattern, 284
Barriers to entry, 197*d*, 197–200
  monopolies
    control of essential resources, 199–200

  Case Study: *Are Diamonds Forever?,* 199–200
    economies of scale, 198, 198*e*
    legal restrictions, 197–198
Barter, 31*d*
BEA. *See* Bureau of Economic Analysis
Behavioral assumption, 8*d*, 10–11
Benefits-received tax principle, 81*d*
Big-bang theory, 480*d*
Binding arbitration, 277*d*
Blockbuster Video, 224*i*
  Case Study: *Fast Forward,* 224
BLS. *See* Bureau of Labor Statistics
Bonds, 302*d*
Bounded rationality, 312*d*
Bretton Woods system, 456–457
Brooking Institution, 363*i*, 458*i*
Buchanan, James, 352*i*
Budget line, 135–136, 135*e*
Bureaucratic objectives, and democracy, 367
Bureaus, 365*d*
Bureau of Economic Analysis (BEA), 443*i*
Bureau of Labor Statistics (BLS), 17*i*
  Occupational Outlook Handbook, 257*i*, 264*i*
Business
  government regulation of, 329–330
Business Week, 297*i*

C

CAB. *See* Civil Aeronautics Board
Caltech's Laboratory for Experimental Economics and Political Science, 190*i*
Capital, 3*d*
  infrastructure, in developing countries, 471
Capital account, 445*d*, 445
Capital gain, 76
Capital goods, 37*e*
Capture theory, 334
Cartel, 230*d*, 230–232, 231*e*
  and cheating, 232
Cash transfer(s), 71
Caterpillar, 284, 284*i*
  Case Study: *Hardball for Caterpillar,* 284
The Cato Institute, 352*i*
Celler-Kefauver Anti-Merger Act (1950), 338
Center for International Comparisons at the University of Pennsylvania, 40*i*

Center for Research on Contracts and the Structure of Enterprise at the University of Pittsburgh, 88*i*

Chamberlin, Edward, 219

Change in demand, 52*d*

Change in quantity demanded, 52*d*

Change in quantity supplied, 56*d*

Change in supply, 56*d*

Cheating
  and cartels, 232

Chrysler Corporation
  Case Study: *Wheel of Fortune,* 83–84

Cimini, Michael, 284

Circular flow model, 84*d*
  flow between households and firms, 84–85, 85*e*
  government-related flows, 86
  international, 86

Civil Aeronautics Board (CAB), 334–336

Civil Rights Act (1964), 407

Clayton Act (1914), 338

Clean Air Act (1970), 384–385

Clean Water Act (1972), 384

Clinton, William Jefferson (Bill), 259

Coase, Ronald, 309–310, 325, 381

Coase theorem, 381*d*
  analysis of externalities, 380–381
  COLLEGE CHOICE program, 26*i*
  College
  costs
    Case Study: *The Opportunity Cost of College,* 26–27
  major, median annual earnings, 13*e*

Collusion, 230*d*
  and oligopoly, 230–232, 231*e*

Command system, pure, 41, 41*d*

Common Cause, 363*i*

Common markets, 432–433

Common-pool problem, 372*d*
  externalities, 372–374
  renewable resources, 372–373
  solutions to, 373–374

Comparative advantage, 30*d,* 30–31, 31*e*

Compensation and Working Conditions, 284*i*

Competing–interest legislation, 358*d*

Competition, 77
  market. *See* Market competition
  perfect. *See* Perfect competition

Complements, 51*d*

Comprehensive Environmental Response, Compensation, and Liability Act (1980) (Superfund Law), 384, 387

Conglomerate merger, 341*d*

Consent decree, 338*d*

Constant-cost industry, 184*d,* 184–185

Constant-elasticity demand, 95–96, 96*e,* 97*e*

Constant-elasticity demand curve, 96*d*

Consumer equilibrium, 119*d*
  at the tangency, 136–137, 136*e*

Consumer goods, 37*e*

Consumer income, 49–50, 50*e*
  changes in consumer tastes, 51
  changes in expectations, 51
  composition changes, 51

Consumer spending
  budget and, 98–99, 99*e*

Consumer surplus, 123–124, 124*d*
  Case Study: *The Marginal Value of Free Medical Care,* 126–127
  and international trade, 424–425, 425*e*
  and market demand, 125–126, 125*e,* 126*e*

Consumption
  and international trade, 421–423, 422*e*
  and time, 289–297, 292*e,* 295*e*

Copyright system, 296–297

Corporate finance
  bonds, 302
  securities exchanges, 302–303
  stock and retained earnings, 301–302

Corporate ownership and control
  managerial behavior of, 303–304
  managerial discretion, constraints on, 304–305
    economics of natural selection, 304
    incentives, 304–305
    institutional investors, 305
    stockholder voting, 305

Corporation, 75*d,* 77*e*

Cost(s)
  average total, 149–150, 150*d,* 150*e*
    and marginal, 150–151, 151*e*
  average variable, 149–150, 150*d,* 150*e*
  distribution of, 358–359
  explicit, 141*d,* 141–142
  fixed, 146*d,* 146–147
    and loss minimization, 173, 174*e*
  implicit, 141*d,* 141–142
  law of increasing opportunity, 36*d*
  in the long run, 152–157
  long–run average, 152–154, 152*e,* 153*d,* 153*e,* 156, 156*e*
  opportunity, 26*d,* 26–29
    Case Study: *The Opportunity Cost of College,* 26–27
  and production, 161–165
  profit and, 141–143, 142*e*
  in the short run, 146–152, 147*e,* 149*e,* 150*e,* 151*e*
  sunk, 29, 29*d*
  total, 147*d*

average total, 149–150, 150*d,* 150*e*
  and marginal, 150–151, 151*e*
  in the short run, 147, 147*d*
  transaction, 56*d,* 74, 309–310
  variable, 147, 147*d*
    average, 149–150, 150*d,* 150*e*

Craft union, 277*d,* 280–281, 280*e*

Cross-price elasticity of demand, 109*d*
  complements, 109–110
  substitutes, 109

Currency appreciation, 448*d*

Currency depreciation, 448*d*

Currency devaluation, 455*d*

Currency revaluation, 455*d*

Current Population Survey, 400*i*

D

Deadweight loss, 209*d*

DeBeers Consolidated Mines, 199*i,* 200*i*
  Case Study: *Are Diamonds Forever?,* 199–200

Decreasing-cost industry, 187*d,* 187–188

Deere & Co., 284

Demand, 46*d*
  changes in, 49–50, 52*d*
    long-run adjustment to, 181–184, 182*e,* 183*e*
  cross-price elasticity of, 109*d*
    complements, 109–110
    substitutes, 109
  derived, 244*d,* 244–245
    Case Study: *The Derived Demand for Architects,* 257
  elastic, 92*d. See also* Cross-price elasticity of demand; Income elasticity of demand; Price elasticity of demand
  income, 106
  income elasticity of, 105–107, 105*d*
    Case Study: *The Market for Food and "The Food Problem,"* 107–109, 107*e,* 108*e*
  inelastic, 92*d*
  market
    and consumer surplus, 125–126, 125*e,* 126*e*
    and resources, 244–245, 245*e*
  and perfect competition, 168–169, 168*e*
  and time, 127–128
  unit-elastic, 96*d*
  law of, 46–47, 46*d*

Demand curve, 47–49, 48*d,* 48*e*
  constant-elasticity demand curve, 96*d*
  kinked, 235*d*
    and marginal revenue, 236, 236*e*
    model of, 235*d*

and oligopoly, 234–237
  price rigidity of, 236–237, 236*e*
linear, 93*d,* 93–95, 94*e*
perfectly elastic, 95*d*
perfectly inelastic, 95–96, 96*d*
price elasticity of. *See* Price elasticity of
  demand
Demand for loanable funds, 294*d*
Demand schedule, 47–49, 48*e*
Democracy
  bureaucratic objectives, 367
  ownership and funding of bureaus,
    365–366
  ownership and organizational behavior,
    366–367
  private versus public production, 367–368
  representative, 365–368
Department of Labor, U.S., 68*i*
Depreciation
  currency, 448*d*
Derived demand, 244*d,* 244–245
  Case Study: *The Derived Demand for
    Architects,* 257
Devaluation
  currency, 455*d*
Developing countries, 463*d. See also* Transi-
    tional economies
  capital infrastructure in, 471
  economic development in, 471–472,
    479–480
  education in, 469
  entrepreneurial ability of, 471
  financial institutions in, 470
  foreign aid in, 475–476
  government monopolies in, 471–472
    Case Study: *Crony Capitalism in Indone-
      sia—All in the Family,* 471–472
  gross national product and, 464, 464*e,*
    465*e*
  health in, 464–468
    birth rates, 467–468, 467*e*
    infant mortality, 465–466, 466*e*
    malnutrition, 466–467
  international trade and, 472–474
    imports versus exports, 473–474
  migration, 474
  natural resources in, 470
  productivity in, 468–469
  technology in, 469
  trade and, 474
  underemployment in, 469–470
  women in, 468
Development. *See* Economic development
Development Economic Research Group
  (World Bank), 468*i*

Discounting, 298*d*
  present value of, 297–300
    Case Study: *The Million-Dollar Lottery,*
      300–301
Discount rate, 298*d*
Discrepancy account
  statistical, 445–446
Diseconomies of scale, 154–155, 154*d*
  Case Study: *At the Movies,* 155
  Case Study: *Billions and Billions of Burgers,*
    156–157
  at the firm level, 156, 156*e*
  long-run average cost curve, 156, 156*e*
Disequilibrium, 63*d,* 63–65
  Case Study: *Toys Are Serious Business,*
    65–66
Dividends, 302*d*
Division of labor, 32*d*
Dumping, 431*d,* 434
Duopoly, 233, 233*d. See also* Oligopoly

E

Earnings
  median annual, 13*e*
  resource, distribution of, 260–261,
    261*e*
  retained, 302*d*
eBay, 180*i*
EconEd (Economics America), 195*i*
Economic analysis
  as art, 5–7
  Case Study: *College Major and Career
    Earnings,* 12–14
  Case Study: *A Yen for Vending Machines,*
    9–10
  marginal, 6
  normative, 7
  pitfalls of faulty, 11
  positive, 7
  resources, 2–5
  as science, 7–14
  theory, 8
Economic choice, 6
Economic decision makers, 4
Economic development
  in developing countries, 471–472,
    479–482
  and transitional econmies, 471–472,
    479–482
Economic growth, 36–38, 36*d,* 37*e*
Economic model, 7*d*
Economic Policy Institute, 259*i*
Economic Policy Network, 370*i*
Economic profit, 143*d. See also* Profit
  maximization

  in the long run, 180–181, 181*e*
  in the short run, 172
Economic regulation, 329*d*
  alternative theories of, 333–337
  Case Study: *Airline Regulation and Deregu-
    lation,* 334–336
Economic Report of the President, 44*i,* 78*i*
Economics, 2*d*
  natural selection of, 304
Economics America, 195*i*
The Economics of Imperfect Competition (Joan
  Robinson), 219
Economics Research Service (USDA), 107*i*
Economic rent, 248*d*
  as earnings, 248–249
  and opportunity cost, 248–251, 250*e*
Economic system, 39*d*
  types of, 39–42
Economic theory, 7*d*
Economies of scale, 154, 154*d*
  and barriers to enter monopolies, 198,
    198*e*
  Case Study: *At the Movies,* 155
  Case Study: *Billions and Billions of Burgers,*
    156–157
  and international trade, 423–424
  and oligopolies, 228, 229*e*
Economies of scope, 315*d*
The Economist, 307*i*
  "Ten Years of the Big Mac Index," 453*i*
Economy
  competitive trends in the United States,
    342–346
    Case Study: *Windows 98 Sold With Mi-
      crosoft Browser,* 346–347
  underground, 364–365, 365*d*
Education
  in developing countries, 469
  and the environment, 390*e*
  and labor supply, 273–274, 274*e*
EEOC. *See* Equal Employment Opportunity
  Commission
Efficiency, 34*d*
  allocative, 188*d*
  and perfect competition, 188–190, 189*e*
    Case Study: *Experimental Economics,*
      190–191
  productive, 188
Elastic demand, 92*d*
Electronic Policy Network, 363*i*
Employment Policies Institute, 259*i*
EmuNet, 461*i*
Entrepreneur, 303*d*
Entrepreneurial ability, 3*d*
  in developing countries, 471

Environment. *See also* Pollution
Case Study: *City in the Clouds,* 385–386
and education, 390*e*
and positive externalities, 389–391
protection of, 384–389
Environmental Protection Agency (EPA), 384, 387
Acid Rain program, 374*i*
New Directions, 374*i*
EPA. *See* Environmental Protection Agency
Equal Employment Opportunity Commission (EEOC), 407–408
Equilibrium, 56–58, 57*e*, 58*d*
consumer, 119*d*
at the tangency, 136–137, 136*e*
firm supply and industry, 177–179, 178*e*
market, 56–58, 57*e*, 168*e*
Euroland, 448–449
Excess capacity, 226*d*
Exchange
foreign. *See* Foreign exchange
medium. *See* Medium of exchange
specialization and, 31–32
Exchange rate, 447*i*. *See also* Foreign exchange
determining, 450–451, 451*e*
fixed, 455*d*
flexible, 455*d*
Excite, 74*i*, 180*i*
Exclusive dealing, 338*d*
Exhaustible resource, 372*d*
Expansion
path of, 164–165, 165*e*
Expenditure(s)
circular flow model, between households and firms, 84–85, 85*e*
Experience, and labor supply, 273–274
Explicit cost, 141*d*, 141–142
Exports. *See also* Imports; International trade
profile of, 418–419
Export promotion, 473*d*
Externality, 78*d*

F

FAA. *See* Federal Aviation Administration
Fallacy of composition, 11*d*
Family Assistance Grant, 410
Farming
Case Study: *The Market for Food and "The Food Problem,"* 107–109, 107*e*, 108*e*
Internet access to, 112*i*
Featherbedding, 281*i*, 281–282
Federal Agriculture Improvement and Reform Act (1966), 359*i*

Federal Aviation Administration (FAA), 335
Federal Reserve Bank of Boston, 132*i*, 241*i*, 307*i*
Federal Reserve Bank of Minneapolis, 12*i*
Federal Trade Commission (FTC)
mergers, guidelines for, 350*i*
Federal Trade Commission Act (1914), 338
Fields, Bill, 224
Firm(s), 73*d*, 77*e*
bounds of, 310–315
and managers, 311–312
minimum efficient scale of, 312, 313*e*
quality of, 312
and suppliers, 313–314
Case Study: *The Trend Toward Outsourcing,* 314–315
circular flow model, between households and firms, 84–85, 85*e*
diseconomies of scale in, 156, 156*e*
economies of scope, 315
equilibrium, firm supply and industry, 177–179, 178*e*
evolution, 72–76
household production
Case Study: *The Electronic Cottage,* 74–75
rationale for existence of, 309–316
and resource demand for, 251–252, 251*e*
and short-run supply curves, 176–179, 177*e*, 178*e*
transaction costs of, 309–310
types of, 75–76
Fiscal policy, 79*d*
Fixed cost, 146*d*, 146–147
and loss minimization, 173, 174*e*
Fixed exchange rates, 455*d*
Fixed-production technology, 375
Fixed resource, 143*d*, 143–144
Flexible exchange rates, 455*d*
Float system
managed, 457*d*
Food stamps, 71, 402*i*
Forbes, 275*i*
Ford Motor Company
Case Study: *Wheel of Fortune,* 83–84
Foreign aid, 475*d*
in developing countries, 475–476
Foreign exchange, 83*d*. *See also* Exchange rate
demand for, 448–449, 449*e*
markets, 83
purchasing power of, 452
Case Study: *The Big Mac Price Index,* 453, 454*e*

rates, 447–455
determining, 450–451, 451*e*
supply of, 449–450
FORTUNE, 224*i*, 244*i*
Freedom to Innovate (Microsoft) Web site, 346*i*
"Free Trade or Fair Trade" (Thomas Klitgaard and Karen Schiele), 440*i*
FTC. *See* Federal Trade Commission

G

Game theory, 233*d*. *See also* Duopoly; Monopoly; Payoff matrix
and oligopoly, 233–234, 234*e*
Gans, Curtis, 364
Gardner, David, 301, 301*i*
Gates, Bill, 346–347. *See also* Microsoft
GATT. *See* General Agreement on Tariffs and Trade
GDP. *See* Gross domestic product
General Agreement on Tariffs and Trade (GATT), 430*d*
General Motors Corporation
Case Study: *Wheel of Fortune,* 83–84
Geographic differences, and labor supply, 276
GNP. *See* Gross national product
Golden rule of profit maximization, 172*d*
Gold standard, 455*d*
Goldman, Marshall, 482
Good(s), 3*d*
alternative, 55*d*
capital, 37*e*
consumer, 37*e*
durable, 72
inferior, 50*d*
nondurable, 72
normal, 50*d*
open-access, 352*d*
price changes, 50–51
private, 352–354, 353*e*
public, 40, 78*d*
quasi–public, 353*d*
Goods and services, 3–4, 39
balance on, 443*d*, 443–444
Government
business, regulation of, 329–330
and circular flow model, 86
growth, 80
income assistance programs, 401–402
and international trade tariffs, 427
monopolies in developing countries, 471–472
Case Study: *Crony Capitalism in Indonesia—All in the Family,* 471–472

objectives, 79–80
revenue sources, 80, 81*e*
role of, 76–79
size, 80
structure, 79–80
tax incidence, 80–82
tax principles, 80–82
Government Accounting Office, 227*i*
Government policy
Case Study: *The McMinimum Wage,* 259
Gradualism, 480*d*
Graphs
basics, 18*e*
curve shifts, 22–23, 23*e*
drawing, 19*e,* 20*e,* 19–20
long-run industry supply curve, 194
marginal analysis, 20–21, 22*e*
slopes of curved lines, 21–22, 22*e,* 23*e*
slopes of straight lines, 20, 21*e*
understanding, 18
Greenspan, Alan, 348
Gross domestic product (GDP), 80
and international trade, 418–419
Gross national product (GNP), 463–464
in developing countries, 464, 464*e,* 465*e*
and transitional economies, 483*e*

H

Hazardous waste, and the Superfund,
387–388
Health
economic development and, 464–468
Health Care Financing Administration, 126*i*
Healthcare, Human Services and Labor Policy Web site (Oregon), 413*i*
Herfindahl index, 339*d,* 339–340, 340*e*
Hidden actions, 319*d*
Hidden characteristics, 319*d*
Holt, Charles, 190
Hong Kong
market economy, 40
Horizontal merger, 338*d*
Household(s)
circular flow model, between households
and firms, 84–85, 85*e*
as demanders of goods and services, 72
evolution, 70–71
production, 73–74
Case Study: *The Electronic Cottage,*
74–75
tax avoidance in household production, 73–74
as resource suppliers, 71, 71*e*
utility, 71
Householder, 70*d*

Household income
and college education, 396–398
distribution of, 396–399, 397*e*
benchmarks for, 398
differences in, 398–399
Housing assistance, 402
Hypothesis, 9*d*

I

Implicit cost, 141*d,* 141–142
Imports. *See also* Exports; International trade
profile of, 418–419
Import quotas, 427–430, 428*e*
Import substitution, 473*d*
Income
circular flow model, between households
and firms, 84–85, 85*e*
consumer, 49–50, 50*e*
distribution of, 260–261, 261*e*
household
and college education, 396–398
distribution of, 396–399, 397*e*
benchmarks for, 398
differences in, 398–399
and international trade, 434–435
and labor supply, 271
median, 398*d*
personal, 71*e*
present value of, 299
real, 47, 47*d*
and substitution effect, 137–138, 138*e*
wage increase, effect on, 270*d*
Income assistance, 401–402, 408–410. *See
also* Welfare reform
dependence on, 409–410
disincentives, 408–409
Income assistance programs, 401*d*
Income effect, 47, 47*d*
Income effect of a wage increase, 270*d*
Income elasticity of demand, 105–107, 105*d*
Case Study: *The Market for Food and "The
Food Problem,"* 107–109, 107*e,* 108*e*
income, 106
Increasing-cost industry, 185*d,* 185–187,
186*e*
Increasing marginal returns, 145*d*
Indifference curves, 133*e,* 134*e,* 135*e*
and utility maximization, 133–138
and utility, 133–138, 133*e,* 134*e,* 135*e*
Indonesia
Case Study: *Crony Capitalism in
Indonesia—All in the Family,* 471–472
Suharto, President, 471
Industrial market countries, 463*d*
Industrial Revolution, 73*d,* 301

Industrial union, 277*d*
Inelastic demand, 92*d*
Inferior good, 50*d*
Information
imperfect, 316–318
implications of, 317–318
optimal, 317*e,* 317
search of
benefit of, 316–317
cost of, 312
Information Revolution, 74–75
Initial public offering (IPO), 302
In-kind transfers, 70
Innovation, 197*d*
Insurance market, and asymmetric informa-
tion, 321
Intellectual property
Case Study: *The Value of a Good Idea—
Intellectual Property,* 296–297
Interest, 3*d*
Interest rate(s), 291*d*
differences in, 295–296
term structure of, 295*d*
Interlocking directorate, 338*d*
International finance
deficits and surpluses, 446–447
statistical discrepancy account, 445–446
International markets, and antitrust activity,
346
International Monetary Fund
"World Economic Outlook," 468*i*
International monetary system
Bretton Woods system, 456–457
Case Study: *The Asia Contagion,* 458–459
development of, 455–459
International Motor Vehicle Program at
MIT, 83*i*
International trade. *See also* Exports; Imports
antidumping and, 434
and circular flow model, 86
and consumption, 421–423, 422*e*
declining industries and, 435–436
in developing countries, 472–474
exchange rates, 83
gains from, 418–424
gross domestic product and, 418–419
income and, 434–435
and infant industry, 433–434
and national defense, 433
production responsibilities without,
419–421, 419*e,* 420*e*
protection of, 436–437
restrictions, 83
Case Study: *Enforcing Trade Restrictions,*
437–438

International trade. *(continued)*
 Case Study: *Wheel of Fortune,* 83–84
 specialization in, 423–424
  differences in taste, 424
  economies of scale, 423–424
  resource endowments, 423
 surplus of, 424–425, 425*e*
Internet
 antitrust issues, 337*i*
 Asian financial crisis, 461*i*
 auctions, 180*i*
 economics of, 195*i*
 economy of, 296*i*
 farming, 112*i*
 labor movement, history of, 278*i*
 lottery information, 301*i*
 merger, guidelines for, 350*i*
 minimum wage, 259*i*
 poverty statistics, 416*i*
 technology resources, 296*i*
"Internet Guide to Colleges and Universities," 27*i*
Investment
 marginal rate of return on, 291*d*
IPO. *See* Initial public offering
Isocost lines, 163–165, 163*e*, 164*e*
Isoquants, 162–163, 162*e*, 164*e*, 165*e*

J

Japan
 international trade
  Case Study: *Wheel of Fortune,* 83–84
 unemployment, 9–10
Job discrimination, 276
Job experience, 271–272
Johnson, Lyndon B., 407
Journal of Economic Literature, 33*i*
Journal of Intellectual Property Law, 297*i*

K

Katz, Jane, 307
Kennedy Round, 431
Kinked demand curve, 235*d*
 and marginal revenue, 236, 236*e*
 model of, 235*d*
 and oligopoly, 234–237
 price rigidity of, 236–237, 236*e*
Klein, Joel, 348
Kornai, Janos, 480
Kremer, Michael, 307

L

Labor, 2*d*
 division of, 32*d*
 specialization of, 32*d*

Labor market, and asymmetric information, 322–324
Labor supply
 Case Study: *Winner-Take-All Labor Markets,* 275–276
 nonwage determinants of, 271–276
  ability, 274
  age, 273–274, 273*e*
  education, 273–274, 274*e*
  experience, 273–274
  geographic differences, 276
  job discrimination, 276
  job experience, 271–272
  market conditions and, 272, 273*e*
  nonmonetary factors, 271
  other sources of income, 271
  risk differences, 276
  taste for work, 272
  training, 273–274
  union membership, 276
  wage differences, 272–273
 and utility maximization, 266–268
  implications of, 268
  time, uses of, 267
  work, and utility, 267
 wages and, 269–271
  backward-bending labor supply curve, 270, 270*e*
  flexibility of hours worked, 271
  substitution and income effects, 269–270
Labor union, 277*d. See also* Unions
 history of, 278*i*
Laboratory for Experimental Economics and Political Science (Caltech), 190*i*
Laissez-faire market system, 40
Land, 3*d*
Law of comparative advantage, 29–30, 30*d*
Law of demand, 46–47, 46*d*
Law of diminishing marginal rate of substitution, 134–135, 134*e*, 135*e*
Law of diminishing marginal returns, 144–145, 144*e*, 145*d*
Law of diminishing marginal utility, 115, 115*d*
Law of increasing opportunity cost, 36*d*
Law of supply, 52*d*
Legislation, 334
 Agricultural Marketing Agreement Act (1937), 359
 Airline Deregulation Act (1978), 335
 antitrust activity, problems with, 345–346
 Celler-Kefauver Anti-Merger Act (1950), 338
 Civil rights Act (1964), 407

 Clayton Act (1914), 338
 Clean Air Act (1970), 384–385
 Clean Water Act (1972), 384
 competing interest, 358*d*
 Comprehensive Environmental Response, Compensation, and Liability Act (1980) (Superfund Law), 384, 387
 Federal Agriculture Improvement and Reform Act (1966), 359*i*
 Federal Trade Commission Act (1914), 338
 per-se illegality and the rule of reason, 339, 339*d*
 Personal Responsibility and Work Reconciliation Act (1996), 410
 on pollution, 383–384
 Resource Conservation and Recovery Act (1976), 384
 Robinson–Patman Act (1936), 217
 Sherman Antitrust Act (1890), 338
 special interest, 358*d*
 Superfund Law (1980), 384, 387
 Trade Agreements Act (1979), 434
Leisure, 267*d*
Liability
 limited, 76
 unlimited, 75
Linear demand curve, 93*d*, 93–95, 94*e*
Loan
 administrative cost of, 296
 demand for, 294*d*
 duration of, 295–296
 risk, 295
 tax treatment of, 296
Loanable funds
 supply of, 294*d*
Loanable funds market, 294*d*
 and time, 294–295, 295*e*
Long run, 144*d*
 perfect competition and, 180–184, 181*e*, 182*e*, 183*e*
Long-run average cost curve, 152–154, 152*e*, 153*d*, 153*e*, 156, 156*e*
Long-run economic profit, 180–181, 181*e*
Long-run industry supply curve, 184*d*
 in constant-cost industry, 184*d*, 184–185
 in decreasing-cost industry, 187*d*, 187–188
 graph, 194
 in increasing-cost industry, 185*d*, 185–187, 186*e*
Loss
 deadweight, 209*d*
 minimization, and fixed costs, 173, 174*e*
Lotteries, 301*i*

M

Macroeconomics, 5*d*
Managed float system, 457*d*
Managerial behavior, corporate, 303–304
Managerial discretion, constraints on corporate ownership, 304–305
　economics of natural selection, 304
　incentives, 304–305
　institutional investors, 305
　stockholder voting, 305
Marginal, 6*d*
Marginal analysis, 6
Marginal cost, 148, 148*d*
　and marginal revenue, 173–174, 175*e*
　total, and curves, 148–149, 149*e*
Marginal product, 144*d*
Marginal product curve, 145, 146*e*
Marginal rate of return on investment, 291*d*
Marginal rate of substitution (MRS), 134
　law of diminishing, 134–135, 134*e,* 135*e*
Marginal rate of technical substitution (MRTS), 162–163
Marginal resource cost, 254*d,* 254–255, 254*e*
Marginal returns
　increasing, 145*d*
Marginal revenue, 172*d*
　and kinked demand curve, 236, 236*e*
　and marginal cost, 173–174, 175*e*
　and monopolies, 200–201
Marginal revenue product, 252*d,* 252–253, 253*e*
Marginal social benefit, 377*d*
Marginal social cost, 376*d*
Marginal tax rate, 81*d*
Marginal utility, 115*d*
　law of diminishing, 115, 115*d*
Marginal valuation, 124*d*
Market(s), 4*d*
　Case Study: *The Market for Professional Basketball,* 62–63
　common, 432–433
　effect of changes in price and quantity, 58–63
　　effect on demand, 58–59, 59*e*
　　impact of changes in supply, 59–60, 60*e*
　equilibrium, 56–58, 57*e,* 168*e*
　foreign exchange, 83
　loanable funds, 294*d*
　supply and demand, 56–58
　　simultaneous changes, 60–61, 61*e,* 62*e*
Market capitalization, 303
Market competition, 343–344, 344*e*
　trends in, 344–345

Market conditions, and labor supply, 272, 273*e*
Market demand
　and resources, 244–245, 245*e*
Market failure, 76*d*
Market power, 220, 329*d*
Market structure, 167*d*
Market supply
　and resources, 246
Market system, pure, 40, 40*d*
Market work, 267*d*
Maturity date, 302
McDonald's, 156*i,* 157*i*
　Case Study: *Billions and Billions of Burgers,* 156–157
　Case Study: *The Reputation of a Big Mac,* 324
McEachern Interactive Web Site, 88*i,* 132*i*
Means-tested program, 401*d*
Median income, 398*d*
Median voter model, 356*d,* 356–357
Mediator, 277*d*
Medicaid, 71, 402*d*
"Medical Savings Accounts for Medicare," 327*i*
Medicare, 71, 80, 401*d*
Medium of exchange, 31
Merchandise trade balance, 82*d,* 443, 444*e*
Merger
　antitrust activity
　　movements, 340–342, 341*e*
　　and public policy, 339–340, 340*e*
　conglomerate, 341*d*
　guidelines for, 350*i*
　horizontal, 338*d*
　vertical, 338*d*
Mexico
　Case Study: *City in the Clouds,* 385–386
　"Urban Air Pollution in Mexico City," 385*i*
Microeconomics, 4*d*
Microsoft, 316*i,* 346*i. See also* Gates, Bill
　case against, by United States Department of Justice, 350*i*
　Case Study: *Windows 98 Sold With Microsoft Browser,* 346–347
Migration
　and economic development, 474
Minimum efficient scale, 156, 157*d*
Minimum wage, 259*i*
Mixed system, 41, 41*d*
Model
　circular flow, 84*d*
　median voter model, 356*d,* 356–357
Monetary policy, 79*d*

Money
　as medium of exchange, 31
Monopolistic competition, 219*d*
　Case Study: *Fast Forward,* 224
　characteristics of, 219
　in the long run, 222–224, 223*e*
　loss minimization in, 220–222
　product differentiation of, 220
　short-run profit maximization in, 220–222, 221*e*
　versus perfect competition, 225–226, 225*e*
　zero economic profit in, 222–224, 221*e*
Monopoly, 77*d*
　allocative and distributive effects of, 209
　barriers to entry, 197*d,* 197–200
　　control of essential resources, 199–200
　　　Case Study: *Are Diamonds Forever?,* 199–200
　　economies of scale, 198, 198*e*
　　legal restrictions, 197–198
　Case Study: *The Mail Monopoly,* 211
　loss minimization in, 206–207, 207*e*
　and marginal revenue, 200–201
　natural, 77*d,* 198
　and perfect competition, 208–209, 208*e*
　and price discrimination, 212–215
　　conditions for, 212
　　examples of, 212–213
　　model, 213, 213*e*
　　perfect, 214–215, 214*e*
　price and output in, 209
　profit maximization in, 203–206, 204*e,* 205*e*
　　long-run, 207–208
　regulation of, 330–333, 331*i*
　resource allocation in, 208–209, 208*e*
　revenue in, 200–203
　　revenue curves, 201–203, 202*e*
　　revenue schedule, 200–201, 201*e*
　shutting down in, 207–208
　subsidizing, 332
　welfare cost of, 209–212
Moral hazard, 321*d*
Most-favored nation clause, 431–432
Motley Fool, 301*i*
MRS. *See* Marginal rate of substitution
MRTS. *See* Marginal rate of technical substitution

N

NAFTA. *See* North American Free Trade Agreement
National Association of Realtors, 316*i*
National defense
　and international trade, 433

National Geographic Society, 385*i*
National Governors' Association, 416*i*
Natural monopoly, 77*d*
   regulation of, 330–333, 331*i*
NBA. *See* National Basketball Association
National Basketball Association (NBA)
   Case Study: *The Market for Professional Basketball*, 62–63
Net unilateral transfers, 444*d*, 444–445
New Republic, 471*i*
New York Stock Exchange, 302–303
New York Times, 346*i*
Nonmarket work, 27*d*
Nonprofit institutions, 76
Normal good, 50*d*
Normal profit, 143*d*
Normative economic statement, 7*d*
North American Free Trade Association (NAFTA), 432–433

O

Occupational Outlook Handbook, 257*i*, 264*i*
Office of the U.S. Trade representative, 440*i*
Official reserve transactions account, 445*d*
Oligopoly, 226*d*
   Case Study: *The Unfriendly Skies*, 227–228
   and collusion, 230*d*, 230–232, 231*e*
   economies of scale, 228, 229*e*
   entry costs, 228–229, 229*e*
   and game theory, 233*d*, 233–234, 234*e*
   and kinked demand curve, 234–237
   models of, 230–238
   and perfect competition, compared, 237–238
     price, 237
     profits, 237–238
   varieties of, 226–230
OPEC. *See* Organization of Petroleum Exporting Countries
Open–access good, 352*d*
Opportunity cost, 26*d*, 26–29
   Case Study: *The Opportunity Cost of College*, 26–27
Oregon's Healthcare, Human Services and Labor Policy Web site, 413*i*
Organization of Petroleum Exporting Countries (OPEC), 83, 230
   OPEC Fact Sheet, 241*i*
Organizational behavior, 366–367
Other-things-constant assumption, 8*d*
Outsourcing, 314*d*
   Case Study: *The Trend Toward Outsourcing*, 314–315
The Outsourcing Institute, 326*i*

Ownership
   and funding of bureaus, 365–366
   and organizational behavior, 366–367
   separation from control, 304*d*

P

Partnership, 75*d*
Patent, 197*d*, 296
Patent Office, 197*i*
Pattern bargaining, 284
Payment
   present value of, 297–299
Payoff matrix, 233*d*, 233–234, 234*e*
Payroll tax(es), 80, 82
Perfect competition, 167*d*
   Case Study: *Auction markets*, 179–180
   demand under, 168–169, 168*e*
   and efficiency, 188–190, 189*e*
     Case Study: *Experimental Economics*, 190–191
   in the long run, 180–184, 181*e*, 182*e*, 183*e*
   loss minimization in, 173–180, 174*e*, 175*e*, 177*e*, 178*e*
   market structure of, 167–168
   and monopolies, 208–209, 208*e*
   versus monopolistic competition, 225–226, 225*e*
   and oligopolies, compared, 237–238
     price, 237
     profits, 237–238
   profit maximization in, short run, 169–172, 170*e*, 171*e*
   in the short run, 173–180, 174*e*, 175*e*, 177*e*, 178*e*
Perfectly discriminating monopolist, 214*d*
Perfectly elastic demand curve, 95*d*
Perfectly elastic supply curve, 103*d*
Perfectly inelastic demand curve, 95–96, 96*d*
Perfectly inelastic supply curve, 103*d*
Per-se illegal, 339*d*
Personal income, 71*e*
Personal Responsibility and Work Reconciliation Act (1996), 410
Plott, Charles, 190
Policy
   fiscal, 79*d*
   monetary, 79*d*
Pollution. *See also* Environment
   air, 384–385
   Case Study: *Destruction of the Tropical Rain Forest*, 379–380
   Coase analysis of externalities, 380–381
   market for rights, 382–384
   optimal levels of, 374–384

   external costs with fixed technology, 375–376, 375*e*
   external costs with variable technology, 376–379, 377*e*, 378*e*
   water pollution, 386–387
Portfolio, 303*d*
Positive economic statement, 7*d*
Positive rate of time preference, 290*d*
Posted-offer pricing, 191
Poverty
   and Affirmative Action, 407–408
   and age, 403, 403*e*
   composition of, 402–409
   and discrimination, 406–407
   and gender, 404–406, 406*e*
   official level of, 399–400, 400*e*
   and public choice, 403–404
   and social welfare programs, 400–402
   statistics, 416*i*
   and women, 404–406
PPF. *See* Production possibilities frontier
PPP. *See* Purchasing power parity
Predatory pricing, 339*d*
Preferences. *See* Tastes
Present value, 297*d*
   of an annuity, 299–300
   and discounting, 297–300
     Case Study: *The Million-Dollar Lottery*, 300–301
   of income stream, 299
   of payment, 297–299
Price
   changes, 47, 50–51
     of alternative goods, 55
     effect on demand, 58–59, 59*e*
     effect on quantity, 58–63, 137, 137*e*
     impact of changes in supply, 59–60, 60*e*
     in number of producers, 55–56
     in producer expectations, 55
     of relevant resources, 55
   and costs
     average, 332
     marginal, 331–332
   differences, temporary and permanent, 246–248, 247*e*
   disequilibrium, 63*d*, 63–65
     Case Study: *Toys Are Serious Business*, 65–66
   income effect, 47
   output and monopolies, 209
   posted-offer, 191
   predatory, 339*d*
   resources, 247*e*

permanent differences in, 247–248
  temporary differences in, 246–247
world, 425*d*
Price ceiling, 64*d*
Price discrimination, 212*d*
  and monopolies, 212–215
    conditions for, 212
    examples of, 212–213
    model, 213, 213*e*
    perfect, 214–215, 214*e*
Price elasticity of demand, 90*d*
  calculation of, 91–92, 91*e*
  Case Study: *Deterring Young Smokers,*
    100–101
  categories, 92–93
  consumer budget and, 98–99, 99*e*
  constant-elasticity demand, 95–96, 96*e,*
    97*e*
  determinants of, 97–100
  elasticity estimates, 99–100, 100*e*
  and linear demand curve, 93–95, 94*e*
  substitutes and, 97–98
  and total revenue, 93
Price elasticity formula, 92*d*
Price elasticity of supply, 102*d*
  categories, 102–104, 102*e,* 103*e*
  determinants of, 104–105, 104*e*
Price floor, 63*d,* 64*e*
Price leader, 232*d*
  and oligopoly, 232–233
Price rigidity
  and kinked demand curve, 236–237, 236*e*
Price searcher, 203*d*
Price taker, 167*d*
Principal, 320*d*
Principal-agent problem, 320*d*
Private goods, 352–354, 353*e*
Private property rights, 373*d*
Privatization, 481*d*
Producer surplus, 190*d*
Product
  marginal, 144*d*
  marginal curve, 145, 146*e*
  total, 144*d*
Production
  and costs, 161–165
  in the long run, 152–157
  private versus pblic, 367–368
  in the short run, 143–152, 144*e,* 146*e,*
    147*e,* 149*e,* 150*e,* 151*e*
  substitution in, 245
  and time, 289–290
Production function, 161
  and efficiency, 161
  representation of, 161*e*

Production possibilities frontier (PPF), 34*d*
  efficiency, 34, 35*e*
  unattainable, 34–35, 35*e*
Productive efficiency, 188
Productivity
  and economic development, 468–469
  in unions, 281
Product market, 4*d*
Profit(s), 3*d. See also* Economic profit
  accounting, 142*d*
  alternative measures of, 142–143, 142*e*
  costs and, 141–143, 142*e*
  economic, 143*d*
    in the long run, 180–181, 181*e*
    in the short run, 172
  normal, 143*d*
  zero, in the long run, 180–181, 181*e*
Profit maximization. *See also* Economic
    profit
  golden rule of, 172*d*
  in monopolies, 203–206, 204*e,* 205*e*
    long-run, 207–208
  short-run, and monopolistic competition,
    220–222, 221*e*
  unregulated, 330–331, 331*e*
Progressive taxation, 81*d*
Proportional taxation, 81*d*
Proprietorship, sole, 75*d,* 77*e*
Public choice, 356–365
  Case Study: *Campaign Finance Reform,*
    363–364
  distribution of costs and benefits,
    358–359
  median voter model, 356–357
  participant goals, 357
  rational ignorance, 357–358
  rent seeking, 362–363
  underground economy, 364–365
Public good(s), 40, 78*d*
  Case Study: *farm Subsidies,* 359–362
  categories of, 353*e*
  market for, 355*e*
  optimal provision of, 354–356, 355*e*
  and private goods, 352–354, 353*e*
Public utilities, 331
Purchasing power parity (PPP), 452*d*
  Case Study: *The Big Mac Price Index,* 453,
    454*e*
Pure command system, 41, 41*d*
Pure market system, 40, 40*d*

Q

Quantity demanded. *See also* Demand
  change in, 52*d,* 58–63
  effect on demand, 58–59, 59*e*

Quantity supplied
  change in 56*d,* 58–63
  impact of changes in supply, 59–60, 60*e*
Quasi-public good, 353*d*
Quota, 83*d*
  import, 427–430, 428*e*

R

Rainforest Action Network, 379*i*
Rainforest Alliance, 379*i*
Rate
  discount, 298*d*
  interest. *See* Interest rate(s)
Rational ignorance, 357*d*
Rational self-interest, 5–6
Rationality, bounded, 312*d*
Real income, 47, 47*d*
Realized capital gain, 76
Recycling, 388*d*
The Region, 132*i,* 241*i,* 327*i,* 352*i*
Regressive taxation, 82*d*
Relevant resources, 55*d*
Renewable resources, 372*d*
Rent, 3*d*
Rent seeking, 210*d,* 362–363
Resource(s), 2*d*
  allocation in monopolies, 208–209, 208*e*
  essential, control of, 199–200
    Case Study: *Are Diamonds Forever?,*
      199–200
  exhaustible, 372*d*
  firm's demand for, 251–252, 251*e*
  fixed, 143*d,* 143–144
  market demand, 244–245, 245*e*
  market supply, 246
  optimal use of, 258
  price differences, temporary and perma-
    nent, 246–248, 247*e*
  relevant, 55*d*
  renewable, 372*d*
  variable, 143*d,* 143–144
Resource Conservation and Recovery Act
    (1976), 384
Resource demand, 243
  Case Study: *The Derived Demand for
    Architects,* 257
  Case Study: *The McMinimum Wage,* 259
  marginal revenue product, 252–253, 253*e*
  shifts in, 255–257
Resource earnings
  distribution of, 260–261, 261*e*
Resource market, 4*d*
Resource prices, 247*e*
  permanent differences in, 247–248
  temporary differences in, 246–247

Resource supply, 243
Retained earnings, 302d
Returns
   increasing marginal, 145d
Revaluation
   currency, 455d
Revenue
   average, 172d
   marginal, 200–201
      and kinked demand curve, 236, 236e
      in monopolies, 200–203
   total, 200
Revenue curves, 201–203, 202e
Revenue schedule, 200–201, 201e
Revenue sources
   governmental, 80, 81e
   total, and price elasticity of demand, 93
Rights, private property, 373d
Robinson, Joan, 219
Robinson–Patman Act (1936), 217
RPA Mall, 217Robinson-Patman Act
      (1936), 217i
Rukeyser, Louis, 301, 301i
Rule of reason, 339d
Russia. See Soviet Union

S

Scarcity, 3d
School lunch program, 402
Scientific American, 297i
Schumpeter, Joseph, 345
Scientific method, steps in, 8–9
Screening, 323d
SDRs. See Special drawing rights
SEC. See Securities and Exchange Commission
Secondary effects, 11d
Securities exchanges, 302–303
Securities and Exchange Commission
      (SEC), 302–303
S-corporation, 76
Selection, adverse, 320d
   asymmetric information, 319–320,
      322–323
Separation of ownership from control, 304d
Service, 3d
Shepherd, William, 343–344
Sherman Antitrust Act (1890), 338
Shortage, 58d
Short run, 144d
   perfect competition and, 173–180, 174e,
      175e, 177e, 178e
   profit maximization in, short run,
      169–172, 170e, 171e

Short-run economic profit, 172
Short-run firm supply curve, 176d,
      176–177, 177e
Short-run industry supply curve, 177d, 177,
      178d
Short-run supply curves, 176–179, 177e,
      178e
Signaling, 323d
Smith, Adam, 40, 56, 329
Smith, Vernon, 190–191
Social insurance, 401
Social regulation, 329d
Social Security, 80, 401d
Social welfare programs. See also Welfare re-
      form
   and poverty, 400–402
Soft budget constraint, 477d
Software and Information Industry Associa-
      tion, 347
Sole proprietorship, 75d, 77e
Solid waste, 388–389
Soviet Union (Russia)
   Case Study: Ownership and Resource
      Use, 478–479
Special drawing rights (SDRs), 445
Special-interest legislation, 358d
Specialization
   Case Study: Evidence of Specialization, 33
   and division of labor, 32–33
   and exchange, 31–32
Specialization of labor, 32d
Speculator, 452d
SSI. See Supplemental Security Income
State of Alaska's Epidemiology Bulletin, 100i
Statistical discrepancy account, 445–446
Stigler, George, 317–318, 334
Stock, 302d
   and retained earnings, 301–302
Stockholder voting, 305
Strategy, 233d
Strike, 277d
Substitutes, 51d
Substitution effect, 47, 47d, 113
   and income, 137–138, 138e
Substitution effect of a wage rate increase,
      269d
Suharto, President (Indonesia), 471
Sunk cost, 29, 29d
Superfund law, 384, 387
Supplemental Security Income (SSI),
      401d
Supply, 52d
   changes in, 54, 54e, 56d
   price elasticity of, 102d

categories, 102–104, 102e, 103e
   determinants of, 104–105, 104e
Supply curve, 52d, 53e
   backward-bending, labor, 270d
   perfectly elastic, 103d
   perfectly inelastic, 103d
   unit-elastic, 104d
Supply and demand, 56–58
   simultaneous changes, 60–61, 61e, 62e
Supply of loanable funds, 294d
Supply schedule, 52–53, 53e
Surplus, 57d
   consumer, 123–124, 124d
      Case Study: The Marginal Value of Free
         Medical Care, 126–127
      and market demand, 125–126, 125e,
         126e
   producer, 190d

T

TANF. See Temporary Assistance for Needy
      Families
Tariff, 83d
   effects on international trade, 425–427,
      426e
Tastes, 51d, 114d, 114–115
Tax(es)
   avoidance in household production,
      73–74
   payroll, 80, 82
Tax incidence, 80–82, 81d
Tax principles
   ability-to-pay, 80d
   benefits-received, 81d
   governmental, 80–82
   progressive, 81d
   proportional, 81d
   regressive, 82d
Tax rate, marginal, 81d
Technological change, 37e, 38, 296i
   and economic development, 469
   and resource markets, 256–257
   and supply curve, 54–55, 54e
   variable, 376d
Technology Review, 9i
Temporary Assistance for Needy Families
      (TANF), 410d, 401
Term structure of interest rates, 295d
Terms of trade, 421d
Theory, in economic analysis, 8
The Theory of Monopolistic Competition
      (Edward Chamberlin), 219
Time
   and consumption, 289–297, 292e, 295e

and demand, 127–128
   loanable funds market and, 294–295, 295e
   optimal investment of, 291–293, 292e
   and production, 289–290
Total cost, 147d
   and marginal, 150–151, 151e
   in the short run, 147, 147d
Total product, 144d
Total revenue (TR), 93d, 200
Total utility, 115d
ToySource, 65i
TR. See Total revenue
Trade Agreements Act (1979), 434
Trade balance
   merchandise, 82d, 443, 444e
"The Tragedy of the Commons" (Garret
   Hardin), 394e
Training
   and labor supply, 273–274
Transactions account
   official reserve, 445d
Transaction costs, 56d, 74
Transfer
   net unilateral, 444d, 444–445
   payments, 71d
Transition, 44i, 468i, 485e
Transitional economies, 476–479
   Case Study: Ownership and Resource Use,
      478–479
   economic development in, 471–472,
      479–482
   gross national product in, 483e
   soft budget constraints and, 477–478
   types of, 476–477
Transparent finances, 481d
Tying contract, 338d

U

UAW. See United Auto Workers
Underemployment
   and economic development in, 469–
      470
Underground economy, 364–365, 365d
Unemployment rate(s), 19e, 44
   in Japan, 9–10
Unilateral transfers
   net, 444d, 444–445
Unions
   Case Study: Hardball at Caterpillar, 284
   and collective bargaining, 277
   craft, 277d, 280–281, 280e
   demand for, 280e, 281–282
   industrial, 277d
   kinds of, 277

labor union, 277d
   history of, 278i
   membership, trends in, 282–283, 283e
   productivity of, 281
   strikes and, 277–278
   and wages, 278–285
   wage floor, effect of, 279e
United Auto Workers (UAW), 284
   Case Study: Hardball at Caterpillar, 284
Unit-elastic demand, 96d
Unit-elastic supply curve, 104d
United Parcel Service (UPS), 211i
   Case Study: The Mail Monopoly, 211
United States Agency for International De-
      velopment (AID), 475
United States Bureau of the Census, 398i,
      399
   Current Population Survey, 400i
   Income and Poverty, 404i
   poverty statistics, 416i
   Trade Data Web site, 424d
United States Customs Service, 437i
United States Department of Agriculture
   Economics Research Service, 107i
United States Department of Energy, 241i
   OPEC Fact Sheet, 241i
United States Department of Justice
   Antitrust Division, 338, 346i
   case against Microsoft, 350i
   Case Study: Windows 98 Sold With Mi-
      crosoft Browser, 346–347
   merger guidelines, 350i
United States Department of Labor, 259i
   Compensation and Working Conditions, 284i
United States Department of Transportation,
      335
United States Environmental Protection
   Agency (EPA), 374i
United States Geological Survey, 120i
United States Postal Service, 211i
Universal Studios Florida, 128i
University of Maryland, 359i
University of Mississippi, 179i
University of Virginia, 190i
UPS. See United Parcel Service
"Urban Air Pollution in Mexico City," 385d
Urban Institute, 411i
Uruguay Round, 430–431
U.S. official poverty level, 399d
Utility, 71d
   analysis, 114–115
   public, 331
   total, 115d
Utility maximization, 266–268

implications of, 268
time, uses of, 267
work and utility, 267
Utility measurement
   Case Study: Water, Water, Everywhere,
      120–121
   conditions of, 119–120
   and indifference curves, 133–138, 133e,
      134e, 135e
   and law of demand, 121–123, 122e, 123e
   maximization of, 117–120, 118e
   units of, 116–117, 116e, 117e

V

Value
   marginal, 124d
Vanderbilt University, 190i
Variable, 8d
Variable cost, 147, 147d
   average, 149–150, 150d, 150e
Variable resource, 143d, 143–144
Variable technology, 376d
Vending machines
   Case Study: A Yen for Vending Machines,
      9–10
Vertical integration, 311d
Vertical merger, 338d
von Hayek, Friedrich, 480–481

W

Wages, 3d
   differences in, 272–273
   income effect of an increase in, 270d
   and labor supply, 269–271
      backward-bending labor supply curve,
         270, 270e
      flexibility of hours worked, 271
      substitution and income effects,
         269–270
   rate increase, 269d
Wall Street Journal, 347i
Wall Street Week, 301i
Warren-Boulton, Frederick, 347
Water pollution, 386–387
Welfare reform, 410–411. See also Income
      assistance; Social welfare
   Case Study: Is Welfare-to-Work Working?,
      411–412, 413e
   Case Study: Oregon's Program of "Tough
      Love," 413–414
   and poverty, 400–402
Winner's curse, 318–319, 318d
Women
   in developing countries, 468

Women, *(continued)*
  evolution of the household, 70–71
  and poverty, 404–406
Work
  market, 267*d*
  nonmarket, 267*d*
World Bank, 44*i*
  Development Economic Research
    Group, 468*i*

Transition, *458*i
World Bank News, *485*i
"World Economic Outlook" (IMF), 468*i*
World price, 25*d*
World Resources Institute, 120*i*
World Trade Organization (WTO), 430,
    431*d,* 431*i,* 439
  Case Study: *The World Trade Organization,*
    431–432

WTO. *See* World Trade Organization

Z

Zero economic profit
  in the long run, 180–181, 181*e*
  and monopolistic competition, 222–224,
    221*e*

Photo Credits

Page 1 © 1998 PhotoDisc, Inc

9 © Paul Chesley/Tony Stone Images

12 © Morton Beebe-S.F./Corbis

25 © Andrew Sacks/Tony Stone Images

26 © Gary Conner/PhotoEdit

33 © Courtesy of Cyberian Outpost/ Feldman & Associates

45 © Connie Coleman/Tony Stone Images

62 © Nathaniel Butler/AllSport USA

65 © Reuters/Joe Traver/Archive Photos

69 © David Hanover/Tony Stone Images

74 © Michael Newman/PhotoEdit

83 © Andy Sacks/Tony Stone Images

89 © Jamey Stillings/Tony Stone Images

100 © Paul S. Howell/Gamma Liaison International

107 © Richard Hamilton Smith/Corbis

113 © Charles Thatcher/Tony Stone Images

120 © Amy C. Etra/PhotoEdit

126 © Steven Peters/Tony Stone Images

140 © David Harry Stewart/Tony Stone Images

155 © Mark Richards/PhotoEdit

156 © Swersey/Gamma Liaison International

166 © Mark Joseph/Tony Stone Images

179 © Xavier Tasteliin/Gamma Liaison International

190 © Thomas Veneklasen/Univeristy of Arizona/Economics Science Lab

196 © Joseph Sohm/Tony Stone Images

199 © Pail Almasy/Corbis

211 © Bonnie Kamin/PhotoEdit

218 © Greg Pease/Tony Stone Images

224 © Porter Gifford/Gamma Liaison International

227 © Dirck Halstead/Gamma Liaison International

242 © Tom Dietrich/Tony Stone Images

254 © PhotoDisc Inc.

259 © Ed Lallo/Gamma Liaison International

265 © Charles Thatcher/Tony Stone Images

275 © Jim Graham/Gamma Liaison International

284 © Barry King/Gamma Liaison International

288 © Deborah Davis/PhotoEdit

296 © Jeff Topping/Gamma Liaison International

300 © Joseph Sohm; ChromoSohm Inc./ Corbis

308 © Ferguson/Katzman/HMS/Tony Stone Images

314 © Michael Rosenfeld/Tony Stone Images

324 © PhotoEdit

328 © Keith Wood/Tony Stone Images

334 © Jeff Christensen.Gamma Liaison International

346 © Tom McCarthy/PhotoEdit

351 © Roger Tully/Tony Stone Images

359 © Mark Richards/PhotoEdit

363 © Peter Dean/Tony Stone Images

371 © Keren Su/Tony Stone Images

379 © Stephanie Maze/Corbis

385 © Stephanie Maze/Corbis

395 © Charles Thatcher/Tony Stone Images

411 © Stephen Ferry/Gamma Liaison International

413 © 1998 PhotoDisc, Inc.

417 © Elie Bernager/Tony Stone Images

431 © Herbert W. Booth III/Gamma Liaison International

437 © Alain Morvan/Gamma Liaison International

441 © Matthias Kulka/The Stock Market

453 © Ron McMillan/Gamma Liaison International

458 © Wolfgang Kaehler/Corbis

462 © Paul Chesley/Tony Stone Images

471 © Nik Wheeler/Corbis

478 © SYGMA